The Complete Book of
British Birds

Credits

Editors: Michael Cady, Rob Hume
Art Editors: Peter Davies, Michael Preedy MCSD, FRSA
Design Assistants: KAG Design Ltd
Picture Researcher: Wyn Voysey

Artists: Norman Arlott, Trevor Boyer, Hilary Burn, Robert Gillmor, Peter Hayman, Ian Jackson, David Quinn, Chris Rose, Ian Wallace, Anne Winterbotham

Writers: Irene Allen, John Andrews, Ian Armstrong, Colin Bibby, Sarah Brennan, James Cadbury, Lennox Campbell, Stan Davies, Ian Dawson, Mike Everett, Chris Harbard, Rob Hume, Mike Langman, Keith Noble, John O'Sullivan, Fay Pascoe, Richard Porter, Tony Prater, Bob Scott, Ken Smith, Carolyn Stowe, Tim Stowe, Stephanie Tyler, Graham Williams, Gwyn Williams, Nigel Wood

Maps produced by and copyright The Automobile Association.

Filmset by Tradespools Ltd, Frome, Somerset, England
Colour reproduction by LC Repro and Sons Ltd,
Aldermaston, Reading, Berkshire
Printed and bound in Italy by Amilcare Pizzi s.p.a.
Published by The Automobile Association, Fanum House, Basing View, Basingstoke, Hampshire, RG21 2EA and the Royal Society for the Protection of Birds, The Lodge, Sandy, Bedfordshire, SG19 2DL.

ISBN 0 86145 663 7
AA Reference 51059

Contents

Foreword

by Magnus Magnusson,
President of the Royal Society for the Protection of Birds

THIS VERY SPECIAL BOOK has been created to mark 100 years of the Royal Society for the Protection of Birds. It is a superb way for the RSPB to celebrate, for, as well as protecting wild birds, it has always been at the forefront of telling people about birds and the environment. Typically, there is nothing self-indulgent about the book; beautiful though it is, its contents will provide a lifetime's interest for any reader.

We often take for granted the wonderful variety of birds that live in, or visit, the British Isles. We watch birds in our garden, or in the local park, but we may know only a few species by name and not much else about them.

This really is a great shame, because a genuine knowledge and understanding of birds and the places where they live can add so much to a family outing or a country drive.

The excellent wildlife programmes which are now a regular feature of our television screens have done much to encourage what I know is a fast-growing interest in birds. But of course there is a limit to what they can do. The essential first step towards enjoyment of birds is the ability to identify them: and it is here that the magnificent spectacle of, say, a sparrowhawk soaring

across our screens can only whet rather than satisfy our curiosity.

That's why the RSPB is delighted to be celebrating 100 years of the Society by publishing this new book with the AA and why I personally find it so valuable.

Here, in superb colour illustrations, are all the birds you are likely to come across, with the birds shown in many different attitudes to give us an overall impression of what they really look like, hopping quickly through the branches of a tree, feeding, in

flight, in flocks – not just in standard field-guide portraits.

The book tells us much about bird behaviour, so that once you have identified your garden visitor, for example, you can go on to learn what it eats, where it nests and how it survives in our glorious climate!

We also learn about the places in which birds live and why some species can be found up on the moors but not down on the heaths, or in the oak woods but not the hedges of our farmland.

Even if you're an old hand at birdwatching I think you'll find a wealth of fascinating and unfamiliar information in this book, and that you will love the unique way in which it combines how to identify, where to go and so much more about birds and their habitats in one volume.

I believe passionately that an understanding and enjoyment of birdlife is the first step towards creating a better world for both birds and people. This book will certainly create, for the next 100 years, a formidable basis for the understanding of birds and of their place in nature.

Magnus Magnusson

Introduction and using the book

BIRDS ARE WONDERFUL. As tiny and fragile a creature as a warbler can survive in the tough outdoors for several years, undertaking migratory flights to and from the middle of Africa. It can find its way there and back without map, compass or artificial aid. Such obvious facts should never be forgotten. The lives of birds, lived at great pace with a phenomenal turnover of energy, are full of events that make our ponderous lives seem dull and dim-witted in the extreme.

REMARKABLE FACTS
The marvellous thing about birds is that the more you learn about them, the more remarkable they prove to be. Intensive long-term studies of birds like blue tits and great tits produce the most extraordinary pieces of information. It is just possible to appreciate that a baby bird could effectively blackmail its parents into feeding it by calling so loudly that it risks attracting a predator to the whole brood, so the parent has to feed it to shut it up. But could you possibly imagine that a baby great tit in a brood of males will have to struggle hard to compete with its brothers and will therefore grow up

big, strong and successful; while a male with nothing but smaller sisters has an easy time, does not learn to stand up for itself and will in all probability be a relatively weak and unsuccessful parent?

Such facts are the results of professional scientific work, but the point is that even the commonest birds become more fascinating with more watching, never less. Do not be misled into thinking that learning about birds makes them somehow less enjoyable. This book is intended to help you enjoy birds by increasing your understanding.

PUTTING NAMES TO BIRDS

The basis of watching birds is identification – simply putting names to things. True, a beautiful bird can be appreciated for the way it looks, behaves or sounds even if we have not got a clue what it is. But once we can give it a name, it becomes much more interesting. It suddenly seems to be more easy to see, because when we have a name for it, we notice it much more. How many people drive by a roadside kestrel without even 'seeing' it? Yet once you know what a kestrel is, you cannot drive past one as it hovers beside a motorway without noticing it and making a mental note.

This book has beautiful bird paintings presented in the clearest possible way, with detailed notes, to help you name the birds you see. Like birdwatching itself, these pages are attractive in their own right, but all the more useful and interesting if you study them. Each species has a map to show where you can expect to see it, and where it is unlikely to be found (which is just as important). A simple column beside each map tells you in which months you can find the bird, and the adjacent text gives details of size, the kind of place where the bird lives, its nest and eggs, food and voice. The silhouette at the top of each map is a further aid to identification.

Some birds have a 'binocular box'. This usually gives field identification hints, but sometimes gives information of a more discursive nature.

BIG, MEDIUM OR SMALL?

Judging a bird's size is fraught with difficulties, but getting a rough idea should not be too hard a job. Try to compare an unknown bird with something you do know – a finch, or a thrush, or a goose. We give size in centimetres, measured from the tip of the bill to the tip of the tail. All birds tend to hunch the shoulders, sink the head and neck into the back feathers and look shorter than the measurements suggest, but use them as a comparison and they will help. We give the wingspan in some cases where it is relevant, and also the bird's weight (minimum and maximum where this may be useful). This is something that is enormously variable – a small bird can put on enough 'fuel' as fat to double its weight before making a migration flight, or lose a third of its body weight overnight in the depths of winter. Nevertheless, the weights, taken with length, give a better idea of a bird's bulk – two species of the same length may be enormously different in weight and one might look 'twice as big' as the other.

The book also looks at the features that together make birds unique. Other animals fly, or lay eggs, or eat worms – but birds have feathers too, and are more easily seen and studied than any other group of wild animals. Many of them sing. But why should a blackbird have such a beautiful song, which each modifies and develops as if to its own 'taste'? If it wanted merely to warn others that it had a territory, or simply to tell females that it was about, it could just as profitably sit on a rooftop all day and make loud screeching noises. It is as well for us that it does not – but why it has such mellow, rich, fluty notes is not easily explained. There are plenty more unanswered questions!

VARIATIONS ON A THEME

Birds are so immensely varied – from those living on mountain tops to those that rarely leave water, from some that eat flesh to others that feed on grass, from some with long legs and bills to sparrows with stubby beaks – that we have tried to explain the reasons behind their innumerable adaptations. So much hinges on food and nest sites that their habitat is of crucial importance.

The book has a series of in-depth examinations of the major habitats in Britain and Ireland, relating their physical characteristics to the life that they support and explaining how it all ties in with the birds.

As well as variety, there is also quite remarkable uniformity among birds. Humans have several colours of skin, eyes and hair, a range of heights, weights and so on. But a robin is a robin. Its size, shape, colour and pattern, even its voice, are repeated millions of times over, so that every robin looks, to all practical purposes, like every other. Because of this, we can group birds into species and families, and a section of this book looks at families of birds according to the basic lifestyle that they adopt. Grebes, coots and tufted ducks all swim and dive – but they are not all ducks. Why is that? How does it help – or does it simply confuse? This book gives some of the answers.

Finally, once you have learned about birds and how they live, and can identify a few, or a lot, you will want to get out to see some. The regional guides will help you to do just that – they contain descriptions of many of the very best birdwatching places throughout Britain and Northern Ireland. Knowing that watching birds is often a family activity, but that some of the family will be less interested than others, we have not neglected the kind of area which offers a good day out for everyone, with enough birds to be of interest. But we have included the 'hotspots' with plenty of birds for the most avid 'bird person' to seek out and enjoy. Locations are given for each place, and there is also a six-figure map reference, which enables the places to be pin-pointed on any map which uses the National Grid.

FUN AND ENJOYMENT

No-one pretends that skill in birdwatching can be acquired overnight. There is never any substitute for experience. But learning is enormous fun. Birds really are wonderful – and they offer the greatest escape from modern life into another, altogether different world that we can achieve. Sit beside a thicket where a nightingale sings; stand above a cliff with a multitude of guillemots and kittiwakes; walk over a downland ridge with corn buntings and kestrels. Keep your eyes and ears open, be prepared to learn, ask yourself questions and probe into the secret life of the birds. Then you will discover the wonder for yourself.

Glossary, bird topography, distribution maps

ABRASION wear and tear on feathers, which can change appearance dramatically. Pale parts wear more easily than dark, *eg* white spots on gulls' wingtips wear off to leave uniform dark colour.

ADAPTATION evolution of feature to fit a certain function, *eg* long bill to probe into soft mud for worms.

ANTING deliberate and well-defined actions of a bird allowing ants to crawl over it or actually putting them into its feathers; formic acid from ants helps rid the feathers of parasites or performs some other useful function still unknown.

CLASSIFICATION the grouping of living things into categories; with birds, based on relationships judged on development from common ancestry, usually producing a list of birds from the most primitive to the most recent (see list on p.382).

COURTSHIP see Display. In order to mate and rear young successfully pairs of most species must first break down their natural instinct to keep their distance, must reduce aggression and maintain a firm relationship, or pair bond, which is created and reinforced by courtship behaviour.

CREPUSCULAR active in twilight.

CRYPTIC usually colouring that makes a bird hard to see – either as protection from a predator, or to allow a predator to approach its prey undetected.

DISPLAY specialised, ritualised actions used in communication – *eg* threatening intruders, courting a potential mate. Many other actions, including submissive postures to reduce aggression from others of the same species, begging for food, dominating bird of lower status within a flock, changing-over ceremonies at nest and so on, are all rather loosely termed 'display'.

DIURNAL active during the day.

ECLIPSE a dull plumage, notably of male ducks, acquired after breeding to reduce conspicuousness (ducks moult all their flight feathers and lose the power of flight for a time while 'in eclipse').

ERUPTION sudden large-scale movement of birds out of an area (*eg* crossbills when cone crop fails); 'irruption' is their arrival into an area (*eg* waxwings erupt from Scandinavia, irrupt into Britain).

FALL sudden (usually overnight) arrival of migrants, caused by bad weather interrupting their migration.

FERAL properly means 'wild', but refers to species or individuals once domesticated or captive but since released or escaped to live in the wild, *eg* feral pigeon, pheasant.

FOOD CHAIN or food web – complicated relationships between plants and animals each of which 'eats' one or more of the others (from fungi growing on decaying plants to birds eating worms to large birds eating small birds and so on).

GAPE the opening or the corners of the mouth; 'to gape' is to hold the bill wide open.

HABITAT environment in which organism lives; usually referred to in terms of a broad habitat type, *eg* muddy estuary, oakwood, lowland heath, but much more difficult to define precisely in order to assess habitat requirements.

HIRUNDINE a swallow or martin.

HYBRID product of parents of different species, also called a 'cross'.

IMMATURE not old enough to breed. With birds usually refers to certain plumage(s), so some such as eagles are sometimes confusingly said to 'breed in immature plumage'. Others, like the fulmar, may not breed for several years even though visually indistinguishable from an adult. Plumage descriptions such as 'first winter',

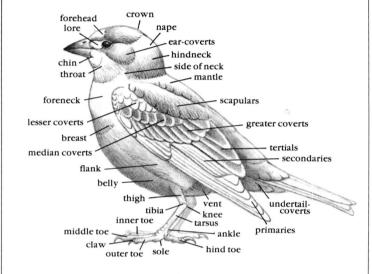

forehead
crown
lore
nape
ear-coverts
chin
hindneck
throat
side of neck
mantle
foreneck
scapulars
lesser coverts
greater coverts
breast
median coverts
tertials
flank
secondaries
belly
thigh
vent
undertail-
tibia
knee
coverts
inner toe
tarsus
middle toe
ankle
primaries
claw
hind toe
outer toe
sole

'second summer' etc, are therefore more accurate and useful, but rarely easy to apply.

INCUBATION maintaining egg(s) at the correct temperature to ensure survival and hatching. Most birds 'sit on eggs' and warm them via a bare patch of skin (brood patch), but others use their feet (*eg* gannet) or other methods (even rotting vegetation in mounds of earth in the case of the megapodes).

INVERTEBRATE animal with no backbone.

IRRUPTION see 'eruption'.

JUVENILE a bird in its first set of feathers, or juvenile plumage.

LEK a communal display ground.

MIGRATION regular, seasonal movements of species, more or less predictable, with a return trip. Irregular movements (*eg* due to hard weather), are usually called 'movements', more predictable ones, (*eg* of young birds spreading away from breeding areas in autumn), can be termed 'dispersal'.

MIMICRY vocal mimicry is simply copying other sounds, whether natural or man-made; the marsh warbler has the greatest range of mimicry of any British bird, copying calls and songs of both British and African species learnt in its wintering areas, but the starling, often making sounds like telephone bells or squeaky gates as well as other birds, is best known.

MOBBING small birds which discover a roosting owl, or a bird of prey, or sometimes a mammalian predator or snake, will flutter around or dive at it, with loud calls, attracting others of mixed species to join in. The purpose is uncertain and suggestions vary from teaching young birds which creatures are dangerous (unlikely to be the main function), to driving the potential predator away (though it often remains and the small birds lose interest), to hopefully attracting some other, bigger animal (*eg* man) which will in turn scare off the predator. Larger birds, *eg* crows, chase birds of prey that are harmless to them, especially buzzards, but also dangerous ones, *eg* peregrines; and small birds such as warblers and pied wagtails often chase other species, *eg* collared doves,

finches, for no obvious reason.

MOULT shedding and replacement of feathers in a regular sequence, which may or may not affect the appearance of the bird. Changes from juvenile to first-year to adult plumage, etc and often from summer to winter or breeding to non-breeding plumage are mostly due to moult. Many species, however, have feathers with dull tips which crumble away in spring to reveal brighter colours beneath.

NEST usually thought of as structure to hold eggs but may be a ledge or cavity. It is not a 'bird's home' though some may roost in nests when they have no eggs or young. Nests may be built by males to stimulate females but not used for eggs.

NIDICOLOUS, NIDIFUGOUS nidicolous young birds remain in the nest after hatching until they can fly. Nidifugous young are more developed when they hatch – downy, able to see, to run and often to feed themselves within hours, *eg* wader chicks, ducklings.

NOCTURNAL active at night.

PASSAGE refers to migrants and to migration – bird 'on passage' is *en route* during its migration; 'a passage' may also refer to series of migrant birds noted at a particular place, *eg* a series, or passage, of greenshanks or other waders at a gravel pit, which are then called 'passage waders'. A 'passage migrant' is a species which appears in spring and/or autumn but does not breed or spend the winter, such as little stint or black tern.

PASSERINE one of a large order of birds, the Passeriformes, which includes the 'perching birds'; others are 'non-passerines'.

PELLET not a dropping (faeces) but a collection of indigestible material passed back up through mouth, *eg* bones and beetle wing cases in the case of owls; also, less obtrusively, produced by many smaller birds.

PLUMAGE the whole set of feathers covering a bird. Also used to describe the different combinations of colour and pattern according to sex, season, age – summer plumage, adult male plumage, etc.

PREDATOR animal which eats others; a blue tit is a predator on (predates) caterpillars; in a bird sense popularly restricted to those birds which eat other birds, eggs or mammals with an arbitrary dividing line – hawks, falcons, owls, etc – or animals, such as mink, which eat birds or eggs. There is no logical reason why a grey heron (which eats fish) or a curlew (which eats crabs) is less likely to be called a predator than a kestrel which is eating beetles, though they would not be termed 'birds of prey'.

RESIDENT a species which remains in a given area all year round.

ROOST 'a roost' is a place where birds gather together in flocks; 'to roost' is to sleep.

SONG voice of a bird in recognisable pattern for its species, be it an irregular flow or a repetitive phrase; intended to identify individual and its species, to proclaim ownership of a territory and/ or to attract a mate. Other vocal sounds are usually termed 'calls' and may be for contact, to sound alarm or to give other information.

SPECIES (same singular and plural) is a 'kind' of organism, basically isolated from others by its inability to crossbreed and produce fertile young. A 'subspecies' is a recognisably different group (because of size or colour) within a species in a defined area, *eg* the wren in Shetland, rather darker and more barred than English wrens but nevertheless still a wren. Apart from subspecies, the remarkable feature of a bird species is the lack of variation within it, in terms of size, colour, pattern, voice, behaviour, food, nest and many other factors which remain remarkably constant.

TERRITORY is an area (or 'home range') occupied by a bird or a pair and which is defended against other individuals of the same species. It may contain all the pair needs to live and rear young (*eg* the territory of a robin) or a much more limited area which may be around the nest or around a special feeding place.

WRECK a 'disaster' occasionally affecting seabirds (*eg* little auks) which become weakened and driven ashore, or even inland, by gales.

Using the bird distribution maps

The column of initials denotes the months – January at the top, down to December. Grey tint in this column indicates in which months the bird is present outside the breeding season; blue tint indicates the breeding season. If there is no blue tint, then the bird does not breed anywhere, or, in the case of one or two very rare birds, it is not practical to show breeding areas. If there is no tint at all, then the bird is absent during those months. Blue on the map shows breeding areas, while grey shows where the bird is to be found during the months indicated in the column, but does not breed. Naturally, there is often an overlap within these areas, since many birds live and breed in the same place.

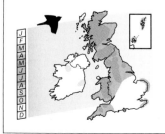

What Birds Are

Archaeopteryx

*Over millions of years birds have developed from
scaly, flying reptiles into some of the most beautiful
and graceful creatures in the animal world. Their
beaks and feet have become adapted to a remarkable
variety of lifestyles, and their feathers are quite
simply amazing*

Birds and their development

THERE ARE ABOUT 9,000 species of birds in the world today. Their variety, beauty and sheer ingenuity have fascinated man for centuries. Yet, this vast variety has probably evolved from a group of 'reptile birds' which lived more than 140 million years ago – of which *Archaeopteryx* was one.

CONTROVERSIAL FOSSIL

Archaeopteryx was about the size of a magpie, with large eyes and well-developed teeth. It had a reptile-like brain and a long reptilian tail. The most interesting features of this prehistoric animal are its wings and feathers – its feathers were just like those of the birds which live today.

There is some dispute as to whether *Archaeopteryx* lived in trees or on the ground. It may have used the claws on its wings for clambering around trees or to help it catch prey. It was probably unable to fly very far at all, possibly just gliding from tree to tree like present-day flying squirrels. Five fossilised specimens of *Archaeopteryx* have been found over more than a century and are now owned by museums in Europe and America, but have aroused fierce controversy in recent years.

CONTINUING CHANGE

Birds have continued to develop throughout the millennia since those first 'reptile birds' existed. Evolution is not something which suddenly stops. It is an ongoing process, with species constantly having to adapt to different situations. Birds are in general highly successful at this and probably use a wider variety of habitats than most other groups of animals: from the ice-cold seas where penguins deep-sea dive to the skies high above the earth which are used as bird motorways on migration; from the baking deserts to the polar caps.

Some habitats are home to larger numbers of birds than others. For instance, the rich forests of South America harbour over 2,500 different breeding species of birds. Much of

This reconstruction of Archaeopteryx *is based on the fossil evidence. No modern bird has teeth, but a very few species have vestiges of the claws on the forewing*

Britain's birds – some record breakers

Biggest – the heaviest bird in Britain is the mute swan – males often weighing over 13 kg (30 lb), with a wingspan of over two metres (seven feet). The white-tailed eagle, with a wingspan up to 240 cm (seven feet 10 inches), has the largest span, almost equalled by the biggest golden eagles. **Smallest** – goldcrest, at 9 cm (3.5 inches) from bill tip to tail tip, weighing 3.8–4.5 g (0.134–0.159 oz). Firecrest equally small, but wren, 9.5 cm long, is twice as heavy. **Fastest** – possibly the peregrine in a stoop (up to 110 mph) but many birds may equal this with a strong tailwind (*eg* ducks); in still air, the fastest so far measured is the eider, at 47 mph.

Highest flier – whooper swans on migration have been spotted from aircraft, at 8,100 metres (27,000 feet) – where it is extremely cold! **Fastest runner** – pheasant, at 21 mph. **Longest migration** – arctic tern (11,222 miles from Anglesey to Australia). **Longest life** – Manx shearwater at 29.82 years. **Largest egg** – mute swan – up to 122 × 88 mm (4.8 by 3.47 inches). **Smallest egg** – goldcrest – 12 mm (0.48 inches). **Most abundant** breeding bird – wren – up to 15–20 million after a good breeding season and several mild winters. **Most widespread** breeding bird – skylark.

The nightjar (left) has become specially adapted to catch flying insects at night. It can open its mouth incredibly wide, and has whiskers on the side of its mouth which increase the capturing area still further. Few birds have such superb camouflage, essential for a creature that wishes to remain undetected in daylight

The puffin's bill may look ridiculous, but in fact it is of considerable benefit in the bird's social life, helping with courtship and with territory protection. It also enables the puffin to be an expert fisherman and an accomplished tunnel-digger

this habitat is still to be explored, so there are probably more species yet to be discovered. Sadly, tropical forest is the most endangered habitat in the world. Many species could be annihilated even before they are known to exist.

In contrast, the Antarctic Circle is home to only 11 breeding species . . . but then a bird has to be tough to live there. The emperor penguin is the only one which has truly mastered the Antarctic winter. It breeds in the winter when temperatures in the colonies can drop to as little as minus 58°F and winds can gust up to 186mph. Incubation is carried out by the male, who carefully rests the single egg on the top of his feet, allowing his pouch-like fold of abdominal skin to cover the egg, providing essential warmth. The same procedure is used to look after the chick once it has hatched.

FLIGHTLESS GIANTS

Birds come in all shapes and sizes. The heaviest bird ever to have lived was *Dromornis stirtoni*, a giant emu-like bird which weighed half a ton. It was one of a group of giant birds that were unique to Australia and lived over 15 million years ago. The ostrich is the world's heaviest bird alive today, weighing up to 156kg (345lbs) and standing up to 3m (nine feet) tall. It is now confined to the more arid areas of Africa where there are several advantages in being such a large bird. But, a bird that cannot fly needs adequate defence. Ostriches are well equipped for this – they have huge, strong legs and have been known to kill humans with just

one of their powerful kicks. Also, ostriches are very fast runners, reaching speeds of about 30mph which enables them to outrun some predators and cover great distances gathering food from a wide area.

THE OPPOSITE EXTREME

From the ridiculous to the sublime, the bee hummingbird, which weighs only 1.6g (0.056oz) and is less than two and a half inches long, is the smallest bird in the world today. It lives in Cuba and the Isle of Pines. It is thought that if it were any smaller it would probably not be able to eat enough to have the energy to feed in the first place. As it is, it must feed almost continuously to maintain its body weight.

THE LONG AND SHORT OF IT

Some birds are beautiful, some are fun, some are ugly and some are strange. But all are fascinating. The beautiful black-winged stilt is rather a strange-looking wader. Proportionately, it has the longest legs of any bird in the world – they make up 60 per cent of its body length. There is, of course, always a reason for such absurdities – the black-winged stilt's long legs enable it to feed in deeper water than other waders, allowing it to exploit a different food source from other waders. On dry land, however, the stilt has to bend its knees to feed, and brooding birds look very peculiar – their extra-long legs forming a large 'V' on either side. This bird is usually only an occasional visitor to Britain, but in 1987 it bred successfully for only the second time in this country.

The shortest legs in the world belong to the swift family. In fact, their legs are almost non-existent.

The family's Latin name, *Apodidae*, means 'lacking legs'. They are the most aerial of all birds and so their legs have become rather superfluous. The strong claws on their short legs do perform a useful function though, enabling the birds to cling to vertical surfaces such as cliffs.

The well-named sword-billed hummingbird has proportionally the longest bill in the world. It lives in Venezuela, Colombia and Bolivia and its bill, which is almost 125mm (five inches) long, is longer than the rest of its body. It has co-evolved with the climbing passion flower which has a corolla tube of 115mm (four and a half inches) and whose nectar the hummingbird exploits. When the hummingbird sticks its long bill into the corolla its forehead, beak and chin become dusted with pollen so that when the bird visits another flower of the same species cross-pollination takes place. This procedure is far better than insect-pollination for the climbing passion flower as hummingbirds outlive insects and travel greater distances.

The shortest bills in the world probably belong to those birds that have very wide gapes, such as the nightjars or swifts. The nightjar's wide mouth which is surrounded by strong bristles, enables it to catch insects in flight at night.

Extraordinarily long legs give the black-winged stilt the edge over other wading birds, since it can feed in much deeper water. It is a rare visitor to Britain, but a pair nested here in 1987

Feathers

EATHERS ARE WHAT make birds unique in the animal world. They are used for camouflage, for advertising, for insulation and for waterproofing. And, of course, without them a bird would not be able to fly.

Feathers come in different shapes and sizes. The largest belong to the crested argus pheasant whose tail feathers can be over 165cm (five and a half feet) long and over 12.5cm (five inches) wide. The smallest feathers are to be found on birds' eyelids.

The colours of feathers can be breathtaking – the iridescent blue of the kingfisher, the garish pink of the flamingo – and serve a whole range of useful purposes.

STRUCTURE

The feather probably developed from the scales of birds' reptile ancestors. Feathers are made from keratin, the same horny material that forms a reptile's scales. They are highly complex structures which combine both strength and lightness.

Feathers are really products of the birds' skin. The skin is made up of two parts – a thick, lower layer containing the blood vessels, muscles and nerves, and a top layer of cells which forms the epidermis. When the outer cells of the epidermis die they become filled with keratin – a feather is simply a mass of keratin sticking together.

The typical feather takes the form of a shaft and a vane, or web. The central shaft, or quill, is made up of two parts – a hollow, cylindrical section at the base called the calamus and a solid, angular shaft called the rachis. The rachis supports the vane on either side. A row of small branches makes up the vane – these small branches are called barbs and they are set at an angle which is inclined towards the tip of the feather. Branching from each barb are two sets of barbules which support barbicels. There are hooked barbules and spoon-shaped barbules. The hooks fit into the grooves of the spoon-shaped barbules and this gives the feather its strength and maintains its shape.

KINDS OF FEATHERS

There are several kinds of feathers. The main ones are the contour feathers, those on the head and body that give the bird its outline. Downy feathers have no rachis; this helps to give them their loose, fluffy texture – they usually lie under the contour feathers and provide insulation. Semi-plumes do have a rachis, but they do not have a firm vane. They are usually shorter than the contour feathers and they, too, provide insulation. Filo-plumes are usually thin, hair-like feathers which are very specialised and may be sensory. Bristles occur around the beak, nostrils and eyes of many birds. Long bristles around the beak in effect enlarge the mouth and so help the bird to capture flying insects. Those about the nose may act as a sift, purifying the air that the bird breathes.

Primary feathers are flight feathers which are attached to the hand (manus) of the wing and secondaries are flight feathers which are attached to the forearm (ulna). These are collectively known as remiges. Each wing feather quill is covered at its base on the upper side of the wing by a greater covert. From the greater coverts to the leading edge of the spread wing are successive rows of smaller and smaller feathers – middle or median coverts, lesser coverts and marginal coverts. Coverts on the underside of the wing are arranged in a similar manner but are less fully developed.

The large feathers of the tail are called rectrices. They are usually of even number. The rectrices are overlain by greater and lesser upper-tail coverts above and a few undertail coverts.

COLOUR

The variety of colour in feathers is produced by pigments such as melanins, carotenoids and porphyrins. Males are often more brightly coloured than females, especially in the breeding season. This is for use in courtship displays and to show aggression to other males. Females are often much duller because their role is usually to incubate and care for the young – it is essential for them to be well-camouflaged. This sort of colouring is known as 'cryptic'. The opposite form to cryptic colouring is 'phaneric' – conspicuous colouring. Uniformly white birds, such as swans and egrets, or uniformly black birds, such as crows, are outstandingly conspicuous. Occasionally, such birds will fluff up their feathers to give the appearance of greater size and ferocity to potential intruders.

Iridescent colours, such as the colourful gloss on a starling or lapwing, are created in two ways: either by the structure of the feather's surface breaking up the light, or by reflections from grains of pigment inside the feather.

FEATHER CARE

It is very important that a bird's feathers are looked after well – its very survival could depend on their condition. A bird does this by preening, 'zipping' the barbs of the feathers together with its beak.

The bird also uses its beak to remove dirt or parasites, and conditions its plumage by using organic oil which it gets from a gland above the root of its tail. A bird may use its feet to clean parts that it cannot otherwise reach such as its head and bill.

Feathers are often warmed in the sun to 'iron out' any twists (especially obvious in big birds of prey) and bathing in shallow water is common. The bird splashes about, flapping its wings and moving its bill from side to side, and its head and breast are often dipped into the water. Dust-bathing is another habit. Fine particles of dry earth or sand are forced through the bird's plumage and it is thought that this helps it to deal with the many parasites that occur in its feathers.

MOULT

Feathers have a limited life – they wear out and need to be replaced. So they are periodically shed and renewed. This is known as moulting. All birds moult at least once a year. Usually the moult occurs after breeding and before migration when brand new feathers are an advantage. Some birds, such as ducks, geese and swans, lose all their flight feathers at once, which makes them flightless for some time. Many feathers are used for display purposes – these obviously have to be renewed for the maximum effect in the following breeding season.

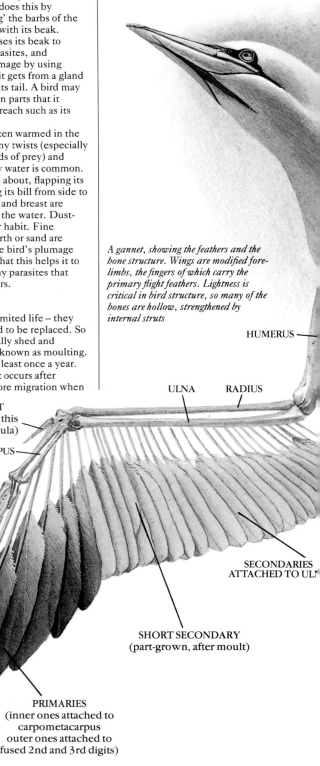

A gannet, showing the feathers and the bone structure. Wings are modified fore-limbs, the fingers of which carry the primary flight feathers. Lightness is critical in bird structure, so many of the bones are hollow, strengthened by internal struts

HUMERUS

ULNA   RADIUS

FIRST DIGIT (feathers from this make up the Alula)

CARPOMETACARPUS

SECONDARIES ATTACHED TO ULN[

SHORT SECONDARY (part-grown, after moult)

MINUTE OUTERMOST PRIMARY

PRIMARIES (inner ones attached to carpometacarpus outer ones attached to fused 2nd and 3rd digits)

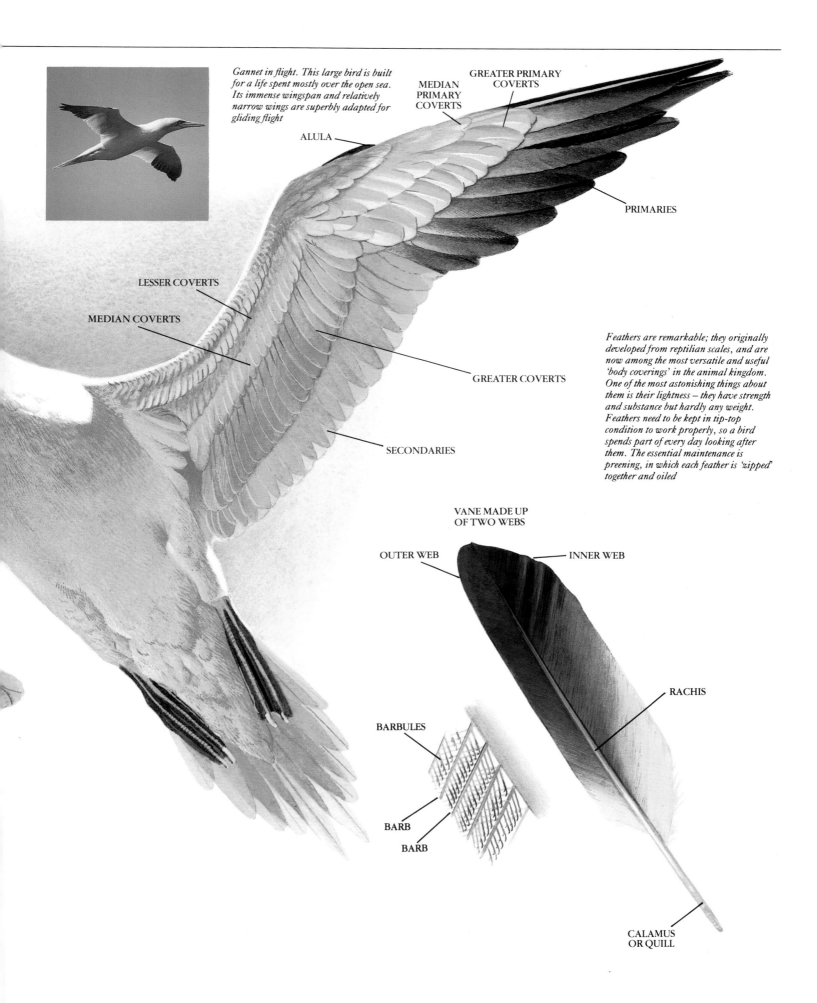

Gannet in flight. This large bird is built for a life spent mostly over the open sea. Its immense wingspan and relatively narrow wings are superbly adapted for gliding flight

GREATER PRIMARY COVERTS

MEDIAN PRIMARY COVERTS

ALULA

PRIMARIES

LESSER COVERTS

MEDIAN COVERTS

GREATER COVERTS

SECONDARIES

Feathers are remarkable; they originally developed from reptilian scales, and are now among the most versatile and useful 'body coverings' in the animal kingdom. One of the most astonishing things about them is their lightness – they have strength and substance but hardly any weight. Feathers need to be kept in tip-top condition to work properly, so a bird spends part of every day looking after them. The essential maintenance is preening, in which each feather is 'zipped' together and oiled

VANE MADE UP OF TWO WEBS

OUTER WEB

INNER WEB

RACHIS

BARBULES

BARB

BARB

CALAMUS OR QUILL

THROUGHOUT HISTORY MAN has envied birds' ability to fly, and many attempts have been made to experience the freedom of the skies. Only recently have we been able to join birds in the air, but only the most expert hang-glider can match even part of the ability of a bird.

Birds fly to reach feeding and roosting places, to escape from predators, to display to potential mates or rivals, to seek a nest site and, it seems, just for fun. Flight allows many birds to exploit food that is out of reach of mammals and, by migrating, to exploit seasonally abundant food supplies.

Flight is very strenuous. Birds have improved their breathing and circulatory systems and reduced their weight in order to produce enough energy to fly efficiently. Their hearts are large, their lungs tremendously powerful, their body temperature high for rapid combustion of fuel, their bones light, often honeycombed, but strong.

Wings are complex, able to spread, fold, flap and twist. Flight feathers provide an unbroken surface which-ever way the wing is folded or warped unless the bird itself wishes to separate them and 'lose' air between their vanes. Tails may add an extra aerofoil, or act as rudders.

TYPES OF FLIGHT

Flapping flight is hard, energy-sapping work. Wing-beats vary with the intention of the bird – taking off, landing, turning – but have a rowing, even figure-of-eight action rather than a simple up-down flap. To save energy a bird can glide, sailing along on outstretched wings. All birds do this to some extent but small ones usually glide very little, whereas some large ones are expert gliders. They take advantage of wind to keep them in the air without flapping their wings, or use the momentum from bursts of active flight to move forwards.

In hot places vultures and others use thermals – rising bubbles of warm air – to carry them aloft and can travel great distances which would be impossible with laborious flapping flight. Such specialised gliding is called soaring.

Birds like the kestrel and terns can maintain position in the air while looking for prey – movements of the body are cancelled out by the flexible neck so that the head, and therefore the eyes, remain motionless relative to the ground. This is called hovering. Gliding, soaring and hovering are strictly speaking quite distinct activities.

WING DESIGN

When a bird flaps its wings it produces lift to keep it in the air and forward thrust to carry it along. A large muscle, the pectoralis, pulls the wing downwards (the deep breastbone and large chest of a pigeon shows its flapping power) and a much smaller muscle, aided by the bird's own weight against the air, pulls it back up. The wing has an aerofoil shape, like an aeroplane's, creating lift as air moves across it.

Different shapes and sizes of wing allow different types of flight so that each species can pursue its own role in life. The long, narrow wings of an albatross allow it to glide for hours on end on air currents rising over steep ocean waves, covering vast distances with little effort. The wandering albatross has a span of almost 4m (12 feet) – but it is not so elegant when it has to return to land to nest and arrives with a great thump!

GOING UP!

Vultures can reach great heights, from which they watch other vultures and scavengers and so detect the whereabouts of a meal. A Ruppell's griffon vulture reputedly collided with an aircraft at 37,000 feet, incredible in view of the intense cold and lack of oxygen at such a height, but certainly 10,000 feet or more must be a regular cruising altitude for such magnificent birds. Even very small birds migrate very high up, where thin air allows faster progress.

COPING WITH SIZE

The heaviest flying bird in Britain is the mute swan, big males at 13.5kg (30 pounds) or more almost getting as heavy as a flying bird can be. They need a long, clear runway across

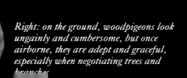

Right: on the ground, woodpigeons look ungainly and cumbersome, but once airborne, they are adept and graceful, especially when negotiating trees and branches.

water to get airborne, but once aloft are beautiful and graceful, their wings making a throbbing hum.

Condors are huge, vulture-like birds which can glide at very low speeds without falling from the sky, spreading their outermost (primary) wing feathers like fingers to reduce turbulence and lower their stalling speed, just like slots in the wings of an aircraft. Should higher speed be needed, they can close the slots by bending the wing. Even tiny birds like warblers have tapered feather tips (called notches and emarginations) of a constant pattern for each species and useful for identifying difficult birds 'in the hand'.

THE FASTEST FLIERS

It is commonly thought that small birds such as swifts fly fastest. The swift, however, despite its perfect aerodynamic shape, catches insects in flight and needs precision rather than speed, and actually flies quite slowly when feeding, but it reaches high speeds in its madcap, round-the-houses displays.

Some of the fastest fliers are ducks, which can move at a great rate, with tremendous roaring from their wings, downwind. The eider is recorded as flying as fast as any bird in direct, steady flight and has the strong wings and muscles needed to face the gusty winds so prevalent on the coasts where it lives.

Hummingbirds have the fastest wing-beats – at least 90 every second. They can tilt their bodies almost vertically and flap their wings backwards and forwards rather than up and down, to keep them in a steady hover while they feed – and they can even fly backwards!

Short, stubby wings allow forest dwellers like tanagers and finches to swerve and dodge through undergrowth. Sparrowhawks have shortish wings and long tails for speed and manoeuvrability in woodland. Peregrines have long wings for fast flight in the open and sweep them back to reach high speeds in a steep dive – the 'stoop' onto prey can be at over 110 mph and exceeds the speed in level flight.

LONG-DISTANCE TRAVEL

Flight allows birds to migrate fast. Migrant mammals move large distances in long, laborious treks, but birds can cover thousands of miles in a few days and take advantage of all that the world offers in terms of food and breeding sites.

The greatest traveller is the arctic tern, breeding in the far north as far as northern Greenland and moving south to the Antarctic Ocean. It can rest on the sea and feed as it goes. After months of ocean travel it returns north for the brief summer and spends both the northern and the southern summers in almost perpetual daylight. Yet the performance of tiny warblers, flying from Europe to Africa south of the Sahara in one go, or the tiny waifs like blackpoll warblers that cross from North America to Europe by mistake, is still more astonishing.

The amount of energy used on these vast journeys is prodigious, but the advantages to the species must be worth the effort and risk involved to the individual.

FINDING HOME

The ability to navigate is even more fascinating than the need to migrate. It is easy to suggest means of finding direction – birds use the stars, sun and moon and even the earth's magnetic field – but man still has no idea how a bird knows where it is on the surface of the earth. If a bird is carried away in a box and released far from its territory, it will fly back home. We can say how it knows which direction is north, east or west – but how can it possibly know which direction to choose?

GROUNDED

The oddest thing about some birds is that they cannot fly at all. For large species like the ostrich, size is an

Main picture: little owl. Taking-off and landing require great skill and co-ordination. When landing, the bird has to slow down without stalling. A group of feathers called the alula, which is attached to the bird's thumb, on the fore-edge of the wing, is specially designed to prevent this happening.

advantage and outweighs the need to fly, especially when they can run at 30 mph to escape from predators. The penguins are adapted to 'fly' underwater using their flipper-like wings, but had to give up aerial flight in order to perfect the technique. The amount of fat they need to survive in extreme cold makes them too heavy anyway.

Unfortunately, some species simply lost the power of flight because it was no longer necessary in the absence of predators on isolated islands. This misplaced faith in the world around them has proved their undoing in the end. Humans introduced rats and cats – and many of these fascinating birds have become extinct or are severely threatened today.

Beaks

A BIRD'S BEAK, or bill, is an extension of its jaw. It has two parts – the upper and lower mandibles – both covered in a horny, protective layer of skin. Like a human's, the lower jaw can move, but the upper is fixed to the skull, though some birds have flexibility in the upper mandible.

The nostrils are usually found in the upper mandible – clearly visible on birds like gulls and ducks, but hidden by bristly feathers on crows and tits. Some, such as the fulmar, have a separate tube on top of the bill through which they breathe. They are known as tubenoses because of this feature. Birds of prey, parrots and pigeons have a fleshy area around the nostrils at the base of the bill, called a cere.

Because it dives headlong into the sea and needs to keep water out of its lungs, the gannet has no nostrils but breathes through its mouth.

BEAKS FOR EVERYTHING

Bills are used for nest-building, preening, eating, even as weapons; and they may have special shapes and colours that are used in display.

The first use is to break out of the egg shell, when a chick uses an egg-tooth, a small, hard growth which falls off soon after hatching.

The main purpose of the bill is to aid feeding. Many sizes and shapes allow birds to feed in different places on different kinds of food.

Herons, egrets and bitterns have dagger-like bills for seizing, not spearing, fast-moving prey in water. The red-breasted merganser holds on to fish as well, but has a saw-edge on its bill to help it.

Wading birds have probing bills of various lengths. Some are straight; some curve upwards; some curve downwards. These variations allow food to be picked from mud or sand, scooped up from shallow water or pulled from deep mud, and several species can live together without competing for the same food because they eat creatures from different levels within mud or water. Food can be detected in deep mud, then grasped, because the bill tip is sensitive and flexible.

LITTLE BEAKS

Small, insect-eating birds such as warblers and flycatchers have small, slender bills, often with bristles around the base to increase the size of the open mouth, or gape, to help catch insects. The treecreeper probes for food in crevices in tree bark and has a thin, curved bill that is best for the job. Swallows and swifts, and the nocturnal nightjar, have tiny bills but huge mouths which they use for catching flying insects while they themselves are airborne.

Then there are the small, seed-eating birds – the finches and sparrows, whose strong, stubby beaks are used to crack open seeds.

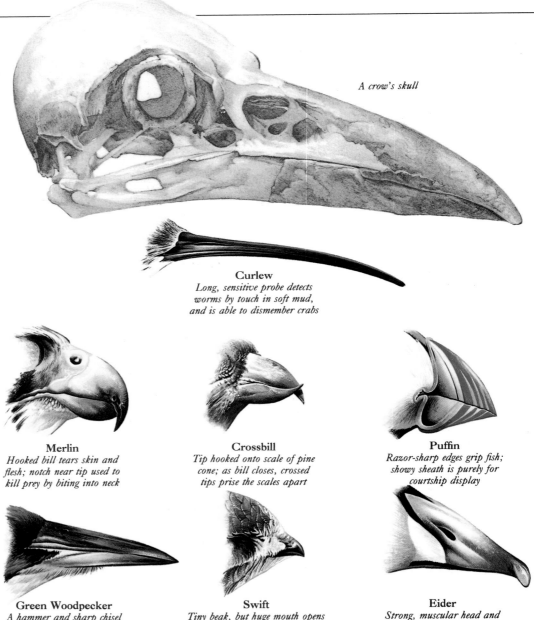

A crow's skull

Curlew
Long, sensitive probe detects worms by touch in soft mud, and is able to dismember crabs

Merlin
Hooked bill tears skin and flesh; notch near tip used to kill prey by biting into neck

Crossbill
Tip hooked onto scale of pine cone; as bill closes, crossed tips prise the scales apart

Puffin
Razor-sharp edges grip fish; showy sheath is purely for courtship display

Green Woodpecker
A hammer and sharp chisel for breaking into wood and digging into ants' nests

Swift
Tiny beak, but huge mouth opens back under eye; bristles enlarge 'trawl' for catching flies

Eider
Strong, muscular head and hooked bill crack open crabs and assorted shellfish

A variety of bird beaks, with the skull of a crow to show the structure

The inside of the beak of several species has a series of interlocking grooves and ridges, to hold seeds firmly while they are crushed, or while they are rolled with the tongue in order to remove unwanted husks.

MUSICAL BEAKS

Woodpeckers have strong bills, cushioned by spongy bone at the base to take the shock of the impact against wood when they are excavating nest holes or bashing off pieces of bark to look for insects underneath. They also use their bills to 'drum' instead of singing – rattling them hard and incredibly fast against a dead branch to produce a resonant, penetrating, drumming noise.

Highly specialised for feeding is the beak of the crossbill – it is literally crossed at the tip. It is used to prise open scales of pine cones so the tongue can scoop out the seeds.

Birds of prey use their bills to tear food. This may be anything from an insect or lizard to a fish or a live mammal, or a carcase of a dead animal. Live prey is caught in the feet; birds like eagles and hawks kill with their strong grip and long claws, but falcons, with a 'notch' in the bill, kill by biting into the victim's neck.

ALL-PURPOSE BEAKS

The puffin has a huge, brightly-coloured bill used to attract a mate, fight off intruders, dig a nest burrow and catch and transport small fish. It holds fish under its tongue while collecting more with its upper mandible. The bright sheath of the bill is shed in winter when display is no longer needed.

A bird's bill is used almost as a human would use a hand. It can carry twigs, weave strips of leaves into nests, preen feathers delicately and place food into the mouth of a chick; but it can also be a weapon.

In small birds the inside of the chick's beak is often brightly coloured or patterned with coloured spots to attract the attention of the parent and stimulate feeding. In other species, such as the herring gull, the parent's bill is marked (in the gull's case with a red spot) and the chick pecks at it to make the parent cough up a meal.

Bills are used in courtship and display and birds may appear to be kissing as they caress bills and feed each other – all part of the process of keeping the relationship of a breeding pair strong and productive.

Feet

BIRDS USE THEIR feet like humans do – for walking and balance – but they are far more versatile than ours. They take on some of the functions of hands in some species, but remain less dextrous in most.

Birds use their feet to cling and climb, to perch on twigs and wires, to dig, to swim and even to kill other animals. A few grasp food while they peck it or lift it to the bill, like parrots.

Like its bill, a bird's foot has adapted to fit in with its way of life, which depends on the habitats where it lives, feeds and breeds. Some feet are covered with feathers or bristles, others with scales, others with leathery skin.

No bird has more than four toes; some have fewer. Usually they have three toes pointing forward and one back.

The swift has all four pointing forwards on its tiny feet, enabling it to cling to rocks and walls. Most of the owl family can turn their outer toe backwards to help them grasp their prey. Woodpeckers have the outer toe more permanently turned back, to give a two-forward two-back format, but the outer one often points out to one side to give a wider grasp on a rounded branch. Kingfishers have the third and fourth toes partly joined, helping them dig out their long nesting burrows.

Birds which run swiftly have fewer toes to lessen the contact made with the ground. The ostrich has only two toes, one scarcely developed, but both have a soft cushion beneath to soften the impact as it runs and to help prevent sinking into soft sand.

CLAWS

The claws on a bird's foot are also highly specialised. Long, curved, sharp ones help the treecreeper in its mouse-like progression up a tree trunk. Stronger, curved talons give a sure grip to birds of prey, and their long toes, especially on bird-eating species, give an extended reach to help them catch their food.

Those birds which feed on the ground and scratch about for seeds have short, strong, blunt claws. Long hind claws help small, running birds like larks and pipits balance as they slip through grass stems.

The jacana, or lilytrotter, a moorhen-like wader with long, spindly legs, has enormously long toes which distribute its weight evenly over floating leaves and prevent it sinking.

Claws and toes are also used for scratching and preening and, as in the heron with its comb-like claw, may be especially adapted for that purpose.

THREE TYPES OF FEET

Within all this variety, there are three main types of feet. They are perching feet, those adapted for walking and wading and those adapted for swimming.

PERCHING

Perching birds include the vast majority of small birds, which have a special tendon along the back of the leg which tightens the toes as the leg is bent, so automatically keeping the bird on its perch as it sleeps. Birds of prey and others also have feet of the same basic design. The osprey has special spines on the soles of its feet to help it grip slippery fish.

WALKING AND WADING

A foot designed for walking and wading does not have the strong grip for perching on a twig, and may even be webbed and lack the hind toe. Webbed feet have the toes joined by a thin membrane. Most waders have long legs and large feet with long, independent toes but a few have complete or partial webs which help on soft mud. As webs prevent a bird sinking into mud, so the feathers on the foot of a ptarmigan act like a snowshoe to stop it sinking into snow.

SWIMMING

Feet adapted for swimming are similar to those webbed feet of waders, but are attached to shorter, stronger legs. Gulls have all-purpose webbed feet on quite long and mobile legs. The ducks, geese and seabirds use their webbed feet as strong paddles for swimming. But grebes and coots swim well with toes equipped with rows of flaps of skin which push against the water on the back stroke but fold neatly out of the way on the forward stroke. To increase their efficiency, they have blade-like legs which present little drag when pushed through the water.

Most webbed feet have just the front three toes joined by two webs, but the cormorants, pelicans and gannets have all four toes joined by webs to give the perfect foot for strong forward propulsion.

COLD FEET!

It might be thought that bare legs would present problems to a bird in cold weather. However, their circulation is controlled so that little blood moves through the legs and feet and heat loss is kept to a minimum. If it is really cold, then the bird can stand on one leg, with the other tucked into its warm belly feathers, or sit down to cover both legs. In flight the coot usually trails its big foot, but in extreme cold will tuck them into its feathers. On the other hand, in extreme heat blood can be pumped into the legs and feet and these are then exposed to the air to increase cooling. Vultures and others often fly with dangling feet to cool off on a hot day. Vultures will even excrete onto their own legs to increase evaporative cooling!

The feet are also used more deliberately in flight to help steer and, more obviously, to help brake before landing – the feet-forward position of a gannet is a classic example of a bird using its air brakes to full effect.

Each species of bird has the design of foot best suited to its lifestyle. So, for example, no perching bird has webbed feet, and no duck or gull has great talons such as birds of prey have

Curlew
Wading in water and walking on dry land requires long legs but unspecialised feet

Merlin
Long toes with rough soles and needle-sharp claws help catch and hold live prey in mid-air

Crossbill
Typical perching foot with extra strength for gripping pine cones while feeding

The skeletal structure of a crow's foot

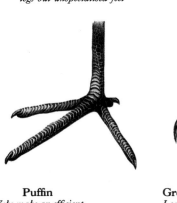

Puffin
Webs make an efficient paddle for swimming; sharp, curved claws help in digging burrow

Green Woodpecker
Long outer toe points back or sideways to improve grip on upright, rounded branch

Swift
All four toes point forwards, so proper perching is impossible; just clings to rough surfaces

Eider
Short, strong leg with broad web between toes ideal for swimming in surging sea

Eggs and nests

A CREATURE THAT flies must weigh as little as possible. Being pregnant would be an impossible burden, so eggs enable birds to have their pregnancies outside their bodies. This allows birds to search for food and escape from predators – to survive. Birds are not the only animals to lay eggs, however – they share this ability with reptiles, amphibians, fish and insects.

An egg basically consists of a yolk, which provides nourishment for the developing chick, the albumen, or egg-white, which protects the embryo, and a tough shell, which protects the egg from damage.

Birds' eggs come in all shapes, sizes and colours. Their shells have to be very strong, but weak enough for the chick to break through from inside. Most eggs are well-camouflaged – their colours and patterns cleverly blending into the background.

Usually the size of the egg is related to the size of the bird. The mute swan lays Britain's largest egg – approximately 120 × 80mm (four and a half inches by three) – and the goldcrest lays the smallest – approximately 12mm long (half an inch by under two-fifths).

A group of eggs is called a clutch. Most species lay one clutch each season and clutch sizes depend on the number of young which can successfully be raised.

INCUBATION

It is essential that eggs are kept warm once they have been laid. The parent birds do this by sitting on the eggs – this is known as incubation. For the eggs to develop properly, a high, even temperature is essential. Most birds develop a brood patch, an area on the breast that loses its feathers and develops a rich supply of blood vessels.

A PLACE FOR THE EGGS

Every bird needs a safe place to lay its eggs – somewhere that provides protection from the environment and from predators. The typical nest is usually a cup-shaped structure delicately woven with pieces of twigs or other vegetation. But a nest need only be a scrape in the ground, a cliff ledge, a hole in a tree or a burrow in the soil. So a nest should properly be described as the place where eggs are laid and remain until they hatch. It is *not* the equivalent of a 'house' because it is only used for holding the eggs and (frequently) chicks. Some species roost in nests at times, however, especially in winter.

The young of birds that lay their eggs in scrapes or on bare ground usually leave the nest at once – they are known as nidifugous and are covered in well-camouflaged down as soon as they hatch. Those that are produced in well-protected nests are known as nidicolous – they remain within the security of the nest until they can fly. Nidicolous chicks are naked and blind when they hatch, and extremely vulnerable.

TERRITORIES

During the breeding season, most birds have territories which they defend avidly. It is usually the male bird that takes on this role. The size of territories varies considerably between different species. One of the advantages of having a territory is that it spreads birds of the same species evenly across large areas, reducing competition for food.

In contrast, many seabirds live in densely-packed colonies. Their territories are not related to the source of food as they feed from the sea where plenty is available for all. These birds' territories are often no more than a small circle around their nest which the parent bird can defend by a jab of its bill.

Coal tit nests are most likely to be in holes in the ground or in tree-holes, but the one above was built in a dustbin! The long-tailed tit's nest (below left) is a marvel of delicate construction; little wonder it sometimes takes 20 days to build. The oystercatcher (below) goes to the other extreme. Its nest is virtually non-existent, but the eggs are almost invisible among the pebbles that surround it

Bird Families

Swallow

The following pages show why it is important to be able to sort birds into their family groupings, and gives practical advice on distinguishing birds in different settings. Also here is an introduction to bird distribution and a look at man's relationship with birds

Bird families

ALL BIRD BOOKS and birdwatchers talk about birds by putting them into categories of one kind or another. It is useful to understand what these are. Without them, birds and other animals would seem to be in a chaotic state, and a book like this would be impossible.

Individual birds vary, and no doubt to other birds they are as recognisable as individual people are to us. But, to our eyes, the variations are so subtle that essentially they are identical within certain groups. Any male blackbird looks much the same as any other male blackbird; an adult grey heron looks just like any other adult grey heron. If they did not, it would be difficult to identify anything.

In addition, many bird species have differing plumages for males and females, young and old, even summer and winter. A framework builds up, within which the birds can be placed. Not only can a particular bird be identified – for instance, a green woodpecker; it can be identified as an adult, or a one-year-old, a male or female – just by looking at it. Many gulls have such a sequence of plumages that they can be distinguished as being one or two or three years old, or older, and in breeding plumage or non-breeding plumage, though sex may be difficult to tell.

It is clear that birds in the garden, in a wood, or on an estuary are not simply random variations of 'bird' but belong to separate species and can be categorised into one of several groups according to age, sex and season. What is most remarkable is that any one of any particular group will look almost exactly the same as another of the same sort. It is amazing how constant colour and pattern can be, throughout millions of birds, over thousands of miles and thousands of years. This gives the basis for any bird identification book and allows expert birdwatchers to 'put a name' to every bird in sight.

SPECIES OR VARIETY?

The idea of *species* has already been introduced. The species concept is an attempt to put living things into 'natural' groups and, for the most part, works very well. Cat, dog, horse, cow, daisy, bluebell, blackbird, robin – all are species. A species is a 'kind' of plant or animal, that is separated from other kinds by being unable to interbreed with them or at least unable to produce fertile young. So the dog is a species, being unable to interbreed with, say, a cat; but alsatian, spaniel, corgi and all other kinds of dogs are simply varieties. Birds of different kinds as discussed in this book are not simply varieties of bird. They are species in their own right. A blue tit will not interbreed with a great tit any more than a cat will mate with a monkey; a curlew is as separate from a godwit as a horse is from a cow.

Species are, however, put together in larger groupings – called families, orders and so on – which leads to misunderstandings. There are often newspaper stories about a 'threatened species' like 'the owl' or 'the dragonfly'. There are, of course, many different species of owls and dragonflies, some threatened, some very common.

ADULT MALE, SUMMER . . .

So now it is possible to put any bird into a number of categories. We can first of all try to tell what species it is, its sex, its age, and its internal condition related to the breeding cycle (which shows through the growth of 'summer' or 'winter' plumage). This may seem very elementary, but it should be clearly understood before going any further.

READ THE CLUES

By learning a little about the species and family groups, we can add a great deal to our birdwatching. Firstly, look at the names written *in italics* after each English bird name in the identification pages of this book. They are based on Latin or Greek words and provide a unique, international name for every living organism. We may talk about a 'robin', but in America or Africa 'robin' means a quite different bird. But *Erithacus rubecula* can mean nothing else but our familiar garden favourite. Now look at the names of the thrushes. The blackbird has an English name that gives no indication that it is closely related – through the history of its evolution – to the song thrush and the fieldfare. But their scientific names all begin with the same word – *Turdus* – which means that all are in the same *genus* and therefore in the same family. Their different second names – *merula*, *philomelos* and *pilaris* – give each a unique combination. By looking carefully at these names it is possible to learn a lot about the relationships of birds (see pp382–384).

They are arranged in a scientific order, rather than a random list, so that species that are closely related – that is, having the same ancestors – are placed together. The list starts with the most primitive birds and ends with the most recent in the development of the evolutionary tree. The main identification pages of this book start with some primitive sea and water birds, such as divers, grebes, petrels and shearwaters, and move on to the finches and buntings that come last in the list, the most recently evolved of all.

Why, then, are grebes not put near the ducks – or the coot? They all swim about on water and feed in similar ways, and they can be hard to tell apart. And why are swifts not next to swallows? They could have been listed close together in this book, making it easier, perhaps, to compare birds that look the same. But that would be to ignore their true relationships. Grebes are *not* ducks; swifts are *not* swallows, and it is better to understand the differences from the start than to put them artificially close in the order. That way, their biology and many facets of behaviour can be appreciated and help identification, and 'classification' – this process of putting order into the birds around us – becomes both useful and fun.

Birds of a feather . . . . left to right are long-tailed tit, blue tit, great tit, coal tit, marsh tit, willow tit and crested tit, with another blue tit at the top of the page

Birds in time and space

Today's pattern of bird distribution is, in effect, a pattern frozen in a moment of time. 'Distribution' is far from a static thing, being the result of millions of years of continuous change. The pattern will change a little during our own lifetimes and the process will continue for as long as there are birds around.

Many factors combine to produce this ever-changing pattern, all of them revolving around a species' evolutionary success – how it has responded to all manner of environmental changes, either long-term or of more immediate impact. How adaptable has a species been, how competitive, or how mobile? What strategies does it have for relating to its food supply, its neighbours, or its predators? Has it been influenced by long-term changes in climatic conditions, or is it affected by short-term weather fluctuations? In the more distant past, what major changes in the earth's physical form (for instance, continents drifting apart, or the formation of isolated islands) have affected its distribution?

THE NEED TO BREED AND EAT

The whole pattern is a very complex one, but it can be simplified by looking at it in terms of the two most fundamental needs of all birds – a reliable source of food, and somewhere to breed successfully. The second is, of course, also totally dependent on the first.

Birds like razorbills and guillemots, for example, require rich supplies of sea food – mainly small fish – so their distribution is governed by its availability: in winter, they are widely dispersed in offshore waters, but in summer they must find suitable nesting places (large ones, since they are highly colonial) close to good fishing grounds. They find these things in parts of northern and western Britain

wherever cliffs and rocky islands coincide with a nearby concentration of food. Red grouse are limited by the presence of heather, their main source of food, so their pattern of distribution is closely linked to that of extensive heather moorland – it is modified, however, by the way in which man treats this habitat: he may destroy it entirely, in various ways, or manage it specifically for the grouse, which is an important quarry species for the sportsman.

EXPANSION THROUGH VERSATILITY

Auks and red grouse are not particularly adaptable birds, so their distribution will always relate to their very specific requirements. On the other hand, some species are clearly much more versatile and this enables them to be altogether more widespread. Those species of gulls that feed inland, on refuse tips or on agricultural land, as well as at the coast where they eat all sorts of scraps as well as fish, are good examples. The tawny owl provides a classic example of this versatility. Originally a woodland bird, feeding principally on small mammals, it has been able to move into many other habitats as well – parks, gardens, squares in towns and cities and so on. Where there is not a good supply of small mammals, it simply switches to other prey, usually small birds. Its distribution, then, shows that it is a successful species – resourceful and adaptable.

THE RISKS OF SPECIALISATION

Being non-adaptable can mean a failure to survive when habitat is destroyed. The present British distribution of the Dartford warbler, for instance, reflects the large-scale disappearance and fragmentation of

its main habitat – the southern heathlands. When they go, it goes too. Many other birds – those heavily dependent on reed beds, for example – also have limited distributions, or recently reduced distributions due to the activities of man.

On the other hand, man has the ability to change distribution for the better by creating or modifying habitats, or by managing the land in an appropriate way. It was imaginative wetland management by the RSPB which restored the avocet as a British breeding bird and led to its expansion and increase; there are numerous other examples. Equally, the provision of nest sites may alter things very markedly – numbers of pied flycatchers breeding in western oak woods where nestboxes have been provided for them have increased significantly, and nestboxes have gained us a new and rapidly increasing breeding species – the goldeneye.

CONTROLLED BY FOOD

The existence of suitable habitat, however it comes about, obviously affects the numbers and distribution of all species, even if some are clearly more catholic than others. But why are some, like birds of prey, so much less numerous than others? The answer lies in the food supply: it is a basic 'rule of nature' that any creature's numbers are primarily governed by its food resources – not vice-versa. Thus, bird predators do not 'control' the numbers of their prey species but are controlled by them. It follows that birds of prey must be much scarcer than their prey species – if they were not, they would soon exhaust their food resources and perish.

Food supplies can fail for various reasons, though – either through severe weather, or through one of the many periodic fluctuations they undergo, often in themselves food-related. Such failures can produce dramatic short-term changes in distribution. Waxwings, for example,

may have had a bumper breeding season, with good weather and excellent food supplies, only to find this coinciding with a failure afterwards in the berry crop in their normal winter quarters. This means large numbers of birds facing a crisis: they solve it by 'erupting' – migrating away to better areas of winter food and producing an 'invasion' in these new areas. Similar things happen when the food-related population cycles of small mammals, such as voles, reach a low point – the raptors and owls which thrived on them while numbers were high have to move out in search of new winter quarters or, if it is the breeding season, adjust to laying fewer eggs, rearing smaller families or not breeding at all.

SHORT-TERM MOVEMENTS

Seasonal changes in distribution are commonplace. Locally, or in the short term, they can be caused by harsh weather, but every year they occur regularly through the phenomenon of bird migration. Migration is all about birds moving into areas of rich and appropriate food supplies and good nesting places for the breeding season and then going elsewhere for the winter – because the breeding areas are no longer suitable. Thus, we see millions of insect-eaters (swifts, swallows, martins, warblers, flycatchers, etc) moving into Britain in summer, but having to migrate south to warmer climes in winter, simply because they cannot survive without insect food. Unlike some resident species – robins and blackbirds, for instance – they cannot switch to a different food resource and stay put. Similarly, winter brings hordes of wildfowl, waders and thrushes which cannot find suitable breeding conditions in Britain but do very well on our winter estuaries, or wetlands, or berry-laden hedgerows and gardens. Still other migrants, both in spring and autumn, come and go in large numbers, using our islands as stop-overs on their long movements northwards or southwards.

Distribution, then, is constantly changing, often within well-established patterns. In the longer term, there have been changes probably related to more subtle factors – like climatic change. This has probably been responsible for bringing in northern colonists like breeding redwings and fieldfares, or birds which are spreading and increasing elsewhere like Cetti's warbler. Sometimes, changing distribution involves something truly remarkable – consider the case of the collared dove, unknown here 35 years ago but now very common in many places – all the result of an amazing range expansion westwards from south-east Europe which began earlier this century. Now what caused *that* to happen . . . ?

Birds by lake and stream

SIT BESIDE A gravel pit in the autumn, and you will see a whole variety of species swimming about on the water or dabbling at its edges. In all probability they will belong to several families. Why are they not all ducks?

Out in the open, frequently slipping quietly under the water, are long-necked birds with pinkish beaks and dark caps. They have glistening white necks and sometimes roll over sideways to preen the belly feathers, showing equally white undersides. These are not ducks, despite the way that they swim and dive. They are great crested grebes – if anything even more tied to a watery environment than most of the ducks themselves. Nearby may be a smaller, darker bird, with the same basic round-bodied shape and with no obvious tail, just a fluffy rear-end. This is the little grebe, or dabchick.

The grebes do not have the flattened, broad bills of most ducks – theirs are slim and pointed. Nor do they have webbed feet – they have lobed toes which fold back into a blade shape on the forward stroke but open out against the water on the backward stroke, making the grebe a powerful swimmer. Grebes build nests of weed on water or anchored among reeds, never hidden away in deep, dry grass, as are ducks' nests. When they leave the nest grebes often cover their eggs with damp weed to hide them. Their young are fed feathers to help them digest fish bones, and they may be carried on their parents' backs.

Grebes rarely come to land. Their legs are set very far back on the body, fine for swimming, but hopeless for walking. They have complicated courtship behaviour, quite unlike anything ducks perform. And in flight they look out of their element, long necks sticking out in front and big feet trailing behind – not like ducks at all.

ROUND AND BLACK

Black, round-backed birds will be coots – swimming, diving, grabbing bits of weed in their beaks, but quite unlike the true ducks. They have lobed feet, like the grebes', but deep, short beaks adapted to feeding on water weeds and grass. They are related to the rails and crakes, and the moorhen is a close cousin. Moorhens have long, thin toes for wading and pattering across floating lily leaves, and they have longer, uptilted tails. They are never confident enough on the water to roll over and preen like ducks and grebes; nor do they sit up on their tails to flap their wings like ducks. Coots often mix with flocks of ducks on water, but moorhens rarely do so. Both are unwieldy in flight, and make sharp, discordant sounds rather than musical whistles and quacks.

UP TAILS ALL

Apart from the white swans, and the long-necked, large-bodied, honking geese, the rest may indeed be ducks! These are swimmers and divers, with males and females recognisably different. Two main groups stand out – dabbling and diving ducks. The first feed from the surface, from floating or bankside vegetation, or even well away from water. They have broad, flattened bills that pluck grasses and leaves, or sieve through water that contains floating seeds and tiny water creatures. The bill has a fine mesh-like structure that lets the water out but keeps the food in – rather like having a mouthful of cornflakes and squeezing the milk out between your closed teeth. Quite good at walking, they have rather centrally placed legs; they swim with their tails held clear of the water. Often they tilt over to submerge the front half of the body, with the tail sticking upwards - 'up-ending'.

The males – drakes – are brightly coloured from early winter until mid summer, then, with no need for mate or territory, go into a dull plumage called the 'eclipse'. All have a patch of colour at the back of the wing called the 'speculum'. Most of the females quack. They spend a lot of time doing nothing – loafing – either on the water or out on a bank. If disturbed, they take flight instantly in a near-vertical take-off; they are fast and agile in flight, changing altitude and direction with ease.

Moorhen chicks have such a bizarre and exotic appearance that they could almost be taken for foreign rarities.

GETTING DEEPER

The diving ducks are more simply patterned, with rounder bodies and tails usually flattened along the water surface. They have a variety of bills according to their feeding habits. The most common ones eat roots, seeds or weeds, or slow-moving water creatures like snails, and have broad, stout bills, but the fish-eaters (mergansers and goosanders) have longer bills, with hooked tips and serrated edges to give a good grip; they are called sawbills. These look more streamlined, more grebe-like, though much longer tailed. All the diving ducks dive from the surface and they have legs placed well back, so they are more upright on land than the dabbling ducks, though not as restricted as the grebes. They have no speculum, but usually a more central stripe of white or grey, or bolder patches of white on the wing. They fly fast, but need quite a run to take off and are far less manoeuvrable in the air than the surface feeders. None of the diving ducks quack – they growl or whistle.

OUT AT SEA

Of course, not all water birds will be seen on a fresh-water lake. There are many diving ducks on the sea – scoters, eiders, scaup – and some specialised ones like the shelduck, which is halfway to being a goose. There are also cormorants and shags, the former much larger than any duck and with a quite different, flat-headed, hook-billed, long-tailed shape. In fact, the cormorant is much more akin to the gannet than to any duck or goose. Cormorants and shags hold out their wings to dry, a pose never taken up by duck, diver or grebe.

The three species of divers are midway between cormorants and grebes – elongated, with lobed feet and pointed bills, legs so far back that they cannot walk, and long, slim wings that take them along at a fast rate but allow very little agility. They are specialised, surface-diving fish-eaters, usually far out on water, often rolling over to preen. They make the strangest, most wonderful noises on their northern breeding grounds.

TURN TO DUCKS

The ducks include some of our most colourful birds. Many become very tame and are easily studied from close range. Yet others perform huge migrations from the Arctic and from continental Europe and Asia to reach Britain's mild winter climate.

Birds from the shore

SITTING ON A headland watching the birds pass by is a kind of birdwatching quite different from any other. It is not possible to walk around and look for birds – they have to come to you. When they pass by on their mysterious way, they are soon out of sight – and will probably not come back. If you do not identify them the first time, there is unlikely to be a second chance.

The variety of birds to be seen on a sea watch is greater than might be imagined. Apart from the passing gulls and terns, there will be ducks, thrushes and starlings on the move in autumn, incoming waders, and surprises like a newly-arriving long-eared owl flopping in over the sea. But the main aim is to see the birds of the ocean and identify them.

It takes years of enjoyable hard work to graduate to expert status in seabird identification. Many are simply hard to find and provide little chance to gain more than a few minutes' experience. It is important to sort out the major groups first – the gulls, terns, skuas, auks, shearwaters and so on – and build on that.

HEADLONG PLUNGERS

An adult gannet poses no problem, so big and spotlessly white that it should not be mistaken. But a mottled or piebald young one is a different matter. Like all seabirds it adapts its actions to suit the elements. In a gale it will glide and bank steeply, careening over and sweeping gracefully down again to skim the waves before the next steep rise. In calm air it has to fly under its own power, beating long, angled, pointed wings regularly in powerful but rather heavy progress. It has the unmistakable gannet shape – long wings set centrally on the torpedo-shaped body, pointed at both ends. It will often pause in its onward flight to rise up a little and glide round in a circle. It may then move on as before, or, if it spies a fish, it will dive in headlong.

FLICKER AND GLIDE

Shearwaters are much smaller and apt to look tiny against the vastness of the sea that they make their home. They are slim, with narrow heads made all the more so by a half-dark, half-white pattern, and they have narrow tails, quite unlike the full-tailed shape of gulls. The gull that flies most like a shearwater in a gale is the kittiwake, but that species always has white on the head and tail and does not have the typical shearwater stiff-winged flickering action. Manx shearwaters are by far the commonest, usually heading somewhere in a determined fashion if seen flying by a headland. They feed far out at sea and rarely hang about or drift aimlessly near the shore like gulls.

Petrels are tiny and almost insect-like in their insignificance on the huge sea. They are rarely seen from the shore, needing a good strong onshore gale to bring them within reach of even a long headland, but a ferry trip will often give a chance of seeing a storm petrel. It is a black bird with a white rump like a house martin and a graceful, swooping flight like a swallow, turning or dipping down every so often to feed in an erratic, engaging way. The Leach's petrel is a speciality of vicious late autumn gales, rarely seen at other times. It looks like a black tern crossed with a shearwater, its erratic progress changing from darting twists and turns to gliding and banking in an instant.

MINI ALBATROSS

Related to the petrels and shearwaters is the fulmar, a bigger, thick-set, more gull-like bird. The resemblance to a gull is merely superficial however, and due to its grey and white appearance. It is more patchy on its wings, a brown-grey and creamy-white, with a bull neck, round white head and broad grey tail, so that at a distance a gleaming white head can be seen,

Arctic skua – most often seen near southern shores from August to October

but no white at the back – quite unlike any gull. It flies heavily in calm weather, flat to the surface, with regular beats of its stiff, straight wings, but given a wind it has no need of such exercise and simply banks and glides exactly like a miniature albatross. Of all the ocean birds the fulmar is the most accessible, as some are usually around the breeding cliffs in most months of the year. They are weak-legged and so unable to stand like gulls, and they are true seabirds, never feeding on the land or even on a beach, though they are quite happy to scrounge a good living around trawlers at sea. They sit high in the water when swimming, often with tails cocked.

Cormorants and shags are always around the coasts, though shags prefer rocks and cormorants are more likely in an estuary. Any sea watch is also likely to produce divers and ducks, though few of the latter are likely to be mistaken for a species of any other group. But the long-tailed duck has a central black stripe with white sides on the rump, and dark wings, making it look rather like an auk in flight.

A WHIRR OF WINGS

Auks themselves include the puffins, razorbills and guillemots. The first two are black and white; the latter

Any suitable cliff along the coast is likely to have at least one or two nesting pairs of fulmars

can look chocolate-brown on top in bright sun. All fly along in a whirr, narrow wings always buzzing, never gliding, bodies looking rather heavy and barrel-like. They swim low in the water, legs set far back like a diver's, bills held horizontally – again, the only duck likely to be confused with an auk is the long-tailed. Auks tend to swim offshore near breeding cliffs or swarm around the nesting ledges, or pass by far offshore in a procession of birds in small groups or long lines, always low over the water. The black guillemot is an exception, but its pattern, small size and round wings with white patches make it fairly easy to identify.

SUPER PREDATORS

Skuas are splendid, piratical seabirds. They can be seen around northern coasts and further south in autumn, especially along the east coast. There will always be scores of gulls for every skua – they are not necessarily rare, but they are never abundant. Arctic skuas come in a variety of colours but have the typical gull-cum-falcon shape, slender and beautiful, with relaxed, gracefully pointed, angled wings and narrow tails. They are usually much more contrasted or more solidly dark in colour than any gull. They have a certain menace about them, especially when one or two spy a tern with a fish. Then they visibly accelerate and overhaul it, chasing it with twists and dives in a breathtaking show of aerobatics. Great skuas are bigger and heavier, solidly dark except for big white wing flashes.

Large birds in the air

Vole's eye view of a kestrel

Partly because of Britain's essentially cool, moist climate, but also because of the history of persecution of birds of prey, we do not enjoy the spectacle of large soaring birds over much of our countryside. In parts of Spain – though things are changing even there – kites and buzzards and vultures soar around all day long in an ever changing pattern.

But, of course, there *are* many birds in the skies of Britain, but few of them are birds of prey. There are gulls and lapwings, and also pigeon flocks and bands of rooks and jackdaws. The crows are a mixed bunch, but the larger species might be taken for birds of prey on first glance. Carrion (and hooded) crows have a steady purposeful flight with regular strong wing-beats, but do not often soar in the true sense of using rising air currents or riding the wind. Rooks are generally in flocks – a giveaway really, as birds of prey here do not flock much – but they can be quite aerobatic, and have special display flights with deep, slow wing-beats and swooping glides.

MASTER ACROBAT

The one crow above all others that looks like a bird of prey is the raven. It is a giant carrion crow, but much more agile in the air, soaring and gliding masterfully, and able to roll over on to its back, or close its wings and plunge down like a stone. Its long wings are often angled in the middle, and when it moults, its gappy flight feathers increase the angled effect; it also has a long, protruding head and a broad, almost diamond-shaped tail matched only by that of the rook at certain angles and only for a moment. The carrion crow has a squarer tail and shorter wings.

The jackdaw is a smaller bird, quicker in its movements and rounder in the wing, and will rarely suggest a hawk or falcon except in a brief glimpse. The classic bird to produce a mistake, if only for a moment, is the woodpigeon. Its rather long tail and wings, small head and fast, even dashing flight, often cause people to stop the car or raise binoculars in the hope of a sparrowhawk or falcon. In fact, the deep chest and narrow neck, and the habit of rising slightly before a descending glide, make the pigeons distinctive.

AIR OF MENACE

A sparrowhawk has a different sort of 'flap and glide'. Its wings seem to snap into place after a few quick beats, remaining rigid and flat for a second or two as the bird glides forwards without losing height, before the next burst of beats. This is different from the more relaxed, almost sluggish flight of the kestrel, with its lazier wing-beats and less dynamic appearance. The sparrowhawk always seems to be sharp and meaning business, whereas the kestrel rarely exerts itself – though, when it needs to, it is quite capable of dashing into a flock of sparrows or starlings and picking one off. The hallmark of the kestrel, of course, is its brilliant hovering.

The other falcons are less likely to be seen by chance from a vehicle or train, but you never know. Merlins nearly always fly low down. Only when they are on a long-distance flight do they seem to lift off the ground more than a few feet. Typically they dash along, swooping up and over hedges or drystone walls in a manner recalling the hunting flight of a sparrowhawk. True hawks – of which Britain only has two species – are round-winged and long-tailed, made for quick pursuit and acrobatic ability within woods. Falcons are longer-winged with much more pointed wingtips. A male sparrowhawk – a third smaller than the female – can look quite sharp-winged, and a merlin can look quite broad across the base of the wings, so they are sometimes confused. But after a few seconds' viewing, the difference is clearer.

POWER DIVERS

Peregrines are rather like giant merlins – big, powerful falcons, much broader in every proportion than the comparatively lightweight kestrel. Their broad shoulders, strong wings and considerable breadth across the base of the large tail give them a solidity and power that smaller birds of prey lack. Peregrines have everything – agility, grace, power and speed – and are quite magnificent to watch. Yet their direct flight has a certain heaviness that distinguishes them from the hobby, at first glance very similar in pattern and shape. Hobbies like trees; peregrines usually avoid them. The hobby is in fact a much more slender bird, with whippy, tapered wings that can curve back rather like a swift's, and its flight is a mixture of merlin-like dash and a graceful swooping and fly-catching that no other British falcon can match. Hobbies fly very quickly after an insect, then slow down, swoop upwards or turn to one side, almost stalling as they put out their feet and spread the tail, to take the insect in one or both feet. They can also go into a long, sloping power-dive into a flock of finches or swallows.

WAVERING GLIDES

Quite the opposite of the falcons are the harriers, which all fly low across open ground (not so slow as they seem) wavering a little from side to side, with steady, flappy wing-beats between glides. When they stop beating their wings, they hold them up in a slight 'V' as they sail onwards, always very distinctive. Harriers need open ground over which to hunt and, although marsh harriers will perch on a tall, dead branch, a harrier will never fly out of a dense tree, whereas a buzzard often will.

RARE TREATS

The red kite is a five-star speciality, somewhat harrier-like in its shape and flight, with lazy wing-beats, but it glides with its wings flat, even drooped a little, and soars high up off the ground. The rusty-red tail, white wing patches and broad, pale bands across the top of the wings make a red kite a very fine bird indeed. The honey buzzard – not a proper buzzard at all – has the most kite-like flight of any other bird of prey, and the rough-legged buzzard approaches it in its relaxed, elastic wing-beats. But both are very rare. Honeys have flat or drooped wings as they soar, rather narrow, lengthy tails and thin heads; rough-legs are long-winged, boldly-patterned and often hover.

Common buzzards are the most likely large birds of prey to be seen over western and northern Britain. They like wooded terrain, but often fly over open hills. Buzzards soar endlessly, circling round and round with wings stretched fully out and raised a little in a 'V'. When they fly off from a perch or from the ground (they often sit on telegraph poles or in fields) they have a rather heavy flight, straight and direct, with quite quick and almost jerky wing-beats, lacking the grace of the other buzzards and the kite. Their loud, ringing, challenging calls often give them away.

GIANTS

Eagles are huge birds, with longer, broader tails than buzzards and longer wings; their heads also protrude more. They also soar with wings slightly raised, but their direct flight is much more gliding, less flappy, and the wing-beats are slow, deep and strong. They have an air of majesty about them, partly due to the deeply-fingered wingtips that act like slots in an aeroplane's wing to reduce turbulence and aid stability, so an eagle sails steadily through the air even in a gale. Golden eagles will usually be high over a mountain, and never on a roadside fence or telegraph pole.

NEVER EASY

With birds of prey it is important to remember that many will always get away, unidentified, even from the expert. Yet, with experience, it is true to say that first impressions are often the right ones – but it is not really safe to rely on them!

Waders

F IND A QUIET sheltered spot beside an estuary, at a place where the birds gather as the tide rises. A place below the skyline will often offer very close views of waders in their thousands. Local knowledge is indispensable – and a tide table is equally vital for a good day.

As with gulls, waders on their own can be very tame, but in flocks they are often wary and unapproachable. They tend to stand facing the wind, so you need to be to one side to see them well. The light needs to be good, with any sunlight coming from behind. The tide also has to be right – not too high, not too low; and bait-diggers, dog-walkers, other birdwatchers or horse-riders will have to be far enough away not to disturb the birds.

Fortunately, the birds will choose the same places year after year, although the shape of an estuary is liable to change over the years as sand and mud is deposited or washed away by the sea. In fact, the different species at a high-tide roost often have a preferred spot and stick to it, so that a flock of oystercatchers always picks the same ridge of sand, with curlews at one end, grey plovers and godwits at the other, redshanks along one edge, dunlins packed in somewhere else, and so on.

VARIATIONS ON A THEME

Many species of waders live in the same area, but can get along together because they are of different sizes, with different lengths of legs and with bills that are adapted to different ways of feeding and preferred foods. This helps identification right away: structure is a good clue to identity.

The big, dark, hunched birds at a roost will be the curlews. At close range, in good light, they look pale, but more often than not, across an open beach on a wintry day, appear to be some of the darkest birds there. Bar-tailed godwits look much smaller, though quite large as waders go, and they have a paler, more buff or fawn appearance. Black-tailed godwits are greyer, taller birds. Both species of godwit are splendid in summer plumage and a lucky birdwatcher may see a few like that before they go in spring, or early in the autumn.

Incoming curlews fly low and steadily, one by one, or come in high up in groups; godwits often arrive more in a rush and 'whiffle' down to the roost, twisting and turning in rapid kinks to lose height quickly.

MIDDLE SIZED

Redshanks are noticeably smaller than the godwits, distinctly 'middle-sized' and usually looking very dark. They feed in small groups or on their own, plodding about quite slowly but with a more lively nature than the big curlews, and they are prone to hysterical bursts of alarm. When they roost they do so in large clusters or lines. The knot is smaller and dumpier than a redshank and looks much paler and greyer in winter. It is a rounded bird with legs and bill rather short for a wader, and with little contrast between upper and undersides. Knots feed in close groups and roost in dense packs, often carpeting the ground even where there are only a few hundred. Where there are thousands they are spectacular and in flight the most remarkable of the waders, twisting like clouds of smoke.

Other shoreline, medium-sized waders are grey plovers. Like curlews, they look rather pale at close range, but usually seem dark and dumpy, hunched down in a dejected stance, on a beach. They feed in isolation and roost in loose parties rather than close-packed flocks.

SMALL AND NEAT

Smaller waders include the dunlin, perhaps the commonest, or most widespread, of all. In winter dunlins are dull brown on top, white below, often with the appearance of a dark breastband. In clear sun they look quite bright, glistening underneath; in dull light, especially on wet mud that gleams under a cloudy sky, they look very dark on top and around the breast and their appearance can be misleading. Their small size, longish bill and shortish legs, and often the fact that there are plenty of them, helps to identify them. In spring many will already be in summer plumage. Much livelier and, in winter, paler, with pure grey upperparts and very clean white underparts are the sanderlings. They show much blacker wings, with a broader white stripe, in flight. They prefer sand to mud.

Rounder and a little larger than dunlins, ringed plovers are often very numerous. They are short- billed, mid-brown on top, white below and strongly patterned with black at the front. They feed in loose groups, but roost in flocks and often mix with the dunlins and sanderlings at high tide. They can be picked out at great range by their stop–start actions when feeding, as they run along, then pause and bend forwards to pick something up.

ROCK BIRDS

Many of these species can also be found on a stony stretch, or a rocky beach, but here they will be joined by turnstones – dark, dumpy, short-billed and bull-necked. Where there are many weedy rocks there may also be small, dark, unobtrusive purple sandpipers. They are often very tame – especially when not with jumpy turnstones.

In winter the noisy, argumentative and beautiful oystercatchers sport white frontal collars, looking rather dull and brownish and having dark bill tips. Come the spring they will all be startling black and white with beaks of the most eyecatching orange; few birds are more glorious.

A WIDE CHOICE

Lapwings and golden plovers are birds of the fields rather than mud flats, though many can be seen on grassier stretches of salt marshes. Snipe visit the beach only in hard weather and prefer the cover of wet meadows and fresh-water marshes or the upper edges of the salt marsh. Greenshanks and a few spotted redshanks do spend winters on the estuaries in a few places, but are never common, and they are more likely to be seen in the autumn on coastal lagoons or in the salt marsh creeks. Ruffs are usually silent. They like wet grassland and muddy pools, not the beach, and can be confusing. Their medium-size, short bill and long legs help. None of these join the big roosts.

The group of small sandpipers – green, wood and common – tend to be fresh-water birds, though common sandpipers are frequent on rocky and weedy shores in summer and autumn. The first two like to feed in rather concealed spots, in ditches and creeks or in hidden pools, rather than on open mud. They are slightly larger and look dark-winged, with contrasting white rumps; the common is quite different in flight, with stiff, rather arched wings, each with a lengthwise stripe of white, and a dark rump with white sides. It bobs its hind end constantly as it feeds. The green sandpiper looks similar on the ground, also a tail wagger, but rather darker; the wood sandpiper is slimmer, longer-legged and more spangled on top. All three have highly distinctive voices, but all are rather solitary and will never be found in a big high-tide roost.

Each autumn, variable numbers of migrant little stints and curlew sandpipers appear, mainly on or near the east coast, but sometimes very widespread. Little stints are tiny, with very short, straight black bills and blackish legs – they are barely more than sparrow-size. Curlew sandpipers are larger than dunlins, more elegant, longer in both legs and bill, and cleaner in their plumage colouring. They are lovely birds and well worth keeping an eye out for in August and September.

ANYTHING CAN TURN UP!

Waders are terrific globetrotters. Practically any species is likely to turn up in Britain at some time. In their non-breeding plumages they are sometimes difficult to identify, not helped by the fact that they feed far out over wet mud. But they are worth the time and effort needed to get to know them. Perhaps the best way is to find a coastal pool or a muddy-edged reservoir, where the numbers will not be too great but the variety will prove adequate. Such places are sometimes visited by very rare visitors, too – the waders are great birds for the rarity hunter. But they have more than their fair share of pitfalls. Above all else, if you want to find rare waders, you must know your common ones inside out first!

The legs of a black-winged stilt. Proportionate to its size, the stilt has the longest legs of any bird. They help the bird when it is feeding, but are a considerable inconvenience when it wishes to sit on its nest

The Gulls and Terns

MOSTLY WHITE, PALE grey and black, set off by a splash of colour on their legs and beaks, adult gulls and terns are clean-cut in colour and shape, made for flight and life on or around water, yet terns do not often swim on the surface and gulls are as often out of water as in it.

Gulls are great opportunists, whereas terns have a much more specialised life-style. The terns' long bodies, short legs and rather long, pointed bills make them poor candidates for running about on land or scavenging at tips or behind tractors. They stand low to the ground, able to walk but never very agile, and are much more at home where they really belong – in the air. They have long, slender wings drawn to narrower points than any gull's, and mostly have tails that end in tapered streamers either side. They dive headlong from the air into water for fish, the streamered tails probably helping them steer.

Gulls are longer-legged, bulky in build, with broader wings – more generalist than specialist in form and life-style. Nevertheless, one only has to sit by the sea on a windy day to appreciate their skill in the air – even the abundant herring gull is a true master of the wind currents above a cliff or over a promenade. Still better, stand at the back of a cross-Channel ferry and watch the gulls in the slipstream – they simply hang in the air hardly even beating their wings. But most gulls are so adaptable that they can feed in fields, on refuse tips, at fish quays and along a beach as well as out to sea. Only the kittiwake has a truly marine life all year round, and the little gull remains a delicate, tern-like creature dipping for food at the water surface.

VISUAL SIGNALS

Young gulls need to look less conspicuous than adults while still inexperienced, so they have a camouflaged and discreet mottled brown plumage. This also helps to avoid aggression from their own parents, who react in a hostile fashion against any white bird at their nest – it is likely to be an intruding adult. The young kittiwake needs no camouflage – it is safe but also immobile in a cliff-ledge nest. It has a black collar that can be presented in 'submission' to its parents in order to reduce the risk of attack.

EASY TO STUDY

Gulls moult in a regular sequence just like other birds, but because they are so large, and young birds replace brown feathers with grey or white as they get older, the process is easy to follow. They leave the nest in their first, or juvenile, plumage but very quickly moult and replace the head and body feathers with new ones. This gives them the plumage of their first winter. Then, in spring,

they repeat the head and body moult to gain their first summer plumage. In autumn the complete plumage is changed gradually, including the wing and tail feathers for the first time. Now they enter their second winter in a completely new set of feathers. The spring partial and autumn complete moults are then repeated every year.

Within this basic sequence are variations according to age and breeding success. If the adult breeds and rears young, it will delay its moult until later. But if it fails to breed, it may start to moult much earlier so that the 'autumn' moult may start early in the summer. For the same reason, the autumn moult is earlier in immatures. The moult is easy to follow. Look at the wing feathers. Each gull has 10 large, outer feathers (primaries) on each wing; the innermost one, just behind the bend of the wing, is the first to drop out in autumn and the first to be replaced; they then work through to the outermost, during which time the rest of the plumage is also moulted. The state of the primaries – seen with surprising ease on a big gull, but hardly noticeable on a warbler unless you catch it – is therefore used as an indication of the stage of moult. In autumn gulls seem to be a very ragged bunch, with many wing feathers missing and irregular patches of white across the wing coverts where fallen feathers reveal white bases of those beneath.

Terns do much the same thing, but the common tern moults half its primaries here in autumn, then migrates before moulting the rest, whereas the arctic tern waits until it has moved south before moulting. A moulting tern with ragged wings in September is, therefore, always an adult common tern, never an arctic.

Gulls tend to have black patches at the wingtips. Black colour indicates a large amount of the pigment melanin in the feather, and melanin adds strength. The wingtips are therefore protected from the worst of the wear and tear that they have to withstand for a year, but by mid summer can be very badly worn – and the colour is faded and bleached by exposure to sun and salt. Gulls are big and approachable so that all this can be seen easily.

Identification is not always easy until the birds are adult; in the larger species this may not be for four years, but in the smallest it may be after just one year. Terns are even more tricky, but not impossible, as is sometimes suggested; bill colour and wing pattern help a great deal. They are inspiring birds – at home over the roughest sea, flying from one end of the world to the other and eschewing any help from man, other than some protection when they nest – always worth watching.

Common terns fishing

Larks, pipits and wagtails

SOME BIRDS ARE very much tied to the ground, and not only the obvious candidates like the gamebirds – pheasants and partridges. The open fields hold other, smaller birds that need careful identification.

Skylarks rarely sit in trees, though now and then one will perch on a bush top or, more likely, a fence post. They inhabit open countryside and even sing from a spot high in the air, in hovering flight, for want of song posts. Woodlarks, however, like woodland edges and heaths with scattered trees. They will sit and sing from a tall tree, but they prefer to launch themselves from a tree and sing as they circle above the ground. They feed entirely on the ground, as do the winter-visiting shore larks on or near the beaches. Skylarks often form flocks – on eastern 'prairie' farmland in winter they may sometimes number many hundreds.

Larks are mostly streaky-brown birds easily distinguished by their superb songs. They are rather stout and broad-winged and have fairly thick, thrush-like bills. Slimmer and altogether more wagtail-like are the pipits, also streaky-brown ground-lovers. The meadow pipit perches in trees from time to time near its nest, calling anxiously until the birdwatcher goes away, but it is the tree pipit that is the real tree bird. It sings from trees, or flies up from a twig into its song flight, singing loudly in the air until it returns to a perch. Its song is not up to a woodlark's, and it is a longer-tailed bird. The meadow pipit has a similar song flight, if an inferior song, but always starts and finishes with its feet firmly on the ground. Tree pipits

walk about in trees, not hopping or leaping like warblers or tits but walking along branches in a most unusual way. Tree pipits have one important characteristic – they migrate south for the winter (so they are of no concern to the British birdwatcher after October or before April!). They are a touch larger, or stouter, in build than meadow pipits, less nervy and shuffly in their actions and more self-assured, striding along in a confident manner. Unlike meadow pipits, which often flock, they are practically solitary birds.

Tree pipits often fly long distances if flushed, quite fast and direct. Meadows flit and dither about in the air, looking weak and hesitant.

Pipits have long, dark tails edged with white, and must not be confused in flight with buntings, which have similar characteristics.

The rock pipit is the dullest and darkest, with dark legs, and is a coastal bird. It likes cliffs and rocks in summer, but visits marshes and estuaries in winter. In early spring and late autumn it may turn up at a reservoir inland. Should you see a large, dark-legged pipit inland in winter, it may be a water pipit. This species – until recently thought of as a race of the rock pipit – breeds in European mountains, but comes to muddy reservoir edges and watercress beds for the winter. The meadow pipit has a shrill, thin, often triple *peet* call; the rock pipit a fuller *pheest*; the water pipit calls somewhere in between! It tends to be a wary bird, hard to approach closely, but in spring you might find one in colourful breeding plumage.

Woodlark

Yellow wagtail

THE BOBBERS

The wagtails are more delicate, longer-tailed – though the yellow is quite pipit-like. The yellow wagtail is a summer visitor, so not to be confused with the grey wagtail, which has yellow under its tail and may visit a lowland stream in winter. Young yellow wagtails are the least yellow, most brownish, with dark patches on their breasts, but are never as streaky as pipits. They run about on grass, wagging their tails and darting forward after flies. Grey wagtails are grey on top and yellowish beneath, have very long tails and are rarely away from water. Pied wagtails have no yellow (except that young ones are yellowy-buff

Rock pipit (below) and meadow pipit (right) are very similar, but their habitats are quite different

underneath at times) and are simply black, white and grey. In spring you may be lucky enough to see a 'pied' wagtail with clean, pale grey flanks and a pale grey back – this will be a white wagtail, the continental version of the same species.

Pied wagtails are likely to be encountered almost anywhere, from crowded suburbia to remote reservoir. They have benefited from new office and factory developments, finding both food and nesting places among the concrete, steel and glass. Grey wagtails and yellow wagtails are much more choosy, and much more shy. The grey prefers fast-flowing upland streams and rivers, while the yellow likes damp meadows in lowland valleys and also, perversely, dry heaths and commons.

Thrushes and chats

THIS GROUPING CONSISTS of a rather mixed bag of sturdy, very small to medium-small birds including the thrushes – represented by such familiar favourites as the song thrush and blackbird – and the chats and their relatives, including wheatear, nightingale and robin. Some have strong colours, or bold patterns, but most are subdued and beautiful for their subtlety more than for their brilliance.

Many of these are fine songsters – nightingale, blackbird and song thrush are well up in the 'top ten'. Some have different male and female plumages, even seasonal changes (for example, wheatear, stonechat and blackbird), while others, such as the robin, are impossible to sex by sight alone. Most have rather spotty-looking young.

All eat insects and worms and are ground-feeders for the most part, but also feed in shrubs and trees, especially on berries in the autumn. The song thrush has the special skill of bashing snails on stones; the nightingale prefers to creep about in the dark places beneath dense thickets, whereas whinchats perch on tall twigs and drop to the ground to catch insects that they spot.

They all hop on the ground, or rush forward in a shuffling half hop, half run. The thrushes stand quietly and tilt their heads to one side, looking and listening for signs of prey. In trees they tend to sit rather motionless or hop heavily about, shaking the twigs and foliage much more than the smaller warblers.

Mistle thrushes (below) are resident in Britain all year round, while their cousins, the redwings (above right) are winter visitors from Scandinavia

LONG-DISTANCE TRAVELLERS

Several of these species are resident, or at least large proportions of their numbers stay put all year round in one spot. They tend to live solitary lives, or gather in small groups – like the thrushes and robins on the lawn. Some are very strongly migratory and often feed and travel in flocks – the winter-visiting fieldfares and redwings for instance. Others migrate over thousands of miles but never flock together – the summer visitors to Britain, such as wheatears and whinchats, redstarts and nightingales. They are often to be seen on migration at places where they do not nest, especially birds such as wheatears and redstarts near the coast in spring and autumn. The ring ouzel is a strong, tough-looking thrush of upland habitats, yet it moves south in winter, just when the delicate-looking redwing is coming to Britain to face the winter.

Robins are among those birds which have taken advantage of human activity, even to the extent of building their nests in such places as a cement mixer's engine!

This is a slightly mixed group, therefore, but they all have sturdy legs and fairly stout, short bills that are not seed-crackers like a finch's nor as slim as a warbler's. They have rather short, broad wings, but lengthy tails. They sing to attract a mate and to defend a summer territory, in which they have to find enough food for themselves and their family. In winter, when they are feeding on food that is widespread or abundant in certain places, they need not necessarily have a territory

– like redwings that gather together to raid the scarlet haws of a bushy hedge or fieldfares that roam the pastures in winter. Robins have winter territories, and males and females separate though very bad weather breaks down the barriers and then you may see two or three together on a bird-table. And that is one other feature of some of the thrushes and chats – they are easy to watch and easy to get to know, though they always keep enough secrets to be just that little bit of a mystery.

Finches and buntings

Chaffinches (left) are among the first birds to begin singing in the spring. The bullfinch (right) is not so familiar, except, perhaps, to those with orchards!

WHAT IS THE difference between a finch and a bunting? Finches are most variable, but all have short, stout legs and triangular bills that are made for splitting and rolling husks from seeds of one sort or another. Buntings are rather more similar in general form, quite slim, small-headed, long-tailed, with superficially finch-like bills.

The finches tend to have multi-syllabic calls, often a regular twitter or trill, from the light, varied spluttering of a linnet to the hard, explosive *chip chip chip* of the crossbill. They call a lot in flight. Two – the chaffinch and the brambling, that make up a close pair of species with many like characteristics – call short, single notes in flight, but also have another of the typically finch sounds, a twangy note based on a *twee* or *tsoo-ee* sound. The greenfinch and redpoll use this note a lot, in their own way, and the twite has it so well developed that it takes its name from it and includes it in its song.

Buntings have short, simple calls as they fly, very occasionally giving a jingling, repetitive twitter or trill.

For instance, the reed bunting has a simple *teu* and the cirl bunting an insignificant *sip*; several others have similar notes, though the snow bunting does have a nice trill too. Yellowhammers have a metallic, sharp note and corn buntings a very distinctive *plip* as they fly.

SPECIALISATION

Chaffinches and bramblings are rather large finches, one being a common bird and the other a winter visitor here. They feed their young on caterpillars, but otherwise eat a mixture of seeds and buds. They hop about on the ground and are unable to hang on to short, weedy plants with seeds at the top in the way linnets and twites do. Goldfinches go one better and feed from seeding dandelions and thistles, using their longer beaks like tweezers.

Goldfinches also bridge the gap to the finches that feed on tree seeds, as they join flocks of siskins and redpolls feeding in alders in winter. Whereas the chaffinch and greenfinch collect in flocks in fields and fly to the hedges if disturbed, redpolls and siskins dash about from tree to tree, bursting out of a tree top in a dense, fast-flying, bounding flock, often to circle round and descend again to the same tree. Goldfinches flit about from thistle patch to thistle patch, in a particularly airy, bouncy flight, usually in a group of half a dozen to a dozen. Linnets live together most of the year, often flocking by the hundred in autumn where there are seeds in abundance (the over-abundant food supply makes territories unnecessary). Crossbills live in conifers, but often buzz about over the trees in small flocks. Often, a finch flock will stop work and simply sit about twittering, as if life is pretty easy and full of the joys of spring – even if it is a mid-winter afternoon!

UNCO-ORDINATED

Buntings do few of these things. Odd ones will certainly join in with finch and sparrow flocks in fields, but you never see a solid mass of pure buntings, though yellowhammers and corn buntings will feed in fair numbers together at times and snow buntings roam the beaches in groups. They lack the co-ordination of the finches, and do not move about from tree to tree in groups, or dash headlong for the nearest hedge in a dense bunch. They may be close together, but they live their own lives. If disturbed they flit away in different directions, flicking tails and dipping up and down as they go. Reed buntings will usually be in odd ones and twos or small groups, but will feed near water in early spring with the first migrating groups of wagtails and pipits. They hop and shuffle about, often flicking their wings and tails in an extraordinarily fast in–out movement. Typical buntings, they cannot manage the acrobatics of the smaller finches and prefer to plod about on the ground.

The buntings all like fairly prominent song posts for their rather indifferent performances. Corn buntings may make do with a mere clump of earth in a cereal field, but they prefer a twig or an overhead wire. Reed buntings like a tall stem in a marsh, where they sit with dangling, untidy, almost loose-looking tails as they go through their endless succession of short jingling songs – each bird has only one version! The finches have more elaborate songs, based on their trilling calls and given in special display flights (such as greenfinch and redpoll); or real songs with repetitive patterns given from high woodland song posts (such as chaffinch and crossbill).

Buntings mostly have longish tails, often edged white (the corn bunting being an exception), whereas finches have more colour, often with a patch each side of the base of the tail as on greenfinch, siskin and linnet. Redpolls have vivid pink and red breasts; linnets have crimson breast and head patches; twites have pink rumps. The finches are a varied lot, none more colourful than the secretive bullfinch with its square of white above the tail; none more exciting than the hawfinch, big and beautifully patterned but hard to see. There is one bunting, however, that on a sunny spring day can look more glorious than anything – the splendid male yellowhammer.

Snow buntings are most likely to be seen on the east coast in winter, but they need careful looking for

Tits and warblers

I F YOU STAND at the edge of a wood in early autumn, there will usually be plenty to see. Small birds, either in the bushes and tree tops or flitting about on the ground, provide endless amusement – but are they all easy to tell apart? Many of them seem, on the face of it, to be almost entirely without distinguishing features.

In the foliage there will be slim, quiet, gentle birds that slip through the leaves and slide about without disturbing the bush at all. These will be the warblers. Leaping about more energetically, swinging like mini-Tarzans on the tips of swaying twigs and creating a generally noisy disturbance, are the tits. By comparison they are stocky, heavy birds, despite their small size.

The tits are mostly solidly built, almost barrel- or box-shaped, with square or chunky heads and short tails. They have stout, almost conical bills and strong legs that can hold them in the most precarious poses, upside down on a twig, hanging half way up a wall or swinging from a peanut bag. They are natural clowns, but clever and quick to learn new tricks. Their feeding habits separate them, even though they may seem at first sight to be doing the same thing in a mixed flock. Coal tits are tiny and blue tits are almost as light, so they can investigate the very tips of the finest twigs. Great tits feed much more on the ground and around the larger branches and trunks, while marsh tits like big, solid boles. Long-tailed tits are not 'real' tits at all and in their communal life-style – even co-operative rearing of young – and year-round sociability they resemble the bird family called babblers – most often found in Asia and Africa.

The tits have strident songs and many thin, high-pitched call notes. If a predator appears they give a very thin whistle which penetrates well, warning that something is afoot, but which is very hard for the predator – and the birdwatcher – to pin down. The rhythmic *tsee-si-si* notes of the blue tit in a mixed autumn flock are, with practice, easy to separate from the strong, but colourless and even *tsee-see-see* of long-tailed tits, and the sibilant calls of goldcrests – despite being impossible to convey on paper!

LEAF WARBLERS

The slender, greenish-coloured warblers with yellower undersides will be *Phylloscopus* warblers – willow, wood and chiffchaff. They look very difficult to identify and some willow warblers and chiffchaffs are a real test to tell apart. Listen for their calls – their songs are unique and easy, but the *hoo-eet* of a willow warbler and *hweet* of a chiffchaff are also quite distinct. They are insect-eaters, leaf-gleaners by trade, but will take a few berries in autumn. Autumn birds often look more stripey-faced and brighter yellow – these are young ones. Look for the leg colour, wing and tail length, head shape, eye stripe and eye-ring – if you can!

Slightly larger, stockier warblers with more irascible natures are the *Sylvia* warblers – blackcap, garden warbler, whitethroat and so on. Most have differences between the sexes; their songs are either scratchy, as in the case of the scrub-lovers of heaths and hedges, or beautifully developed to carry far through the dense structure of a wood. The acoustic qualities and carrying power of

warblers' environments and songs make fascinating studies. *Sylvia* warblers are prone to turn up at odd places in autumn – many gardens with honeysuckle or other berries have visits from them, often unseen. Listen for the short, sharp chacking notes that give them away.

There are other warblers, of course. Reed and sedge warblers live in swampy places, though they forage in bushes. Reed warblers sing to defend small nesting territories in reed beds but move out to feed. They have strong feet to clasp upright stems. Grasshopper warblers are different, with long, rounded tails, tiny bills and softly streaked plumage; they behave almost like mice in low grass and scrub.

IMPOSSIBLE JOURNEYS

A most extraordinary feature of these tiny birds is that they migrate. Imagine a willow warbler, a scrap of a few ounces, feeding up one autumn day. It gets dark; a clear starry night. The bird that seems to take all its time simply flying across an open space will suddenly fly up, through the trees, on over the fields, climbing higher and higher until it is truly in the realm of aeroplanes, on through clouds and rain, on and on through the night surrounded by nothing but black emptiness. It is hard to credit this event that takes place millions of times every year. What self-confidence the tiny creature has, setting out to cross land and sea to some unknown, unseen destination. How much more incredulity must we have if it is an old bird that has done it several times before – and will return to the very same tree next spring!

Rare warblers are outside the scope of this book, but it has to be said that there is another kind of magic here: to get out early one October morning, to a wood where there were few birds the day before, and to see a newly-arrived rarity from Siberia is little short of miraculous.

CRESTS

Goldcrests are tiny, dumpy warblers, or kinglets, that stay all year round. They have contact calls rather like the tits', high and thin, not like the whistle of the willow warbler or the hard *tak* of the *Sylvia* group. They move about quietly and often hover momentarily up in the tops of trees, or feed lower down in dense bushy places and thick hedges in winter. Like warblers, and unlike tits, they are neither hole nesters, bird-box users nor bird-table clients.

An autumn hedgerow. Inset (left to right): goldcrest, blue tit, great tit, whitethroat

MORE BESIDES

There is quite an assortment of other birds around a bushy place or in a wood. The woodpeckers are distinctive enough, of course, but treecreepers are unobtrusive and almost mouselike as they creep about rough bark. Shuffling about quietly, usually going unnoticed though they have sharp calls and quite attractive songs, the dunnocks are in a group of their own. They seem dull little birds, but have a racy life-style that belies appearances. Close up, their orange legs, stripey backs and beautiful hazel eyes can be seen.

In summer a pale, upright little bird will be found periodically flying out, twisting after a fly, and returning to its look-out – a spotted flycatcher.

Birds and man

Modern man has the ability to impose far-reaching and sometimes catastrophic changes on bird numbers and distribution. He can change or totally destroy a habitat and even quickly reduce a species to extinction. On the other hand, he also has the ability to act more positively and to preserve, protect and restore. Bird conservation is a relatively new concept (although simple 'protection' is not) and represents a new chapter in man's relationship with birds. Ornithology in its modern sense, and even birdwatching, as we know it, are fairly new developments.

HUNTING AND DOMESTICATION

Man's general relationship with birds is, of course, as old as man himself. It is such a broad and diverse subject that it deserves several books all to itself. It begins with a very basic thing – the use of birds for food, originally simply through hunting. Interwoven with this use of birds as a 'natural resource' are a multitude of strands of religion and folklore, all part and parcel of the way in which man once lived (and in less 'developed' parts of the world still lives) in harmony and balance with wildlife. Then comes domestication, in effect the controlled production of birds, largely for food. Pigeons were among the earliest animals to be domesticated (they have been so for at least 5,000 years) – again largely for food: racing pigeons are a much more modern phenomenon. Fowl, probably all descended from wild Asian species, date from some 3,000 years ago. Birds kept as pets must date back at least as far. Nowadays, the vast majority of the birds we eat in Britain are of domesticated origin, despite the fact that gamebirds and wildfowl are still eaten quite widely.

BIRDS IN THE HOME

Captive birds provide company and colour for millions of people. In Europe huge numbers are kept caged, from small finches to partridges. In Britain most are now captive-bred stock and no native species is kept as a pet – canaries and budgerigars have taken over. But many species are kept for show purposes, including wild-caught parrots, exotic finches, even sunbirds. National cage-bird shows have an array of chats, wagtails, thrushes, warblers, even waders in cages and many British species, especially the finches, are captive-bred in aviaries. It is, of course, illegal to trap and keep captive birds from the wild.

KILLING FOR SPORT

Bird hunting gradually became a very sophisticated business; it involved, among other things, the art of falconry, popular in medieval times and shortly afterwards and now enjoying a new vogue. The widespread use of firearms brought enormous changes (this can be dated roughly from the early to middle part of the 19th century) and much more possible impact on wild birds. It was not long before specific land management began for birds like the red grouse and others, like the pheasant, became the subject of intensive rearing and release programmes. The shooting of birds today has as much, if not more, to do with sport and enjoyment as with hunting for the pot. Sportsmen, unwittingly at first, but now much more consciously, have done a lot to preserve certain types of habitat, such as woods and grouse moors, but they also saw birds of prey and owls as unwanted competitors – vermin, in their jargon – and slaughtered them in vast numbers last century and well into this century. Sadly, even in these much more enlightened times, when many sportsmen and landowners value and help conserve birds of prey, some of this senseless and illegal persecution persists.

Introduced by the Romans, pheasants are entirely naturalised in Britain, but their numbers are constantly boosted by birds released for shooting

AGRICULTURAL PESTS

Competition has also led to some conflicts between birds and agricultural man. British farmers do not have to contend with queleas or red-winged blackbirds, like their African and American counterparts respectively, but they do face problems with woodpigeons. The position regarding rooks – another 'pest species' – is much less clear-cut, and on balance the rook may well do much more good than harm. Big flocks of winter geese can cause problems on crops, but farmers and conservationists working together are now devising ways of solving these, through providing alternative feeding areas, which do not mean wholesale slaughter of the birds. Similarly, possible problem species like herons, sawbills and cormorants are now being investigated in a co-operative way – compromise rather than needless 'vermin killing' being the best way forward.

Birds undoubtedly face many threats from man and the effects of his increasing 'civilisation' and technological power and efficiency – but at the same time birds are better understood and appreciated than ever before. We should not need to live in conflict with them at all: we have the means *not* to do so and if we have the will there is no reason why the future for our birds should not be a good one.

Birds In Their Setting

Kingfisher

Britain has a remarkably diverse variety of bird habitats for so small an area. Each one has its own special history, landscape and birds. Ten principal types of habitat are described here, along with some of the typical birds that might be found in them

ALTHOUGH THE BRITISH ISLES ARE SMALL, THEY HOLD A REMARKABLE VARIETY OF BIRD HABITATS. THE REASON LIES IN THE INTERACTIONS BETWEEN THE CLIMATE, THE GEOLOGY, AND HUMAN MANAGEMENT OF THE LAND. THESE ARE THE FACTORS WHICH DECIDE WHAT PLANTS CAN GROW WHERE, AND PLANTS ARE THE BASIS OF THE FOOD CHAINS ON WHICH BIRDS AND ALL OTHER ANIMALS DEPEND.

MILD AND MOIST

For the last few thousand years Britain's climate has been kind. The Atlantic weather system and the Gulf Stream continue to give mild, moist summers and some protection from extreme continental cold in winter. The growing season for plants is quite long, even in the north, and trees can grow over almost all of the land, except the mountain tops.

Britain's geology is very varied and this is important because it controls the shape of the land and the fertility of the soil. The high ground of the north and west is very exposed to Atlantic rain and winds, and the soils are mostly thin and poor, so plant growth is restricted and the range of food for birds is limited. Snow covers Scotland's high tops almost all year round and, in winter, conditions are exceptionally severe, with sub-zero temperatures and high winds, which only ptarmigans and golden eagles can tolerate.

By contrast, the south and east of Britain have deep, fertile soils and are protected from the worst of the rain and wind by the western hills. The productivity of the land is high and the greatest variety of breeding birds is found here. In the mild conditions of coastal Dorset, Dartford warblers can survive year round.

As well as controlling the habitats which developed for land birds, the climate and geology also produced a diversity of wetland habitats. Among the features created were tumbling upland streams, with few plants but many aquatic insects – ideal places for birds such as dippers; the great fens of East Anglia, where rivers fretted their way through vast reed beds alive with wildfowl; and the estuaries with their flocks of waders probing for food in the mud. Last, but not least, the waters round the long, indented coastline teemed with food for many kinds of seafowl.

THE INFLUENCE OF PEOPLE

For several thousand years man lived among these riches as a hunter, leaving little trace and having little effect on land or water. However, about 6,000 years ago Neolithic settlers began to clear the forest for grazing and crops. They started a process which was greatly to increase the variety of habitats available to birds and in some way to change the natural character of almost every inch of land and water. Some birds gained from this. Others lost.

The need to find food is of paramount importance to birds. Most of their physical adaptations have evolved to make them more efficient at it – in other words, to be able to feed with the least possible expenditure of energy and the least exposure to danger. And by specialising in the type of food they eat and the places where they seek it, birds can minimise competition from other species. For instance, honey buzzards are the only British birds which can dig out wasps' and bees' nests to eat the grubs. So they enjoy a rich food resource, abundant in the wild forest, with competition only from badgers. The drawback of such extreme specialisation is that the bird becomes highly dependent on one special set of habitat conditions. So, when the forest is cleared, honey buzzards are in trouble.

By the time the Romans came, half or more of England's tree cover had probably been destroyed and replaced by farmland, and the honey buzzard, together with most other woodland birds, must have declined along with the trees. But there would have been winners too. Birds such as rooks would still have had ample trees to nest in, plus a lot of new open farmland to feed over. Perhaps it was about this time that grey partridges, stone-curlews and great bustards first bred here, having spread westward from the steppes as Europe's forest cover was stripped away.

Some of the new farmland was on such infertile, hungry soils that it quickly turned to heath, good only for common grazing, but much appreciated by linnets, whinchats and pipits. Where the rainfall was high and frequent, through much of Ireland and the British uplands, ground cleared of trees became moorland, clad in heathers, where red grouse, golden plovers and hen harriers spread and thrived.

DRYING OUT THE LAND

Before the Roman legions withdrew, much of the fens had been drained, but the new grasslands may well have been a bonus for snipe, nesting in the lush tussocks and probing the damp soil for worms. Wetlands in general probably absorbed more nutrients and produced richer habitats because tree clearance and ploughing would have allowed the rain to wash fertile soil into lakes and rivers. Much found its way to the estuaries, creating vast new expanses of mud flats – perfect wintering grounds for the waders which breed around the Arctic.

Throughout the Dark Ages and medieval times, the general picture was of farmland expanding and forest in retreat. Only the Black Death briefly reversed the process, with trees recolonising abandoned fields and much land allowed to revert to pasture – good hunting grounds for barn owls and kestrels. Then, as the human population recovered, so pressures on birds' habitats began anew and the steady intensification of human influence was to proceed for several centuries. Almost all the woodlands which remained were managed to provide fuel and

Views towards the Black Mountain near Abergavenny, a perfect combination of hedgerow and hill, 'tamed' and 'wild'. Bluebells (inset left) flourish best where woodlands are actively managed, as do many species of birds. The heron may not know it, but most of what it sees has been shaped by man

Birds in their Setting

building materials. Very few of them still held big, old trees, so nest sites for the many birds which use holes were probably in short supply, affecting stock doves and jackdaws, tits, flycatchers and lots of others. At the same time, woods which were coppiced and cut every decade or so will have benefited nightingales and those other birds which like dense thicket conditions and do not need tall trees.

Slowly at first, farming systems changed to increase production. The big open fields, such as those in the English Midlands, probably held few nesting species except skylark, lapwing and partridge. But a major change was to come with the expansion of the enclosure movement in the 18th and 19th centuries, the new hedges allowing today's farmland songbirds – dunnock, yellowhammer, whitethroat and blackbird, for example – to spread across the countryside.

DRAMATIC CHANGE
At the same time, the Industrial Revolution was gaining momentum. Cities were growing, air and water pollution began to affect birds and industrial development began not just to change but to obliterate habitats. In this century, we have seen more rapid and widespread change than ever before. The draining of wetlands continues unabated. Huge conifer forests have altered the face of the uplands, and farming technology makes much of the lowlands a difficult place for birds to live in. The countryside in which our birdlife exists today is very different from its origins 6,000 years ago. Pressures on it are greater than ever before; the rich variety of habitats and birds that remains is a testimony to the tenacity and adaptability of so many species in the face of human pressure, coupled with the more recent growth of environmental awareness and the conservation movement. The challenge that faces us now is to respond to the persistence of the wildlife by ensuring, in return, that it is treated with greater respect in the future. We are still offered the chance to respond, but we must work hard to ensure that we take it.

SOMETHING TO EAT AND SOMEWHERE TO NEST
Birds have two main requirements from the habitats in which they live – food and nest sites. Many species also need shelter from bad weather, especially in winter. They have evolved adaptations in their physical structure and behaviour in order to become most efficient in exploiting the available resources.

WINTER HARDSHIPS
The problems of finding food change with the seasons, but never become very easy to solve. Winter is the most obviously difficult time. Plants have stopped growing and the autumn production of seeds, berries and fruit is being steadily reduced by a variety of consumers – birds, mammals, insects, slugs and snails. Some plants set their fruits up to be eaten – elderberries and hawthorn for instance – so that the seeds will be dispersed in birds' droppings, but most seeds

disappear from view under leaves, into grass tussocks or down cracks in the soil.

Invertebrates are also increasingly hard for birds to find in winter. They, too, lack plant food and they reduce their activity accordingly. Many overwinter not as adults, but as eggs or pupae. Of those which do pass the winter as adults, many hibernate. Even those which remain active slow down or stop as the weather gets colder. The ones that live in the soil, such as earthworms, burrow deeper at the onset of frost.

Frost is a physical problem too: freezing fog can coat twigs and branches with ice – beautiful to see on a crisp, clear morning, but disastrous for birds like tits trying to forage for insects. Snow likewise can coat tree limbs, or the ground, with an impenetrable coat. Many birds die then.

LESS TO EAT – HARDER TO CATCH
Predators such as owls and hawks face the difficulty in winter that the amount of prey grows less day by day. Perhaps, too, the survivors are older and smarter, so less easy to catch. Of course, if conditions are really bad, prey may be very weakened but inevitably by then it is thin and less nutritious!

As the days get shorter, there is less feeding and hunting time for most birds, and the freezing nights get longer. Birds are superbly insulated by their feathers, but heat loss does occur, especially at night, so to survive, birds must keep reasonably well fed and, if possible, roost in a protected spot where wind cannot ruffle feathers and reduce their insulating effect. Wildfowl and seabirds are well adapted to tolerate cold water, but ducks will move under a lee shore on rough nights and even auks and gulls try to move to sheltered waters when gales blow up.

Winter can be beautiful, but it kills many birds. Their food may be hidden by snow, or trapped beneath ice; prolonged intense cold may freeze birds to death.

Man has transformed the land, affecting the life of every bird in Britain. Their adaptability means that some will live in landscapes such as those at Pitstone (below)

In winter waders move to estuaries where there are rich food supplies. In spring they disperse to suitable breeding grounds

MIGRATE OR STAY PUT?

Some species anticipate winter's problems and leave before it begins – though migration itself is a demanding and risky business. But insect-eaters like swallows and warblers could not survive Britain's winter. They have no choice but to embark on movements of thousands of miles every autumn, to return again in spring. Others, of course, arrive in Britain in winter from colder areas in the north. Many upland birds move downhill. Even the upland woods are almost devoid of birds in winter when the wind and rain cut between the bare trees day after day. Some species, such as blue tits, become nomadic; they form into flocks and roam from wood to wood, seeking food. Others will stay put until frost forces them to move – then lapwings leave their fields and, as ice spreads, waterfowl desert their lakes to move westward and south seeking open conditions.

SPRINGTIME REVIVAL

At winter's end, many birds have died, but now comes the breeding season and the chance to rebuild populations. By March, conditions are much easier. Buds are swelling and many more insects are on the move. Day length is greater, beginning to reverse the disadvantages of winter's long nights and short days. Feeding is easier, but no less important because birds must get into condition for the challenges ahead. The males must establish territories, keeping out other males and attracting a mate. Many woodland species use song as a means of declaring possession of desirable real estate – they need suitable song posts. In open country, where no perches exist, larks and pipits sing in flight – an extra drain on energy. Other birds, such as grouse and some birds of prey, have vigorous displays, on the ground or in flight.

While males are claiming territory, females build up their reserves ·for egg production and incubation. They seek the most nutritious foods and, in some species, courtship feeding by the male aids the process.

THE ESSENTIAL NEST SITE

Each territory must contain a good nest site, providing shelter for eggs and young, and either concealment from predators or inaccessibility. Some birds tackle the problem by building splendidly camouflaged nests; many waders lay cryptically marked eggs on bare ground.

Most seabirds choose nest sites on offshore islands or cliff ledges where eggs and young, though easy to see, are hard to get at for all predators except other seabirds, such as skuas. But most birds hide their nests in deep cover or in tree holes, which provide a splendid mix of shelter, concealment, and difficulty of access for predators.

The great increase in food resources that comes with warmer weather is sufficient to support not only winter's resident survivors but also the returning summer migrants. Most of these are invertebrate feeders and even the resident seed-eaters largely rear their young on invertebrates, which become very abundant and are high in protein.

Despite the amount of food available, there is a lot of competition for the best items. For example, caterpillars are much sought by woodland songbirds, sand eels by many seabirds, earthworms by many waders. This is because the ideal food item for chicks is large, easy to find and easy to carry. However, it can sometimes be a better strategy to compromise, for instance by collecting more, smaller items if they happen to be abundant. The more versatile a bird is, the better its chances of success.

By late summer, bird numbers are at their peak, swollen by the new crop of young. Many adults moult, replacing worn plumage. Most do it by stages, but wildfowl lose all their flight feathers at once. Before it happens they move to places which offer plentiful food, plus safety. There they stay until able to fly once more. So, habitat is again of crucial importance – these birds are entirely dependent on a safe place with sufficient food.

NEW OPPORTUNITIES

The new habitats which man created across the British Isles as the landscape changed were all good places for birds of one sort or another. Even though they were used to graze animals, grow crops or produce timber, there were plenty of wild plants, seeds and invertebrates on which birds could feed year round, and usually plenty of suitable cover for nesting and shelter. Often, one small area would contain a variety of habitats – woodland, fields and ponds perhaps – so the local bird community must have been very abundant and diverse.

But, as the human population has grown, man has constantly sought ways of increasing the productivity of the land. He is now better able to do that than ever before. Farming and forestry can maintain output not only with fertilisers, but by using chemicals, which destroy weeds and invertebrates on which many birds depend. Another effect is the process of specialisation, which means that whole areas of the countryside grow only a limited range of crops and may not contain livestock and pasture at all. This reduces habitat diversity and the range of feeding and nesting opportunities for birds. The third problem is the destruction of 'old-fashioned' habitats like moor and heath, reed beds and estuaries, by the expansion of conifer forests, farmland and industry. All this has happened in the last 50 years – a period during which the face of the countryside has been changed more than it had been during the previous 50 centuries.

BRITAIN'S VITAL ROLE

What variety of habitat remains in the British Isles today and how important is it to birds? Many of the birds that live here are

This wren will only build its nest where there is a suitable site and where there are good food supplies. Caterpillars form an essential part of the diet of many baby birds

widespread in other parts of Europe, but four British habitats are important on an international scale because they hold a large proportion of the total European or world populations of certain species. These four are: seabirds on the cliffs and islands, waders on the estuaries, wildfowl on inland waters and estuaries, and birds of prey on the moors and mountains.

ALONG THE CLIFFS

From Yorkshire up round Scotland, down north-west England and Wales round to Dorset, most of the coastline is rocky, and often tall cliffs rear above the sea. Much of the western and northern coasts of Ireland are rocky too, and off Scotland in particular lies a profusion of islands and stacks. Along these coasts, vast colonies of seabirds gather each spring to nest, returning from a winter spent at sea, where many species have travelled far into the Atlantic, even to Antarctica. The auks – guillemots and razorbills – need cliffs with ledges on which to nest. Puffins dig burrows in the soft ground of the clifftop. Terns gather on high shingle beaches or even grazing land near by.

For tawny owls snow is bad news, but not as bad as loss of hunting grounds

Cormorants like the tops of rocky stacks, but their near relatives, the shags, prefer sea coves and tumbled boulders. For a few weeks the big seabird colonies are alive with activity, but by midsummer birds are already moving away, some to spend months out of sight of land until spring draws them back again.

ESTUARIES AND LAKES
Even as these seabirds leave, the first migrant waders start to arrive in Britain, returning from their breeding grounds in the Arctic where the short summer is soon over. Through the autumn, huge numbers appear on the mud and sand flats of the estuaries, some to refuel on the myriad worms and shellfish before moving on again to warmer shores, but many to stay right through the winter. Some of Britain's breeding waders may be among them too, dropping down to the coast from nearby hills. Now their lives will be governed not by day and night, but by the rhythm of the tides.

When water covers the mud flats, waders must roost on high salt marsh or nearby farmland. They flock closely together and

Scotland is one of the principal European strongholds of the golden eagle. Eagles need vast hunting territories covering thousands of acres of wild uplands – and such areas are disappearing fast

though many seem to sleep, others are vigilant – quick to call in alarm and take wing at the approach of danger. As the tide turns, birds begin to move out to feed, each species concentrating on just a few kinds of prey. Curlews probe for worms, oyster-catchers prise open cockles and mussels, sanderlings scurry after the retreating waves, picking food from near the surface of sand or mud.

On many estuaries, flocks of ducks and geese also gather, though they feed mainly on plant material such as eel-grass, which grows between the tide lines. They, too, have bred in the north and will stay only for the winter. Other wildfowl move inland – geese and wigeon to graze on pasture or winter cereal crops, others mostly to dabble or dive in lakes, reservoirs and gravel pits throughout the lowlands. If these freeze, they will concentrate on the bigger waters

which stay open longest, or move south and westward hoping to find milder weather. Upland lakes have few birds in winter – they are too infertile, cold and windswept.

ON THE UPLANDS
In fact, few birds of any kind stay in the uplands in winter. Golden eagles are among those that do, their flying and hunting skills enabling them to feed under most conditions and their large size giving them the physical reserves necessary to sit out the worst days of storm or mist. The expanses of the Scottish Highlands hold many of Europe's golden eagles and, in summer, they are joined by hen harriers and merlins which have probably wintered in the valleys or at the coast, hunting among the small bird flocks. In fact, both these birds of prey are more widespread in the British Isles than eagles are, and may be found in most upland blocks where heather still grows, providing them with nest cover and good hunting conditions.

Heather is vital too for the red grouse – a bird found nowhere else but Britain and Ireland. The upland fields of rough grass hold many of Europe's breeding curlews. The other upland waders – dunlin, golden plover and greenshank, for example – are common in Scandinavia and Iceland, but some of them are now very rare in Britain because of destruction of their habitats by overgrazing and by new afforestation. The uplands are, therefore, a national conservation priority.

So too, sadly, are many other habitats. Reed beds with their bitterns, bearded tits and marsh harriers; heathland with its Dartford warblers; native pine woods with crossbills and crested tits; sessile oak woods with pied flycatchers and wood warblers; wet grassland with snipe and black-tailed godwit. The future of all these uncommon birds rests with our willingness and ability to protect their habitats. The absurdities of draining land to produce yet more surplus milk, of grant-aiding the planting of alien trees in places where they will not grow, or the insensitive use of land that produces no economic return must be resisted by those of us who care.

Woodlands

Autumn in a Surrey wood

WOODLAND IS A WONDERFULLY INTRICATE AND ANCIENT HABITAT, ONE THAT HAS BEEN PRESENT IN BRITAIN FOR SUCH A HUGE LENGTH OF TIME THAT IT HAS EVOLVED A VARIETY OF FORMS, ALL OF WHICH HAVE THEIR CHARACTERISTIC BIRDS. WOODLANDS CHANGE WITH THE SEASONS, PARTICULARLY THOSE OF BROADLEAVED TREES, WHICH ARE GREEN AND LUXURIANT IN SUMMER, BUT COLD, BARE AND DIFFICULT TO LIVE IN DURING THE WINTER MONTHS. THE BIRDLIFE IS ALSO VERY MUCH INFLUENCED BY THE WAY THE WOOD IS USED BY PEOPLE — FOR EXAMPLE TO PRODUCE TIMBER, TO SHELTER LIVESTOCK, TO REAR PHEASANTS, OR AS A NATURE RESERVE.

The story of Britain's woods begins with the end of the latest Ice Age, about 20,000 years ago. As the glaciers retreated and the temperature rose, a few hardy plants and dwarf shrubs spread over the cold, wet ground, helping to dry it out and to build up soil as they decayed, so that conditions became suitable for trees. Willows, birch and pine were probably the first tree colonists, having seeds that spread far on the wind, the ability to grow in difficult ground, and tolerance of low temperatures. Hazel was among the early colonisers too; the importance of this modest tree in the development of the countryside is often overlooked.

Gradually both the soil and the climate improved. Oak trees arrived and spread north as far as the Highlands, which remained, as it still does today, the province of birch and pine. In Ireland, elm with hazel was the dominant tree community except in the west where oak and pine seem to have been more abundant. Wales and western England held oak and elm, and oak also covered the north of England. On the richer soils of the lowlands – the Midlands, East Anglia and the south – lime was probably the most numerous tree. There must have come a time when all the land which was not too wet or too high was covered by trees.

EXPANDING VARIETY

As the forest community developed, so a diversity of birds would have begun to appear in the British Isles, expanding into land long denied them by ice and snow. The wildwood which greeted them would have been very different from modern, managed woods. A variety of trees and shrubs, the presence of many ancient and giant trees, the simple extent of the forests, and the activities of wild mammals such as boars and bears must all have had important consequences for birds. The presence of grazing animals – deer, sheep, cattle and pigs – has also had a great effect on the well-being of woods and consequently the bird life within them. Although different regions had different species of dominant tree, a diversity of other kinds would also have grown in smaller numbers, at least in the richer, warmer lowlands.

RANGE OF OPPORTUNITIES

No two kinds of tree have the same value for birds. There are three reasons for this. One is that they support different communities of insects and produce different kinds of fruit or seeds – so the food resource is different. For example, oak trees are attacked in summer by great numbers of caterpillars of certain moths which eat the leaves and are in turn eaten by many birds and taken to feed their young. By contrast, elm is a far less useful supplier of insects. Oak produces acorns, eaten avidly by jays; alder has tiny cones with seeds taken by redpolls and siskins; ash keys are important to bullfinches, and so on.

The second factor influencing birds is that differences in the physical structure of bark, branches and leaves of trees means that they offer a varying range of nesting and sheltering places. For example, rough-barked trees like oak provide far more living and hiding places for insects and spiders than smooth trees such as cherry, so they are much better foraging places for treecreepers. Birch, quick growing, short-lived and with a tendency to rot while standing, is ideal for birds which excavate their own nest cavities.

Finally, the food and the nest sites available to birds are different under different varieties of tree because the trees control the kinds of herbs and shrubs that grow beneath them – the understorey. Thus, ash comes into leaf late in the season and casts only a light shade so other plants can grow well beneath it, while a tree such as beech, which casts a dense shade, will have only shade-tolerant plants growing with it. In general, the richer the understorey, the more birds will be present. However, a few birds, such as wood warblers, like the open conditions under beech and many species feed on beech-mast in winter.

Beech trees (right) provide food in the form of beech-mast. Jays (below) eat the mast, but acorns form a more important part of their diet

AVAILABILITY OF FOOD

It is obvious from this that a wood containing several different sorts of tree is likely to attract the greatest variety of birds, but there is a second important value in woodland diversity and this concerns the availability of food year-round. Different trees, shrubs and plants produce their crop of seeds or invertebrates at different seasons, so continuity of supply is assured. Studies in an Oxfordshire wood show that marsh tits take beech-mast as well as aphids from sycamore, and maple seeds in autumn; in winter they forage on oak trees looking for insects, but also eat spindle berries and the flowers of wych elm when they appear in February; hazel buds and birch catkins are used in spring, and the birds also hunt for insects on ash trees and in hawthorn; oak again becomes important in summer because of the abundance of insects that live on it. In addition, marsh tits eat honeysuckle berries, burdock and maple seeds, and various leaf buds. In fact, few birds can rely on the same kind of food year-round, so for residents at least it is essential to change diet with the seasons, exploiting whatever is abundant.

THE VITAL DEAD WOOD

Another important feature of the wildwood must have been its abundance of huge old trees, decaying hulks and fallen timber. For woodpeckers this would have been ideal, because for much of the year they feed mainly on the larvae of insects that bore in rotten wood. It will also have suited the many species of bird which nest in holes or cavities, which provide shelter, conceal-ment and some safety from predators such as magpies, though weasels and squirrels can often gain access. Potentially there is a lot of competition for nest holes, but this is somewhat reduced by individual species' preferences. Marsh tits, for instance, like to nest near the ground, perhaps in a stump; great tits usually nest higher than this at four metres (12–25 feet) up; blue tits prefer the highest and smallest cavities. In fact, birds nest in the layer of the forest where they do most feeding. But this rule is by no means hard and fast in modern woods where nest cavities tend to be in short supply and birds must take what they can get. Putting up boxes helps to reduce the problem and permits breeding by 'surplus' birds which have failed to find natural sites.

Tawny owls need big, old trees with holes in them in which to build their nests

A SHAFT OF SUNLIGHT

Though many native trees are very long lived, eventually there comes a time when they die, decay and collapse. Others are overtaken by catastrophes such as the gales so graphically brought to our attention in October 1987. Depending on the kind of tree, a successor generation may already be growing up beneath it, but it may not be until sunlight reaches the forest floor that this process begins. So, some parts of the wildwood would have contained a mix of trees of different ages, and in other places a stand of trees all of the same age and size may have extended for many miles. Birds' adaptations not only determine what they eat, but also where they seek food and nest sites. This means that different ages and mixtures of trees are used by different birds. Tree pipits like clearings where little re-growth has begun, but need a few saplings or nearby trees from which to launch their song flights. Nightingales nest in dense thickets of young trees or scrub, and feed only on the bare ground beneath them where they find abundant ants. Many species like the edge, where forest gives way to a clearing or a riverside. Some, such as the nuthatch, stick mainly within areas of big, old timber. The vast, continuous extent of the wildwood would have meant that every sort of condition existed somewhere.

ROOM TO SURVIVE

For large birds, extensive forest areas are essential not because they need special structural conditions but to support suf-ficient prey. Raptors such as golden eagles, goshawks and honey buzzards would have been widespread throughout the natural forest. So too, probably, was that massive gamebird, the capercaillie.

The forest's extent may also have been important, especially to resident songbirds, because of its sheltering effect, especially in cutting down the impact of wind. This means less heat-loss, so birds can survive on a smaller intake of food. It may also mean that the forest plants and insects become active sooner in spring and persist longer in autumn, so extending the breeding season. In some places native evergreens – ivy, holly and yew – would also have added to the cover and shelter, and may well have attracted flocks of bird to roost as they do today. For small songbirds, winter may well also have been made easier by the activities of the large mammals. Wild cattle – the aurochs – and wild boar were themselves seeking food and disturbing the ground, breaking up snow cover and kicking or rootling over the leaf litter. The robin which follows you confidingly in the garden learnt the value of this trick long ago at the heels of the wild pigs.

Nuthatches are usually found among mature trees, on the larger limbs

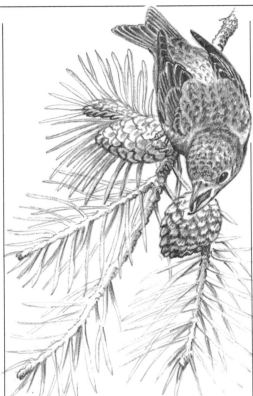

The crossbill has become so specialised that it can only live where there are conifers

HUMAN INFLUENCE

For several thousand years, man had little effect on the wildwood except as a nomadic hunter and gatherer, but in the Neolithic period, about 6,000 years ago, he began to clear the trees so that he could graze livestock and grow crops. This was the start of a process of forest clearance which was to continue until about 500 years ago, by which time the population was actually short of certain kinds of timber for building and wood as fuel. Long before that point, probably in prehistoric times, woodlands had been taken into management. Many kinds of tree will shoot from the base when cut down and this attribute was turned to advantage – by cutting, or coppicing, the shoots every ten years or so a constant supply of wood was guaranteed. This new habitat attracted the birds which like scrub and thickets, such as garden and grasshopper warblers, yellowhammers and nightingales. Often it included some standard trees – those which had been left uncut and allowed to grow on to provide timber for structural uses. Here, blackcaps and willow warblers, tree pipits, finches and others would have found homes. Wild cattle and pigs were by then extinct and livestock was excluded from young coppice because it browsed the new shoots, but in some areas wood pasture had come into being, with stock grazing beneath pollard trees, which were those whose limbs were cut periodically from a 'crown' well above the ground rather than coppiced at ground level. Many of the spreading trees in parkland, and most riverside willows, are pollards. The old boles develop cavities suitable for redstarts, tits, flycatchers, stock doves and owls.

A CHANGE OF SCALE

Fortunately, most woodland birds hold fairly small territories so the much reduced and fragmented woods could still support them, provided the range of food and physical structure was suitable. But the larger birds were less fortunate – eagles were pushed back into the Highlands, honey buzzards became rare, and goshawks and capercaillies were made extinct (though both these species have now been re-introduced).

For centuries the situation changed little. The creation of hedgerows across the lowlands benefited birds which like woodland edges or scrub habitat – blackbirds, whitethroats, dunnocks and linnets for instance. Then, quite suddenly, the economic importance of woodlands declined as coal replaced coppice and as cheap hardwood imports replaced standards. Many woods were destroyed; others became pheasant coverts in which magpies and crows, sparrowhawks, buzzards and owls were wiped out. The last 60 years have seen the creation of vast new conifer forests in the uplands, providing habitat for many bird species, and in just the last few years the destruction of lowland broadleaf woodland seems to have come to a halt. For most woodland birds, the current outlook is good. Britain is still, nevertheless, poorly wooded in the main and a greater concentration on the planting of lowland broadleaved woods would undoubtedly bode well for the long-term outlook for many birds.

BIRDWATCHING IN WOODLAND

Birdwatching in woodland can be most frustrating. There is so much cover that birds are hard to see and will often quietly move away before you even know they are there! In spring, song and calls reveal most species, but learning them is not easy – and in late summer the calls of young birds are even more difficult to sort out. In winter you can spend hours in a wood and see almost nothing, as many birds have migrated south and several of the residents are in flocks which can easily be missed. But, with the knowledge of what to look for, where and when, a woodland becomes a much more rewarding place to visit.

First some general facts. For climatic reasons more species of bird occur in the south and east than in the woods of the west and north. On average, sites of about 100

Highland pine woods are home to birds not seen elsewhere in Britain

acres will hold up to 40 breeding species, but small woods have fewer simply because they offer only a restricted range of habitat diversity and food. Almost all broadleaved woods, however small, have song thrushes, mistle thrushes and blackbirds, robins, wrens and dunnocks, blue and great tits, willow warblers and chaffinches. The majority of broadleaved woods also hold wood-pigeons, coal and long-tailed tits, treecreepers, bullfinches, starlings, jays and crows. Great spotted woodpeckers do not occur in Ireland; chiffchaffs and blackcaps are uncommon there and in northern Scotland, but elsewhere all of them are widespread.

THE VALUABLE OAK

Most lowland woods contain a lot of oak, widely planted for timber and fuel. Until oak reaches about 100 years of age it is not much good for birds, but after that its value is great. The foliage supports many caterpillars; rot holes have begun to develop and provide nest sites, and there is usually a good understorey of shrubs and herbs; the acorn crop is eaten by pigeons, jays and small mammals – which in turn are food for tawny owls. Because of the diversity of food sources and the abundance of big timber, marsh tits and nuthatches are often present.

THE VIRTUES OF BEECH

By contrast, beech woods are less good in summer. Widely planted on free-draining chalky soils where oak does not thrive, beech casts a deep shade in which little understorey can grow. This attracts wood warblers, which feed in the canopy and nest on the ground among dead leaves, usually where a low-hanging limb or solitary sapling gives them a 'covered pathway' along which they can travel up and down. But few other species find food or cover here. The virtue of beech is its production of great quantities of seed or mast about every third year, providing winter food for marsh tits, chaffinches and bramblings. Winter visitors to Britain, bramblings sometimes occur in massive flocks concentrating on the rich supply of seeds.

TWO WOODLAND SPECIALISTS

An uncommon or, at least, elusive woodland seed eater is the hawfinch. Famed for their ability to crack cherry stones, hawfinches actually take a wide range of tree fruits, including those of hornbeam, beech, sycamore, maple and wych elm (now sadly almost gone from the British landscape, at least for the time being). When these are exhausted they turn to hawthorn berries, rosehips and other shrubby fruits and, in late winter, eat the newly fattening buds of trees. Large insects are taken in summer. As most of their feeding is done in the canopy and the birds are shy, they are hard to see. A good place to watch for them is at a woodland pool, where many other species will come to bathe and drink.

Woodcocks, too, are elusive birds, spending the day roosting on the ground and moving out to feed at night. However, their courtship or territorial flight – roding – takes place at dusk among the tree tops, so a visit at this time of day can be rewarding. Many birds also sing at dusk, though the best song is in the early morning. For birdwatching, afternoons are the worst time as activity and song are at a low ebb.

TRADITIONAL MANAGEMENT

Today, few woods are coppiced; this entails cutting trees, in rotation, almost at ground level to produce a thicket of slender 'poles'. Some nature reserves are managed in this

way, mainly to benefit plants and insects. A springtime visit to such a wood may find garden warblers, nightingales and, in the standard trees, a good range of common species. Wood pasture, the other traditional management system, is still widespread in the uplands, where the oak woods are grazed by sheep which largely prevent the understorey from developing. This suits pied flycatchers, which catch insects in the open air space below the canopy. Redstarts are present here too, as they feed largely on the ground and like the bare open areas created by heavy grazing. Both need holes for nesting and these too are plentiful in the old oaks. Wood warblers and tree pipits also thrive here, buzzards remain common and, in Wales, red kites nest.

CONIFERS

Much of the uplands and some lowland areas now carry conifer forests, with a distinctive bird community of their own. When first created they hold many of the species that colonise any new planting, such as grasshopper warblers and whinchats, but also sometimes woodlarks in the lowlands and black grouse in the uplands. As they grow up, goldcrests and coal tits colonise, seeking insects among the needles. Later, common crossbills come to feed on the cones.

NATIVE PINE

In the Spey Valley, remnants of the ancient native pine forests still clothe the slopes of the Cairngorms. Here the rare Scottish crossbill feeds on the cones and crested tits excavate their nest cavities in rotting trunks of old pines. Reintroduced after its extinction in Britain, the capercaillie now finds its main stronghold here.

Throughout their long history, the woods have seen and suffered many changes. In many areas the pitiful fragments which remain give little idea of the glory that must once have been there. The glorious and productive woods of Caledon – the ancient Scots pine forest of the Highlands – remain under the most serious threat. But it is still possible to find birds of great variety within British woodlands and to enjoy the special pleasures of watching wildlife within the depths of a forest.

Woodcocks are unlikely to be seen during the day since their plumage blends beautifully with the woodland floor. The best chance of seeing them is at dusk in spring, when they glide among the tree tops in ghostly courtship flights

COVERING ALMOST HALF THE TOTAL LAND AREA OF THE BRITISH ISLES, MOUNTAINS AND MOORLANDS MAKE UP A SCENICALLY DIVERSE AND VARIED GROUP OF HABITATS. THEY ENCOMPASS THE WILDEST AND MOST REMOTE PARTS OF THE COUNTRYSIDE, WHERE MUCH THAT IS SPECTACULAR IN BRITAIN IS TO BE FOUND, WHERE IT IS STILL POSSIBLE TO WALK FOR A DAY WITHOUT SEEING ANOTHER PERSON AND WHERE A SENSE OF WILDERNESS PERSISTS.

Although difficult to define precisely, mountains and moorlands are easily recognised as including all areas above or beyond the normal limits of enclosed and cultivated land. At first sight, it may be difficult to accept that they have much else in common. The frost shattered rocky ridge of Liathach near Torridon, the rolling heather-clad North Yorkshire Moors or the sodden bogs of central Caithness, seem poles apart. But they are all largely dominated by three or four of the same major environmental factors: poor soil, low winter temperatures, high precipitation (snow as well as rain) and man.

The present-day distribution and structure of the mountains and moorlands is a result of underlying geology and reflects the presence of older and harder rocks, which have persisted despite successive periods of glaciation in the 'Ice Ages'. These are concentrated in the north and west. There are no mountains or moorlands south and east of a line from Scarborough to Exeter. North and west of this line, mountains and moorlands become increasingly predominant as one moves northward until, in Wester Ross and Sutherland, other habitats are mainly restricted to narrow coastal strips or ribbons running up the main river valleys. These resistant rocks are mostly acidic and non-calcareous and they give rise to soils of generally low productivity.

LOW BUT EXPOSED

British mountains are not particularly high (Ben Nevis, the highest peak, is only 4,406 feet above sea level). However, increasing altitude always results in increased exposure to wind, increased precipitation and a decrease in mean temperature of about one degree Fahrenheit for each 270 feet. Even these modest hills, therefore, provide opportunities for British birdwatchers to see truly Alpine – or arctic – species. Low winter temperature, with regular frost and persistent and extensive snow cover, is a major characteristic of mountains and moorlands. Temperature also decreases with latitude, and low temperatures come into effect at increasingly lower altitudes as one goes north. Thus, while in much of the south of Britain moorland areas may be confined to land over 1,000 feet, in the north of Scotland and Shetland moorland habitat is found very close to sea level. The presence of ptarmigans above 2,500 feet in central Scotland, but almost down to sea level in the north, illustrates the point vividly.

Lying on the edge of the Atlantic and subject to the warming effects of the North Atlantic Drift, a trans-Atlantic offshoot of the Gulf Stream, the climate along the west

Ben Lawers. Inset is a merlin at her nest. Merlins are most often found on moorland

coast is strongly oceanic and rainfall is not only high but relatively evenly spread throughout the year. A hundred or more inches of rain per year is not unusual in many mountain and moorland areas. This effect tends to diminish as one moves away from the west, so easterly mountains and moors tend to be somewhat drier.

DIVERSITY IN EXTREMES

High rainfall, low temperatures and poor soil combine in different areas to produce a variety of upland habitat types. On the highest and most rugged mountain tops, where climatic conditions are most extreme, frost and water in winter combine to fracture and erode exposed rock, which is then washed or blown away. Soil is confined to small cracks and crevices and vegetation has to fight to retain a foothold. Opportunities for birds are inevitably limited. On flatter mountain ridges and plateaux, such as those in the Cairngorms, where beds of snow carpet the ground for much of the winter and spring, more substantial soils develop, providing more opportunities for those plants able to withstand the extremes of exposure to cold and high winds. In these mountain areas, the vegetation has much in

Mountains and Moorlands

common with that found in arctic and tundra regions elsewhere in northern Europe and they remain to a large extent natural and unaffected by man, despite increasing pressures from skiers and other recreationists. The birds are very special, with ptarmigans, dotterels, the occasional snow bunting and, from time to time, a pair or two of unexpected breeding birds such as shore lark and Lapland bunting.

On lower and flatter ground exposure and temperature are less extreme and a wider range of plant species is able to become established, particularly where drainage is good. Shrubs and trees are able to grow and water plays an increasingly important role in

determining vegetation type. Regular rainfall leaches nutrients from the soil and further reduces its productivity and where drainage is slow or impeded, the soil may be perpetually waterlogged. This encourages the accumulation of dead vegetation which forms deposits of peat; these may be particularly extensive and form blanket bogs, such as those in Caithness and Sutherland.

THE IMPACT OF MAN

These lower lying areas have been substantially influenced by man over the last 2,000 years. The majority were once covered in trees and the present predominance of

heather and grass is the result of centuries of management, most recently for sheep, deer and grouse. Where grazing pressures from sheep are low and grouse are favoured, heather is encouraged by systematic burning, but elsewhere management is more haphazard. Increased sheep stocking levels and uncontrolled burning results in the replacement of heather by coarse moorland grasses. In extreme cases, like parts of the Peak District, overgrazing and excessive trampling has led to extensive losses of vegetation and erosion. More recently large areas of moorland have been planted with exotic conifers, reintroducing tree cover, but in a totally alien form.

PATCHWORK OF HABITATS

Much diversity is added to mountain and moorland areas by the presence of smaller patches of other habitat types, each of which may have populations of characteristic birds more widespread elsewhere. Lochs, streams and rivers are all integral parts of the upland environment, and on steeper slopes, in narrow gorges or on islands in lochs, areas of woodland or scrub may persist which have escaped the worst effects of grazing and burning and which give some indication of what the natural vegetation might have looked like before the intervention of man.

For much of the year, mountains and moorlands do not provide a hospitable environment for birds and very few species depend on them exclusively. Food is a major constraint and although there may be an abundance of invertebrates in summer, low winter temperatures, snow cover and high winds mean that only herbivores, predators and scavengers have any real chance of surviving as year-round residents. The remainder migrate within the British Isles to spend the winter in habitats where conditions are less extreme, or move south away from Britain altogether.

MAKING THE BEST OF IT

The winter residents are therefore an exclusive group, among which the ptarmigan endures the most extreme conditions, wintering on the highest ridges where the vegetation on which it feeds is kept free of snow by the wind. Its white winter plumage helps to reduce the chances of it being taken by predators. Red grouse and black grouse are also resident, but at lower altitudes in much less exposed places where they find shelter in and feed on heather and other persistent vegetation. The golden eagle, raven and that irrepressible related pair, the hooded and carrion crows, also remain throughout the winter, each depending to a greater or lesser extent on the availability of the carcasses of deer, sheep and other victims of winter weather. A reduction in stocking levels would reduce overgrazing, but at the same time limit the numbers of these scavengers, including Welsh red kites. Other predators, such as buzzards, peregrines and kestrels, may stay on moors in some areas, but most usually move out, particularly if the snow cover is heavy or the temperature very low. Small numbers of a variety of other species such as wrens, dippers and grey herons eke out a precarious winter existence on or around the moors, but many die if conditions become at all severe.

SOFTENING WITH SPRING

With the advent of warmer weather in spring, mountains and moorlands assume a more friendly face and the desolate stillness of winter is replaced by the songs of larks and displaying curlews. But moods change rapidly and even in the middle of summer falls of snow, heavy rain and sudden drops in temperature regularly occur causing nests to be deserted and young to die of exposure or drowning. Life is never easy here!

On the mountain tops the resident ptarmigans are joined by species such as wheatear and golden plover, and two other mountain species, the rare snow bunting, which breeds in areas of scree and shattered rock, and the dotterel, which nests on the flatter ridges. Although the breeding season is relatively short, it is still appreciably longer than that available to these species in arctic regions elsewhere. Dotterels are often back on their Scottish nesting grounds before Scandinavian birds appear farther south, still on their way north to where spring, as yet, has not arrived.

A male hen harrier performing his display flight

On the lower ground, as temperature rises and the snow cover vanishes, plant and invertebrate food starts to become more plentiful and a variety of birds returns to breed. A few species, notably red grouse, golden plovers, meadow pipits and skylarks, are widespread on moors throughout Britain while others, such as dunlins, curlews, lapwings and snipe, are more restricted and

have substantial populations on other lowland habitats. Marshes and lochs, as well as being generally important for many wader species, also attract breeding wildfowl, such as wigeon and teal.

In the north, moorlands attract a variety of species, which properly belong to habitats of the arctic and boreal zone – the band of forest in the cold north of Europe and Asia. They include greenshanks, whimbrels, red-throated divers, common scoters and rarities such as wood sandpipers. The moors of the north are also the breeding grounds for more marine species such as arctic skua and great skua, and many dunlins.

Although many are of great interest, the total number of species is not large. Overall densities are generally low, but the sheer extent of moorland and mountain habitat means that overall populations of some of these species may be high. Many of these summer visitors depend heavily on the seasonal abundance of invertebrates, and feeding is often concentrated around marshes, pools, lochs, streams and rivers. However, even in summer some species, such as golden plover and curlew, nest on moorlands but prefer, where the opportunity exists, to feed in richer agricultural areas near by. Greenshanks may even walk their newly hatched young several miles to better feeding areas. Most of these species are ground nesters and have no difficulty finding suitable places to nest. Larks and pipits, which conceal their nests in grassy tussocks or under heather, have ample opportunities, even on the most heavily grazed hillsides. Breeding waders, such as golden plovers and lapwings, will happily nest in a wide range of situations from totally bare ground through to tall heather and grass, but snipe and curlew tend to prefer more well-covered areas. Only where the vegetation is really rank are species of birds such as these likely to be prevented from nesting.

SURFEIT OF FOOD
Resident and returning birds of prey and scavengers inevitably benefit from this general influx of breeding birds and, in areas of poor husbandry, from the carcasses of lambs and sheep. Ravens are the earliest to nest, clutches being laid in February, and their young hatch at the time when such food starts to become abundant. Eagles benefit in the same way and also nest early, but others, such as merlin, may still find that food is scarce when they return to nest and may be forced to rely on woodland birds and other species using habitats adjacent to the main moors, until newly fledged pipits and larks become available. Birds of prey and scavengers have relatively large and conspicuous nests and young and prefer sites on cliffs and in trees that are safe from

Water Tor, Dartmoor. Meadow pipits (above) are usually the most numerous birds in such places

ground predators. In mountainous areas such as the west of Scotland cliffs and crags are widespread and eagles, peregrines and ravens may have several alternative nest sites, but where cliffs are scarce they may be forced to nest on low cliffs, in trees or even on the ground. Hen harriers and short-eared owls are ground nesters and need dense vegetation such as rushes or heather. Merlins also nest on the ground in areas of long rank heather, but where such heather is lacking, as in much of Sutherland, they nest in old crows' nests in trees in birchwoods or in isolated trees on vegetated islands.

Soil fertility has an important effect on the abundance of invertebrates and moorland bird densities are conspicuously greater on the more productive moors and hillsides. The highest recorded densities of golden plover are on limestone areas in the Pennines, and high densities of grouse on the richer moors of eastern Scotland contrast with those in the unproductive west.

IMPROVEMENT BY FIRE
Equally important are the effects of differing land management regimes, which can have a major impact on both the type and density of moorland birds. Planned burning to produce a mosaic of differing ages of heather not only provides shelter and food for grouse and an income through shooting for the landowners, but also promotes a habitat that is favoured by moorland waders and birds of prey, albeit that the latter may suffer from ill-informed individuals and illegal persecution. Overgrazing and overburning, which lead to the replacement of heather by grasses, favour a few species such as skylark at the expense of grouse, golden plovers and merlins. Large areas of the southern uplands in the Scottish borders, which consist of almost birdless, grass covered hills, serve as a warning as to what the uplands could become. Equally worrying are the inroads being made into moorlands by plantations of exotic spruce and pines. These have their place, but too many recent plantations have destroyed sites of major wildlife interest.

Despite their apparent inhospitability and their relatively restricted avifauna, British mountains and moorlands are the haunts of some of the most spectacular and rarer British birds. In such areas the birdwatcher still has a chance to feel that each encounter with a bird is a unique experience, unshared by the teeming masses elsewhere in the British Isles.

If moorland disappears under conifer plantations, golden eagles have nowhere to hunt, so large-scale forestry threatens their survival

Lowland Heaths

TREES COVERED MOST OF BRITAIN AFTER THE RE-TREAT OF THE ICE, BUT THEY WERE CLEARED BY MAN, OFTEN STARTING WITH THE LIGHTEST AND MOST EASILY WORKED LAND. ON FREE DRAINING, SANDY SOILS, THIS LEADS TO A RAPID LOSS OF NUTRIENTS, WHICH DISSOLVE IN RAIN WATER AND GET CARRIED DEEPER THAN THE REACH OF MOST ROOTS. FEW PLANTS GROW IN SUCH POOR CON-DITIONS, AND HEATHER CAN BECOME DOMINANT.

WASTED OPPORTUNITIES

The literary travellers of the 18th and 19th centuries recorded the heather moors as wastelands. And they are wastelands in the sense that they represent land whose poten-tial for human exploitation has been wreck-ed by mismanagement. But they have been around long enough to acquire special inter-est of their own. It is worth remembering that forest clearance continues today in areas where trees represent the most pro-ductive use of the land, leading to rapid loss of soil fertility. In the tropics, and especially in rain forests, this process is generally deplored.

Lack of fertility and human origins are key aspects of heaths. Given the chance, trees – either pine or birch – will rapidly re-invade. Left alone, they will form woodland which in time will tend towards oak domina-tion. But historically they have not been left alone, and grazing and burning have con-tinued, preventing accumulation of soil fer-tility and development of tree cover.

Heaths are thinly scattered throughout lowland Britain. The most extensive tracts remain in a belt from Surrey through the New Forest to Dorset, where there is a band of geologically recent sands. Heaths have recently been devastated by human in-fluences different from those which created them. Large areas have been turned into conifer forests, poor farmland and housing land. Paradoxically, much has also been lost through neglect. If burned frequently, heather may be replaced by bracken and birch is often a vigorous invader after fire.

POOR AND SIMPLE

The key features of heaths are their soil poverty and their simplicity. Extensive tracts of heather may be broken by scattered patches of gorse or the occasional birch or pine tree. Simple structure means few dif-ferent niches in the scheme of nature which bird species can occupy and a small variety of birds. Poor soils lead to a low production of plant growth and insect life. As a result, the birds that do occur are not very numer-ous, just as on the rather similar moorlands. Indeed, the separation of moors and heaths is rather arbitrary.

The heather itself can vary in depth and thickness depending on age and soil con-ditions. Its most characteristic bird is the meadow pipit, which is a long-legged ground-feeder. Like other open country species, such as the skylark, it sings from the air with a fluttering flight. Meadow pipits tolerate thicker ground vegetation than skylarks. On grassy heaths the skylark is often more common. It can conceal its nest in the smallest of hollows on open ground, often covered with no more than a wisp of vegetation. Meadow pipits use more cover for nesting and are slimmer and more agile as they feed over and under the heather. These common brown birds each have a scarcer counterpart associated with woodland margins or scattered trees. It is quite extraordinary how the presence of even a few trees can attract tree pipits. Tree and meadow pipits are very similar in ap-pearance, though the songs differ. Tree pipits perch and often feed in trees and frequently make their song flights from them. They treat branches just like the ground as they walk along them, quite unlike the flitting and perching actions of a tit or warbler.

Heaths are among Britain's most threatened habitats, yet they are beautiful and support such rare and delightful birds as the Dartford warbler (below)

SPLENDID SONGSTERS

Woodlarks are also brown and not very distinguished looking. They do, however, have a distinct and wonderful song. Woodlarks need scattered tree cover and, like skylarks, a reasonably open ground vegetation. Ideal features on heaths are generally created by fires, and sometimes by ploughed or otherwise disturbed soil. These habitats are ephemeral, so woodlarks may come and go – in recent years they have become quite a rare and exciting find.

Heather is rarely deep enough to support those birds which favour scrubland. Sometimes wrens creep about, mouselike, in the very deepest parts of the thickest heather bushes. An interesting feature of the heather is the number of pygmy shrews and lizards, both of which are common, and locally the presence of the rare and declining sand lizard. These mammals and reptiles outnumber the insect-eating birds in such places, but even where they are numerous they are usually frustratingly elusive. In winter, insect life in heather is very poor, and if it snows the whole surface is readily blanketed. Little wonder that the larks and pipits usually move out at this season.

THE RICHNESS OF GORSE

The most common shrublike plant of the heaths is gorse. Gorse is a legume, related to peas and beans, and capable of fixing its own nitrogen. Even on poor soils, it can grow very palatable foliage. In spite of its thorns, it is remarkable to see the enthusiasm with which New Forest ponies browse it. Gorse also supports a good supply of plant-eating insects, while many spiders make use of its varied structure. Wrens are often the most abundant exploiters of this food supply, while robins may skulk on the ground below the very open-structured bushes.

In parts of Dorset, Hampshire and Surrey, the rare and special bird to look out for in the gorse is the Dartford warbler. It is small, even as warblers go, and a great skulker. A buzzy *churr* or the deceptively weak-looking flight of a rather long-tailed bird are often all you can make out. Dartford warblers probe for spiders and insects in the evergreen gorse throughout the year and may nest there too. In winter they can use the cover. Even when snow lies thickly there is often shelter beneath the gorse where spiders and insects can still be hunted. This is an unusual warbler as practically all Britain's other species migrate south for the winter. Periodically it suffers a severe reduction of numbers after a cold spell – it is quite clearly near the limit of its climatic tolerance in southern England. Given a few good winters Dartfords can bounce back quite quickly, roughly doubling every two years. In spring they often look as if they are eating the flowers of gorse, dismantling the petals with vigour. In fact they are after the caterpillars of a tiny moth. Later in the summer a small weevil infests the flowers to lay its eggs in the developing seed pods and is another favourite food of the Dartford warbler.

GOOD COMPANIONS

Where there are Dartford warblers there are often stonechats too. Indeed the two species often go together in a way that looks more than chance. The warbler perhaps welcomes the vigilance of the stonechat, which always has a good vantage from a high perch and vigorously *chacks* on sight of disturbance. The stonechat goes for larger, active food, sometimes in an aerial chase, but more often in a sweeping descent to the ground. It sits several feet up on gorse, bracken or a small tree to watch out for such prey. Stonechats will tackle things as large as emperor moths.

Once, red-backed shrikes fed in a similar way on heaths throughout Britain. These are fierce birds equipped with a hooked bill, and reminiscent of a diminutive falcon in structure and behaviour. They might pounce on grasshoppers or large beetles but also have the size and ferocity to go for small birds, mammals or reptiles. Sadly the shrike has declined enormously in northern Europe, almost certainly for natural reasons, and by 1987 only one or two pairs remained in England. This is only the second species of regular British breeders to go in the last 50 years. The red-backed shrike is a summer migrant to Britain. In winter, great grey shrikes sometimes stay on the heaths. This is a larger species, preying much more on small mammals and birds. Both shrikes share the somewhat gruesome habit of impaling prey on thorn bushes or spiky twigs. This habit is used both to help in dismembering prey and also as a larder for temporary storage.

The hobby is a real falcon. It is found on heathland, and also in other sorts of habitat. Hobbies feed on dragonflies from the boggy areas and nest in old crows' nests, especially in pines. They also feed on birds; they are agile enough to catch swallows, house martins and even swifts. With a diet like that, hobbies are necessarily migrants to Britain and retire to Africa for the winter.

THE NIGHT SHIFT

Flying insects are also the fare of nightjars. Nightjars rest during the day, quietly camouflaged on a low bough, or covering their eggs on a small bare patch of ground. By night they come into their own with their strange churring song, evocative calls and curious wing-clapping display flights. They feed on night-flying insects, especially moths and beetles, which must be a precarious life, especially in periods of cold or wet weather which suppresses insect activity. Nightjars haunt the edges of woodland where scattered trees provide some shelter but leave enough space for these agile fliers to hunt. The variety of vegetation is probably important in providing a reliable supply of prey to cover the different flight periods of several species. Nightjars sometimes

Hobbies are often seen on heaths; dragonflies can form part of their diet

gather at temporarily good feeding areas, from bogs to individual large oak trees.

Boggy areas of heaths have features of their own. They add a variety of plant communities with sundews on carpets of sphagnum mosses and small pools. The wetter areas are favoured by dragonflies, which in southern England include several rare and localised species. Sometimes they attract breeding waders like snipe, redshank

and curlew, though these species occur in greater numbers on wet meadows and in the uplands. Bog pools are too poor in productivity to attract many ducks either in summer or winter – there is nothing for them to eat.

THE BIRDLESS MONTHS

In winter the poverty of the heaths is shown by their poor ability to support birds. Wrens and Dartford warblers stay and may be joined by influxes of coal tits and goldcrests, especially in the gorse. The odd bird of prey such as a peregrine or merlin may come from the north. Hen harriers may switch their moorland breeding areas for the similar but more benign heaths for the winter. Harriers forage widely by day, but sometimes gather in small communal roosts for the night in the safety of open heathland.

Much heathland has been planted for forestry, usually with pines. A mature pine wood supports a similarly poor but very different bird community from the open heath; woodland species such as coal tit and goldcrest predominate. When the trees are felled and replanted open conditions reappear for a few years. These conditions may attract many of the heathland birds. As many woodlarks and nightjars now live in these habitats as on the heaths, which are older, but only slightly less artificial.

A CLOSE-CROPPED TURF

Heather is a dominant feature of most heaths, but this is not the whole picture. In places with more base-rich soils, often shallow glacial drifts, grassy vegetation may be dominant. The most extensive area of such grass heathland is in the brecks of Norfolk and Suffolk. The brecks have many similarities with the chalk grasslands on thin soils on downland. Both these areas are dependent on high levels of grazing by rabbits or sheep. They develop a scrub cover of birch or hawthorn very quickly if grazing is reduced. This happened to a great area in the 1950s after myxomatosis devastated rabbit populations.

Ground-living birds characterise these open areas. Most exciting is the furtive stone-curlew, a rather peculiar wader. Stone-curlews feed on large invertebrates, mainly by night when their prey is more active. Much of their food is most abundant on grazed pastures fertilised by sheep or rabbit dung. Other waders, especially lapwings and, now rarely, ringed plovers, favour similar conditions. A counterpart of the stonechat in the more open conditions of brecks or downs is the wheatear. Apart from the connection through grazing, wheatears also go with rabbits to the extent that burrows often provide the birds' nest sites.

SEASIDE HEATH

Another rather special and distinct kind of heathland occurs in western coastal areas from the Lizard in Cornwall through Wales to the western islands of Scotland. These coastal heaths do not harbour Dartford warblers, woodlarks or nightjars, but meadow pipits and skylarks are still characteristic. Nowhere is the stonechat more at home. These areas have very mild winters with rare snow falls, which allows the stonechat to be more sedentary than is the case in places like Surrey. The special bird (though sadly gone from the south-west) is the chough; a most unusual crow with a curved red bill. It probes for insects in short turf, but in winter may feed on the tideline or on farmland. Choughs generally nest on sea cliffs, especially favouring caves. The combination of all these requirements together is not common, and it is therefore no surprise that neither is the chough.

Heathland very quickly reverts to woodland if given a chance. Birch and pine are usually the first colonisers

Yellowhammers often sing from heathland gorse

Lakes and Gravel Pits

WATER ATTRACTS BIRDS. THEY USE IT FOR FEED-ING, DRINKING, BATHING, NESTING, ROOSTING AND MOULTING. FOR THE BIRDWATCHER AREAS OF OPEN WATER OFFER THE PROSPECT OF AN INTERESTING TIME OUT. FOR THE NOVICE THEY ARE GOOD PLACES TO START BIRDWATCHING AS LAKES AND RESERVOIRS ARE USUALLY ACCESSIBLE, EASY TO VIEW AND HOLD LARGE, BRIGHTLY COLOURED BIRDS THAT ARE REASONABLY EASY TO IDENTIFY. OF COURSE THERE ARE EXCEPTIONS: DUCKS, DURING THEIR ECLIPSE PERIOD IN LATE SUMMER AND EARLY AUTUMN WHEN THEY HAVE LOST ALL THEIR DISTINGUISHING PLUMAGE, OFFER A DAUNTING CHALLENGE TO THE UNINITIATED!

There is a wide variety of open fresh waters throughout Britain, both natural and man-made. It has been estimated that there are over 81,000 areas of fresh water in Britain, varying from small ponds of under an acre to extensive lakes such as Loch Lomond, many thousands of acres in extent. Many of these provide valuable habitats for birds. Of course not all lakes are alike; they differ considerably in water quality, the nature of their shoreline, their depth and bottom profile, their size, altitude and exposure to wind. Their geographical location will also affect the birds present. Such factors control the types and numbers of birds that an area of water can support. The most significant factor, however, is the 'trophic' condition – or productivity – of the lake. Water bodies are usually classified according to their cal-cium carbonate content. Most are either 'oligotrophic' (low calcium carbonate concentration and low productivity) or 'eu-trophic' (high calcium carbonate concen-tration and high productivity).

UNPRODUCTIVE LAKES
Oligotrophic lakes are acidic waters, low in nutrients and generally found in the upland areas of western and northern Britain. They are poor in nutrients because they are fed by water gathered from infertile upland catch-ments underlain by old, acidic rocks. Usual-ly they are of natural origin, filling valleys and depressions created during the last Ice Age. Most of the lochs in the glacial valleys of upland Scotland, such as Loch Maree in Highland Region, are firmly in the oligo-trophic group. In recent decades some man-made lakes of this kind have been created as upland valleys have been dammed to cap-ture water for water supply and hydro-electric power generation. Examples are the Elan Valley lakes in mid-Wales, built at the end of the 19th century to supply water for Birmingham.

A BLEAK PROSPECT
The combination of high altitude, lack of shelter, low nutrient status and deep water means that oligotrophic lakes are usually of low biological productivity and that they support relatively few plants and animals. Indeed, such a lake is best recognised by its rather bleak aspect with a stony shore and

Lowland lakes are the richest in wildlife. Bankside vegetation can provide shelter for many species of bird, including the great crested grebe (inset)

lack of water plants growing from the shal-lows. A lack of nutrients for plant growth combines with wave action to destabilise the lake bed so vegetation can rarely find a footing. Those few birds that do occur feed on invertebrates or fish. Breeding birds include red-throated and black-throated divers, goldeneyes, red-breasted mergan-sers and goosanders, although the first three are restricted to Scotland. Also in Scotland ospreys may be seen hunting for fish during the summer months. At the water's edge, common terns, common gulls and common sandpipers may nest among the stones of the shore, or on small islands. Outside the breeding season, oligotrophic lakes may attract a few migrant wildfowl or waders, but not in great numbers or variety. In winter, however, they are cold, bleak, in-hospitable places and are usually deserted by the birds.

THE OPPOSITE EXTREME
In total contrast, eutrophic lakes are produc-tive waters, high in calcium carbonate and nutrients. Located in lowland areas, gener-ally in southern and eastern Britain, they are fed by water from fertile catchments under-lain by nutrient-rich rocks. Often the natu-ral nutrient supply is enriched from artificial sources. Consequently, these waters are of high biological productivity, rich in plant-life and invertebrates and attractive to birds. Natural lakes of this kind in lowland Britain are rare. Some have been drained for agri-culture. Whittlesey Mere near Peter-borough, for example, was once the second largest lake in England. Over 1,000 acres in size, it was drained in 1851 to create arable farmland. Today, the main areas of natural lakes in England are the meres of Cheshire and Shropshire and in the brecklands of East Anglia. Many new areas of water have been created in lowland Britain by the construction of reservoirs to supply drinking water, the creation of lakes as fishponds and as amenity features, the extraction of sand, gravel and peat and subsidence caused by coal mining and brine pumping. The crea-tion of new man-made waters in areas where lakes were previously few has extended the range and increased the numbers of aquatic birds in many regions of lowland England.

SEASONAL CHANGE
The bird community of lowland lakes varies considerably by season. During the spring and summer months breeding waterfowl may include great crested grebes, little grebes, mute swans, Canada geese, mal-lards, tufted ducks, coots and moorhens. Reed, sedge and grasshopper warblers and reed buntings may nest in reeds and scrub around the edge. As summer moves into autumn, some lakes hold moulting great crested grebes and ducks. For a few weeks during this period they are flightless and vulnerable to predators and they seek a secure site with abundant food in which to moult and replace their flight feathers. Male ducks also take on their dull eclipse plum-age, similar to the females, before re-moulting into their full bright breeding plumage during autumn, ready to display

and pair up. Large numbers of swallows, house martins and sand martins may also be seen hunting for insects over water, building up their food reserves ready for migration.

As autumn turns to winter, hard weather forces waterfowl to migrate from their breeding grounds in Greenland, Iceland, Scandinavia, eastern Europe and arctic Russia, in search of warmer conditions to the south and west. Britain's oceanic climate buffers the impact of hard weather: water freezes less readily than in continental Europe and, by January, Britain provides a home for thousands of ducks, geese, swans and waders. Lakes, reservoirs and gravel pits, in particular, attract mallard, teal, wigeon, shoveler, tufted duck and pochard and, less commonly, gadwall, pintail, goldeneye and goosander. In parts of the Scottish lowlands, sheltered lochs frequently provide safe night-time roosts for pink-footed geese and greylag geese, which fly out to feed on the surrounding fields during the day.

READING THE CLUES

A lake, reservoir or gravel pit is made up of a series of micro-habitats, each of which play a part in supporting birdlife.

Open water is important to wildfowl for roosting. A lake needs to be large and deep enough to provide security from predators. Shelter is also required to protect the birds from excessive wind and waves. Many ducks, such as mallard, wigeon, teal and pintail use open waters for roosting during the day, and fly out to nearby feeding areas – often on pasture or stubble – at night. Night-time feeding is normal with ducks as it helps them to avoid the disturbance they would suffer if they attempted to feed by

day. As described earlier, the reverse is the case, oddly enough, with geese. The location of feeding areas usually controls the choice of roost site or vice versa: wildfowl rarely fly more than five miles between roost and feeding sites. Large numbers of gulls may also fly in to lakes and reservoirs to roost overnight, often covering much greater distances – less romantic but almost equally spectacular. Grebes, diving ducks such as tufted duck, pochard and goldeneye, and fish-eating ducks such as goosander and red-breasted merganser use areas of open water for feeding, diving below the surface in search of food. Diving ducks normally descend to around four metres (13 feet) in search of food, propelling themselves by their powerful legs and occasionally opening their wings to aid in steering. Tufted ducks are animal feeders, and search on the lake bottom among leaves, stones and aquatic plants for crustaceans and insect larvae. In contrast, the pochard has a broader bill. It is better adapted to feeding on the stems and leaves of water plants, although seeds and small water animals are also taken.

Areas of shallower open water are favoured by dabbling ducks, such as mallard, teal, gadwall and shoveler, for feeding. They 'dabble' through the water, filtering it through finely-meshed bills to extract seeds, plant material and invertebrates. This form of feeding is especially well developed in the shoveler. Mute swans plunge their long necks under water in search of submerged water plants. Coots and gadwalls often feed in association with mute swans, searching out the plant fragments that the swans leave. Each wildfowl species has developed its own strategy to obtain food, so that direct competition for food between species is reduced as far as possible.

OUT OF THEIR DEPTH

The depth of water is clearly crucial in determining whether a lake attracts dabbling ducks, or diving ducks and grebes, or both groups of birds. Gravel pits are of particular interest in this context. Initially, gravel extraction was inefficient because of the limited reach of the excavators and the use of water pumps that were not effective in keeping the workings dry. This limited the depth of digging and meant that many spits and islands had to be left at the end of extraction. Now water-filled, many of these pits have matured to become varied and attractive habitats for wildfowl – especially dabbling ducks. Modern gravel extraction is more efficient. Heavy machinery and effective pumping equipment means that nearly all of the available gravel is removed. A deep, steep-sided and regularly-shaped pit is usually left with few, if any, islands and spits, unless specific steps have been taken to introduce special features for wildlife. These newer pits are usually more attractive to diving ducks than to the dabbling species.

Acid lakes such as Pen-y-garreg in Wales are usually poor in wildlife. Bearded tits (left) are dependent on reed

THE WATER'S EDGE

A characteristic feature of productive lakes is the fringe of aquatic plants such as the common reed, reed mace and bur-reed, which provides secure nest sites. Great crested grebes, little grebes, mute swans and coots build their floating nests, anchored by the stems of aquatic plants. The reed warbler builds a nest of dried grasses, woven among stems of common reed. Ducks, too, frequently locate their nests in dense vegetation at the water's edge. In the autumn, flocks of wagtails, swallows and martins roost in reeds.

If the water level fluctuates there may be a band of bare mud along the shoreline: a feeding area for passage and wintering waders such as redshanks, dunlins, greenshanks and common and green sandpipers. Water supply reservoirs are frequently 'drawn down' during times of high water demand, which can provide ideal conditions for waders. If the water level is lowered for a long time during the summer months the mud will be colonised by opportunistic weedy plant species, such as grasses and docks. When the water level rises again, the seeds of these plants are released, providing plentiful food for dabbling ducks. Of course, fluctuating water levels can also be harmful to birds; in the breeding season nests may be flooded or, alternatively, be left high and dry and exposed to land-based predators such as foxes and hedgehogs.

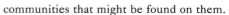

Snipe thrive in damp areas

OUT ON DRY LAND

Habitats beyond the water's edge also have an important influence upon the bird community of the lake. Areas of bare shingle, usually associated with gravel excavation, attract nesting little ringed plovers and ringed plovers. Grassland, particularly short, well fertilised pasture, provides herbivorous species such as wigeon, Canada goose, mute swan and coot with places to feed. There is evidence that these grazing species choose the best grasses according to the strength required to break the grass. Nutritious grasses containing plenty of nitrogen have a higher water content and break more easily! Areas of marshy wet grassland with tussocks are potential nesting places for lapwings, redshanks, snipe and yellow wagtails. Bramble, willow and hawthorn scrub, especially when associated with plants growing from the shallows, is attractive to breeding sedge and grasshopper warblers and reed bunting.

Mature trees, as well as attracting woodland birds, also provide mallards and moorhens with unexpected nest sites. The crown of a willow pollard, for example, frequently hides a mallard nest. Herons also nest in the tops of mature trees. The hanging branches of willows, where they meet the surface of the lake, may support the nests of aquatic species such as coot and great crested grebe. Trees also supply food. Siskins often feed in waterside alders during autumn, and dabbling ducks tear at the leaves of low-lying branches. Leaves and invertebrates – especially aphids – fall into the lake from trees to supply fish and invertebrates with food.

THE BIGGER THE BETTER?

The size of lakes is a fundamentally important factor in determining the kinds of bird communities that might be found on them.

In general a larger lake will support a greater number of birds than a small one of the same productivity. A greater diversity of species will also be found on a larger site than on a smaller one of the same type. Not only is a bigger range of habitats likely to be represented in a larger site (attracting a higher number of species), but some species only live on the larger areas. For example, the great crested grebe will only be found on larger lakes with sufficient fish to support a hungry family.

MIDDLING TO POOR

There are a few lakes of intermediate productivity, between the extremes so far described. An example is Esthwaite Water, Cumbria. Frequently, these 'mesotrophic' lakes are poor waters enriched by the addition of farmland run-off and sewage effluent. They usually support the commoner birds of productive lakes such as mallards, moorhens, coots, tufted ducks and grebes, but also retain species of more acid sites, such as common sandpipers. 'Dystrophic' lakes, on the other hand, represent the poorest end of the scale, being of exceptionally low productivity, associated with blanket peatlands, with brown peat-stained water. Due to their small size, vertical peaty sides and low productivity, birds are scarce. In Scotland, however, red-throated divers favour nesting on such pools, the *dubh lochans*, but the adults fly many miles to find their food at sea or on other lakes containing fish.

THE HEAVY HAND OF MAN

Man's activities have dramatically affected the bird communities of open waters. Reservoir construction and mineral extraction have widened the distribution of water birds. The use of upland lakes for water supply or river regulation may exacerbate fluctuations in water levels, so disrupting nesting birds. Many water birds are sensitive to disturbance from recreational activities such as sailing and water-skiing. Intensive use can cause birds to leave a lake altogether. During the breeding season birds may be prevented from nesting or be caused to desert. In winter, feeding is interrupted and energy expenditure increased just at a time of year when, if the bird is to survive the winter, it is essential that every moment is used for feeding and that energy losses are minimised.

Pollution is another important factor. Many lakes are enriched artificially from sewage effluent and run-off from agricultural operations, especially ploughing and use of fertiliser – a process known as 'eutrophication'. Already productive lakes may become over enriched. The production of phytoplankton is stimulated causing smelly and unsightly algal blooms. Plants die back and the variety of invertebrates is reduced as the water loses oxygen and increased water turbidity reduces the light available for water plants. In extreme cases, as in some areas of the Norfolk Broads, the diversity of species and total numbers of birds is markedly reduced.

THE CHARACTER OF A RIVER VARIES GREATLY AC-
CORDING TO ITS UNDERLYING GEOLOGY, GRADIENT
AND ADJACENT LAND USE. THE IMPRESSION OF A
FAST-FLOWING, TUMBLING UPPER REACH AND A
SLOW-FLOWING, SLUGGISH LOWER SECTION IS MIS-
LEADING. IN FACT THE AVERAGE SPEED OF A RIVER
IS MUCH THE SAME THROUGHOUT ITS LENGTH,
ESPECIALLY IN FLOOD CONDITIONS, AS THERE IS A
BALANCE BETWEEN THE GRADIENT OF THE RIVER
AND THE RESISTANCE, THROUGH FRICTION, OF THE
BANKS AND BED.

A TURBULENT START

The mountain stream hardly wears away its
bed but the sides of its valley slip and creep
and add material directly to the river. Lower
down, a broader valley plain comes between
the slopes and the river and less material is
deposited directly into the water. As the
river begins to meander in wide swings from
side to side, the outer parts of the bends are
eroded and form cliffs, while at the inner
edge the water is slower and deposits sand
and mud in broad banks. Already there are
enhanced opportunities for birds, such as
kingfishers and sand martins nesting in the
earth cliffs and moorhens foraging in the
shallows. Mountain streams tend to have
steep gradients, clear, turbulent water and
waterfalls, rocky pools and riffles, where
shallow water passes over a bed of pebbles.
Their average speed is not great, but in
places the water squeezes through narrow
spaces between rocks or cascades over
sudden falls in a burst of speed that would
sweep away a moorhen or a duck. Moss-
covered boulders, clumps of ferns and scattered birch or rowan trees cling on beside
the water. Below the surface there are
aquatic mosses and liverworts.

EASING OFF

Downstream, the river flows more smoothly, and there may be patches of rocks and
pebbles and shallow riffles, but also mud
and silt where plants such as water crowfoot
can become established. Lower still there is
often more luxurious vegetation, unless it
has been cleared by river engineers in the
course of straightening the channel. There
may be overhanging willows and alders,
deep pools, shallows and earth cliffs.

Different watercourses support characteristic communities of invertebrates and
fish. Generally, rivers flowing through limestone, chalk or other calcareous strata have a
greater diversity of aquatic animals than the
more acidic rivers. Rivers draining recently
afforested catchments in Wales and Galloway support few species of invertebrates
because they have become more acid, and
trout can no longer survive in such waters. It
is these ecological factors that determine
which birds you will find on a given stretch
of river. You would not, for example, expect
to see a dipper on a lowland river in eastern
England; neither would you expect to see a
moorhen on a mountain stream in Wales.

*High Force in Teesdale. Birds such as the
elegant grey wagtail (right) search for
insects among the rocks and at the edges of
fast-flowing upland rivers such as the Tees*

A DIVING SONGBIRD

The headwater streams tumbling down
from mountains and moorland are the haunt
of two characteristic birds – the dipper and
the grey wagtail. The dipper is remarkable
for its aquatic lifestyle, obtaining much of
its food by diving down to the river bed and
searching there for prey. Stonefly and
mayfly nymphs live among the rocks on the
river bed, and caddis larvae, in cases of tiny
stones or fragments of wood, cling to the
rocks or hide in webs between the pebbles
in the riffles. Although dippers commonly
nest on streams at altitudes of up to 300
metres (1,000 feet) or more, they may breed
down to sea-level. On lowland rivers at the
edge of the range, weirs or mill-streams can
provide suitable conditions.

In severe winters some dippers move
down from high altitudes, even appearing
on the coast; however, most birds remain on
their breeding grounds provided that some
holes occur in the ice through which they
can dive to find food. Dippers nest on rock
ledges, often by or behind a waterfall, or in
the stonework of old bridges. Many pairs
have two clutches, although those breeding
at high altitudes on more acidic streams lay
later and only produce one brood in a
season. It is an exciting experience to watch
a dipper dive into a rushing torrent, surface
with a beakful of food and then fly up to its
nest on a spray-drenched ledge.

ELEGANT WAGTAILS

There can be few more attractive sights
than a pair of grey wagtails feeding by a
mountain river, flying up to catch a passing
insect, or hopping from rock to rock. Grey
wagtails are found mainly on upland rivers
in the north and west of Britain in the spring
and summer. Unlike the dipper, they are
equally at home on New Forest streams, the
chalk rivers of Wiltshire and Dorset, mill
streams of East Anglia, by locks on canals,
or even on small streams around London,
especially where there are weirs. Their only
requirements are some rapidly flowing

Rivers and Streams

water, a nest site in a rock face, bank or wall, and a supply of insect food. They do, however, prefer those watercourses that are fringed by broadleaved trees, which may provide caterpillars and other insect food. In the winter, grey wagtails desert higher ground, some moving to southern Europe. Birds that remain in Britain or visit here from Europe may feed at sewage works, around farms, by ditches and lowland rivers, or even by lakes and ponds, where they have been recorded catching sticklebacks. Some will even appear briefly at puddles in car parks or on flat roofs.

The pied wagtail occurs alongside the grey wagtail on many streams and rivers. This familiar black and white bird is not a true river bird and is as likely to be found nesting away from water. In north-west Britain it is, however, associated with tree-less, rocky streams and roadside cliffs. Like its more colourful relative, it feeds largely on insects.

THE MIDDLE REACHES

The tree-lined middle reaches of rivers in the north and west of Britain are suitable for goosanders. These attractive fish-eating ducks have colonised this country since the end of the 19th century. A few pairs now breed in Devon. Goosanders select a stretch of clear water that provides good fishing, and a nearby old hollow tree for a nest hole. In areas where they are illegally persecuted because of their liking for young salmon and trout, they may be very wary and quickly take flight as soon as an observer comes into sight. Females with broods require cover under an overhanging bank or in thick foliage. Tidying up banks and felling old trees is disastrous for the goosander. Some goosanders will remain throughout the year on those rivers on which they breed, but fly off at dusk to roost on large pools or lakes. Others, perhaps immigrants from further north, winter on lower reaches of rivers, large lakes and reservoirs outside their breeding range.

As the river drops down from the hills, the waterfalls, rocks and riffles give way to smoother water, edged by sand cliffs and pebble shoals. Other species of bird now appear. The eroding cliff banks are exca-vated by sand martins, which may nest in colonies of only a few pairs, or up to one or two hundred pairs. Having wintered in the Sahel region of Africa, these migrants return as early as March to breed along river banks, occasionally in drainpipes in walls, or in sand and gravel quarries.

Kingfishers select similar river cliffs for their nest holes but, unlike sand martins, are solitary nesters. The lowering of earth cliffs into a smooth, tidy bank, so often a feature of river management, removes all suitable sites for these species. Each pair patrols a two to three mile stretch of river, on which there will be overhanging trees from which the birds can fish. Despite their brilliant blue and orange plumage, king-fishers can be surprisingly inconspicuous when perching on a leafy willow branch. Kingfishers may be found on unpolluted rivers throughout England, Wales and

southern Scotland. From April to August, they are largely restricted to rivers which provide both a plentiful and accessible supply of fish, and suitable banks in which they can excavate a nest burrow and rear two or more broods of noisy young. In the autumn, though, young birds may appear on upland rocky rivers, while in the winter birds may occur on canals, at lakes and garden ponds, in estuaries and around the coast.

RIVERSIDE WADERS

Pebble shoals along northern and western rivers are often frequented in the spring and summer by common sandpipers, pairs nest-ing at intervals of half a mile or more. Nests may be concealed in thick vegetation away from the water or among pebbles on an exposed shoal. The young feed on beetles, worms and other small prey among the rocks and pebbles or in nearby grassland.

Other waders may sometimes share the pebble banks. One is a relative newcomer to Britain, the little ringed plover. Low water levels in the spring and exposed shoals encourage some pairs to nest on rivers in Wales and England, but the usual haunts are gravel pits and reservoirs. A close rela-tive, the ringed plover, replaces the little ringed plover on northern rivers. Perhaps better known as a bird of shingle beaches by

the sea, it also nests in scrapes among pebbles by rivers, relying on the markings on the eggs to camouflage them.

A much noisier and more conspicuous bird of shingle by northern rivers is the oystercatcher or 'sea-pie'. Equally at home on rocky shores and beaches, in recent years it has taken to nesting by rivers and on farmland. Although it eats cockles and mus-sels when by the coast, it will probe with its strong red bill into mud and soil, or between pebbles, for earthworms and other inverte-brates at inland sites.

In the winter, few waders are to be found on rivers; a visitor from northern Europe may, however, be found at this time on southern, lowland rivers. The green sand-piper feeds in the mud by the river edge, in shallow water among stones on the river bed, or often in tidal creeks and at water-cress farms. Snipe, too, probe into mud at the river edge during the winter, zig-zagging up when danger approaches. From July to September, many other waders, such as greenshank, redshank and dunlin may migrate down the river corridors from their breeding grounds to the coast, stopping briefly to feed on the shoals and mud.

LUSH BANKS

In its lower course, a river is frequently fringed by trees and by a luxuriant band of

The unspoilt upper reaches of the River Loddon, in Hampshire. This stretch of the river has not had its banks scoured or its course straightened to make it flow faster. Its lush bankside vegetation of reeds, sedges, grasses and flowering plants provides nest sites for moorhens (inset right). Branches act as hunting perches for kingfishers (inset left)

vegetation, with great willow-herb, purple loosestrife, meadowsweet, reed-grass and sedges. This bankside vegetation by rivers and canals provides ideal cover for moorhens and coots. Both build their nests among emergent plants, where they may be vulnerable to feral mink. Some moorhens will nest well above the water in willow branches. Where rivers have been unsympathetically 'canalised' the moorhens and coots have disappeared.

Other species, such as reed buntings and sedge warblers, conceal their nests low down in vegetation by rivers and canals, even by small ditches. Where common reeds (*Phragmites*) fringe larger lowland rivers, reed warblers may also occur, suspending their deep cup nests between reed stems. In the winter months, the warblers are absent but reed buntings, moorhens,

coots and mute swans are still dependent on these waterways. Wash from boat traffic on canals and rivers can destroy the riverside plants and swamp nests.

In wet pastures or in cereal crops in the broad river valley, another species of wagtail may breed. The migrant yellow wagtail is pipit-like in its feeding behaviour, walking about on the grassland or at the river edge catching small insects, and nesting on the ground. It is scarce in upland Britain, but occurs in parts of southern Scotland and the Welsh borders as well as in lowland England.

Grey herons may be encountered on any stretch of river, whether in the uplands or lowlands, provided that eels and other fish

are available and accessible. Their heronries, usually sited in woods or even in single trees, are commonly close to the river. In Scotland, though, they may be on cliffs or in low scrub near the coast.

DUCKS

The best-known and most common duck throughout Britain is the mallard. This dabbling duck nests in pollarded trees and tall vegetation by any river with abundant aquatic weeds and invertebrates for food. One newcomer is the Chinese mandarin duck, which has escaped from waterfowl collections and established small breeding colonies on a few lowland reaches of rivers in England and Wales, nesting in holes in trees. Two other species of duck may be encountered on the lowest reaches near the sea. The shelduck commonly breeds around the coast of Britain in rabbit burrows and holes in banks. Sometimes pairs may breed several miles inland, but when the young hatch, the parents lead them down to the sea to mud flats where they feed on small snails. The other duck encountered in river estuaries and sea lochs is the red-breasted merganser, a sawbill related to the goosander. It breeds in clumps of heather or other rank vegetation near the water's edge, mainly on the west coast of Scotland and around the Welsh coast. Some pairs do breed on rivers well inland in mid Wales but it seems that as the goosander has spread, so the smaller merganser has been pushed down to the estuarine sections of rivers. In the winter months, other ducks – mallard and teal, and diving ducks such as tufted duck, pochard, goldeneye and even scaup – may all turn up on rivers, particularly on deeper lowland reaches.

A WATERY WOOD

The importance of the strip of woodland found along many rivers must not be forgotten. This woodland corridor provides habitat for many woodland and hedgerow birds, but perhaps the most noteworthy are lesser spotted woodpeckers and willow tits, both of which excavate nest holes in alders by the river, and pied flycatchers nesting in tree holes by streams in Wales. Seeds in the alder cones are an important food source for wintering finch flocks of goldfinches, redpolls and siskins. Wrens, too, are very much birds of the river bank. In the winter, riverine wrens survive better than those further away because the running water always keeps some ground at the water's edge unfrozen so that insect food remains accessible to the small birds.

Goosanders, often seen on northern rivers

THE ALL EMBRACING TERM 'WETLAND' HAS BEEN COINED TO DESCRIBE A WIDE RANGE OF WATERY PLACES FROM UPLAND PEATLANDS TO RIVERS, REED BEDS, WET GRASSLANDS AND ESTUARIES. DESCRIBED HERE ARE TWO PRINCIPAL BIRD-RICH LOWLAND WETLAND HABITATS: LOWLAND BOGS AND FENS, AND WET GRASSLANDS.

LOWLAND BOGS AND FENS

Peatlands – collectively known as mires – are permanently wet places, where waterlogging prevents the complete decomposition of dead plants and peat develops as a result. In general, the greater the degree of waterlogging, the more rapid is the rate of peat formation. In consequence, the deepest peats tend to be found on the wettest sites. Peatlands are popularly known as bogs or fens. More precisely, bogs generally form in areas where the water is poor in nutrients and slightly acidic, and fens where the water is nutrient rich and slightly alkaline.

Fens form where the local topography aids peat development and the water table is permanently high: for example, in a continually waterlogged depression. The vegetation present, however, varies according to the nutrients in the water. Fens are widespread in lowland Britain. The shallow edges of lakes and rivers are colonised by aquatic plants such as reed-mace and common reed, which grow in the shallows and spread outwards. As these plants die, peat develops and a reed swamp forms. Gradually, the landward side of the swamp becomes drier as the peat builds up, allowing woody species – especially water lovers such as willow and alder – to invade and form a type of woodland called carr. At the water's edge, peat accumulation causes the reed swamp to extend into open water, as areas of deep water become shallow enough to permit reed colonisation. Open water is succeeded by fen vegetation and eventually woodland with trees such as oak.

Fens also once covered the flood plains of most lowland river valleys. Drainage, however, has massively reduced their area. The extensive fenlands of East Anglia, for example, have been reduced to a few isolated remnants, such as Wood Walton and Wicken Fen in Cambridgeshire, less than one per cent of fen present in 1600. Ironically, some of the best fens now found in Britain were created by man! Examples include the Norfolk Broads, developed as a consequence of medieval peat digging, and Stodmarsh, Kent, an extensive reed bed formed in coal-mining subsidence pools.

Many kinds of bird breed in fens. At the water's edge, coots, moorhens, little grebes and ducks nest. In the deeper reed-swamp, water rails, mallards, reed warblers, reed buntings, sedge warblers and moorhens are typical. If the fen is grazed, species of more open habitats such as breeding waders will be found. As reeds blend into scrub and carr, these species are joined by typical scrub and woodland birds, such as dunnocks, wrens, pheasants, whitethroats, willow warblers, blackbirds, robins, blue tits and great tits, and reed warblers which nest in the reeds feed in the bushes, taking inexperienced birdwatchers by surprise.

BEDS OF REEDS

Large stands of common reed are rare in Britain and they support some of our rarest birds. Reed beds are concentrated on the coasts and Broadland areas of Norfolk and Suffolk, the Humber, in Anglesey and on the south coast of England. Large reed beds provide marsh harriers with secure nest sites, although they also require nearby areas of open land for hunting. The bittern, with the male's deep, resonant 'booming' voice, favours extensive reed beds with wetter areas in which to hunt for prey – mainly fish, amphibians and aquatic insects. Bearded tits are also confined to large reed beds. In summer they feed at the water's edge on aquatic insects, but in winter, due to the scarcity of invertebrates in reed beds, they switch to a staple diet of reed seeds. Bearded tit numbers may fall sharply during hard weather if ice and snow smothers the reed litter and cuts off their food supply, but their ability to raise large families means they usually recover fairly rapidly. Retention of extensive reed beds is dependent upon water management to stop them from drying out and to prevent the invasion of scrub. Reed cutting, which can provide thatching material, is a valuable means of maintaining stands of pure reed.

REFUELLING STATIONS

Outside the breeding season, fens are of great importance for sedge and reed warblers which feed within the reeds and put on enough weight to fuel their migratory flights. Other warblers, such as willow warbler, blackcap, chiffchaff and whitethroat, also exploit areas of willow scrub for feeding. Reed beds also provide important pre-migratory roosts for swallows, sand martins and yellow wagtails, in late summer. In winter, redpolls and siskins are attracted to alder carr. Moorhens, water rails, mallards, herons, teal and kingfishers are typical of the wetter, swampy areas of fen. Towards dusk, small birds gather in reed beds to roost. These might include corn buntings, yellowhammers, reed buntings, starlings and pied wagtails. A reed bed is always an exciting place to watch birds.

Cold, acidic and nutrient-poor lakes are not productive enough to develop the lush fen vegetation typical of eutrophic nutrient-rich lakes. Instead 'poor fens' develop, dominated by sphagnum moss and sedges. Where the peat dries out sufficiently to permit shrub colonisation, bog myrtle, willow and eventually birch invade. Although extensive areas of poor fen can be found – such as at the Insh Marshes, in the Highland Region of Scotland – it is usually found in small patches fringing the edge of lakes in north and west Britain. The birds of this community are discussed in the chapter on lakes, beginning on page 55.

BOGGY GROUND

The acidic, nutrient-poor conditions under which bogs form tend to favour the growth of sphagnum moss and sedges. Three types of bog are of special ornithological interest. Blanket bogs develop in places with high rainfall where surface drainage is impeded;

Lowland Wetlands

they are characteristic of the British uplands (see pages 46–49). Raised bogs are also rain-fed mires, found on the flood plains of river systems and estuarine plains. Often they develop on ground-water-fed fens, but as peat accumulates peat development becomes less dependent on ground water and more dependent on rain water, so the nutrient supply is reduced and the growth of bog vegetation encouraged. Sphagnum tends to draw up the water table, permitting the upward growth of the bog, producing its characteristic convex profile with a raised centre where growth is most active. Deep and very extensive deposits of peat may develop in this manner.

THE BIRDS OF BOGS

Numbers of breeding birds on raised bogs are low; meadow pipit, skylark, mallard, curlew and snipe are typical species. Many raised bogs have been changed by burning, peat cutting, drainage and grazing. This dries out the peat and reduced sphagnum cover lets grasses and scrub invade. This may benefit species such as nightjar, tree pipit, whinchat and stonechat which prefer open spaces, with scattered bushes and trees to use as song posts. Complete scrub cover causes the loss of all of these species. Peat cutting may create open water areas, attracting moorhens, coots and reed and sedge warblers. In winter, raised bogs are used as feeding areas and, if small pools are present, roosting areas by geese. Greenland white-fronted geese are typical, although in recent years they have tended to use cereals and grassland for feeding as well. In Scotland and northern England, greylag and pink-footed geese also make extensive use of raised bogs, mainly as roosts or daytime resting places.

In the southern heathlands of Surrey, Hampshire and Dorset, some of the acidic valley bogs are of considerable bird interest. They may hold substantial numbers of breeding lapwings, snipe and redshanks. Curlews often feed on these bogs, but breed on nearby dry heath. Other wetland birds such as moorhens, mallards and reed buntings may also breed. The bogs can provide an important source of food for other species too: nightjar and hobby may be seen hunting moths and dragonflies.

WET GRASSLANDS

Usually found in the lowlands of Britain, on neutral soils derived from clays or loams, wet grasslands are among the most important habitats for birds in Britain. Unfortunately, they are also rapidly disappearing as a result of drainage schemes. As their name suggests, wet grasslands are poorly drained and may be subject to flooding, especially during the winter months. This restricts their agricultural use, usually to the summer grazing of sheep and cattle and the cutting of grass for hay.

Reeds are always valuable for birds. Reed warblers (inset left) are common even where the reeds form only a narrow strip, but bitterns (inset right) require much larger reed beds

COASTAL GRAZING

There are four main types of wet grassland. Coastal grazing marshes fringe much of the low-lying coasts of south and east England, especially in estuarine areas. They were created by the enclosure of high salt marsh by sea walls to protect them from tidal flooding, a process started by the Romans and largely completed by the Victorians. After enclosure, the influence of salt water declines and the salt marsh vegetation is lost, to be replaced by plants more typical of fresh water grassland. Typically, coastal grazing marshes are brackish close to the sea wall, where the saline influence is strongest, grading to fresh-water marsh in inland areas. Some grazing marshes extend far inland, where the saltiness would always have been limited except after major tidal flooding.

Today, coastal grazing marshes are areas of rough pasture, intersected by a network of sinuous drainage channels – the old salt marsh creeks known as 'fleets' – with a high water table. In summer, the water in the fleets is often dammed or 'penned' at a high level, acting as wet hedges to enclose sheep and cattle. Because of the construction of sea walls and flood-banks, major flooding is rare. Small areas of grazing marsh may flood, however, by sea water over-topping sea walls, by flood water draining from nearby upland areas, or by the collection of surface water. Ornithologically, the more important grazing marshes include the Broadland marshes of Norfolk and Suffolk; the coastal marshes of Essex, including Old Hall and Langenhoe Marshes; the North Kent Marshes, including Cliffe Marshes and the Sheppey Marshes; Romney Marsh, Kent; Pennington and Keyhaven Marshes, Hampshire; Exminster Marshes, Devon; the Somerset Levels and the Gwent Levels.

RIVERSIDE FLOODS

Flood meadows are river valley meadows, usually with high water tables in summer and regularly flooded in winter. They may also flood in the summer months, as the river overtops its banks after heavy rain. In some areas of the country, such as South-lake Moor, Somerset, fields were deliberately flooded in winter, so that the silt carried in the water would be deposited on them as a valuable fertiliser.

Water meadows were a widespread man-made type of wet meadow, found in the chalk stream valleys of southern England. An elaborate system of sluices and ditches was constructed to irrigate the meadows in spring. The water raised the temperature of the pasture and encouraged earlier grass growth. The system was labour intensive, however, and today only one or two systems are still operated.

Washlands are also man-made. They are areas of river valley meadow, bounded off by flood-banks, which can be used to store water in times of flood to prevent it from spilling over nearby agricultural land or urban areas. Perhaps the best known example is the Ouse Washes, in East Anglia, constructed by Dutch engineers during the 17th century under the direction of Vermuyden. Water draining from the catchment of the Great Ouse in normal conditions flows directly into the tidal Great Ouse and thereby into The Wash. In times of flood, however, surplus water is directed into the Ouse Washes, for later release into the tidal river when conditions permit. Construction of the Ouse Washes allowed the surrounding fenland to be drained and converted to arable farmland as it was freed from the threat of regular flooding. A remnant of the Fens, the Ouse Washes continue as a major

Flooded fields and meadows often attract hundreds, or even thousands of wildfowl, waders and gulls, which roost on lakes and reservoirs each evening. Graveney Marshes (below), in North Kent, are of great importance for such birds

focus for wetland birds. In winter, the combination of shallow flooding and wet pasture usually attracts over 30,000 wildfowl to the Washes. In summer, the washland meadows support well over 1,000 pairs of breeding waders, including lapwings, snipe, redshanks and the rare black-tailed godwit, and some 1,500 pairs of ducks, including mallards, shovelers, gadwalls and tufted ducks. The scarce garganey also breeds. In recent years many washland areas have been built to protect urban areas from flooding; examples are washlands upstream of Skipton, Yorkshire, in the Aire Valley, and of Par, Cornwall, in the valleys of the rivers Par and Treesmill.

THE DAMP MEADOWS IN SUMMER

The breeding bird communities of wet grasslands are determined by a combination of water conditions and grassland management. At one extreme, dry grasslands support only skylarks; at the other, wet grasslands attract a wide variety of ducks, waders and other wetland birds. Typical breeding waders are lapwings, redshanks and snipe. Wet grasslands in Britain north of a line from Southampton Water to The Wash may also hold curlews. A handful of sites – mainly the East Anglian washlands – sup-

port black-tailed godwits and ruffs. Breeding waders, especially snipe, require high water tables, where the soil is soft enough for them to probe for food – usually small invertebrates. Most wet grasslands in Britain are too dry and do not have sufficient standing water to support breeding ducks other than mallard. Exceptions are the East Anglian washlands, where temporary and permanent pools of flood water are common, and areas of coastal grazing marshes, where the inlets attract pochards and shovelers.

THE NEED FOR LIVESTOCK

The bird interest of wet meadows has developed under the influence of their traditional use for pastoral agriculture – primarily summer grazing for cattle and sheep, or hay cutting followed by grazing. This maintains the meadows as pasture and prevents succession (that is the gradual change to drier habitat types leading towards woodland); lack of grazing or cutting produces a rank sward and, eventually, willow and alder carr develops. In consequence, breeding wildfowl and waders are lost in favour of scrub-nesting passerines. On the other hand, very intensive grazing creates a low, even sward with few nest sites. The ideal is a variety of grazing intensities, which produces a patchwork of fields with different lengths of grass. Breeding waders, especially lapwing and black-tailed godwit, tend to prefer fields with short grass. Mallards, tufted ducks and gadwalls nest in lightly grazed fields, while shovelers and pintails favour more heavily grazed areas. The ditches and fleets associated with wet meadows support their own breeding bird community, including little grebes, moorhens, coots, sedge warblers, reed warblers and reed buntings.

WINTER WILDFOWL

Water also influences the use by birds of wet grasslands in winter. Wildfowl quickly find washland and river valley floods. Dabbling ducks and coots feed in the shallows on invertebrates and the seeds, leaves and stems of aquatic plants. Areas of deeper flooding may attract the diving ducks, tufted duck and pochard. Drier areas of pasture provide feeding for grazing species – wigeons, European white-fronted geese and Bewick's swans. If the area of flooding is deep enough and extensive enough, wildfowl may roost on the flood waters. Failing this, they will commute to and from a nearby lake or reservoir. Flooded grasslands are also attractive to feeding waders, especially lapwing, snipe and ruff.

Over time, extensive works have been carried out to protect coastal grazing marshes from tidal and fresh water inundation. Now they tend to flood less frequently and less extensively than inland washlands. They may attract large flocks of grazing wildfowl to feed, notably of wigeons, European white-fronted geese, bean geese and, increasingly, dark-bellied brent geese. Typically these birds fly out to a nearby estuary to roost. Other dabbling and diving ducks are usually restricted to the fleets.

Waders may use well-grazed coastal grazing marshes adjacent to inter-tidal areas for roosting during high tides. Grazing marshes are also important feeding grounds for curlews, lapwings and golden plovers.

REFUGE MANAGEMENT

Human disturbance, especially from shooting, is a major factor affecting the use of flood waters by waterfowl. Usage of the Ouse Washes by wigeon, for example, increased markedly in the late 1960s, after conservation bodies bought effective no-shooting refuge areas; the maximum count was over two and a half times higher in 1969–1977 than in 1951–1959 and the amount of time spent on the Washes by wigeons was more than five times higher. The timing of use also changed. Before reserves were available, wigeon numbers were highest in March, after the end of the shooting season; subsequently they peaked in January. Wet grasslands are now among Britain's most threatened bird habitats. They have been progressively drained to increase their agricultural productivity; flooding has been reduced and water tables lowered through river engineering and flood protection works. Between 1935 and 1982 over 35 per cent of the North Kent Marshes was drained and converted to arable farmland and 55 per cent of the East Essex Marshes was converted in the same way.

THE THREAT OF DRAINAGE

Almost invariably, drainage improvements are detrimental to wetland birds. Not only does the land become too dry to support them, but drainage increases the intensity of agriculture. Increased herbicide and fertilizer use, ploughing and re-seeding of pasture, increases in grazing and conversion of pasture to arable are all hostile to breeding wetland birds. In recent years, however, the value of wetlands for wildlife and landscape has been increasingly recognised. In Britain at least, government policy no longer encourages the drainage of wetlands and conservation bodies have also established many wetland nature reserves, ensuring that at least some of the best areas should be conserved for the future.

Wood sandpipers might be seen on some marshes during migration periods

ESTUARIES, WHERE RIVERS FLOW OUT INTO THE SEA, ARE AMONG THE MOST IMPORTANT HABITATS FOR WILDLIFE AND MOST EXCITING PLACES FOR BIRDWATCHING. MANY ARE OF INTERNATIONAL IMPORTANCE FOR WILDFOWL AND WADERS. BRITAIN'S COASTLINE HAS 133 ESTUARIES, AND THERE ARE AT LEAST ANOTHER 36 IN IRELAND. THEY ARE PART OF A NETWORK OF BIRD FEEDING SITES LINKED WITH NESTING PLACES IN THE ARCTIC AND WINTERING GROUNDS AS FAR AS THE SOUTHERN TIP OF AFRICA.

THE UNCEASING TIDES

A feature of most estuaries is extensive inter-tidal flats formed from sediments brought down by rivers and washed in from the sea. The turbulence at the mouth of estuaries is such that only the heavier sediments settle, forming shingle and sand beaches. The finer silt is carried into the inner parts of estuaries to form mud flats. On The Wash, for example, the holiday beaches are at the outer corners, at Hunstanton and Skegness, leaving the mud flats and salt marshes within the bay to those who gather cockles, lugworms and samphire – as well as to the birds.

Unlike the Mediterranean and Baltic, the seas around Britain's coast have a considerable tidal range. In the Severn Estuary the maximum tide range is 12 metres (39 feet), while in Poole Harbour (Dorset) it is less than two. The range is greatest on spring tides, on a 28 day cycle. The highest and lowest tides coincide with the equinoxes in March and September. High water on most estuaries occurs at intervals of rather over 12 hours, with the tide ebbing to low water six hours after high tide. High tides get later by about one hour each day. The time of high tide varies around the coast (so local tide tables are valuable) and the height is also influenced by wind direction and strength and atmospheric pressure.

WADERS ON THE MOVE

The ebb and flow of tides have a major influence on the activities of waders on an estuary. They determine when the birds have access to their food, which is out of reach at high tide. At high water, especially on spring tides, shore birds usually have to stop feeding for several hours and congregate at roost sites, often in flocks of spectacular size. Roosting places are used year after year and the different species even use the same patch of beach every season. Waders choose undisturbed places, such as islands or spits, with a good all round view for safety. Where there are large salt marshes, they frequently roost on the seaward edge, but on the highest spring tides, when the saltings are immersed, the birds may fly inland to pastures and arable fields from which crops have been harvested, or which are bare after ploughing. All this has a great influence on anyone wishing to watch the birds.

In estuaries, salt water from the sea mixes with fresh water from rivers. The point where salt mixes with fresh water moves (either seaward or upstream) according to the state of tide and how much fresh water is flowing down. Moreover, since salt water is denser (therefore heavier) than fresh water, it penetrates the estuary *below* the inflowing river water on the surface. Water salinity affects the variety and the distribution of estuarine flora and fauna, especially the invertebrate animals.

ESTUARY VEGETATION

In Britain's estuaries, the only plants apart from seaweeds that are almost continually submerged, or exposed only for short periods at low tide, are three species of eel-grass, *Zostera*. Eel-grass and the green seaweed *Enteromorpha* are important foods of wintering brent geese and wigeon. Where there are rocks and boulders, brown seaweeds such as the wracks are common. They are not grazed by birds, but harbour invertebrates eaten by certain waders.

On many estuaries, salt marshes (or saltings) form above the high-water mark on neap (smallest) tides. Some salt marshes, such as those on The Wash, Morecambe Bay and the Solway, are very extensive. They are often a dangerous wilderness of large creeks and small channels, up which

Estuaries

the water flows on a rising tide, bringing a load of silt to be deposited on the marsh. Some salt marshes are rising and extending as a result of this process. On others, such as on the Essex coast, the marshes are eroded and broken up into numerous steep-sided islands. On many salt marshes, such as that on the Dee, in North Wales, there are shallow pools or 'flashes' in depressions that are too salty or poorly drained for plants to grow.

The vegetation of salt marshes is a neat patchwork of different communities of maritime plants, each adapted to a different degree of submergence and drainage. Characteristic of the lowest zones are pioneer colonisers of mud flats: cord-grass *Spartina*, succulent annual marsh samphires (gathered as a vegetable delicacy on the East Coast) and sea aster (a relative of the Michaelmas daisy). *Spartina* has been introduced to many estuaries around the coasts. Its roots and extensive underground stems help to trap and bind silt. This vigorously growing grass has spread rapidly on some mud flats such as on the Dee, Ribble and at Lindisfarne, seriously encroaching on the feeding areas of estuarine birds. The fine-leaved salt marsh grass *Puccinellia* is predominant over most salt marshes. It forms extensive 'lawns' where grazing by livestock and geese is intense. Where grazing is light, as on many east coast marshes, sea aster

(usually the form with rayless flowers) and the low, grey-green bushes of sea purslane are frequent in the mid-marsh. Sea purslane often covers the banks of channels.

The upper parts of salt marshes, less frequently covered by the tide, have a greater variety of plants. The flowers of some make an attractive display: white scurvy-grass (a cress with fleshy leaves rich in vitamin C) in May, pink thrift and sea spurrey in June and blue sea lavenders in July and August. Less striking, yet typical of the turf of upper salt marshes, are sea milkwort, sea plantain and sea arrow-grass. Red fescue tends to take the place of salt marsh grass and spiky tussocks of sea rush are sometimes prolific. Such high, ungrazed salt marsh is a feature of the north Norfolk coast, but on The Wash the upper marsh is largely missing as a result of a succession of enclosures to claim land for agriculture. Along the edge of salt marshes, often at the foot of the sea wall, there is a drift line where flotsam and jetsam accumulates at the upper limits of the tide. Here dark-green-leaved oraches, aromatic sea worm-wood, sea beet (a close relative of sugar beet), the white-rayed daisy flowers of may-weed and coarse blue-green tussocks of sea couch grass flourish. Such plants are not often praised for their beauty, yet seen close-to they have subtle and delicate charms.

BREEDING BIRDS

On average, only nine or 10 species of bird are to be found breeding on a British salt marsh, less than a quarter of the number in a large broadleaved English wood. Some of the less accessible salt marshes have some of the largest colonies of black-headed gulls in Britain, often joined by colonies of terns. Excluding such colonial birds, the most abundant breeding species are often red-shanks, skylarks, reed buntings and meadow pipits. Redshanks are numerous on most British salt marshes, except those in south-west England and South Wales, and the small marshes on the head of sea lochs on the west coast of the Scottish mainland. The numbers breeding on Britain's salt marshes are of considerable importance in European terms.

Birds tend to nest on the upper half of salt marshes. Even so, there is the risk of flooding on spring tides in May and June. This may have disastrous effects on gull colonies, but redshank eggs, in deeply cupped nests among tussocks of salt marsh grass, do not float away, and often still hatch after being flooded for an hour or two. The mobile and buoyant chicks are also able to cope with flooding.

The Solway, whose great expanses of mud attract huge numbers of waders, including the curlew (inset)

Oystercatchers are present on most estuaries

GRAZERS AND SEED-EATERS

The sward of fine-leaved grasses is grazed by wildfowl in winter and spring: wigeon, brent geese in East Anglia, white-fronted geese around Slimbridge on the Severn and barnacle geese on the Solway. These tend to seek areas already cropped by livestock.

Salt marsh plants such as marsh samphire, orache and sea aster, may produce large crops of seeds which provide winter food for teal, skylarks, reed buntings and flocks of finches, notably twites (a speciality of East Anglian saltings) all in turn attracting birds of prey. In winter, twites tend to feed on marsh samphire and sea aster seed on the outer edge of the marsh, but parties commute to drink in puddles behind the sea wall. On east coast salt marshes in winter, rock pipits replace meadow pipits, having territories along the creeks and borrow pits beside the sea wall, where they feed on small invertebrates.

MOLLUSCS BY THE MILLION

Only invertebrates that can stand changing salinities can inhabit estuaries. Hence, by comparison with the sea and rocky shores on the open coast, the variety of species is limited. On the other hand, those that are there can be extraordinarily abundant in the nutrient-rich, inter-tidal mud. It is largely for this reason that estuaries attract such vast numbers of waders and wildfowl. The feeding habits of these birds and their distribution within estuaries are related to the ecology and availability of their food. The main food of any one species of bird may vary from estuary to estuary at different times of year.

Dunlins and redshanks live mainly in the inner, more muddy parts of estuaries. Minute snails called *Hydrobia* and a burrowing shrimp called *Corophium* are their favoured food and can be present in astonishing numbers (sometimes over 24,000 in a square metre). The small snails are one of the main foods of shelducks and, on a few

estuaries such as the Mersey and Dee, of large flocks of pintails. Ragworms, important food of many waders, particularly grey plovers, curlews and bar-tailed godwits, are also often abundant on the inner mud flats. Shore crabs live in creeks where they are sought by curlews. Knots, which form huge flocks on The Wash and estuaries such as Morecambe Bay in north-west England, feed on molluscs, particularly the Baltic tellin, a small bivalve, whose small pink shells are often found on beaches.

Nearer the mouth of estuaries, where the mud flats become sandier, lugworms occur in great numbers. They burrow and, as well as being used as bait by sea anglers, are the food of long-billed waders such as bar-tailed godwits and curlews. Oystercatchers concentrate to feed where cockles are abundant on muddy sand banks and on mussel beds on rocky outcrops in estuaries. Well-camouflaged turnstones also frequent such rocky places and shingle banks, foraging among seaweed and crevices for small crustaceans and snails; they even prise barnacles and small limpets off the rocks. Within estuaries it is only on the sandy beaches, at the outer extremities, that parties of sanderlings can be seen scurrying along the shore close to where the waves break. These active little waders, usually in their grey and white non-breeding plumage, feed on flies and small crustaceans such as sand-hoppers.

The bill length of many waders is related to the depth at which their main food lurks in the mud. Avocets, found on a few estuaries in Britain (the Alde in Suffolk and the Exe and Tamar in the south west), use their fine up-turned bills to capture shrimps in shallow water and liquid mud. Greenshanks, which frequent estuaries in relatively small numbers on passage, but increasingly in winter, actively chase fish, as well as shrimps in creeks and brackish pools. Large and dense flocks of sea ducks occur in winter in the shallow, relatively sheltered waters of a few estuarine bays such as the firths on the east coast of Scotland and Carmarthen Bay in South Wales. Sea ducks feed largely on molluscs which they obtain by diving. Whereas scoters tend to frequent sandy bays, eiders are associated with mussel beds on rocks.

FISHY FOOD

The flounder, a flat-fish, is tolerant of brackish water and is therefore found well up estuaries, which are also important nurseries for more marine fish such as sand eels and sprats. Complex food webs exist on estuaries, extending from the plants and detritus, through the invertebrates that feed on them, to the fish and both herbivorous and carnivorous birds. The picture would not be complete without mention of the predators at the top of food chains. Flounders are the main food of the cormorants that winter on estuaries, notably on the firths of Forth and Tay and Poole Harbour in Dorset. The fish also attract grebes, grey herons and red-breasted mergansers in winter; common seals, gulls, terns and (very locally) ospreys in summer and autumn. In

winter, the numerous small waders and other birds provide food for merlins, hen harriers, sparrowhawks and short-eared owls. Many estuaries now have one or two wintering peregrines which feed on waders, gulls and ducks such as teal.

One of the reasons why British and Irish estuaries are so important for wintering wildfowl and waders is that the shores rarely freeze over. Prolonged, severe conditions which birds cannot survive are rare. Even so, in cold winter weather, when invertebrate food can be hard to get, shore birds may need to feed during every moment that the mud flats are exposed in daylight, if not at night. Shelducks, grey plovers and redshanks appear to be the species that suffer most in severe conditions.

MOULTING AND ROOSTING

Late summer and autumn is the time of year when adult estuary birds moult their plumage. Birds from some populations do so *en route* to their winter quarters. Moulting birds concentrate at sites with rich food supplies. Wildfowl, which moult their flight feathers almost simultaneously, are flightless for sev-

THE IMPORTANCE OF ESTUARIES

Regular counts for the 'Birds of Estuaries Enquiry' and 'National Wildfowl Counts' provide a good picture of the numbers and distribution of wildfowl and waders in the estuaries outside the breeding season. Almost one and a half million waders spend the winter on British estuaries, representing 40 per cent of the total wintering in Europe. In addition, huge numbers use them as essential stop-over sites for 'refuelling' and moulting when on long migrations between their northern breeding grounds and southern wintering areas in Spain, Portugal and West Africa. The number of wildfowl wintering on the estuaries varies according to the severity of winter weather in north-west Europe. At times there may be as many as half a million ducks, geese and swans when inland sites are frozen. At least 24 estuaries in Britain and Northern Ireland are each used by more than 20,000 waders in winter, and at least 38 sites have more than 10,000 wildfowl. These estuaries meet established criteria as sites of international importance for water birds. Others are of international importance for individual species, regularly having at least one per cent of their western European wintering populations. British estuaries have more than one third of the north-west European wintering populations of five species of wildfowl: shelduck, wigeon, teal, pintail, and two races of brent goose; and of six species of wader: oystercatcher, grey plover, knot, dunlin, black-tailed and bar-tailed godwits. It is estimated that about 17,500 pairs of redshanks nest on the salt marshes of British estuaries. This is about 20 per cent of the European breeding population and half those in Britain.

The great majority of birds using these estuaries in winter are not from British breeding populations, and birds from widely separated regions occur on the same estuaries. For example, knots and turnstones from Canada and Greenland come to The Wash together with redshanks from Iceland, oystercatchers from Norway, curlews from Sweden and Finland, dunlins from north Scandinavia and the USSR and bar-tailed godwits from arctic Russia and west Siberia.

THREATS

There has been a long history of claiming land from estuaries such as The Wash for agriculture. Industrial developments, including those related to oil, ports, road and rail bridges, rubbish tips and marinas have all encroached on Britain's estuaries and continue to do so. In the early 1970s there were plans for barrages on estuaries for water storage; now barrages are being considered to harness tidal power for electricity generation (on the Mersey and Severn) and for amenity lakes (on the Taff and Ely at Cardiff). Many estuaries have been severely polluted by industrial effluent and sewage.

The responsibility which the United Kingdom has for its large and international assemblage of water birds makes it all the more important that the estuaries are protected from further destruction and unnecessary damage. It will be a difficult task.

eral weeks at this time, and need sites that are safe from predators. Many of Britain's adult shelducks migrate to moult in the German Waddenzee; some, however, remain on estuaries such as The Wash and the Dee. Canada geese which breed in Yorkshire migrate to salt marshes on the Beauly Firth in east Scotland to moult.

Mud flats, sand banks and sheltered water within estuaries provide relatively safe nocturnal roosts for gulls and wildfowl. Gull flocks tend to fly along rivers when approaching their roosts and peak numbers are seen on east coast estuaries in early autumn. As dusk approaches during the winter months, parties of gulls, often in formation, can be seen flying to their roosts from their feeding grounds inland. Skeins of pink-footed geese fly off the Solway, the Firth of Tay and The Wash at dawn to feed on arable fields inland and return at nightfall, unless it is a clear, moonlit night. At such times their contact calls add a tingling magic to the darkness. Large numbers of mallards resort to the safety of estuaries during the day, but at dawn and dusk they fly inland to feed.

Low tide at Sunderland Point, on the River Lune in Lancashire. Estuary mud is full of invertebrate food for waders

Slavonian grebes fish in some estuaries in winter

Coasts, Cliffs and Islands

THE COASTLINE OF BRITAIN EXTENDS FOR ALMOST 17,000KM (11,000 MILES) COVERING A WIDE RANGE OF DIFFERENT HABITATS, FROM PRECIPITOUS CLIFF FACES TO PICTURESQUE BAYS OF SILVERY OR GOLDEN SANDS.

The type of coastal habitat is determined by several related factors. For example, the rock and soil types, together with the height of the land, will influence whether there are cliffs or gently sloping beaches. The geographical position will determine how exposed the shore is both to pounding by the sea and to the influence of the weather. Coastal erosion in areas of soft soils may be as much the result of rainfall washing away the cliffs as the activities of the waves and currents. Like all other habitats in Britain, coasts, too, have their legacy from the past. Coastlines have been altered over thousands of years by changes in the sea level, especially after the last Ice Age, when melting ice released more water into the sea and removed a vast weight from the land allowing it to slowly rise or tilt, flooding some areas while exposing others. Although barely perceptible, these changes are still taking place.

As the physical features of the coastline vary, so too do the kinds of birds to be found there. One special type of coast, the estuary, is described on page 66. Described here are the other coasts, which fall into two contrasting categories: those with solid cliffs or rocky, boulder strewn beaches, most commonly found in northern and western Britain, and those derived from 'soft' materials, such as sands and shingle.

SEABIRD CITIES

Cliffs along rocky shores may reach over 300 metres (1,000 feet) in height. Where the cliff face is bare rock with horizontal ledges, there may be suitable breeding sites for seabirds such as fulmars, kittiwakes, guillemots and razorbills, for whom the cliffs are their only point of contact with land. Fulmars have spread widely this century and are now found on almost all cliff coasts. The distribution of the other species is more restricted, often to large colonies which may comprise tens of thousands of birds in northern and western Britain and must be counted among the finest bird spectacles in Europe. Kittiwakes and guillemots in particular make use of ledges on the cliffs, often nesting in long, tightly-packed lines. The ledges are formed where the rock is sufficiently strong not to crumble, and where the rock beds, formed millions of years ago, are still almost horizontal. Where the rocks have been tilted by movements in the upper part of the earth's crust, the ledges become unsuitable. Boulders fallen from the cliffs are used by shags and black guillemots which nest in the crevices beneath, while at the top of the cliffs herring and great black-backed gulls nest on the flatter ground.

The varied coastline – sand dunes and cliffs at Dunnet in Scotland. The turnstone (inset) is likely to be found on almost any kind of shore where it might find a meal

ISLAND HAVENS

On many rocky coasts, there are steep grassy slopes above the cliffs. The grass is usually kept short by grazing animals, and by poor soils, salt spray and strong winds. Here there are nesting opportunities for hole-breeding species, such as the tiny storm and Leach's petrels, Manx shearwaters and puffins. The steep slopes do not deter predators, so not only are the nests of these four species in danger but the adults themselves may be taken. It is not surprising, therefore, that, excluding puffins, which can nest in crevices on the cliff faces, all colonies of these species are on islands which are virtually free from mammalian predators. Gannets nest in the open on flatter rock surfaces, but the threat of predation by mammals has led to all but one of the British gannetries being on islands where such predators are absent.

RICHES OF THE SEA

Although the cliffs and islands provide safe nest sites, the birds depend on the sea for food. The seas around Britain vary in quality. To us, the most noticeable differences are probably temperature and the clarity of the water, but the waters also vary in their chemical composition. Water brought by currents from the Atlantic differs from water in the North Sea which receives large quantities of fresh water from rivers. Where water bodies of different temperature, salinity and density meet, vertical mixing takes place. Such areas are often rich in plankton, which are food to cephalopods and fish. The birds may feed on the plankton, the cephalopods or the fish, exploiting the rich supply. Auks and shags swim under water to catch food, whereas the others feed on the surface or make shallow plunge dives. The upwelling and mixing of sea water may also be caused by physical features such as promontories and headlands. The coincidence of the major cliff systems containing safe nest sites, which occur in north and west Britain, with the areas of vertical mixing, which occur where the North Atlantic Drift meets the waters of the North and Irish Seas, accounts for the location of most major colonies of cliff breeding seabirds.

SPECTACULAR LAND BIRDS

The cliffs are also nesting places of specialist land birds such as peregrines and choughs. These, too, exploit the safe nesting sites afforded by the precipices. Peregrines may also benefit from the abundant supply of seabirds for food close at hand. Choughs, on the other hand, feed on maritime heath, a rare and threatened habitat, which occurs on the flatter ground and certain soil types above the cliff top. Choughs are now confined to parts of Wales and Ireland, the Isle of Man and the west coast of Scotland, all places where maritime heaths have not been eroded or claimed by agriculture. Other cliff dwellers include the rock dove, the ancestor of the feral pigeon now so common in many of our towns and cities. Today the only rock doves of truly wild stock are probably confined to the more remote outer islands of northern Scotland.

Gannets can often be seen fishing quite close to the shore; they make spectacular plunge-dives into the water

ROCK POOLS AND BOULDERS

Away from cliffs, rocky shores comprise small pools, patches of sand, and rocks and boulders. These are often covered with shells, colourful seaweeds or algae. In the pools a variety of marine life is trapped as the waves recede, until freed by the next tide, and the plants here are home to a variety of invertebrate life. Nesting is not possible in this temporary habitat, but there is much food for birds if they can get at it. Most common are wading birds with long bills capable of probing and digging. Purple sandpipers are particularly fond of rocky shores in the winter. Turnstones, oyster-catchers, redshanks, ringed plovers and cur-lews are all commonly found, although their numbers vary with the season and geo-graphical location. Apart from waders a few other birds can feed here. Rock pipits feed all year round in this habitat, but they are not the only small birds to be found along rocky shores in winter. In south-west Eng-land, small numbers of black redstarts spend the winter along the rocky shores, feeding on the insect life. They survive because there is sufficient food in the milder climate, but they may move south in colder weather. Occasional advantage of the food supply is also taken by parties of starlings looking for insects and even by the odd song thrush breaking winkles open against a rock.

AT HOME IN THE DUNES

Few species of birds use sand dunes. This habitat is unsuitable because nests may quickly be covered by blown sand. The main vegetation and primary stabilising in-fluence is marram grass, but this is home to few insects which might be food for birds. However, shelducks have learned to exploit sand dunes, nesting in holes in the more stable, firmer sand under the dune. Lesser black-backed and herring gulls and, in a few places, Sandwich terns also nest among the more stable dune systems, often in large colonies. In winter, especially on the east coast, snow buntings forage among dunes in small flocks, never staying long in one place, searching for seeds on the sandy surface. Behind the dunes, or even above the less exposed cliff slopes, where the coast begins to grade into the next habitat, areas permanently covered in denser vege-tation, notably bracken, brambles and haw-thorns, provide greater opportunities for the bird community. Typical birds of this habi-tat in summer are skylarks, meadow pipits, stonechats and yellowhammers. Where the scrub is thicker, whitethroats may sing from the tops of the bushes, whereas in more open, rocky areas wheatears are found. Such areas are often grazed to a close sward by rabbits, providing suitable areas for birds to forage on the ground. The scrub, often dense and prickly, is an ideal nesting place for small birds, and if there is sea buck-thorn, the berries are ideal for newly-arrived migrant thrushes.

THE OPEN BEACH

Sand and shingle beaches form another habitat which has a special group of breed-ing birds. The beach itself offers little protection by way of vegetation or shelter to hide the nest from predators. All species which nest here simply make a small scrape in which to lay their camouflaged eggs. Their young are covered in sandy coloured down to make them difficult to spot, and are able to move away from the nest scrape soon after hatching to reduce the risk of the whole brood being eaten. Pure sand and shingle holds few invertebrate foods for birds. The shingle nesters tend to feed elsewhere, either out to sea in the case of the terns, or on the tideline and wrack, or in other habitats in the case of oystercatchers or ringed plovers. All the terns feed on small fish caught by plunge diving, so they need to nest on beaches near areas of reasonably clear water in order to see their prey, though they are not as particular as the auks, since they do not travel far under the surface.

Beach nesting species are particularly vulnerable to accidental disturbance by human visitors. The little tern is often badly affected, but fortunately, due to areas being fenced off and people being asked to take care, many colonies still survive. Sandwich, common and arctic terns also nest on shingle, although the last two species nest in a range of other coastal habitats. In winter, and during migration periods, the beaches are sometimes frequented by large numbers of waders. Shingle beaches alone are not popular, but especially on beaches in north and west Britain, waders such as turnstones, oystercatchers and redshanks search for food among the piles of tidewrack brought ashore by the wind and waves. Probably the commonest wader on sandy beaches is the sanderling, which runs along the edge of the wavelets, picking at inverte-brates on the surface. Dunlins and ringed plovers are also found, with longer-billed species, too, on beaches where the sand covers muddy silts that contains large amounts of food for the birds.

Rock pipits are very good at hiding; often only their calls give them away

SHALLOW BAYS

The sands which cover the beaches often extend below the tideline out to sea. Shal-low, sandy-bottomed bays are home to a variety of flat-fish and other fish species, as well as some crustaceans. Off the rockier coasts where the water is clear, other bottom dwelling fish and invertebrates such as mus-sels may be found in abundance. These all provide food for diving birds. In winter, birds such as great crested grebes or red- and black-throated divers, which nest inland on fresh water, spend much of their time at sea, often feeding in the shallower and more sheltered bays. Wintering sea ducks such as scoters, scaups, goldeneyes and long-tailed ducks, as well as eiders, which also breed along the rocky shores, also favour areas of relatively shallow water. Here they can reach food on the sea bed with comparative ease.

OPPORTUNIST GROUP

In winter one group of birds, the gulls, occurs in all coastal habitats. Herring gulls and black-headed gulls are probably the most widespread, but common gulls are also found in large numbers. Being scavengers, they frequent coastal towns, particularly fishing ports, where there is often a good supply of food. In some towns the gulls nest on rooftops, a habit which is becoming increasingly common.

Kittiwakes nest on ledges which look terrifyingly precarious

EXCITING MIGRANTS

Promontories and small islands can be exciting places during spring and autumn, when large numbers of migrating land birds pass overhead. Many birds arrive on the coast tired and hungry from their long flight, and may land and feed furiously, sometimes becoming quite tame. Some species which occur on passage are seldom found breeding, for example bluethroats and wrynecks, whereas others which do breed, such as pied flycatchers and wheatears, which may be coming from farther north, are taking a refuelling stop before continuing their migration. The sudden occurrence of large numbers of migrants is called a *fall*, and occurs more on the south and east coasts, which are closer to the main migration routes. The features of the coast which attract the birds have less to do with habitat than with geographical position. Often these places are the first the migrants catch sight of as they come over the sea, and their arrival is highly dependent on the weather.

Promontories and headlands are also ideal places to watch seabird movements off the coast. Again the feature which makes such places good is not the habitat, but the geographical position, which forces birds to come close inshore, when otherwise they would be too far out to sea to observe. Seeing such movements is also dependent on the weather, and usually requires strong onshore winds. In the right conditions, shearwaters, gannets, arctic and great skuas, gulls, kittiwakes and auks may all be seen in large numbers. Sea watching, as watching birds flying over the sea is commonly called, requires much patience, and sometimes considerable skills at identifying fast moving dots on the horizon – not a rewarding activity for a beginner.

FARMING IS THE DOMINANT LAND USE THROUGH-
OUT BRITAIN. IT HAS CREATED MOST OF THE PAT-
TERN OF THE COUNTRYSIDE, INCLUDING THAT ON
THE HILLS, WHICH MAY NOT LOOK FARMED, BUT
OWE MUCH OF THEIR PRESENT ASPECT TO SHEEP
REARING. OPEN MOORLANDS ARE SO SPECIAL AND SO
SEPARATE FROM THE REST OF THE FARMED LAND
THAT THEY HAVE A SECTION OF THEIR OWN IN
THIS BOOK (ON PAGES 46-49). THE INFLUENCE
OF AGRICULTURE ON BIRDS DIFFERS GREATLY
BETWEEN AREAS SUPPORTING GRAZING ANIMALS
AND THOSE GROWING CROPS.

GROWING GRASS
Grass is one of the things that grows best in
the relatively cool and wet climate of Britain. It is for climatic reasons that the main
pastoral areas are to the west and north,
while arable agriculture predominates in the
warmer and drier regions. Grass is no use as
a human food. Sheep or cattle are used to
convert it into products of use to humans –
meat and dairy foods – especially in areas
where the direct growing of food is less
easy. Many grasses are resistant to grazing,
and can be bitten down and keep their flat
growing leaves while spreading underground. On all but the poorest soils, grass
dominated vegetation is the natural consequence of continued grazing after the removal of trees. Traditional pastures would
have been created thus, though nowadays
artificially sown and nurtured mixtures of
higher yielding cultivars are more commonly used. Because grass does not grow in
the winter, but the animals still have to be
fed, some of the summer crop is conserved
for the winter. Traditionally this was mown
and dried as hay. Commonly it is now cut
earlier and fermented as silage. The pastoral
landscape in summer thus consists of some
fields grazed short by the stock and some
allowed to grow tall for hay or silage.

BIRDS ON THE GRASSLANDS
Grazed pastures are home to ground-feeding
birds. Most widespread, though fast declining, is the lapwing, which feeds on surface-
dwelling invertebrates and nests in the
open. Lapwings often nest in loose colonies
with birds combining forces to protect their
vulnerable nests by driving off predators or
grazing animals which might crush eggs.
Especially on the upland margins, curlews
are abundant, using their long bills to probe
for worms or buried insect larvae. Oystercatchers have recently spread inland, mainly
in the north, making a remarkable shift in
diet from coastal molluscs to earthworms.

Cattle and sheep dung supports a lot of
flies and other potential food. The yellow
wagtail exploits these, often feeding under
the feet of grazing animals to seize anything
they flush. Dairy farms always have swallows nesting in the outbuildings and foraging in the pastures, while spotted flycatchers sally out from trees at field margins.
These landscapes are also haunts of starlings, which can open their bills underground to lever out leatherjackets and similar items. Equally characteristic are rooks,
which also use their bills for hunting soil
invertebrates. They have declined in numbers in areas where crops have replaced cattle.

PROBLEMS IN THE HAY
Fields of growing hay are less good for birds,
with the cover generally being too dense
and wet after rain or dew. The corncrake is a
specialist hayfield bird which can skulk
about unobserved in the thick cover. From
being widespread it has retreated steadily to
the north and west, where it now only
survives in places with the least technically
advanced agriculture. It appears that the
corncrake cannot survive modern machinery
and more intensive grass production. Young
are vulnerable to modern mowers, and grass
is cut earlier than was once the case.

In days before modern drainage and river
engineering, riverside meadows were especially attractive to birds. Winter floods
fertilised the fields by depositing silts, and
water meadows were specially managed
both to provide summer grazing and hay and
to contain winter flooding. In winter, these
areas, which are now uncommon, used to
support geese and especially ducks. In
summer, they were often wet enough to
provide nesting places for waders such as
snipe and redshank. Although the Ouse
Washes is a rather specially engineered
example, it is salutary to remember that
such places owe their history and their
future to agriculture even though these are
now often maintained by nature conservation organisations. Without summer grazing
and mowing, the vegetation grows rank.
Both winter wildfowl and breeding waders
prefer shorter swards, though particular
species vary in their preferences and reserve
management has to take this into account.

GRASS AS A FOOD
Grass is a poor food because of its bulk in
relation to nutritional value. Plant eaters
need large guts in which to process enough
grass to stay alive. This is difficult for a bird
which also needs to be light enough to fly.
There are not, as a result, many grazing
birds. Their number includes geese and
swans, with the mute swan being about as
heavy as a flying bird can be. Mute swans
prefer aquatic vegetation and breed by
water, but sometimes graze on adjacent
meadows. Large numbers of geese from the
north, spend the winter in Britain. Many of
the species now rely on agricultural land,
especially the most fertile grasslands. In
spring they can be pests as they compete for
the 'early bite' which is so critical for stock.
Barnacle and white-fronted geese in the
north, and recently brent geese in East
Anglia and the south, gather in large grazing
flocks on grassland. These geese migrate to
the arctic to breed and only just have time to
do so while the weather is good enough.
Their breeding success can be influenced
by their condition in spring, which is determined by the quality of their foods in late
winter and on migration. No wonder they go
for the best pastures.

*Devon landscape – the ancient patchwork
of fields, hedges and woods is good for birds
and beautiful to look at. Neither pheasant
(inset left) nor red-legged partridge (inset
right) is native, but they prosper just the
same*

Farmland

GOING FOR WORMS

Other birds use grasslands in winter. In the north and west common gulls gather in flocks and feed primarily on worms. Black-headed gulls are more widely abundant and may steal worms from lapwings and golden plovers instead of catching their own. The plovers derive some benefit from the vigilance of the gulls, but not enough to make this piracy an attractive prospect. The interactions between gulls and plovers seeking their foods in winter are interesting enough to be the subject of a book!

Stock rearing areas had two traditional features of particular value to wildlife: ponds to water the animals and hedges to contain them. Ponds harbour water birds such as mallards, moorhens or sedge warblers, which exploit animal and plant foods provided by the high level of production in wet places. But farm ponds are increasingly rare, grown over through neglect or filled in. The substitutes in the form of piped water and troughs provide no bird habitats.

THE TRADITIONAL HEDGE

Hedges provide a completely artificial habitat resembling both woodland and scrub. Most hedgerow birds also occur in these other habitats, but would not be nearly so widespread or abundant without hedges. Until its numbers were reduced by drought in its Sahelian winter quarters, south of the Sahara, the whitethroat was the characteristic hedgerow bird, giving its scratchy song

Grey partridges are native to Britain, but they are not doing very well in today's modern landscapes. The winter flocks, called coveys, are now neither so big nor so widespread as they once were

along any decent hedge. Trees in hedges have a huge benefit to birds, allowing many woodland species to breed widely in the farmed countryside. Sadly, many of these trees were elms which died in the Dutch elm disease epidemic. Large dead trees or those with dead limbs do, however, provide nesting places for several species requiring holes. Barn owls, jackdaws and stock doves are among the birds for which these are important habitat features. Hedges are not only important to farmland birds in summer. The most common hedgerow tree, hawthorn, provides an abundant source of fruit. This is mainly consumed in the early part of the winter by thrushes from the north, especially fieldfares, redwings and blackbirds. Hedges also provide cover for flocks of finches exploiting seeds on winter stubble. These birds are wary of ambush by predators like the sparrowhawk and prefer to feed near hedges where they can dive for cover.

In cereal growing areas, hedges are even more important because the rest of the agricultural fabric is more hostile to birdlife. Although the hedges might be less carefully maintained, having lost their stock controlling function, they can support a very high proportion of all the birds breeding on a cereal farm. Hedges managed in different ways support differing bird communities. Tall overgrown hedges, especially double ones along lanes, might support species of tall scrub like lesser whitethroat or even blackcap. Hedges with adjoining herbaceous vegetation, such as along a ditch side, are especially good.

HOSTILE CORN

The most commonly grown cereals are barley and wheat. Traditionally, they were sown in the spring and harvested in the autumn with the stubble being left over winter and cultivated before spring sowing. They are now more commonly sown in the autumn right after harvest. Modern cereal farming relies on artificial fertilisers and a battery of chemical treatments to suppress competing weeds and kill insect pests or fungal diseases. Either way, cereal growing provides a very unstable environment for wildlife with the sudden changes at harvesting and especially at cultivation. With such a simple environment it is not surprising that rather few species live there.

Characteristic of so much open country, the skylark can be abundant throughout the year, taking a mixed diet of seeds, invertebrate and plant material. When the crop is thick and growing, skylarks are among the few birds to occur other than at the margins. A consequence of the shift to autumn sowing is that growth now starts much faster in the spring and there is barely time for birds to breed before the crop is too thick. This is a problem for species such as the lapwing, which risk finding that conditions have deteriorated by the time they complete their incubation. With the soil being exposed at autumn cultivation, there is a brief period of plenty for invertebrate feeders. Flocks of black-headed gulls or lapwings can move in for a while.

EATING THE SEED

The cereal itself can provide food for seed eaters both as it ripens on the plant and more so as spilled seeds after harvesting. Annual weeds used to be common as a result of frequent soil disturbance. As a result, seed-eaters from finches, sparrows and buntings to rooks would be supported in abundance on stubble throughout the winter. This opportunity is declining as crops become cleaner of weeds as a result of effective herbicides, and exposed seeds are covered by autumn cultivations. Seed-eaters such as linnets, yellowhammers and corn buntings are still characteristic breeding birds in the hedges, but appear to be declining in numbers.

Grey and red-legged partridges are economically valuable birds. The interest in shooting game has been responsible for habitat maintenance which might not otherwise have been contemplated on many

cereal farms. Grey partridges have been extensively studied because of their value and because numbers have declined drastically throughout the northern hemisphere. They need dry grassy banks for nesting. The chicks feed on insects, many of which themselves feed on the weeds of cereal crops. The indirect effects of removing weeds and the direct effect of removing insects by pesticides have been disastrous for partridges. Experiments by the Game Conservancy have, however, shown that leaving a narrow, unsprayed margin around the edge of the field can have quite disproportionate benefits to the breeding success of partridges at little cost to cereal yield. This might be one simple and obvious way of reducing unwanted cereal production while enhancing bird populations on farmland, though benefits to other sorts of birds have yet to be fully investigated. The barn owl is one possible beneficiary.

Lapwings are among those birds which have suffered as a result of the dramatic changes in British agriculture. Though still quite common in some areas, in others they have all but disappeared

THE DANGER OF CHEMICALS

The widespread use of insecticides on cereals has had other effects on birds. In the 1950s powerful and persistent new insecticides were widely introduced. These organochlorines had devastating secondary effects on bird-eating raptors, even affecting populations from the remoter uplands as a result of winter movements. Numbers of sparrowhawks and peregrines are now recovering strongly since farm insecticides have become more poisonous, but less persistent. While most arable farming is rather hostile to birds, a few species have done spectacularly well as a result, none more so than the woodpigeon. This bird has a wide diet, taking seeds and leaves, especially of clover and brassicas. In spite of laying a clutch of only two eggs, it breeds at a great rate as a result of a prolonged season. Woodpigeons can be serious pests when they descend in thousands on vulnerable crops. Starlings can also be costly pests, especially when their numbers are swollen in winter by immigration from the continent. These bold birds will enter cattle sheds to feed on the expensive diets of indoor wintered stock. House sparrows are very numerous, nesting around buildings and flocking to glean seeds in the fields, though being small, they are rarely serious pests except when they foul stored foods indoors. Abundance of just a small number of species is characteristic of a simple environment offering rather few niches, which is very much what most arable farming has become. In general, mixed farming supports the greatest variety of birds because it provides opportunity for a variety of lifestyles.

Looking to the future, new crops may become attractive to farmers seeking ways of avoiding growing unwanted cereals. It is unlikely, however, that these will offer new opportunities for birds.

One oak tree and one crow in a sea of young corn. Landscapes such as this have an austere kind of beauty at certain times of year, but their value for birdlife is minimal. There are signs now that the rush for greater farming 'efficiency' is over, and that there will be changes in the way the countryside is used. But will those changes be any better for wildlife, or will they simply be cosmetics to cover the real squandering of the land?

BRITAIN'S TOWNS AND CITIES AND THEIR ATTEND-
ANT PARKS AND GARDENS ARE BEING INCREASINGLY
APPRECIATED FOR THE WILDLIFE THEY HOLD,
ESPECIALLY BIRDS. FEW PLACES CONTAIN AS MANY
VARIED NICHES FOR BIRDS AS THE URBAN LAND-
SCAPE, AND ALTHOUGH THERE ARE NO NATIONAL
RARITIES BREEDING IN TOWNS, EXCEPT FOR BLACK
REDSTARTS, ABOUT 50 SPECIES OF BIRDS REGULARLY
DO SO.

Consider the habitats within one major
built-up area in mainland Britain. Large
parks simulate open woodland, often with
the bonus of shrubberies (scrub) and some
open water. A semi-wild park like Richmond Park on the edge of London has
practically all the likely breeding species to
its credit alone. These are mainly woodland
birds, like nuthatches, treecreepers and the
woodpeckers that thrive on the insect food
available in the older trees, but also include
grassland and heathland species such as
stonechat, tree pipit, skylark and even grey
partridge. Two large artificial ponds add

aquatic species such as great crested grebe,
tufted duck and Canada goose, and a reed
bed has a reed warbler colony which is
parasitised by cuckoos. Richmond may be
the best example of its kind, but smaller
and more gardened parks often have a wide
variety of species, like the Royal Botanical
Gardens in Edinburgh, which has breeding
hawfinches and sparrowhawks, or Singleton
Park in Swansea with its winter redwings,
bramblings and siskins. Belfast is no exception. The wild park of the Laggan Meadows
boasts breeding snipe, the Bog Meadows
harbour the corncrake, whose habitat has all
but disappeared, and the ponds of the
'Waterworks' have dippers.

Other grassland or heathy areas to be
found in towns are playing field complexes,
railway marshalling yards, abandoned allotments and disused or reclaimed slag-tips. In
areas like these, especially on the fringes of
some northern and Welsh industrial towns,
can be found meadow pipits, whinchats and
skylarks, even the odd lapwing.

AN ADDITIONAL RESOURCE
The bonus of water, especially in these
places on the edge of the uplands, brings
grey wagtails and, where the water is clean
enough, the odd dipper. Pied wagtails and
the occasional kingfisher are likely elsewhere, and mallards and moorhens seem to
find a home on any scrap of water. Larger
areas of water, especially reservoirs, have a
much wider variety of wildfowl, particularly
in winter, when the rarer grebes or even a
diver may be found among the pochards,
tufted ducks, coots and gulls that throng
them. With the addition of the extra birds
that a coastal or estuarine town can muster,
the number of species can go up to 50 or
more, and all this without considering passage birds. Wading birds are the most poorly
represented species in towns, and yet, even
so, spring and autumn bring a flush of these
birds – common sandpipers on river-banks,
ruffs, redshanks, and ringed plovers on the
reservoirs and green sandpipers at the few
remaining old fashioned sewage farms.

Gardens, Parks and Towns

THE ADAPTABLE PIGEON

In the canyons of the modern city, some pioneers from natural cliffs have established bases – herring gulls on rooftops, black redstarts on gantries and gas cylinders, jackdaws and kestrels, and that well adapted bird, the feral pigeon. Some would prefer to call this bird the rock dove, because it is descended from the wild rock doves that our ancestors domesticated.

In towns tens of thousands of these birds give great pleasure to some people, but concern to not a few town halls worried about the corrosive effect of their accumulated droppings on buildings and statuary. But they are a gift to the birdwatcher. They are common, reasonably large and relatively tame, and perform their courtship displays throughout the year. They are vocal, their nest sites are easy to locate, and they rarely stop 'behaving'. In the micro-climate of the big conurbation they thrive, and are able to breed throughout the year. Like their ancestors, they may travel out to the fields to feed, but they return to the ledges each night to roost. In the winter they remain in the cities, feeding on scraps that they find in the streets, or devouring bread put out by well-wishers.

NEWCOMERS

Collared doves are also associated with urban centres and the food found in them. Unknown in Britain before the early 1950s, they have since spread to occupy all but the highest and most westerly places. But they show a strong affinity to man, and tend to flock round wharves and grain stores where they can find spilt grain. In the suburbs they favour large gardens, especially those with some conifers, and seek out food near stables and chicken runs. Their monotonous cooing is now familiar to most city dwellers, though the harsh cry uttered in flight is less well known. The collared dove's relative, the woodpigeon, is equally familiar in parks and large gardens, and is frequently quite tame as a result of being fed and not knowing the sound of a gun.

Carrion crows, jackdaws, magpies and even jays are all much tamer (and sometimes commoner) in towns than the countryside for exactly the same reasons. Jackdaws in particular will use buildings as nest sites, using crevices and cracks to enter larger spaces and even blocking chimneys by dropping nest materials down them. Carrion crows, too, will nest on buildings, notably at Heathrow Airport where the main bulk of one particular nest was constructed almost entirely of heavy wire! Pylons and other high structures will also be utilised, although the most likely place for the nest is still a large tree.

FASCINATING TIPS

Crows, pigeons, and gulls in plenty can be seen at rubbish dumps. One thing attracts

The urban landscape: Birmingham. Inset are two well-loved birds of town and garden – goldfinch (left) and blackbird (right). Starlings (top) get a mixed reception!

the birds – food – and they tend to ignore both men and machinery as they scramble for the best pickings.

Several species of gull are likely to be seen together on tips, which does not happen that often elsewhere, and those birds will probably show every kind of plumage – from first-year through to full adult. Such gatherings can be very useful for the birdwatcher.

Late summer often brings parties of young starlings to the rubbish dumps, where they may fall prey to kestrels, hunting sparrowhawk fashion and appearing suddenly over a rise in the ground to snatch the victim before it gains speed and height. Like their parents, these starlings may travel quite long distances to find food, but each evening they head toward the safety of the city, picking up other groups of birds on their way, until thousands arrive noisily in the city centres, like commuters in reverse, to seek the warmth and shelter of the ledges. Like the pigeons, they arouse both the wrath of the custodians of public buildings and the sympathies of those others who feed them.

UBIQUITOUS

Bracketed with the starlings are the house sparrows, even more closely dependent on man for their nest sites and food. Apart from a period in summer when they may leave the town to feed on grain in the fields, adult birds rarely travel. Their main enemies are cats and cars; from a pair and five young it is estimated that usually only one adult and one young will survive to the next year. Despite this, their immense adaptability allows them to thrive, and they exploit every available food source and nest site, including the nests of the house martins. Quite a large percentage of the cup-shaped nests of this neat black and white bird is taken over during winter and never relinquished, and sometimes they are even annexed by sparrows as the martins complete them. But the presence of house martins in the major cities is largely a happy story. Before the Clean Air Act of 1956 the air in most cities was too polluted to support the insects on which house martins feed. However, the martins returned to inner London in 1966, the first time that they had done so in 77 years.

TOWNS AS WOODS

The typical birds of the garden – blackbirds, song thrushes, blue tits and so on – are really woodland birds that have adapted successfully to urban living. Viewed from above, an area of gardens may not be that different from a small, open wood, and may be blessed with more nesting opportunities than the natural habitat, as such a large proportion of it may be made up of boundary hedges, shrubs and climbers. With the addition of nestboxes and an abundance of food, territories can be small, and most suburban gardens have more songbirds than an equivalent area of woodland.

Although bird mortality can be high, with the automobile as the chief instrument of death, winter feeding and the slightly higher winter temperatures experienced in towns may well balance things out. The city streets, parks and gardens constitute a vast area where birds are rarely molested and where they should continue to thrive. Urban sprawl is certainly Britain's least endangered habitat!

Not leaves, but starlings!

The Birds

Peregrine

Over 240 British birds are described on the following pages. They are arranged in their family orders, which usually means that birds which look alike are close together. Each bird is illustrated in painstaking detail, and its lifestyle, habitat, range, voice, nest and eggs are described in the text

Red-throated Diver

Red-throats take off more easily than other divers and can take advantage of smaller pools, but are restricted to areas with very little human disturbance. The range has expanded recently to south-west Scotland. The nest is a mere cushion of aquatic vegetation, often so close to water that on larger lochs, where strong winds can whip up large waves, eggs are often swamped. Adults are very ungainly on land, but young have been recorded moving in short leaps over dry ground between pools, encouraged by a calling parent. Young birds and adults from the far north start moving south in late August, usually appearing in the south in September. They stay until April, even May, often in large, loose groups but more usually in ones and twos. By May many birds will have acquired their smart summer plumage, a sight not often seen outside Scotland. They are then distinguished from other divers by their unpatterned backs, but a close view shows delicate striping on the nape and sides of the neck; the white breast is more obvious. In summer they are seen in flight more often than the black-throated, as they move from their breeding loch to and from their feeding places on the coast, usually calling loudly as they go.

Gavia stellata
53–69 cm; 1,200–1,600 g
Where to look: breeding birds are confined to lochs and small fresh water pools on moors. In winter widespread around UK coasts, off both rocky and sandy shores. **Nest:** a flat pad close to water. **Eggs:** 1 or 2, dark, speckled brown. **Food:** nearly always fish, but some crabs, shrimps. **Voice:** only in breeding season, wailing and rhythmic goose-like calls; loud, deep quacking in flight, rapidly repeated *kwuk-uk-uk*.

Except in very good light, the red throat patch appears dark, almost black. It is the last part of summer plumage to be lost in autumn.

On water the general appearance is of a slim, long-necked bird, low in the water, with head and bill uptilted. Swims long distances under water.

Regularly flies from breeding loch to fish in the sea, calling in flight. Wings raised higher than other divers' in flight and wing-beats are quicker.

A flying red-throat in winter is best identified by its slim build and pale head and neck, with the white face often obvious. Feet look smaller than other divers'.

In winter, adults have paler face and neck than juveniles, with the dark eye obvious against white background. Upper parts have fine white speckling, not seen on other divers. Longer body and thicker neck distinguish it from grebes.

In territorial disputes rival males glide across surface of water, calling loudly, in 'snake', 'penguin race' and 'plesiosaur' ceremonies.

Red-throated: pale bird; small and slender; upward tilt to bill.

Black-throated: dark upper parts, greyer nape, white flank patch.

Great northern: bulky, broad bird with heavy bill; dark cheeks and neck patches.

Great Northern Diver

In flight, big feet give as much length behind as in front of wings; broad, dark flank stripe; large wingspan and goose-like action may help identification.

Summer birds are spangled and have black heads, not grey.

Gavia immer
69–91 cm; 3,000–4,000 g
Where to look: rocky coasts and sandy bays. **Food:** mostly fish but also molluscs, crabs and shrimps. **Voice:** wailing calls – rarely heard outside breeding sites.

The scaled pattern of the great northern diver is appropriate for a bird that spends more time under water than on top when it is feeding – not helpful for the birdwatcher! Most birds in Britain in winter come from Iceland, where the wonderful, strange wailing calls can be heard from the lonely lakes where they breed. This is the largest of the divers and has a heavy bill well-suited to catching flatfish and to manipulating and cracking the shells of crabs and molluscs before they are swallowed. After a good feed, divers go through a rigorous preening process to keep all their feathers in good condition – essential for a bird that never leaves the water except to fly. The roll preen is often seen, as the diver rolls over, often with one leg raised, and shows the pure white underside as it preens its belly feathers. In May, divers in full summer splendour move east along the English south coast before migrating north, and lucky observers may be treated to small parties passing favoured headlands. An odd bird on a reservoir inland is not unusual in winter. Where a reservoir is large enough, with plenty of fish, a diver may stay for weeks at a time, but such birds are often surprisingly elusive and may take a lot of finding!

From behind, looks broad-beamed. Head blacker than back, with angular, lumpy shape; dark cheeks and neck patches and large, pale bill aid identification; back may be more or less barred.

Black-throated Diver

Like all divers, the black-throated faces many potential dangers all year round. Because it feeds in the larger lochs where it breeds, instead of flying to the sea, it has been persecuted by man in the past. Now the problem is disturbance by boats or noisy groups of people which cause the sensitive divers to desert their nests. Even on ideal lochs, breeding density is low because each pair needs a territory of up to 350 acres. And whereas red-throated divers can breed on acidic, peaty pools and feed out at sea, there is some evidence that black-throats have been affected by acid rain reducing fish stocks in the large lochs they use. In autumn and winter all divers can fall victim to fishing nets in inshore waters, or to oil. Despite these problems, the British population, though small, seems stable after a decline prior to the 1940s. Breeding birds may be helped by the provision of artificial, floating islands, which removes the problem of flooding of nests, though this idea, which seems a very good one on the face of it, has yet to be proved successful.

Gavia arctica
58–73 cm; 2,000–3,000 g
Where to look: breeding birds on large Scottish lochs; in winter moves south, to both sandy and rocky coasts. **Nest:** beside water, often on island. **Eggs:** 1 or 2, olive-brown with black spots. **Food:** almost entirely fish. **Voice:** raven-like croaking, often repeated, and wailing calls building up to loud, far-carrying climax.

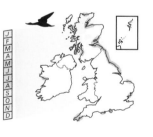

Dark back, paler hindneck and narrow body distinctive in winter when back may show scaly pattern. Club-shaped head.

Territorial displays may involve spectacular rushes across water, with wings raised, then bird rears up with neck arched back.

Divers dive smoothly without forward leap of shag. Young cormorants have pale undersides but longer tails. In flight, divers look hump-backed, legs trailing. Black-throats form small groups, have pale, horizontal, dagger-like bills and white flank flash; red-throats have uptilted bills; great northerns look much heavier.

Contrasted black and white; shallow wing-beats.

Great Crested Grebe

The display of the great crested grebe is as incredible as its history. In the mid 19th century these beautiful grebes were the height of fashion, when skinned and converted into ladies' hats. So much so that by 1860 the UK population had been reduced to just 42 pairs. Today, after a steady increase, the population is standing at approximately 5,000 pairs. This remarkable recovery has been aided by the flooding of many old gravel pits which, after a few years, provide an ideal habitat with overhanging bank vegetation in which the grebe can nest. The extraordinary springtime display was first recognised and documented in the early 20th century. 'Cat display', 'penguin dance', 'habit preening' and 'head shaking' are all parts of the ritual in early spring. The fluffy, striped young are regularly carried aboard the parents' backs soon after they are hatched. It is thought the young do not recognise their parents by sight during the first six weeks as they have been known to follow anything that moves – including boats! The first two weeks of a great crested grebe's life are especially hazardous as they often fall prey to large fish like the pike.

A new menace in the shape of escaped mink, which are versatile hunters, at home on land, in water and in trees, threatens eggs and young birds. The increasing recreational use of many lakes has forced grebes to move to less suitable areas which has resulted in the UK

Podiceps cristatus
46–51 cm; 800–1,400 g
Where to look: inland lakes, especially gravel pits, occasionally on slow-flowing rivers and often off sandy stretches of coast in the winter. **Nest:** often floating heap of aquatic plants anchored by surrounding vegetation. **Eggs:** 3–4, white but often stained by water plants on nest. **Food:** small fish, insects, molluscs and sometimes vegetable matter. **Voice:** barking *rah-rah-rah* and a clicking *kek*; loud whistles from chicks.

The head feathers of the great crested grebe are raised, making the colour as obvious as possible during the head-shaking display.

population not being as high as it might have been. Powered boats create enough wash to swamp grebes' nests and chicks, and the birds are unable to fish, display or rest if they are disturbed by boats too often. Ideally they like peace and seclusion throughout spring and summer. Grebes are not particularly worried by people on shore, but there is a risk that their eggs might be taken by crows if the grebes are disturbed and leave their nests.

Grebes move long distances under water and can be frustrating: after a long dive they come up far from where you expected.

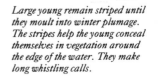

Large young remain striped until they moult into winter plumage. The stripes help the young conceal themselves in vegetation around the edge of the water. They make long whistling calls.

Young birds the size of their parents will continue to plead for food until they are driven off the territory or the parents leave the area. Families usually split into two, each parent feeding its 'own' chicks.

With beaks full of vegetation the grebes begin the 'penguin dance', raising themselves from the water breast to breast, with furiously paddling feet, while swinging their heads from side to side.

This bird is best identified in flight by its vivid wing pattern; the long neck and trailing feet reduce possible confusion with mergansers which have similar white patches. A moulting bird can be mistaken for a red-necked grebe but the black crown never extends as low as the eye.

This is the largest and most often seen grebe in Britain. Like all grebes it loses its splendid summer dress in the autumn. In winter plumage it is a long-necked, slim and pale bird, although a group can loaf about in all sorts of strange positions, making identification difficult. The use of reservoirs by water-skiers and speed boats in winter exhausts flocks of grebes as they continually have to fly to quieter areas.

Large groups congregate on inland reservoirs in winter as their smaller breeding lakes become frozen. Others move to the coast.

The head ruffs are lost during the winter. The pink bill is specific to the great crested grebe.

Great crested grebes are often far out on large lakes and size is misleading; they can look as big as divers or as small as moorhens! The thin bill, gleaming white breast and foreneck and rounded, stumpy-tailed body usually identify them. A grebe with a pink bill, a thin black cap and a line of white over the eye will be this species. Red-necked grebes have a rounder, deeper black cap to eye level and yellow on the bill; beware young coots with white on the neck and face; cormorants are much larger and longer-tailed; ducks have broader, blunter bills.

Little Grebe

From a dumpy little puff ball on the surface the little grebe transforms to a sleek, highly developed hunter beneath water. All of its features are geared to fast movement when submerged. Its legs are set well back on the body to allow as much movement as possible. Its tail is reduced to mere bristles so as not to collide with its thrusting feet. The toes, with wide lobes, can be folded over each other on the forward stroke, and even the bones in the leg are flattened to give extra propulsion on the backward stroke but less resistance on the forward stroke. Beneath water the little grebe appears silver because air bubbles are trapped under its feathers. This helps to keep the grebe warm and also enables it to float to the surface while concentrating on holding on to its prey – often diving beetles and sticklebacks.

Little grebes, or dabchicks, are found on tiny ponds and narrow rivers, but also on the bigger, more open waters that larger species inhabit, especially in winter. Then they look smaller than ever.

Notice the pale spot by the bill.

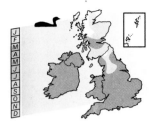

Because of their small size and ability to hide, little grebes are able to occupy waterways well used by man. The rich burgundy sides to the face and neck show well.

Young birds have unusually striped heads. They dive to find their own food at a very early stage.

Tachybaptus ruficollis
25–29 cm; 140–230 g
Where to look: shallow-edged lakes, small ponds and slow-moving rivers. **Nest:** floating tangle of aquatic vegetation attached to larger plants. **Eggs:** 4–6, white, but often stained. **Food:** small fish, shrimps and many types of aquatic insects. **Voice:** distinctive, high-pitched, tittering giggle.

As with all grebes, it is really only the face and neck colours which fade away in the winter plumage.

In flight its very small size and upperwing with no white make this bird easy to distinguish from other grebes.

Red-necked Grebe

Flight views show less white on upperwing than great crested. In summer it is easily identified by white cheeks and chestnut neck.

Its smaller size and stockiness clear when seen with great crested grebes.

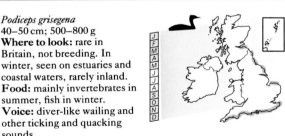

More black on nape than on the smaller Slavonian.

Looking like a thick-set, dark great crested grebe, the red-necked grebe can also appear quite diver-like in winter. A feeding bird can be guessed at from some distance since it often jumps from the surface before each dive. Its size and shape can be misleading; sometimes it looks like a black-necked or Slavonian grebe and at other times more like a great crested grebe though it rarely appears so slim. Although it does not breed in Britain, it can be seen in its summer plumage in September and October when the first individuals reappear, on reservoirs and more particularly on the east coast. During periods of very harsh winter weather many birds are forced to move from the Baltic and Dutch coasts to Britain's milder, more sheltered coastline and lakes. They occasionally mix with parties of great crested grebes, but more often mingle with parties of scoters or eiders on the coast. Like Slavonian and black-necked grebes, this species has a wide distribution and is also found in North America. It is never a common bird, however, unlike the more numerous black-necked in southern Europe.

Podiceps grisegena
40–50 cm; 500–800 g
Where to look: rare in Britain, not breeding. In winter, seen on estuaries and coastal waters, rarely inland. **Food:** mainly invertebrates in summer, fish in winter. **Voice:** diver-like wailing and other ticking and quacking sounds.

The cleanliness of the cheek patch varies from bird to bird.

Black crown extending below the eye, dusky neck, dusky-whitish cheeks and black-tipped yellow bill are the best features of a winter-plumaged bird. Some look whiter-faced than others.

Often very active, staying on the surface only for short periods. Usually solitary but occasionally with other grebes or diving ducks. Dull overall plumage, stocky build with dagger-like bill help with identification.

Black-necked Grebe

Groups are sometimes joined by more solitary Slavonian.

The dusky cheek and neck separate from 'cleaner' Slavonian.

Black-necked grebes are usually only seen in their black, white and grey winter plumage. Head and bill shape help. From September to March they may be found fishing in the breakers on the coast, floating buoyantly over the waves.

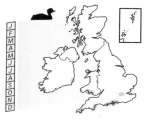

Podiceps nigricollis
28–34 cm; 250–400 g
Where to look: well vegetated, undisturbed, shallow ponds in the breeding season. Moves to the sea or large reservoirs in winter, often found in groups on open areas of water particularly in spring and autumn. **Nest:** floating or grounded heaps, often in loose colonies. **Eggs:** white, but soon stained by weeds. **Voice:** chittering trill.

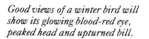

The ups and downs of breeding black-necked grebes in Britain are not fully understood. The first breeding record was in Wales in 1904; several other cases followed in Ireland, Scotland and England, often involving colonies. One colony in Ireland numbered up to 250 pairs from 1929 to 1932. These birds have now all but disappeared. Other small colonies have been started in Britain, but their fate remains to be seen. The large pre- and post-breeding flocks will no doubt continue to appear on their traditional sites. Staines Reservoir in Surrey can often hold good flocks of birds, many of which are still in their smart summer plumage. Traditional sites are also kept on the coast in winter, although birds move around to find sheltered bays during bad weather. Stray birds can turn up at any time of year on small lakes and ponds inland, and sometimes one will linger in spring to give a rare view of its rich summer colouring. It appears a little less colourful than the Slavonian on glancing at a book illustration, but the plumage has a sheen and depth of hue that makes it an exceptionally attractive bird in reality.

Good views of a winter bird will show its glowing blood-red eye, peaked head and upturned bill.

The summer-plumaged bird with its black neck is easy to identify.

Slavonian Grebe

The spectacular golden-yellow eye stripe and tufts are only present during the summer when they are used in great crested grebe-like displays. It is during these displays that the North American name, horned grebe, seems more appropriate. A penguin-like dance varies from the great crested grebe's in several ways. Aquatic plants are gathered from the bottom of the pond and the birds surface to face each other as though to start the dance. When raised out of the water the two grebes immediately turn parallel to each other and race across the surface together. This ceremony is termed the 'weed rush'. Like the black-necked grebe, the first records of Slavonian grebes nesting in Britain were in the early 1900s. Today they are still increasing and spreading slowly, with about 60 breeding pairs. During the winter they move from the coast or estuaries only when the weather is too bad for them to fish easily. The stocking of lakes with trout causes some concern for the well-being of these rare grebes. The ecology of the lake is changed by the great numbers of voracious trout, to the detriment of the grebes.

The well-defined black and white plumage and sleek appearance help to separate this grebe from the black-necked; occasionally found in small groups.

Podiceps auritus
31–38 cm; 350–450 g
Where to look: rare breeder in the highlands of Scotland. In winter almost exclusively found around the coast, particularly in sheltered bays and estuaries. **Nest:** made of floating weed anchored by surrounding vegetation. **Eggs:** white, but soon stained by vegetation used to cover the nest as the adult bird leaves. **Food:** Fish.

The Slavonian is told from black-necked by 'cleaner' appearance and two white wing patches.

With experience, observers can tell red-necked, Slavonian and black-necked grebes apart fairly easily, although single birds at a distance are enough to throw the best observers into confusion. Shape is always a good pointer, but when the birds are resting they all look very similar. Birds in moult are even more difficult.

Summer plumage unmistakable.

Manx Shearwater

Puffinus puffinus
30–38 cm Wingspan 76–89 cm
Where to look: mainly off west coast, spring to autumn. Ashore only at colonies at night. **Nest:** in burrows on islands. **Egg:** 1, white. **Food:** small fish, squid. **Voice:** excited cackles.

Stiff-winged cruciform silhouette of birds flying past, flashing alternately black and white as they tilt from side to side.

The Manx shearwater has remarkable navigational abilities: a bird released in Boston, USA, took just over 12 days to return the 3,200 miles to its nesting burrow on a Welsh island. Even to feed they may travel more than 200 miles. Perhaps the most remarkable colony in Britain is 2,000ft up on a mountainside on the Hebridean island of Rhum. The birds are vulnerable to predators on land, and so gather at dusk in rafts offshore before coming into their burrows in darkness.

Like other members of the shearwater family, the adult abandons its young in the nest burrow, where it lives off its fat reserves for two weeks, and then finds its own way to the sea, and winter quarters 5,000 miles away off the South American coast.

The Western Mediterranean race, the Balearic shearwater, is browner above and dusky below, lacking the sharp contrast of Manx. Small numbers appear off British coasts in late summer. There is some discussion about the status of these birds, which may be classified as a separate species eventually.

A few rapid stiff-winged flaps interspersed with glides, close to the surface, the lower wingtip almost cutting the water. They revel in strong winds, flying in higher arcs, gliding even more.

Sooty Shearwater

Larger than Manx, with longer, more pointed wings; appears all dark at any distance.

Characteristic stiff-winged flight, with few flaps, followed by long glide on slightly swept-back wings. Rather heavy cigar-shaped body and long, thin bill.

Puffinus griseus
40–51 cm
Wingspan 94–109 cm
Where to look: off all coasts, though rare SE England; in onshore winds in late summer and autumn, often out on horizon. Scarce. Does not breed in UK. **Food:** squid, fish. **Voice:** silent in Britain.

The sooty shearwater is one of the world's most abundant seabirds. Along with its cousin, the great shearwater, it is unique among British birds in being a non-breeding summer visitor to the northern hemisphere, nesting during the southern summer on the Falklands, Tierra del Fuego, and in huge numbers in the South Pacific. Numbers in the Atlantic are much smaller, and it is always an exciting sight in Britain, though more often seen in inshore waters than the more numerous great shearwater. It is essentially a cold water species, travelling in a huge, clockwise movement up the west side of the Atlantic, then across to the east in late summer, reaching as far north as the Arctic waters of Iceland, and down into the North Sea.

Its favourite squid and fish are caught at the surface, where it swims buoyantly, or in shallow dives. Small numbers of birds are sometimes attracted to fishing boats by oily fish waste thrown overboard.

The dark, sooty-brown plumage is relieved by a variable pale stripe the length of the underwing, which frequently catches the light as the bird banks, though often invisible at long range. Care must be taken not to confuse it with the rather smaller, more compact Balearic shearwater, nor even with distant immature gannets. At extreme range birds may only be visible when soaring stiff-winged above the horizon, disappearing when down against the background of the sea. Sooty shearwaters are practically always seen on the move, flying past a headland and not coming back. To see them needs a special effort (usually with a telescope to hand) to watch for birds low over the sea—they are unlikely to be noticed 'by accident'.

Storm Petrel

Hydrobates pelagicus
14–18 cm
Wingspan 36–39 cm
Where to look: at sea, off west coast during gales. Following boats. **Nest:** in holes, burrows on islands. **Egg:** 1, white. **Food:** plankton. **Voice:** churring from burrow.

It is a memorable sight to see Britain's smallest seabirds, only sparrow-sized, battling against a fierce autumn gale, apparently at the mercy of the elements. However, the weak-looking, bat-like flight with rapid wingbeats and very short glides is deceptive, for much of their life is spent far out of sight of land, and birds 20 years old have been recorded. They only come to land, after dark, to breed in colonies. Inland records are quite exceptional.

Their habit of following ships, fluttering back and forth across the wake, has made them familiar to sailors. Large numbers can be attracted by 'chum' – a mixture of fish oil and offal; within minutes, an apparently empty sea is dotted with tiny black fluttering birds heading purposefully low over the surface towards the slick, attracted by the smell.

Petrels are named after St Peter from their habit of apparently walking on water. In fact they simply flutter and patter with their feet or merely lower their legs to stabilise themselves above the waves.

> Boat trips in late summer, or seawatching in autumn gales can be very exciting. Huge numbers of kittiwakes and gannets may pass; petrels and the rarer shearwaters are keenly sought. Identification of distant 'tubenoses' rests largely on their flight action – a few stiff-winged flaps and long glides of shearwaters, weak fluttering of storm petrels, and graceful, bounding, erratic flight of Leach's.

The pale underwing bar can show well. At a distance recalls a sea-hugging house martin. Feeds by dipping to surface with bill, wings raised, legs dangling.

Leach's Petrel

Oceanodroma leucorhoa
19–22 cm
Wingspan 45–48 cm
Where to look: off west coasts, Norfolk, in onshore autumn gales. **Nest:** in burrows on a few remote islands. **Egg:** 1, white. **Food:** plankton, small fish. **Voice:** churring and hiccoughs from nest at night.

Leach's petrel is perhaps the most difficult to see of all Britain's breeding birds, with less than 10,000 pairs, and the most accessible colony on St Kilda! However, millions breed on the west side of the Atlantic, and other races occur in the North Pacific. The right conditions in autumn will bring small numbers within sight of land, and more are blown inland than storm petrels – perhaps because they remain in British waters later, to be caught by autumn gales *en route* for their winter quarters in the Gulf of Guinea and off Brazil. Occasional incidents cause many birds to be picked up exhausted or dead after gales: in 1952 more than 7,000 were involved in such a 'wreck' in Britain and Ireland.

Leach's petrels are usually solitary at sea and do not follow boats. Their manner of progress is really quite remarkable – recalling a small shearwater one moment, a tern the next, then suddenly darting off on a different tack, leaping erratically along the surface, before hanging almost motionless in the wind.

Like other petrels, their nostrils are tubular. They drink salt water and excrete the salt through the tubes, though these may have other functions too.

Petrels and shearwaters have tubes at the base of the upper mandible to aid the removal of excess salt.

The pale grey-brown upperwing coverts, forming a broad diagonal bar across the wing, are usually very obvious. A slightly browner bird overall than storm petrel.

The fork in the tail is often not visible in the field.

Leach's are noticeably larger than storm petrel, with longer wings. Bounding flight is stronger and more graceful, with erratic changes of pace and direction.

No pale bar on underwing. Wings held angled at 'wrist' joint. Wing-beats often deep. Does not patter as habitually as storm, though legs may be dangled.

Fulmar

Fulmarus glacialis
45–50 cm
Wingspan 102–112 cm
Where to look: present
round entire coastline where
cliffs suitable, all year except
late autumn. Non-breeders at
sea. Very rarely inland. **Nest:**
in colonies on cliff ledges, less
often unused buildings, sand-
dunes; grass or soil preferred
to bare rock. **Egg:** 1, white.
Food: offal, crustaceans,
carrion, refuse, small fish,
usually taken from surface.
Attends trawlers in large
numbers. **Voice:** loud,
excited cackling and crooning
at nest, grunts and cackles in
feeding flocks, otherwise
silent.

Fulmars are perhaps Britain's longest-lived birds,
many probably reaching 40 years of age. Immature birds
remain at sea for several years, not breeding until nine or
10. Young birds looking for future nest sites are
sometimes trapped in old roofless buildings: in three
years 274 were found on North Ronaldsay, Orkney.

In the last 200 years there has been a spectacular
spread from Icelandic stock, with birds first recorded
breeding in Britain, away from the ancient colony of St
Kilda, on Foula in 1878. In 1969/70, the British and
Irish breeding population was 305,000 pairs, with
40,000 on St Kilda. This increase is thought to have
resulted from the availability of whaling and trawling
offal as food. The St Kilda population has remained
stable and still has a diet largely of plankton; it also
behaves differently, avoiding ruined buildings, so it is
possible that a new adaptable type of fulmar arose on
Iceland, capable of exploiting man's fishing waste – just
as the collared dove has spectacularly extended its range
more recently by filling a vacant niche.

Fulmar-oil is a foul smelling liquid, ejected by both
adults and young as a form of defence, though also used,
mixed with regurgitated food, for feeding the young. It
is rich in vitamins A and D. The smell of fulmars is said
to stay on oil-stained clothing for many years.

*Heavy body, straight wings, lack
of neck distinguish from gulls
such as herring gull (right).*

*From the high Arctic, the 'blue
fulmar' is rare in British waters.*

*The stout, hooked bill is made up
of several plates, topped with a
prominent pair of nostril tubes.
The dark patch of modified
bristly feathers in front of the eye
may help to reduce glare.*

*The pale patch on the inner
primaries is especially noticeable
in worn plumage. No British gull
has a grey tail.*

*Fulmars swim buoyantly, and
may spend much of the day
resting on the water. They feed
from the surface, and also
occasionally by shallow plunge-
diving.*

*Fulmars are faithful to their
mate and nest site. They wave
their heads and bow and cackle at
their mates and rivals. The inside
of the bill, shown in display, is a
striking mauve or purple.*

*The nest site is vigorously
defended, though once incubation
has started the adults are rarely
together.*

*The downy white chick is attended
constantly for the first two weeks.
Later, the parents only visit
briefly to feed the chick.*

*At fledging, the young bird
resembles its parents. Despite the
long period of immaturity, there
are no plumage differences with
age, sex or season.*

Superficially gull-like, the fulmar is easily identifiable, with its stiff-winged, effortless, sail-planing
flight, thickset, neckless appearance, and short, chunky,
'broken' bill. The ivory-white head and body contrast
with the brownish- and silvery-grey of the rest of the
plumage. Along cliffs, it flies in long glides on straight,
slightly bowed wings, hanging on updraughts, stalling,
then dropping away, using tail and feet to steer and
brake. The stronger the wind, the more this mini-
albatross seems to enjoy it.

Gannet

Britain and Ireland now hold 189,000 pairs of this largest and most spectacular seabird of the North Atlantic, a large proportion of the world population. It was formerly taken for food by sea-fowling communities; the fat, unfledged young or 'guga' providing considerable quantities of protein and fat. The inflated, dried stomachs were used on St Kilda as containers. Cessation of most persecution has enabled numbers to increase to a new peak, doubling between 1949 and 1969, and still rising, with several new colonies.

Gannets have no brood patch, so the egg is incubated under the large webbed feet, and the newly hatched chick brooded on top of the webs. Another special adaptation is the lack of external nostrils, enabling the birds to dive head-first into the sea from up to 30 metres (100ft), reaching 100kph (60mph) as they hit the water.

Each young gannet eats about 30 kilos (65 pounds) of fish before leaving the colony. After 13 weeks, they jump off the cliffs and flop-glide to the sea below, unable to take off again for a week or more, until their excess fat reserves have been used up. They move south to waters off the West African coast and may remain there for two years, before returning north.

Sula bassana
87–100 cm
Wingspan 165–180 cm
Where to look: breeds mainly on rocky islands in north and west, but seen off all coasts, less numerous in winter. Vagrant inland. **Nest:** pile of seaweed, vegetation, earth. In large, dense, noisy colonies. **Egg:** 1, pale blue, chalky, turning white, then staining. **Food:** fish, especially mackerel and herring, caught in spectacular plunge-dive; also offal. **Voice:** *arrr, urrah.*

Gannets take about four years to attain full adult plumage, each stage being recognisable. First-years have white underparts, head and neck, but otherwise are all dark above; second-years have largely white forewings but still have dark flight feathers.

Third-years resemble adults, but retain some black feathers on the inner wing and tail. They hang around the colony edge in 'clubs'.

The magnificent adult is gleaming white with black outer wing, and rich buff head and nape.

Distant birds of all ages are identifiable by their shape.

The central, long, thin, angled wings, long, pointed bill and tail give characteristic silhouette.

In flight the body is often angled above the horizontal.

One or other parent is always in attendance at the nest to defend it and to tend the downy, white chick. As it grows older, dark juvenile feathers replace the down. When fledged, juveniles are black to avoid being taken for trespassing adults.

Steady, powerful wing-beats.

Fishermen may use the spectacular sight of fishing gannets to locate fish shoals.

Cormorant

In full breeding dress they are very handsome; black, glossed blue and bronze, with a white throat and thigh patch, flashed in courtship display. A few white plumes adorn the loosely crested nape formed of elongated feathers, though the Continental race sinensis *has extensive white on the head. Outside the nesting season adults are much duller, and lose most of their white.*

Phalacrocorax carbo
80–100 cm
Wingspan 130–160 cm
Where to look: breeds round all coasts, but large gaps in east, otherwise widespread on estuarine and inland waters, especially winter. **Nest:** pile of twigs, seaweed, lined with finer material, in loose colonies on cliff ledges. Abroad, also in trees, reed beds inland. **Eggs:** 3–4, chalky white. **Food:** fish, especially bottom-dwelling species, eels. **Voice:** guttural croaking at nest and roost.

Cormorants seem to spend much of their time doing nothing, sitting like bottles, upright in rows on a sand bank, on buoys or other man-made structures, or trees, unlike shags which prefer rocks.

Rather goose-like in flight, even as far as adopting loose 'V' formation when in a flock.

Fly with steady wing-beats and occasional glides. Circle inland waters before landing in shallow glide. Laboured take-off.

The thick neck is often held kinked in flight, rather than fully extended, accentuating the reptilian appearance.

Usually bring fish to the surface to shake or toss before swallowing. Eels are a favourite, but may present quite a problem.

Bill held at an upward angle. At a distance may be confused with divers, which are always very white underneath in winter.

Chicks hatch at intervals and at first are fed on regurgitated liquid. Later they take solid food from parents' throats.

Cormorants are widely distributed over five continents. They eat a variety of fish, many of no commercial value, but fishermen, who see them as competitors, have long persecuted them. Their fishing ability is turned to man's advantage in the Far East, where trained birds, fitted with a neck collar to prevent swallowing, are sent fishing on a lead. In Britain, too, the cormorant was exploited, and King James I had a Master of Cormorants on the Thames.

Some foresters also dislike the cormorant because the acid droppings rapidly kill off trees regularly used as perches. Although tree nesting is very rare in Britain, there are many inland tree roosts which bear testimony to the power of cormorant guano.

The cormorant uses its large, webbed feet to incubate its eggs, carefully placing them under the eggs, so they are warmed between the feet and body. The young are born blind and naked, and look distinctly reptilian at this stage. They were formerly eaten in the Netherlands, where some tree colonies are very large: the famous Nardermeer colony has 3,800 nests.

Cormorant feathers have modified barbs which allow air to escape and water to penetrate the plumage. This makes for more efficient underwater swimming. However, it also means the bird becomes waterlogged and must dry its plumage in the well-known heraldic posture, which may also aid digestion in some way, as in vultures, which stand in a very similar pose.

Immature brown with varying amount of white underneath.

Shag

The dapper, spring adult with its dark, oily green plumage, yellow gape, and comic, upturned crest is easily distinguished from the larger cormorant. At other ages and seasons, more reliance must be put on shape and structure.

Phalacrocorax aristotelis
65–80 cm
Wingspan 90–105 cm
Where to look: rocky coasts, absent from much of east and south England. Immature birds disperse more widely in winter. Not inland except after gales. **Nest:** heap of weed, vegetation, on sheltered ledge, sea cave, among boulders. **Eggs:** 3, pale blue, with chalky deposit. **Food:** fish, mainly sand eels and herrings. **Voice:** grunts and clicks.

In flight shows proportionately shorter and less pointed wings, and more rapid wing-beats, with the neck usually fully extended. They hug the sea more closely.

Both shag and cormorant may spring clear of the water when diving, though the lighter, more graceful shag does so more often. It is more at home in rough water.

Fresh material is added to the nest throughout the breeding cycle. Adults vigorously defend young against predators.

Atlantic race immature birds are pale brown below, white only on the chin (but white belly on birds in the Mediterranean).

In all plumages the shape of the feather line around the gape is a clue. Lores (eye to bill) feathered on shag, bare on cormorant.

Shag smaller and more finely proportioned than cormorant, but beware sexual and racial size variations. Bill thinner and of more even width with a less strongly hooked tip, head shape rounder, with steeper forehead, less angled nape, more 'snaky'.

The shag, or green cormorant, like most British seabirds, has been steadily increasing this century, despite periodic disasters. It is highly susceptible to paralytic shellfish poisoning, contracted from a natural toxin produced by a small marine organism, and concentrated by the fish the shags feed on. In 1968, 82 per cent of Farne Island breeding birds died within a few days. However, the following year, numbers were rapidly replaced by incoming young birds, which had dispersed from the colony. Shags take four years to mature, and, once adult, have a high life expectancy. Young birds are prone to disorientation in adverse weather and may end up inland in considerable numbers. Such influxes are called 'wrecks'.

More of a deep water bird than the cormorant, and often rather solitary, flocks of several hundred shags will gather to exploit a large surface shoal of fish.

It is an early breeder, nesting usually timed so that the young are in the nest when most sand eels are available in May and June, but occasional nests have been found in winter. The long fledgling period of 53 days is followed by a further four weeks during which the adults still feed and tend the young. The female chick loses her voice after five weeks, able only to hiss and click!

The shag is confined to European Atlantic coasts as far south as Morocco, and the Mediterranean and Black Seas. It is largely resident, with little more than local dispersal from most colonies, so they must be sought near rocky coasts all year round.

Grey Heron

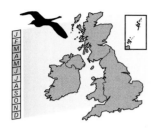

Ardea cinerea
90–98 cm; 1,100–1,700 g
Where to look: ponds, lakes, rivers, marshes and other fresh water sites, sometimes seen at coastal localities, particularly in winter. **Nest:** large stick construction in tree-top colonies, although occasionally singly or on ground. **Eggs:** 4–5, pale blue. **Food:** varied, fish, small mammals and birds. **Voice:** a loud, harsh and distinctive *frank;* young birds chatter or give a pig-like squeal, especially before being fed.

A heron standing motionless beside a river or pond is a very familiar sight, and the actions of a hunting bird that has succeeded in catching an eel are truly spectacular as this most accomplished of fishermen tries to swallow the most agile of fish. Frequently the eel actually knots itself around the heron's bill. So successful is the heron at fishing that for many years it was thought that the legs of the bird produced some magical substance which attracted fish as it stood in the water. Anglers were not slow to capitalise on this belief by scattering pieces of herons' legs around a fishing ground. There is, of course, no foundation to the idea.

The grey heron population of England and Wales is probably better known than that of any other bird. First counted in 1928, there has been an annual monitoring ever since, and the population now numbers some 4,000 breeding pairs (plus a further 1,000 or so in Scotland). The largest colony is at the RSPB Northward Hill reserve, Kent, where in most years the colony totals some 200 pairs. Fears that the death of the elm trees in which they nested would seriously affect this colony were ill founded, as the birds simply moved to the neighbouring oaks. The grey heron, usually so silent, is an aggressive and noisy bird at the nest.

In both flapping flight and when gliding and soaring, the heron is immediately identified by the broad, rounded wings, 'kinked' neck and long, trailing legs.

The large, dagger-shaped bill is a highly efficient tool for fishing. Normally yellow, but turns bright pink when breeding.

The unmistakable heron is a large bird with heavy bill, long legs and neck. The black and white patterning on the head and neck contrasts with the grey body.

When nesting, groups of 'off-duty' birds can be found near the colony on the 'standing-ground'.

Sunbathing herons adopt a posture that allows the sun to warm the maximum surface area of the body. A similar pose is taken when bathing in heavy rain or sheltering small nestlings.

Herons have special, powdery down on the sides of their chests. They rub any feathers (usually head and neck) that have become sticky or scaly against the down after feeding, and the powder soaks up the fish slime, making the feathers much easier to clean.

The claw on the third toe has a serrated edge which enables the plumage to be preened clean.

Hunting herons adopt two very different techniques. One is to stand completely motionless and 'wait and see'; the other involves a careful stalk of prey.

The breeding season in a colony is very protracted, first eggs in mid-February, the last young in early September. From egg laying to first flight takes three months.

Throughout the breeding cycle birds indulge in displays which maintain the bond between the breeding pair. Formal greetings accompany arrival at the nest.

The same nest is used and added to each year, eventually getting so heavy that one winter it falls.

Male and female herons are indistinguishable; young birds lack the striking black and white markings of the adults. Young move south, returning to the colony to breed when two to three years old. One British ringed nestling was recovered in Morocco.

Bittern

Botaurus stellaris
70–80 cm; 900–1,500 g
Where to look: reed beds, except in cold weather. **Nest:** on ground among reeds.
Eggs: 5–6, olive-brown.
Food: almost exclusively fish. **Voice:** male has deep, resonant boom, repeated 3–4 times in 5–6 seconds.

Although a member of the heron family, when seen in flight the brown plumage with rounded wings can give the impression of a giant woodcock or owl.

Drainage, and persecution in the 19th century, has resulted in a very restricted British bittern population, now probably numbering less than 30 nesting pairs each year, the majority confined to only two or three sites. East Anglia is still the stronghold of the species, but some of the best views of bitterns are to be obtained from the hides of the RSPB reserve at Leighton Moss, Lancashire.

In most winters the population is swollen by immigrants from Europe, forced out by freezing conditions. At that time of the year, bitterns may appear at almost any site in eastern England. The chance of seeing the brown mottled bird, however, is slight, for this is a secretive species. It has the ability to 'freeze' in an upright posture, when the striped markings on the neck make it very difficult to see against a background of dead reed.

The presence of bitterns in spring is best established by hearing the distinctive territorial 'booming' call of the male. This strange noise, although not loud, is far-carrying and may be heard up to three miles away, most frequently at dusk in April or May.

The skulking and secretive nature of the bittern, the camouflage of the mottled and barred golden-brown plumage, together with the motionless stance, can make it extremely difficult to observe.

Mute Swan

Cygnus olor
145–160 cm; 8–13 kg
Where to look: shallow lakes, slow rivers, marshes, wet meadows, sheltered coasts. **Nest:** beside water, huge heap of vegetation with shallow depression. **Eggs:** 5–8, huge, chalky, greenish, April–June. **Food:** aquatic vegetation obtained by dipping head and neck or up-ending; grasses taken when grazing on meadows or salt marsh; some snails, worms. **Voice:** hoarse, strangled trumpeting, snorting and hissing calls; wings noisy in flight.

Downy chicks will often ride on female's back until 10 days old, sometimes later; less so on male.

Adult pulls up food and passes it to chick on one side, using same action as in nest-building; foot movements attract chicks and stir up food particles for them.

In flight the wings of a mute swan make a unique humming, throbbing sound that replaces the contact calls of other species.

Downy chicks call noisily, with head upstretched, if they are lost, cold or hungry. They clamber onto the hen's back with no active help from her.

Up-ending allows the mute swan to exploit deeper water than geese or dabbling ducks, using its longer neck to full advantage.

Juveniles are uneven, dirty grey-brown at first, growing more white feathers during their first winter, when the bill brightens.

Big, white swans are symbols of grace, elegance and serenity, but also strength and power. Adult humans enjoy their beauty and shapeliness; children prefer to ask if it is really true that a swan can break a leg with one swipe of its wing! Probably not, but they are certainly big and impressive, and a very characteristic part of the British scene. Numbers have declined in central England where they seem most obviously at home. Associated with an increase and spread in western Europe, mute swans in Britain became much more numerous early in the 20th century and by 1955/56 there were 3,500–4,000 breeding pairs and another 11,000 non-breeding birds. Hard winters, increased disturbance by boats and the effects of lead poisoning from lost fishing weights combined to cause a decline, though it has been most marked in central England and balanced by increases in the north. By 1983 there were 3,150 pairs and 12,600 non-breeders, but some of the most famous herds, on the Thames and at Stratford-upon-Avon, have declined almost to the point of disappearance. Swans used to be kept for food, but their need for water and the problems of feeding, then catching, such big birds eventually caused a change-over to domestic geese.

Aggressive males will chase off intruders, flying and then swimming quickly towards them.

This spectacular behaviour is called 'busking', with arched wings, breast thrust forwards, head curved back and neck feathers fluffed out; serious fights sometimes develop.

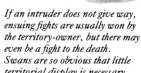

If an intruder does not give way, ensuing fights are usually won by the territory-owner, but there may even be a fight to the death. Swans are so obvious that little territorial display is necessary.

Bewick's Swan

Cygnus columbianus
115–125 cm; 4–8 kg
Where to look: flooded meadows, salt marshes, shallow lakes and reservoirs. **Food:** roots, shoots, aquatic plants, grain and waste potatoes. **Voice:** varied soft or loud and far-carrying, musical, bugling calls.

In flight Bewick's call loudly, but their wings simply 'swish', without the hum of the mute's.

Adults have rounded yellow side patches on otherwise black bill; young birds are dingy grey with pink and black on the bill.

The typically thick, goose-like neck can be raised erect, and then appears long and thin.

Bewick's swans used to be common in west Scotland and rare in England, but since the 1930s the opposite has been the case. They breed in remote tundra at the far northern edge of Siberia, from which only a few thousand come to Europe each winter. In England the main flocks are found on the Ouse Washes and at Slimbridge, where artificial feeding brings them close to observation hides; normally they are very shy. Their appearance on these Wildfowl Trust reserves is predictable, but the big flocks remain spectacularly beautiful. Elsewhere it is an exciting event to discover a newly arrived party of these wild and wonderful swans on a frosty November day. They are noticeably smaller than other swans when seen side by side, but the shorter, straighter neck, black and yellow bill and shorter, less pointed and, when swimming, less elevated tail are the best distinctions from the familiar mute swan. Whooper swans are much more like them, but with a longer, flatter head profile and more yellow on the bill.

Whooper Swan

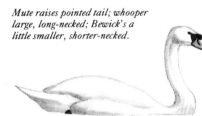

Mute raises pointed tail; whooper large, long-necked; Bewick's a little smaller, shorter-necked.

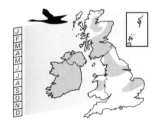

Cygnus cygnus
145–160 cm; 8–14 kg
Where to look: wet meadows and stubble fields by rivers and estuaries, upland pools, large lochs. **Food:** leaves, stems and roots of aquatic plants, waste grain and potatoes. More often on dry land in recent years. **Voice:** loud, trumpet-like or bugling call, stronger than Bewick's.

Plumages are like Bewick's, but longer bill and flatter forehead often obvious; notice that the yellow extends forward in a point on the side of the bill.

All swans are prone to reddish staining from oxides in water, but whoopers perhaps show it most often. They, and Bewick's, walk more freely than the waddling mute and are slightly quicker to take to the air.

Small, quiet lochs in the Scottish hills, grassy fields beside the mouth of a river, or wild, remote farmland with meadows and stubble not far from a lake make the ideal winter home for whooper swans. In some places, especially at the Wildfowl Trust reserve on the Ouse Washes, all three swans mix together in winter, but it is generally true to say that whoopers prefer the north and west of Britain to the softer south. Most of Britain's winter whoopers are from Iceland, where there are 5,000–7,000 birds, though only a small proportion nest in any one year. Like other swans and geese, the numbers here in any winter depend very largely on the breeding success of the previous season. As young birds are obvious and family parties stay together all winter, the productivity of the whooper swan is easily studied. The weather in Iceland also plays a part in how many come to Britain and Ireland, as more will stay there in a mild winter, but a spell of bad weather even in mid-winter can trigger off a new movement south and flocks can cross to and from Iceland at almost any time from September to April. They can migrate at enormous heights, presumably in very cold air indeed.

Wild Geese

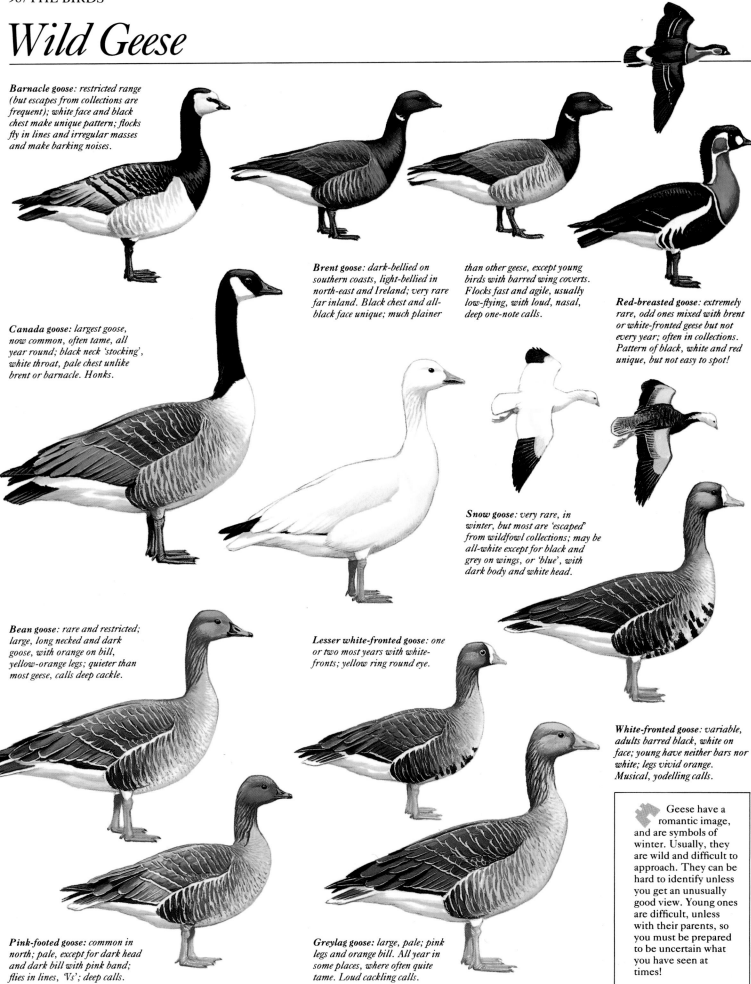

Barnacle goose: restricted range (but escapes from collections are frequent); white face and black chest make unique pattern; flocks fly in lines and irregular masses and make barking noises.

Brent goose: dark-bellied on southern coasts, light-bellied in north-east and Ireland; very rare far inland. Black chest and all-black face unique; much plainer than other geese, except young birds with barred wing coverts. Flocks fast and agile, usually low-flying, with loud, nasal, deep one-note calls.

Red-breasted goose: extremely rare, odd ones mixed with brent or white-fronted geese but not every year; often in collections. Pattern of black, white and red unique, but not easy to spot!

Canada goose: largest goose, now common, often tame, all year round; black neck 'stocking', white throat, pale chest unlike brent or barnacle. Honks.

Snow goose: very rare, in winter, but most are 'escaped' from wildfowl collections; may be all-white except for black and grey on wings, or 'blue', with dark body and white head.

Bean goose: rare and restricted; large, long necked and dark goose, with orange on bill, yellow-orange legs; quieter than most geese, calls deep cackle.

Lesser white-fronted goose: one or two most years with white-fronts; yellow ring round eye.

White-fronted goose: variable, adults barred black, white on face; young have neither bars nor white; legs vivid orange. Musical, yodelling calls.

Pink-footed goose: common in north; pale, except for dark head and dark bill with pink band; flies in lines, 'Vs'; deep calls.

Greylag goose: large, pale; pink legs and orange bill. All year in some places, where often quite tame. Loud cackling calls.

Geese have a romantic image, and are symbols of winter. Usually, they are wild and difficult to approach. They can be hard to identify unless you get an unusually good view. Young ones are difficult, unless with their parents, so you must be prepared to be uncertain what you have seen at times!

Barnacle Goose

Branta leucopsis
60–70 cm; 1.5–2 kg
Where to look: meadows and stubble beside salt marshes and on islands. **Food:** leaves, stems, seeds and roots of grass and other vegetation. **Voice:** short, sharp bark, often repeated in yapping chorus from flocks.

With its beautiful barring, glossy black chest and immaculate appearance, always spick and span and impossibly perfect, the barnacle is perhaps the most lovely of all geese. The neat little beak and, for a goose, rather long legs, add a distinctive touch at close range. Barnacles that breed in Greenland spend the winter in west Scotland, especially on the island of Islay, and in Ireland. There will usually be over 20,000 of them. Another group breeds in Spitsbergen and these spend the winter only on the Solway Firth; these have increased to over 10,000 birds. A third group breeds in the northern USSR and spends the winter in the Netherlands, but some reach England each winter, especially Norfolk and Kent. On Islay they have been the cause of great controversy, because they prefer to eat the rich, green grass of meadows improved for sheep rearing, to the detriment of the sheep. An RSPB reserve is managed in order to attract the geese away from other farms on the island in an attempt to reduce the conflict. The success of the scheme remains to be evaluated.

The black chest and white belly make an obvious contrast; from above, the rump is eyecatching.

Grazing flocks look greyest of all geese in dull light, sharp contrasts in sunshine.

Young bird duller than adult with mottled face, greyer chest; adults glossy and splendid.

Brent Goose

Branta bernicla
55–60 cm; 1.2–1.5 kg
Where to look: muddy estuaries and adjacent salt marshes and pastures; sandy bays. **Food:** grazes and up-ends to feed on eel-grass, green algae, growing cereals and marsh plants. **Voice:** deep, rolling bark.

On a dark, misty winter's day in south-east England, only the comfortable sounds of the brents' deep, nasal, *rronk-rronk* calls, echoing around the marsh, may give them away. The flock may be hidden in the gloom, or tucked away in a muddy creek or out of sight behind the sea-wall, but these little geese are as much a part of the wilderness of Britain's low-lying coasts as the life-giving mud and marsh on which they live. They feed and roost in tight-packed groups, even when they fly to the fields, an increasing habit of recent years, so that counting them is a hard job. Dark-bellied birds come here each winter from the northern tundra of the USSR, to feed in the southern estuaries; pale-bellied birds from Greenland visit Ireland and others from Spitsbergen come to Lindisfarne. Both races are rare in world terms. The pale-bellied birds number some 20,000 in Ireland and 3,000 in Northumberland. When eel-grass was reduced by disease in the 1930s, numbers of dark-bellied brents fell by at least 75 per cent. The population of this race is enormously variable depending on breeding success, but recently has reached over 80,000 with careful protection, in turn renewing calls for their control.

Though only as long as mallard, brents look larger, heavier in flight, with white rump obvious. Flocks usually shapeless masses or lines, low and fast-flying.

Dark birds browner beneath, black chest less contrasted than on pale race; sometimes hard to tell.

Black neck, chest, face, marked only on sides of neck, unique; juvenile has no neck patches at first, and barred wing coverts.

Dark chest contrasts less than on barnacle, especially on dark-bellied birds; flight quite agile.

Canada Goose

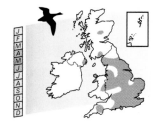

Branta canadensis
90–100 cm; 4–5 kg
Where to look: ornamental lakes, flooded gravel pits, reservoirs, and nearby meadows. **Nest:** on ground near water, often below tree or bush; a pile of leaves, grass, reeds. **Eggs:** 5–6, cream or white, March–April. **Food:** roots, stems, leaves and fruits of water and waterside plants; mostly grazes, also up-ends in water. **Voice:** loud, resonant honking calls, usually obviously two notes – *gor-rronk*, etc. Also various loud, quicker and shorter honking and trumpeting notes in display or alarm.

Brown-barred back, creamy chest (often striking at a distance) and black neck and head, with white 'chinstrap', make it easy to identify this large goose.

In North America the Canada goose is a highly-migratory species with many distinct races and traditional migration routes and wintering grounds. It is odd that such a bird was so successfully introduced into Europe (to Britain in the 17th century) and remained content to live all year round on the lakes where its ornamental qualities were required. Nevertheless, the lakes and pools of Britain's stately homes, surrounded by ample, flat, grassy expanses for easy grazing, proved ideal and the adaptable birds soon became established and familiar. So long as food is readily available, Canada geese seem content to settle anywhere, even on a city-centre lake; if food is insufficient to support them, they simply fly elsewhere. By the late 1960s there were over 10,000 birds in Britain and their increase continues. In favoured sites in central England it is possible to find flocks of several hundred birds in late summer and autumn, which undoubtedly look spectacular and allow everyone to enjoy the sight and sound of 'wild geese', but they somehow lack the romantic associations and appeal of their truly wild relatives, which would not be seen dead in a town! Consequently, they are rather neglected, even despised, by many birdwatchers.

Only the female incubates eggs; male stands on guard.

Females on nest lower head and neck and face intruders, making the white throat patch as inconspicuous as possible.

Canada geese in Britain are not migratory as they are in America. Some, however, have developed regular movements to sheltered estuaries to moult in late summer.

Pairs – formed at about two years old – remain together for life; young tended by both parents but driven away next spring.

Both parents tend the young, which are able to feed themselves.

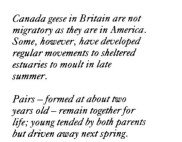

As on other geese, the 'stern' is strikingly white – clearly an obvious mark for other birds to follow, especially in flight.

Chicks use frequent contact calls and perform greeting displays after accidental separation.

Chicks leave nest on hatching and are vulnerable to predators; they fly after seven weeks.

Winter flocks are well organised, with much aggression; large families dominate small ones, which dominate pairs, with single birds at the bottom of the 'peck order' in every respect.

Young birds (right) are duller than adults at first but soon become indistinguishable except by their lighter build. Moulting adults are flightless for a time.

There are several smaller races of Canada goose; occasionally they escape from collections and very rarely cross from North America.

White-fronted Goose

Anser albifrons
65–78 cm; 1.5–2.5 kg
Where to look: meadows in broad river valleys, beside estuaries. Very restricted, in reduced numbers, mostly in Gloucestershire, Kent, Hampshire. Greenland race in wilder places, very rare in Wales, more widespread Ireland, Scotland. **Food:** grass, roots. **Voice:** most musical of geese, with ringing, laughing, yodelling quality to flock calls; usually high-pitched *lyo-lyock*, *klik-klek*, etc. Hissing and yapping calls on ground and 'creaking' wings on taking flight.

To many people in the south of England this was once the most familiar of the wild 'grey geese', as greylags and pink-feet are more northerly in their distribution. Nowadays, however, flocks of introduced greylags are much commoner, while, coincidentally, wild white-fronts have declined dramatically. Only in the North Kent Marshes, the Avon Valley of Hampshire, the Tywi Valley of South Wales and on the Severn Estuary around Slimbridge, are there now regular flocks of birds from the Siberian tundra, and all have declined in numbers. In the north and in Ireland, darker birds from Greenland appear, around 20,000 all told in an average year. White-fronts are fascinating to watch, like all geese, and the hides at Slimbridge in mid-winter offer the best views. They are noisy, busy and quarrelsome, quick to take alarm and difficult to approach except behind the Slimbridge screens. In flight, white-fronts *en masse* are unparalleled, as they cross the sky in huge 'Vs', lines and chevrons; in full voice they create a yapping, squeaky, babbling chorus that can be quite deafening from a really big flock – in the Netherlands it is often possible to see 10,000–15,000 together. The calls of geese are difficult for a beginner to identify, though each species has its characteristic tone and pattern. The calls of white-fronts have a distinctive 'catch' to them.

In flight shows white rump and some grey on forewing above. More agile in flight than greylag, especially landing and taking off.

Usually wary and difficult to approach, but gets used to hides, as at Slimbridge.

Adult of USSR race has pink bill, variable barring; can look strongly contrasted or plainer.

Immature birds best recognised by plain, brownish colour, orange legs, dull, pinkish bill, and parents!

Those that winter in southern England and South Wales come from Siberian tundra; as more stay all winter in Netherlands, so fewer are seen in Britain.

Greenland birds are darker and have orange bills; they prefer rushy places, often near field edges, and are timid and agile.

Lesser white-front is extremely rare; a small, dark goose with neat, round head, tiny pink bill; yellow ring round eye; only adult has the large, white forehead.

Lesser white-front

Greenland race

Russian race

Bean Goose

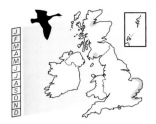

Anser fabalis
65–80 cm; 2–4 kg
Where to look: pastures and arable land. **Food:** in Britain grazes mainly on grassy fields, but on the Continent also in stubble. **Voice:** generally quieter than other grey geese, resembles deep pink-footed, without the higher-pitched notes.

Only in south-west Scotland, where a very few birds appear each winter, and in Norfolk, where a reduced but recently recovering flock can be found, are bean geese regularly seen in Britain. Most winters one or two will be found mixed with Russian white-fronts, but otherwise only irregular parties appear from time to time. At the traditional wintering places they are creatures of habit, seeking out the same preferred fields year after year. Britain's wintering birds breed in the birch scrub and coniferous forest south of the north European tundras. Beans are big geese, though not so heavy as greylags, and their lengthy proportions – especially the long neck – give them a special elegance. Adults are particularly cleanly barred above, but have none of the blue-grey cast so often evident on pink-feet, nor do they show the same fawn-buff colour on the breast. Choosing open spaces in winter, with a wide view, bean geese are shy and unapproachable birds, always exciting to see.

Dark upperwing, long, rather slender neck and deep calls are helpful features in flight.

Bean has longest neck and head profile of grey geese, unlike round-headed, short-billed pink-foot; head and neck look dark.

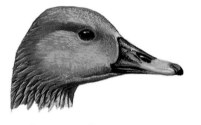

Bean

Pink-foot

Greylag

Beans look dark, only bright sun adding warmth to their plumage; among white-fronts pick them out by bill colour and pale barring.

Bean has longish, orange and black bill; pink-foot has short bill with pink band; greylag has paler head, massive orange bill with paler tip, no black.

Pink-footed Goose

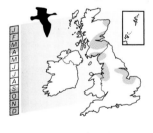

Anser brachyrhynchus
60–75 cm; 1.8–3.3 kg
Where to look: estuaries, salt marshes, lakes, nearby arable and pasture land. **Food:** grass, spilt barley and other grain, waste potatoes. **Voice:** musical, deep di- or tri-syllabic honking; also high-pitched, sharp *wink-wink*.

Forewing shows blue-grey, more than white-front but darker than greylag. Flight action fast, aerobatic; head and neck small.

White-front (left) and pink-foot.

In central and southern Scotland, where it mixes with greylags, and in northern England, especially on the Lancashire mosses, this is the most abundant winter goose. In late 1985 the number wintering in Britain reached a new record of 128,000. They come from Iceland and east Greenland and, like other northern geese, are very dependent on good weather during the short summer at such high latitudes. In a bad season, they may rear virtually no young at all and fewer are seen in Britain as a result. At places such as the north shore of the Solway Firth it is one of the great birdwatching experiences to stand between the inland feeding grounds and the estuarine roost at dusk, when stream after stream of noisy geese fly overhead. After many years with reduced numbers, the traditional Norfolk flocks have recently recovered, and it is now often possible to see several thousand there, too – much to the delight of more southern birdwatchers. The reason for the increase – in 1950 there were only 30,000 – seems to be largely to do with improved food supplies and better refuges in Britain rather than changes in the breeding grounds, which are threatened with development.

Barred, greyish back, pale buff forebody and very dark head and neck; rounded head, short, dark bill, legs pale to deep pink.

This is perhaps the prettiest, most attractive grey goose. It may have white around the bill.

Greylag Goose

Greylag geese can now be found in many parts of England due to recent introductions on to ornamental lakes and flooded gravel pits near arable land.

Grey geese have leg and bill colours in different combinations, their own wing patterns in flight, and their own distinctive shapes and proportions, but most are shy and hard to see closely – they are usually difficult!

Wild breeding pairs frequent remote lochs; 'feral' birds, introduced but now living wild, may be much tamer and breed on quite small, even well-wooded, pits in unlikely places.

Chicks quickly follow their parents and soon learn the rank of the family within the flock.

Anser anser
75–90 cm; 3–4 kg
Where to look: open arable land, marshes and lakes. Feral birds in more enclosed spaces. **Nest:** on ground in sheltered hollow or in reeds. **Eggs:** 4–6, creamy-white, April–May. **Food:** grass, spilt potatoes and grain; moving to growing cereals in late spring. **Voice:** clattering clamour in flight, less bugling or trumpeting than other geese, more rattling in effect.

Like all geese, greylags have a strict social order and have many calls and displays used to keep individual distance, to defend territories and to greet mates.

Usually only the female broods small chicks, while the male keeps guard close by.

A flying greylag shows a very pale area on the forewing both above and below, more obvious than on any other grey goose; it is heavier, slower and larger-headed than pink-foot.

Greylags are much the heaviest of the wild geese, but still show remarkable aerobatic ability that should not be underestimated.

Males often 'attack' a real or imagined intruder, then return to their mate with neck outstretched and calling loud, staccato notes.

Both then lower their necks and cackle, but they avoid a 'beak to beak' confrontation if they can.

This is the 'triumph ceremony' seen at any time of the year in pairs or courting couples.

The large, bright orange bill, generally pale appearance and loud, rather rattling calls (without the musical quality of many other geese) help to identify the greylag. Visiting birds in winter have pink legs; but some of the wild breeding stock, and some feral birds, have orange legs, though it must be admitted that orange and pink may be hard to distinguish at a distance! Old birds have a few spots of black on the belly and chest, but never so much as a white-front. All geese vary greatly in appearance according to the light. Greylags are essentially pale birds, but strong sun can create sharply contrasting highlights and shadows, and swimming birds can often look misleadingly dark-headed as their barred backs catch the light. Britain's winter-visiting greylags – in record years there may be up to about 100,000 of them – come from Iceland in October, mainly to Scotland, where they need a safe, quiet roost on water and undisturbed feeding places. The greylag is not generally long-lived, studies showing that average adult life expectancy is under four years. Pairs form for life and will be together all year round, and families remain together during the winter within the spectacular flocks. To us, their voices sound similar, but they vary enough for geese to recognise each other's.

Much more active than a goose in the farmyard, but the ancestor of domestic stock, with a similar range of noisy calls. Flocks spend most time feeding quietly.

Juveniles are duller and more irregularly barred above.

Shelduck

Tadorna tadorna
60–70 cm; 1–1.8 kg
Where to look: sandy and muddy shores, dunes, flooded gravel pits, reservoirs, marshes. **Nest:** in burrow, hole in tree, haystack. **Eggs:** 8–10, white, April to June. **Food:** molluscs, insects, crustaceans dug or sieved from wet mud or from water. **Voice:** male whistles; deep, quick quacks from female.

Almost any hollow will serve as a nest site, even in an old tree.

The nest site is chosen by female, with male in attendance. The eggs are incubated only by the hen, for 29–31 days. The chicks leave soon after hatching and may face a long walk to water.

They leave the nesting territory for a special feeding territory.

For 15–20 days the family stays in the feeding territory, then the chicks join with others in a crèche up to 100 strong. The crèche is often looked after by adults that have failed to breed. The young fly after seven weeks.

Young are independent as soon as they can fly; females breed when two years old, but males may not do so until they are four or five. Few chicks reach maturity.

Survival of chicks is best in middle-sized families of six–ten; with fewer or more, a greater percentage die before fledging.

Parents attack strange young; if they happen to be of the same size, they then attack their own!

Most pairs persist from year to year, and move to territorial feeding places on the shore by late March. At the same time they look for nest sites, often miles away, visiting them each morning. Nests may be close together, with no territories around them. When the young hatch, the family goes to a new, nursery area, with a 'mobile territory' centred around the chicks.

Males in spring are glorious, with brilliantly red bill topped by a large knob; females have no basal knob and show white facial marks, less black below.

Large size and goose-like shape unlike other ducks; unmistakable.

An attacking bird chases others from its territory with head held low; the intruder runs off with its head raised and plumage sleek.

If the intruder does not run away, there may be a vicious fight, with beating wings and jabbing of partially-open beaks.

Flying birds show such a striking pattern that they are hard to miss.

After breeding, the adults moult, starting in late June; between July and October they moult flight feathers and cannot fly for 25–30 days.

Most fly to German Waddenzee to moult, though some moult in Bridgwater Bay; non-breeders moult first, failed breeders next, successful birds last.

'Moult migration' is made by flocks in a single flight.

Young birds dive, but adults are content to upend in the shallows.

When asleep on mud flats, they may be overlooked among gulls; drake shovelers have white breasts but darker underparts, the red extending to the flanks.

Females lead the families of young chicks, with the males in close attendance, ready to repel other shelducks and predators.

The broad, short bill is ideally suited to sieving through wet ooze and dealing with molluscs.

Shelducks are quite frequent inland on migration, and recently have begun to breed inland, especially by flooded pits.

Courtship and pursuit flights are frequent, especially in spring; unpaired males may chase females, which are defended by their mates; unpaired females may be chased by up to eight drakes, with much calling. As with other wildfowl, courtship postures are rigidly defined.

Downy chicks start to cheep as they hatch; later they have high-pitched piping noises, with the same rhythm as the female's quack.

Once fledged, the young shelduck looks pale and gawky, with little of the elegance of its parents; it has much white on the face and no chestnut band around the chest, but its proportions, pink-grey bill, grey legs and white underparts help to identify it.

Shelducks are startlingly white, even on the dullest day, exaggerating their size and making them stand out from all the duller birds around. On a sunny day in summer, the brightness of the bill is almost unreal, and the sharp, clean lines of the plumage are equally breathtaking. Numbers have increased this century and by the early 1970s there were thought to be 12,000 pairs nesting in Britain and Ireland. Because most of the shelducks of north-west Europe go to the same place to moult, this figure is small compared with the great gatherings in the Waddenzee. At least 100,000 gather there, safe for the dangerous period when they shed all their flight feathers at once – a characteristic of all ducks and geese – and are unable to fly. Their distribution abroad is quite wide, though largely limited in Europe to the coasts of France, and those countries bordering the North Sea and the Baltic, but shelducks nest in scattered places in the Mediterranean and then eastwards beyond the Caspian into central Asia. This sporadic distribution shows a liking for rather warm climates and a need for productive shallow-water habitats. In the past the range was probably more complete and the isolated remnants have survived through their adaptability to changing conditions. It certainly seems odd to find the same species on a cold Scottish mud flat and on a hot, reed-fringed Mediterranean marsh!

Exotic and Domestic Ducks

Ducks have had a close association with man for many centuries. Several species have been domesticated, hybrids are not unusual and exotic species are kept as ornamental waterfowl on many lakes. All cause identification problems for the birdwatcher.

Muscovy: large species from South America. Common. Black with varying amounts of white.

White mallard: an albino variety, common at farms and on town ponds.

Cayuga mallard: domesticated form now common in wild populations. Black body with varying amounts of white on breast of male.

Khaki campbell: commonest form of domesticated mallard. Uniform pale brown with deep body shape.

Hybrid mallard × pintail: one of the most frequent hybrids. Males show features of both.

Ruddy shelduck: Asiatic species, perhaps rare visitor to Britain, but escapes from collections.

Wood duck: North American species very similar to mandarin (p.114). Wild population not yet fully established in Surrey.

Bahama pintail: South American species breeding readily in captivity. Escaped birds can include the albino form.

Red-billed whistling duck: from South America, the commonest captive 'tree duck'. Stands very upright on long, pink legs.

Comparing Ducks

With over 120 species in the world, ducks come in a range of shapes, sizes and colours. In general, males are more colourful than the brown females, which are dull so that they can remain hidden while incubating eggs. There are two basic types of duck, the surface feeding, or dabblers, and the diving species.

Teal: *the smallest duck, only garganey (p.110) similar size. Leaps straight from water to fly.*

Wigeon: *short-necked, rather dumpy species with tiny bill. Flocks 'graze' when feeding.*

Mallard: *the largest, commonest and most familiar of the surface feeding species. The 'basic' duck.*

Gadwall: *often an overlooked species, commonest in eastern England. Female mallard-like, but greyer, with white in wing.*

Shoveler: *the squat, low-in-water appearance, with short neck and huge bill, makes this the most distinctively shaped duck.*

Pintail: *a long-necked, slender duck, the pointed tail of both sexes most obvious in flight.*

Pochard: *fresh water diving duck, often in flocks with tufted. Has hump-backed, tail-less shape.*

Tufted duck: *the commonest of the diving ducks. Striking male, dull all-brown female.*

Goldeneye: *rather small, but large-headed duck, found on both fresh and salt water. Both sexes have white panels in wings.*

Goosander: *the largest of the 'sawbills'. A long, low body with largish head and long, thin bill present very distinctive shape. Female resembles merganser (p.121).*

Wigeon

Short-necked appearance in flight. Male has white forewing. Underwing and belly very pale.

Anas penelope
45–51 cm; 600–900 g
Where to look: shallow, fresh water when nesting, salt marsh or pasture in winter.
Nest: on ground in cover.
Eggs: 6–12, pale buff. **Food:** vegetable, mainly algae and eel-grass. **Voice:** whistling *whee-OO*; grating purr.

The British breeding population of wigeon rarely exceeds 500 pairs, but in the winter months birds from Iceland, northern Europe and the USSR move south, and as many as 200,000 are present during the January peak. The main wintering sites are coastal, apart from the Ouse Washes, where the creation of reserves to prevent disturbance, and the establishment of a water management regime on grazing meadows, has resulted in a dramatic increase to over 25,000 birds at a peak. The most evocative sound of a salt marsh is the whistle of a male wigeon. Feeding flocks move forward in dense groups; good sunlight reveals their beautiful colours.

Small size and steep forehead. White and black undertail of male. Grey legs and small bill.

A highly gregarious duck, between mallard and teal in size, with a short neck and tiny bill used for cropping vegetation. In flight, often with complex aerial manoeuvres, the distinctive whistle and prominent white patch on the upperwing of the male, plus the short pointed tail, are all distinguishing features. The overall impression is of a small, light duck with a dark head.

Eclipse males resemble females, but retain white forewing.

In close flocks, individuals often show threat display.

Teal

Small size with rapid wing-beats and twisting flight. Whitish underparts hard to see.

Anas crecca
34–38 cm; 240–360 g
Where to look: shallow waters. **Nest:** on ground in cover. **Eggs:** 8–11, off-white. **Food:** seeds, invertebrates. **Voice:** distinctive high-pitched, chirping *krick*.

Creamy and black undertail very obvious during take off, which is vertical. White underwings.

Very active when feeding, but resting birds can remain motionless for long periods. Preening birds show the striking green and black speculum with white edging, a useful pointer.

In a group or 'spring', teal leap vertically from the water and then dash about the sky over a pool, so active that, although in shape they resemble small wigeon, they will often give the impression of a party of dark waders. By contrast, when walking they are, if anything, rather clumsy and less agile than the larger mallard. The smallest of the wintering ducks, only a third the weight of a mallard, the 100,000 or so that are present in December are to be found at both inland and coastal sites, with over 20,000 on the Mersey Estuary alone. The favoured areas are where shallow water only a few centimetres deep covers soft mud into which the birds can easily thrust their bills, for they rarely feed by up-ending as do the larger species. In areas where they are not disturbed, they become extremely tame and are often found feeding very close to observation hides. Normally, however, they tend to be rather wary and difficult to see, looking very dark and dull except for the horizontal white bar across the males.

Mallard

Anas platyrhynchos
50–65 cm; 950–1,300 g
Where to look: almost
anywhere with water. **Nest:**
usually on the ground, can be
high in tree. **Eggs:** 9–13,
bluish-green. **Food:** variable;
opportunistic feeder. **Voice:**
female gives familiar quack,
male a weak nasal note.

*In flight, female shows brown
belly. Both sexes have blue or
purple-blue speculum on wing.*

*Feeding birds frequently up-end
to reach submerged vegetation,
showing bright orange legs.*

*The brown plumage of the female
provides camouflage so that she
remains hidden among vegetation
while incubating eggs.*

The commonest, most widespread of all ducks, the
mallard needs no introduction, being encountered
everywhere from the town park to the village pond,
from the reservoir or gravel pit to the wildest sea loch or
estuary salt marsh. Except for her yellowish bill and
orange legs, the female is a rather undistinguished
brown colour. This contrasts sharply with the male,
with his striking bottle-green head and curled feathers
above the tail. There are few sounds more familiar than
the *quack* of a female mallard; the male has only a weak
rasping *raehb*.

The press seems regularly to feature a female mallard
leading her brood across a major road, usually under the
protective eye of a policeman. Highly adaptable,
mallards often nest well away from water, high in a tree
or on a building, and newly hatched young face a
perilous journey. The British breeding population is
difficult to estimate, but it could exceed 150,000 pairs,
which together with an arrival of European birds,
provides a winter count in excess of 700,000.

Mallard drakes tend to defend territories around a
small headland or other feature.

*Active and capable of swimming
from hatching, ducklings are
quickly escorted to water.*

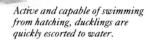

*Although pairs form in late
autumn, males take no part in
the incubation of eggs or rearing
of young. Parties of displaying
males gather in the early spring,
and are markedly promiscuous.*

The commonest duck, probably needing little in
the way of identification details, for this is the
'basic' duck. However, because of domestication and the
frequency of hybrids, many strange-looking individuals
can be encountered even in the most unexpected
localities (p.106). Males have dark green head, white
neck ring, purple-brown breast and grey back. Females
are brown, with blue speculum, and 'quack'.

*In July and August the eclipse
plumage males resemble females,
but appear darker and more
uniform; bill remains yellow.*

*Out of water the birds walk easily,
their bodies parallel with the
ground. Both sexes show orange legs.*

Gadwall

Anas strepera
46–56 cm; 600–900 g
Where to look: inland lakes and marshes, usually well vegetated. **Nest:** on ground beside water. **Eggs:** 8–12, pale pink. **Food:** seeds, plants and insects. **Voice:** a quiet quack from female, a nasal *mair* from male.

In flight, gadwalls show white underwing and belly and clearly visible white speculum together with yellow legs and feet.

Feeding gadwalls can form close association with diving coots.

Easily distinguished from female mallard when speculum visible.

The very first gadwalls to nest in Britain were a pair trapped in Norfolk in the mid-1800s which were released after wing-clipping. From this pair the population increased and spread northwards, although the large numbers at Loch Leven, Scotland and Tresco, Isles of Scilly, are of less certain origin. The numbers are continuing to increase and the present breeding population probably exceeds 500 pairs, with a wintering peak of some 5,000 birds, mainly from mainland Europe, still very much concentrated in East Anglia. Further introductions in the 1960s and 1970s have established groups in Gloucestershire and Lancashire.

Rather drab-looking birds, gadwalls can be overlooked among other ducks, where they may be dismissed as females, for the male lacks the bright plumage of other dabbling species. The best distinguishing features are overall greyness, black undertail of male and the white speculum of both sexes. Female gadwalls have obvious orange sides to the bill and plainer heads than mallards.

The male appears very grey with contrasting black tail, steep forehead and fine black bill.

Garganey

Anas querquedula
37–41 cm; 320–500 g
Where to look: shallow flood water. **Nest:** on ground in thick tussock. **Eggs:** 8–9, light brown. **Food:** insects and aquatic vegetation. **Voice:** main call is a mechanical-sounding rattle by male; females quack quietly.

In eclipse the males resemble the females, although brighter on wing.

Distinctive flight characteristic is blue-grey upper forewing; dark leading edge to pale underwing; dull speculum edged white.

Usually in pairs in spring, with the male's distinctive head pattern and pinkish plumage aiding identity. Female shows face-markings with pale spot near bill; no bright green on wing (see teal).

Unique among British ducks, the garganey is a summer visitor and hence its alternative name of 'summer teal', for in size it is closest to the more numerous teal. Although a very common duck in world terms, the garganey is scarce and decreasing as a British species, with less than 50 pairs present in most years and all confined to the south and east. The continual loss of shallow floods and water meadows suggests the population is likely to decrease further.

One of the earliest of the summer migrants to arrive in spring, appearing on the south coast in late March, the male is immediately identifiable by the prominent curved white stripe from above the eye to the back of the lower neck. The overall impression is of a pinkish-brown and pale grey duck with fine mottling. The female resembles a rather pale teal, but shows very strong facial markings with a pale spot at the base of the bill and very pale throat. In flight, the white bar across the mid-wing is less obvious than a teal's, but the rear edge is more so, giving two parallel lines as on a mallard.

Pintail

Anas acuta
51–66 cm; 750–1,000 g
Where to look: open areas
with shallow water. **Nest:**
rare, usually in open. **Eggs:**
7–9, yellowish. **Food:** variety
of plant and animal matter.
Voice: quiet whistle from
male, short quacks from
female; silent in flight.

*White neck stripe and breast of
male is distinctive.*

*In flight looks long and thin with
pointed tail. Underside pale,
upperwing dark with pale line on
trailing edge.*

Subtlety of colour and an elegant form make the
pintail one of the most attractive ducks. The gleaming,
distinctively coloured, slightly off-white breast of the
male is visible from a considerable distance when no
other details may be obvious. In flight the shape is
unmistakable; even the female shows a long pointed tail
and long slender neck.

Less than 50 pairs breed in Britain, almost all
confined to Kent and the fenlands of East Anglia, but, in
winter, birds from Iceland, Scandinavia and Russia
concentrate on some of the west coast estuaries, with
counts of over 15,000 birds on the Mersey. Only here
and on the Dee Estuary do counts regularly exceed
5,000. On these coastal sites they feed on the tiny snail
called *Hydrobia*, but increasingly the species has
developed night flighting away from the more traditional coastal sites to exploit the stubble and potato
fields of inland farms. They are much quieter birds than
mallards and most people see them far less often, and
usually in very small groups.

*When up-ending to feed –
more common in females
than males – the tail is
angled down.*

*Female looks pale, greyish-brown
with blue bill and pointed tail.*

*In eclipse, the male resembles
female, but somewhat darker.
Differs from female mallard in
slimmer build, longer neck and
more speckled appearance.*

Display: tails raised upright.

Shoveler

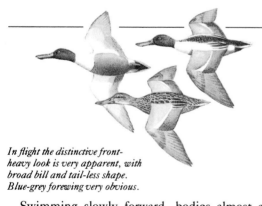

*In flight the distinctive front-
heavy look is very apparent, with
broad bill and tail-less shape.
Blue-grey forewing very obvious.*

*May feed in close groups, leaning
forward with bill submerged.*

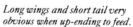

*Long wings and short tail very
obvious when up-ending to feed.*

Anas clypeata
44–52 cm; 400–850 g
Where to look: shallow
water. **Nest:** on ground.
Eggs: 9–11, buff. **Voice:**
quiet *tuc* by male, female
quacks.

Swimming slowly forward, bodies almost awash,
shovelers filter water through their big, broad bills,
pushing it out through the sides and trapping food
particles with the special serrations that line the edges.
Feeding in this manner will often involve small groups
which appear to work in unison. To be successful this
technique requires a rich food source – seeds and
invertebrates – suspended in shallow water.

The male shoveler is distinctive both in shape and
colour, while the brown-plumaged female shows the
similar distinctive short neck and large bill. Both sexes
show striking blue areas on the leading edge of the wing,
although these are duller in the female. Especially as
they take off, the wings of shovelers make a loud, deep
'woofing' noise, quite unlike mallards'.

Something like 1,500 pairs may breed in Britain,
mainly confined to the south-east, with the largest
concentrations on the Ouse Washes. In the winter,
populations from eastern Europe move westward and as
many as 10,000 reach Britain.

*In all plumages the shape of body
and size of bill is distinctive.
Eclipse male differs from female
in redness of plumage.*

Scaup

Very like tufted duck in flight, but male's grey back and female's white face often conspicuous. Female looks larger, broader, paler than female tufted.

Male looks black fore and aft, pale in middle – white flanks and grey back, unlike tufted duck of either sex or any age.

Juvenile hard to tell from tufted but bulkier, no crest. Summer female has pale ear patch.

Male in eclipse.

Aythya marila
42–51 cm; 900–1,200 g
Where to look: shallow coastal waters, bays and estuaries. Does not breed in UK. **Food:** mainly molluscs, also waste grain. **Voice:** harsh *karr – karr* while flying.

Scaup are principally sea-ducks in winter, many of them coming to Britain's shores from Iceland. At present, probably only 5,000–10,000 winter here, widely scattered around the coast, but most numerous in the Forth, the Dornoch Firth, Islay, the Solway, on the Cheshire Dee and at Carlingford Lough, Northern Ireland. Gone are the days when up to 30,000 could be seen in the vast flock which wintered off Leith in the Forth, attracted by waste grain from breweries and distilleries and by the small worms which lived on the raw sewage. Fewer grain discharges and better sewage treatment led to its abrupt disappearance. Males are easily distinguished from similar ducks. Females are not difficult, but beware of female tufted ducks with white face-marks; scaup are slightly larger and broader-looking, as well as much less dark in appearance. Their bills are longer and broader and, except on young birds, the white is always much more extensive. Tufted ducks have broad black tips to their bills; scaup have only a narrow black mark, useful on dull-faced juveniles.

Pochard

Aythya ferina
42–49 cm; 800–1,200 g
Where to look: well vegetated lakes and pools in summer and open fresh water in winter. **Nest:** on ground near water. **Eggs:** 8–10, greenish. **Food:** water plants, seeds and invertebrates. **Voice:** harsh growling notes.

Although one of the most familiar diving ducks, the pochard is actually a very scarce breeding bird in Britain. There are no more than 200–400 pairs, mainly in south-east England, with important concentrations in the North Kent Marshes and the Norfolk Broads. Most of the birds which come to Britain and Ireland are winter visitors from central Europe and as far away as the USSR. The wintering population may be as high as 80,000. About 85 per cent of their food is plant material, including many seeds, which is obtained by diving in shallow fresh water, hence the birds' preference for shallow and well-vegetated lakes and gravel pits. Reservoirs and other deep-water sites are more often used for roosting and resting. The males, with their chestnut heads, black breasts and sterns and greyish bodies, are usually unmistakable, but females sometimes cause confusion – especially when asleep. They have quite pale, greyish-brown bodies with warm brown breasts and heads, the latter showing pale marks at the eye and the base of the bill. The bill, when visible (pochards sleep for much of the day), has a broad pale band around the middle and a black tip.

Characteristically rounded shape and uniform tone, except for black breasts of males.

In flight, female looks very plain, but note pale belly. Neither sex shows prominent wing markings.

Tufted Duck

Males obviously black and white in flight, females dark brown and white, both with conspicuous white bellies and white wing stripes.

After the ubiquitous mallard, the tufted duck is the most widespread and best-known duck, often occurring on park lakes and on rivers in towns and cities, where it soon becomes very tame. It is a remarkably successful species which has been quick to make use of the many new artificial water areas created by man, including gravel pits and reservoirs. In a mere 25 years the breeding population in mainland Britain has trebled to its present level of about 7,000 pairs; there are at least 2,000 more in Ireland. Similarly, the winter population has increased over the same period (by about 50 per cent) with a mid-winter peak of over 60,000 birds. Scottish birds are known to go to Ireland in winter, but those in Ireland and the rest of Britain apparently do not move far. Large numbers reach the British Isles from Iceland, northern Scandinavia and Russia, arriving from late September onwards to stay until early spring. Being so common and often so tame, tufted ducks can be watched and 'learned' thoroughly in all their plumages, which makes it that much easier for the birdwatcher when a scaup appears among them! They are more lively than nearby pochards during the day, as pochards are more nocturnal feeders. Tufted ducks are sociable, often displaying together in groups.

Aythya fuligula
40–47 cm; 600–1,000 g
Where to look: areas of open water, including rivers. **Nest:** well hidden, near water. **Eggs:** 8–11, greenish-grey. **Food:** some aquatic plant material, but mainly molluscs, insects, etc. **Voice:** various harsh growling notes.

Female tufted duck is a small, dark bird with pale flanks and always some suggestion of a crest. Can look very uniform in distance. First winter males are duller, especially on the flanks, while eclipse males have greyer sides. Female scaup is larger, broader, paler, with bigger white face patch. Beware hybrids from time to time, which can look like scaup with crest.

Dives normally last 15–20 seconds, rarely much longer, generally to a depth of about 2.5 metres (8 ft). Up to 100 dives per hour are common, with pauses of about 10 seconds between dives.

Some females show white on face, but never as much as female scaup. White undertail is not uncommon, but not as striking as on smaller, richer-coloured ferruginous duck.

Male is strikingly black and white; long, drooping crest.

Male in eclipse resembles female but has pale grey flanks. Usually still shows white mark behind the black tip of the bill, as in summer.

Male in its first winter like adult with shorter crest and greyer sides. Cleaner black and white plumage develops as the bird moults during winter.

Often associates with other ducks, especially pochard. Scaup is rare, but regular, on fresh water, and may join tufteds, when different shape is often first pointer.

Characteristic plump, angled look on shore. Note white bellies.

Mandarin

Aix galericulata
41–49 cm; 500–650 g
Where to look: lakes, ponds
and rivers with well-wooded
edges. **Nest:** hole in tree.
Eggs: 9–12, white. **Food:**
mainly vegetable, including
seeds; some insects and
molluscs. **Voice:** call most
often heard is short whistle.

*Often sit in water, rest or perch
under bushes, well hidden and
surprisingly inconspicuous.*

*In flight, small with short neck
and long tail. Note white belly.
Springs clear of water and flies
fast with great agility.*

*Being a perching duck, uses logs
and branches freely. Moves easily
on land. Appears compact, drake
looking very large-headed.*

The exotic-looking drake mandarin is unlikely to be
mistaken for anything else, but the female is rather dull
and puzzling on her own. The small bill, crested head,
white chin and white 'spectacles' are helpful features. A
native of the western USSR, China and Japan, the
mandarin is a naturalised 'escape' in Britain, found
mainly in south-east England, especially in Surrey and
Berkshire. It is appearing more and more elsewhere and
there is a well-established population on the Tay at
Perth. It can be helped by providing nestboxes, though
it is not always eager to use them. Old trees with large
cavities are its chief requirement. The most recent
estimate puts total numbers at 850–1,000 pairs, but it is
a highly secretive bird, easily overlooked even where it
is quite numerous, and it is also rather neglected by
most birdwatchers. For some time there have been
disturbing reports of a continuing decline in its natural
range in Asia, so Britain's population may now be of
considerable international importance. It therefore
merits much more careful investigation in future.

*Drake unlikely to be confused,
but female requires care.*

Ruddy Duck

*Displaying drake 'chest beating'
and rattling open bill.*

Oxyura jamaicensis
35–43 cm; 500–700 g
Where to look: lakes, ponds,
reservoirs, gravel pits. **Nest:**
well hidden, near water.
Eggs: 6–10, whitish. **Food:**
mainly insect larvae, seeds.
Dives. **Voice:** largely silent.

*Female has brown cap with pale
cheeks crossed by dark stripe.*

*Summer male is bright chestnut
with white cheeks contrasting with
black cap. Note blue bill and
stiffly cocked dark tail.*

In the late 1950s, about 20 unpinioned young ruddy
ducks escaped from the Wildfowl Trust reserve at
Slimbridge. From their original strongholds on reservoirs in Somerset and Staffordshire these North
American 'stifftails' spread quite rapidly, having nested
in the wild for the first time in 1960. There are now
probably some 3,000 birds, mainly in the southern half
of England, but with records from Wales (including
Anglesey) and Northern Ireland. The species has also
bred in one area in Scotland. Males in breeding dress are
unmistakable, but winter males, females and immature
birds need to be compared with various other ducks and
also grebes which have dark crowns and white or pale
cheeks. Look for the long tail, often held in a stiff,
cocked position, and the rather long, broad bill. When
breeding, ruddy ducks prefer shallow waters with good
surrounding vegetation, but in winter they use more
open water and may occur in large flocks. Already
several sites have become 'traditional' places and attract
as many as 400 birds each year.

*In winter, male closely resembles
female, but still has clear white
cheeks and black cap. Bill
becomes greyish. Note typical
shape and posture (tail not
always cocked). Bill is large and
broad. See smew.*

Ferruginous Duck

Aythya nyroca
38–42 cm; 500–650 g
Where to look: shallow, well vegetated lakes, pools, marshes. Does not breed in Britain. **Food:** dives for aquatic seeds, plants, some invertebrates. **Voice:** female's high, repeated *karri* is distinctive.

Like slim tufted duck in flight, reddish colours often still apparent. Striking white wing stripe – longer than in tufted.

Smaller, slimmer than tufted, distinctly redder. White stern very conspicuous, white eye obvious – eye on tufted is clearly yellow.

Ferruginous with tufteds.

The ferruginous duck breeds in southern and eastern Europe and is a rare but fairly regular visitor to Britain. As with other rare wildfowl, its true status is difficult to assess, as really wild ones are impossible to tell from most 'escaped' birds that fly free from collections. Given reasonable views, the male is easily identified, being a rich, dark reddish brown, almost mahogany in good light, blacker on the back and around the very striking white stern. Females are drabber and dark-eyed, but the gleaming white patch under the tail is still very distinct and much larger and more sharply defined than any white patch on a female tufted duck. The long, narrow bill, sweeping up into a sloping forehead and high crown also make the bird distinctive and in flight the white wing stripe is really striking. This bird is quite at home where there are only small patches of open water between tall stands of reeds, behaving more like a small grebe than most of the ducks, which prefer larger open spaces. Nevertheless, in Britain most associate with tufted ducks or pochards on larger pools.

Drake has inconspicuous dark collar and white chin spot.

Red-crested Pochard

Netta rufina
53–57 cm; 900–1,200 g
Where to look: fresh water with extensive cover, but in winter often gravel pits, reservoirs. Introduced birds nest in Britain. **Food:** mostly vegetation. Dives and dabbles on surface. **Voice:** generally silent.

In flight, white underwing obvious. Broad white wing stripes. Pattern of head usually clear in both sexes. Note male's black underparts.

Eclipse drake like female, but bill red.

White side patches obvious on male.

Red-crested pochards are larger than most fresh-water diving ducks, and might almost be thought of as surface feeders – not really so far-fetched since they represent a halfway point between dabblers and divers, the two main groups of ducks. The handsome male is unmistakable; even in eclipse, when he looks very like a female, he retains his bright red bill. The female is most likely to be confused with a female common scoter (occasional on fresh water), but is larger and paler, sits higher on the water and has a differently shaped head and bill. The red-crested pochard has a wide but scattered distribution across Europe, where it is typically a bird of rich, well-vegetated wetlands. Its status in Britain is confused by the fact that it is widely kept in captivity and frequently escapes and wanders. Thirty years ago there was evidence of genuinely wild birds in winter, from Denmark, where it has since declined. Perhaps some still do originate from the wild, but most are probably feral, including those which have nested in recent years. It is a pity that such suspicion should be attached to sightings of this bird, which is always an exciting find among the commoner ducks.

At a distance, female's pale cheeks sometimes conspicuous. White sides contrasting with black breast and stern obvious in drakes.

Larger than pochard – drake clearly very different; female similarly nondescript, but with obvious pale cheeks, dark cap.

Eider

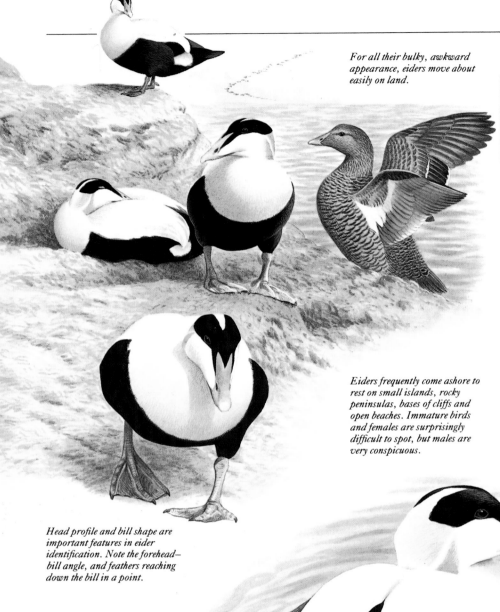

For all their bulky, awkward appearance, eiders move about easily on land.

Eiders frequently come ashore to rest on small islands, rocky peninsulas, bases of cliffs and open beaches. Immature birds and females are surprisingly difficult to spot, but males are very conspicuous.

Head profile and bill shape are important features in eider identification. Note the forehead– bill angle, and feathers reaching down the bill in a point.

Somateria mollissima
50–71 cm; 1,500–2,500 g
Where to look: coastal waters, usually close to shore. **Nest:** on ground, often exposed. **Eggs:** 4–6, greenish-grey. **Food:** dives (or feeds from surface) mainly for molluscs. **Voice:** except when courting, rather silent.

Even at very long range, an adult drake eider, uniquely white on top and black beneath, is easy to identify. Young males, passing through a variety of piebald plumages as they grow older, can be more tricky, but at least the bill shape and their size and bulk are distinctive. Very often the white is most obvious on the breast of a patchy young male eider. Only the velvet scoter has the generally dark look, and flat head profile, of a female eider, but the scoter's facial marks and wing patches can be seen given patience. Eiders occasionally turn up inland and small numbers occur around all Britain's coasts, but they are essentially birds of the northern and north-western seaboards. They are usually close inshore, riding the swell in a sandy bay or out beyond the breaking waves on a rocky beach, often strung out in long lines. Some come into harbours and families often paddle about among seaweedy rocks allowing very close observation. The crèches of youngsters with their attendant 'aunties' may be seen running over mud in some northern estuaries, where they can be in danger of being snatched up by large gulls. A herring gull will make short work of a duckling.

Adult male is only duck with combination of white breast and back with black underparts and stern. Note also heavy, broad-bodied appearance.

'Eiderdown' has long been famous and no artificial substitute has been found to better it. The down from a single nest may be worth as much as £3. It comes from the breast of the female and the best quality down is that taken a few days before the eggs hatch. There is a long history of such exploitation in Iceland, where some colonies are enlarged to as many as 10,000 pairs by artificial nest sites.

Mature male unmistakable, but this plumage not attained until about fourth year. Crisp green markings on head and pink flush on breast can be very obvious, even far off and in poor light.

Courtship begins in late winter, as with many wildfowl. The cooing and crooning calls of the beautiful drakes are familiar sounds along favoured coasts well into spring. Female eiders nest singly or in loose colonies, sometimes in quite open spots but often in a crevice between big rocks. Many nest in gull and tern colonies, where they derive some protection as their more aggressive neighbours combine to chase away predators. Eiders are increasing, and perhaps as many as 25,000 pairs breed in Britain and Ireland, while the winter total is estimated at 72,000 birds. This is but a small proportion of the total European wintering population, which is around two million birds. The big flocks in the Baltic have been counted using radar! Eiders eat slow-moving, bottom-living creatures, mainly molluscs, which they take in dives from the surface. They use their feet to swim underwater, but half-open their wings as they roll forward to dive. Feeding activities vary according to the tide – low tide being favoured, when food is easier to reach – but they also tend to feed most in the morning and evening if the tidal range is small. To watch a group of eiders feeding in a seaweedy bay, diving in turn and reappearing with crabs or shellfish, rolling gently in the swell, is a restful and enjoyable experience. Their approachability, and the sharp, intricate patterns combined with a subtle delicacy of colour, make them well-loved favourites of many holidaymakers and birdwatchers alike.

Looks heavy and ponderous in flight, with slightly drooping head and neck. Flies low over water, often in long lines.

Sequence of moults from female-like immature through various piebald phases. Eclipse drake dark, much white on back.

Female best told by rather plain, barred appearance, pale line over eye at close range, size and distinctive bill.

Ducklings, uniformly greyish brown, can dive readily. More than one brood may accompany one female, or large parties may assemble with several females in attendance.

Nests singly or in loose group, sometimes well hidden, but often out in open.

Long-tailed Duck

Clangula hyemalis
40–47 cm; 600–800 g
Where to look: sea coasts.
Does not breed in Britain.
Food: dives, mainly for
animals, especially
crustaceans and molluscs.
Voice: unlike many sea
ducks, very vocal – drakes
have musical calls.

*Very fast, agile flight with wings
wholly dark above and below.*

Even where it is common and fairly easy to see, the
long-tailed duck remains a blue riband species for the
birdwatcher. Fortunately, despite plumage variations,
it is not a difficult bird to identify. It occurs off many
coasts in small numbers, wherever there are shallow
waters offshore, but is commonest from Northumberland northwards to Shetland, and in the Outer
Hebrides. It can be seen close inshore in some areas, but
often remains well out to sea, flying around a great deal.
It is perfectly at home in the roughest conditions. It was
only comparatively recently that realistic estimates of
wintering numbers became available, following work
on sea ducks in the Moray Firth area. This revealed that
the Moray Firth regularly held 10,000–15,000 birds,
which must be at least three-quarters of the total for
Britain and Ireland. In the sandier inlets of the Firth,
displaying groups in spring are at their liveliest and give
the most delightful birdwatching.

*Winter male is a spectacular
white bird with dark cheek-mark,
black on back, wings, breast and
also on very long tail. Small bill
distinctly two-coloured, dark
with pinkish band.*

*Winter female much duller,
browner than male and lacks
long tail. Note pale sides of body
and dark breast, dark crown and
nape and white face with dark
mark below cheeks. Greyish bill.*

*No other sea duck has
combination of small size, small
bill, black, brown and white.
Male's long tail is unique
(plumage totally unlike pintail,
which may also be seen on sea).
Marked change in summer when
male becomes very dark brown
with whitish face and sides.*

*Juvenile resembles female, while
first winter males are generally
less well marked, but with
drake's two-colour bill.*

Common Scoter

Flies in lines or dense packs. Male wholly black; pale cheeks on female visible at long range.

Best known as bulky, dark ducks flying low over sea in small groups, with paler flight feathers and pale cheeks of females the only obvious marks; also inland, especially in summer, swimming quietly far out on large reservoirs; usually gone next day. Beware young birds with very dull cheeks; females with pale, bleached feathers on back in late summer.

Common scoters breed on a few fresh-water lakes in Scotland and Ireland. In some areas, even in central England, they appear regularly on large reservoirs in late summer. Mainly, though, they are known as sea ducks, winter visitors from Scandinavia and Russia. There are big concentrations in the Moray Firth and Carmarthen Bay. It is often worth looking through flocks in the hope of discovering a few grebes, velvet scoters or long-tailed ducks. Scoters always give the impression of extraordinary buoyancy, and when the males raise their pointed tails and very slender necks, they belie their heavy build. On rare calm days the sounds of courting birds carry far across the water, a chorus of rippling, piping calls that spread infectiously through the flock.

Forms close-packed, often very large, rafts on sea, diving under frequently. Pale cheeks of female conspicuous. Often swims with tail cocked.

Melanitta nigra
44–54 cm; 700–1,300 g
Where to look: coastal waters. **Nest:** well hidden near water. **Eggs:** 6–8, cream to buff. Rare breeder. **Food:** dives for molluscs.

Male is only totally black duck. Black and yellow bill can often be seen at very long range. Female has obvious pale greyish cheeks and is otherwise rather uniform. No other duck – or grebe – showing pale cheeks is as dark.

Velvet Scoter

Melanitta fusca
51–58 cm; 1,200–1,800 g
Where to look: coastal waters, mainly north-east and east. Sometimes occurs on fresh water inland. Does not breed in Britain. **Food:** dives; in winter feeds mainly on molluscs. **Voice:** away from breeding areas largely silent.

The velvet scoter is both bigger and bulkier than the common scoter, and is closer to an eider in size. Females and immature birds can be difficult to identify, especially at any distance, but at some stage the characteristic white wing patches will be seen. Eiders have different bill shapes and those which are as dark as velvet scoters will usually show much more white. The female's pale head markings are actually visible even at quite long range in reasonable light.

While individuals turn up quite regularly inland, most velvet scoters are seen on the sea, sometimes very close inshore and quite tame. They have been suspected of breeding in Britain in the past, but are essentially winter visitors from Scandinavia and western Siberia. Numbers are very variable from year to year: as many as 10,000 have been recorded, but the more normal total is probably 2,500–5,000. Recent work on winter sea duck populations has shown that the Moray Firth is as important for velvet scoters as it is for common scoters and long-tailed ducks. It is always a pleasure to be able to watch a selection of these attractive marine species close to the shore.

Looks heavy-headed and bulky in flight. Note white wing patches.

Often occurs in small flocks on its own, but also (above) mixes with common scoter. Is noticeably larger and bulkier. Bill colour more orange on drake. White on wing often obvious; red legs.

Immature male has little colour on bill, no white below eye. Compare with adult male.

Male usually readily identified. Female is large, bulky scoter with pale head patches, white on wing and red legs and feet.

Goldeneye

Small, short-necked; drake very distinctive. Both sexes at all ages show obvious white wing patch. Rapid flight, wings with distinct whistle.

Drakes display in late winter, silently or with faint calls.

Bucephala clangula
42–50 cm; 800–1,100 g
Where to look: fresh water and inshore at coast. **Nest:** hole in tree or nestbox. **Eggs:** 8–11, bluish-green. **Food:** dives for molluscs, crustaceans, insect larvae. **Voice:** mainly silent; creaky display note.

Despite the recent welcome rise of the Scottish breeding population, the goldeneye is still best known as a winter visitor to Britain and Ireland, apparently from Scandinavia and western Russia. The peak winter population is 10,000–15,000 birds, widely distributed over inland waters (where it is most numerous on some of the largest reservoirs) and also along the coast.

The drakes are among the most handsome and distinctive of winter wildfowl, strikingly black and white, but females and first winter birds are both less obvious and less distinctive, looking hunched and dark.

Through the provision of large numbers of nest-boxes, goldeneyes have colonised Scotland in the last 20 years; in 1986 there were 44 successful nests, with 381 ducklings seen. Planned and supervised by the RSPB, this highly successful conservation operation also owes much to co-operative landowners.

Short-necked and small with tail sometimes cocked. Whiteness of drake most distinctive; females and immature birds grey with brown heads.

Look for a small, mainly grey duck, with or without a white collar below the brown head, showing a white flash on the side. Goldeneyes dive continually and are usually nervous and easily put up: watch for the white wing patches; listen for the distinctive wing noise.

Note characteristic head shape and small bill. Females and immature birds may show white flash on side.

Smew

Mergus albellus
38–44 cm; 600–900 g
Where to look: fresh-water lakes, reservoirs, gravel pits. Does not breed in Britain. **Food:** dives; a 'sawbill' which uses serrated bill edges to seize and hold small fish. Usually brings fish to surface. **Voice:** silent in winter.

Takes to flight readily and then shows rakish outline, but rather short neck and noticeably small bill. Drake's largely white body contrasts with striking pattern of upperwing and dark underwing. Female and immature bird show much white on inner part of upperwing; obvious white cheeks.

Even at their regular haunts, smews can be very mobile and frustratingly elusive: this, and their scarcity, makes them rather special birds – for the birdwatcher. Most European smews breed in northern Russia; they are rare in northern Scandinavia. Most of these birds winter in the Netherlands, and in normal winter weather only 100 or so reach the British Isles. The majority occur in southern and south-eastern England. Females and young birds, collectively called 'redheads', which tend to winter further south than the adult drakes, are in the majority. Thirty years ago, three times as many smews wintered here on a regular basis, so there has been a considerable decline in their numbers during that time. The London reservoirs are no longer the prime site for smews that they once were. Nevertheless, severe weather in their Dutch wintering grounds (where there may be up to 20,000 birds) causes many birds to move out, and in these circumstances large influxes are experienced in Britain. As many as 350 have occurred here in recent hard winters. They are great birds to find, unexpectedly, on a local lake during a spell of arctic weather, rewarding the hardy!

Adults (below) are strikingly different: male largely white with black and fine grey markings; female darker and much greyer with fine, short, dark bill, red-brown cap and conspicuous white cheeks and chin.

Winter group active on water, with much diving. 'Redheads' usually outnumber males.

Red-breasted Merganser

Rakish flight outline. White inner wing on drake, patch on female.

Males have spectacular displays, often performed in late winter.

Mergus serrator
52–58 cm; 900–1,200 g
Where to look: inland lochs, rivers, also coastal waters.
Nest: on ground, well hidden. **Eggs:** 8–10, buff to olive. **Food:** as other sawbills, fish caught by diving and pursuit under water.
Voice: mostly silent.

Female is smaller, darker and more obviously crested than goosander. Note lack of clear-cut division between head colour, throat and neck.

Male unmistakable – fine red bill, wispy crest, white neck-band, orange-brown breast.

Although they now breed in north-western England and in parts of Wales, mergansers are most commonly associated with Scotland and Ireland. While many nest well inland on lochs and rivers, the majority breed along the coast, especially in inlets and sea lochs with an abundance of small islands. Some remain on fresh water in winter, but most move to coastal waters, occurring right around the eastern and southern coasts of England as well as their western and northern haunts. Many of these more southerly birds come from Scandinavia, while birds from Iceland join those in Scotland and Ireland. The total winter population is perhaps as high as 11,000 birds.

Seen well, males are unlikely to be confused with other sawbills, but 'redheads' (females and immature birds) can be tricky; they are always thin-billed, darker and generally more brown than 'redhead' goosanders, lacking the clear-cut head and throat markings of the latter. The facial expression is different, with almost a 'smile' compared with the stern goosander.

Goosander

Large, long and rakish in flight, drake very white with dark head. 'Redhead' more uniform, but head darker and white wing patches.

Eclipse male closely resembles female. Moves freely ashore.

Mergus merganser
58–66 cm; 1,100–1,700 g
Where to look: fresh-water lakes and reservoirs, locally on sheltered coasts. **Nest:** usually hole in tree, also in ground or nestbox. **Eggs:** 8–11, whitish. **Food:** fish.
Voice: silent except during display.

The goosander is the largest of the three sawbills found in Britain and Ireland; there is little risk of confusion with smew, the smallest species, but 'redhead' (female and immature) goosanders and red-breasted mergansers require care. With practice, they are not actually too difficult to identify and the goosander's clear preference for inland fresh water in winter is a useful extra clue. It haunts fish-rich lochs, lakes and rivers in the breeding season and is very much a bird of large areas of open water, including reservoirs, in winter. Only locally (such as in the Beauly Firth, where there may be as many as 1,500 birds) does it winter regularly on sheltered coasts. Not long ago, the goosander bred only in Scotland, but it is now established in parts of northern England and has also colonised Wales and Ireland in very small numbers. The population appears to be fairly sedentary and, except when hard weather brings influxes from Europe, is not added to by migrants. About 8,000 spend the winter here. They are best sought on traditional sites, albeit often rather modern reservoirs, and are relatively rare away from these regular wintering places.

Note long, low appearance in water.

Female goosander is rather larger than female merganser, much more uniformly grey, with clearly demarcated red-brown head and neck, well defined white chin and throat and less wispy crest. Immature similar.

Male unmistakable. Black, white and pink.

Comparing Birds of Prey

Birds of prey (raptors) are among the most difficult groups to identify. Views may only be brief or distant. This makes familiarity hard to achieve. Wing shape and position, and tail length, are important to distinguish families, but then one should concentrate on plumage, especially wing patterns.

Red kite: *the forked, reddish tail and white wing patches are the main characteristics. A rare bird for which a journey to Wales must be made.*

Buzzard: *large-sized raptor with broad wings raised in shallow 'V' when soaring. Note wing pattern and compare with the rare honey buzzard, which has longer neck and tail and soars on flat wings. Commonest in western and northern Britain.*

Golden eagle: *much larger than buzzard, with longer wings and tail and powerful bill on well-protruding head. Soars on wings raised in shallow 'V'.*

Male hen harrier

Male

Marsh harrier: *like all harriers, soars and glides on raised wings. Note male's wing pattern and rusty body. Female brown, often with yellow head and wing markings.*

Hen harrier: *like all harriers, males and females differ in plumage. Female difficult to distinguish from female Montagu's, but note head pattern. In male look for white underparts, grey head and upper breast, black tips to wings and dark trailing edge, white rump.*

Female hen harrier

Female marsh harrier

Osprey: *long wings bowed when gliding and soaring, and white body with large black patches at bend of wing make this easy.*

Peregrines

Hobby chasing swift

Peregrine: *large falcon with thick-set body, broad-based pointed wings and rather short tail. When chasing prey its speed is impressive. Note the large black 'moustache', white cheeks.*

Hobby: *small falcon with long, narrow, pointed wings and silhouette not unlike large swift. Streaked black underparts, small 'moustache' and reddish undertail-coverts are characteristic.*

Falcons are small to medium-sized raptors with rather long tapering wings and medium-length tails, their shape designed for fast flight and rapid acceleration enabling pursuit of their prey – flying birds in open country. The kestrel is the exception, locating its prey on the ground by hovering or watching from a vantage post. **Hawks** have short, rounded wings and long tails and are woodland dwellers, their wings shaped for manoeuvrability between trees and branches.

Female merlin

Merlin: *the smallest falcon, with shorter wings than other species, and bold dashing flight. Note blue-grey upperparts and black tail band of male (above).*

Sparrowhawk: *note short rounded wings, long tail and flight: rapid wing-beats interspersed with glides. Secretive woodland dweller.*

Female

Kestrel: *persistent hovering is the most characteristic feature of this common bird of prey. Often seen over roadside verges.*

Male kestrel

Golden Eagle

Soaring majestically on outstretched wings over a wild, mountainous landscape, the golden eagle is a genuinely thrilling sight. Like many of Britain's rarer raptors, its home is in Scotland, where it nests on crags and hunts over moorland and bare hillsides. Therein lies one of the main threats to its future, for such areas are becoming the target for forestry plantations. As blanket coniferous forests start to swathe the Scottish glens and moors the eagle's vital feeding grounds are lost.

Around its eyrie, a golden eagle hunts over a 'home-range' which can vary from 8,000 to 18,000 acres. Much of its food is carrion, particularly in winter, when dead sheep can form nearly half its diet. Otherwise it feeds on medium-sized mammals and birds, notably mountain hares and red grouse.

The eagle has declined in many countries and Scotland is no exception. During the last century it was intensely persecuted; during World War II numbers rose, only to be reduced again by killing on grouse moors. Then followed reduced breeding success through eating sheep carrion contaminated by dieldrin sheep dip. Today the illegal use of poisonous baits is almost certainly having its effect on the eagle population, and nests are still robbed by egg collectors. Scotland has 420 pairs of golden eagles, one of the highest numbers in Europe. This gives Britain an international responsibility to ensure that poisoning, egg collecting and, particularly, blanket afforestation are kept in check.

Aquila chrysaetos
75–85 cm
Wingspan 200–220 cm
Where to look: wild mountainous country in Scotland; with luck in the Lake District. **Nest:** remote crags, occasionally Scots pine. Eyrie with extensive views; pair often has 2–4 alternate nest sites. Bulky nest of branches lined with grasses. **Eggs:** 1–3 (usually 2), whitish or blotched red-brown. **Food:** hares, rabbits and grouse, also carrion; hunts over vast area ('home range'). **Voice:** thin yelp at nest and whistling *twee-oo* alarm.

Golden eagles and buzzards both soar on raised wings, so caution needed at a distance. The eagle is much larger with more protruding head; longer wings are often 'pinched-in' at the body.

Immature birds readily identified by conspicuous white patches in the wing (less extensive above) and white at base of tail, with broader black terminal band. The white is gradually lost, through moult, as the bird matures and adult plumage is attained after about six years.

When seen close to, the massive bill, accentuated by the flat crown, is impressive. The crown and rather shaggy hind neck are washed golden-yellow.

Young covered in white down at first; usually only one survives — flies at about 11 weeks old.

Sunny days in early spring best time to see display: circling to a great height or tumbling rolls with the pair presenting talons. More typical is switch-back display: diving head-first on half closed wings only to sweep up before falling into next dive. Up to 20 undulations performed.

From below, the adult is dark brown, though the bases of flight and tail feathers are slightly paler grey-brown, in good light accentuating the darkness of the wing-coverts and body.

Britain's largest bird of prey, with a two-metre (seven-ft) wingspan. Over 400 pairs nest in Scotland. Adult brown, but young distinctive, with white flashes in wings and tail. Forestry plantations are reducing hunting areas. This is the main problem for its future conservation. Contrary to some beliefs, it rarely kills lambs.

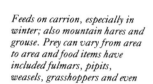

Feeds on carrion, especially in winter; also mountain hares and grouse. Prey can vary from area to area and food items have included fulmars, pipits, weasels, grasshoppers and even salmon and pike. One pair studied fed mainly on puffins!

White-tailed Eagle

Haliaeetus albicilla
70–90 cm
Wingspan 200–240 cm
Where to look: west coast of Scotland, but very rare. Its haunts are kept secret. **Nest:** bulky, of sticks in tree or cliff ledge. **Eggs:** usually 2, white. **Food:** carrion, seabirds, mammals, fish.

Broad, door-mat-like wings, short tail and well protruding head give characteristic silhouette. Unlike golden eagle, soars on flat wings.

Adult brown with white tail, variable whitish feathers on head and upper breast, yellow bill.

Huge, with long, broad wings, held flat when soaring. White tail of adult distinctive. Very rare; only found on west coast of Scotland where reintroduced in 1976. Continental birds occasionally occur in southern England in winter and may stay for several weeks. Population decreasing in Europe.

The last truly wild British white-tailed eagles nested on Skye in 1916, the population then becoming extinct through persecution. Because white-tailed eagles are largely resident and, like all large raptors, have difficulty in making long sea crossings, the chance of them returning to breed naturally was remote. Therefore, in 1968 the RSPB tried to give them a helping hand and four young birds were brought in from Norway. That attempt to reintroduce them was unsuccessful. In 1976, the Nature Conservancy Council carried out a large-scale reintroduction programme in western Scotland, bringing over, at yearly intervals, a total of over 80 young eagles, again from Norwegian eyries. This time the project was successful and 1985 saw the first young white-tailed eagle fly from a Scottish eyrie for nearly 70 years. The RSPB and NCC are now involved in monitoring the population and protecting vulnerable nests, of which several are discovered each year. Their whereabouts are a closely guarded secret because of the risk of theft by egg collectors, but the long-term hope is to find a suitable eyrie for public viewing. This would surely rival Loch Garten's ospreys!

Squarer-cut wings than golden's.

Juveniles more difficult to identify, lacking obvious white tail of adult. Dark brown plumage relieved by whitish breast streaks, bar on wing coverts and patch on 'armpits'; spread tail shows white streaks.

Buzzard

The fate of the buzzard in Britain has been dictated by two main factors: gamekeepers and rabbits. At the turn of the century it was a relatively rare bird, but with a decline in persecution and in the collection of specimens and eggs, and with rabbits still common and widespread, an increase took place up to the 1950s. An interesting aspect of this was the way buzzards spread eastwards during the two world wars – when keepering was reduced or non-existent in many areas. Between 1952 and 1955 myxomatosis struck Britain's rabbits, resulting in their near elimination. This in turn had a drastic effect on buzzards, which depend largely on rabbits during the breeding season. The buzzard population may have been reduced by half from about 25,000 birds. Today there are signs that it is spreading its range once again.

The buzzard continues to be persecuted, though at a much lower level than in former times. It is particularly vulnerable to poisoned baits and more buzzards are killed by them than any other raptor in Britain.

Buteo buteo
50–55 cm
Wingspan 115–130 cm
Where to look: hilly country and wooded farmland. **Nest:** trees and crags, bulky. **Eggs:** 2–3, white or bluish, with reddish-brown blotches. **Food:** rabbits, earthworms, carrion. **Voice:** mewing *peeioo*.

Wings raised when soaring, but flat in glides. Compact, well proportioned with broad head and thick-set neck. Soars with tail fanned, often to edge of wings.

Commonest large bird of prey to be seen in western Britain, the Lake District and Scotland.

Wings look broader and tail shorter than honey buzzard, which soars on flat wings. Viewed from above, buzzard-types look basically brown and then structure is important for identification. Though raptors are usually seen in flight they spend most time perched.

Rough-legged Buzzard

Note white base to tail with black terminal band; also characteristic dark belly patches.

Uncommon winter visitor. Larger and longer winged than buzzard with more elastic wing-beats. Typical colouration dark and white: whitish underwing and white-based tail contrast with black carpal patches, dark area on belly and black band on tail.

Buteo lagopus
50–60 cm
Wingspan 120–150 cm
Where to look: a wintering species found from Scotland down east coast to East Anglia in marshes, moors, heaths, downs and dunes. Numbers vary annually. Arrives October, departs March–April. Breeds Scandinavia east to Urals. **Food:** chiefly rabbits, and other small mammals. **Voice:** similar mew to buzzard, but louder and lower.

The rough-legged buzzard is the only raptor that regularly spends the winter in Britain (though not in large numbers) but does not breed here. It is the buzzard of the arctic *taiga* woodland and tundra and its fortunes are allied to the abundance of its main prey: lemmings and voles. These mammals normally have three- or four-year cycles of abundance – characteristic of small rodents living in harsh climates. The rough-legged buzzard is affected by these cycles. A good population of rodents in the spring means that many buzzards will breed and lay large clutches. If the rodent numbers remain high the bird will rear large broods. If rodent numbers are low the converse will occur.

The rough-legged buzzard is a regular but erratic visitor to Britain. In some winters only a few birds are seen, while in other years there may be 100 or more, mostly in the eastern counties. These invasions, or irruptions, are almost certainly linked to a food shortage on the Continent.

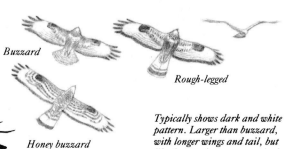

Buzzard

Rough-legged

Honey buzzard

Typically shows dark and white pattern. Larger than buzzard, with longer wings and tail, but like that species soars on raised wings; frequently hovers.

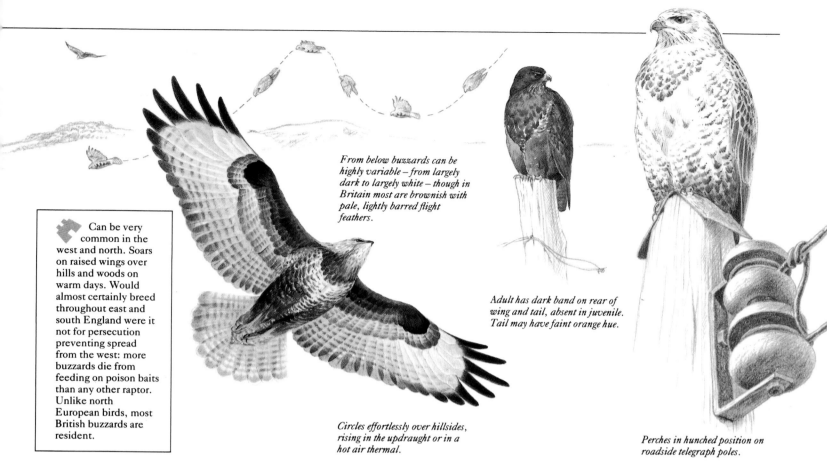

From below buzzards can be highly variable – from largely dark to largely white – though in Britain most are brownish with pale, lightly barred flight feathers.

Can be very common in the west and north. Soars on raised wings over hills and woods on warm days. Would almost certainly breed throughout east and south England were it not for persecution preventing spread from the west: more buzzards die from feeding on poison baits than any other raptor. Unlike north European birds, most British buzzards are resident.

Adult has dark band on rear of wing and tail, absent in juvenile. Tail may have faint orange hue.

Circles effortlessly over hillsides, rising in the updraught or in a hot air thermal.

Perches in hunched position on roadside telegraph poles.

Honey Buzzard

The honey buzzard is one of the commonest large raptors breeding in Europe, so why is it so rare in Britain? Part of the answer must lie in its diet of bee, wasp and insect larvae – the numbers of which can be seriously affected by the wet summers of Britain's Atlantic climate. Another factor is its type of migration. Honey buzzards spend the winter in Africa and do not like making long sea crossings. So they migrate where the sea is at its narrowest – places in Europe like the Bosphorus and Gibraltar. The English Channel, therefore, could act as a serious barrier to those that might otherwise reach our shores.

The few that nest in Britain do so from Hampshire to Scotland, but the population is probably less than 30 pairs. They can occasionally be seen on migration in late spring and autumn when care should be taken not to confuse them with the commoner buzzard: note the honey buzzard's small protruding head and neck, long tail, flat wings when soaring and characteristic tail and wing pattern.

Pernis apivorus
50–60 cm. Span 135–150 cm
Where to look: uncommon migrant in south and east. Rare breeder in mixed open mature woodland. **Nest:** in large tree, often built on an existing nest. **Eggs:** 2, whitish with red or chocolate markings. **Food:** bee and wasp grubs, other large insects, small mammals.

Varies in pattern below from whitish through to chocolate brown. Typically barred with dark patches on fore-wing and characteristic lines on flight feathers. Bars on tail also a clue to identification.

Soars on flat wings, unlike buzzard and rough-legged buzzard; soars less than those.

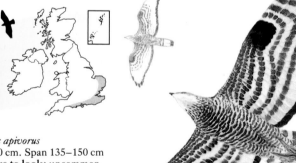

Note well-protruding cuckoo-like head and long tail and narrower wings which readily distinguish it from buzzard in silhouette. Upperparts brownish, but note bars on tail when close.

You must be lucky to see the rare and secretive honey buzzard. Headlands on the south and east coast can produce migrants in May, returning from their African wintering grounds. Look for buzzard-type with protruding head and long tail that soars and glides on flat wings. Breeding areas are kept secret as they are easily disturbed and the eggs are sought by illegal collectors. Spectacular 'butterfly' display over nesting wood.

Marsh Harrier

Like many raptors, the marsh harrier suffered from persecution in the last century and actually became extinct as a breeding bird. Then, just before World War I, a pair nested and heralded the recolonisation of Britain. At first this was slow, but with increased protection in the 1950s numbers grew to 15 pairs in 1958. This success was short-lived, however, because they succumbed to pesticides, and the population crashed to just one pair in 1971. Subsequently, with voluntary bans imposed on the use of the more persistent kinds of pesticides the situation greatly improved, and a quite dramatic recovery took place, with over 30 pairs raising nearly 100 young each year in the late 1980s. Many nest in the safety of reserves or under RSPB protection. Furthermore, birds are spreading from their traditional nest sites in East Anglia, though the best chance of seeing this grand bird of the reed beds is still at RSPB reserves such as Minsmere in Suffolk and Titchwell in Norfolk.

Circus aeruginosus
55 cm. Wingspan 115–130 cm
Where to look: reed beds, though often hunts over nearby fields. **Nest:** bulky, among reeds and vegetation in water. **Eggs:** 4–5, bluish-white, often stained. **Food:** mainly frogs, birds and small mammals. **Voice:** a plaintive shrill *kweeoo*.

Male and female harriers differ in plumage, readily separated.

The dark brown female usually has a creamy crown, throat and shoulders. The brown tail is unbarred.

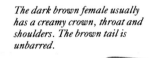

Note the tricoloured wings of male above; below, shows russet-streaked body, whitish underwings with black tips. Flight leisurely with glides on raised wings.

Look for marsh harriers soaring and gliding on raised wings over East Anglian reed beds. Increasing in England, with nearly 100 young raised each year. Some (mostly juveniles) migrate to southern Europe and North Africa; others remain in winter.

Red Kite

Milvus milvus
60–65 cm
Wingspan 175–195 cm
Where to look: mature oak woods in steep valleys and nearby hill country in central Wales. **Nest:** of sticks and mud in tall trees. **Eggs:** 3–4, whitish, variably marked. **Food:** small mammals, birds, worms, carrion. **Voice:** shrill, quavering *weoo-weoo-weoo*.

Soars on slightly bowed wings held forward. Graceful flight, forked tail constantly manoeuvred.

Colouration distinctive below with rusty body and underwing coverts, whitish head, reddish tail and noticeable white wing-patches, black wing-tips.

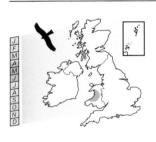

In good light, rusty-red tail very obvious. Note distinctive buff band on upperwing.

Majestic and agile in the air. Wings outstretched, slightly bowed and tail constantly twisted. Protection in Wales has helped increase to nearly 50 breeding pairs. Several have been killed by illegal poisoned baits.

Strict security surrounds Britain's red kite breeding area in central Wales. Once a common scavenger (even in towns), its population gradually dwindled as hygiene improved, and fewer animals died to provide it with carrion. Persecution also took its toll. The Welsh population now numbers nearly 50 pairs, and under careful protection has slowly increased from just 12 birds at the turn of the century.

What problems does it face now? Several succumb each year to the illegal activities of egg collectors, and for this reason nests are guarded. Poison continues to produce victims: poison baits set for crows and foxes (an illegal act in itself) are indiscriminate and can easily kill kites. On one occasion two were found dead on a poisoned carcass. Sadly, about two-thirds of all known kite deaths investigated have been directly attributable to human action. A natural hazard is bad weather in May, which can seriously affect chick survival. The hanging oak woods in which it nests will remain vital.

Hen Harrier

Typically seen over moorland in summer and marshes in winter.

Males

Male is pale grey, white and black below. Note grey hood and dark trailing edge to wing. Dramatic switch-back display over breeding area.

Circus cyaneus
45–50 cm
Wingspan 100–120 cm
Where to look: moorland and bracken-covered hills, newly afforested areas, but marshes and farmland in winter. **Nest:** on ground in heather, lined with rushes and grasses. **Eggs:** 4–5, bluish-white, occasionally with reddish marks. **Food:** small birds and mammals. **Voice:** rapid, chattering *ke-ke-ke-ke* in nesting area.

Harriers fly low over open ground, more quickly than often imagined, wings often held up in a slight 'V'. Female and young hen and Montagu's harriers are very similar and, in spring and autumn when they are most likely to overlap, many are simply noted as unidentified 'ring-tails'. The hen harrier is the larger of the two, broader in the wing (especially near the tip which is particularly long and slender in Montagu's) and the head pattern is a little different with a less bold cheek patch on the hen harrier. Juveniles look like females except that young Montagu's have unmarked rufous underparts – a useful point.

Many hen harriers breed on heather moorland and come into conflict with shooting interests because grouse can form an important part of their diet. Whether they cause any reduction in the numbers available for shooting is a matter of debate, though certainly where grouse numbers are healthy, scientists have shown hen harriers have little or no effect on the population.

Female very similar to female Montagu's, but larger with different head pattern: compare the two.

Female and juvenile

Montagu's Harrier

Wintering in Africa, Montagu's harriers arrive on their breeding grounds in April and May. They are not uncommon on the Continent, with perhaps 1,000 pairs in France and 6,000 in Spain, but in Britain they are rare birds. The highest numbers this century were in the 1950s, when some 40 pairs bred, mainly in Devon and Cornwall. A period of decline followed with a 'low' in 1975 when none bred. There has been an improvement since and now several pairs regularly nest in southern England. But there has been a change of habitat. Traditionally they nested on heaths, reed bed fringes and new conifer plantations, but now all the nests are in corn or rape fields. Therein lies a problem. When the fields are to be cut, the young are still in the nest and earlier spraying operations can flatten them. Thus, nests have to be located and protected from farming activities and, if necessary, an area around them left uncut until the young fly. This is a case where farmers and conservationists have worked closely together.

Circus pygargus
40–45 cm
Wingspan 105–120 cm
Where to look: cereal and rape fields in southern England, previously in reed beds, moorland and young forestry. A very rare summer visitor. **Nest:** in crops, lined with grasses etc. **Eggs:** 4–5, pale bluish-white with obscure rusty markings. **Food:** small mammals and birds. **Voice:** high-pitched *yik-yik-yik* over breeding area.

The main features to look for on the male are dirty-grey plumage, black wing tips, bars on underwing.

Female Montagu's and hen harrier are similar and have a white band at base of tail.

Juvenile

A 'ring-tail' from November to late March must be hen. In summer both species possible – take care!

Britain's rarest breeding harrier. Less than 10 pairs nest annually and all are given protection by the RSPB. Delicate raptor seen with luck on migration on south and east coast in May and autumn. Nest sites kept secret, but many have been in crops such as barley and rape.

Female

Osprey

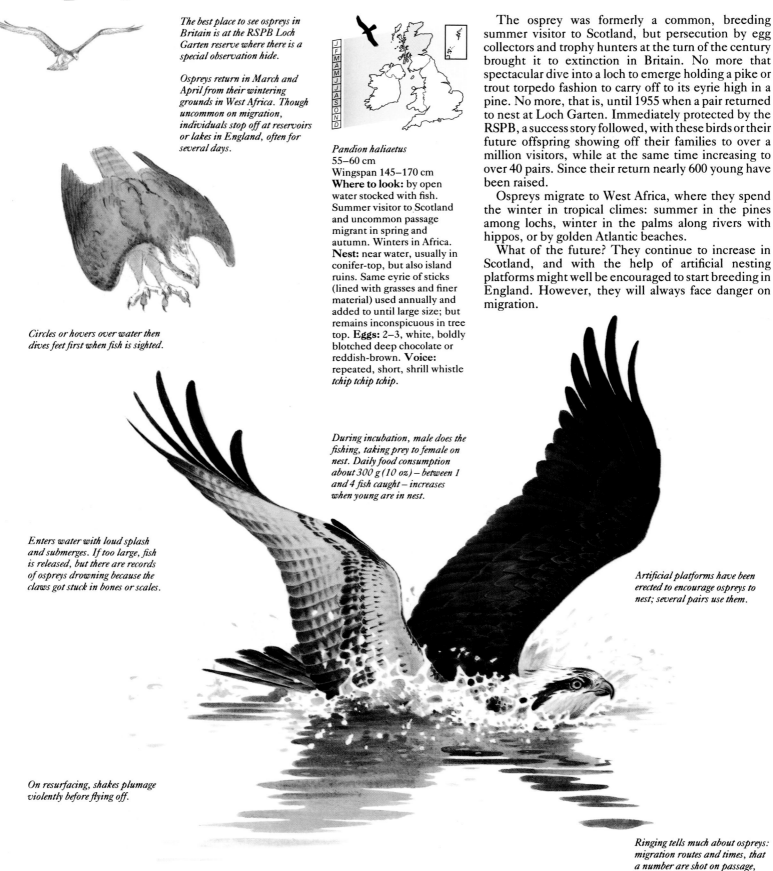

The best place to see ospreys in Britain is at the RSPB Loch Garten reserve where there is a special observation hide.

Ospreys return in March and April from their wintering grounds in West Africa. Though uncommon on migration, individuals stop off at reservoirs or lakes in England, often for several days.

Circles or hovers over water then dives feet first when fish is sighted.

Pandion haliaetus
55–60 cm
Wingspan 145–170 cm
Where to look: by open water stocked with fish. Summer visitor to Scotland and uncommon passage migrant in spring and autumn. Winters in Africa. **Nest:** near water, usually in conifer-top, but also island ruins. Same eyrie of sticks (lined with grasses and finer material) used annually and added to until large size; but remains inconspicuous in tree top. **Eggs:** 2–3, white, boldly blotched deep chocolate or reddish-brown. **Voice:** repeated, short, shrill whistle *tchip tchip tchip.*

The osprey was formerly a common, breeding summer visitor to Scotland, but persecution by egg collectors and trophy hunters at the turn of the century brought it to extinction in Britain. No more that spectacular dive into a loch to emerge holding a pike or trout torpedo fashion to carry off to its eyrie high in a pine. No more, that is, until 1955 when a pair returned to nest at Loch Garten. Immediately protected by the RSPB, a success story followed, with these birds or their future offspring showing off their families to over a million visitors, while at the same time increasing to over 40 pairs. Since their return nearly 600 young have been raised.

Ospreys migrate to West Africa, where they spend the winter in tropical climes: summer in the pines among lochs, winter in the palms along rivers with hippos, or by golden Atlantic beaches.

What of the future? They continue to increase in Scotland, and with the help of artificial nesting platforms might well be encouraged to start breeding in England. However, they will always face danger on migration.

During incubation, male does the fishing, taking prey to female on nest. Daily food consumption about 300 g (10 oz) – between 1 and 4 fish caught – increases when young are in nest.

Enters water with loud splash and submerges. If too large, fish is released, but there are records of ospreys drowning because the claws got stuck in bones or scales.

Artificial platforms have been erected to encourage ospreys to nest; several pairs use them.

On resurfacing, shakes plumage violently before flying off.

Ringing tells much about ospreys: migration routes and times, that a number are shot on passage, that most juveniles remain in Africa for their first summer and that the oldest known osprey is 32!

The male often sits near the nest when the female is incubating.

Nest, added to each year, is usually built in top of pine tree, but despite size can be inconspicuous among foliage.

Long-winged with shortish tail. In most positions wings are decidedly angled which, with colouration, gives appearance of large gull.

Unmistakable from below; white body and wing linings contrast with greyish flight feathers, black wrist patches. Note breastband.

Adaptations for capturing fish include strong legs and feet, long claws, spiny scales on underside of toes and reversible outer toe.

Small head and relatively small bill with a long hook for dealing with bony fish. White head, with brown eye stripe, contrasts with all-brown upperparts.

Fish are held head-first in torpedo-like manner. It is possible that prey up to 3kg (6½lbs) in weight might be carried by adult. Occasionally two fish are caught in one dive.

Ospreys breed at three years of age, though adult plumage is attained before then. Immature birds have pale, scaly edgings to feathers of upperparts and less obvious breastband.

Long-winged, almost gull-like in flight and always found near water. Over 40 pairs nest in Scotland, but in spring and autumn several Scandinavian breeders migrate through Britain. With the present rate of increase in Scotland, and helped by artificial nesting platforms, ospreys could soon be breeding in England. Visit the RSPB Osprey Viewpoint at Loch Garten in Speyside.

Sparrowhawk

The male is one of the smallest British raptors, with short rounded wings and long tail. White below closely barred orange, but appears deep orange at distance.

The female is much larger than the male and double its weight. She is duller and browner than the male with grey brown barring below and grey brown above, not so bluish as adult male. Her eye is yellow, whereas that of male is orange.

Woodland dweller, spends most time perched in thick cover. Wing and tail shape adapted for flying between trunks and branches.

Fairly widespread in Britain, but commoner in the north and west. The secretive nature, however, means it is not commonly seen.

Males only half weight of females. In all raptors female is larger, but the most marked difference is shown by those which feed on fast-moving prey.

Open flight is a brief series of rapid wing-beats interspersed with long or short glides.

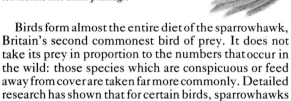

The juvenile sparrowhawk resembles the female in being brown above, but with a rufous wash which can be obvious in good light. The whitish underparts are spotted and blotched brownish forming ragged bars. Juveniles moult after about ten months into adult plumage.

A good way to spot a sparrowhawk is to look for mobbing birds: thrushes 'chacking' in a hedgerow or a group of crows reeling round.

Birds form almost the entire diet of the sparrowhawk, Britain's second commonest bird of prey. It does not take its prey in proportion to the numbers that occur in the wild: those species which are conspicuous or feed away from cover are taken far more commonly. Detailed research has shown that for certain birds, sparrowhawks may account for more than half their total mortality.

Like most raptors, sparrowhawks were seriously affected by the introduction of DDT and other chemicals, such as dieldrin and aldrin, to control insects and other invertebrates that are harmful to agriculture. During the late 1950s and early 1960s a population decline started and sparrowhawk numbers were reduced by 50 per cent in western Britain. In the east, where agriculture was more intensive, the bird was practically wiped out. With the voluntary and legal bans on the use of pesticides the situation is now improving. Once again sparrowhawks can be seen over the woods and fields of East Anglia, Kent and Sussex; indeed in some areas they may be as common as kestrels, though few would realise this because of the sparrowhawk's secretive behaviour.

Once heavily persecuted, and illegal destruction continues on a few estates. Ringed hawks reported shot have declined, while number killed on roads and by hitting windows increases.

After killing, the prey is taken to a stump or log to be plucked – remains give useful data on diet.

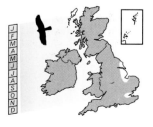

Accipiter nisus
30–40 cm
Wingspan 60–80 cm
Where to look: widespread resident, but less common in south-east England; coniferous and mixed woodland, farmland with hedgerows; look for displaying birds in spring, or soaring birds at any time.
Nest: built of sticks, sometimes uses foundation of old nest of another species, high in conifer near trunk.
Eggs: normally 4–5, whitish, many without markings.
Food: small birds caught on the wing in swift dashes.
Voice: harsh *kek-kek-kek-kek.*

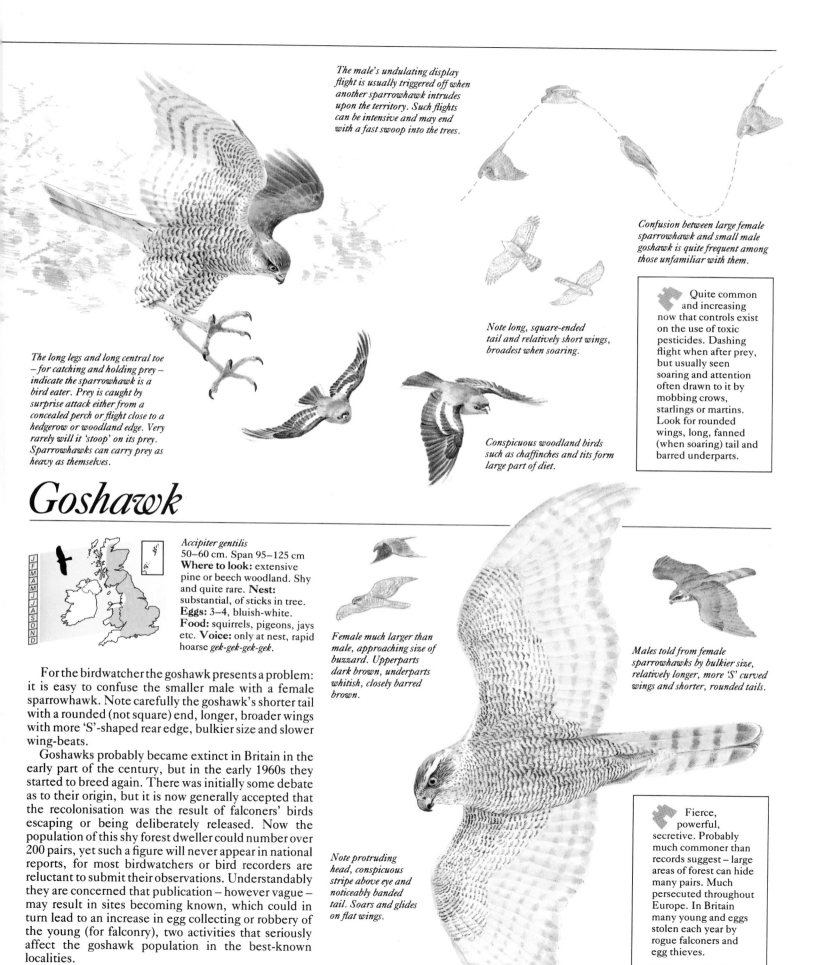

The male's undulating display flight is usually triggered off when another sparrowhawk intrudes upon the territory. Such flights can be intensive and may end with a fast swoop into the trees.

Confusion between large female sparrowhawk and small male goshawk is quite frequent among those unfamiliar with them.

Note long, square-ended tail and relatively short wings, broadest when soaring.

Quite common and increasing now that controls exist on the use of toxic pesticides. Dashing flight when after prey, but usually seen soaring and attention often drawn to it by mobbing crows, starlings or martins. Look for rounded wings, long, fanned (when soaring) tail and barred underparts.

The long legs and long central toe – for catching and holding prey – indicate the sparrowhawk is a bird eater. Prey is caught by surprise attack either from a concealed perch or flight close to a hedgerow or woodland edge. Very rarely will it 'stoop' on its prey. Sparrowhawks can carry prey as heavy as themselves.

Conspicuous woodland birds such as chaffinches and tits form large part of diet.

Goshawk

Accipiter gentilis
50–60 cm. Span 95–125 cm
Where to look: extensive pine or beech woodland. Shy and quite rare. **Nest:** substantial, of sticks in tree. **Eggs:** 3–4, bluish-white. **Food:** squirrels, pigeons, jays etc. **Voice:** only at nest, rapid hoarse *gek-gek-gek-gek.*

Female much larger than male, approaching size of buzzard. Upperparts dark brown, underparts whitish, closely barred brown.

Males told from female sparrowhawks by bulkier size, relatively longer, more 'S' curved wings and shorter, rounded tails.

For the birdwatcher the goshawk presents a problem: it is easy to confuse the smaller male with a female sparrowhawk. Note carefully the goshawk's shorter tail with a rounded (not square) end, longer, broader wings with more 'S'-shaped rear edge, bulkier size and slower wing-beats.

Goshawks probably became extinct in Britain in the early part of the century, but in the early 1960s they started to breed again. There was initially some debate as to their origin, but it is now generally accepted that the recolonisation was the result of falconers' birds escaping or being deliberately released. Now the population of this shy forest dweller could number over 200 pairs, yet such a figure will never appear in national reports, for most birdwatchers or bird recorders are reluctant to submit their observations. Understandably they are concerned that publication – however vague – may result in sites becoming known, which could in turn lead to an increase in egg collecting or robbery of the young (for falconry), two activities that seriously affect the goshawk population in the best-known localities.

Note protruding head, conspicuous stripe above eye and noticeably banded tail. Soars and glides on flat wings.

Fierce, powerful, secretive. Probably much commoner than records suggest – large areas of forest can hide many pairs. Much persecuted throughout Europe. In Britain many young and eggs stolen each year by rogue falconers and egg thieves.

Kestrel

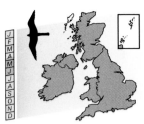

Falco tinnunculus
33–36 cm
Wingspan 70–80 cm
Where to look: many places, even in city centres; can be most easily observed over roadside verges. Most widespread bird of prey in Britain. **Nest:** hole in tree, crevice in wall or cliff face, ledges (even on buildings) and other structures; may use old crow's nest. **Eggs:** 4–5, white with red-brown markings, laid in mid-April in scrape with no lining. **Food:** usually field voles, mice, insects, worms; urban kestrels, especially, take small birds. Hunts by hovering or perching in readiness to pounce on prey. **Voice:** *kee-kee-kee-kee* generally at nesting area.

The commonest raptor in Britain, most frequently seen hovering over motorway verges or perched on roadside telegraph poles.

Pointed wings and hovering flight when hunting instantly distinguish it from sparrowhawk, the second commonest raptor in Britain.

Handsome male has chestnut back and wings spotted black, blue-grey head and faint black 'moustache'. The blue-grey tail has a conspicuous black band.

The female is much duller than the male, being dull chestnut brown above, heavily barred blackish. Colour relieved sometimes by tinge of greyish in head and tail.

Some females have such a strong blue-grey wash to the head and especially tail that they can be mistaken for males, but females always show bars on the tail. Juveniles are similar to females, but never show grey in tail.

Few people can fail to notice kestrels hovering over roadside and, particularly, motorway verges. This, Britain's commonest and most familiar bird of prey, can be seen on most days by anyone with the opportunity to look for it. Kestrels require open areas to hunt over, particularly grassy meadows and banks; and safe nest sites, such as holes in trees and quarry ledges. They readily take to nestboxes and are also venturing into towns, where they nest on ledges on buildings. The RSPB knows that a number of kestrels are taken illegally each year as chicks, which are then reared in captivity. The would-be falconers may attempt to fly the birds, but more often the birds are abandoned, which inevitably means that they will die.

Kestrels have been less affected by pesticides than other raptors, but nonetheless they became scarce in the intensively farmed arable land of eastern England during the late 1960s and early 1970s. Now numbers are back to their former levels, and the population is estimated at about 70,000 pairs. Now that the pesticide problem seems to be under control, the future conservation of the kestrel lies with the maintenance of its food supply, notably voles and mice. Conversion of rough grazing land to cereals and stubble burning can seriously affect the abundance of these small mammals. The removal of old or dead trees from hedgerows is also to the kestrel's detriment, though this can, to some extent, be overcome by the provision of nestboxes, even on isolated poles.

In Britain adult kestrels are largely resident, remaining close to their breeding site, but young birds move away in random directions, some crossing the Channel to Europe. If they survive they will return to nest near the area where they were raised. They have a difficult few years ahead of them, before they are really expert at finding food in unfamiliar areas.

Birds of prey have excellent eyesight, and thus the kestrel hovering over a meadow or bank can easily detect small movements in the grass which indicate the presence of its main prey – the field vole; stooping on half closed wings, it captures it in its talons.

Kestrels will readily use nestboxes, and in areas where nest sites are few their provision can increase the population.

Kestrels eat about a fifth of their body weight a day. Much is known about their diet from the study of pellets (the undigested bones, feathers and fur of their prey) that they regurgitate at roosting sites.

Vigorous courtship displays are performed in the spring. The male dives at the female, either in flight or when perched, uttering a shrill scream and, in flight, she will present her talons to him.

Rather long, pointed wings and tail. Flight is a series of fast shallow wing-beats irregularly interspersed with glides, but is most frequently seen hovering.

Male below is deep or pale buff, spotted lightly with black; underwing coverts are buffish-white also lightly spotted black. Pale grey tail has black band.

Voles form the bulk of the diet, these and other small mammals forming about 70 per cent of the prey. Fewer kestrels breed successfully in poor vole years. In towns the diet is mainly birds.

Though mammals are the main prey, kestrels will readily feed on slugs, worms and insects.

It is illegal to kill or take a kestrel or any bird of prey. It is also unlawful to possess one unless it is registered with the Department of the Environment.

Black flight-feathers contrasting with chestnut upperparts are a good feature at a distance.

Hovering flight and agile movements. Often perches for long periods spying grass for prey. Commonest falcon, well adapted to life in lowland Britain, even venturing into towns. Feeds on wide range of prey: small mammals, birds, insects, worms. Collect pellets from roost sites, soak in water and identify prey from the bones and insect wing-cases.

Merlin

Compact falcon with relatively long, square-cut tail and rather broad-based pointed wings, shorter than those of other falcons.

Female is brown above, sometimes with a little white on hind neck and rusty edges to mantle. Tail is most obvious feature: dark brown with whitish or cream bands.

Merlins hunt by low dashing flights, grasping their prey – small birds – in mid-air.

Falco columbarius
27–32 cm
Wingspan 50–70 cm
Where to look: uplands, especially moors and fells in Scotland, northern England and Wales. Quite rare. In winter, coastal marshes and farmland. **Nest:** scrape in cover of heather on lower slope of moor. Will use old nest of crow. **Eggs:** 3–6, usually 4, cream stippled with red-brown spots. **Food:** small birds, especially meadow pipits, chaffinches and tits, which are caught in flight. **Voice:** a rapid, grating chatter *quik-ik-ik-ik*, when nest site intruded upon.

In winter small waders may be hunted; frequent sight on estuary is merlin 'bombing-up' dunlins.

In early spring, before pipits return to moors, chaffinches and tits form large part of diet.

Female is creamy-white below, heavily streaked reddish brown. Underwing is similar to male's.

The tiny merlin has a certain dash and energy about it which gives it a special appeal. It is a bird of the upland heather-covered moors and therein lies one of the main problems it faces. These areas are under threat from forestry planting or conversion to grass through sheep grazing or re-seeding. True heather moors are disappearing at an alarming rate and their future protection as habitat for the merlin is closely connected with them continuing for grouse shooting. But grouse numbers are falling and this, coupled with the high cost of running moors, is encouraging some owners to move towards an income from trees and sheep – two things definitely detrimental to merlins.

Merlins are not persecuted, and keepers enjoy having them on their moors as much as birdwatchers do. Problems through the use of pesticides are probably largely over and so habitat destruction is almost certainly the major cause of their decline. Another interesting but worrying prospect for the merlin's future is also connected with the encroaching forestry problem. Research has shown that sparrowhawks – which are forest dwellers and increasing in numbers – are predators of merlins. So Europe's smallest bird of prey may not be facing too rosy a future.

Male is pale rusty below with dark streaks, the underwing coverts are whitish-buff streaked reddish brown and the flight feathers whitish with dark bars.

Above, the male – which is noticeably smaller than female – is slate-grey with blackish flight feathers and black terminal tail-band. When close note faint 'moustache' and rusty sides of face.

Smallest falcon in Britain and declining in numbers. Bold, dashing with more active and determined flight than other falcons. Also soars less. Blue-grey male has black band on tail while brownish female has dark and white banded tail. Summer haunts are upland moors, the conservation of which is vital for its existence. In winter often hunts waders over estuaries, finches over lowland fields.

Hobby

The graceful hobby is a trans-Saharan migrant which spends the winter in Africa and is present in Britain for about five months in the summer. It arrives in May, and the breeding season is late, with young in the nest from mid-July onwards, coinciding with the appearance on the wing of young swifts, swallows and martins, which are easily caught by the parent hobbies. Look out for hobbies at swallow and martin roosts in early autumn. In addition dragonflies and other insects are taken in flight – dexterously grasped in an outflung talon, they are quickly transferred to the bill for plucking and devouring.

Hobbies are secretive, and a nesting pair can easily go undetected, especially on farmland. As a consequence, informed opinion now believes the population may be as high as 500 pairs, well above the often quoted figure of 100–150 pairs. Unlike many of Britain's birds of prey the hobby does not seem to be under threat from habitat destruction, pesticides or human persecution, though a few clutches go to egg collectors each year.

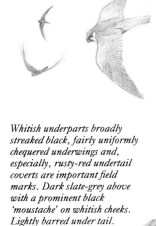

Whitish underparts broadly streaked black, fairly uniformly chequered underwings and, especially, rusty-red undertail coverts are important field marks. Dark slate-grey above with a prominent black 'moustache' on whitish cheeks. Lightly barred under tail.

Falco subbuteo
30–35 cm
Wingspan 70–85 cm
Where to look: heaths and downs in southern England, also farmland. **Nest:** old crow's nest, does not build. **Eggs:** 2–3, yellowish with red-brown blotches. **Food:** birds, especially martins; insects. **Voice:** rapid *kew-kew-kew*, musical for falcon.

Often catches insects such as dragonflies in flight, holding them in talons to dissect and eat.

Small slender falcon whose narrow scythe-like wings give shape not unlike swift; tail relatively short and square-cut. Larger female has broader wings.

A summer visitor mostly to southern England and thus only likely to be confused with kestrel – the only other similarly shaped raptor present. Look for hobbies over heathland, around gravel pits and farmland with conifer clumps.

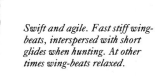

Swift and agile. Fast stiff wing-beats, interspersed with short glides when hunting. At other times wing-beats relaxed.

Small, agile falcon. Summer visitor. Quite rare, but most easily seen over heathland in southern England, especially New Forest. Will prey on starlings and martins at reed bed roosts in autumn. Skillfully catches insects in flight. Heavily streaked below, reddish under-tail coverts and black 'moustaches' on white cheeks.

Peregrine

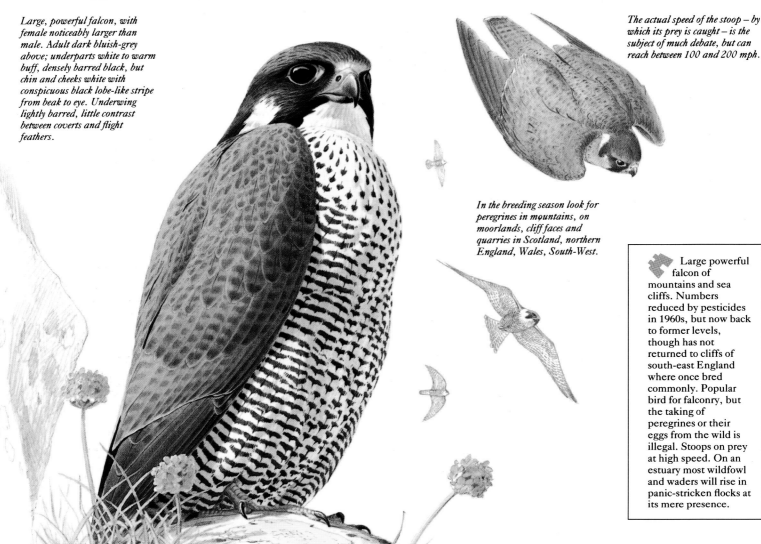

Large, powerful falcon, with female noticeably larger than male. Adult dark bluish-grey above; underparts white to warm buff, densely barred black, but chin and cheeks white with conspicuous black lobe-like stripe from beak to eye. Underwing lightly barred, little contrast between coverts and flight feathers.

The actual speed of the stoop – by which its prey is caught – is the subject of much debate, but can reach between 100 and 200 mph.

In the breeding season look for peregrines in mountains, on moorlands, cliff faces and quarries in Scotland, northern England, Wales, South-West.

Large powerful falcon of mountains and sea cliffs. Numbers reduced by pesticides in 1960s, but now back to former levels, though has not returned to cliffs of south-east England where once bred commonly. Popular bird for falconry, but the taking of peregrines or their eggs from the wild is illegal. Stoops on prey at high speed. On an estuary most wildfowl and waders will rise in panic-stricken flocks at its mere presence.

Juvenile birds are dark brown above, rusty-buff below, streaked (not barred) dark brown, 'moustache' thinner than adult's.

The life and times of the peregrine are among the best documented of any bird. Before World War II it was heavily persecuted by keepers and collectors; during the war it was shot to protect pigeons carrying messages; after the war it was hit by pesticides and then subjected to high levels of theft of its eggs and young. It was the use of pesticides that was the most damaging, reducing the population to an all time low in the early 1960s. Quick action by conservationists in studying just why peregrines were starting to lay thin-shelled eggs (which therefore broke) or failing to raise young resulted in the discovery that levels of pesticides were building up in their tissues through eating prey that had fed on contaminated insects. Being persistent, these chemicals accumulated in 'top' predators like the peregrine. Once discovered, action was swift and voluntary bans on the manufacture and use of these dangerous substances were introduced. So, in many ways, the peregrine was a barometer of the health of the environment, and for that we should be grateful.

Falco peregrinus
40–50 cm
Wingspan 80–115 cm
Where to look: mountains, moorland and sea cliffs, but not in south-east England in breeding season. Estuaries and coasts in winter. **Nest:** ledge or crevice on cliff or quarry face; may use old raven's nest. **Eggs:** 3–4, lightly dappled tawny to reddish brown, laid in bare scrape. **Food:** medium-sized birds such as pigeons, crows, seabirds, grouse; taken on wing in powerful stoop; also mammals. **Voice:** in breeding season a shrill chattering *kek-kek-kek-kek*, harsh *kaark*.

Many spend the winter near their breeding sites. In early spring they perform spectacular aerial displays, soaring together and stooping at high speed only to swoop up again to a great height. Sometimes a pair will engage talons and often displays are accompanied by calling.

When the population 'crashed' through pesticide poisoning, peregrines became vulnerable to the illegal activities of egg collectors and chick thieves. Over 80 eyries were robbed in some years in the 1970s and early 80s.

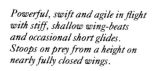

Powerful, swift and agile in flight with stiff, shallow wing-beats and occasional short glides. Stoops on prey from a height on nearly fully closed wings.

Can have shape of short-stemmed anchor, with wings swept in even curve; late summer adults show notch near wingtip as flight feathers moult in sequence.

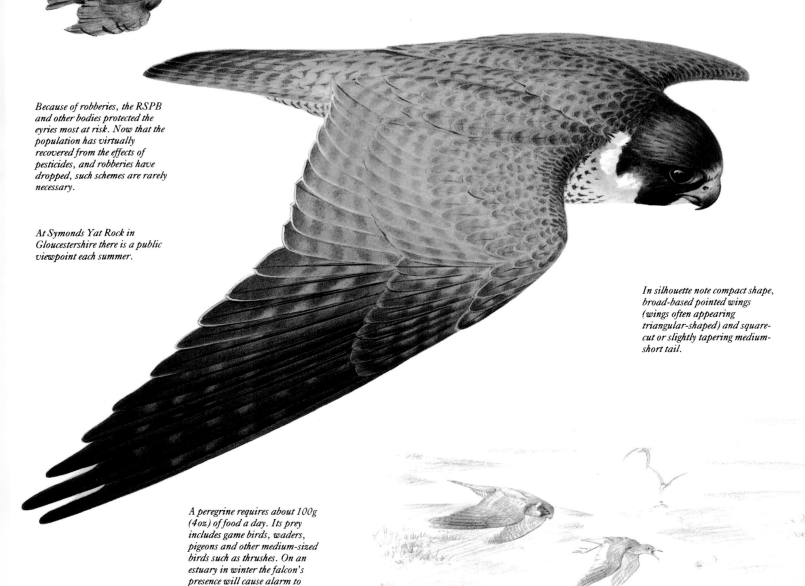

Because of robberies, the RSPB and other bodies protected the eyries most at risk. Now that the population has virtually recovered from the effects of pesticides, and robberies have dropped, such schemes are rarely necessary.

At Symonds Yat Rock in Gloucestershire there is a public viewpoint each summer.

In silhouette note compact shape, broad-based pointed wings (wings often appearing triangular-shaped) and square-cut or slightly tapering medium-short tail.

A peregrine requires about 100g (4oz) of food a day. Its prey includes game birds, waders, pigeons and other medium-sized birds such as thrushes. On an estuary in winter the falcon's presence will cause alarm to wildfowl and waders.

Red Grouse

Lagopus lagopus
37–42 cm; 550–690 g
Where to look: moorland
with good cover of heather;
also on damp cotton-grass or
sedge. **Nest:** on ground.
Eggs: 4–9, cream, blotched
brown. **Food:** heather, seeds,
berries. **Voice:** explosive,
rapid barking notes.

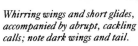

*Whirring wings and short glides,
accompanied by abrupt, cackling
calls; note dark wings and tail.*

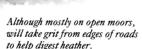

*Although mostly on open moors,
will take grit from edges of roads
to help digest heather.*

*Males are more rusty-red than
buff-speckled females.*

The head-to-toe feathering of the red grouse enables
it to withstand the frequently appalling weather
conditions of Britain's moorlands. Regularly feeding
beneath snow, this dark, rusty-coloured bird avoids its
predators – peregrines and eagles – but faces months of
hardship. The closely related willow grouse, of Scandinavia, actually changes to white plumage in winter
like the ptarmigan. The red grouse was once unique to
Britain, but has been introduced to other parts of the
world; it has also lost its status as Britain's only unique
species, being reclassified as a race of the willow grouse.
The 'Glorious Twelfth' is 12 August, the start of the
grouse shooting season, and most grouse are on ground
maintained by keepers. Management of heather by
burning allows fresh new growth with succulent shoots
– ideal food – but over-burning and over-grazing destroy
the heather which the grouse rely on. When flushed, the
grouse utters a rapid staccato call which changes to a
distinct 'go-back go-back' – probably good advice as the
mist and clouds roll in over the high, exposed moor.

*'Go-back' call often given on
alighting, when well-marked
underwings may be seen. Darker
than partridges, without rufous
tail; wings plainer, dark brown.*

Ptarmigan

*Black tail, white wings all year,
only body feathers change colour.*

*Rarely seen below 2,000ft except
on northern coastal hills.*

The snow lies thick on the high Scottish mountains
for three months or more and the ptarmigan in their
smart white winter dress crouch unnoticed. As spring
begins to melt the snow, and rocks and vegetation show
again, they develop mottled plumage to merge with the
new background. When all the snow has gone in midsummer, ptarmigan disappear against the lichen-
covered rocks with grey-brown and black plumage
patterns. These mountain grouse really are masters of
disguise, but despite their superb camouflage many still
fall prey to the golden eagle. In late autumn and winter
large parties of ptarmigan may gather, using the theory
that many pairs of eyes are better than one. The largest
flock recorded in Scotland was of 470 birds! Normally,
flocks number several dozen at most, with males and
females in different groups. The males put themselves
in the front line against predators and harsh weather by
feeding in the more exposed places. If many males die,
in the following spring the remainder become highly
polygamous, often having three or more mates.
Ptarmigan seem oblivious to humans and are often
surprisingly approachable.

*Hiding perfectly on mountain
screes, only movement and
blinking white eyelids give them
away. Never so rich brown as red
grouse; males often quite grey or
patchy in summer, females more
buff. In winter all white except
for tail, but male has red wattle,
black eye patch.*

Lagopus mutus
34–36 cm; 400–600 g
Where to look: Scottish
mountains, lower in extreme
north. **Nest:** on ground.
Eggs: 5–9, cream with brown
spots. **Food:** heather, other
plants. **Voice:** quiet, rattling
karrrrakakaka, belching *AAr-
aa-ka-ka.*

Black Grouse

As a silvery dawn breaks, with dew heavy on the ground, male black grouse gather to display at favoured, traditional sites called leks. In Britain, groups may number up to 40 birds, but in the USSR leks may hold 200. The curious ritual is practised throughout the year except for a break in late summer and autumn, when the birds are moulting. Males fluff up their white undertail coverts and raise their lyre-shaped tails, inflate their blue necks and make a bubbling, dove-like cooing in a regular, repeated pattern. The males – blackcocks – bustle about in mock fights, while the females – greyhens – watch nearby. The display will continue even without greyhens present – and so vain are the blackcocks that they will even strut about alone! Although the black grouse has disappeared from many of its old haunts, due to over-shooting and loss of habitat, its population is increasing in a few parts where new conifer plantations provide temporary havens.

Female greyer than red grouse; has slightly forked, paler tail and faint pale wingbar.

Male is always unmistakable.

Tetrao tetrix
40–55 cm; male 1,300 g
female 1,000 g
Where to look: typically edges of moor or heath near trees; bogs, plantations.
Nest: on ground in long grass. **Eggs:** 6–10, buff with brown spots. **Food:** buds, shoots of birch, pine.
Voice: far-carrying dove-like bubbling; hissing sneeze.

Feeds mostly on buds, often in trees; at dusk, gathers in pines or birches beside the moor.

Males at the lek.

Capercaillie

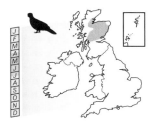

Tetrao urogallus
60–87 cm; male 4 kg
Where to look: old conifer forests of north Scotland.
Nest: on ground near tree.
Eggs: 5–8, buff speckled brown. **Food:** pine needles, buds, also seeds, berries.
Voice: male – clicking song; female – pheasant-like crow.

These giants of the forest, though the size of turkeys, can be elusive, disappearing into the pines away from a frustrated observer – either clattering through the branches or creeping silently away on the ground. A quiet observer may be lucky enough to see one crash out of a tree to fly off on large, rounded wings. In the early spring, dripping water may stimulate the male's song, which starts with a similar *pelip-pelip* sound and continues into a fast *plip-plip-plip-itit-t-t klop*! The last note sounds like a cork popping from a bottle. The turkey-like display attracts females and keeps other males at bay, indeed even other animals. Occasionally an unpaired male will become over-territorial and will display to anything that moves, even cars! Many people have been attacked by raging male capercaillies. The species became extinct in Britain in the late 18th century due to over-hunting and loss of habitat. Today's population of several thousand birds has built up from a few birds introduced from Sweden in the 1830s. Most are found north of the River Forth, generally preferring old forest to plantations. It is a bird that shows the value of ancient pines as opposed to plantations.

The cock's black and brown plumage glistens green in good light. The white shoulder patch and pale bill are often obvious.

May be flushed from clearings in forest where juniper and bilberry provide good feeding.

Displaying males are solitary or, where common, in small groups.

Large size and broad, fanned tail separates hen from other grouse; note orange breast and richly coloured plumage with many black bars. Male is unique.

Pheasant

The vivid plumage of the splendid male serves to attract females – up to 18 have been recorded in one harem. The male scuttles around each hen, trailing the near wing, twisting over his tail and inflating his facial wattles to show off his finery. Once the females have settled down on a nest the male appears to ignore them. This is for the best – his colours would soon attract the attention of predators such as fox or stoat, whereas the female and young are well-camouflaged. Although introduced to Britain, probably before the Norman Conquest, pheasants are now a familiar and characteristic part of the British landscape – even favourite Christmas card birds! It seems odd to think that they are not 'British' at all.

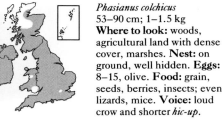

Phasianus colchicus
53–90 cm; 1–1.5 kg
Where to look: woods, agricultural land with dense cover, marshes. **Nest:** on ground, well hidden. **Eggs:** 8–15, olive. **Food:** grain, seeds, berries, insects; even lizards, mice. **Voice:** loud crow and shorter *hic-up*.

Released by gamekeepers in thousands, young birds stay together until spring if they survive the guns. Old males are very obvious; females less so.

Long-tailed male quite unlike any other British bird; more likely to run than fly from danger.

Smaller, short-tailed females like big partridge but pointed tail never rusty; beware half-grown young birds that can already fly and can cause confusion.

Quail

Short, quick flights on rather long wings characteristic.

May stand higher to peer over short vegetation.

Small size makes confusion unlikely with other gamebirds except half-grown, but flying, young partridges which have rusty tails. Usually crouch.

Female lacks facial markings and chestnut streaks of male.

Coturnix coturnix
16–18 cm; 70–150 g
Where to look: arable land on limestone or chalk; open downs. **Nest:** scrape on ground. **Eggs:** 7–12, buff, variably blotched brown. **Food:** shoots and seeds, also insects. **Voice:** loud, liquid *whic whic-ic*; doll-like *mama*.

A rare breeding bird, appearing sporadically, mainly in southern counties, the quail has periodic 'good years' which bring more to nest here. A decline noted during the early years of this century was thought to be due to over-persecution by egg collectors and shooters rather than any agricultural changes. Today it is much more a characteristic bird of rolling cereal fields shimmering in the heat of Spain or southern France, where the dawn and dusk chorus of penetrating, triple calls can be quite dramatic. If flushed – not an easy thing to accomplish – the quail flies on relatively long, narrow wings before dropping back into the vegetation with a lark-like flutter, as much like a big lark or small snipe as a partridge. Usually quails will scurry away through dense vegetation without ever being detected, and they are nearly always 'heard but not seen'. This is Britain's only migrant gamebird, and most move to central and southern Africa after the breeding season. On migration European quails suffer enormous losses to trappers and gunmen in North Africa, especially in Egypt and Libya. It is difficult to judge just how damaging this is to the long-term well-being of the quail population.

Red-legged Partridge

Less secretive than grey partridge, happy on open ground, heaths and rough places near gravel pits; sturdy legs carry it very fast when threatened.

Introduced into Britain nearly 200 years ago and now common, particularly in southern and eastern England where harsh calls are familiar.

Flies with long glides between bursts of whirring wing-beats, showing rusty tail and plain sandy-buff upperparts.

Uniform buff-brown back, well-marked face and red bill and legs all distinctive.

Crouching bird looks like a clod of earth; surprisingly large when seen well.

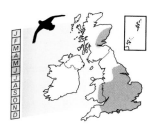

Alectoris rufa
32–34 cm; 500 g
Where to look: often drier arable land, heaths, dunes. **Nest:** on ground in dense vegetation. **Eggs:** 10–15, spotted brown. **Food:** shoots, seeds; also slugs, insects. **Voice:** harsh, loud, chuffing *CHUkaarr . . CHUkaarr.*

There are as many red-legged partridges as there are grey, but the red-legs are less widespread. Red-legs are much easier to see, as flocks up to 20 strong wander over ploughed fields and open pastures. Despite their rather bright colours, however, they can conceal themselves remarkably well even on open ground. Crouched low into a depression, the black and white face and striped flanks help to break up the outlines of the birds and make them less eyecatching. When approached they will run away rather than fly, but if taken by surprise at close range, they burst into the air with whirring wings, then glide down to the ground before scampering away on bright red legs. Watch them walk over rough ground and you will see that the head remains very steady while the legs and body act as a 'suspension', absorbing all the irregularities – better for seeing food and possible danger. Red-legs often perch on high objects – walls, haystacks, even old farm buildings, an unlikely thing for a grey partridge to do. The 'French partridge' is often more familiar than the grey these days.

Grey Partridge

Although feeding predominantly on plants, during the first few weeks of its life insects form a vital part of every partridge's diet. A mixed diet of animal and vegetable helps chicks to develop more quickly. Unfortunately, many of the insects they eat are crop pests, like aphids, weevils and sawfly larvae. In cereal crops these have been greatly reduced by effective use of pesticides – and so the partridge has declined. Other changes in farming practice have not helped. Loss of hedges reduces nesting places, herbicides kill off food plants like grasses and chickweed, and more efficient harvesting leaves less waste grain in fields. Because the numbers have declined many have been imported from Europe for shooting and in some places so many have been released that it is difficult to class the bird as 'native'. Other species of partridge, especially the chukar, have also been introduced in hundreds – surely not the best way to protect wild birds that are already under pressure. Autumn coveys (or flocks) give an idea of the breeding success – up to 20 birds at times, but after a bad year as few as three or four. Without its partridges, the countryside would be the poorer.

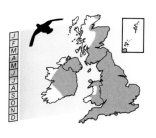

Perdix perdix
29–31 cm; 350–400 g
Where to look: arable land, lower moorland edges, rough pasture. **Nest:** in thick cover. **Eggs:** 12–19, olive-buff. **Food:** mostly vegetable, but chicks eat insects. **Voice:** loud, like creaky, rusty gate *SKERrr-ik*; *ik-ik-ik* in flight.

Whirring flight, frequent glides; streaked back, rusty tail.

Takes to flight rather than running if threatened, usually with short, clicking calls.

Often well hidden in tall plants.

Smaller than red-legged, with orange face, speckled upperparts and less bold flank stripes. Creaky calls quite different. Male has more obvious horseshoe mark on belly than female.

Water Rail

A winter cold spell of four or five days' duration is usually enough to drive this normally very secretive bird out of a frozen reed bed to areas of unfrozen running water. The true shape of the water rail cannot be appreciated during winter as it fluffs up its striped flanks to retain body heat. The skeleton illustrates how incredibly slim it really is; looking almost as though it had been squashed from both sides, it enables the bird to slip between reed stems quickly and quietly.

The long red bill is used to probe into mud or shallow water for grubs, but can be turned on unsuspecting small birds and mammals with deadly accuracy. Water rails have been observed eating larger dead birds like moorhens, which had probably frozen to death.

Flying as a last resort, water rails will normally dart into a clump of vegetation and will only move when virtually stepped on. Sometimes one gives an unexpectedly clear view when it hides its head behind a stem, leaving the rest of its body exposed!

Even a brief view shows the silhouette, with its long, slightly down-curved bill, short neck and cocked tail, quite unlike any other British bird. Better views reveal richly-marked plumage, with lovely colours.

Rallus aquaticus
23–28 cm; 90–150 g
Where to look: thick reed beds and marshes; also overgrown ditches, older thickets. **Nest:** in very dense cover of dead reeds and other aquatic vegetation. **Eggs:** 6–11, buff, with a few grey or brown spots and blotches. **Food:** mostly insects and grubs, but also berries and seeds. Larger prey such as fish, small mammals, eggs, birds and carrion also eaten. **Voice:** varied pig-like squeals and grunts; other calls include whistles, squeaks and hisses.

After breeding, adults may move if the marsh dries out, but they pause to moult in a safe place before migration. All the flight feathers are shed at once, so they are flightless for three weeks.

Moves swiftly through the densest cover with high-stepping stride.

Its slim body glides between reed stems without touching them, so that not even a twitching reed head will point a hungry marsh harrier in the right direction.

The buff undertail is shown when the tail is jerked up. Brown horizontal streaks on upperparts and vertically striped flanks help to hide the bird in vegetation.

More often heard than seen, the strange squeaks, hisses and squeals will give away its presence. These noises inform other water rails of its position; the calls become quieter and die away as birds meet in the cover of a reed bed. A quiet, still, patient observer may be rewarded by good views.

When forced into the open by frost they can be quite confident, strutting around conspicuously. Notice the glowing red eye.

Long toes prevent feeding birds sinking into deep mud.

The distinctive shape is the best identification feature. The long red bill, blue-grey underparts, streaked brown upperparts and striped flanks help to tell it apart from other British crakes. Remember to listen for the pig-like squeals or the sharp *kikk-ik-ik* calls giving its presence away in the densest marsh.

Although capable of long distance migration, the flight of a rail when flushed appears weak, with legs dangling.

Spotted Crake

The dumpy little bird is carried into the air on fluttering wings with legs trailing.

From behind, the orange-buff undertail coverts are the best identification feature, together with size and shape.

A quiet observer, seated near a marshy-edged reed bed in September, may be treated to superb views of this otherwise secretive little bird. Advancing around the edge of the marsh, not sensing any danger, it may stroll within inches of the lucky watcher, showing off the tiny, pearly speckles on the breast and mantle which give the bird its name. In spring and summer it is very rare and becomes much more secretive; only the whip-crack-like calls inform a careful listener it is there.

About the size of a starling, the spotted crake is the smallest of the crake family breeding in Britain. The short bill is used to peck at insects and grubs on the surface of the marsh, or the bird may clamber up reed stems to grab at craneflies or seed heads. All crakes are scarce and hard to see, and have a weak-looking flight, but they are great wanderers and can turn up almost anywhere on migration, always good birds to find on a regularly-watched local patch.

Porzana porzana
22–24 cm; 60–100 g
Where to look: uncommon autumn migrant in dense, damp marshes; rarely breeds here. **Nest:** of reeds, grasses and other vegetation, usually in a tussock. **Eggs:** 8–12, olive with a mixture of dark brown and pale grey speckles.

Food: mostly water insects and larvae; also seeds. **Voice:** clock-like *tik-tok* and whiplash *kwIT-kwIT-kwIT*.

It is only at very close quarters that the pretty spots and stripes on this handsome bird are seen.

About the size of a starling. Best points to look for are orange undertail feathers and yellow bill with red base. Beware small young moorhens which are a paler brown.

Corncrake

The future of the corncrake in Britain seems now to be in the hands of farmers. Strangely, it was the farmers who first helped it spread its range. As forests were felled centuries ago, giving way to cultivated grassland, corncrakes rapidly moved in, taking advantage of the newly created habitat. The introduction of mechanical grass cutters and the repeated cuts of grass to make silage have forced the corncrake out of many areas in recent decades; changes in Africa's climate may also have been disastrous though the habitat remains good.

The rasping call would have been familiar to all country dwellers in the early 1900s. Today it is only a few crofters farming in traditional ways in western Ireland and the Hebrides who hear the corncrake summoning spring after its long-distance migration from wintering grounds in central Africa. The call which gave the corncrake its Latin name is likened to the teeth of a comb being drawn rapidly across the edge of a matchbox twice, but at close range is a much louder, harder sound.

Crex crex
27–30 cm; 150–200 g
Where to look: hayfields, iris beds. Formerly common throughout Britain, now rare. **Nest:** hidden in dense tussock. **Eggs:** 8–12, creamy with brown blotches. **Food:** mostly insects, worms; a few seeds. **Voice:** distinctive, repeated *crek-crek*.

Very skulking, but easier to see soon after its arrival in May when vegetation is still low.

Also called the landrail, the corncrake resembles a moorhen in shape, but its striped buffish plumage with greyer head and its habitat (especially hay meadows) are good identification pointers.

In flight, rounded rufous wings obvious; legs are trailed behind like other crakes'.

Moorhen

Moorhens are very adaptable birds, being able to climb trees, walk or run on flat ground, swim, wade and clamber through undergrowth. Yet they never appear to be quite at home, often moving awkwardly or cautiously with their big feet getting in the way. The long, spread toes enable them not only to wade on marshy ground without sinking, but also to swim confidently – they are among the few British birds able to swim well without webbed or lobed toes. Their cautious nature is exaggerated by jerky movements and frequent stops to survey the surrounding land. At the first sign of danger the tail is flicked to warn other birds, before an ungainly waddling exit, with head held low, into the nearest area of dense cover. A moorhen caught out by a predator on open water will dive and stay submerged by clasping on to underwater plants until the threat has gone. Two or three broods are reared each year. The black, downy young follow their parents persistently, waving tiny wings as though rowing through the air, trying to attract attention. They may be fed by older brothers and sisters from earlier broods.

Gallinula chloropus
32–35 cm; 200–400 g
Where to look: fresh water from small pools to large lakes or rivers, always requires good plant cover. Feeds on wet meadows. **Nest:** floating heap of vegetation, or up to 5 metres (15ft) high in trees or bushes beside water. **Eggs:** 5–11, glossy buff with brown and black blotches. **Food:** water weeds, seeds, fruit, grasses, insects, worms and larvae. **Voice:** variable, often urgent *kittik*, a loud, abrupt or metallic *kaak* and *kic-kic-kic*.

At close range the bright bill, brownish back, black head and slaty underside look very different from the 'black and white' of a distant bird.

Although moorhens regularly use trees to roost and even nest in, unwary observers are often caught out by finding this 'water bird' in a tree or even a hedge.

The long legs and toes (typical of the crake family) allow easy movement on moist ground.

When swimming, the head and tail move in a jerky, deliberate fashion. The bird's tail is held nearly as high as the head, unlike the more horizontal body of the coot. Notice the flank streaks.

Juveniles have browner backs, buff underparts, and greenish bill (quite unlike the adult).

Groups venture away from the waterside to feed, but at the first sign of danger they scamper back into cover, much more mobile than coots; often forage on turf.

In flight, the legs trail behind. They are much more likely to run than fly, unless crossing a pond or stream in a panic.

Before moorhens clash in territorial border disputes they go through special displays, showing off their red bills and white undertail feathers. If this fails and an intruder does not give way, they fight noisily and vigorously, clawing with their long toes.

Coot

The huge lobed feet are very obvious in flight or on land. Pale rear edge to wing.

Large gatherings, even thousands, bustle around on inland lakes in winter, concentrated more by cold weather when smaller lakes freeze.

Fulica atra
36–38 cm; 400–800 g
Where to look: larger areas of open water with plenty of vegetation. Also town park ponds. **Nest:** aquatic plants, floating, but anchored to safe foundation. **Eggs:** 6–9, buff with small dark spots. **Food:** shoots of reed, roots, algae; also insects, eggs. **Voice:** *kep* or *coot* call, loud and abrupt.

Downy black and red chicks pester the adult birds continuously for food; older juveniles are grey with white face and breast.

During the breeding season coots do not tolerate each other's company, often fighting viciously with their long, sharp claws. With head almost flat on the water and wings bunched high over its short tail, a coot will drive off birds much larger than itself – even swans and geese. Noisy calls and splashing fights are frequent in summer wherever there are coots.

Large winter flocks, often several hundred strong, will gather on favourable waters to dive for food. When on the surface the broad body appears unsinkable, but air is pushed out of the feathers by flattening them and a leap well clear of the water before submerging helps the coot dive to depths of seven metres (20ft). The lobed grey feet are quite unlike the moorhen's and enable it to swim and dive very efficiently.

Coots spending the winter on ponds near humans will become very tame, even taking food from the hand. Their urge to feed will often lead to a squabbling mass of black and white as they clamber over each other. Moorhens are always far more timid, pushed out to the edge of the bustling, self-important coots.

Coots quarrel over boundaries by slashing at their opponent's breast with long sharp claws.

The silky black plumage helps to show off the white bill and frontal shield; glowing red eye is common feature of nearly all European crakes and rails.

Hastily retreating coots combine a mixture of running and flying across the surface of the water. When threatened by predators flocks dive in a shower of spray.

Wings raised to make itself look bigger, an aggressive coot will menace an intruder by showing its white bill and shield. It is turned away in courtship.

Oystercatcher

Haematopus ostralegus
40–46 cm; 500–600 g
Where to look: on all coasts, some on coastal fields. Also breeds in river valleys. **Nest:** simple scrape. **Eggs:** 2–3, pale buff, spotted brown. **Food:** mussels, cockles, ragworms; worms inland. **Voice:** clear, sharp *KLEEP*.

This big, boldly coloured bird is a familiar sight on estuaries and rocky shores all round the coast, equally characteristic of cold, bleak mud flats, sunny sandy beaches, beautiful Scottish sea lochs and tangy mussel beds. After a steady rise in numbers, at least 280,000 now spend the winter in Britain, many from the Faroes, Iceland and Norway, although 40,000 pairs breed here. Some winter concentrations are huge – in Morecambe Bay alone there can be 50,000 – and to see them pouring in to their high-tide roost, landing on the run and crashing into those already settled, is a noisy and memorable experience. Numbers in an estuary vary according to the food supply – a good cockle year means more oystercatchers. Unlike most waders, the oyster-catcher collects food and takes it to its chicks, because they have yet to learn the specialist feeding techniques that make this bird so successful. Many stalk their prey, waiting for a chance to strike the bill into an open shell; others simply find a shellfish and hammer it open with the powerful, chisel-tipped bill.

Large, with heavy orange bill and red eyes. White patches make dazzling pattern in flight.

Summer bird glossy black above, in winter duller with white collar. Stout, pale pink legs.

Noisy when in piping display or quarreling for food in winter.

Avocet

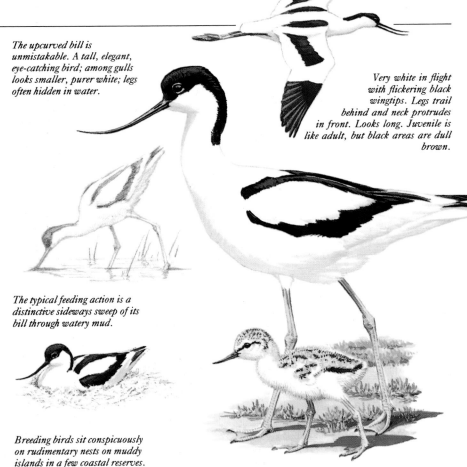

Recurvirostra avosetta
42–45 cm; 300–400 g
Where to look: muddy coasts in south and east England: breeds mainly on East Anglian coastal lagoons. **Nest:** scrape, little lining. **Eggs:** 3–4, buff, spotted. **Food:** small shrimps and worms. **Voice:** *klute*.

Active protection and habitat management are the main reasons why the avocet has managed to gain a strong foothold in Britain. In 1947 two groups totalling 28 pairs were discovered breeding on land flooded as part of war-time defence measures. The areas were purchased by the RSPB and sophisticated systems were developed to improve the nesting and feeding con-ditions, including controlling the salinity of the water. Those areas, Minsmere and Havergate Island, remain the principal breeding places, although birds have spread to many other areas, particularly in north Norfolk. The total number of pairs in Britain is now over 200 and rising. They require brackish water which can support very high numbers of small shrimps, the main food in summer. Up to 300 avocets remain in southern England during the winter, mainly near Havergate, or on the Exe and Tamar estuaries in Devon. Avocets often swim, up-ending to catch their food and looking remarkably like shelducks or gulls. In some places they even roost on the water like ducks. Despite their fragile bills and delicate build, they are very aggressive near the nest, viciously attacking intruding shelducks.

The upcurved bill is unmistakable. A tall, elegant, eye-catching bird; among gulls looks smaller, purer white; legs often hidden in water.

Very white in flight with flickering black wingtips. Legs trail behind and neck protrudes in front. Looks long. Juvenile is like adult, but black areas are dull brown.

The typical feeding action is a distinctive sideways sweep of its bill through watery mud.

Breeding birds sit conspicuously on rudimentary nests on muddy islands in a few coastal reserves.

Stone-curlew

Burhinus oedicnemus
40–44 cm; 400–500 g
Where to look: rare summer migrant to sandy heaths in the Breckland and chalk in south England. **Nest:** simple scrape. **Eggs:** 2, pale, blotched. **Food:** mainly earthworms, beetles. **Voice:** wailing *cur-lee*; whistles.

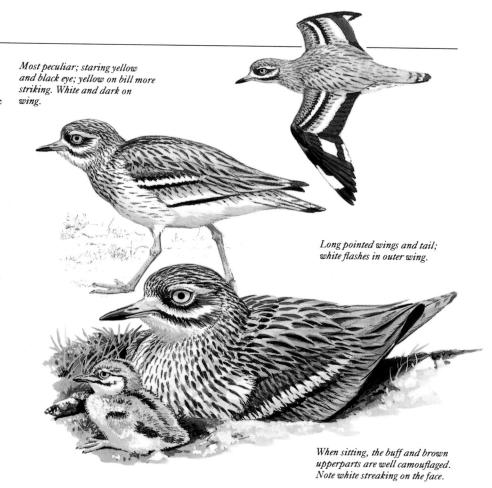

Most peculiar; staring yellow and black eye; yellow on bill more striking. White and dark on wing.

Long pointed wings and tail; white flashes in outer wing.

When sitting, the buff and brown upperparts are well camouflaged. Note white streaking on the face.

Secretive and inconspicuous, the stone-curlew is one of Britain's least familiar birds. Ideally, it requires large, open spaces where grass is kept very short by grazing, and where bare ground can be found. Such conditions are now only found in East Anglia's Breckland (where two-thirds of the 120–150 pairs of British stone-curlews breed) and to a lesser extent the upland chalk of southern England. It will also live on agricultural land which has areas of bare earth, but if it does it needs the active help of the farmer in not ploughing up its nest or eggs. It is inactive for much of the day, sitting or standing quietly by patches of taller vegetation. As dusk approaches so it comes to life, searching grass, open soil or dung piles for earthworms, burying beetles and other invertebrates. Even small mice and nestling birds are taken. Activity is intense through the night, and it is then that the extremely varied calls can be heard. These are a mixture of wailing and slurred curlew-like calls interspersed by oystercatcher-like piping. The large eye is adapted to its nocturnal habits.

Dotterel

Charadrius morinellus
20–22 cm; 90–110 g
Where to look: mountain tops in northern Britain; migrants mainly in eastern England. **Nest:** usually unlined scrape. **Eggs:** 3, buff, heavily spotted. **Food:** mainly beetles and flies. **Voice:** a trill or *kwip-kwip*.

Pale stripe over eye, and breast line clear in winter and on juveniles. Sandy-buff and brown above. No white on wing or rump in flight. Often tame.

Superb in summer; clear, very long, white stripe over eye; chestnut and black belly; pale line across the breast. Legs yellowish. Males are duller than females.

As the winter snows melt on the mountain tops of northern Britain, so these spectacular little plovers appear. They will have spent the winter on poor agricultural land around the lower slopes of the Atlas mountains in northern Africa, and in late April and early May they move north, stopping for a day or two at a number of traditional sites, many in eastern England, before reaching the breeding grounds. At least 150 pairs nest in Britain, but they can be extremely elusive. Although brightly coloured, their patterns provide excellent disruptive camouflage against broken backgrounds. Dotterels are among the few waders where the female is more intensely coloured than the male. Her crown is dark brown, not streaked, and the stripes over the eyes (which meet on the back of the head) and breastband are sharply white. Females tend to take the lead in display and very rarely incubate the eggs or look after the young. The sex roles are, therefore, almost entirely reversed. By the time autumn migrants appear in late August the adults have already almost lost their breeding plumage. Dotterels are usually extremely tame, allowing an approach to within a few yards.

Ringed Plover

Charadrius hiaticula
18–20 cm; 56–70 g
Where to look: sandy parts of estuaries, beaches, gravel pits. **Nest:** scrape, little lining. **Eggs:** 3–4, buffish or bluish, spotted; April–August. **Food:** small shrimps, snails, worms and insects. **Voice:** mellow, rising *too-li*.

The very distinctive stop-go action when feeding provides an easy way of separating this species from other small coastal waders. Like other plovers, it uses sight to locate prey moving on the surface of the sand. For this reason strong winds, heavy rain or very cold weather make finding food difficult. When feeding in slightly muddier areas it often rapidly trembles a foot; this disturbs invertebrates – which then reveal themselves. About 8,600 pairs breed in Britain; the greatest concentration is on the sandy agricultural land (the machair) of the Western Isles, where over a quarter of the total is found. Elsewhere they are mainly on coastal beaches, but increasingly inland on reservoirs, gravel pits or rivers in northern Britain. Males have a striking display flight in which they hold their wings stiffly and flap slowly, calling loudly with a continuous, piping *leea*. In winter some 23,000 are present in Britain, most of which are native breeders and their young. In spring and autumn many more pass through on migration, and they are then frequent inland.

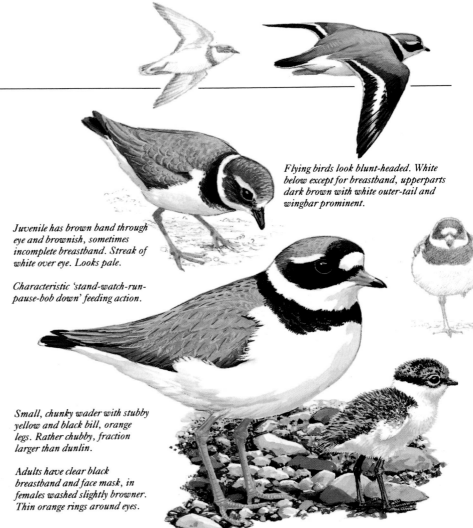

Flying birds look blunt-headed. White below except for breastband, upperparts dark brown with white outer-tail and wingbar prominent.

Juvenile has brown band through eye and brownish, sometimes incomplete breastband. Streak of white over eye. Looks pale.

Characteristic 'stand-watch-run-pause-bob down' feeding action.

Small, chunky wader with stubby yellow and black bill, orange legs. Rather chubby, fraction larger than dunlin.

Adults have clear black breastband and face mask, in females washed slightly browner. Thin orange rings around eyes.

Little Ringed Plover

Charadrius dubius
14–17 cm; 35–45 g
Where to look: inland waters; scarce on migration on coastal lagoons. **Nest:** simple scrape. **Eggs:** 3–4, April–July; buff to green-blue with small spots. **Food:** insects, other invertebrates. **Voice:** a clear *peeoo*, sharp *pew*.

The expansion in gravel extraction over the last 40 years has aided this species considerably. Breeding was first recorded in Britain at Tring Reservoirs, Hertfordshire, in 1938; since then the numbers have rapidly increased so that in 1984 over 600 pairs bred. Initially, nearly all birds were in south and east England, but they have now spread into Wales and Scotland. The majority breed on gravel pits and banks of reservoirs, but some are on their typical continental habitat of shingle river beds. As ringed plovers increase inland, it seems that little ringed plovers find it difficult to compete with the more aggressive, larger species and are being forced away from traditional sites. The two look very similar at first sight, but careful observation will reveal many differences. Perhaps this species will be picked out first by its slightly faster feeding action and relatively small size, then positively identified by its thin, mostly black bill and clear yellow eye-ring. In flight the dark wing without a white wingbar and sharp calls would dispel doubts. It is an early summer migrant, returning in March and April from wintering grounds in tropical Africa and quickly settling into nesting territories.

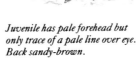

Juvenile has pale forehead but only trace of a pale line over eye. Back sandy-brown.

Breastband of juveniles often incomplete in centre of the breast and is pale brown.

Yellow eye-ring clear at close range in juveniles. They feed faster than ringed plovers.

Legs of adults more pinkish, but in juveniles yellowish.

In flight looks small, dark; note no white wingbar; calls also characteristic.

Very bold yellow eye-ring is characteristic in adults; single black breastband is narrower than on the ringed plover.

Similar to ringed plover, but subtly different. Bill thinner, mostly black; legs longer, more yellow or pinkish. Slightly smaller, longer, slimmer.

Golden Plover

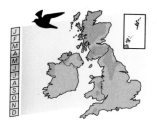

Pluvialis apricaria
26–29 cm; 150–250 g
Where to look: winter – on
permanent grassland,
cultivated land; summer – on
moorland. **Nest:** depression
in peat. **Eggs:** 3–4, buff,
blotched brown, April–June.
Food: insects, some seeds.
Voice: clear, whistled *tooeee*.

*In flight, darkish or golden above
with small whitish patches in the
middle of the wing. Below, the
'armpits' are always white.*

*Northern race is very black below
with white streak on side.
Southern birds are less well
marked in summer.*

A musical, but sad, rising whistle is often the first clue
that a flock of golden plovers is about. Searching the sky
should then reveal this fast-flying species, looking
almost like small white crosses from below. They wheel
around in a tight flock, then, on banking, the dark
golden brown upperparts show as they almost funnel
down and seem to disappear on landing. When on the
ground the flock slowly spreads over the chosen grass
field, each bird showing the typical plover run-pause-
bob feeding action. Watch one and you will see that it
sometimes cocks its head sideways, apparently listening for prey and sometimes clearly watching a spot for
movement. It is estimated that about 250,000 spend the
winter in Britain. These not only include Britain's
breeding birds but also some from Iceland and others
from Scandinavia. About 27,500 pairs breed in Britain,
mainly on moorland, where their complex aerial display
and almost melancholic song seem to suit the open
landscapes. The few breeding on Dartmoor are the
most southerly birds of their species in the world.

*In winter, golden spotted breast
and white belly. In summer, belly
black; face, neck variably black.*

*A medium-sized bird, standing
upright. Always with golden
spotted upperparts, prominent
dark eye and short dark bill.
Fairly wary.*

Grey Plover

Pluvialis squatarola
27–30 cm; 200–250 g
Where to look: nearly all are
on estuaries, mainly in the
southern half of Britain. Does
not breed in Britain. **Food:**
summer – insects; winter –
marine worms, shellfish.
Voice: a flat *TLEE-oo-EE*.
Wistful but far-carrying.

*Long-winged in flight and shows
a clear white wingbar and square
white rump. Characteristic black
mark on the 'armpit' contrasts with
white underwing from below.*

Grey plovers in summer plumage are stunning in the
contrast between their black underparts and silvery-
white and grey upperparts. There can be few birds as
striking as these, which appear during April/May and
July/August. Most seek out large, muddy estuaries in
southern and eastern England. They are of a similar size
to redshanks, but stand out on the mud flats because of
their pale grey plumage and hunched, dejected stance,
combined with a rather slow feeding action. Sight is the
sense which is used when feeding. They watch for tiny
movements on the surface, then lunge to catch the
worms or molluscs before they retreat into the mud.
Because they feed on items at the surface, bad weather
(low temperature, high wind, rain) may affect their
feeding rate significantly. Typically, grey plovers
spend the winter in warm climates, but during recent
years the numbers wintering in Britain have doubled to
21,000. The Wash, Chichester Harbour and the area
around Foulness in Essex have over 2,000 birds each.
Very few are noted inland, even during migration. All
the grey plovers seen in Britain come from breeding
grounds on the tundra of northern Siberia.

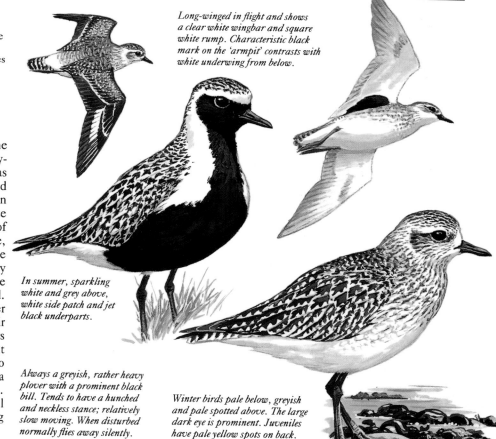

*In summer, sparkling
white and grey above,
white side patch and jet
black underparts.*

*Always a greyish, rather heavy
plover with a prominent black
bill. Tends to have a hunched
and neckless stance; relatively
slow moving. When disturbed
normally flies away silently.*

*Winter birds pale below, greyish
and pale spotted above. The large
dark eye is prominent. Juveniles
have pale yellow spots on back.*

Lapwing

Vanellus vanellus
28–31 cm; 150–300 g
Where to look: found in many areas in winter; mainly on grassland, some on ploughed fields. On coasts in severe weather. In summer on wet meadows, moorland and spring cultivated land. **Nest:** scrape on dry land, little lining. **Eggs:** 3–5, pale brown, blotched dark; March–June. **Food:** wide range of adult and larval invertebrates, many worms, some plant material. Many food items eaten would harm crops. **Voice:** a rising, two-note, thin, slightly harsh *wee-ip* or *pee-wit*.

The flight silhouette is characteristic; the broad, rounded wings and shortish, blunt tail give it an appearance unlike any other British bird. The outer half of the wing bows down slightly.

Manoeuvrable in flight – seen very clearly as they chase magpies or crows away from the nest.

The English names for the lapwing show how well known it is. Lapwing itself describes the flapping, broad-winged flight, green plover the correct plumage colour, while peewit is an excellent description of its call note. In winter it can be found throughout Britain, shunning only the cold mountains and uplands. No accurate figures exist for the numbers present in winter, but there are certainly more than a million. These include not only British breeding birds, but birds from Scandinavia and western Europe east to western USSR. The lapwing is almost always found in flocks, and flocks often number several thousands. In very severe weather, when the food it takes from the surface is almost impossible to find, huge daytime movements take place, with birds seeking milder southern and western feeding grounds. In exceptionally harsh conditions birds can be seen feeding on road verges in towns or even in gardens. Many may die at such times. Territories are taken up during late February and March in southern Britain, but into April further north. It is then that the spectacular display flight can be seen. Britain's breeding population has been estimated at 181,000 pairs. However, numbers have slumped in recent years as agricultural intensification has changed the landscape.

Flies with distinctive, jerky, almost intermittent flaps. This is enhanced by the wings being sharply kinked at the 'wrist'.

Mobbing is started by the male; with practice he can be told from the female by his broader wings which bulge out more on the outer half (the primary feathers).

The spring display flight of the male is spectacular. He rises slowly before suddenly diving down, twisting and turning as if out of control before pulling up.

During the display flight his wings seem to creak under the pressure and he repeatedly utters a complex medley of distinctive harsh, shrill and wheezing notes.

On alighting he often holds his wings up for a second or two.

Flying birds, especially when disturbed or mobbing, can be very noisy, calling loudly.

The male attracts the female to a nest site by scraping. He shows his chestnut undertail feathers and utters a low wheezing call.

Look for the wispy, black crest, which is unique in Britain. At long range looks black and white, but is dark green above. Feeds by typical plover 'stop-go' method. In flight has a jerky flapping action and broad, rounded wings. Then it is very black and white and seems to flicker as it flies. Gregarious, but usually wary.

In summer, adult males are easy to identify by the all black chin, throat and breast. The long black crest is longer than in females.

In very cold weather flocks often fly high and purposefully in a south or south-westerly direction.

Adult females in summer have some white speckling on the chin and throat. Crests are shorter than males' and wings glossed blue-green, not dark blue.

The white-naped chicks feed close to the adults, who stand guard.

Flocks of lapwings are a familiar winter sight. The typical form is a loose flock, often breaking into irregular lines as the birds turn to land. A gregarious species.

The boldly marked male stands on guard, the dull female sits tight until he calls her off the nest.

A fairly large, rounded wader with a distinct wispy crest. No other British bird has this plumage feature.

At a distance they look black and white but close views show the 'black' is really a dark bronze-green. The legs and shortish bill are dark and the eye prominent.

Winter adults have a white chin and throat; breastband is black.

Lapwings feed mainly by sight and use the 'stand-run-a-few-steps-pause-bob' technique. Sometimes listen for prey movement.

Successful feeders often chased by gulls trying to steal worms.

Juvenile is distinctive in autumn with short, stubby crest and much white on the chin and throat. The upperparts are scaled with neat buff-fringed feathers.

Knot

Calidris canutus
23–25 cm; 110–170 g
Where to look: large, mostly sandy estuaries; rocky coasts. Does not breed in UK. **Food:** summer – insects; winter – mainly small molluscs.
Voice: a quiet *knutt* or double *knuup-knuup*.

Juvenile looks slightly slimmer than adult. Has distinct pink-buff wash on breast and browner upperparts with fine curved lines near feather tips. Legs tinged a yellowish-green.

Look for pale grey rump and indistinct wingbars in flight. Flocks usually look very dense.

When seen singly, the knot's bulky size and mainly grey colour make it distinctive, but it is a very gregarious wader more often found in flocks of many thousands. Although 250,000 spend the winter in Britain, few occur away from areas with larger, sandier estuaries, such as Morecambe Bay and the Wash, or the rocky coasts of north and east Scotland. They form extremely tight flocks, which carpet the ground, giving rise to the descriptive name of 'a pack' of knots. As the tightly-packed flocks turn in their complex aerial manoeuvres, the colour changes as first the upper, then the lower parts of the birds come into view. Knots are among Britain's most spectacular migrants. Most come from north-east Canada and Greenland; others, which breed in Siberia, are only seen in May and autumn *en route* from and to Africa. A very restricted range of food is taken, consisting almost entirely of small cockles and, especially, Baltic tellins, which are obtained by probing. Tiny mussels help the birds put on weight before migration, for which fat is the essential fuel.

A bulky, smallish wader with short greenish legs and straight bill. Looks low-slung. In winter very grey with paler underparts: pale face. Legs more greyish.

Transformed in summer to brick red below and blacker above.

Sanderling

Calidris alba
20–21 cm; 50–60 g
Where to look: sandy beaches and outer part of estuaries. **Nest:** only on the tundra of the high arctic. Does not breed in UK. **Food:** summer – mainly insects, winter – tiny shrimps. **Voice:** a quiet, positive *twick*.

Frenzied activity is the sanderling's hallmark as it dashes up and down the beach picking up small shrimps exposed by each wave. The 14,000 that spend the winter in Britain are highly localised, many beaches being apparently unsuitable. The Western Isles are favoured. The pale winter dress is very obvious, even where the bird mixes with other waders at roost. Sanderlings breed on tundra near the Arctic Ocean and can be found wintering on beaches all around the world as far as the extreme southern tips of Africa and South America. Those coming to Britain breed mainly in north-east Canada, Greenland and Siberia. Summer plumaged birds are often mistaken for other waders, but the large white wingbar is always distinctive and the belly is always spotlessly white.

Large white wingbar prominent, dark line down centre of rump. Flicks low along shoreline. In summer reddish back and breast.

Usually very active in front of waves in small groups.

Strikingly pale in winter; pearly grey above, white below with dark shoulder patch; black legs.

Dunlin

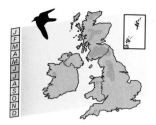

Calidris alpina
16–22 cm; 40–60 g
Where to look: widespread on muddy estuaries, lake shores. **Nest:** in deep vegetation near northern wetlands. **Eggs:** 4, buff, variably marked. **Food:** invertebrates. **Voice:** a slurred, slightly harsh *treeep*.

Variability in size and plumage makes this the most likely species to be confused with other small waders. As it is the most numerous wader on the coast, (approximately 430,000 spend the winter in Britain) it is usually best to assume a small wader is a dunlin unless you can prove to the contrary. Muddier estuaries are favoured, although groups can be found on sandy shores and rocky coasts. Small ragworms and the snails called *Hydrobia* are perhaps its favoured food. When worms are extracted they are often taken to the nearest water and washed before being eaten. Severe weather places much stress on small waders, and at those times dunlins crowd along the tideline where food is most easily found. Those wintering in Britain breed in Siberia and northern Scandinavia, but others from Iceland and Greenland pass through to spend the winter in south Europe and north-west Africa. There they are joined by the 9,000 pairs which breed in northern Britain. Males have a beautiful song, a descending reedy trill which seems to blend into the wild moorland and marshes.

In flight looks quite brown, but with distinct, fairly narrow white wingbar. Black line running through pale rump and grey tail.

Juveniles are often very tame and allow a close view of their neat plumage. Frequently seen inland.

Flocks in flight twist and turn, often changing shape, but usually forming thick, tapering lines. Distinctive call given in flight.

Often a fairly hunched wader with a longish, slightly drooping dark bill and black legs. Active and gregarious. This is the species most likely to be seen on coasts.

Dunlins come in many sizes; those from the east are long-billed, but birds from Greenland have much shorter, straighter bills.

Juvenile has dark spots and streaks on belly; neat lines of pale fringed feathers on back. Breast and head suffused buff.

When feeding keep their heads down and probe into the mud very rapidly. They run quickly between feeding sites; often quarrelsome.

Flocks suddenly take flight for no obvious reason, wheel around and drop down again to feed.

In spring the back of the neck of male is grey, but in female it has a strong reddish tinge.

No other small wader has a black belly in summer plumage. Has chestnut markings above which wear to become darker.

Dull in winter, with grey-brown upperparts, white underparts and breast suffused grey, forming a breastband at a distance. Then more easily confused with other small, much scarcer, waders.

A common species, seen anywhere. Look for the longish bill drooping at its tip, and the black legs. Small and round-shouldered in shape. Black belly in summer, but in winter a dull grey-brown and white. An active bird when feeding, probing deep into the mud. Almost always in very mobile large flocks. Breeds mostly on moorland, spends winter on the coast.

Little Stint

Calidris minuta
12–14 cm; 20–30 g
Where to look: exposed mud inland, some on estuaries. Mostly seen in autumn. Does not breed in UK.
Food: small invertebrates, mainly insects. **Voice:** a quiet but clear *tip-tip* or *stit-stit*.

Two winter stints with dunlins.

Chequered red, buff and dark brown upperparts in summer with chestnut on head and neck.

A tiny wader, much smaller than dunlin and with a diminutive straight bill and black legs. Feeds with very rapid pecks from the mud surface. Often tame.

Muddy lagoons, especially those just behind sea-walls, attract most little stints, although any inland wetland might be used. They are less frequently seen on estuaries, but this is due to the difficulty of spotting them. Once seen, their tiny size, thin straight bills, crouching stance and tendency to remain in a small area for some time are distinctive. Often, small dunlins cause confusion, but a genuine little stint should leave no doubt. Most occur between September and November and are the strongly marked juveniles, blown west by easterly winds over the Continent. Normally these Scandinavian and Siberian birds migrate through central Europe to overwinter from Africa to India. Very few (under 20) spend the winter in Britain, and only scattered, chestnut-faced adults in breeding plumage are seen in May or late July/August while on passage. In order to ensure as many young as possible are raised, females often lay two clutches, the male incubating one and the female the other, so that two adults rather than four can in effect rear two complete families.

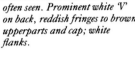

Juveniles in autumn are most often seen. Prominent white 'V' on back, reddish fringes to brown upperparts and cap; white flanks.

In flight looks small; narrow white wingbar and dark line over white rump and grey tail.

Curlew Sandpiper

Calidris ferruginea
18–23 cm; 55–70 g
Where to look: mainly coastal lagoons and muddy estuaries: some inland. Most in autumn. Does not breed in UK. **Food:** wide range of invertebrates, especially worms. **Voice:** a gentle rippling *chirrup*.

When feeding, curlew sandpipers often wade out into quite deep water and probe vertically, submerging their heads. Others probe for worms on mud flats. Females have longer bills than males, enabling them to probe more deeply. The neatly-patterned juveniles are seen from late August to October and greatly outnumber adults. In exceptional years, with strong persistent easterly winds after a good breeding season, up to 3,500 have been seen in Britain, but 500–1,000 is more usual. These breed in central north Siberia and over-winter throughout Africa; others fly to New Zealand for the winter, often in large numbers.

Dark chestnut-red underparts characteristic of breeding adults; seen in May and July/August, but often only patches of red on moulting birds.

Flying birds show a prominent square white rump and a short-tailed, long-winged shape. A clear white wingbar.

Like tall, long-legged dunlin with longer, downturned bill. On juveniles note pale stripe over eye, scaly back, pink-buff breast.

In winter grey above, white below (shown with dunlin here).

Usually noticed first because of its elegant appearance, or long down-curved bill. Closer views reveal long black legs, and in most plumages a distinct pale stripe over the eye. Not very vocal, but sometimes can be picked out in a flying flock of small waders by its soft call. Often feeds with dunlins, but wades further out into deeper water, up to its belly. In flight white rump obvious during banking or landing.

Purple Sandpiper

Superb camouflage helps the purple sandpiper to merge perfectly into a background of dark, wet, seaweed-covered rocks. This habitat is preferred, but in many areas artificial structures such as groynes, piers or outer harbour walls hold small flocks. In total about 16,000 spend the winter in Britain, with the great majority on the flat rocky coasts of Shetland, Orkney, east Scotland and north-east England. Britain's birds come from breeding areas in Norway and, probably, Greenland. Most arrive in October and November. There have been up to three pairs breeding in Scotland since 1979, making a welcome addition to the list of breeding birds. Relying on their camouflage, they allow a very close approach. They are so tame that their behaviour can be studied in detail as they peck among the seaweed, taking many small periwinkles and a range of other invertebrates. Early in the winter juveniles can be identified by buff edges to the upperwing feathers. Females have noticeably longer bills than males, and there may be tiny differences in the way they feed.

Calidris maritima
20–22 cm; 55–80 g
Where to look: rocky coasts especially in the north-east, often on piers and harbours. **Nest:** on ground in moorland. **Eggs:** 3–4, buff, blotched brown. **Food:** small marine invertebrates. **Voice:** low, single or double *whit*.

Dark in flight; neat white wing-bar and sides of rump stand out. Tends to fly low over the water.

Slightly paler, more spotted in summer, reddish on back. Legs and base of bill more orange.

Chunky, neckless, slaty-brown with pale chin, eye-ring, belly. Bill drooping, yellowish at base.

Pale, yellowish legs characteristic.

Most often found in small flocks, feeding inconspicuously near the tide line. Very easy to overlook.

Turnstone

Arenaria interpres
21–25 cm; 80–150 g
Where to look: rocky coasts, outer parts of estuaries: rarely inland. **Nest:** mostly on arctic tundra, moorland. **Eggs:** 4, green, streaked brown. **Food:** wide range of coastal invertebrates. **Voice:** clear rattled *trik-tuk-tuk-tuk*.

Although most abundant on the rocky coasts favoured by purple sandpipers, turnstones are also frequently seen on mussel beds, rocky outcrops or even shingle beaches where drifts of seaweed occur. They are very scarce inland, even when migrating. The birds seen in Britain are from two distinct areas – Scandinavia and Greenland/Canada. Those from Scandinavia pass through in autumn and spring on their way to and from wintering grounds in central and southern Africa, while the Canada/Greenland birds mostly spend the winter in Europe. About 45,000 of those remain in Britain. Turnstones are aptly named, for with their strong bills and necks they move over feeding grounds turning small stones, lifting up patches of seaweed or digging furiously in sand; the invertebrates there dash for cover, but are rapidly caught. In addition many small periwinkles are eaten and limpets prised off rocks. Turnstone camouflage is excellent and thus feeding birds are confident and can be very approachable. In breeding plumage, males have much more white on the head than females. Occasionally pairs may breed in Scotland, but turnstones have not colonised Britain.

Short, chisel-shaped bill and orange legs. In summer, strikingly white-headed and chestnut-backed.

Transformed in flight by white wing patches and white back. Flies low, usually calls loudly.

Sturdy, thick-set; in winter, head dark, back brown and black.

Snipe

As the drainage of lowland grassland and its conversion to intensive agriculture has taken place, so the lowland populations of snipe have decreased substantially in Britain and elsewhere in western Europe. Even so, taking into account the upland breeders, there are probably about 30,000 pairs remaining in Britain. In winter many more flood into the country, especially from Scandinavia and Iceland. Winter totals are not known, but must be much higher. Snipe love flooded grassland where worms have been forced to the surface, and where the ground is soft and there is plenty of vegetation to provide camouflage. In general they rely for protection on being hidden, but fly up if approached too closely. Sometimes they feed out on open mud beside reservoirs. In very cold winters most of their feeding grounds become unsuitable and then they can turn up in gardens, on roadsides and other unlikely places. Many die or become so weak they can be caught by cats or hit by cars. A flock of snipe is given the collective name of a 'wisp', perhaps due to its rapid twisting and turning before the birds drop down again.

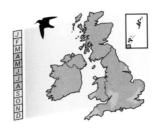

When flying high overhead looks rather jerky, with fast flickering wing-beats. Wings sharply pointed triangles, short tail, but long bill held slightly angled down.

Gallinago gallinago
25–27 cm; 90–150 g
Where to look: around edges of fresh-water areas where mud meets vegetation; marshes, wet fields. **Nest:** in tussock of grass or rush in wet meadows; lined with grass. **Eggs:** 4, olive, blotched brown. **Food:** mostly worms; insect larvae, other invertebrates. **Voice:** harsh *scaap* when startled.

When flying up, parallel buff lines on back often noticeable. Thin white line along rear of wing. Some white on the tail.

On warm summer evenings the males dive in aerial display; the outer tail feathers are spread and they vibrate to give a characteristic tremulous or drumming sound.

Beautifully camouflaged, subtly marked with lines and patches of buff, brown, pale chestnut and black. Strongly striped head and very long bill provide instant recognition; often seen first when flushed or in diving aerial display flight. Look for white trailing edge to wing and white sides of tail, both most obvious as it brakes on landing. Listen for the harsh *scaap* call (like tearing cloth). Mainly found on wet grassland and by inland waters.

Displaying birds often choose to stand on posts or lumps of soil and utter the distinctive chipa-chipa call note. Agitated adults with young will stand on posts, calling in alarm if danger near.

Appears to feed in small groups or singly, but camouflage is so good they are difficult to see.

Note the pale belly; the brown bill darker at its tip and the legs yellow- or greyish-green.

Feeding birds remain in the same spot probing a small area rapidly. The bill is held vertically and inserted to its base. Disturbed, they remain motionless but alert.

The long bill, almost twice the length of the strongly striped head, and the striped and mottled back make it very distinctive.

Woodcock

Large, dark brown; long bill.

Display (roding) low over woods at dusk in regular circuit; calling with whistle and croak; flickering wings.

Relying on camouflage, remaining still until almost trodden on, this bird is rarely seen unless driven into the open by severe weather, but it is worth a look at dusk at the edge of a wood on a fine spring evening. Then you may see its distinctive roding flights, and hear its strange calls. If put up, the large size, broad wings, rusty colour and noisy wing-beats make identification easy as the bird flies fast through the trees; the long bill and dark crown bars are distinctive if seen. Up to 40,000 pairs breed, in both coniferous and broadleaved woods, and many more come to Britain from western Europe in November and December. If one is lucky enough to watch a bird feeding, in a boggy glade or in damp leaf litter, it has a peculiar to-and-fro rocking action with the head kept remarkably still. The woodcock has a most extraordinary and endearing habit – the adult flies with small young held between its legs when danger threatens. Several trips are needed to move a whole family to safety.

Scolopax rusticola
33–35 cm; 290–320 g
Where to look: put up from ground in woods, but easiest in spring display flight over trees. **Nest:** on ground.
Eggs: 3–5, blotched brown.
Food: worms, insects, grubs.
Voice: sharp *pitz* or *tswik*, alternating with deep croak.

Jack Snipe

Lymnocryptes minimus
17–19 cm; 40–70 g
Where to look: in marshy areas where small wet, open patches are found among vegetation. Does not breed in Britain. **Food:** mostly invertebrates, many worms.
Voice: normally silent in Britain, but sometimes a weak *gah* when flushed.

Although widely distributed, this small snipe is scarce and very difficult to see. It may be picked out when feeding among snipe or in vegetation by its remarkable up-and-down rhythmical bouncing action, which is quite unlike any other species. Why it does this is not known. Otherwise it is only flushed from wet marshland when almost trodden upon. Occasionally one may be seen flattened against the ground just in front of the advancing boot! If a good view is obtained look for the dark centre to the crown and the dark, purple tinged back. Birds arrive in Britain in late autumn from their Scandinavian breeding grounds and return during early spring. Considering how weak its flight appears to be when flushed, it is remarkable that it undertakes quite substantial migrations each year. Perhaps one summer a pair will remain to breed in Britain.

A small snipe. When flushed shows prominent pale buff lines on the very dark, glossy back.

Bill is short, just longer than striped head. No white in tail.

Flushes from underfoot and drops back into cover very quickly.

Relies on keeping very still and its almost perfect camouflage.

Black-tailed Godwit

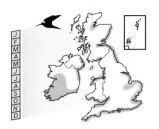

Limosa limosa
36–44 cm; 250–350 g
Where to look: winter –
muddy estuaries in southern
England; summer – wet
meadows. **Nest:** hollow in
grass. **Eggs:** 3–5, olive,
blotched brown. **Food:** range
of invertebrates. **Voice:** quiet
tuk, noisy when breeding.

*Very long, almost straight bill;
long legs give a tall, elegant
appearance. Flight distinctive
with large white wingbar and a
square white rump. Legs trail far
behind: like a slim flying cross.*

*Neck and breast red in summer;
flanks barred, belly white.*

The outer third of the bill of the black-tailed godwit is packed with sensory cells, enabling it to follow underground movements of its prey. In any flock some birds will be resting their bills on the surface while others will probe deeply. Another characteristic feeding action is seen in shallow lagoons, where the head is thrown back quickly to swallow items caught under the surface. Only 50–60 pairs breed in Britain, nearly all on wet meadow nature reserves such as the Ouse Washes in Cambridgeshire. When breeding, they have a complex aerial display and are very vocal with loud, nasal, slightly harsh *grutto-grutto* and *wicka-wicka* calls. Recolonisation of Britain took place in 1952, but despite optimism its hold is still precarious. Winter numbers have increased greatly over the last 50 years, but have remained at about 4,800 since 1970. The wintering birds breed in Iceland and form a distinct race. Birds breeding in Scotland also belong to this race, but those in eastern England are from the continental race; these migrate to Africa for the winter.

*Winter birds have an even
brown-grey wash to back and
breast, stripe over eye distinct.*

*Alarm and display calls given
from fence posts when breeding.*

Bar-tailed Godwit

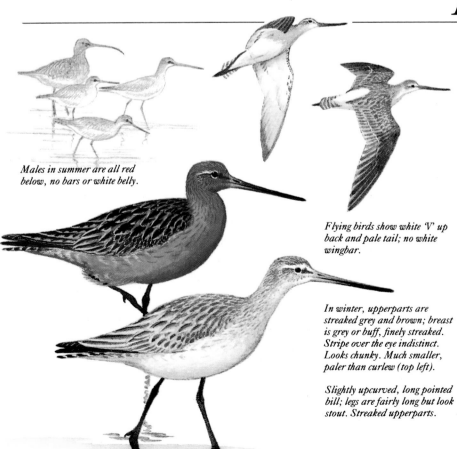

*Males in summer are all red
below, no bars or white belly.*

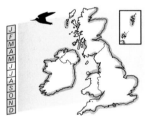

*Flying birds show white 'V' up
back and pale tail; no white
wingbar.*

*In winter, upperparts are
streaked grey and brown; breast
is grey or buff, finely streaked.
Stripe over the eye indistinct.
Looks chunky. Much smaller,
paler than curlew (top left).*

*Slightly upcurved, long pointed
bill; legs are fairly long but look
stout. Streaked upperparts.*

Limosa lapponica
37–41 cm; 200–350 g
Where to look: large sandy
areas, mainly on estuaries.
Does not breed in UK. **Food:**
many coastal invertebrates,
mainly lugworms. **Voice:** a
low barking *kirruc-kirruc*.

There tends to be a clear separation in habitats used by the two godwit species. The bar-tailed is found in sandier areas, while the black-tailed will be inland or on muddier sections. The largest bar-tailed flocks are on major estuaries such as The Wash or Morecambe Bay, where they gather on sand flats rich in lugworms. They scan the surface looking for worms coming up to make their distinctive coiled casts and then they probe deeply to catch them before they withdraw out of reach. Flocks are often at the tide edge where lugworm activity is greatest. One of the spectacular sights of migration is of bar-tailed godwits sweeping east along the coast of south-east England during late April. The dark brick-red males with their relatively short bills can be picked out from the long-billed females, which have only a tinge of red on their underparts. These birds have come from wintering grounds in West Africa and are on their way to breeding areas in arctic Scandinavia and Siberia. British wintering birds breed there as well and arrive here in October and November. When coming in to roost they often plummet down, twisting and turning as they drop to the sand in an action called 'whiffling'.

Curlew

Very long, gently down-turned bill is unmistakable. A very large brown and buff streaked wader. Bland face pattern with no eye stripe.

Large white 'V' on back. Leisurely flight action.

Numenius arquata
50–60 cm; 700–1,000 g
Where to look: estuaries and coastal meadows in winter. Summer – moors, farmland edge. **Nest:** grassy hollow. **Eggs:** 3–5, spotted. **Food:** wide range of invertebrates. **Voice:** melodic *cur-lee*; bubbling song.

The curlew's bubbling song, given mainly during the hanging display flight, seems to express the nature of the lonely, open spaces where it breeds. Most of Britain's 35,000 pairs nest in the north and west, where some are under pressure from modern agricultural methods. Many of the birds which breed in Britain move to Ireland and France for the winter, while British estuaries are filled with 91,000 birds which breed mainly in Scandinavia. These immigrants start arriving very early in the season; it is not unusual for the first birds to be back by August. When feeding they take a wide range of invertebrates: inland, earthworms are favoured, but on mussel beds and rocky coasts it is not unusual to see them eating small crabs. They break off the legs before swallowing them. High tide roosts are formed on salt marshes or on fields, but as the species is very wary, they are easily disturbed.

Scattered when feeding, probing deeply after worms. May search for fish or crabs in rockpools.

Whimbrel

Numenius phaeopus
40–46 cm; 350–450 g
Where to look: on migration wet meadows, salt marshes. **Nest:** partly lined hollow. **Eggs:** 3–4, olive, blotched. **Food:** mostly invertebrates; berries in summer. **Voice:** mainly a rippling *bibibibibibibi*.

'Heard before seen' could be the motto for the whimbrel. Its characteristic rippling note carries a long way and is given frequently. One of its colloquial names is the 'seven whistler', as the single note is often given about seven times. Just to create some confusion, it also gives a *cur-lee* reminiscent of a curlew's call. A very small breeding population of about 400 pairs is found in northernmost Scotland; there the bubbling display song, recalling the curlew, can be heard. However, over most of Britain it is a relatively scarce migrant. Small flocks, rarely more than 50, may be encountered on the edges of estuarine marshes at high tide or seen flying along the coast. The speed of the wing-beats is closer to that of godwits than of the slower curlew. April and early May is when spring migration is at its peak. Some birds stop on coastal grassland at night. One spectacular flock of over 1,000 builds up on Stert Island in Bridgwater Bay, Somerset. These are on the way from sub-Saharan Africa to breed in Iceland; Scandinavian breeders pass through eastern Britain. They are not familiar birds to most birdwatchers, but at the right time on suitable coasts are not particularly rare.

Flying birds usually give distinctive rippling calls.

General colour a dark oily brown, lightly spotted above and darker than curlew. In small parties.

White 'V' on back clear in flight. Beats wings faster than a curlew.

Like dark curlew, but smaller, with a shorter, more sharply down-turned bill. Head pattern distinctive, with prominent pale stripe over eye between two dark stripes. Narrow crown stripe.

Compact, dark wader, larger than most, but dumpier than curlew; faster flight, shorter bill, tittering call make it distinctive, but hard to see head pattern unless very close. 'Bent' bill may be more useful. A bird to watch for during short spring and longer autumn migration periods, often inland, but usually simply flying over, calling.

Ruff

Britain is on the western edge of the breeding range of the ruff, and fewer than 10 pairs breed here each year, mainly on wet meadows in East Anglia. The males' communal dancing display (called lekking) is a complex ritual carried out on traditional leks (display grounds). Females watch and then choose with which male to mate. They then depart and bring up the young alone. The ruff is unusual not only in its display, but also in appearance. In many ways (size, shape, feeding action) it resembles a redshank, but it is actually more closely related to the dunlin. In the autumn, migrants from Scandinavia and the USSR pass through Britain, some staying for the winter. About 1,500 remain, most on the Ouse Washes, and at Pagham Harbour, in Sussex. However, several million winter south of the Sahara in Africa. Interestingly, most wintering in Britain are males, but in Africa most are the smaller females.

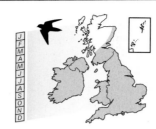

Philomachus pugnax
26–32 cm; 75–200 g
Where to look: edges of lakes, shallow, flooded grassland; in summer wet meadows. **Nest:** in grass tussock. **Eggs:** 3–4, pale grey–green, boldly spotted; May–June. **Food:** small invertebrates.

Long, broad wings with indistinct wingbar. White oval patches on side of rump are distinctive. The flight action is rather languid. Rarely calls.

An unusually shaped bird. Long legs but shortish, slightly down-curved bill. Head seems too small for the longish neck. Usually has pot-bellied, hump-backed shape.

Juveniles have underparts strongly washed deep buff; the upperparts look neatly scaled with pale outlined dark feathers. Bland face. Legs are greenish.

In summer, males are extraordinary, with huge variably coloured ruffs and head tufts. Main colours are white, chestnut-brown, purplish-black. Legs of adults are reddish. Ritualized display at lek.

Males are very much larger than females; the sexes can be told apart easily in mixed flocks.

Winter birds are whitish below with mostly grey upperparts. The face is very pale and in some the whole head and neck is white.

In summer, the females lack the colourful plumage of the males. The upperparts are mottled brown, grey and chestnut. Prominent blotches on flanks.

Spotted Redshank

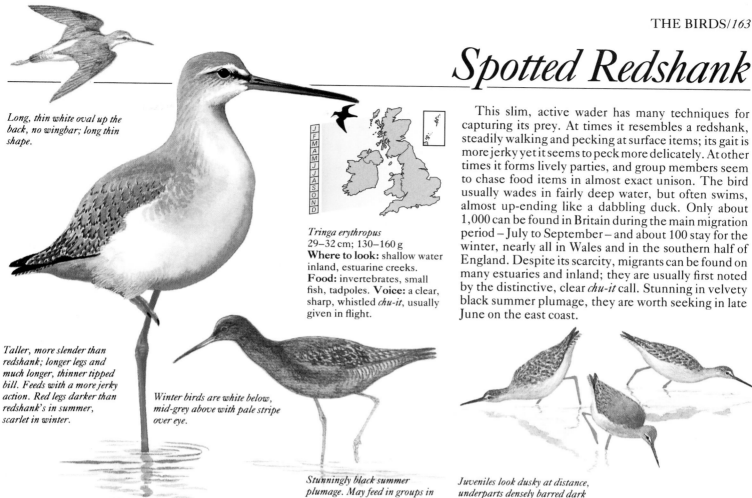

Long, thin white oval up the back, no wingbar; long thin shape.

Tringa erythropus
29–32 cm; 130–160 g
Where to look: shallow water inland, estuarine creeks.
Food: invertebrates, small fish, tadpoles. **Voice:** a clear, sharp, whistled *chu-it*, usually given in flight.

This slim, active wader has many techniques for capturing its prey. At times it resembles a redshank, steadily walking and pecking at surface items; its gait is more jerky yet it seems to peck more delicately. At other times it forms lively parties, and group members seem to chase food items in almost exact unison. The bird usually wades in fairly deep water, but often swims, almost up-ending like a dabbling duck. Only about 1,000 can be found in Britain during the main migration period – July to September – and about 100 stay for the winter, nearly all in Wales and in the southern half of England. Despite its scarcity, migrants can be found on many estuaries and inland; they are usually first noted by the distinctive, clear *chu-it* call. Stunning in velvety black summer plumage, they are worth seeking in late June on the east coast.

Taller, more slender than redshank; longer legs and much longer, thinner tipped bill. Feeds with a more jerky action. Red legs darker than redshank's in summer, scarlet in winter.

Winter birds are white below, mid-grey above with pale stripe over eye.

Stunningly black summer plumage. May feed in groups in deep water.

Juveniles look dusky at distance, underparts densely barred dark brown; clear pale stripe over eye.

Redshank

Tringa totanus
27–29 cm; 100–160 g
Where to look: winter–muddy and sandy coasts; summer–wet meadows, marshes. **Nest:** lined cup in tussock, well hidden. **Eggs:** 3–5, variable colour, spotted; April–May. **Food:** creatures from mud. **Voice:** loud *TEU-hu-hu.*

The title 'Sentinel of the Marshes' is most apt for this widespread, wary and noisy wader as it flies off yelling a warning to other birds. On the face of it, this is an adaptable species, being found on all types of coasts and on inland marshes in winter. However, though 75,000 still winter here, numbers have been dropping in the 1980s. Many that have bred in Britain remain for the winter (although often their young move down to southern Europe) and are joined by birds which bred in Iceland. Most of the time they feed on small shrimps, snails and worms found on the surface, but they will take a very wide variety of food. A rhythmical, even-paced walk with steady pecks is the typical and distinctive feeding action. By April, most of the British birds are back on their breeding territories. About 32,000 pairs breed in Britain, the favoured habitats being estuarine salt marshes, wet meadows and rough pastures. Drainage of inland wetlands poses problems for inland breeders. The song, given in a hanging flight, on quivering wings, echoes beautifully over the marshes – but noisy alarm calls have an hysterical ring to them as redshanks dive at potential predators.

Bright red legs characteristic. Bold dark spots in summer.

Brownish-grey wash to upperparts; little sign of pale stripe over eye.

Immature birds more brown/buff. Always have streaked and grey-washed breast, slight streaks on belly. Steady walk.

Striking white rear edge to dark wings, white 'V' up back distinctive. Calls loudly in flight.

Greenshank

The loud, clear trisyllabic call draws attention to the greenshank, for these notes penetrate through other wader calls. In flight it gives the impression of being rather thick-set compared with similar species. Perhaps as many as 1,500 pairs breed in Britain, but they are restricted to northern Scotland, and choose some of the most beautiful, yet wildest countryside. In winter up to 400 remain here, almost all on western coasts, with at least as many again in Ireland. They are scattered in small muddy estuaries or on sea-lochs. For most of the time birds feed with a fairly steady, elegant walk, pecking at the surface, but at times they chase small fish in shallow water, running erratically with the bill held slightly open. The largest numbers are found in autumn, when Scandinavian migrants pass through to Africa.

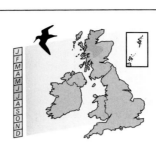

Tringa nebularia
30–34 cm; 170–200 g
Where to look: peat bogs, lakes, estuaries. **Nest:** hollow on ground. **Eggs:** 3–4, olive, spotted dark; May–June. **Food:** worms, fish. **Voice:** a ringing *tu-tu-tu*.

Very dark wings and contrasting white blaze up the back. Noisy.

Solid, upcurved bill; longish green legs distinctive.

Summer birds with dark spotting on breast, heavily streaked head.

Very white in winter, with pale grey upperparts. Active feeder.

Wood Sandpiper

Tringa glareola
19–21 cm; 55–80 g
Where to look: edges of lakes and pools, floods. **Nest:** on ground among sparse trees, sometimes in old nests in trees. **Eggs:** 4, buffish, boldly spotted; May–June. **Food:** invertebrates. **Voice:** high, thin *chiff-iff-iff*.

This is one of the species to seek out in eastern counties of Britain, for it is very scarce on the west coast. Small numbers are seen in August and September, with most appearing on east winds which have blown them across from Scandinavian breeding grounds. Although resembling a green sandpiper, redshank or ruff, the yellowish legs, pale stripe over the eye and the slim, neat shape help to separate it.

Normally, wood sandpipers eat small invertebrates, but just occasionally are galvanised into action by tiny fish. Most of the time they wade in shallow water, especially where low vegetation is emerging, and walk steadily, pecking from the surface. They are quite wary and fly away rapidly, climbing quickly with peevish calls. Nearly all spend the winter in Africa, south of the Sahara. In spring a few are seen on passage and fewer than 10 pairs remain to breed in Scotland. Here they give the melodic whistled song, delivered in a wing-quivering display flight, which is interspersed by glides on down-curved wings. Like many other waders nesting in wet, open woodland, they frequently perch in trees but are remarkably elusive.

In summer, stripe over eye distinctly white. Bird rather greyish, with large white and brown speckles. Bars usually distinct on flanks.

Underwings are pale, buff-brown; note the relatively slim wings.

Mid-brown above, square white rump. Feet extend past tail.

Relatively slim and delicate for a medium-sized sandpiper; bill straight and rather short; legs longish, especially above knee. Bobs less than its relatives.

Juveniles are warm brown above with bright buff spots and buff wash to finely-streaked breast.

Common Sandpiper

The rhythmical, bobbing walk makes the common sandpiper one of the most distinctive small waders. It feeds along the edge of lakes, rivers, even sea-lochs and rocky shores. Food is usually pecked from the surface of the mud, but sometimes the bird can be watched stalking insects with head held horizontally and slowly extended before a sudden snap to catch the prey. The bird is nearly always found singly or in very small groups. Many are seen on migration, especially in autumn, but only about 50 spend the winter here, mainly in south-western Britain; most migrate to sub-Saharan Africa. Breeding birds are found in upland areas of Wales, northern England and Scotland, and about 18,500 pairs breed in Britain. The flickering, down-curved wings, combined with the penetrating whistled call, given almost continuously in flight, are distinctive.

In winter, breast markings form isolated side patches; greyer.

Pale buff bars on closed wing distinguish a juvenile.

Actitis hypoleucos
19–21 cm; 40–60 g
Where to look: summer – upland rivers, lake sides; passage – water edge anywhere. **Nest:** hidden in hollow near water. **Eggs:** 3–5, buff, dark spots; May–June. **Food:** invertebrates. **Voice:** noisy; a thin piping, penetrating *tsee-wee-wee.*

Slight stripe over eye, and glossy green-brown above in summer.

Dark with white wingbar; flies on strongly bowed, stiff wings.

Dark; white point between breast patch and wing, legs green-grey.

A horizontal wader with a long tail and short, straight bill. Walks with strong bobbing action.

Green Sandpiper

Looks very black in flight, with square white rump, white belly. Flickering flight, broad wings.

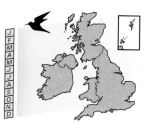

Tringa ochropus
21–24 cm; 60–100 g
Where to look: by edges of inland waters, in winter some on estuary creeks. Does not breed in Britain. **Food:** mostly insects, other invertebrates. **Voice:** a rapid high-whistled *Tuwit-wit-wit.*

Juveniles have breast washed dark grey and small buff-brown spots on back.

Relatively bulky for a smallish wader; always very dark above and white below; complete, but diffuse breastband. Small white stripe in front of the white eye-ring. Legs dull; often bobs.

A dark wader with white underparts seen walking steadily in shallow water inland is most likely to be a green sandpiper, for they are widely distributed across Britain during late summer and autumn. Nowhere do flocks of more than 30 appear, but in autumn the total number in Britain may be as high as 2,000. When feeding, they walk steadily, pecking at surface items, but with an occasional bob; if agitated they will bob vigorously before dashing away, calling very positively. In flight the black lining to the wings is an instant identification feature; the flight itself is very snipe-like with sharp flicks of the wings. They are often picked up by their calls when flying overhead.

Between 200 and 300 remain for the winter, most having departed for Africa. In Britain, they seek fresh-water springs, chalk streams, or where rivers enter inner estuaries; all places where water rarely freezes. They have only bred twice in Britain. When breeding, they seek old nests in trees, the young having to leap to the ground. They migrate back very early, and by late June many autumn passage birds are already in Britain; they seek the rich mud of sewage farms or reservoirs.

Waders

Bar-tailed godwit: *more stocky than black-tailed godwit; bill stouter, pointed, slightly upcurved. Back streaked.*

Black-tailed godwit: *tall and slim with a long, almost straight bill. Breast with an even, pale wash. Clear stripe over eye.*

All the waders shown on this page are in their first autumn and winter plumages.

Redshank: *clear red legs, reddish bill base. Fairly dark, many fine streaks on underparts, breast darkish. Noisy.*

Greenshank: *very white; long greenish legs. Upcurved stout bill.*

Dunlin: *small, brown-grey and white with dull greyish breast. Dark bill is distinctly down-curved. Very common. This one is autumn juvenile gaining grey winter feathers.*

Knot: *smallish, but chunky. Grey. Legs greenish.*

Little stint: *tiny, with a small straight bill. Richly brown and chestnut above with distinct white 'V' on back. Usually seen in autumn in juvenile plumage like this one.*

Sanderling: *small. Very white below. Back is mostly grey (all pale grey in adult). Big black eyes, black legs.*

Curlew: *very large with a long, strongly down-curved bill. A dark and pale brown, streaked bird. Very wary.*

Golden plover: *rounded shape with many yellow spots on upperparts and breast. White belly. Big, dark eyes. Inland.*

Dotterel: *long whitish stripes over eyes meet on nape. Pale breast line. Usually very approachable.*

Grey plover: *a pale greyish, stocky wader of coasts; always looks distinctly spotted above. Big dark eyes, heavy bill.*

Lapwing: *wispy crest very characteristic. Looks black and white at a distance. An inland and gregarious species.*

Oystercatcher: *large. Sharply black and white. Large orange bill, pale pink legs. Noisy.*

Turnstone: *thickset, smallish wader, mostly blackish and white. Orange legs. Chisel-shaped bill. Often approachable.*

Ringed plover: *small, chubby wader. Brown above, with clear dark breastband and face mask. Legs orange. Bill short.*

Grey Phalarope

Summer females are magnificent; dark chestnut below, white face patch and mostly yellow bill.

Young birds in autumn (below) show some dark feathers among the grey of the back. Often a little yellow on bill base. Note fairly thick bill and stocky appearance.

Summer male is duller than female. The species is usually very approachable.

White wingbar prominent against large, dark wings and grey back.

Pale and buoyant on water in winter; prominent dark eye patch.

Nearly always on water, often among waves near rocks. Spins around or paddles when feeding.

Phalaropus fulicarius
20–22 cm; 40–60 g
Where to look: only likely to be seen on the sea or coastal lagoons in late autumn or early winter. **Nest:** arctic tundra. **Eggs:** 3–4. **Food:** wide range of invertebrates, mainly from water surface. **Voice:** a positive, shrill *whit*.

The grey phalarope lives a mysterious life far out to sea for almost all of the year, seeking rich feeding grounds off western Africa and eastern South America. At first this seems to be an unlikely life-style for a small wader. However, the short, strong legs and large, rounded lobes on each toe show that it is adapted for swimming, while it is obviously extremely buoyant when sitting on the water. Indeed, it seems to have no difficulty in feeding in rough inshore waters when persistent onshore winds drive birds on to the coast. Very few are blown inland. Severe westerly gales from late September to early November are most likely to bring a few birds, especially to south-west Britain. When sitting on the water phalaropes are easy to recognise by their mostly grey and white appearance, with the striking dark mark through the eye, but care is needed to separate this from the rarer red-necked. The bill is a good guide, being stouter from the side and remarkably broad from above. If it has any yellow at the base of the bill then identity is confirmed.

Red-necked Phalarope

Sadly, the beautifully marked red-necked phalarope is now very rare in Britain, with only 30 pairs breeding, all in the far north of Scotland where they seek out well-vegetated lochans. A few appear at other times, mainly in eastern England after north-east winds in autumn. Huge flocks gather in winter in the Arabian Sea, and it is probably there that the British breeding birds go. It is an unusually late migrant in spring, with few arriving before June; most return south from late July onwards. Most sex roles are reversed; it is the male who incubates the eggs and looks after the chicks, so he is less brightly marked and better camouflaged than the female. Juveniles and summer-plumaged birds have characteristic golden lines down the back, but in winter plumage they are very like grey phalaropes. Subtle points such as bill shape, body size, flight action and call need to be assessed. The bird is very approachable.

White wingbar; flight fast and erratic; broad wings.

Phalaropus lobatus
18–19 cm; 30–40 g
Where to look: a very few breed on pools in northern Scotland. Coastal pools in autumn. **Nest:** in grass by water. **Eggs:** 3–4, buff, blotched brown; June. **Food:** invertebrates. **Voice:** fairly low-pitched *twit*.

Very thin, black bill; small size. Autumn young (below) show thin, golden edges on the dark back feathers.

Breeding adult with red and grey neck, white chin. Female brighter.

Winter adults are very like grey phalarope – grey with dark eye patch. Most occur far out to sea.

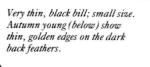

Great Skua

Chases many seabirds, can kill gulls, auks, ducks.

Size of herring gull but heavier build. No white on body, tail short, wings broad but pointed. No pale phase, but some paler than others; tawny-brown in bright sun. Large wing patches visible at great range are best feature.

Raised wing pose used in display and aggressive encounters.

Often called 'bonxies', the traditional Shetlanders' name, great skuas are not easy to see in the south, though relatively familiar in northern coastal waters and from eastern headlands in autumn. Shetland had 10 pairs in 1774, but that number had actually declined by the 1860s. However, with protection they survived, and birds spread to Orkney in 1915, the Outer Hebrides in 1945 and a few to mainland Scotland from 1949. There are now over 5,400 pairs in Shetland alone. Great skuas chase seabirds and terrify them into disgorging food, which they then eat. They also kill many birds in summer. They are bold enough to bring down a gannet, and aggressive enough to dive at humans (and sheep) with repeated headlong rushes that sometimes end with a severe clout from the bonxie's feet – so they are not popular with crofters! After breeding they leave for the mid-Atlantic and South American and West African coasts. Three-year-olds disperse most, spending summers far to the north; by five years old they are more attached to the colony and travel less widely in winter.

Stout, hooked, dark bill; triangular, capped head.

A heavy bird; broad wings with big flashes of white visible at great distance; may look more or less tawny or paler around neck.

Stercorarius skua
53–58 cm; 1,300–2,000 g
Where to look: at sea and on coastal moors in far north.
Nest: on ground. **Eggs:** 2, blotched dark brown. **Food:** mainly fish stolen from other birds; also birds and eggs.
Voice: rather quiet calls in colony; silent at sea.

Arctic Skua

Lazily drifting over the sea, well offshore, the dark shape of the arctic skua suddenly raises its tempo, accelerating in pursuit of a tern, which it then harries relentlessly, following each desperate twist, until the tern drops a fish. Few birds have the exciting aura about them that this skua has, and few have such elegance of form. Arctics are far more widespread in northern parts of the world than great skuas, but only about 2,500 pairs breed in Britain, 1,600 of these in Shetland. In winter they go as far as South Africa. Arctic skuas chase terns, kittiwakes and puffins, whereas great skuas chase mostly guillemots and gannets. Nearly half their attacks on terns end in success, whereas a far smaller proportion of chases after larger birds yield food, so most skuas prefer to follow the terns in autumn. This takes them into the North Sea rather than south along the Atlantic coasts where terns are fewer. They kill fewer birds than great skuas, but human intruders at the nest are equally likely to be attacked, in fast, elegant, swooping dives at the head, though contact is rarely made.

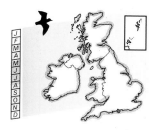

Stercorarius parasiticus
41–46 cm; 350–550 g
Where to look: northern isles and coasts, headlands in autumn. **Nest:** on ground. **Eggs:** 2, brown. **Food:** fish. **Voice:** loud wail, short bark.

Immature birds warm brown with paler bars, buffish wing patches, short tail projection. Pale adult has dark cap, white belly, often slight breastband; dark phase uniform brown. All show wing flashes, tail spike.

Calm weather: direct flight, easy and relaxed; in wind glides and tilts like shearwater; at colony often reaches great height.

Comparing Gulls

Gulls are familiar by the sea and almost everywhere inland, from central London to the highest tops of Snowdonia and the Cairngorms. Too often they are taken for granted, passed over on the way to 'more interesting' birds, or thought to be too difficult to identify. All those shown here are in winter plumage.

Black-headed gull: *small, agile, widespread and common.*

Bright red legs and bill are good clues; head is white in winter!

Herring gull: *typical of beaches and harbours. Pale back.*

Young herring gulls are mottled brown, like most other species.

Great black-backed gull: *a giant among the others.*

The drab plumages of young gulls change as they grow to adulthood, taking several years in big species. The changes are in a regular sequence, not random, and allow unique opportunities to study moult and ageing.

Common gull: *like small, slim herring gull, with no red on smaller bill, and dark eyes, it has 'gentler' expression.*

Great black-backed gull: *strong beak and aggressive look.*

Black-headed gull: triangle of white on front of each wing – instant recognition!

All gulls are buoyant swimmers and masterful fliers. They feed on practically anything, but each species has its favoured way of making a living.

Black-headed gull: slim and lightweight, only has dark hood in breeding plumage – from late winter through to mid summer.

Herring gull: strident, ringing calls are part of any seaside trip – but unwelcome on the guest-house roof at sunrise.

Black-headed Gull

Whether flying from a nest in a marsh to protest noisily at intrusion, following a plough to snap up worms, stealing bits of sandwich at the seaside or dipping into the fountain in Trafalgar Square, the black-headed gull is almost everywhere. A long drive in winter shows that it is one of the few birds so obvious in the landscape that it cannot be missed – gleaming white flocks in fields or thousands of them scrambling for food at rubbish tips catch the eye a mile away. Many breed inland, though the largest colonies are on coastal marshes and they are common on beaches all year round. Consequently, while many live on worms from the fields, others have a diet of fish scraps from harbours, all kinds of edible refuse from tips, and whatever awful food they get from sewage outflows. Britain's breeding population is much higher than a century ago, perhaps up to 300,000 pairs, but in winter there may be three million of them – two thirds from the Continent (especially the Baltic countries) and well over a million of the overall number living inland.

Below the wings is a dark patch before a translucent stripe near the tip. Young birds have much brown in the wing, with a dark trailing edge, but still have the blaze of white on the outer primaries and coverts that is so characteristic of black-headed gulls.

Usually stands and swims head to wind, wingtips looking long and thin. Very young birds have blunt wings and look dark brown.

Larus ridibundus
34–37 cm; 200–300 g
Where to look: almost anywhere. **Nest:** on island or by pool from coast to upland moors. **Eggs:** 2–3, blotched, brown or blue. **Food:** worms, grubs, fish, scraps. **Voice:** long squealing calls, short, repeated yapping notes.

Juvenile birds have tawny back and neck for a short time in summer.

Breeding adult has dark brown hood, dark red legs and bill; white primaries tipped black.

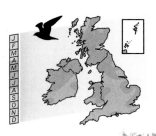

To appreciate the agility of the species, watch a flock behind a plough. The flashes of white on the wingtips are distinctive.

Flight is quick and active, though bird will soar and glide and even catch flying insects.

Colonies are found in grassy or rushy places, from a couple of pairs up to many thousands.

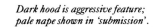

Dark hood is aggressive feature; pale nape shown in 'submission'.

In its first winter, it has a neat pattern of brown on the wing coverts, a dark tail band and pale orange on the bill and legs.

Pigeon-size; long white triangle on wings, dark hood or white head with black ear-spot make identification easy. Red beak and legs shared only by rare gulls; this one has thinnest, sharpest bill. Often mixed with other species, when it looks palest of all. May have flush of pink.

Of all the familiar gulls, this is the palest. The wingtips show mostly black when closed.

Adults in winter have a dark spot behind the eye; bright red bill tipped black and bright red legs, unlike any other numerous gull.

Little Gull

The little gull is not very common, though sizeable flocks are regular in a few places. It is chiefly a passage migrant in spring and autumn, but it can be seen almost anywhere at almost any time of year. It is always a good find, especially at an inland reservoir where the young birds often turn up in autumn in their 'zigzag' plumage, with a black 'W' across their wings in flight. They have to be distinguished from young kittiwakes. These are bigger birds with clear grey backs and pale rumps (both of which may be dark on a little gull) and sharp, narrow, black collars (moulting young little gulls have a broader dusky band across the neck, often going onto the sides of the breast). Smart, adult little gulls are sadly much scarcer, but are among the most attractive of gulls. They breed in north-eastern Europe and across into central Asia, with odd colonies along the Baltic and North Sea coasts. But they can be seen outside the breeding season on practically all the shores of Europe and Asia Minor. Why they are sometimes quite numerous in north-west England and in the Irish Sea is a mystery!

Tiny gull; buoyant flight. Adult has jet-black head in summer, grey and white in winter. Upperwing grey with white border (some show small black marks at tip); underwing black with white rim.

Juvenile bird very dark on back. Neat, with extremely short legs, tiny bill. Wingtips largely black at first, but it wears off to show streaks of white by spring.

Larus minutus
25–27 cm; 90–120 g
Where to look: lakes, reservoirs, coasts and coastal lagoons, mostly spring and autumn. Does not breed in Britain. **Food:** insects taken from surface of water or marsh. **Voice:** *kuk-kuk-kuk*, not often heard.

Young birds, more often seen than adults, have black zigzag across wings like young kittiwake.

At first has blackish back (young kittiwake never has); dull collar in autumn soon lost; secondaries dark; dipping, tern-like flight.

One-year old (above)

Mediterranean Gull

Adult has pearly upperwing and eye-catching, white underwing; jet black hood, white eyelids, red bill in summer; ghostly pale, dusky mask, dark bill in winter.

Larus melanocephalus
36–38 cm; 300–400 g
Where to look: beaches, gull roosts. Rarely nests in Britain. **Food:** fish, insects, offal.

Spotting a Mediterranean gull is a real test, but it is worth the effort. An adult in breeding plumage is one of Europe's most handsome birds. Its scarlet bill contrasts with a hood of jet black (the bill and hood of a black-headed gull are all of one tone). If it takes flight, the whiteness of the wings is much more striking than might be expected. The young birds are difficult to identify, but their big-chested, heavy-billed, bold character is distinctive once learnt. On the ground they look like bulky black-headed gulls, but in the air the lack of a white forewing flash separates them. Likely places to find this rare species are on the south coasts of England and Wales and in parts of Kent, East Anglia and the north-east, but any large gull flock is always worth searching for such unusual birds. Young birds are most often seen in April and May, but adults move through Britain early in spring and also spend the winter in a few places; a pair or two may nest in some years, but more often a male will pair with a black-headed gull.

Young like young common gull but back paler, pale midwing; white marks on blacker primaries; mask.

Often with black-headed or common; aggressive; note head band, pale back. All have same character.

Like stocky, round-headed black-headed gull; stouter, blunt bill, deep chest, longer legs. In winter has 'pirate's' eye patch.

Adults very pale; white primaries often stand out, but head pattern useful; bill red, orange or buff tipped black, or all black.

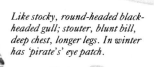

Common Gull

Looking like a small, gentler version of the herring gull, the common gull is far less widespread as a nesting bird and only found over most of England and Wales outside the breeding season. It is not at all common in some inland areas, though often abundant on the coast and in some eastern counties, frequenting pastures and sports fields, where flocks spread out in search of worms. They are now seen more often in towns and on housing estates in winter. The greenish legs and bill, with no red spot, confirm that an adult is no herring gull, though in practice even at long range the slim shape, dark eye and darker back give it a quite distinctive look. Young birds have neat and attractive bands of brown, pale-edged wing coverts, and at first a scaly brown back, but this turns grey by the autumn; by the following spring the grey is often darker than the sun-bleached wings, which can be almost cream-coloured with pale, brown tips (on a young Mediterranean gull the back is always very pale). In winter, adults have the head and upper breast heavily soiled with grey-brown streaks.

Middle-sized; round head, small bill. Young bird has white tail with black band. Like adult in second year of life with more black on wing, dark band on bill, greyish legs.

Juvenile

First winter

Wingtips have large black and white patches, more black than herring gull beneath; fluent flight.

Larus canus
40–42 cm; 350–450 g
Where to look: lakes, coasts, farmland, tips. **Nest:** on ground near coast or on moor. **Eggs:** 3, blotched olive–brown. **Food:** insects, worms, fish, scraps. **Voice:** high, squealing calls shriller than larger gulls.

Smaller than herring gull, back a shade darker with bolder white patches; greenish bill; long wings.

Lesser Black-backed Gull

As a breeding bird, the lesser black-backed gull is best known on Welsh islands, northern moors and thickly-vegetated areas above cliffs; it is less of a cliff-ledge breeder than the herring gull and is more likely to be surrounded by bluebells and campion as it sits on its eggs. Many leave Britain in winter, though now thousands do stay to feed at Midland tips and to roost on large reservoirs. On most coasts it is simply a passage migrant. The summer adult, with soft slate-grey back, and legs and beak of vivid yellow, is a most handsome bird and an elegant addition to the summer coastal scene. Juvenile birds are very dark and black-billed; in the winter they have all-dark flight feathers, unlike young herring gulls, and by the following autumn they are dark grey on the back like their parents, though still brown-winged and with black tail bands. In winter, adults have grey-brown heads and much duller yellow legs. A few birds from the southern Baltic may be seen in autumn, recognisable by their long wings, blacker backs and unstreaked white heads.

Larus fuscus
50–52 cm; 600–1,000 g
Where to look: islands, lakes and reservoirs, coasts, tips. **Nest:** on ground, on islands and moors, colonial. **Eggs:** 3, blotched brown. **Food:** fish, offal, worms, eggs, seabirds. **Voice:** deeper, more throaty calls than herring gull, abrupt *ow-ow-ow, kyoww*; longer wailing notes and squeals.

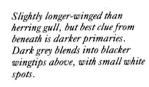

Slightly longer-winged than herring gull, but best clue from beneath is darker primaries. Dark grey blends into blacker wingtips above, with small white spots.

First winter has all-dark flight feathers, black bill. Second-year gains grey back, paler bill.

Longer-winged, shorter-legged than herring gull. Slim, low-slung; legs yellow; red ring round eye, spot on bill. In autumn moult shows white patches.

Follows ships further out to sea than most gulls; more predatory behaviour at seabird colonies.

Herring Gull

Rooftop nesting increasingly frequent at seaside resorts; also rests on roofs in factory estates, dockyards, but rarely suburbia.

First-year in flight largely pale brown with dark tail and wingtips, but inner primaries (behind bend of wing) paler than outer ones.

Bill of first-year has pale base; plumage fades with age.

Second-year begins to get pale grey back, whiter head and body, paler bill; third-year more like adult.

Plumage changes with a head and body moult each spring and a complete moult each autumn, which begins earlier (June) with young birds and failed breeders.

In winter, adults streaked with grey-brown on head and breast; darker-backed birds frequent.

Large gull. Young bird mottled brown; pale grey back when one year old, but mottled wings and brown tail; gradually loses brown until fourth year, when adult. Plain grey above with clear-cut black wingtips; bill dark at first, then brown with dark tip, then yellow except for red spot.

Adults clean grey and white in summer with sharply defined black wingtips spotted white; pink legs, unlike lesser black-back's.

The herring gull is so common and approachable that it is worth using as a standard against which to compare others. The plumage sequences can be worked out easily and, once the pearly-grey begins to appear on the back, it is not hard to identify. Because young gulls are brown and get progressively paler as they mature, it is possible to work out their age much more easily than with most birds, the changing patterns being obvious at a glance. Larger, darker birds come here in winter from north Scandinavia – Britain's breeding birds are the smallest and palest in Europe – and on some southern coasts dark-backed, white-headed, yellow-legged birds from the Mediterranean can be found. These may even be of a different species, but the relationships of these large gulls are notoriously difficult to work out clearly. Winter flocks resting on fields or roosting on reservoirs are often wary and require care and patience for close views; quite unlike those that dive for scraps at your feet at any summer seaside resort, or wait in line on railings at fish quays, ready to pounce and fight for fish heads, guts or spilled herrings.

Larus argentatus
52–55 cm; 750–1,200 g
Where to look: cliffs, all kinds of coasts, reservoirs, tips, farmland in winter. **Nest:** on ground, cliff ledge or building. **Eggs:** 3, spotted brown. **Food:** fish, offal, refuse, eggs. **Voice:** loud squealing, wailing and laughing notes; deep *kyow-yow-yow*; short barks. Young birds have thin whine.

Refuse tips attract flocks all year on coast, in winter inland.

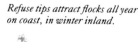

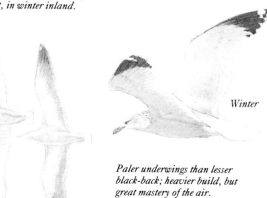

Winter

Paler underwings than lesser black-back; heavier build, but great mastery of the air.

Herring　　　　*Lesser black-back*

Iceland Gull

Young birds pale creamy fawn, with wingtips and tail palest.

First year   Second year   Third year

Bill brown, blending to dark tip in first year, later paler.

On water, wingtips look very long and slim, body dumpy and rounded, 'chinless' head.

Adult very pale with wingtips all white. Shows large area of primaries at rest, giving 'droop-winged' effect; head rounder, eye larger than glaucous gull; bill short and stubby. Head streaked in winter. Legs short; dark pink.

Size of herring gull, but rounder head, smaller bill, give gentler expression than glaucous gull. Tips of wings longer, flight less heavy; bill darker on youngest birds.

Despite its name, the Iceland gull breeds in Greenland and northern Alaska, though most spend the winter in Iceland. With hard weather there, and perhaps also due to the decline of the Icelandic fishing industry, between 100 and 300 will move on to the north and west coasts of Britain and Ireland, in 'good' years, even reaching the extreme south-west. Oddly enough, it is regular on a few Midland reservoirs, especially after Christmas and through until late March, and a few individuals have returned year after year to the same wintering site. Among hundreds of herring gulls, the white wingtips will be more readily spotted by a practised eye than might be supposed, and the ghostly paleness, at all ages, is very striking as a bird takes flight. The problem is to decide whether the bird is an Iceland gull or the more frequent glaucous – look for the shape of the head and bill, then the length of the closed wingtips. Because of its rarity and its remote summer home, the Iceland gull has a certain romantic aura about it, and is always a very good find.

Larus glaucoides
50–52 cm; 750–850 g
Where to look: rubbish tips, reservoir roosts, beaches, harbours and outflows, usually with gull flocks.
Food: worms, fish, offal, refuse, scraps. **Voice:** rarely heard in winter, higher than herring gull's.

Glaucous Gull

The glaucous gull is common all around the Arctic and a number breed in Iceland, where it is a familiar bird around the docks and rocky shores. Predatory in summer, in winter, when between 300 and 500 are scattered through Britain and Ireland, it is still a dominant presence among the mixed gull flocks. However, few are as big as a great black-backed gull, the average being rather larger than a typical herring gull. It is almost always bigger and more heavily built than an Iceland gull. Sometimes large flocks appear in the northern isles, probably associated with stormy weather to the north-east, and in other years there may be more in the south and west – these probably coming direct from Greenland. They can be found with gull flocks just about anywhere, though most are coastal. Inland they are most frequent on the rubbish tips and on the nearby reservoir roosts of the north and west Midlands of England. This wide spread makes them worth searching for – rare birds, but always likely to repay the careful gull watcher.

Larus hyperboreus
62–68 cm; 1,500–2,200 g
Where to look: fish docks, outflows, refuse tips, gull flocks. **Food:** offal and refuse, fish, crabs, shellfish. **Voice:** quiet in winter, short yapping and wailing notes, high-pitched.

Adult looks like large herring gull with white patch at back.

First-year neatly barred brown and cream, wingtips palest.

Second-year (left) paler still, often fading to almost creamy white. Bill pale pink with sharp black tip in first year, not blended like Iceland gull's, later losing black and gaining yellow. Flight relatively ponderous.

Standing bird has primaries more hidden than Iceland gull's, their tips extend less beyond tail. Bill longer and heavy, head often flatter, eye smaller.

Great Black-backed Gull

Male gulls are larger, with bill and head bigger, than females, but their plumages are alike. This species is biggest gull of all and blackest on back; legs pale pink.

Big, dominant gull of north and west coasts, but in winter also found on eastern estuaries and increasingly inland. Length a little greater than lesser black-back but its bulk can make it look 'twice as big' (see weight); breadth of body is striking when standing or swimming head on.

Young birds in flight look like young herring gull in pattern, with pale patch behind bend of wing; head paler, tail more clearly banded. In second and third year black blotches increase on wings (never on herring gull).

In winter adults stand out due to size, white head, black back; young have large black bill, pale head, chequered upperparts.

Typical nest site is on isolated stack or clifftop knoll, always overlooking the sea.

Compare immature birds with herring gull and darker young lesser black-backed gulls; once black shows there is no problem.

In flight shows large, white wingtip spots; wings broad and body heavy, yet still graceful.

Wingspan almost equals gannet's, but tail and neck shorter than young gannet. Action is slower than other large gulls'.

Huge size always evident, but in flight over clifftops close views reveal giant size most clearly. May glide low over sea, even the cause of occasional optimistic reports of a passing albatross!

Larus marinus
62–65 cm; 1,500–2,000 g
Where to look: rocky coasts, beaches in winter, refuse tips and nearby fields, reservoirs, harbours. **Nest:** pad of grasses, in hollow on clifftop. **Eggs:** 3, blotchy. **Food:** offal, fish, birds, eggs, dead animals and rubbish. **Voice:** deeper version of herring gull's wails and squeals and deep, barking *owk, uk-uk-uk.*

Characteristic of a windswept clifftop, under blue summer skies and surrounded by sea pink and campion, the great black-backed gull is one of Britain's most impressive birds, in a land of predominantly small species. It does not, however, meet with universal approval, especially where it may eat a puffin or be seen feeding on a dead sheep. Even in winter a marauding great black-back will swoop at flocks of teal and coots, and it is quite capable of swallowing a big rat or a rabbit whole!

A flock of gulls resting in a field – which they do for hours at a stretch even in the shortest days of winter – may look a motley bunch, but when a great black-back flies down it simply dwarfs the rest, like a great bomber among lightweight fighters. On water, it is clearly the battleship of the fleet! About 25,000 pairs breed in Britain. In the north of Scotland, flocks of hundreds bathe in coastal fresh water lochs and fly off to feed around passing trawlers. In winter it is very widespread, with over half of the European population on the shores of Britain, especially on the east coast.

Kittiwake

At any great seabird colony the most numerous species is likely to be the kittiwake. Vast ranks of gleaming white birds on ridiculously tiny, precarious nests, and hundreds more wheeling over the sea, create an eye-catching spectacle and a great volume of noise, all the birds calling their name (or perhaps it's 'sorry I'm late') in yodelling, nasal tones. It seems unlikely that a kittiwake will be misidentified, even when it goes to bathe or find nesting material at a nearby lake. But, from time to time, kittiwakes are seen inland, usually adults in early spring, or immature birds in autumn or winter after gales, and they frequently pass headlands a long way offshore. The bounding, banking flight (if there is a good wind), the mid-grey back fading out towards the wingtips, and protruding head and neck (looking brilliant white in summer) then make an adult identifiable a mile away – even if you cannot see the black legs and wingtips that would confirm it. Real birds of the sea, kittiwakes – unlike many gulls – do not scrounge at refuse tips or feed on beaches.

Larus tridactyla
38–40 cm; 350–425 g
Where to look: at sea; in summer on cliffs, beaches; in winter, harbours. **Nest:** on sheer cliff. **Eggs:** 2, spotted. **Food:** fish, offal from trawlers – not a tideline scavenger. **Voice:** quiet mew and ringing *kitti-way-ake*.

Colonies found on sheer cliffs with nests on tiny ledges, often thousands of pairs; constant noise and activity make kittiwakes unmistakable.

One-year-old birds around colony look very dull, faded, with wing pattern bleached and worn away leaving hint of brownish 'W'.

Adult has grey back, paler towards solid black wingtips; grey neck, ear spot in winter.

Some near-adults have grey neck, black marks on bill in spring.

In winter only 1,000 or so around Britain's coasts, the rest far out at sea; close to half a million pairs breed. Black legs, yellow bill and 'dipped in ink' tips of wings identify adult; dark eyes, round shape, give head gentle expression; the young have no need of the brown camouflage mottling of most gulls because they are out of harm's way on a cliff, but their collar prevents parental aggression.

Winter

Summer flocks often stand on flat rocks or sandy beaches; short legs and tail-down shape obvious.

Unless at colony, such faded birds can confuse; legs often brown.

After leaving nest and through first winter, young birds are very handsome, neatly patterned black, white and grey with 'W' on wings, black collar and ear spot.

Sabine's Gull

All have basic three-triangle wing pattern — black outer, grey inner, white rear; no black diagonal.

The rare Sabine's gull breeds on islets and marshy tundra in arctic Greenland, Alaska and the north coasts of Siberia. Little wonder that it is a special and exciting bird to see, never an easy task, on its way south to little-known wintering grounds off the coasts of Africa. Appearing in the Western Approaches from August to November, it takes a good gale to bring them close inshore. There are even fewer in the North Sea. Like many seabirds, they present a problem of identification, made worse by the fact that they usually fly by and never come back. The birdwatcher has to be quick to look carefully for the crisply-marked triangles on each wing. These can be suggested by a faded or distant young kittiwake, but the kittiwake's black inner wing diagonal and collar instantly rule out Sabine's if they are seen. Young Sabine's have brownish upperparts and a black tail band; adults are clear lead-grey on top and the tail, though still notched, is pure white; on the underwing a smudge of grey across the coverts can often be seen.

Sabine's gull with kittiwakes.

First winter

Larus sabini
27–32 cm; 160–210 g
Where to look: off headlands of north-east and west coasts in autumn; at sea especially off south-west. Most often after northerly or westerly gales. **Food:** fish, floating offal, crustacea. **Voice:** not heard in Britain.

Ring-billed Gull

Adult paler than common with less white between black and grey; eye pale; bill thicker; body stouter with more tail-down shape.

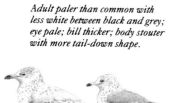

First-year

First-year common

Second-year

First-year (left) has more contrasted wings than common gull, but smudgy tail band; pale grey back is good clue. Second-year less like adult than common gull, with marks on tail, hindwing always obvious.

Common gull often has dull band on bill, which is not so broad or sharp; ring-billed's greenish in winter, yellow in summer; immature bird's pale with black tip at first, later ringed.

The ring-billed gull is common and very widespread in North America and in recent years numbers have dramatically increased in some eastern areas. This has coincided with its first appearance in Britain, as recently as 1973, and a subsequent increase to such an extent that, at least in South Wales, Cornwall and parts of Ireland, it is scarcely considered a rarity nowadays! Nevertheless, there are still only a few dozen a year in Britain and Ireland and it is far from easy to identify, so it is unlikely to be encountered without a visit to a favoured place in the south-west. But you never know – there have been odd ones in such unlikely spots as a park lake in the Potteries! Because it is much like a common gull in appearance and behaviour, and usually associates with common gulls on this side of the Atlantic, it is possible that it might begin to nest in a common gull colony, or even hybridise with the common gull. However, that idea has been suggested before for frequent visitors from the New World, so far without foundation. Hybrid gulls would be very hard to detect.

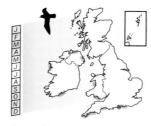

Larus delawarensis
43–47 cm; 500 g
Where to look: with common gull flocks, west and south coasts, autumn through to spring. Very occasionally inland or on east coast. Does not nest in Europe, but may do so in future. **Food:** worms, shellfish, scraps. May feed on beaches, tips, fields. **Voice:** usual gull squeals, yapping notes.

Adult has spotted head in winter. Eye yellow, but not easy to tell at long range; nevertheless helps give 'meaner' look than common gull. Wings broad-based, but sharply pointed, more angular than common gull with more black, less white on the tips.

Sandwich Tern

The Sandwich tern is the largest of the terns found regularly in Britain, and when flying over the sea or standing on a beach is noticeably the palest. Its whiteness is the best identification feature, along with the yellow-tipped black bill. The rhythm of the quick, double, or nearly triple, call is also an instant pointer that the first Sandwich terns are back in late March or early April, after their long winter in West Africa. Most birds reared the previous summer will spend their first year of life in the winter quarters, sometimes as far as South Africa (even on the east coast). In 1962 nearly 6,000 pairs bred in Britain and Ireland, then the highest 20th-century figure, but since then numbers have increased and by 1979 there were over 15,000 pairs. They are greatly helped by protection of their colonies on coastal dunes and lagoons, though they have a tendency to shift site for no very obvious reason after several years. Like all terns, they seem highly-strung, unpredictable birds, quick to take alarm and easily disturbed by insensitive intruders.

Sterna sandvicensis
36–38 cm; 210–250 g
Where to look: all coasts; dunes, coastal lagoons. **Nest:** on ground, scrape in sand; in large colonies. **Eggs:** 1–2, mottled. **Food:** small fish, such as sand eels. **Voice:** rasping *kierr-ink* or *kirrick* is distinctive; short *kik*.

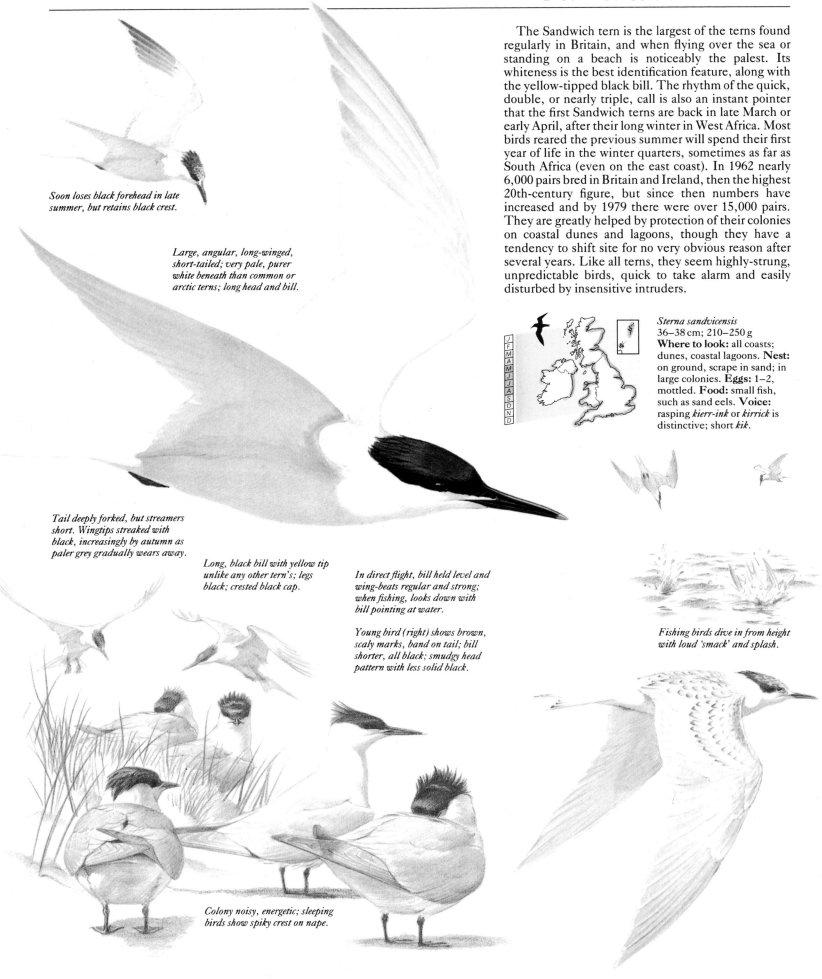

Soon loses black forehead in late summer, but retains black crest.

Large, angular, long-winged, short-tailed; very pale, purer white beneath than common or arctic terns; long head and bill.

Tail deeply forked, but streamers short. Wingtips streaked with black, increasingly by autumn as paler grey gradually wears away.

Long, black bill with yellow tip unlike any other tern's; legs black; crested black cap.

In direct flight, bill held level and wing-beats regular and strong; when fishing, looks down with bill pointing at water.

Young bird (right) shows brown, scaly marks, band on tail; bill shorter, all black; smudgy head pattern with less solid black.

Fishing birds dive in from height with loud 'smack' and splash.

Colony noisy, energetic; sleeping birds show spiky crest on nape.

Little Tern

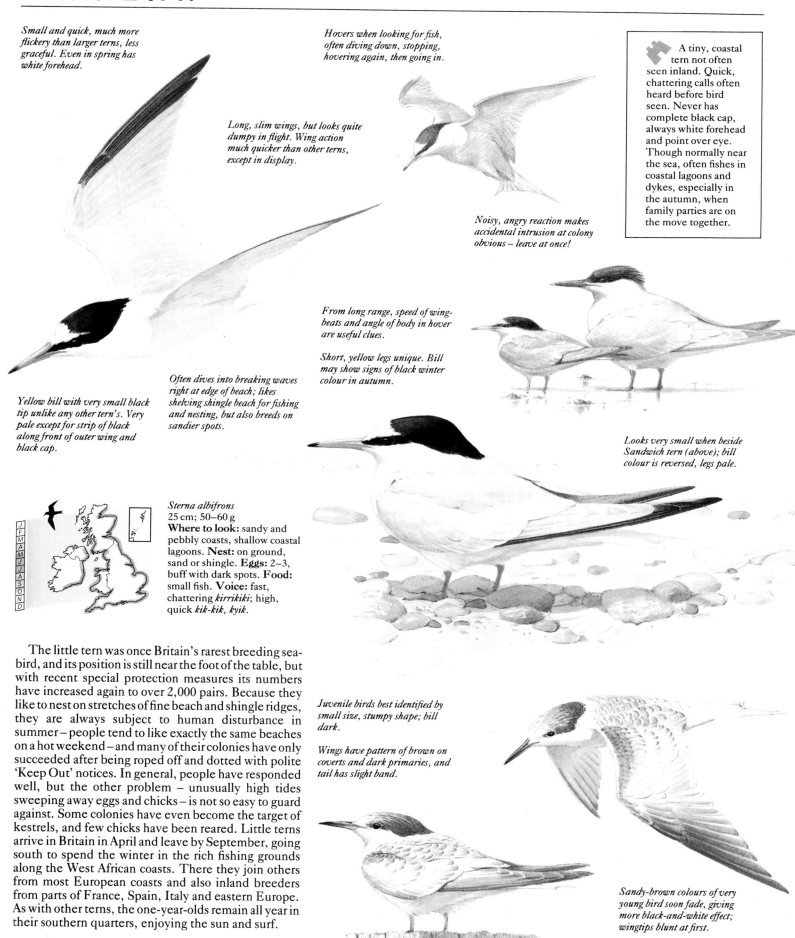

Small and quick, much more flickery than larger terns, less graceful. Even in spring has white forehead.

Hovers when looking for fish, often diving down, stopping, hovering again, then going in.

A tiny, coastal tern not often seen inland. Quick, chattering calls often heard before bird seen. Never has complete black cap, always white forehead and point over eye. Though normally near the sea, often fishes in coastal lagoons and dykes, especially in the autumn, when family parties are on the move together.

Long, slim wings, but looks quite dumpy in flight. Wing action much quicker than other terns, except in display.

Noisy, angry reaction makes accidental intrusion at colony obvious – leave at once!

From long range, speed of wing-beats and angle of body in hover are useful clues.

Short, yellow legs unique. Bill may show signs of black winter colour in autumn.

Yellow bill with very small black tip unlike any other tern's. Very pale except for strip of black along front of outer wing and black cap.

Often dives into breaking waves right at edge of beach; likes shelving shingle beach for fishing and nesting, but also breeds on sandier spots.

Looks very small when beside Sandwich tern (above); bill colour is reversed, legs pale.

Sterna albifrons
25 cm; 50–60 g
Where to look: sandy and pebbly coasts, shallow coastal lagoons. **Nest:** on ground, sand or shingle. **Eggs:** 2–3, buff with dark spots. **Food:** small fish. **Voice:** fast, chattering *kirrikiki*; high, quick *kik-kik, kyik*.

The little tern was once Britain's rarest breeding sea-bird, and its position is still near the foot of the table, but with recent special protection measures its numbers have increased again to over 2,000 pairs. Because they like to nest on stretches of fine beach and shingle ridges, they are always subject to human disturbance in summer – people tend to like exactly the same beaches on a hot weekend – and many of their colonies have only succeeded after being roped off and dotted with polite 'Keep Out' notices. In general, people have responded well, but the other problem – unusually high tides sweeping away eggs and chicks – is not so easy to guard against. Some colonies have even become the target of kestrels, and few chicks have been reared. Little terns arrive in Britain in April and leave by September, going south to spend the winter in the rich fishing grounds along the West African coasts. There they join others from most European coasts and also inland breeders from parts of France, Spain, Italy and eastern Europe. As with other terns, the one-year-olds remain all year in their southern quarters, enjoying the sun and surf.

Juvenile birds best identified by small size, stumpy shape; bill dark.

Wings have pattern of brown on coverts and dark primaries, and tail has slight band.

Sandy-brown colours of very young bird soon fade, giving more black-and-white effect; wingtips blunt at first.

Common Tern

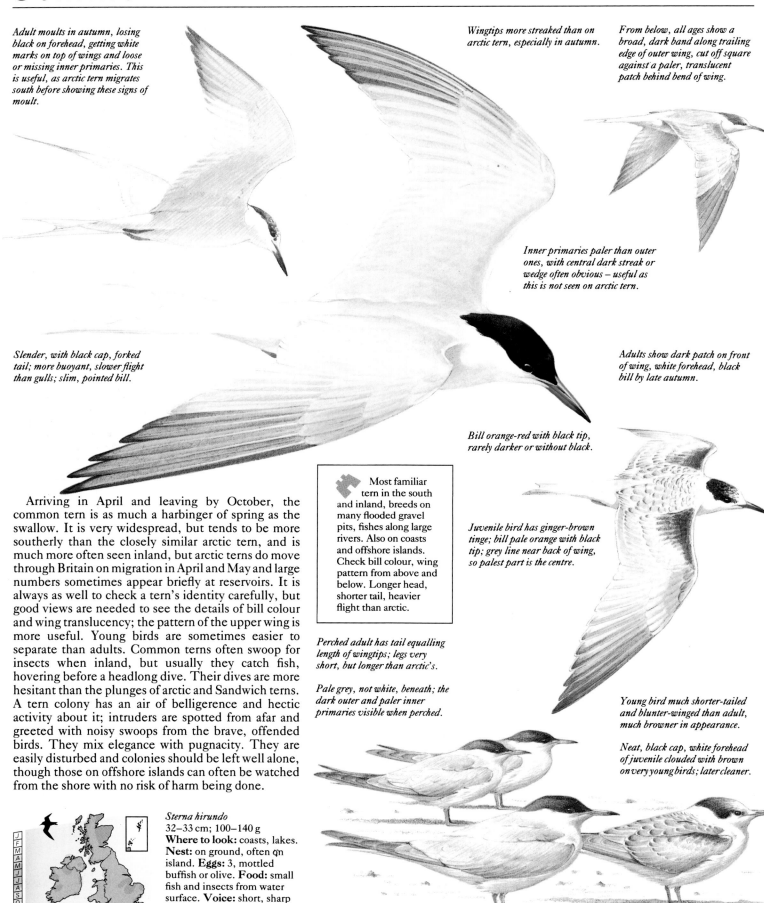

Adult moults in autumn, losing black on forehead, getting white marks on top of wings and loose or missing inner primaries. This is useful, as arctic tern migrates south before showing these signs of moult.

Wingtips more streaked than on arctic tern, especially in autumn.

From below, all ages show a broad, dark band along trailing edge of outer wing, cut off square against a paler, translucent patch behind bend of wing.

Inner primaries paler than outer ones, with central dark streak or wedge often obvious – useful as this is not seen on arctic tern.

Slender, with black cap, forked tail; more buoyant, slower flight than gulls; slim, pointed bill.

Adults show dark patch on front of wing, white forehead, black bill by late autumn.

Bill orange-red with black tip, rarely darker or without black.

Most familiar tern in the south and inland, breeds on many flooded gravel pits, fishes along large rivers. Also on coasts and offshore islands. Check bill colour, wing pattern from above and below. Longer head, shorter tail, heavier flight than arctic.

Juvenile bird has ginger-brown tinge; bill pale orange with black tip; grey line near back of wing, so palest part is the centre.

Arriving in April and leaving by October, the common tern is as much a harbinger of spring as the swallow. It is very widespread, but tends to be more southerly than the closely similar arctic tern, and is much more often seen inland, but arctic terns do move through Britain on migration in April and May and large numbers sometimes appear briefly at reservoirs. It is always as well to check a tern's identity carefully, but good views are needed to see the details of bill colour and wing translucency; the pattern of the upper wing is more useful. Young birds are sometimes easier to separate than adults. Common terns often swoop for insects when inland, but usually they catch fish, hovering before a headlong dive. Their dives are more hesitant than the plunges of arctic and Sandwich terns. A tern colony has an air of belligerence and hectic activity about it; intruders are spotted from afar and greeted with noisy swoops from the brave, offended birds. They mix elegance with pugnacity. They are easily disturbed and colonies should be left well alone, though those on offshore islands can often be watched from the shore with no risk of harm being done.

Perched adult has tail equalling length of wingtips; legs very short, but longer than arctic's.

Pale grey, not white, beneath; the dark outer and paler inner primaries visible when perched.

Young bird much shorter-tailed and blunter-winged than adult, much browner in appearance.

Neat, black cap, white forehead of juvenile clouded with brown on very young birds; later cleaner.

Sterna hirundo
32–33 cm; 100–140 g
Where to look: coasts, lakes.
Nest: on ground, often on island. **Eggs:** 3, mottled buffish or olive. **Food:** small fish and insects from water surface. **Voice:** short, sharp *kit, kikik*; high, grating, emphatic *KEEY-yah*!

Arctic Tern

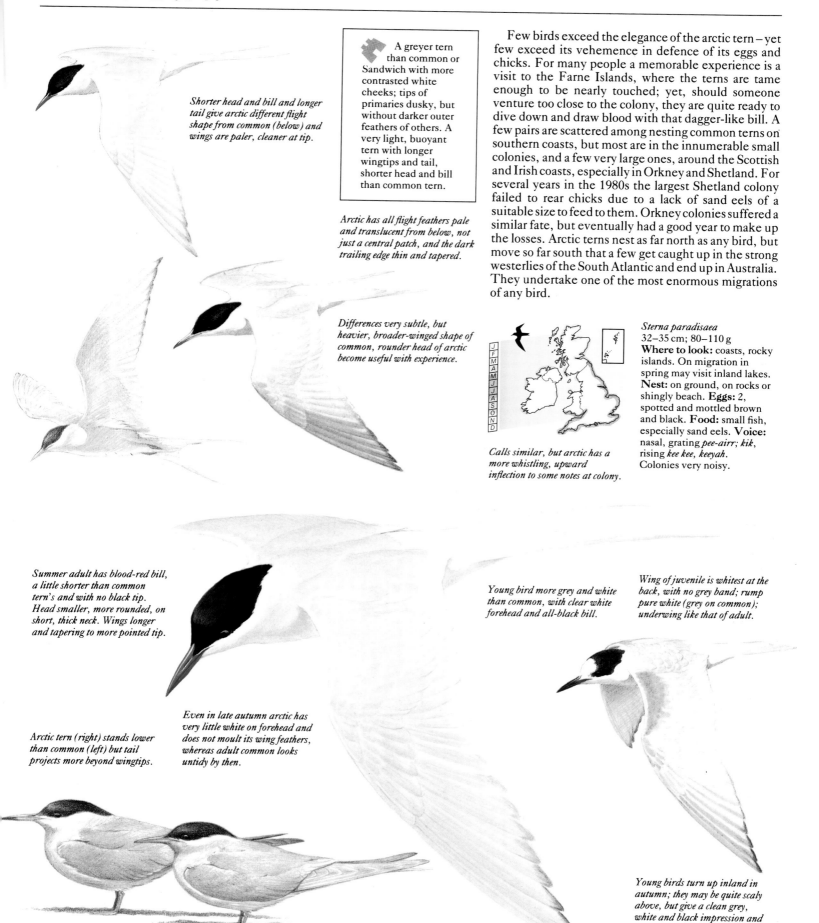

A greyer tern than common or Sandwich with more contrasted white cheeks; tips of primaries dusky, but without darker outer feathers of others. A very light, buoyant tern with longer wingtips and tail, shorter head and bill than common tern.

Shorter head and bill and longer tail give arctic different flight shape from common (below) and wings are paler, cleaner at tip.

Arctic has all flight feathers pale and translucent from below, not just a central patch, and the dark trailing edge thin and tapered.

Differences very subtle, but heavier, broader-winged shape of common, rounder head of arctic become useful with experience.

Few birds exceed the elegance of the arctic tern – yet few exceed its vehemence in defence of its eggs and chicks. For many people a memorable experience is a visit to the Farne Islands, where the terns are tame enough to be nearly touched; yet, should someone venture too close to the colony, they are quite ready to dive down and draw blood with that dagger-like bill. A few pairs are scattered among nesting common terns on southern coasts, but most are in the innumerable small colonies, and a few very large ones, around the Scottish and Irish coasts, especially in Orkney and Shetland. For several years in the 1980s the largest Shetland colony failed to rear chicks due to a lack of sand eels of a suitable size to feed to them. Orkney colonies suffered a similar fate, but eventually had a good year to make up the losses. Arctic terns nest as far north as any bird, but move so far south that a few get caught up in the strong westerlies of the South Atlantic and end up in Australia. They undertake one of the most enormous migrations of any bird.

Calls similar, but arctic has a more whistling, upward inflection to some notes at colony.

Sterna paradisaea
32–35 cm; 80–110 g
Where to look: coasts, rocky islands. On migration in spring may visit inland lakes. **Nest:** on ground, on rocks or shingly beach. **Eggs:** 2, spotted and mottled brown and black. **Food:** small fish, especially sand eels. **Voice:** nasal, grating *pee-airr; kik,* rising *kee kee, keeyah.* Colonies very noisy.

Summer adult has blood-red bill, a little shorter than common tern's and with no black tip. Head smaller, more rounded, on short, thick neck. Wings longer and tapering to more pointed tip.

Even in late autumn arctic has very little white on forehead and does not moult its wing feathers, whereas adult common looks untidy by then.

Young bird more grey and white than common, with clear white forehead and all-black bill.

Wing of juvenile is whitest at the back, with no grey band; rump pure white (grey on common); underwing like that of adult.

Arctic tern (right) stands lower than common (left) but tail projects more beyond wingtips.

Young birds turn up inland in autumn; they may be quite scaly above, but give a clean grey, white and black impression and look especially small, dainty.

Roseate Tern

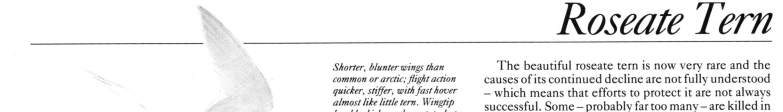

Shorter, blunter wings than common or arctic; flight action quicker, stiffer, with fast hover almost like little tern. Wingtip has blackish marks on top, but a white edge, no black, beneath, unlike common or arctic terns.

Long bill, round head and long tail give recognisable profile.

Bill black in spring, dark red at base in summer, then half red.

Juvenile heavily marked on back; forehead dull; bill, legs black.

Shape similar to Sandwich with long bill and black cap smoothed down over nape, rather chesty appearance – subtly different.

In mixed group roseate stands out very much paler than common terns.

The beautiful roseate tern is now very rare and the causes of its continued decline are not fully understood – which means that efforts to protect it are not always successful. Some – probably far too many – are killed in winter in Ghana, where small boys catch them in snares and with baited hooks on fishing lines. At the colonies in Britain they are killed by peregrines, foxes and rats. In Ireland some colonies have been deserted, for no clear reason. Yet there may be some other, unknown cause for a long-term decline in many parts of the wide range of this tern. It is a lovely bird, especially in spring, with extremely long tail streamers and a pink flush on the otherwise very white underparts. The very pale back and whiteness of its breast help to pick out individuals in mixed tern flocks, and bill colour (though with nearly as much bright red as a common tern's in late summer), flight action, wing pattern and other subtle differences help to confirm the identity of an adult. Juveniles are coarsely marked and have dark foreheads, black bills and black legs.

Sterna dougallii
33–38 cm; 95–130 g
Where to look: rare away from colonies on rocky islets. **Nest:** in hollow, crevice, or under vegetation on ground. **Eggs:** 1 or 2, cream, blotched darker. **Food:** small fish. **Voice:** distinct rasping *aakh* and whistled *chiv-y, chewit*.

Black Tern

A breeding bird of eastern Europe and western Asia, with many scattered colonies in west European river systems and marshes, the black tern is known only as a migrant in Britain. It passes through in quite large numbers in some years, often in a concentrated passage, with many places having flocks of up to a hundred or more, all on, or about, the same day in May, or from late July to September. Then they are gone, leaving just odd birds for the rest of the period. The flocks that pass through are small compared with the numbers that build up in the Netherlands and on some Baltic coasts in autumn, when assemblies of many thousands are normal. They move south to the West African coast, being much more marine in winter than in summer, when they prefer shallow fresh water with plenty of waterside and floating vegetation. Their lazy, erratic progress over marshes and lakes, even during migration, is quite unlike the more direct flight of the 'sea terns' (all the others in this book), though they are capable of migrating at a great height and can sometimes be watched soaring up and away from a reservoir where they were feeding.

Small, short-tailed, grey-rumped tern, never white on top of tail. In spring has black body, in autumn can have black and white mottles before getting white underparts and black cap of winter.

Flight light and erratic, often dipping to surface of water; most often in small groups over lakes.

Juvenile has brown tinge to back, dark brown on front of wing, spot on side of breast, grey tail.

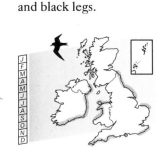

Chlidonias niger
22–24 cm; 60–80 g
Where to look: lakes and reservoirs, calm coastal waters. Mainly spring and autumn. **Food:** insects in summer, otherwise fish, from surface of water in dipping flight. **Voice:** quiet, but may give squeaky *kik-keek*.

Autumn adult like greyer juvenile with breast spot distinctive; in summer sooty-grey, blacker head, white under tail, pale underwing.

Black Guillemot

Cepphus grylle
30–32 cm; 340–450 g
Where to look: on cliffs,
boulder-strewn shores or on
the sea. **Nest:** in a crevice or
among boulders, occasionally
under driftwood. **Eggs:** 2,
white. **Food:** mainly fish.
Voice: a variety of high-
pitched whistles.

*In summer plumage, a striking,
black, pigeon-sized auk, with
white wing patches and red feet.
Flies fast and low over water.*

*The vermilion gape is only likely
to be seen during threat or
courtship displays.*

*In winter, appears pale grey, but
retains the white wing patches.*

*Bright white patches on both
sides of whirring wings.*

The black guillemot, or tystie, as it is also known, is
the most sedentary of Britain's auks, and the only one
with white wing patches. It is widespread along the
rocky shores of north and west Scotland and Ireland. In
Wales it breeds only in Anglesey, and in England only at
St Bees Head, Cumbria. Tysties are usually seen singly
or in small groups. They do not nest together in large
numbers like the other auks. They dive for food,
usually submerging for up to a minute, and prefer the
shallower inshore waters. The white patch on the wings
makes it possible to follow diving birds underwater if
watched from a clifftop using binoculars. Butterfish and
sand eels are the most frequently taken foods. Only one
fish at a time is brought to the chicks, and this is usually
carried crosswise in the bill. Occasionally, a parent
bringing food may be robbed by another parent from a
neighbouring nest. Tysties are vulnerable to oil
spillages near the shore and their eggs and young may be
eaten by introduced mink, but are otherwise fairly free
to enjoy their seaside existence.

*At long range, winter birds may
resemble sea-ducks or small
grebes.*

*At close range, the adult's bright
red feet are even visible through
the water when the bird is
swimming or diving.*

Little Auk

*In summer, upperparts, head
and chest black, underparts
white.*

*Takes flight from water without
running across surface. Flight
low with rapid wing-beats. Has
paler underwing than puffin.*

*In winter, breast, chin and sides
of neck are dirty white, leaving a
dark patch below the eye. Dives
frequently for food.*

*Note the relatively large, heavy
head and the small black, stubby
bill. Head is raised only when
alarmed or excited; more usually
birds have a hunched
appearance.*

Alle alle
17–19 cm; 140–170 g
Where to look: out to sea
from vantage points in late
autumn and winter. Erratic in
occurrence, most commonly
seen during or after stormy
weather. **Food:** plankton.
Voice: usually silent away
from breeding grounds.

Little auks are hardy, starling-sized seabirds which
breed among boulder screes on high arctic islands such
as Greenland and Jan Mayen Island. They are only seen
in Britain in the winter, when the pack-ice covering the
arctic seas drives the birds south in search of open water.
Most birds remain at sea to the north and west of Britain,
but every year small numbers occur in the North Sea.
They are especially prone to being displaced from their
usual wintering areas by severe northerly and westerly
gales. They feed on tiny crustaceans at or near the
surface. During storms their food probably descends
below their reach, forcing them to seek food elsewhere.
In extreme conditions some birds may be blown inland
and may turn up almost anywhere – on roads, in fields or
in gardens! Sometimes these movements, or wrecks,
may involve many hundreds of birds, but more
commonly small wrecks occur each year on the east
coast, particularly in October and January. Birds are
most often seen a day or two after the gales have
subsided, either flying back north, fast and low over the
sea, or sitting hunched-up in calmer waters, frequently
looking rather miserable or sick.

Guillemot

Uria aalge
38–41 cm; 750–1,000 g
Where to look: cliffs and sea
at breeding colonies (March
to July); otherwise out to sea.
Nest: on cliff ledge, less
often among boulders. **Egg:**
1, extremely variable colours.
Food: mainly fish. **Voice:**
prolonged whirring *aaargh*.

Guillemots usually nest on narrow, densely packed ledges in colonies sometimes numbering tens of thousands of birds. The ledges are often so densely occupied that birds may be in physical contact with several neighbours, thereby defending the smallest-known nest area territory of any bird. The colonies are all action, the birds noisy and aggressive, stabbing at neighbours with their dagger-like bills. This appears vicious, but they seldom seem to be injured. In contrast, paired birds commonly preen their partner's head and neck feathers most delicately (this is called allopreening). Like razorbills, guillemots are strong, but not agile, fliers, and are superbly adapted for life in the sea. Underwater, they are strong swimmers, propelled by feet and wings, and capable of diving to depths of over 50 metres (160 ft). Like razorbills, the largest colonies are in northern Britain, particularly in Scotland. The numbers of birds have increased at many northern and eastern colonies in recent years, but the western colonies have shown little change. In the smaller colonies in the south, the declines recorded earlier this century appear to have halted. The breeding population of Britain and Ireland exceeds 700,000 birds, but guillemots are always vulnerable to oil-spills.

At colonies, breeds on tightly packed ledges, sometimes numbering hundreds of noisy, squabbling and sparring birds. How do they find their mates?

Birds with white 'spectacles' (above) are known as 'bridled' guillemots. Their frequency increases from south to north, but the reason is unclear.

In summer, adults in southern Britain have warm chocolate-brown upperparts, gradually becoming darker in colour further north, almost black in Shetland.

Egg shape may have evolved to prevent it rolling off ledges, or perhaps as a consequence of the size and shape of the adult's body.

At about 20 days, the flightless chicks jump from ledges at dusk, landing on rocks or in the sea.

The male parent jumps after its chick, lands on the sea, and calls to it. When reunited, father and young head out to sea.

Birds are gregarious when fishing, often swimming in lines or sometimes encircling shoals.

In winter, chin, throat and sides of neck are white. Note the dark line running back from the eye.

Told from razorbills in flight by dagger-like bill and longer neck. Often flies in small parties of 10–20 birds, sometimes travelling over 30 miles to fishing grounds.

Razorbill

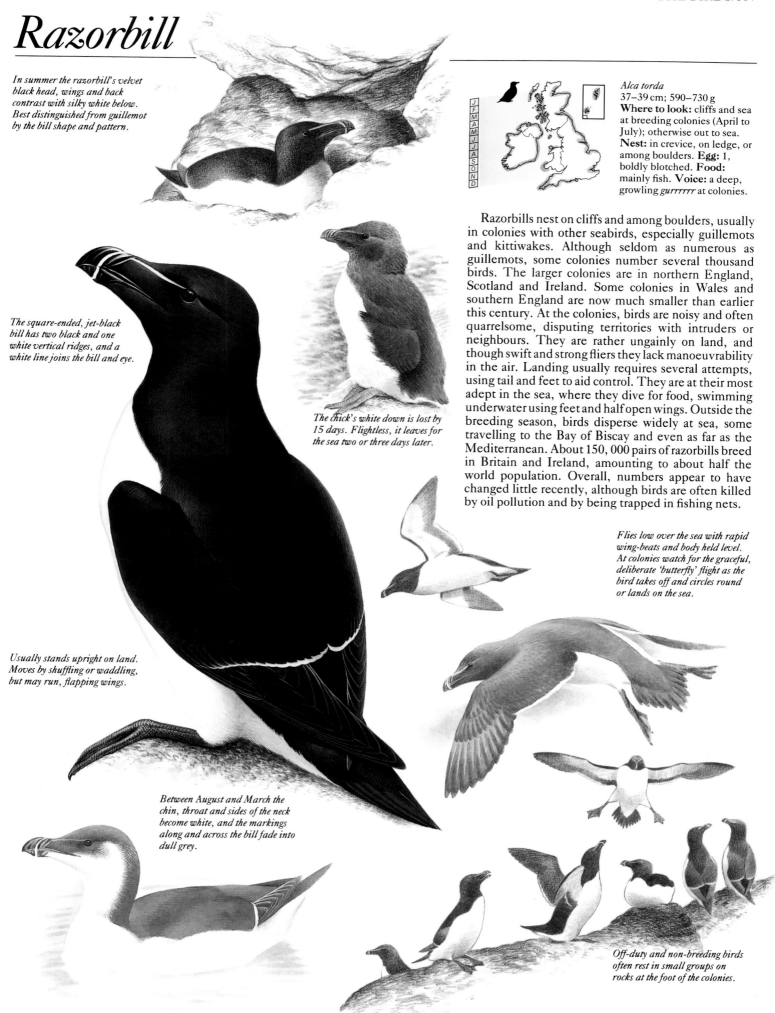

In summer the razorbill's velvet black head, wings and back contrast with silky white below. Best distinguished from guillemot by the bill shape and pattern.

Alca torda
37–39 cm; 590–730 g
Where to look: cliffs and sea at breeding colonies (April to July); otherwise out to sea. **Nest:** in crevice, on ledge, or among boulders. **Egg:** 1, boldly blotched. **Food:** mainly fish. **Voice:** a deep, growling *gurrrrrr* at colonies.

Razorbills nest on cliffs and among boulders, usually in colonies with other seabirds, especially guillemots and kittiwakes. Although seldom as numerous as guillemots, some colonies number several thousand birds. The larger colonies are in northern England, Scotland and Ireland. Some colonies in Wales and southern England are now much smaller than earlier this century. At the colonies, birds are noisy and often quarrelsome, disputing territories with intruders or neighbours. They are rather ungainly on land, and though swift and strong fliers they lack manoeuvrability in the air. Landing usually requires several attempts, using tail and feet to aid control. They are at their most adept in the sea, where they dive for food, swimming underwater using feet and half open wings. Outside the breeding season, birds disperse widely at sea, some travelling to the Bay of Biscay and even as far as the Mediterranean. About 150,000 pairs of razorbills breed in Britain and Ireland, amounting to about half the world population. Overall, numbers appear to have changed little recently, although birds are often killed by oil pollution and by being trapped in fishing nets.

The square-ended, jet-black bill has two black and one white vertical ridges, and a white line joins the bill and eye.

The chick's white down is lost by 15 days. Flightless, it leaves for the sea two or three days later.

Flies low over the sea with rapid wing-beats and body held level. At colonies watch for the graceful, deliberate 'butterfly' flight as the bird takes off and circles round or lands on the sea.

Usually stands upright on land. Moves by shuffling or waddling, but may run, flapping wings.

Between August and March the chin, throat and sides of the neck become white, and the markings along and across the bill fade into dull grey.

Off-duty and non-breeding birds often rest in small groups on rocks at the foot of the colonies.

Puffin

Fratercula arctica
26–29 cm; 310–490 g
Where to look: at colonies on grassy slopes or cliffs or on the sea from March to August. Attendance can be erratic, especially early in the season. Birds most numerous in early evenings in July. **Nest:** in a burrow 1–2 metres (3–6 ft) long, less often in crevices on cliffs. **Egg:** 1. **Food:** mainly fish, but also crustaceans. **Voice:** a low nasal *kaa-arr-arr* at the colonies, silent elsewhere.

The large, powerful bill is slightly hooked to help hold slippery prey. The feet are strong and used for swimming, for extra control when flying and for excavating burrows.

Puffins walk, and sometimes run, standing upright on their feet alone, rather than using their legs and feet like other auks.

Standing on a grassy slope outside its burrow, the puffin is unmistakable. It is Britain's most colourful seabird, comical to watch and naturally inquisitive. The main colonies are in northern Scotland, the largest on St Kilda, west of the Outer Hebrides. Last century, St Kilda may have held over one million pairs, but now there are probably about one fifth that number. Numbers also declined earlier this century at other colonies, especially in southern England and Wales. The decline now appears to have halted, and some northern colonies may be increasing. The decline was probably caused by climatic change influencing sea temperature, which affected the distribution of fish. Pesticides or oil pollution were probably not the cause. About 700,000 puffins now breed in Britain and Ireland. Most nest in burrows, many of which are regularly occupied from year to year. The birds may excavate the burrows themselves, or use those of Manx shearwaters or rabbits, with whom they sometimes share a common entrance. Early in the breeding season thousands of birds may be present on one day and almost none on the next. July is the best month to watch them. By mid-August they have left the colony, not to return to land until the following March.

The triangular red, yellow and blue bill, white face, curious eye markings, black head, back and wings, white undersides and bright red feet make puffins quite unmistakable. Amusing to watch, they walk with a waddle, display, fight each other, and cock their heads to one side to watch you watching them.

In winter puffins are far out to sea, and rarely seen from land.

Unmistakable, with large bright bill, white face, red feet. Often appears comical, angling head and hopping around burrow. Flies low and fast over the sea. Seldom seen in winter.

The 'billing' display commonly occurs between paired birds. The male may become so excited that he pushes the female downhill.

In flight, the large head and bill give a rounded profile to the front. The underside of the wing is darker than other auks'.

For the first three weeks of life the black-brown, downy chick remains in the darkness of its burrow.

By four weeks the down is lost and the bill is longer. The chick may exercise wings at burrow entrance, usually at night.

Adults may suddenly take flight, circling the colony in wheeling flocks of thousands of birds.

At five or six weeks the youngster is deserted in the burrow by its parents. It leaves the burrow at night and flies out to sea.

Puffins are highly gregarious in summer, often gathering in large 'rafts' under the colony. They roost at sea, sleeping with the bill tucked under the wing.

Adults carrying fish to their young may be chased by gulls or skuas. They often escape by crashing into the sea.

The bill of a first-winter, immature bird begins to take the shape and colour of the adult, but is still smaller and duller.

Puffins are superbly adapted to catching fish underwater, often at depths of 15 metres (50 ft). When feeding young, birds may catch several fish in one dive, holding them crosswise in the bill.

In winter, the adult's face is dark grey. The bill is deeper than an immature bird's but not as large or as bright as it is in summer.

Rafts under the colony may include many immature and non-breeding birds. When feeding, flocks are usually small, most commonly of two or three birds.

In summer, the enlarged bill is bright red, yellow and blue. Note the red eye ring, blue above and below, and swollen yellow gape.

Woodpigeon

Large, heavy, deep-chested pigeon with long, broad tail. Bigger-bodied, smaller-headed than falcons and sparrowhawk.

Crescents of white on wing and adult's neck patch unique. Tail has pale central band, dark tip.

Underwing soft grey; head well forward on thin neck.

Shot in thousands, woodpigeons are reluctant to allow man too close. Yet when unmolested, in a town park or public grounds, they quickly become approachable. Only then does the full beauty and size of this pigeon become apparent. The dash and agility shown in a sudden, noisy escape flight through a shrubbery should hardly fail to impress — but pigeons are pigeons, and usually ignored! Town woodpigeons start to nest in February, with a peak in April and May. Rural birds start later, peaking from July to September. This is due to the different availability of food. These pigeons have been thoroughly studied. They are very agile in trees, but feed mainly on the ground. Flocks have subordinate birds in front, with slower pecking rates than the dominant pigeons. Their feeding rate increases to a peak just before they fly to roost, but most food is taken in the afternoon. In the autumn stubble, only five to 10 per cent of the daylight is spent feeding; but in winter 95 per cent is spent feeding on pastures, and a little less in richer habitats.

Columba palumbus
40–42 cm; 480–550 g
Where to look: farmland with trees, woods, parks.
Nest: thin platform of sticks in tree. **Eggs:** 1–2, white.
Food: leaves, seeds, berries, buds, grain. **Voice:** *coo COOO coo, coo-coo,* in series, last with extra *oo* at end.

Display flight often seen in full or in reduced intensity — high, steep climb followed by one or several whip-cracks of wingtips, then downward glide with fanned tail.

Looks grey at distance, but close views reveal browner back, pink breast, attractive eye and bill colours, smooth appearance.

Take-off quick and agile, with noisy clattering of wings; very high upstroke and deep downbeat give instant power for escape.

Feeding birds look long-bodied, short-legged; very quiet, calling only when singing from perch.

Pigeons often seen high up, easily taken for hawk. Woodpigeon largest, long-tailed, long-winged; stock dove rounder in head and wing shape, dumpy; rock dove has white rump, more pointed wings; racing pigeons have longer neck, swept-back wings set farther back.

Juvenile bird dull, with wing marks, but no white neck patches.

Feeding flocks easily disturbed, but incoming woodpigeon causes no panic despite hawk-like shape; wing patches may allay fear.

Rock Dove/Feral Pigeon

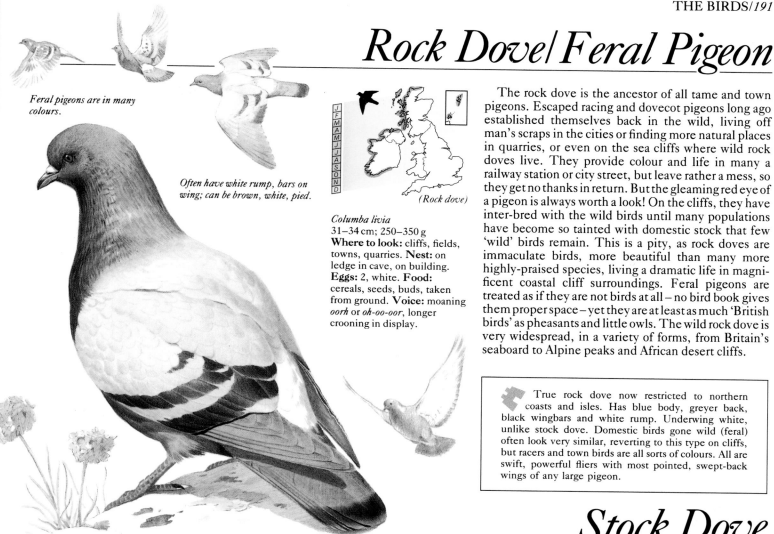

Feral pigeons are in many colours.

Often have white rump, bars on wing; can be brown, white, pied.

(Rock dove)

Columba livia
31–34 cm; 250–350 g
Where to look: cliffs, fields, towns, quarries. **Nest:** on ledge in cave, on building. **Eggs:** 2, white. **Food:** cereals, seeds, buds, taken from ground. **Voice:** moaning *oorh* or *oh-oo-oor*, longer crooning in display.

The rock dove is the ancestor of all tame and town pigeons. Escaped racing and dovecot pigeons long ago established themselves back in the wild, living off man's scraps in the cities or finding more natural places in quarries, or even on the sea cliffs where wild rock doves live. They provide colour and life in many a railway station or city street, but leave rather a mess, so they get no thanks in return. But the gleaming red eye of a pigeon is always worth a look! On the cliffs, they have inter-bred with the wild birds until many populations have become so tainted with domestic stock that few 'wild' birds remain. This is a pity, as rock doves are immaculate birds, more beautiful than many more highly-praised species, living a dramatic life in magnificent coastal cliff surroundings. Feral pigeons are treated as if they are not birds at all – no bird book gives them proper space – yet they are at least as much 'British birds' as pheasants and little owls. The wild rock dove is very widespread, in a variety of forms, from Britain's seaboard to Alpine peaks and African desert cliffs.

True rock dove now restricted to northern coasts and isles. Has blue body, greyer back, black wingbars and white rump. Underwing white, unlike stock dove. Domestic birds gone wild (feral) often look very similar, reverting to this type on cliffs, but racers and town birds are all sorts of colours. All are swift, powerful fliers with most pointed, swept-back wings of any large pigeon.

Stock Dove

The stock dove is best-known as a bird of farmland and parkland with old trees, which give it nest sites in cavities and holes where branches have been wrenched away in gales. But it is also at home wherever a cliff ledge or cavity gives it room to lay its glossy eggs, so long as this is within easy flying distance of suitable feeding grounds. So, it can be seen, rather unexpectedly, high up on moorland crags or even on sea cliffs. The stock dove often visits open pools, such as new gravel pits, to drink at the water's edge. It is much less likely to become tame or to live in a park than the woodpigeon.

Stock doves are often overlooked, but become easy to spot with practice – in flight they look neat, rounded pigeons, without the speed and dash of a racing pigeon, but far less ponderous, shorter-tailed and rounder-headed than the bigger, more numerous woodpigeon. On the ground, they are likely to be seen in pairs rather than huge flocks (though occasionally up to a hundred or two may gather together), and in good light they look a lovely shade of slightly purplish blue. The call is also a give-away, especially from the depths of a big tree or from an overgrown quarry face. It has a loud, almost booming quality about it, with a rhythmic pattern quite unlike the lazy crooning of the woodpigeon. The name 'dove' is more or less interchangeable with 'pigeon', but if there *is* a difference then in the case of rock and stock doves it is wrongly applied: 'doves' tend to be the smaller, lighter, longer-tailed species, which makes the rock dove and stock dove both undeniably 'pigeons'.

Flight is fast; quicker action than woodpigeon.

Upperside shows pale centre and blackish edges to wings; no white, but two small bars near body.

Columba oenas
32–34 cm; 290–330 g
Where to look: fields, woods, open spaces near gravel pits. **Nest:** hole in tree, ledge of cliff or building. **Eggs:** 2, white. **Food:** seeds, leaves, buds, flowers. **Voice:** deep series of *ooo-uh* or *orr-wump* calls, second note abrupt.

Looks a darker, bluer bird than woodpigeon on ground, with shorter tail, rounder body and neater shape.

Collared Dove

Small, slim dove with long, broad wings and long tail, held closed in normal flight, but fanned in display or when braking to land. Flight active, with quick, rhythmic wing-beats, wings quite bowed or arched. Round head, steep forehead, thin, dark bill and dark eye in plain face.

Pale grey-fawn with pink breast and thin black half-ring on neck.

Head paler, wingtips darker than basic colour; tail rather long, with white corners on top, black base with broad white tip below.

Display flight from roof, tree or lamp post; steep rise before long glide down; note grey on wings.

Small round head on slim neck helps separate from kestrel at a distance; plainer back than turtle dove; slimmer than pigeons.

Readily comes to gardens and any places with spilt grain, seeds, scraps; large flocks around docks, distilleries and farms.

Juvenile bird pale and dull, with no collar at first. Tail pattern and length still distinctive.

The collared dove arrived in Britain in the 1950s. Its spread across Europe, from ancestral dry, hot habitats in India, to a cooler, damper environment closely connected with man and spilt grain has been well documented. By 1964 about 3,000 pairs were breeding in Britain; by 1972 there were between 30,000 and 40,000 pairs, but the increase was beginning to ease off. The north-westward spread took the bird to the Faroes and Iceland, but the cause of the phenomenal expansion has not been fully explained. Collared doves are gregarious and good feeding sites attract flocks even in the breeding season. Town centres and open country where other pigeons are common are usually avoided, but gardens, shrubberies, allotments and farms are eagerly sought; these doves often come to bird-tables. Unless persecuted, they become very approachable, but the monotonous *ku-koo-kuk* calls can be tiresome just after dawn in midsummer, and are also the chief cause of over-optimistic reports of early cuckoos! The breeding season is very prolonged and there may be three, sometimes even six, broods of two young each reared by a single pair each year.

Streptopelia decaocto
31–33 cm; 150–220 g
Where to look: suburbs with conifers, parks, farms. **Nest:** in tree, near trunk. **Eggs:** 2, white. **Food:** grain, seeds, fruits. **Voice:** *ku-KOO-kuk*, abrupt at end; nasal *kwurr* or *ghee-gheee* in alarm and in gliding display.

Turtle Dove

As the pleasant cawing of rooks epitomises spring in wooded parkland and the bubbling of the curlew is the essence of early summer in the hills, so the long, rolling, deep song of the turtle dove means high summer in the country lanes of southern England. The main problem for the turtle dove, other than cool, wet summers that reduce breeding success, is that the tall, ancient hedges which it loves so well are often grubbed out, so that there is less room for it than ever before. It needs big hawthorns, unkempt elders and small trees, in farmland or on the edge of a broken, sunny wood if it is to survive in the face of agricultural change. Though happy to forage in the quiet lanes of a village, it is unlikely to nest close to human habitation and is far less of a garden bird than the collared dove. In the winter it makes for the Sahel, south of the Sahara, where the droughts of recent years, compounded by loss of forest and scrub, may also affect its numbers, but in some African areas huge concentrations still occur. Sadly, huge numbers are illegally killed in southern Europe each spring.

Small, slim dove with thin neck and protruding round head, deep chest, giving typical pigeon-like form, but rather long, wedge-tipped tail and swept-back wings. Flight characteristic, with flickering, jerky wing-beats, irregular short glides, sometimes tilting from side to side. Lands with a flurry of wings, tail fanned and showing broad white edges. A summer visitor, April or May to September; absent in winter.

Agile dove, quick to fly off if disturbed, quieter than pigeon, but some clatter of wings; has no flight call, unlike collared.

Pattern recalls kestrel, but flight and shape quite different.

Compare underside of tail with that of collared dove. This is a neater, shorter-tailed dove.

Upperside neatly patterned with light orange-brown and black; head pink. Note blue on wing.

Streptopelia turtur
26–28 cm; 130–180 g
Where to look: woodland edge, lowland farmland, hedges. **Nest:** in hedge or tree. **Eggs:** 1–2, white. **Food:** weed seeds, buds, leaves, cereals. **Voice:** purring song *coorrrr-coorrrr*, rather deep, lazy.

Often seen in flocks in late spring, migrating along coasts; then in feeding parties in late summer on arable land.

Perches on wires, but mostly out of sight in hedges or thickets, not so obvious as collared dove.

Typical late summer group on wires above stubble field, with one much larger woodpigeon.

Note pattern of dark rump and tail with white sides and tip.

Sides of neck have barred or striped patch. When calling, throat and breast puffed out.

Juvenile duller, browner, with no striped neck patch, but still easy to identify given good view. Song is good clue to adult.

Cuckoo

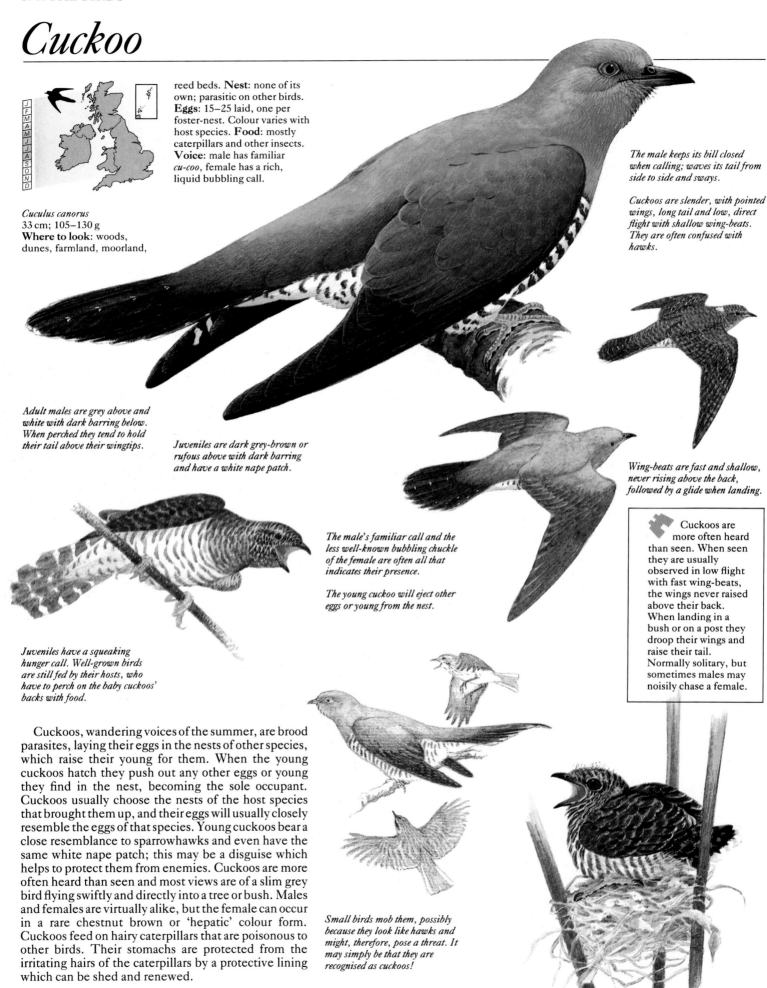

reed beds. **Nest:** none of its own; parasitic on other birds. **Eggs:** 15–25 laid, one per foster-nest. Colour varies with host species. **Food:** mostly caterpillars and other insects. **Voice:** male has familiar *cu-coo*, female has a rich, liquid bubbling call.

Cuculus canorus
33 cm; 105–130 g
Where to look: woods, dunes, farmland, moorland,

The male keeps its bill closed when calling; waves its tail from side to side and sways.

Cuckoos are slender, with pointed wings, long tail and low, direct flight with shallow wing-beats. They are often confused with hawks.

Adult males are grey above and white with dark barring below. When perched they tend to hold their tail above their wingtips.

Juveniles are dark grey-brown or rufous above with dark barring and have a white nape patch.

Wing-beats are fast and shallow, never rising above the back, followed by a glide when landing.

The male's familiar call and the less well-known bubbling chuckle of the female are often all that indicates their presence.

The young cuckoo will eject other eggs or young from the nest.

Cuckoos are more often heard than seen. When seen they are usually observed in low flight with fast wing-beats, the wings never raised above their back. When landing in a bush or on a post they droop their wings and raise their tail. Normally solitary, but sometimes males may noisily chase a female.

Juveniles have a squeaking hunger call. Well-grown birds are still fed by their hosts, who have to perch on the baby cuckoos' backs with food.

Cuckoos, wandering voices of the summer, are brood parasites, laying their eggs in the nests of other species, which raise their young for them. When the young cuckoos hatch they push out any other eggs or young they find in the nest, becoming the sole occupant. Cuckoos usually choose the nests of the host species that brought them up, and their eggs will usually closely resemble the eggs of that species. Young cuckoos bear a close resemblance to sparrowhawks and even have the same white nape patch; this may be a disguise which helps to protect them from enemies. Cuckoos are more often heard than seen and most views are of a slim grey bird flying swiftly and directly into a tree or bush. Males and females are virtually alike, but the female can occur in a rare chestnut brown or 'hepatic' colour form. Cuckoos feed on hairy caterpillars that are poisonous to other birds. Their stomachs are protected from the irritating hairs of the caterpillars by a protective lining which can be shed and renewed.

Small birds mob them, possibly because they look like hawks and might, therefore, pose a threat. It may simply be that they are recognised as cuckoos!

Nightjar

Secret and mysterious birds of bushy heaths and rough gorsy commons, nightjars are never easy to observe. Unless it is a clear, calm, warm evening there is no guarantee that they will be seen or heard, but late twilight on a midsummer evening is the best time to seek them. You may have to be content with hearing the sustained churring song, but with luck a pair will hunt for moths against the dim light of the sky, or come twisting and swirling around a birdwatcher's head as they would an isolated bush. During the day they sit along a log or on a patch of bare ground, almost impossible to find. They arrive here in May and leave for Africa in August and September, when several may migrate together. The British population is small and declining due to habitat loss and disturbance (sometimes by birdwatchers), pesticides and climatic change, a combination which is difficult to resist.

Nightjars are best seen at dusk when they begin to call. They fly silently after insects with many sudden twists and glides.

Wings clapped loudly in display flight; also glide with wings raised and tail spread.

Males have conspicuous white spots near the wingtips and on the outer tips of the tail. Females and young lack these.

The churring song is loud and vibrant at close range, far less high and metallic than song of grasshopper warbler.

Caprimulgus europaeus
27 cm; 75–100 g
Where to look: heathland, felled woodland, new plantations, moorland and dunes with bracken and scrub. **Nest:** on bare ground. **Eggs:** 2, mottled grey. **Food:** flying insects, mainly moths and beetles. **Voice:** song is a loud churring trill which rises and falls, given by perched male. Both sexes also have a deep *kooick* flight call.

Barn Owl

Tyto alba
33–35 cm; 250–350 g
Where to look: mainly farmland, field edges, rough grassland. **Nest:** hole in tree, sometimes in quarries, or in ruins, barns or other outbuildings. **Eggs:** 4–7, white. **Food:** mainly rodents. **Voice:** snores, shrieks.

Appears exceptionally pale above; white face and underparts; long, but rounded wings.

Barn owl often hunts in flight, low over ground, flapping and gliding, with frequent changes of direction and occasional hovering. Often drops briefly to ground.

Also hunts from exposed perch at no great height above ground, on fence posts, walls, banks, etc, looking and listening before pouncing.

The barn owl's extraordinarily well-developed sense of hearing may be more important in hunting than vision: prey located by ear can be caught in total darkness.

Long, white-feathered legs often obvious, lowered while hunting in readiness for the kill.

Road verges often provide ideal habitat for voles and other small mammals — sometimes even along main roads. Hunting barn owls frequently become traffic victims.

The barn owl is one of the most widely distributed birds in the world. Those in Britain are at the extreme north-west edge of the range in Europe, and Scottish barn owls are probably the most northerly in the world. Sadly, in many areas the barn owl is now very scarce, or has gone altogether. This decline is known to have been going on for over 50 years, but it has clearly accelerated in the last 25 years or so. It is not known whether any long-term factor such as climate is involved, nor is it easy to be totally clear about other, more short-term causes. But it seems highly likely that the enormous changes in agriculture, especially in arable farming, during the last 20–30 years are at the root of the matter. The loss of prey-rich field edges and corners, rough pastures and similar areas has been critical; this habitat loss has been exacerbated by pesticides and also by the loss of nest sites as hedgerow trees disappear and farm buildings are pulled down, modernised or converted. Persecution has probably been minimal: barn owls have long been welcomed as neighbours on farmland. More research into barn owl habitat needs, and co-operative work with farmers, may provide some answers and some remedies. However, until we understand and can correct environmental problems captive breeding and release is a waste of time. Unfortunately, attempts to put barn owls back into places that have become unable to support them inevitably fail, but get much media attention, focussed on the 'cuddly owl', which does little to put the problem into true perspective.

Seen well, a barn owl is unmistakable. Note large, round-topped head with characteristic heart-shaped face and dark eyes, very long legs (looks 'knock-kneed' when seen from front). Always looks extremely pale and flashes ghostly white in car headlights — but beware deceptively pale look of all owls in headlights at night. Very rare snowy owl is much bigger, bulkier; male all white, female and young barred; yellow eyes.

Owls have relatively long, muscular legs; in most species (all those in Britain) these are feathered to the base of the toes — the reason for this is not fully understood.

The toes are powerful and equipped with long, sharp talons. The outer toe is reversible, giving better grip on prey.

Soft-toothed feather edges help reduce noise in flight.

The kill: a short, headlong plunge with wings up and back and feet swinging in at moment of impact. Prey is seized and killed in the talons, often picked up in bill.

The call of the barn owl is popularly described as a blood-curdling shriek, but is not familiar to many people. A variety of snores and hisses come from the nest site.

Prey may be carried in bill as owl flies up, but is usually quickly transferred to one foot while carried to nest; then passed to bill again on arrival.

The vole or mouse usually has no idea what hit it.

Sometimes, however, there may be a short chase on the ground.

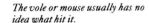

Eggs are laid at intervals of 2–3 days, but incubation begins with first egg laid: this results in a staggered hatch — first owlet in family eight days older than 5th.

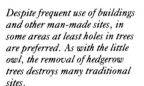

Despite frequent use of buildings and other man-made sites, in some areas at least holes in trees are preferred. As with the little owl, the removal of hedgerow trees destroys many traditional sites.

The characteristically large black pellets of undigested prey remains accumulate in large amounts at nests and roosts. Many studies throughout Britain show that small mammals (voles, mice, rats, shrews) form about 90 per cent of prey taken, but although voles and wood mice often predominate there is much variation according to habitats and seasons.

Nesting barn owls require freedom from disturbance: nest visits are illegal without licence.

No nest as such: bird lays on floor, ledge, beam in building etc.

While some are partly diurnal (out in daylight), owls, essentially nocturnal hunters, effectively take over from day-hunting birds of prey after dark. As a group, though, they have not specialised as some of the day-hunters have: for instance, there are no owls which exist mainly on carrion, or by taking bats on the wing. It is not quite true that owls can 'see in the dark' – at least, not in complete darkness – but their extremely large, specially constructed eyes help them to see very well at very low levels of light. Contrary to popular belief, owls can see perfectly well in daylight. They have phenomenally efficient ears: hunting owls rely on their sense of hearing far more than is generally realised and several species, including barn and long-eared owls, are known to be able to locate and then capture prey which they cannot see at all. Many, such as the tawny owl, have dense, soft plumage and soft-fringed wing feathers – giving silent flight, a great advantage to an owl. Bright colours and striking plumage patterns are not appropriate to night birds and indeed owls tend to have camouflaged plumage instead – but this is not necessary for barn owls, which roost in holes and buildings. Many owls have very loud voices with which to proclaim territories, warn rivals and attract mates.

Little Owl

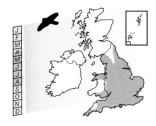

Athene noctua
21–23 cm; 150–200 g
Where to look: farmland, field edges, semi-open habitat with scattered trees, quarries, waste ground, etc. **Nest:** hole in tree, bank, cliff or ground. May use nestbox. **Eggs:** 2–5, white. **Food:** small mammals and birds, but also many insects and other invertebrates, including earthworms. **Voice:** song is repeated, plaintive *kiu*. Call is loud, ringing *werro*.

Though very short, it is dumpy and heavily built and looks quite a large bird in flight.

Over much of central and southern England, the little owl is much the most likely owl to be seen by the average birdwatcher. Although it does much of its hunting after dark, it is often abroad well before dusk, especially in summer. Other owls occasionally sit out in the open by day, but the little owl is the only one to do so as a matter of course, often using the same perch (often a most conspicuous one) very regularly. This is not a native British bird, but owes its presence here to a series of introductions during the latter half of the 19th century. Its spread has been limited by bouts of persecution, by occasional severe winters and by the use of agricultural pesticides. It may also have lost some ground in areas where intensive arable farming has caused widespread changes in habitat and, especially perhaps, the loss of old hedgerow trees. While it is a common and widespread bird in other parts of Europe, its distribution here is much more confined to the lowlands and – a direct reflection of the high proportion of insects and other invertebrates in its diet – is clearly also related to climatic conditions, especially winter temperatures. The loud, clear calls of this owl are not familiar to most people, yet give one of the best means of locating a pair in spring. They have a distinctive, clear quality and carry far, yet even experienced birdwatchers are often left puzzled by the sound.

Relaxed little owl has squat, big-headed shape, but when alarmed or curious will stretch tall, jerking body from side to side, bobbing head up and down. May shock observer by suddenly turning head upside down!

Characteristically perches out in open, almost immobile for hours.

In flight, is dumpy and thickset with blunt head and rounded wings. Quick wing-beats, characteristic heavy, bounding flight action.

Preferred nest site, if available, is often hole low in old or pollarded tree, often at field edge or in hedgerow. May be used for years and adults often have regular perches close by.

Little owl was one of the first British birds of prey whose diet was studied in any detail, after widespread complaints that it was killing many gamebird chicks: it was completely vindicated — study revealed high invertebrate content of diet and almost no gamebirds.

Small pellets often accumulate below favourite roosts and nest sites. Look for beetle wing-cases and other insect remains: precise identification of prey difficult.

Small size, rather broad and flat-topped head readily distinguish little owl. Usually looks squat and dumpy — yellow eyes very obvious. Habit of using conspicuous daytime perches good identification point.

Tawny Owl

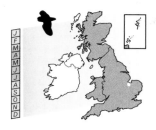

Strix aluco
37–39 cm; 350–500 g
Where to look: woods, parks, gardens, villages, towns – any area with trees. **Nest:** in hole in tree, sometimes in ground or in building. Will use nestbox. **Eggs:** 2–5, white. **Food:** usually small mammals, but versatile enough to switch to birds in towns. **Voice:** the commonest call is loud *kewick*. Song is loud, far-carrying musical *hoooo . . . hoo-hoo huhoooo.*

May have regular, conspicuous perch on nightly rounds, used as song post to hunt from. In towns often uses roofs, chimneys, walls – as well as steps on telegraph poles.

Adaptability can be the key to a species' success; this is certainly the case with the tawny owl. Originally purely a woodland bird, it has moved out into many man-modified habitats in the lowlands and, despite being absent from Ireland, is easily the commonest and most widespread of Britain's owls. It even lives in parks and large gardens in the hearts of cities. Woodland tawny owls feed mainly on wood mice and bank voles, but elsewhere they adapt readily to whatever small mammal species are available; in towns and cities they have switched to preying on small birds.

Tawny owls are thoroughly nocturnal and are thus seldom seen in daylight, unless found at a roost, where their presence may be revealed by the mobbing behaviour of small birds. After dark, they can often be found on the regular perches on their nightly 'beat', but are usually hard to see in treetops and other thick cover where they spend much of their time. They are much more often heard than seen: the commonest call is a loud *kewick*. The tremulous, far-carrying song, so beloved of TV sound effects men, is almost too well-known to require description. The word 'hooting' scarcely does it justice, however. Occasionally an owl will hoot in the middle of the day, a rather incongruous sound then, but the full performance is reserved until well after dark.

Superb camouflage helps to hide tawny owl at (often regular) roosting place. Presence may be given away, however, by gathering of small birds mobbing owl and alarm-calling continuously.

Flying tawny owl looks quite bulky, with big head, short tail and broad, medium-long wings; flies with soft (and silent) flapping, often with short glides. Can appear very pale in car headlights.

Downy juvenile: young owls are mobile well before they can fly and call continuously to be fed.

Plumage variable, but 'tawny' is misnomer. May be more chestnut than shown, or much greyer. Note big rounded head, black eyes and stocky appearance.

As with other owls, undigested parts of prey – bones, teeth, fur, feathers, etc – regurgitated in pellets found under perches.

For obvious reasons it is very difficult to see what owls catch and eat. Pellets provide many clues and enable long-term food studies to be made: these show seasonal changes in diet and explain changes in abundance or breeding success. The tawny owl was among the first to be studied in this way.

Long-eared Owl

Asio otus
35–37 cm; 220–300 g
Where to look: plantations, woods, copses, etc. **Nest:** old nest of magpie, crow; in some areas in cover on ground. **Eggs:** 3–5, white. **Food:** mainly voles, also other small mammals and birds. **Voice:** song is low, quiet cooing.

In flight, long-winged, but darker on underparts than short-eared.

Uses old nest of other bird (or squirrel drey) in thick cover.

Very often the first clue to the presence of this elusive bird is the 'squeaky gate' call of the young waiting to be fed. Breeding long-eared owls easily escape detection – the song period is short, and the low, cooing song quiet. Even the male's aerial display flying and wing-clapping can pass unnoticed. The birdwatcher's task is made no easier by the bird's strongly nocturnal habits and the fact that it chooses to nest in dense cover, generally preferring plantations and copses, but also using larger woods, shelterbelts and thick, tall scrub or bushes. Winter roosts, often in traditional sites, usually provide the best chance of seeing these owls, although birds feeding young may appear well before dark (and after dawn): hunting takes place over open areas, not in thick cover. The ear-tufts can be raised or lowered and the facial discs opened or closed, according to mood; alarmed birds often assume a characteristically slim, upright posture. In a tangled willow thicket or hawthorn scrub they blend in amazingly well; even in a green pine they are surprisingly hard to spot.

Facial discs are mobile, giving different expressions: open with ear-tufts erect when alarmed, shut and tufts down when relaxed.

Impressive threat posture used by young when threatened.

Short-eared Owl

In flight, typically looks pale and long-winged, moving buoyantly; perches on posts or level ground.

Pale underwing very like long-eared owl, but upperwing looks more barred, underparts whiter.

Yellow eyes surprisingly obvious, even on flying bird.

Ear-tufts very small, seldom seen except on wary or alarmed bird.

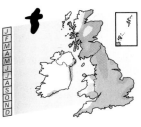

Asio flammeus
37–39 cm; 280–350 g
Where to look: open moorland, rough pastures, marshes, coasts. **Nest:** none made. **Eggs:** 4–8 (or more), white. **Food:** principally voles. **Voice:** least vocal of owls, but rasping and barking calls, deep *boo-boo-boo*.

Always nests on ground in thick cover. Like other owls, male hunts for family and female remains at nest with young.

Unlike the long-eared owl, this bird is not too difficult to see. It is often abroad in full daylight and can be very conspicuous as it hunts over the open moors, heaths, rough grasslands and young plantations where it breeds, or the coastal marshes where it is often found in winter. The principal prey of the short-eared owl is, in most areas, the short-tailed vole. It is the abundance or otherwise of this small mammal which governs both the numbers and the breeding of the owl: in years when voles are plentiful, short-eared owls will lay large numbers of eggs and rear large families. Similarly, the amount of prey available in winter quarters dictates how many owls will be in an area, or whether, as often happens, they will be absent altogether. The classic relationship between the predator and its prey is strikingly illustrated by this species. It shows too how the effects can be very marked with such a specialised predator: they are much less obvious with a more versatile bird like the tawny owl. In late winter and spring the short-eared owl may fly high up in display, calling with hollow, booming notes and clapping its wings rapidly beneath its body.

Swift

Rapid, winnowing wing-beats alternate with short glides.

Parties of screaming swifts chase low over roofs on fine evenings.

Swifts are sometimes confused with those other aerial insect eaters, the swallows and martins. As well as larger size, distinguishing features are all dark plumage (pale underneath in the others) and the very long, narrow, crescent- or bow-shaped wings, held more stiffly, without obvious 'elbow' (actually wrist) bend. In fine weather, swifts feed high in the sky, circling on flickering wings, followed by long glides, often tilting. In rapid flight, they may give the illusion of beating their wings alternately.

Although the bill is small, the gape is enormous to help catch its insect food.

Adults are dark sooty brown, appearing black, with pale chin. Young show more white on throat and forehead, visible in flight.

Groups can be watched spiralling up out of sight into a clear evening sky to sleep on the wing.

Non-breeding swifts may undertake journeys of 100 miles or more to avoid heavy rain.

The tiny legs are almost useless, though the four strong claws allow the bird to cling to vertical surfaces.

Exceptionally long primary feathers and short inner wing create the familiar crescent shape, ideal for rapid sustained flight.

The swift is a very remarkable bird: it is the only insectivorous bird whose young hatch at staggered intervals, thus ensuring that at least the oldest survives. Moreover, both eggs and young can survive long periods of chilling if the weather prevents the adults from feeding close by. Adults, too, are able to enter a state of torpor, and remarkable clusters of birds, clinging to walls like swarms of bees have, very occasionally, been recorded.

On leaving the nest for the first and only time, a young swift heads south immediately without its parents, and may remain on the wing non-stop for two or three years! Swifts not only feed, bathe and 'sleep' aloft, but even on occasions mate on the wing. Only when nesting do they roost 'normally'. They may fly well over a million miles in their life of maybe 10 years or more.

They probably eat more animals than any other British bird. Analysis of 12 food-balls intended for the young revealed more than 300 species of insects and spiders. One bird may catch 10,000 individual insects in a day. Although it does fly fast, a feeding swift takes insects in slow, steady glides.

Shallow-forked tail usually closed, used for greater control.

Every swift seems to carry more than its fair share of parasites, including the large, green, flightless louse-fly.

The hobby is the only regular predator on the swift; it may resemble a large swift in shape.

Apus apus
16–17 cm; 35–50 g
Where to look: in the summer sky, anywhere.
Nest: hole in eaves, thatch, towers, rarely in cliffs; shallow cup of feathers and saliva. **Eggs:** 2–3, white.
Food: insects, spiders.
Voice: loud, shrill scream.

Although British by birth, they spend only about one third of their lives in Britain.

Kingfisher

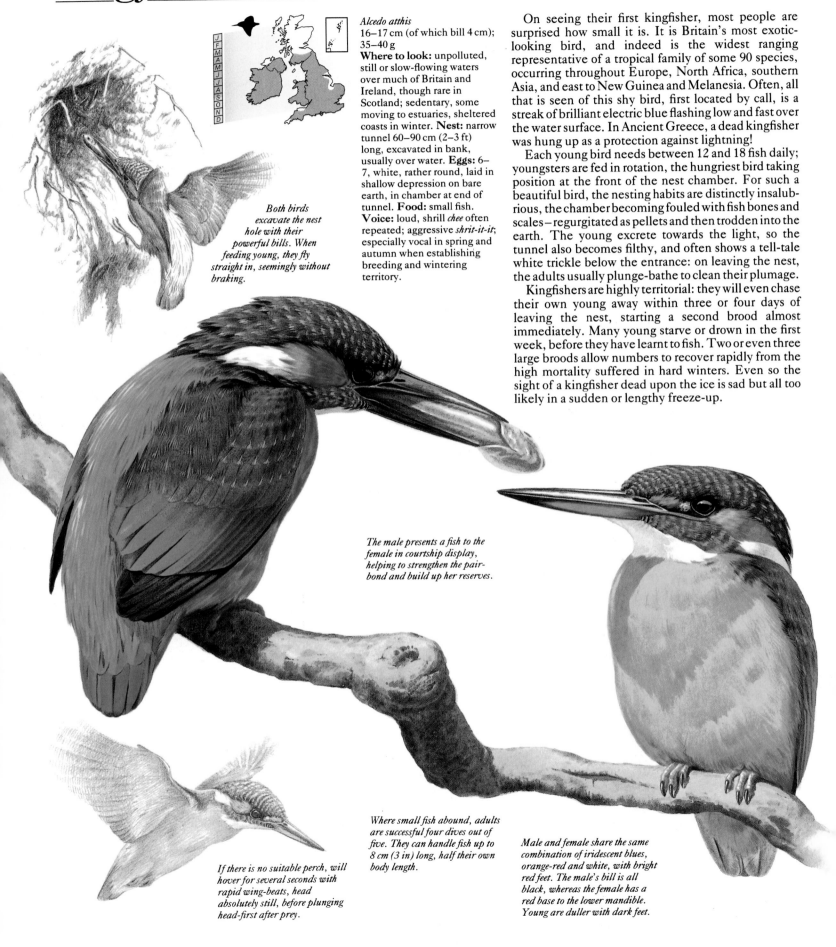

Alcedo atthis
16–17 cm (of which bill 4 cm); 35–40 g
Where to look: unpolluted, still or slow-flowing waters over much of Britain and Ireland, though rare in Scotland; sedentary, some moving to estuaries, sheltered coasts in winter. **Nest:** narrow tunnel 60–90 cm (2–3 ft) long, excavated in bank, usually over water. **Eggs:** 6–7, white, rather round, laid in shallow depression on bare earth, in chamber at end of tunnel. **Food:** small fish. **Voice:** loud, shrill *chee* often repeated; aggressive *shrit-it-it*; especially vocal in spring and autumn when establishing breeding and wintering territory.

On seeing their first kingfisher, most people are surprised how small it is. It is Britain's most exotic-looking bird, and indeed is the widest ranging representative of a tropical family of some 90 species, occurring throughout Europe, North Africa, southern Asia, and east to New Guinea and Melanesia. Often, all that is seen of this shy bird, first located by call, is a streak of brilliant electric blue flashing low and fast over the water surface. In Ancient Greece, a dead kingfisher was hung up as a protection against lightning!

Each young bird needs between 12 and 18 fish daily; youngsters are fed in rotation, the hungriest bird taking position at the front of the nest chamber. For such a beautiful bird, the nesting habits are distinctly insalubrious, the chamber becoming fouled with fish bones and scales – regurgitated as pellets and then trodden into the earth. The young excrete towards the light, so the tunnel also becomes filthy, and often shows a tell-tale white trickle below the entrance: on leaving the nest, the adults usually plunge-bathe to clean their plumage.

Kingfishers are highly territorial: they will even chase their own young away within three or four days of leaving the nest, starting a second brood almost immediately. Many young starve or drown in the first week, before they have learnt to fish. Two or even three large broods allow numbers to recover rapidly from the high mortality suffered in hard winters. Even so the sight of a kingfisher dead upon the ice is sad but all too likely in a sudden or lengthy freeze-up.

Both birds excavate the nest hole with their powerful bills. When feeding young, they fly straight in, seemingly without braking.

The male presents a fish to the female in courtship display, helping to strengthen the pair-bond and build up her reserves.

If there is no suitable perch, will hover for several seconds with rapid wing-beats, head absolutely still, before plunging head-first after prey.

Where small fish abound, adults are successful four dives out of five. They can handle fish up to 8 cm (3 in) long, half their own body length.

Male and female share the same combination of iridescent blues, orange-red and white, with bright red feet. The male's bill is all black, whereas the female has a red base to the lower mandible. Young are duller with dark feet.

There is no mistaking that flash of pale blue, so brilliant that other colours often do not register with the eye. The flying bird always seems to be hurrying, low to the surface, wings rapidly whirring, not even slowing down to take a bend in the river.

In winter, many young kingfishers disperse to the coast to find food. Here they are much less aggressive and territorial.

Perched motionless among vegetation, can be surprisingly difficult to see, the strong colour contrast breaking up the bird's outline. When fishing, often bobs head nervously.

Struggles free of the water with strong wing-beats, returning to the same perch to beat its prey before swallowing it head-first. The dive is over in a trice.

Flies, rather than drops, to the water, and is carried under by impetus, bill open, eyes closed, success depending on correct prior calculation.

Green Woodpecker

The green woodpecker is more often heard than seen; its loud almost laughing *yaffle* call carries a great distance, yet the bird itself is often shy and elusive. Britain's largest woodpecker, it is about the size of a jackdaw, and when seen is unmistakable, with green plumage, striking red crown and yellow rump. In flight the pointed shape of the head and tail and the short bursts of flapping interspersed with long swooping glides are characteristic. At rest it can be difficult to locate, often perching motionless for many minutes, occasionally giving an alarm call. In trees it will usually perch on vertical branches and has the habit of hiding from view behind a limb. It can usually be found in areas of mature woodland and open parkland, heaths and commons.

Old pasture and heaths are favoured feeding areas, for it is here that the bird finds the ants which are its staple diet. It uses its stout beak and long tongue to extract ants and pupae from galleries deep within the nest. The tongue can be extended up to 10 cm (4 in) and is used to explore the galleries, while the sticky tip is used to catch the prey. At most times of the year the birds are seen singly, but the young accompany their parents for a few weeks after fledging in July and such family parties can often be located by the loud begging calls of the young. Although they sometimes occur in well-wooded gardens, green woodpeckers are extremely shy birds and on the slightest hint of disturbance they fly off, calling loudly in alarm with shouted, rapid notes, more screeching than the pleasant yaffle.

Near the nest the birds are very secretive and may fly off a long way to collect food.

In both the male and female the crown and central nape are deep crimson mottled with grey.

The nest is a cavity excavated in the trunk, or large limb, of a tree and can be up to 15 metres (50 ft) above ground. The entrance hole is just big enough for the adults to squeeze in; 6–7 cm (2½ in) in diameter. Oak and birch are the favoured trees, and although most nests are within woodland many are in isolated hedgerow or parkland trees.

The back is uniform yellow-green, with the primary feathers showing brown with white spotting. The undersides are an unmarked grey-green.

Moustachial stripe of male has red central streak, difficult to see in poor light.

Dark cheeks and pale eye-ring are readily seen in the field.

The main food throughout the year is ants and their pupae. The signs of green woodpecker attacks can often be seen on ant hills.

The female has the same crimson crown and nape as the male, but lacks the red moustachial stripe.

In flight, the pointed head and tail and brilliant yellow rump are striking.

Picus viridis
30–33 cm; 190 g
Where to look: deciduous woods, parkland, heaths and commons. **Nest:** deep cavity excavated in trunk or large limb of mature tree. Unlined. **Eggs:** 4–7, glossy white, laid on wood chippings. **Food:** mainly ants and their pupae. **Voice:** loud, laughing *yaffle*.

In spring, male and female chase in courtship, and display with beaks held up and much head swaying.

Immature birds have the red crown and nape, but with more grey and black than the adults. Immature males already have the red moustachial stripe.

Occasionally perches on manmade structures!

All birds, including immatures, grow a new set of feathers in autumn, and from then on adults and juveniles look the same.

Like all woodpeckers the green has zygodactyl toes — two facing forwards and two back — to help it climb rounded vertical surfaces.

On the ground, birds hop clumsily, sit upright and remain very alert.

Immature birds have a more mottled appearance, with pale spotting on the back, distinct dark barring on the underside and black and grey flecks on the head and neck.

Great Spotted Woodpecker

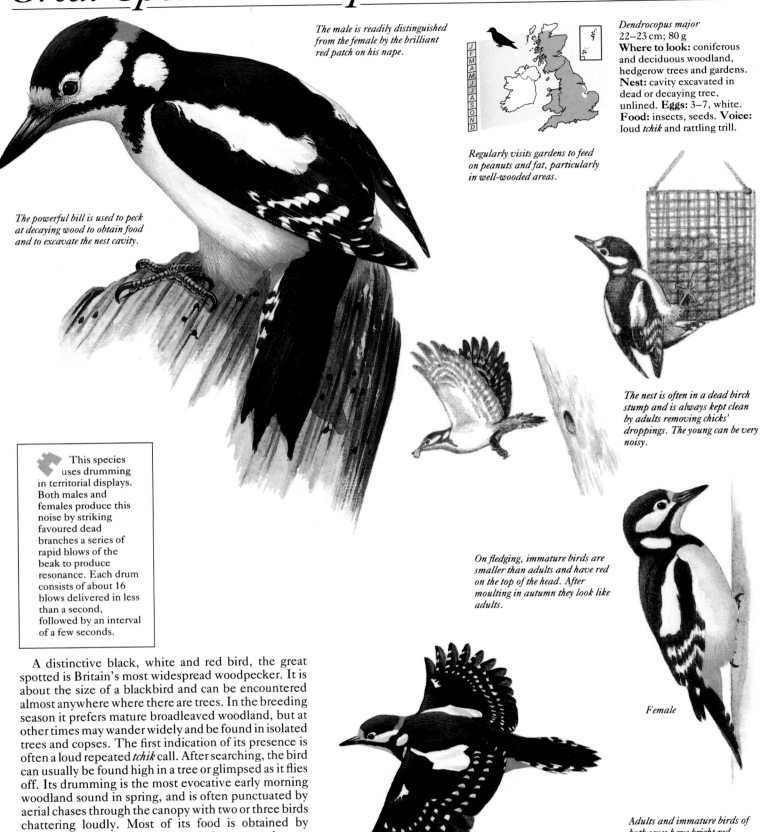

The male is readily distinguished from the female by the brilliant red patch on his nape.

Dendrocopus major
22–23 cm; 80 g
Where to look: coniferous and deciduous woodland, hedgerow trees and gardens. **Nest:** cavity excavated in dead or decaying tree, unlined. **Eggs:** 3–7, white. **Food:** insects, seeds. **Voice:** loud *tchik* and rattling trill.

Regularly visits gardens to feed on peanuts and fat, particularly in well-wooded areas.

The powerful bill is used to peck at decaying wood to obtain food and to excavate the nest cavity.

The nest is often in a dead birch stump and is always kept clean by adults removing chicks' droppings. The young can be very noisy.

This species uses drumming in territorial displays. Both males and females produce this noise by striking favoured dead branches a series of rapid blows of the beak to produce resonance. Each drum consists of about 16 blows delivered in less than a second, followed by an interval of a few seconds.

On fledging, immature birds are smaller than adults and have red on the top of the head. After moulting in autumn they look like adults.

Female

A distinctive black, white and red bird, the great spotted is Britain's most widespread woodpecker. It is about the size of a blackbird and can be encountered almost anywhere where there are trees. In the breeding season it prefers mature broadleaved woodland, but at other times may wander widely and be found in isolated trees and copses. The first indication of its presence is often a loud repeated *tchik* call. After searching, the bird can usually be found high in a tree or glimpsed as it flies off. Its drumming is the most evocative early morning woodland sound in spring, and is often punctuated by aerial chases through the canopy with two or three birds chattering loudly. Most of its food is obtained by pecking at dead and decaying wood to extract insects and larvae – crevices and decayed spots are attacked with rapid blows of the beak. In spring, the young are fed on caterpillars. A new nest cavity is usually excavated each year and this can take the birds one or two weeks depending on the hardness of the chosen tree. Dead birch stumps and oaks are preferred.

In flight the large white wing flashes, white-barred primaries and brilliant red undertail coverts are obvious.

Adults and immature birds of both sexes have bright red undertail coverts.

Lesser Spotted Woodpecker

Dendrocopus minor
13–14 cm; 20 g
Where to look: deciduous woodland, parks, orchards and gardens. **Nest:** cavity excavated in decaying wood, unlined. **Eggs:** 3–8, white. **Food:** insects. **Voice:** slow, nasal *pee..pee..pee..pee*; weak *chick*.

Distinguished from great spotted woodpecker by small size, barred black and white wing pattern without any large white flashes and lack of red vent. Immature birds have red crown; female is less bright.

Male has distinct red crown which is absent in female.

This small woodpecker is only the size of a house sparrow. It spends much of its time high in the tree canopy feeding among the smallest branches; with a rapid sewing machine-like action of its beak it searches out its insect food. In winter it often joins mixed feeding flocks of tits. For a few weeks in early spring its *pee..pee..pee..* calls, conspicuous butterfly-like display flights and weak drumming betray its breeding areas. The drumming is much softer than that of the great spotted woodpecker, and each burst lasts for well over a second. Both male and female drum, usually from high in the crown of a tree. The nest cavity is excavated by both birds and can be between one and 25 metres (3–75 ft) above the ground, often placed on the underside of a dead limb. The entrance hole is only 3 cm (1 in) in diameter, distinguishing the nest from those of other woodpecker species. The nest is usually very inconspicuous and difficult to find.

Usually high in woodland trees, but will also feed close to the ground in hedgerows and scrub.

When feeding, flutters more like a perching bird than a woodpecker.

Wryneck

Jynx torquilla
15–16 cm; 32 g
Where to look: a rare breeding bird in semi-natural pine forests in Scotland; in England and Wales only seen on passage in spring and autumn. **Nest:** any cavity, including nestbox, unlined. **Eggs:** 7–10, white.

Food: ants and other insects. **Voice:** weak *quee..quee..quee*, similar to lesser spotted woodpecker.

Flies hesitantly, rather like a small song thrush.

The mottled brown back and barred tail are distinctive.

The wryneck is a close relative of the woodpeckers. Like the green woodpecker, it feeds almost exclusively on ants and uses its long mobile tongue to scoop them up. Unlike woodpeckers, it is seen mainly on the ground, does not often climb up vertical limbs and only rarely excavates dead wood. For a nest site it uses any available cavity, including artificial boxes. Another difference from Britain's true woodpeckers is that it is migratory, spending the winter in sub-Saharan Africa. At a distance it looks like a rather dull, long songbird, but close views reveal complex brown and lilac patterning on the back with two lilac and one blackish band running down from the nape. The undersides are barred and spotted and the tail has complex transverse patterning – all reminiscent of a small nightjar. In England the breeding population has declined to extinction in recent decades and now the only birds seen are occasional migrants in spring and autumn. These birds often appear in the most unlikely places, including suburban gardens, feeding on ants. A small number now breed in Scotland; these are thought to be an offshoot of the large Scandinavian population.

The wryneck twists its neck right round to look behind it.

When displaying, the wryneck stretches out, pointing its beak at the opponent, raising its crown feathers and tail.

On the ground it hops clumsily and collects food with a darting tongue. It often remains motionless for long periods collecting ants that pass by.

Skylark

These familiar birds of the open countryside are often visible only as small specks in the sky as they hang in the air, singing non-stop. They are numerous throughout the country in the breeding season, but in winter many leave the bleaker upland areas for more hospitable lowland fields. Large numbers of skylarks from northern Europe arrive here in October and November to spend the winter. During very severe winters Britain's skylarks may move south to warmer parts of the Continent. Skylarks give their glorious song all year round, but tend to go quiet in August and September when they moult. They have probably benefited more than any other birds from the advent of arable farming and the deforestation of the countryside, which has provided the open cultivated areas that the species prefers. They rarely even feed close to a tall hedge.

The aerial song is a familiar sound, with the bird often too high to be seen. The song flight can last for anything up to 5 minutes.

The crest is not always easily seen, but can be raised when the bird is excited or alarmed.

Continuous flow of rapid song is unlike any other songbird.

Stouter bills and stockier build distinguish skylarks from pipits.

When disturbed they flutter for a short distance. When flying further they have a strong, undulating and 'floppy' flight.

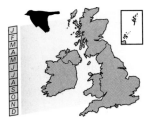

Alauda arvensis
18 cm; 33–45 g
Where to look: open fields, moors, dunes and salt marshes. **Nest:** on ground in grass tussocks with fine grass/hair lining. **Eggs:** 3–5, white with heavy brown markings. **Food:** insects, seeds and worms. **Voice:** loud, clear, very rapid warbling in flight. Call a liquid *chirrup*.

In flight, the white trailing wing edge, white outer tail feathers and loud chirrupping call help to identify them.

Skylarks from northern Europe gather in winter flocks which may have several hundred birds. Local birds remain separate.

They land some distance from their nests and run unseen through the grass to reach them.

When not singing, they spend most of their time on the ground. They walk rather than hop and crouch down when alarmed.

Woodlark

Lullula arborea
15 cm; 24–36g
Where to look: heathland with scrub, plantations. **Nest:** fine grass lining in sheltered hollow. **Eggs:** 3–4, pale, brown-speckled. **Food:** insects and seeds. **Voice:** melodious descending song phrases; *tloo-ee*, *titlOOeet* calls.

Short tail and more rounded wings help to distinguish woodlarks from skylarks in flight. Stouter build, marks on wing and pale stripe over eye are good features on ground. Superb song and call unlike skylark's.

Small crest and clear buff-white stripes over the eyes which meet at the back of the head.

Black and white mark at bend of wing is visible when perched.

Woodlarks are very patchily distributed in southern and eastern England with, until recently, a few in Wales. They are often difficult to find, feeding inconspicuously on the ground, but they perch on the tops of trees and bushes. They sing beautifully through most of the year, especially from March to June, and often at night. The song flight is different from a skylark's, with the male circling at a constant height with a more fluttering action. In flight, the short tail, undulating flight and call – *titlooeet* – help to distinguish them from skylarks. They are particularly fond of forestry plantations where trees have been felled or recently planted. Their numbers have been declining both in Britain and on the Continent. It is thought that habitat loss combined with climatic change may have caused this. It is very sad that their lovely song is now so rarely heard.

In flight shows very short tail with brown sides; broader, more rounded wings than skylark's.

Shore Lark

Eremophila alpestris
16 cm; 33–45g
Where to look: stony mountain tops in summer; shingle and coastal fields in winter. **Nest:** grass cup on ground. **Eggs:** 4, pale, lined and speckled. **Food:** seeds and insects. **Voice:** skylark-like song and shrill *tseee* call.

Flight is more undulating than skylark. Call is pipit-like.

Shore larks are scarce winter birds in Britain, although pairs occasionally breed in Scotland. The numbers wintering here fluctuate from a few score to more than a thousand birds in some winters. The highest numbers are recorded in late autumn as northern European birds arrive, many of them moving on to the Continent as the winter progresses. They prefer a specialised habitat in winter, and are found only on salt marshes with nearby shingle and dunes. The north Norfolk coast is one stronghold. Here they can be found feeding on the saltings and fields in exciting mixed flocks in the company of snow and Lapland buntings. Shore larks appear to be expanding their range on the Continent and the number of birds visiting has been increasing. They may become established as regular breeders, although given their tundra breeding requirements they will almost certainly be confined to the mountains of Scotland. Shore larks are known as horned larks in North America, where they fill a niche very similar to that occupied by Britain's skylark, and are common in open lowland areas. Perhaps Britain's shore larks will one day adopt a less spartan life-style!

Black and yellow head pattern in spring and summer, duller in winter.

Seen in winter flocks, often with snow buntings. Tail is dark with brown centre and pale edgings. Walks and runs along ground.

Swallow

Swallows are glossy blue-black above; below they vary from nearly white to orange-pink, with a blue band across the breast. The throat and forehead are a rich, deep red. The dark tail has oval white spots.

Females have shorter tail streamers than males. Young are duller, with more orange foreheads and throats.

Swallows will sometimes take food while perched, but they are predominantly aerial feeders.

Their long tails give them great manoeuvrability near ground or water and around obstacles, such as grazing animals.

Britain's swallows winter in Africa, as far south as the Cape, and return from March to May to take up territories around buildings, in less urban areas than house martins. The male sings from a wire or on the wing, and soon the pair will be dashing through an open shed door, a broken window, even the observation slit in a birdwatching hide, to build their mud-saucer nest. A chimney-stack or old mine-shaft may also be used: one nest in Cornwall was 17 metres (53 feet) below ground. A nest may be occupied several years in succession by the same birds — a tribute to amazing navigation skills. Food-balls of small insects and individual larger ones are brought to the young. When they have fledged, the young sit in a prominent spot, often a branch, and wait to be fed; they must soon learn to feed themselves and to drink and bathe on the wing. A classic autumn sight is of swallows gathering on wires; at the same time reed-bed roosts may hold thousands of birds. Swallows melt away south in September and October, with stragglers in November.

Hirundo rustica
18–20 cm; 18–19 g
Where to look: open country. **Nest:** of mud and dry grass on a ledge in an outbuilding. **Eggs:** 4-5, white, dark-speckled. **Food:** insects taken on the wing. **Voice:** *tswit-tswit*; alarm *tswee*; prolonged song of calls and a rolling trill.

A typical nest; sometimes old nests of other species are used, even artefacts (eg a hat!).

Swallow, house martin, sand martin and swift easily confused when colours cannot be seen. Swifts all dark, fly rapidly on stiff, curved wings. Swallows long-tailed, relaxed, fly low in purposeful straight line. House martins dumpier, feed higher, flap faster with frequent changes of direction. Sand martins slimmer, less confident and dashing.

House Martin

Adults are blue-black above with white rump and underparts; white feathering on the short legs. Young are browner above and below.

Parents feed fledged young both in the air and perched on wires.

Delichon urbica
12.5 cm; 18 g
Where to look: around houses, over open areas and wetlands. **Nest:** of mud pellets and a little dry grass, under eaves, occasionally on bridges and cliffs; often colonial. **Eggs:** 4–5, white. **Food:** insects taken in flight. **Voice:** *chrrrp*; alarm a shrill *treep*.

Before men built houses, house martins nested on cliffs. A few still do so, but most now build under eaves (or other sites such as street-lamp shades) in villages, towns and city suburbs. Some have even nested on sea-ferries (including a cross-Channel vessel), the adults feeding the young between voyages and raising them successfully! Nesting may be delayed by drought, as mud is the main building material. The adults gather this in their bills and apply it with trembling movements of their chins. The bird is social and some sites have dozens of nests: why some houses are chosen and others not is still not clear. Old nests may be repaired and re-used and artificial nests may encourage birds to colonise. Fledglings of earlier broods often help feed the latest young. Unlike the swallow and sand martin, which make up the trio collectively called the hirundines, this bird rarely roosts in reed beds; it may use trees mainly, or sleep on the wing, but this, and precisely where it spends the winter in Africa, is still mysterious.

Sand Martin

Sand martins brown, house martins black and white, but beware young house martins with brownish rumps. Sand martins look frail, with jerky, flicking wing-beats; house martins plump and purposeful.

The sand martin is often the first summer migrant to arrive in the spring, beating the swallow by several days. Flicking low over some reservoir or gravel pit in March, it was once perhaps taken a little for granted. No more. Catastrophic declines in sand martin numbers have followed the long drought (aggravated by man) in the southern Sahara, the Sahel, where the bird spends winter. Some long-established colonies are empty, those still active are at a low ebb; it remains to be seen whether the species can make a come-back. Sand martins are the smallest of Britain's hirundines and rather delicate-looking, yet in excavating their burrows in sand or soil, they may dig in two metres (six ft) or more (usually half this) and move stones four times heavier than themselves. Living in colonies has several advantages, notably 'safety in numbers' and more eyes to spot predators. The bird has a special alarm call to warn of birds of prey; nevertheless many are taken, particularly by hobbies. Migrants roost in reed beds, often with swallows.

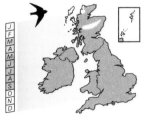

The nest colony, with holes old and new, not necessarily all in use.

Swallows and martins have wide gapes for collecting food, water and nest material on the wing.

Riparia riparia
12 cm; 13–14 g
Where to look: fresh-water wetlands, especially near mineral workings. **Nest:** in colonies, in a tunnel in a bank or cliff, occasionally in man-made holes, *eg* pipes. **Eggs:** 4–5, white. **Food:** insects taken in flight. **Voice:** a dry, hard *chrrp*; alarm sharper; song a series of call-notes.

Young birds have brighter edges to the feathers of the upperparts.

Perches freely on wires, branches and on ground, where it may drink, and even bathe in, dew.

Plain brown above, off-white below with a brown band across the breast. Tail only slightly forked.

Tree Pipit

The song is given after an upward flight from a tree during a 'parachute' drop.

Anthus trivialis
15 cm; 20–25g
Where to look: plantations, heaths, scattered trees and scrub. **Nest:** grass cup with fine lining in tussock or bank. **Eggs:** 4–6, variable with dark spots. **Food:** insects and seeds. **Voice:** loud song with trills. Call a hoarse *teez*.

Breast lightly streaked and yellower than a meadow pipit's.

Solitary, perching on trees, but feeding on ground. Stronger bill, stouter build, bolder actions and different call from meadow pipit.

As their name suggests, tree pipits make more use of trees than other pipits, especially in the lovely display flight. They feed on the ground, but when disturbed they will fly up into a tree or bush. They are summer visitors, arriving from April to June and leaving for tropical Africa from late July to October. Males usually arrive first and take up territory, announcing their presence with spectacular song flights; they fly upwards from a tree perch and begin to sing as they reach the top of their ascent, descending with wings open and tail spread. The birds need song posts for display, as well as clear ground to feed on, and so choose heathland, commons and pasture with scattered trees or woodland edges. Newly-planted conifers are readily used and recently felled areas with some trees still standing are favourite sites. Tree pipits have spread north in Scotland during the last 100 years, and now breed extensively in mature birch woods. They are still absent as breeding birds in Ireland and only occur there as rare migrants.

Rock Pipit

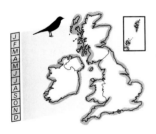

Anthus petrosus
16 cm; 21–30g
Where to look: rocky coasts and salt marshes. **Nest:** in rock crevice. Grass cup, lined with hair. **Eggs:** 4–5, white with grey/brown spots. **Food:** seeds, marine animals and insects. **Voice:** loud musical song. Call – strong *feest*.

Habitually perches on rocks. Often seen in small parties feeding on the shoreline.

Call fuller, less thin than meadow pipit's; song stronger.

Big, dark, dull, dark-legged pipit – usually beside the sea.

Almost exclusively coastal, rock pipits search for food among rocks, seaweed and shore vegetation. They always make their nests close to the shore, in sheltered gullies and coves. Breeding usually begins in April and two broods are not uncommon; in some areas they are a host species for cuckoos. Lack of suitable rocky coastline from North Humberside to Kent means that they are absent from that whole stretch of coast. They are difficult to spot among the rocks, and their presence is often first noticed as they fly up, calling as they go. In winter they may eat more than 15,000 small molluscs and larvae each day. They are usually solitary and territorial, but may form flocks in winter and can be quite approachable. Rock pipits are resident and most do not move far from their home territories, although in winter birds are found on coasts where they do not breed and in March and October, especially, a few turn up by reservoirs inland. Birds of the Scandinavian race migrate south and appear regularly on the east and south coasts of England. In spring they can be distinguished from Britain's rock pipits by their browner upperparts and whiter belly.

A heavy-bodied pipit with dark olive upperparts and buff underparts with poorly defined breast streaks. Dark legs and grey outer tail feathers.

Meadow Pipit

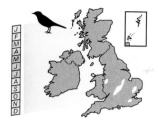

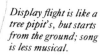

Anthus pratensis
14 cm; 16–25 g
Where to look: moors, meadows and dunes. **Nest:** on ground in tussock of grass with fine lining. **Eggs:** 4–5, white with grey/brown spots. **Food:** insects and seeds. **Voice:** accelerating song with trill. Call high *tseep* repeated.

Display flight is like a tree pipit's, but starts from the ground; song is less musical.

Meadow pipits are classic 'little brown birds'. Often only seen as they fly away from rough grass, the best clue to their identity is the thin, squeaky call, repeated persistently. They are often hard to see when on the ground, as they run between clumps of grass, occasionally pausing in the open. They are widely distributed throughout the country in the breeding season, but in winter leave the high ground for lowland areas, often feeding in urban parks and gardens and living secretively in weedy fields. Many of Britain's northern birds migrate south to southern and south-western England and Ireland and some will travel as far south as Spain. Migrants from northern Europe arrive here each autumn and may spend the winter. Meadow pipits are important hosts for the cuckoo, especially in Ireland. They make up a large part of the prey of species such as hen harrier, merlin and kestrel, too!

The squeaky call and white outer tail are distinctive in flight.

Always prefers ground to trees.

The upperparts can vary from grey to olive-buff. Underparts yellowish to pale grey; pale legs.

Water Pipit

Anthus spinoletta
17 cm; 21–36 g
Where to look: lakes, watercress beds in winter and spring. Does not breed in Britain. **Food:** insects and seeds. **Voice:** song similar to meadow pipit. Calls are a sharp *dzit* and a short *drrt*.

Bold stripe over eye, white outer tail, dark legs, white throat all year.

In winter, browner, plainer above than rock pipit, white wingbars, belly.

In spring, the water pipit is a very attractive bird, with a brown, almost unstreaked back, greyish head and unstreaked underparts which have a warm, pinkish flush. The white tail sides are not easy to see, but the bold, pale stripe over the eye and wingbars stand out. Water pipits breed in the mountainous regions of Europe; they leave the upland pastures between August and November, moving down to lowland regions, often dispersing some distance. The nearest breeding birds to Britain are probably in the Alps. No more than a hundred are recorded in Britain each winter, usually between October and April. They like watercress beds, coastal fresh water, inland marshes and rivers. Most are seen in southern and eastern England. They are often hard to see well, as they fly up at a distance and may move several hundred yards before settling again. After a while they will be found back at their preferred feeding place. Until recently, water pipits were regarded as a race of the rock pipit, but the two have been split into separate species along with the American water pipit, or buff-bellied pipit, a rare accidental visitor to Britain.

Faded in summer.

In summer, breast is pinkish and unstreaked. Head is grey.

Bigger, browner, shyer than meadow pipit, with dark legs.

Pied Wagtail

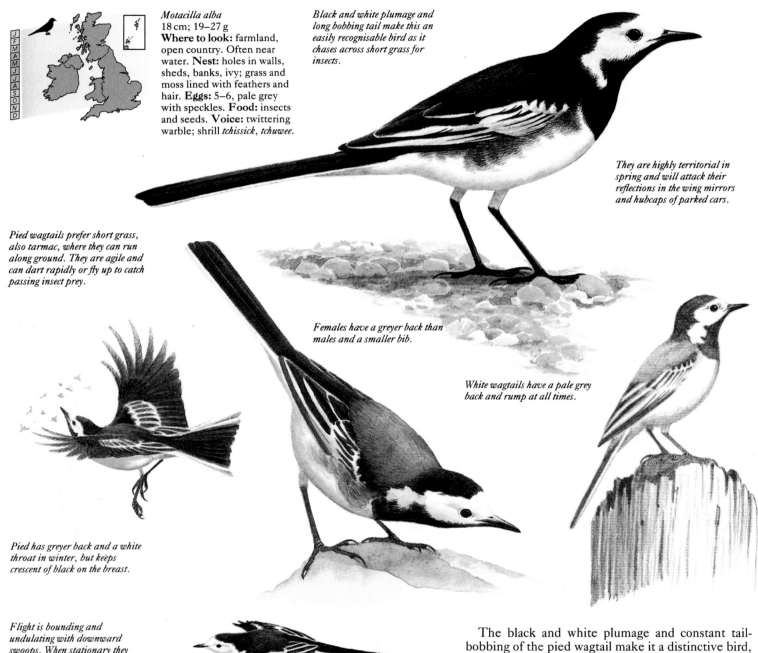

Motacilla alba
18 cm; 19–27 g
Where to look: farmland, open country. Often near water. **Nest:** holes in walls, sheds, banks, ivy; grass and moss lined with feathers and hair. **Eggs:** 5–6, pale grey with speckles. **Food:** insects and seeds. **Voice:** twittering warble; shrill *tchissick, tchuwee*.

Black and white plumage and long bobbing tail make this an easily recognisable bird as it chases across short grass for insects.

They are highly territorial in spring and will attack their reflections in the wing mirrors and hubcaps of parked cars.

Pied wagtails prefer short grass, also tarmac, where they can run along ground. They are agile and can dart rapidly or fly up to catch passing insect prey.

Females have a greyer back than males and a smaller bib.

White wagtails have a pale grey back and rump at all times.

Pied has greyer back and a white throat in winter, but keeps crescent of black on the breast.

Flight is bounding and undulating with downward swoops. When stationary they habitually wag tails up and down.

Pied wagtail nests are often parasitised by cuckoos, which can successfully mimic their eggs.

Juveniles are brownish-grey above with a double breast band. White parts have a yellow tinge which may remain into winter.

The black and white plumage and constant tail-bobbing of the pied wagtail make it a distinctive bird, found commonly in open country, especially farmyards, parks and gardens. It can be seen in paddocks and fields, trotting along the ground and dashing after insects scared up by the horses or cattle. Small groups may be seen flying over towards dusk, making their way to a communal roost, where hundreds noisily gather on a tree before flying to a reed bed, bush or even a building ledge for the night. They breed over the whole country with the exception of the Shetland Islands. In winter, northern birds move south to spend the winter in central and southern England, although many go to France, Spain and even Morocco. Pied wagtails are a race (*ie* subspecies) of the white wagtail and only breed regularly in Britain and Ireland. White wagtails breed from Iceland to the Mediterranean and are seen in Britain on passage in spring and autumn, especially on the west and north coasts. There have been records of white wagtails breeding in England and of hybridisation between the two races.

Yellow Wagtail

Motacilla flava
17 cm; 16–22 g
Where to look: water meadows, pasture, moors and lakesides. **Nest:** on ground in grass. Roots and grass lined with hair. **Eggs:** 5–6, buff with darker spots. **Food:** mainly insects. **Voice:** a loud *tswee-ip*; warbling song.

Male mostly bright yellow; long, spindly legs, fast walk, wingbars, unlike any other yellow bird.

Female is paler yellow with browner green upperparts.

Yellow wagtails are among the most colourful summer visitors, the males shining out from grassy meadows like buttercups. They arrive from March to May and leave in August and September. There are occasional reports of overwintering birds, but care must be taken not to confuse them with grey wagtails. Yellow wagtails are a race of the blue-headed wagtail and breed only in England and Wales, except for a few pairs in Scotland and even fewer in Ireland. Blue-headed wagtails breed from Scandinavia eastwards into Asia and are seen as rare passage migrants in Britain in spring and autumn. Males can be distinguished in spring by their blue-grey crowns and ear-coverts with a white stripe over the eye and a white chin. Odd ones turn up now and then in spring wagtail flocks.

Found in damp meadows and fields by water, often feeding on insects disturbed by cattle.

Long white-edged black tail is a useful feature in flight.

Feed in flocks in spring, roost communally in autumn.

Juveniles are brown above with a blackish bib, yellower than pied.

Grey Wagtail

Grey wagtails live up to the family name more than the others as their longer tail accentuates the vertical wagging motion. They delight in the rush and tumble of upland streams and rivers, perching on boulders and flying out after passing insects. They also feed on the ground, running quickly and pumping their tail up and down each time they stop. In winter they leave the upland areas and move to lower ground, frequenting lakes, reservoirs, farmyards and sewage farms. Some birds travel south, even as far as France and Spain. Britain's residents are joined by northern European birds which arrive here for the winter. Grey wagtails suffer badly in severe winters, in common with other birds which feed by fresh water that becomes frozen.

Grey crown and back, yellow underparts, yellow-green rump, long white-edged tail; very sharp call.

Often mistaken for yellow wagtail, but legs pink.

Male in summer has black throat.

Often seen perched on rocks and overhanging trees near streams.

In winter, male and female are similar with buff-white throat.

Motacilla cinerea
18 cm; 15–23 g
Where to look: fast rivers and streams. **Nest:** ledges, holes in walls and banks near water. Moss, grass and leaves, hair lining. **Eggs:** 4–6, buff with grey/brown marks. **Food:** insects. **Voice:** infrequent warble, call a high *tzitzi* sharper than pied's.

Waxwing

Bombycilla garrulus
18 cm; 50–55 g
Where to look: anywhere with berry-bearing bushes or trees, from country lanes to city centres. **Food:** in winter almost entirely berries, *eg* rowan, hawthorn, cotoneaster, rose, viburnum. **Voice:** a long, silvery trill.

Every winter, British birdwatchers hope for an invasion of these gorgeous birds. Such 'irruptions', caused by overcrowding and food shortages on their normal wintering grounds in northern Europe, occur irregularly and may be becoming less frequent. Nevertheless, in most winters there are at least a few along the east coast of England and Scotland and, in some years, they are more numerous and get as far as the west, Wales, and even Ireland. Waxwings are remarkable in many other ways: they turn up regularly in gardens and parks and allow a close approach. This will show their handsome plumage, including the secondary feathers with their extraordinary red blobs of 'sealing wax' at the tips, which give the bird its name. Very occasionally the buttercup-yellow end of the tail will show these tips too. Waxwings feed acrobatically among the branches of berry-bearing shrubs and trees, sometimes gorging themselves to a state of total inactivity. At other times, they will fly up on to aerials (a good place to check for them if you know they are around), or chase insects in the air like flycatchers – although this is more common in the breeding season than in winter. The same is true of courtship-feeding, when birds will pass berries or other objects back and forth to each other. Waxwings are gregarious birds, but single birds often occur in winter. They may stay until they have eaten all the berries available, or leave suddenly and unexpectedly.

All waxwings show features such as grey rumps and cinnamon undertail coverts; some markings vary in extent and brightness, such as yellow tail-tip, marks on the primaries and the number and size of waxy red tips to secondaries. These are related to age and sex, but separating, for instance, young males from adult females is not straightforward.

Gregarious and tame, waxwings may feed in one bush for some days.

Immature birds are duller than adults, especially on wings.

Pink-brown, with obvious crest, black mask and throat, grey rump, colourful wing and tail patterns.

Females tend to show less intense black bibs and less bright yellow and red markings on the wings and tail, but sexing is not easy.

Like starling in flight shape and action, but lighter coloured.

Dipper

In winter, the south-east sometimes has Continental dippers.

Cinclus cinclus
18 cm; 60–65 g
Where to look: fast-flowing upland streams; less often lowland rivers, mill-races, weirs. **Nest:** under bridge, bank overhang, tree roots, behind a waterfall. Domed. **Eggs:** 4–6, white. **Food:** aquatic invertebrates; some small fish, tadpoles. **Voice:** piercing, rasped *zit* or metallic *chink*; song a long warble of liquid and grating notes.

They fly low and fast on short, whirring wings, following the course of the stream or river.

Portly, smooth shape, with short tail, sometimes cocked like a wren's.

Brown head, slate-grey back, with dark 'scaly' markings only visible at close range.

Brilliant white chin, throat and breast, separated from dark belly and undertail by a chestnut band. White eyelid obvious when blinked.

Dippers are unique among songbirds in feeding underwater. Despite unwebbed feet, they swim very well.

They walk deliberately into the water, or dive from a rock or the air, and bob back to the surface.

Juveniles are greyer above and white dappled with grey below. By late autumn they look more like adults, but with pale tips to the wing and belly feathers.

Living chiefly in the north and west of Britain, dippers love fast, shallow water. A bird will stand on a rock in mid-stream, 'curtseying' every few seconds as if on springs, then slip beneath the surface and walk along the stream-bed, or 'fly' underwater – tricks that no other songbird can do: the plumage is soft and dense for good insulation in the water. Dippers sometimes perch on trees or wires, and they even search house gutters for food at times! Usually solitary or in pairs, several birds may roost together in winter, in a sheltered spot such as under a bridge. In winter, too, some birds move to lowland rivers or even to the coast, and some reach the south-east – although a winter dipper there may well be of the 'black-bellied' race from Europe, which lacks the chestnut of British birds. A hazard for upland dippers could prove to be acid rain, which may reduce populations of their animal food.

The white may be obvious against a dark background, but dippers are often surprisingly hard to see.

Wren

Most British and Irish wrens look the same as European ones, red-brown and buff, barred darker. However, there are four other subspecies on British islands – on St Kilda, on Fair Isle, in the Hebrides, and in the Shetlands. The first two races are greyer than mainland birds, the last two darker. One day they may form different species: at present, they all share the restless and excitable nature of the familiar woodland wren, and its explosive calls and song.

Few people would name the wren as the commonest British bird, and yet in many years it is exactly that, with perhaps 10 million pairs. Its ability to survive and breed from southern heathlands to northern sea-stacks is the reason for its success in these years. But hard winters are murderous for the species: sometimes seven out of 10 are killed. Some wrens combat severe weather by moving to better feeding places. Some roost communally in natural or artificial holes, and over 60 have been watched at dusk going into a standard-size nestbox! Special roosting nests are occasionally built, or old

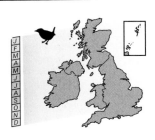

Troglodytes troglodytes
9.5 cm; 10 g
Where to look: low cover anywhere from gardens to remote sea cliffs, but especially in woodlands. **Nest:** domed, usually low in tree, ivy or crevice. **Eggs:** 5–6, white, spotted red. **Food:** insects, spiders. **Voice:** a hard *chiti*; dry rattle. Song is startlingly loud outburst.

Tiny; red-brown above with darker bars; buffish below. Short, cocked tail. Both sexes, and young birds, look alike.

Wrens thread invisibly through the undergrowth, then pop up to sing or to scold the observer.

Normal flight is whirring, direct and low, the bird quickly diving back into cover again.

Wrens sometimes roost communally for added warmth in winter.

breeding nests may be used. How the birds all learn of such roosts is a mystery. Their live-food diet is one reason for wrens' winter vulnerability, but they can be helped by sprinkling grated cheese under hedges and in other likely places. When spring comes, the male builds several nests (up to 12 have been known) and encourages a female, or females, to select one. A monogamous male will help to raise the young, but a polygamous male may be too busy defending his property!

The male builds several nests and the female (or females when the male is polygamous) lines one with feathers. A second brood may be reared in the same nest.

Wrens often spend winter in odd places such as reed beds.

Dunnock

'Still waters run deep', the proverb says, and the dunnock is a perfect example. Sober in colouring and demeanour, it has a reputation among birdwatchers for being a bit boring, and yet it has an enormously interesting sex life! A male may have a single mate, two or even three; a female might have two or three males; and sometimes several males are associated with several females. The commonest arrangement is a simple pair or a female with two males. Because of these complications, it is a biological advantage to a male to ensure that he is the one to fertilize the eggs: to do this, before mating he uses his bill to stimulate the female to eject sperm from any previous mating. In a two male/one female relationship, one male tends to be subordinate and may be prevented from mating: if so, he will not help to feed the young. Despite these intricacies, dunnocks often raise young that are not even of their own species – they are frequent victims of the cuckoo, the speckled eggs of which they are unable to distinguish from their own unmarked ones.

Adult dunnocks are a rich brown above, streaked with black, slate grey on the head and underparts. They have a thin, buff wingbar.

Once commonly known as the hedge sparrow, the dunnock is sparrow-like in colouration, but with a quite different lifestyle.

Juveniles are browner, especially on the head, and more spotted and streaked below.

Dunnocks have the fine bill of an insect-eater, though they mostly eat small seeds in the winter.

They hunt for food under hedges, on lawns, along field borders and in root-crops and weed-patches.

'Wing-waving' is a distinctive display linked to breeding: up to 10 birds may be involved.

Dunnocks are not usually sociable, but in winter loose feeding flocks of a hundred or more birds may gather at food-rich sites.

Dunnocks have a distinctive gait, hopping slowly and deliberately, body close to the ground.

Prunella modularis
14.5 cm; 20–22 g
Where to look: gardens, woodland, hedges, open spaces with bushes. **Nest:** low in hedges, bushes, often in evergreens. **Eggs:** 4–5, turquoise. **Food:** insects; mainly seeds in winter.
Voice: a piercing *peep*; song is a high, pleasant warble, like wren's, but weaker, more rambling.

Robin

As Britain's 'national' bird, the robin must be familiar to everyone. Its association with Christmas dates from the 1860s, when greetings cards became fashionable and postmen wore red tunics and were known as 'robins'. Britain's robins are resident, and are joined by paler northern European immigrants in the winter. These European birds are less confiding and more skulking than Britain's birds – perhaps due to the continuing massacre of migrant birds in southern Europe. Robins may live to be as much as 10 years old, but only a quarter of all robins manage to live beyond their first birthday. The greatest enemies of robins are domestic cats and traffic, which both take a heavy toll. When nesting, the male robin defends the territory and responds to almost any small patch of red – a red flag to a robin would be a better saying than a red rag to a bull. Fights between males can be extremely vicious and may even be to the death. The perky little chap that waits on the spade handle for worms is really quite a nasty piece of work!

They are bold and friendly, but aggressively defend their homes.

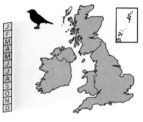

Erithacus rubecula
14 cm; 16–22 g
Where to look: gardens, woods and hedges. **Nest:** in bank, ledge or nestbox. Leaves and moss, domed, with hair lining. **Eggs:** 5–7, white with red spots. **Food:** insects, worms and berries. **Voice:** fine song; call *tic-tic-tic*.

During severe winters robins relax their territorial nature and several birds can be seen feeding at a bird-table together.

They are highly territorial and will display their red breasts vigorously to any intruders.

Seem to disappear during the late summer: they are undergoing their post-breeding moult and become very shy and silent.

Though mainly insectivorous, they will eat fruit and seeds. They are particularly fond of mealworms and can become hand tame if fed with them.

Male and female robins look the same and will sing in autumn to mark out winter territories. The autumn song is quieter and less forceful than in spring.

Young robins are spotted and have no red breast. They moult into adult plumage in autumn.

Robins pair up from late December to early March. The female chases the male until she is accepted and once paired the male feeds her as part of courtship.

They stand very upright, bobbing their heads and flicking their wings and tail when excited.

Nests are usually concealed in a bank or hole; they will use garden sheds and even old tins.

Robins keep warm in winter by fluffing out their feathers.

In spring, males sing loudly to proclaim their territory and to attract a mate. Song is a rich, rambling warble, less powerful than blackbird's with longer, more wistful notes.

Usually sing from a hidden spot in a hedge, bush or tree.

A small bird with upright stance. Hops along the ground; when alarmed it bobs and raises its tail. Brown back and orange-red breast identify it. Sings throughout the year, sometimes at night by a street lamp. Highly territorial and will even chase off larger birds from a winter territory. Frequently tame and confiding, taking worms from recently-dug earth, and sometimes entering houses. Young birds are brown with golden spots, showing no red breast at first, red patches later.

Nightingale

Nightingales have acquired a place in British folklore, not for their looks or familiarity, but for their voice alone. One of the earliest outdoor radio broadcasts included a nightingale from a Surrey wood. In fact, they can be extremely difficult to see as they are generally skulking birds whose brownish plumage hides them well in the dense vegetation that they prefer. Very much a species of south-east England, nightingales are scarce in the west and north even as migrants.

Returning as a summer migrant from wintering grounds south of the Sahara, the nightingale's far-carrying, rich and varied song fills some English woods from mid-April onwards, peaking during the first half of May. Contrary to popular belief, the nightingale does not only sing at night. Indeed, as a songster it is equally vocal in daylight, and can often appear to survive without sleep, as the singing will continue day and night during warm spring periods. By early June it is more sporadic and the brief song period soon comes to an end.

In southern Europe, nightingales are not only more numerous, but appear less secretive and are consequently more visible, often singing from exposed perches. Although the warm brown plumage lacks distinctive features, when the bird is seen clearly the contrasting rusty-red tail, often held in a cocked position, is characteristic and gives the general impression of a rather oversized robin. The similar red tail of the redstart differs in having dark central feathers. Plainness in looks can be easily forgiven, though, when the bird has such a wonderful voice!

Luscinia megarhynchos
16 cm; 18–26.5 g
Where to look: scrub and dense thickets such as overgrown coppice woodland. **Nest:** among vegetation close to ground, made of leaves, lined with grass and hair. **Eggs:** 4–5, heavily speckled on bluish-green background. **Food:** insects, found on ground, plus some fruit and berries in autumn. **Voice:** song rich, varied and vigorous, delivered day and night. Alarm a harsh, hard *tack tack*; grating croak; loud *hweet*.

The juvenile bird's tail is the bright chestnut of the adult's, but the body has pale spots.

The rather long, broad tail with its distinctive bright chestnut-red coloration is often the clue to the bird's identity as it disappears into cover.

An extremely difficult bird to see, the uniform plumage blending with the shadows when well hidden in the foliage. Watch carefully for movement and look for the distinctive large black eye.

On the ground, nightingales are active, hopping with tail raised and holding their bodies slightly upright on long black legs.

Singing birds are often in dense cover, but the song is remarkable for its carrying ability, speed and variety of rich, full-bodied fluty notes and phrases. Beware robins singing near street lights at night.

Principally a ground feeder, often sitting on a perch among the lower branches of scrubby bushes with head cocked on one side, carefully watching the ground below for movement. It will then drop onto any insect. Once on the ground, moves easily among the dead leaves and other foliage with a very agile hopping motion as it flicks tail and wings.

Most easily located by song, but a patient search will often be rewarded by a view of a bird with rich, warm brown upperparts and looking like a large robin, but lacking a red breast. The underparts are a creamy buff, and only the tail shows a deep reddish colour. The dark eye is large and appears to dominate the face, while the stance is frequently distinctive with tail well cocked over the back. The long black legs carry the bird's body in an upright stance well above the ground when it is hopping among vegetation.

Redstart

Phoenicurus phoenicurus
11.5 cm; 12–19.5 g
Where to look: old woods or parkland. **Nest:** hole in tree, will use nestbox. Nest of grass lined with feathers. **Eggs:** 5–7, unmarked pale blue.
Food: mainly insects. **Voice:** brief warbling song and plaintive call note *hweet*.

Male in mottled autumn plumage.

Young are reared on small oak-feeding caterpillars that are abundant when the eggs hatch.

Robin-like speckled young.

Although widely distributed throughout Britain, redstarts are very much birds of the western and northern oak woods. The older trees provide the holes and cavities that make ideal nesting sites, and the open spaces and leaf-litter give good feeding.

Among the earlier returning summer migrants, many redstarts are back from their African wintering grounds by the middle of April, when their arrival is announced by the distinctive song issuing from high on an exposed woodland perch. They are very active birds, constantly flitting and hovering through the branches. When perched, they bear some resemblance to robins, which are of a similar size.

In all plumages, redstarts differ from all but black redstarts in having contrasting dark central tail feathers in a chestnut-red tail that is continually moved up and down in a characteristic quivering motion. The adult males with their strikingly patterned plumage of black, white, red and blue-grey must be among the most distinctive and most beautiful of all British birds.

Appearance rounded or sleek.

Lacking the bright plumage pattern of the male, females retain the tail coloration.

Black Redstart

The greyness of the female is good camouflage when on the nest.

Phoenicurus ochruros
14 cm; 14–19.5 g
Where to look: towns and buildings. **Nest:** hole in wall; grass, lined with feathers.
Eggs: 4–6, white. **Food:** mainly insects. **Voice:** quick warbling and rattle.

The black body plumage of the adult male contrasts with the white wing panel and red tail. Young males can closely resemble females – but they may sing, hold territories and breed.

The song is delivered high above the city noise and is only clearly audible early in the day.

Until the middle of the 20th century, the black redstart was considered a migrant species, occurring in both spring and autumn on the south and east coasts of England. It was rare in the north and west, and on the few occasions when a pair remained to nest it was usually at rocky coastal sites in Kent. Following World War II, a remarkable colonisation took place at the London bomb sites and the black redstart became an established British breeding species. Since that time the numbers have increased, and although still very much of south-east distribution the bird can now be encountered in towns and at such places as power stations far from central London. Railway yards and canal wharves are often appreciated!

The presence of breeding pairs is easily overlooked, for although the brief song is distinctive (the final phrase has been likened to a handful of metal balls shaken together), the birds are inevitably in a noisy urban setting and only in the very early morning before the town awakens can the song be easily heard.

Whinchat

Saxicola rubetra
13 cm; 16.5–23.5 g
Where to look: open country with bushes. **Nest:** on ground, of grass, lined with hair. **Eggs:** 5–6, bluish, finely speckled brown. **Food:** mainly insects. **Voice:** a sweet warbling song; mimics other species. Call note a whistle and a *tap-hweet-tak*.

A summer visitor from wintering grounds in tropical Africa, the whinchat is rather patchy in its distribution through Britain. Most numerous in the open countryside of the north and west, it definitely favours the open hillsides and edges of moorland where isolated bushes or fence posts provide suitable look-out points and song posts. It is extremely easy to locate within its territory.

For differences from the closely related stonechat see below, but the whinchat always shows a pale stripe above the eye and pale patches on either side at the base of the tail. The streaked upperparts contrast with the warmish flush of pink or buff on the underparts, and the male presents a contrasting white flash in the wing. Somewhat resembling a rather short-tailed robin in shape, the whinchat sits very upright on long black legs. When perched on the ground it can be mistaken for a wheatear, particularly when facing the observer, but it regularly bobs its body and flicks both wings and tail.

Ever alert, the whinchat lives on its nerves, perhaps aware of its dangerously exposed position.

In flight, the male shows striking white wing flash and tail panels.

Autumn juveniles are like female, but still show the pale stripe over the eye that is distinctive at all ages. Short tail and upright stance are characteristic.

Slimmer than similar stonechat, upright stance on long black legs. Favours exposed perches such as fence posts.

Less well marked, the female still shows the streaked back and pale stripe above the eye.

The striking and contrasting plumage of the male is distinctive, particularly the black face mask.

Stonechat

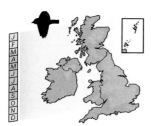

Saxicola torquata
12.5 cm; 14–17 g
Where to look: open country with gorse, and near coast. **Nest:** on ground; grass, lined with hair. **Eggs:** 5–6, greenish, speckled with rust. **Food:** chiefly insects. **Voice:** song series of double notes, call harsh *tsak, whee-tsak-tsak*.

The number of stonechats in Britain is highly variable, a result of their susceptibility to cold winters, when local populations may be eliminated. Although some individuals are migrants (there are records of British ringed stonechats being found in the Mediterranean in winter), the majority remain here all year, although they spread more widely around the coast. Even in winter they are strongly territorial and remain in pairs, always thinly spread.

Slightly shorter and rounder than the whinchat, the stonechat has a less streaked back and never shows the pale stripe over the eye of the whinchat. The distinctive male in breeding plumage has a black head with a contrasting white collar and very red breast. There is usually a clear area of white on the rump and a white flash on the wing. Females and young birds are less well marked, but retain the round-headed appearance with a large dark eye and at least a trace of a dark chin.

The stonechat has a clear attachment to gorse, which the male will use as a song perch and from which he will launch into the characteristic song flight, when he appears to dance in the air.

Rather robin-like in general appearance, with large rounded head, long legs and upright stance. The brightness of the red breast in the male may enhance this appearance. Always perches in an open position on top of a bush or fence post and has a close affinity with gorse bushes.

In flight, the male shows prominent white patches on wings and rump.

The distinctive pattern of the male is visible in subdued coloration on the female.

The speckled plumage of the juvenile is very robin-like.

Wheatear

Oenanthe oenanthe
14.5 cm; 17–30 g
Where to look: open country, particularly upland areas. **Nest:** in hole, ground or wall; grass, lined with hair and feathers. **Eggs:** 5–6, blue. **Food:** chiefly insects. **Voice:** song scratchy, often in flight, call a harsh *chack*.

The more northerly breeding wheatears from Greenland and Iceland pass through Britain on migration. They are larger and more richly coloured than Britain's birds. They also stand more upright, often on higher perches.

The longer wings of the northern wheatears, 10.8 cm (4½ in) compared with 9.5 cm (3½ in), are an adaptation to enable them to undertake the long over-sea migrations necessary to reach their African wintering grounds. Southern birds migrate overland.

The song is frequently delivered from a hovering flight.

When flying away, all wheatears show the distinctive white rump and black 'T' shape on tail.

Wheatears are typically birds of open country, from mountain tops to moorland, from heaths to sandy coastlands. They are ground-living birds with long legs and short tails. Highly active and very distinctive, as they fly away when disturbed they display the gleaming white rump and base of the tail. A frequent perch is the top of a stone wall or exposed fence post, but as a substitute they will hover some distance above the ground giving their harsh warning alarm note.

They have a wide distribution, from Greenland across Europe and Asia to Alaska. Throughout the range they are summer migrants, all individuals migrating south each winter to tropical Africa. Some of the migratory flights are particularly spectacular: a regular crossing from Iceland to northern Spain, for example. They are among the earliest of the returning spring migrants, the first individuals reaching the south coast of England before mid-March. The sudden surprise of a flashing white rump announces the return of what, for the moment, seems the prettiest bird of spring.

Breeding throughout the British Isles, from the south coast of England to the Shetland Isles, the wheatear demonstrates how a population can vary in plumage and size. The males of the southern birds are smaller and paler, being almost pure white on the underparts compared with the rich buff further north. The northern birds are also bigger and heavier.

Spring males are clean, clear cut, handsome birds.

Spring females are a uniform, rich buffish-brown.

The long, black legs and upright stance are characteristic.

In upland areas, wheatears favour sites with drystone walls, which not only provide suitable look-out points and song posts, but also contain the holes and crevices in which to build their nests. These bleak, open moorland sites contain very few breeding species; the wheatears share the habitat with meadow pipits and skylarks, two other species which regularly deliver their song in flight. At such times they are likely to fall prey to hunting merlins.

Perches on ground or exposed post. Very active; upright stance. Male with blue-grey back, black wings and mask. Prominent white rump and base to short tail. Female and young more uniform buffish-brown, with white rump. Bows and bobs while flicking tail.

In autumn, females and juveniles are similar.

In autumn, the male loses his striking markings, except for shadows of the spring finery.

Blackbird

A common and familiar bird in town centres, gardens and the open countryside. The adult male, with jet-black plumage and contrasting bright orange-yellow bill and eye-ring is unmistakable. The loud, fluty song is always delivered from a prominent perch, such as the top of a tall tree or television aerial, while the continual *pink pink* call often heard at dusk is a pre-roost or alarm note.

Turdus merula
25 cm; 80–110 g
Where to look: dense woodland to open moorland, common in gardens. **Nest:** a little way up, in trees and hedges, sometimes in buildings. Constructed of mud and moss lined with grass. **Eggs:** 3–5, bluish-green, speckled brown. **Food:** insects summer, berries winter. **Voice:** rich fluty song, rattling alarm.

Berries and fruit form a major portion of the winter diet. If the ground remains soft, worms predominate.

There can be few places in Britain where it is not possible to find the blackbird throughout the year. The British breeding individuals are resident, but each autumn large numbers of migrants from northern Europe arrive on their way south to milder winter grounds. Spectacular arrivals on the east coast can be seen in late October and November, when, at times, hundreds of blackbirds, accompanied by other thrushes, may drop from the sky.

Many of these migrants remain in Britain throughout the winter, joining the resident birds at communal feeding grounds (orchards with waste apples being a particular favourite), and at traditional roosting sites that may be used year after year.

Blackbirds are very susceptible to albinism and individuals often have substantial numbers of white feathers. On such dark birds these feathers are particularly obvious and at times may resemble the crescent shape on the ring ouzel.

The song, delivered from a very prominent song post, consists of loud clear notes combined to make phrases, which last for some six seconds with a pause between of similar length. They sing between March and June, whereas the mistle thrush starts in late December and has short phrases repeated over and over again.

Males' wings look paler when flapped and catch the eye. Females are sooty brown, much darker than song thrush, but throat can be very pale, with dark streaks. Legs are dark, unlike thrushes'.

Young males, in their first year, have dark bills turning yellow in spring. They keep the brown wing feathers grown in the nest, which contrast with the black body.

A blackbird searching the lawn for worms is a familiar sight. Mainly ground-feeders, they move about in a series of short hopping runs, pausing to cock their head as if listening (in fact looking) for food. The struggle between blackbird and worm as the prey is slowly but steadily drawn from the ground is a familiar garden sight.

Although the flight never looks particularly strong, the blackbird is capable of covering great distances on migration. The flight usually seen is low to the ground and only covers short distances.

The speckled juvenile is often the cause of confusion and claims of blackbird × thrush hybrids.

One of the most distinctive blackbird postures is the wings down and tail cocked up position that is adopted as the bird lands on an open perch.

Strongly territorial when breeding, but genuine fights are rare. Occasionally two males may come to 'blows'.

Like all thrushes, blackbirds enjoy sunbathing and adopt a posture to 'catch' the sun.

Ring Ouzel

The ring ouzel spends winter in the Mediterranean region, with some British breeding birds reaching North Africa. It is the only thrush that is a summer visitor to Britain. It is an early arrival, the first individuals reaching southern England in early March, and they are quickly back in the hills, where they occupy wild, open country.

Its upland breeding areas have earned the species the alternative name of 'mountain blackbird', and the differences between ring ouzel and blackbird are not always striking. The white breast crescent is only obvious in the adult males, but in all plumages the ring ouzel has a greyer look, caused by the pale fringes to the feathers. Paleness on the wing feathers results in a distinctive pale area visible on the upperwing as the bird flies.

Ring ouzel flight shows a somewhat similar quality to that of the blackbird, but it appears stronger on the wing and is rather erratic. The flight is accompanied by a deep, throaty, chattering call. The song is a simple, loud piping, audible over very long distances.

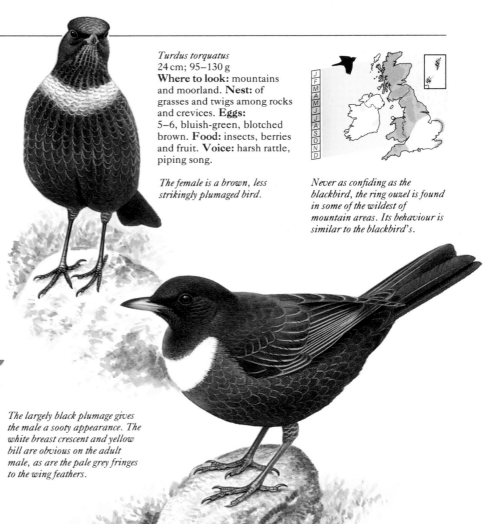

Turdus torquatus
24 cm; 95–130 g
Where to look: mountains and moorland. **Nest:** of grasses and twigs among rocks and crevices. **Eggs:** 5–6, bluish-green, blotched brown. **Food:** insects, berries and fruit. **Voice:** harsh rattle, piping song.

The female is a brown, less strikingly plumaged bird.

Never as confiding as the blackbird, the ring ouzel is found in some of the wildest of mountain areas. Its behaviour is similar to the blackbird's.

The erratic flight is achieved with deep wing strokes that show off the pale upperwing panels.

The largely black plumage gives the male a sooty appearance. The white breast crescent and yellow bill are obvious on the adult male, as are the pale grey fringes to the wing feathers.

Mistle Thrush

Turdus viscivorus
27 cm; 110–140 g
Where to look: gardens and woodland. **Nest:** in fork of tree, built of roots and grass. **Eggs:** 3–5, variable colour, but well spotted with brown. **Food:** fruit, berries and insects. **Voice:** loud, far-carrying blackbird-like song. Harsh, churring flight call.

The largest of the common thrushes, the mistle thrush is the earliest to start nesting. The song, often delivered from the top of a tall tree in very windy conditions (the bird's alternative name is 'storm cock'), can be heard from December onwards, and this is one of the few birds in full song at the beginning of the year. Eggs can be laid as early as February and young may have left the nest by the end of March.

When breeding, the mistle thrush can be very aggressive, showing a complete lack of fear in driving cats and dogs away from its nesting area. Some individuals will even attack man to the extent of regularly striking at the head and preventing people from entering their own gardens!

This is the greyest of the speckled thrushes, most readily identified by the large size, large round spots on the underparts, very upright stance and pure white underwing that is easily visible in flight (when very distinct undulations are also apparent).

Two identification features visible when the bird is in flight are the gleaming white underwing (obvious) and the whitish tips to the outermost tail feathers (less so).

The song is always delivered from a very exposed position and consists of up to six blackbird-like phrases repeated again and again in regular sequence.

General appearance is very grey compared with brown song thrush.

The underparts are very boldly marked with broad black spots.

On the ground, the stance is very upright and birds move about with strong hopping, almost bounding, leaps. In winter the birds can often appear larger and rounder in contrast to the sleeker summer appearance.

In juvenile plumage the back and wing feathers are covered with white marks on the feather tips, creating a patterned effect.

A ground-feeder, with upright stance, slightly drooped wings and occasional tail flick.

Small parties gather in autumn, but usually in ones and twos.

Song Thrush

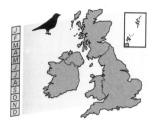

Turdus philomelos
23 cm; 70–90 g
Where to look: hedgerows, gardens and woodland. **Nest:** made of leaves and twigs, lined with mud. **Eggs:** 4–5, blue, spotted with black. **Food:** worms, snails, fruit and berries. **Voice:** alarm rattle; thin *sip* in flight.

Although this is principally a resident species, to be found in towns and gardens throughout the year, some British song thrushes move south for the winter, to be temporarily replaced by arrivals from Scandinavia and northern Europe. Many of these birds, which are seeking the milder maritime winter climate, will pass on through Britain to spend much of the winter in western France or Spain. Most of the arrivals take place in October and are usually slightly in advance of the true 'winter thrushes' – the redwing and the fieldfare.

The presence of a song thrush in an area is often indicated by the discovery of a thrush's 'anvil', the site where snail shells are broken against a prominent stone or the concrete of a garden path to gain access to the soft, nutritious body inside. This behaviour is unique to the song thrush, although other species, notably the blackbird, have developed the habit of robbing the thrush as soon as the work of opening the snail has been completed, and flycatchers have occasionally been known to break a snail open.

Mainly a ground-feeding species, moving with short runs or hops.

Winter food may be obtained from bushes and hedges, but most is collected on the ground – largely earthworms and snails, but also a wide range of insects, fallen fruit and berries.

Song thrushes are regular visitors to bird-tables and garden 'feeding stations', preferring to collect items dropped beneath the table rather than using the table itself. They can be attracted with fruit or grated cheese.

The adult song thrush is a familiar garden bird; it was once more numerous than the blackbird, but this situation has now been reversed. The warm-brown upperparts of the adult, together with the buffish underparts covered in small narrow black spots, distinguish it from the other thrushes. The stance is upright, but the body is more horizontal when running.

The superb song is delivered from a lower perch than that of the mistle thrush, a low bush or building being typical.

Compared with most British ones migrants from the east are greyer, birds from western Scotland are darker brown. Sexes are identical.

The long-legged, upright stance is typical of all ground-feeding thrushes. The birds are usually solitary, but will roost communally in cold weather.

The familiar and common resident speckled thrush. Brown upperparts and buffish underparts with rather narrow spots distinguish this species from the much larger, greyer mistle thrush. The similar-sized redwing is a winter visitor which differs in having reddish, not buffish-yellow underwings and a broad pale stripe over the eye.

Although resembling the adult, the juvenile plumage differs in the very speckled appearance of the upperparts. Back feathers have pale buff streaks and dark tips, and wing feathers have distinct yellowish tips.

Each song phrase of two or three syllables is repeated 2–4 times.

In flight, usually low, the creamy buff underwing is easily seen, distinguishing the song thrush from the redwing (tawny-red underwing) and mistle thrush (gleaming white).

Fieldfare

In flight, note the white underwing and contrasting upperparts.

The birds feed in loose, scattered flocks over the open ground, moving systematically forward, occasionally stopping in a very upright alarm posture. If they take flight the entire flock will usually alight on nearby trees facing into wind; further alarm and they fly off downwind.

Fieldfares first nested in Britain in 1967, when a nest with fledged young was discovered in the Orkneys, but the subsequent colonisation has not been particularly dramatic. It is rare for more than 10 pairs to have been recorded nesting in any one year, and these have almost always been in Scotland. The species has been steadily extending its breeding range westward through Europe, but this expansion may now have ceased.

Traditionally looked upon as a winter visitor, fieldfares may begin to arrive as early as August, but peak numbers are not reached on the east and south coast until late October or November. In suitable weather conditions, flocks of several hundred at a time will cross the southern North Sea, often arriving exhausted. Of all the winter visitors, the fieldfare is one of the latest to depart, with small parties regularly seen well into May.

Mixed thrush flocks in winter tend to be dominated by fieldfares and redwings, which behave in a noisy, nomadic fashion. Although fieldfares are usually found in the open countryside feeding on farmland and playing fields, cold weather will rapidly drive them into gardens where fruit and any remaining berries will be readily eaten and where they will join other birds at tables and feeding stations. Prolonged frozen conditions will force a further southward migration with many birds leaving Britain, although a number may become too weak for the journey and not survive.

Turdus pilaris
26 cm; 80–130 g
Where to look: parkland, open country. **Nest:** in fork of tree, made of grasses and twigs. **Eggs:** 5–6, speckled greenish-blue. Rare and erratic nesting species in Britain. **Food:** mainly worms, insects, but fruit and berries in hard weather. **Voice:** nasal *ee-eep*; harsh *cha-cha-cha-chack* flight call. Song rather weak, blackbird-like.

Winter food will be largely insects if the weather remains mild and the ground unfrozen.

Flocks gather around food supplies.

Flocks will suddenly arrive on berry bushes and remain until the supply is exhausted. Rotting fruit in orchards is eaten if weather is cold. Stubble and ploughed fields are also frequented.

Note red-brown back.

The most colourful of the thrushes, with contrasting plumage pattern. Grey head, reddish-brown back, grey rump and black tail form a distinctive rear-view picture. Underneath, the orange-buff of the breast contrasts with the white belly. Usually found in flocks, often mixed with redwings and exploiting berry crops on hedgerows.

On the ground, behaviour is typical of all thrushes, with an upright stance and hopping run.

The yellow base to the bill and contrasting plumage pattern, with smooth grey head and rump, makes the fieldfare the most elegant of all the thrushes.

Redwing

Of the winter thrushes the redwing appears the most susceptible to mortality in cold weather. Freezing conditions force southerly movements, but many individuals seem to succumb in hard frosts and deep snow.

Behaviour on the ground is typical of all thrushes.

Highly gregarious when not breeding, often mixed with parties of fieldfares and song thrushes, feeding in open fields and parkland.

Clear nights in October are ideal for migration and the high calls of redwings can often be heard from the blackness overhead.

Although a ground-feeder, flocks will gather on berry bushes such as hawthorn or ivy and feed until the supply is exhausted.

A standing bird will show distinctive lines of streaks on an almost white breast. Dull red flanks are usually visible. Note pale stripes on face.

Turdus iliacus
21 cm; 55–75 g
Where to look: open country and gardens. **Nest:** grasses and twigs in trees or bushes. **Eggs:** 5–6, greenish, with red-brown markings. **Food:** worms, insects, but also berries in winter. **Voice:** simple fluty song. Call distinctive *seeip*.

The British breeding population of redwings is usually confined to northern Scotland, where nesting was first recorded in 1925. The population increased slowly, and now numbers some 100 pairs in most years. There is little evidence of a westward spread in range and it is speculated that Britain's breeding birds are migrants which have simply failed to return to Scandinavia, rather than being the vanguard of an extensive colonisation. Isolated breeding has been recorded as far south as Kent.

Two distinct populations reach Britain each winter, one from Scandinavia, the other from Iceland. The Icelandic birds spend winter in the west, around the Irish Sea, the Scandinavian birds in the east. Although at first glance the two populatons are very similar, the Icelandic birds are in fact distinctly darker and larger. The greater size gives longer wings, necessary to carry them on the lengthy, over-sea migration. The Icelandic birds have recently colonised the Faeroes and may also be responsible for some of the British breeding birds.

In flight, the smallness of this species can at times make it appear rather lark-like, particularly in a migrating flock. The tawny-red underwing can be very obvious and quite unlike the yellow-buff of the song thrush.

Smallest of the typical thrushes and distinctive because of the tawny-red underwing – just visible on the flank of a standing bird – and the prominent pale stripe above the eye. Solitary when nesting, but usually seen in mixed flocks with fieldfares in winter. Readily visits gardens during cold weather when may even be attracted to bird-tables.

Slightly smaller and darker than the song thrush, the distinctive shade of olive on the upperparts is a good feature once noted.

Usual food consists of worms, snails, etc, but berries and fruit are often taken. In gardens they will be attracted to soft fruit, apples, and pears, but will also feed on grated cheese.

Comparing Warblers

Lesser whitethroat: *quieter, more unobtrusive than whitethroat, found in taller, thicker vegetation. Key features: white throat, dark ear-coverts, dark legs, no rust colour in wings, basically grey and white. Song hardly worthy of the name.*

Whitethroat: *lively and excitable; horizontal posture. Key features: rusty-coloured wings, contrasting white throat, pale legs, long white-edged tail, peaked crown. Scratchy song.*

Blackcap: *fairly active and lively, medium-sized. Key features: sharply defined black or brown skullcap, no white in tail. Beautiful, rich, fluty song.*

Garden warbler: *secretive. Key features: compact build, gentle expression, soft browns, rather pale overall. Mellow song.*

Chiffchaff: *very active. Key features: very like willow warbler, but shorter-winged, duller, stripes above eyes less obvious, dark legs. Bright, repetitive song.*

Willow warbler: *very active. Key features: small, slim, well-proportioned, longer-winged than chiffchaff, greenish and whitish, often with extensive yellow; fine bill, palish legs. Delightful song.*

Cetti's Warbler

Named after an 18th-century Italian Jesuit (and pronounced *chetty*), this is a most unusual bird. As well as its uniquely coloured eggs, and remarkable, powerful song, it is the only European passerine with 10 tail feathers, rather than 12; it also boasts the biggest size difference between the sexes, with males up to 30 per cent heavier than females. There are more females (they may be better able to survive hard winters), so each male may have up to three mates, leaving the entire rearing process to them alone. Incubation and fledging, at around 16 days each, are unusually long for a small bird, and the female may feed the young for up to a month after they have fledged.

Spreading from the Mediterranean, this warbler was first recorded in Britain as recently as 1961, and it did not breed until 1973. Like the Dartford warbler, it is resident and vulnerable to hard winters: indeed, the population in the original British stronghold in east Kent was wiped out in the mid-1980s.

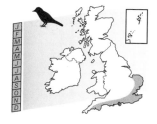

Cettia cetti
13.5–14.5 cm; 12–18 g
Where to look: dense, low scrub close to water. South and east England, very local. **Nest:** deep cup of leaves and grasses, low in thick vegetation. **Eggs:** 4, brick-red. **Food:** insects, spiders. **Voice:** loud, explosive bursts of song from dense cover.

Cetti's warbler can prove very difficult to see. Successive bursts of song are intermittent and rarely from the same spot. The first glimpse will probably be of a dark, rather stocky warbler with short wings and a full, rounded tail, diving for cover. With patience, a good view will reveal dark, red-brown upperparts and soft white and grey underparts, and often a flicked and cocked tail. Beware confusion with the nightingale, which has a longer, more red-brown tail.

Dark, thick-set, whiter beneath; dark bars under rounded tail.

Grasshopper Warbler

A rather mysterious bird, the grasshopper warbler is probably often overlooked, for the song, though carrying considerable distances under favourable conditions, is too high for many ears, and when not singing the bird is seldom seen. Though singing from cover, it may be in full view, often in a hawthorn or bramble, with the whole bird vibrating in time to the song.

Analysis of the dry, insect-like song (hence the name) reveals between 23 and 31 triple pulses per second. It is given in bursts of a minute or more, especially at dusk and dawn, though often also at night. It is perhaps better likened to a distant, small, tinny, muffled alarm clock or the rapid ticking of a freewheeling bicycle.

When disturbed at the nest, the adults may display to distract predators, rather as some waders do.

A nocturnal migrant, the numbers arriving in Britain fluctuate markedly from year to year. Because of its secretive behaviour, the main wintering grounds are something of a mystery, though some birds apparently remain around the Mediterranean, while others cross the Sahara to West Africa.

The long, slender bill and slim head give this bird rather a mean look. Soft streaking on dull olive-brown above, underparts whitish or yellowish. The long, streaked undertail coverts are revealed when the full, graduated tail is cocked.

The singing bird, beak open, turns its head from side to side. The volume and tone of the song appear to alter, producing a ventriloquial effect, and making the singer frustratingly difficult to pinpoint.

Perhaps Britain's most mouse-like bird in its movements. Will drop into low vegetation when disturbed, and run and creep in preference to flying.

Locustella naevia
13 cm; 11–15 g
Where to look: scrub, marsh, plantations. **Nest:** cup of grass, leaves, moss, in low vegetation. **Eggs:** 5–6, glossy white, speckled purplish. **Food:** insects, spiders. **Voice:** reeling song.

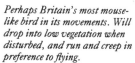

Sedge Warbler

Acrocephalus schoenobaenus
13 cm; 10–13 g
Where to look: waterside
vegetation, cereal fields,
plantations. **Nest:** deep cup
of grass, sedge, low in
brambles, etc. **Eggs:** 5–6,
pale olive, well speckled.
Food: insects, larvae, aphids.
Voice: impatient chatter of
harsh and sweet notes.

*Inquisitive, often sidling up
vertical stems to investigate an
intruder or strange noise.*

Old country names for the sedge warbler include
mock nightingale and Scotch nightingale, for this lively
summer visitor sings night and day when it first arrives
back in Britain. A mass overnight arrival can be very
exciting, with singing birds occupying every riverside
bush where the previous day there were none. Often a
bird will suddenly emerge from the depths of the
vegetation where it has been feeding low down, and
burst into its exuberant song, full of mimicry, seldom
repeating itself, suddenly halting, then tearing off
again, always sounding vaguely irritated. He may also
fly up vertically and spiral down, with fluttering wings
and spread tail, singing excitedly.

Normally weighing only about 10 g (⅓ oz), the sedge
warbler feeds avidly on plum-reed aphids before
migration and puts on large fat deposits which may
double its weight. This enables it to cross the Sahara in
one hop from France or Spain, a distance of some
3,800 km (2,400 miles). The Sahel drought in West
Africa has caused a decline in numbers since 1968, as
returning birds use this zone for feeding prior to spring
migration.

*Often seen in jerky, low flight,
tail spread and depressed. May
perch horizontally, looking
rather furtive.*

*The yellower juveniles show a
paler, streaked, central crown-
stripe, and may be confused with
the rare aquatic warbler.*

The broad,
creamy stripe
over the eye, streaky
back, and unstreaked
tawny rump identify,
though worn plumage
more uniform grey-
brown.

Reed Warbler

On the edge of its range in Britain, the reed warbler
has spread west and north to occupy most suitable reed
beds in England and Wales. Large numbers may nest in
one reed bed, though the birds themselves are not
social, and are highly aggressive to others of their kind.
Along with the meadow pipit and dunnock, this bird is
the main host of the cuckoo in Britain. Studies have
shown that the proportion of reed warbler nests
parasitised has more than doubled in recent years, and
that 'reed warbler cuckoos' are significantly more
successful in having their young reared to maturity than
those using other hosts. Because of high cuckoo
predation in reed bed colonies, nests outside reed beds
are, paradoxically, more successful from the warblers'
viewpoint. For such small birds, reed warblers are long-
lived. Ringing studies have revealed several 10 and 11-
year-old birds.

The song may recall that of the sedge warbler at first,
and like that species includes mimicry, but it is much
more repetitive, with a steadier rhythm. Unlike the
neurotic sedge, the reed warblers' song sounds rather
'laid-back', perhaps in keeping with drowsy summer
days by the waterside.

*Seasonal and age variation in
plumage colour, though always
with warm red-brown hues,
especially on the rump.*

*Though nesting in reed beds, they
regularly forage in nearby bushes,
especially willows. Often seen far
from water on migration.*

*The neat, woven nest has living
reed stems incorporated into its
structure.*

*Very agile. Clings to vertical
stems with both feet, or to
adjacent stems, thereby doing the
splits! Moves up and down in
jerks, or hops and flits from
plant to plant.*

Acrocephalus scirpaceus
13 cm; 10–15 g
Where to look: southern
reed beds. **Nest:** deep cup of
grasses woven around reed
stems, over shallow water.
Eggs: 4, greenish-white,
mottled darker. **Food:**
insects. **Voice:** like sedge
warbler, but more relaxed,
each phrase repeated.

Marsh Warbler

Not shy when singing. Avoids large reed beds.

Olive hues of spring adult. Juveniles very like reed warbler.

Singing birds may show contrast between yellow gape and orange mouth, or look like reed – but song is uniquely beautiful.

Reed and marsh warblers both have long bill and legs, long undertail coverts and rounded tail. Voice only reliable distinction, but marsh paler, with colder, more olive hues above in spring, paler legs.

Subtle shape difference: fuller bodied and heavier, bill slightly shorter, crown more rounded, wing-point a little longer than reed.

Usually the last summer migrant to arrive back, in late May or early June, the marsh warbler was not recognised as a British bird until 1871. Numbers in its Worcestershire stronghold are fast declining, and there is now serious cause for concern over its future as other than a sporadic nester in the 1990s. As well as habitat destruction and drainage, climatic factors are probably at work. By contrast, 10,000 pairs were breeding in Sweden by 1977, and yet the first nesting only took place there in 1930.

In its preference for a drier habitat, usually with meadowsweet, nettle and willowherb, and in its nest construction, this species differs from its visually almost identical cousin, the reed warbler. However, the chief distinction lies in the song, which is much richer and more varied. The marsh warbler is the master mimic, and analysis of song recordings has revealed elements of the song or call of no less than 99 European and 133 African species, with an individual average of 31 European and 45 African!

Acrocephalus palustris
12–13 cm; 11–15 g
Where to look: in lush vegetation and damp places, but very rare. **Nest:** attached to surrounding plants by 'basket handles'. **Eggs:** 4–5, pale grey, spotted dark. **Food:** insects. **Voice:** very rich, varied and sustained song.

Dartford Warbler

Until recently Britain's only resident warbler, this entirely insectivorous bird is badly hit by hard winters, and by fragmentation of its specialised heathland habitat. It was first described from Bexley Heath, near Dartford in Kent, in 1773, but has not occurred in that county for many years, other than as a vagrant. Nowadays it is confined mainly to Hampshire and Dorset, with outlying groups in Surrey and Devon. Wandering birds which occasionally appear elsewhere probably come from the French population.

Often hard to find, because they skulk and (for a small bird) have large territories, the males may sing from the tops of gorse bushes, or ascend in a song flight. At other times the birds usually reveal their presence by a soft churring call, almost a buzz, which, once learnt, is very characteristic. A bird may appear briefly on top of a gorse bush, tail cocked and flicked, and crown feathers raised, before diving abruptly out of sight, leaving the observer excited but anxious for more.

The male builds a series of flimsy 'cock's nests', but the actual nest, often decorated with spider cocoons, is built mainly by the female.

Sylvia undata
13 cm; 9–12 g
Where to look: resident on southern heaths with gorse and heather. **Nest:** cup of dead grasses, moss. **Eggs:** 4, pale, speckled grey. **Food:** insects, in winter mainly spiders. **Voice:** scratchy warble. Call a soft *tchirr*.

Identified by distinctive flight silhouette and jerky action, together with restricted habitat.

A restless, agitated bird, its long tail constantly cocked, fanned and flicked.

Note relatively large, angular head, and pale-based spiky bill.

Both sexes appear all dark at any distance. Male is dark chocolate-brown with slate-grey head above, and dark wine colour below with white belly, the pale throat spots invisible except at close range. His mate is paler, greyer; young greyer still.

Often, all that is seen is a small dark shape in weak flight on short whirring wings, followed by a long, bobbing, white-edged tail, cocked on landing.

Whitethroat

In spring, the male is a very smart bird with grey head, white throat and beautiful, pinkish wash across his breast.

Easily told in all plumages from lesser whitethroat by the rusty fringes to the flight feathers, pale legs, longer tail and large headed, often rather unkempt appearance.

His mate is rather duller, with a browner head. Note also the white eye-ring and pale eye.

The autumn juvenile is more subdued, with fewer contrasts, but still shows a white throat, and rufous patch in the wing.

In the spring of 1969 birdwatchers were asking 'where have all the whitethroats gone?'. Until then they had been among Britain's most abundant birds. Subsequent analysis showed that less than one in four birds had returned, and that the factor responsible was the disastrous drought in the arid thorn-scrub zone of the Sahel, south of the Sahara, which holds Britain's whitethroats in winter. The population has never recovered, though the rather tetchy song remains a characteristic summer sound. The old country name of 'nettlecreeper' reflects the bird's favourite nesting site.

The males return a fortnight before their mates to set up territory. They are restless birds, forever complaining, raising their crown feathers, or fanning the rather long, prominently white-edged tail. The song may be given while on the move inside bushes, from an exposed perch, or (especially where there are no trees or taller features in the territory) in a jerky, dancing, short song-flight, the bird bouncing as if on an invisible piece of elastic.

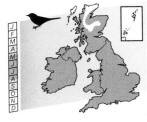

Sylvia communis
13–15 cm; 12–18 g
Where to look: low hedgerows, scrub, woodland edge. **Nest:** low cup of dry grass, roots. **Eggs:** 4–5, blue/green, spotted grey. **Food:** insects, berries. **Voice:** vigorous, scratchy warble. Calls include *whet-whet-whet*.

Lesser Whitethroat

One of a small group of birds which migrates southeast to spend the winter in north-east Africa, mainly in the Sudan and Ethiopia, lesser whitethroats take different routes in spring and autumn. Ringing recoveries have shown that British birds pass through northern Italy *en route* to Egypt, where they follow the Nile, but when returning north, they pass to the east of the Mediterranean, through Cyprus and Turkey.

Lesser whitethroats are rather retiring birds, but once their song has been learnt, it will reveal the species to be quite common over much of England. Care must be taken not to confuse the far-carrying, rattled song with that of the now rare cirl bunting. Birds often sing while on the move, almost always from within a thick hedge, or concealed in the canopy of a tree. At close range, a soft, inward whitethroat-like warble can be heard preceding the song proper, which is a simple, quick rattle sounding like 'chakakakakaka'.

In autumn, young birds may be seen in gardens, diligently searching bushes for insects, or taking berries. Their presence may be announced by a hard *tac* or occasionally, a high-pitched squeak.

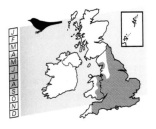

Sylvia curruca
14 cm; 10–16 g
Where to look: tall, thick hedgerows, scrub. **Nest:** flimsier than whitethroat's, higher above ground. **Eggs:** 4–6, cream, speckled darker. **Food:** insects; fruit in autumn. **Voice:** unmusical, loud rattle. Call hard *tac-tac*.

The song makes up for its lack of musicality by its carrying power.

In flight, shows less white in outer tail than whitethroat.

Male and female similar. Not shy, but often stays well concealed.

Young bird browner than adult, with ear-coverts less contrasting. Much cleaner looking than whitethroat.

Dark face and lower edge to ear-coverts.

Neat, sleek, and shorter-tailed than whitethroat, greyer above, whiter below, with dark legs, grey-brown wings, grey ear-coverts contrasting with white throat. Less excitable.

Garden Warbler

No outstanding features, other than beautiful voice.

A gentle-looking bird, with a rounded head, short stout bill, and large dark eye in a rather plain head, and plumage of soft shades of brown and palest buff. Lack of obvious distinguishing features is best clue to identity! In flight, note stockier build than blackcap, relatively shorter tail.

In flight, note shortish square-ended tail without 'white outers', longish wings and rather plump appearance.

When in full song, it has few rivals, and must rank in the British 'top ten' songsters. Note greyish-brown sides of nape and hind neck, and, in close view, narrow pale eye-ring.

On migration, may be seen in hedgerows, eating berries. Rather secretive. In worn plumage, upperparts greyer-brown, paler buff below, throat white, grey neck spot. Moults in winter quarters.

The nondescript garden warbler more than makes up for its lack of looks with its beautiful song. It is always with a feeling of satisfaction that one catches sight of the songster to confirm the sound identification, for it can be tricky to separate the songs of garden warbler and blackcap. The former sings longer phrases with shorter intervals, and the song is quieter and mellower, more rapid and even, without the almost abrupt outburst of the blackcap.

The garden warbler arrives later than the blackcap. Competition between the two species is largely avoided by the garden warbler's preference for feeding in lower vegetation. The male builds several 'cock's nests' of dried grass before the actual nest site is chosen.

In autumn, late migrants hang on well into October, and then turn to fruit and berries to supplement the basic insectivorous diet. Like many birds, the garden warbler is rather inappropriately named, rarely occurring in the average garden, and unfamiliar to most garden birdwatchers. Only small numbers breed in Ireland, and it is scarce in the north of Scotland.

Sylvia borin
13–15 cm; 16–23 g
Where to look: woods, scrub, overgrown hedgerows. **Nest:** loose cup of dry grass, usually low. **Eggs:** 4–5, white or buff, blotched darker. **Food:** insects, larvae, fruit. **Voice:** rich, sustained, even warbling. Call *check-check*.

Blackcap

Sylvia atricapilla
13–15 cm; 14–20 g
Where to look: woods, parks, gardens, bird-tables in winter. **Nest:** compact grass cup. **Eggs:** 5, pale, spotted brownish. **Food:** insects, berries, also fat and scraps in winter. **Voice:** beautiful loud, rich, pure warbling.

Although (like other warblers) they are primarily summer visitors, increasing numbers of blackcaps now spend the winter in Britain. At this time they most often live in gardens, where they feed on bird-table scraps, fat, bread and, not infrequently, even peck at hanging nut bags. British breeding birds migrate to the Mediterranean and North Africa; those seen in Britain in winter have come from eastern Europe. The habit of overwintering is not new, but it is growing, with perhaps 2,000 birds now, some regularly as far north as Aberdeen. Although smaller than many other garden birds, blackcaps are usually very aggressive, and may be the dominant bird present at the 'feeding station'. They often puff out their feathers to appear larger than they really are, as an added protection against the cold.

The full song consists of short phrases, often with a terminal flourish of loud, clear notes, and is regarded by many as equal to the nightingale in quality. By contrast, the call is a *tac-tac*, harder than that of the garden warbler. However, the softer, more rambling subsong is very garden warbler-like and many people feel happiest to identify them by sight, not sound.

In autumn, blackberries are regularly and greedily taken; in winter, ivy and holly berries. Rather clumsy feeder.

Often sings from high in an oak tree in spring. In jerky flight from tree to tree, the longish tail shows no white, ruling out whitethroats.

Juvenile more rusty-brown, less olive-brown above, yellower below, with orange-brown or dark brown cap.

At bird-table, beware confusion with tits. Black cap in male only to eye level, unlike marsh tit. Female unmistakable with bright, red-brown cap.

Willow Warbler

Gilbert White, of Selborne fame, was the first to distinguish the three species of 'willow wren' – willow warbler, chiffchaff and wood warbler – noticing that their songs were quite different.

The first real feeling of spring comes with the overnight arrival, in early April, of willow warblers – their effortless, beautiful cascade of sweet, liquid notes coming from still leafless trees and bushes. They are the commonest summer visitors, with some three million pairs in Britain and Ireland, their huge range stretching right across northern Eurasia. East Siberian breeding birds undertake a 10–11,000 km (6–7,000 miles) journey twice a year to and from their winter quarters in East Africa – an astonishing journey for such tiny bundles of feathers. Their resilience is further evidenced by the record of a bird, alive and well, but completely transfixed by a thorn which must have pierced it some time previously, for dead skin surrounded the thorn.

Willow warblers are the only British birds to undergo two complete moults annually – once in summer, and again in West Africa in late winter: a remarkable fact considering the extra energy requirements needed to form a complete new set of feathers.

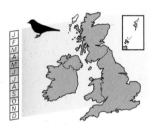

Phylloscopus trochilus
10.5–11.5 cm; 6–10 g
Where to look: woods of all types, scrub. **Nest:** dome of grass, lined with feathers, on ground. **Eggs:** 6–7, white, speckled red-brown. **Food:** small insects, larvae. **Voice:** falling cadence of pure notes. Call soft *hoo-eet*.

Male chases female in courtship, waving one or both wings slowly while perched close by. Normal behaviour includes much nervous wing flicking.

Raises crown feathers in aggression, like many warblers.

Migrant birds from Scandinavia and many Scottish breeders are brown and white, rather than olive and yellow.

Freshly arrived adult brown-olive above, whitish buff below, with yellowish breast and stripe over eye. 'Brighter' plumage than chiffchaff.

Call distinctly nearer two syllables than chiffchaff's hweet.

Juvenile bright primrose-yellow below. Often misidentified as icterine warbler.

On arrival, feeds actively on early insects at willow flowers.

Legs usually pale in willow warbler, dark in chiffchaff, but not always! Much variation in both species, but willow warbler less drab, sleeker and usually with clearer and longer stripe above eye. Call different.

May hover briefly, or sally out after flying insects, like a flycatcher.

Chiffchaff and willow warbler are small, neat, active birds, seldom still for long, diligently inspecting twigs and foliage for tiny insect morsels, frequently flicking their wings, and often singing as they forage. Flight is rapid and dodging.

Many silent birds will remain unidentifiable 'willow-chiffs'.

Chiffchaff

Like the cuckoo, the chiffchaff derives its name in many European languages from its rather monotonous, but unmistakable, song – *chiff chaff chaff chip chap chiff chep*. Many who recognise the song have little idea of the appearance of the singer, for this tiny bird, the first summer songbird to arrive back, in late March, usually sings from high in a tall tree. Most spend the winter around the Mediterranean, with small numbers braving the British winter, mainly in the south-west, and often at sewage farms. These residents may occasionally include the greyer Siberian-race birds, with their different, chick-like call. Bright autumn days may cause migrants to burst into unseasonal song.

The males play little part in the nesting cycle, leaving nest building, incubation, and most of the feeding of the young to the female.

This short-haul migrant has shorter, more rounded wings than the long-winged, tropical-wintering willow warbler.

Phylloscopus collybita
11 cm; 6–9 g
Where to look: woods, scrub with trees. In winter, often by water. **Nest:** grass dome, just above ground. **Eggs:** 5–6, white, lightly marked darker. **Food:** small insects. **Voice:** repeated *chiff-chaff*. Call emphatic *hweet*.

Brownish-olive upperparts, dirty white underparts with yellow tinge on breast. Rounder-headed, dumpier than willow, with clearer eye-ring.

Though requiring more mature trees than willow warbler, it also feeds more regularly on the ground, especially on migration and in winter, hopping in an agile way, flicking its wings and tail frequently.

Juvenile browner above and yellower below than adult, less bright than young willow warbler.

In worn plumage in midsummer, becomes browner and whiter.

Wood Warbler

Clear yellow stripe above eye; yellow throat and upper breast sharply divided from white lower down.

Unmistakable in spring, with bright, contrasting green, yellow and white plumage. Plump-bellied, long wings drooping either side of shortish tail, wings not flicked. Pale legs often obvious.

Adults become duller, browner above as season progresses.

Largest of the green warblers, the wood warbler is peculiar in having two totally different songs. Only the willow tit shares this characteristic. A beautiful, silvery, shivering trill, uttered with head thrown back, causing the whole bird to vibrate, is the regular song, but interspersed less frequently in these phrases is a powerful, rather melancholy repetition of the call note *pew*. Though nesting on the ground, it spends more time in trees than the willow warbler or chiffchaff. The beautiful spiralling courtship display flight of the male in and below the canopy attracts attention in the open woods with little undergrowth which are its favoured habitat.

Wood warblers are seldom seen on spring passage as they head straight for their breeding grounds. In autumn, like the lesser whitethroat, they move south-east through Italy to their equatorial wintering grounds in central and eastern Africa.

Unlike other leaf warblers, wood warblers do not give their nests a cosy feather lining. The parents are kept busy feeding their young for a month after fledging, and thus only have a single brood.

Yellow fringes to tail and wing feathers, forming paler panel.

Bright colours harmonise with fresh greens in late spring sun.

Phylloscopus sibilatrix
12–13 cm; 7–12 g
Where to look: oak and beech woods with sparse ground cover, local. **Nest:** dome of dead leaves, grass on ground. **Eggs:** 5–7, white, speckled reddish. **Food:** insects. **Voice:** accelerated shivering trill, or repeated *pew-pew*.

Goldcrest

Lively actions, hovering or flycatching like a leaf warbler, flicking wings while carefully searching the tiniest twigs and pine needles.

Large, beady black eye in bare face, gives a rather 'surprised' expression. Yellowish feet.

Pugnacious birds, crown stripe flared in anger, even at own reflection. Juveniles lack the black and yellow crown markings.

Along with the similar but much rarer firecrest, this is Britain's smallest bird, weighing only as much as a 5p coin. It is a sobering experience, on the east coast in late autumn, to spot a minute dot heading over the waves towards land, at last pitching into a bramble, where the lively actions and thin high call note reveal its identity. That such a tiny, entirely insectivorous bird not only survives the British winter, but chooses to migrate here from Scandinavia, is one of nature's wonders. In Yorkshire, it was known as the 'woodcock pilot', arriving at the same time as that species, and in Norfolk it was even thought that they sometimes hitched a lift on the backs of short-eared owls!

Often joining tit flocks in winter, the restless and confiding goldcrest keeps in constant touch by means of its thin contact call. Along with the coal tit, it may be the dominant species in conifer plantations, both in summer and winter. Its ability to exploit these alien trees has resulted in a huge increase in numbers.

Regulus regulus
9 cm; 5–7 g
Where to look: woodland, parks, gardens with conifers. **Nest:** tiny suspended cup of moss, cobwebs. **Eggs:** 7–8, white with faint spots. **Food:** tiny insects. **Voice:** thin, high, rhythmical song, ending in flourish.

Firecrest

It is always a tremendous thrill to see this tiny gem, surely one of Britain's most beautiful birds, and rare too! Formerly only a rare visitor on migration and in winter, mainly to the south and south-west coasts, breeding in Britain was not recorded until the early 1960s; numbers have slowly increased, and small colonies are now scattered over a number of English and Welsh counties, though breeding remains sporadic. These initial attempts at colonisation follow an increase in western Europe this century. The song has similarities with that of the goldcrest, and it is likely that the bird is often overlooked. Evidence of the close relationship of these two species is shown by reports of cross-breeding.

In Britain, at least, Norway spruce is usually present where firecrests nest, with some deciduous trees and often holly too. Firecrests often feed closer to the ground than goldcrests. On migration they frequent bracken, bramble and sea buckthorn. The thin call is very similar to that of the goldcrest, but to the practised ear sounds harder and slightly lower-pitched, a repeated *zit*, the last note rising a little in pitch.

A little jewel, much brighter than goldcrest, with a striking head pattern. Usually first located by call; both 'crests' are very active.

Bright orange sheen on shoulder patches, greener above, whiter below than goldcrest. Males have richer, fiery orange central crown stripe, best seen in display.

When displaying, males flash their brilliant crowns at a potential mate or intruder.

Juveniles lacking striking head pattern, though identified by suggestion of adult markings.

Regulus ignicapillus
9 cm; 5–7 g
Where to look: less reliant on conifers than goldcrest; woods, coastal scrub. **Nest:** like goldcrest. **Eggs:** 7–11, white or pinkish, faintly marked. **Food:** tiny insects. **Voice:** song – simple, repeated crescendo of one note, without end flourish.

Spotted Flycatcher

So great is its dependence on insects that the spotted flycatcher is among the last of the summer migrants to return to Britain from Africa, since it needs to be quite sure of the supply of its food. One day in late May it will be back, sitting erect on a dead bough, post or wire. It launches out in agile pursuit of some insect, catching it (sometimes with an audible snap of its bill) and perches again, often in the original place, with a flick of its wings. It pursues most flying insects, including butterflies, bees and wasps, and it strikes large and dangerous victims against its perch to subdue them. In cold or wet weather, it will hunt among branches for aphids and the like. The female will also eat snails and woodlice for the calcium she needs to form egg-shells. To avoid competing with each other, males and females may feed in different parts of their territory. A favourite nest site is a climbing plant against a wall or tree trunk, but spotted flycatchers will nest anywhere from an old nest to a corpse hanging on a gamekeeper's gibbet! Open-fronted nestboxes will often attract them to breed.

Seen briefly, female and young pied flycatchers resemble spotted, but pied is dumpier, more fidgety, and the calls are different. White in wings and tail will show clearly when pied turns or flies.

Adults are grey-brown above, with blackish, pale-edged wings; off-white, streaked with grey, below, noticeably pale.

The bird flies out in pursuit of passing insects, often returning to its original perch.

Muscicapa striata
14 cm; 15–16 g
Where to look: woodland edges, clearings, parks and gardens. **Nest:** in natural and man-made crevices and ledges, creepers, etc. **Eggs:** 4–5, white, blotched red. **Food:** chiefly insects. **Voice:** thin, high calls and song.

Juvenile birds are truly 'spotted' on the breast and 'scaly' above.

The bird perches in a distinctive upright pose in a prominent place.

Pied Flycatcher

Ficedula hypoleuca
12.5 cm; 13–14 g
Where to look: mature deciduous woods. **Nest:** in a hole, usually in a tree; nest-boxes. **Eggs:** 5–9, unmarked pale blue. **Food:** mainly insects. **Voice:** a sharp *squick* or a soft *wheet*. The song is a short, sweet warble.

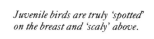

Although they do take prey in the air, pied flycatchers frequently pick food from leaves, branches and also the ground.

This is a classic bird of wooded hillsides in the west and north of Britain. In spring, the male calls attention to himself with his repeated, musical song and his flashing plumage. The female is much more discreet and she incubates the eggs alone. The male is sometimes bigamous and may then hold territories up to 3.5 km (2 miles) apart, perhaps in order to convince the second female that he is unattached! But if both the clutches hatch, he will only help feed the young of the first. Many broods are raised in nestboxes, and the provision of these has undoubtedly helped the bird to maintain or increase its numbers in some areas. Feeding among leaves, on trunks and branches, and on the ground, pied flycatchers take a good deal of non-flying prey, particularly caterpillars, and occasionally even worms. Snails are also eaten and the bird has been seen hammering one on a road, in the manner of a song thrush. Once the young have fledged, the family moves up into the canopy and becomes silent and difficult to find. In autumn they depart and, at the same time, the east coast of Britain may receive 'falls' of Continental pied flycatchers on migration.

The male in spring is most striking. Females, young birds and males in autumn are grey-brown above and white below, with obvious white patches in the wings and on the sides of the tail.

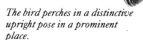

Pied flycatchers do not sit bolt upright like spotted flycatchers: they appear more restless, flicking a wing, or wings, and waving their tails.

Some males in autumn retain the white forehead and some black on the wings and tail. A spring moult restores the pied plumage.

Bearded Tit

Panurus biarmicus
16.5 cm; 15–16 g
Where to look: reed beds.
Nest: low in reeds. **Eggs:** 5–7, white speckled with black.
Food: mainly insects in summer and small seeds in winter. **Voice:** unique and memorable: a metallic *ching* and a hard *tik*, repeated.

The fascinating 'beardie' is not a tit at all, but belongs to an Asian family, the parrotbills. It lives in reed beds, climbing with agility among the stems and often perching with a different reed in either foot. In windy weather it keeps low, but a chorus of unmistakable ringing calls will give away a flock, or the birds may fly, like tiny pheasants, just above the reed tops. Sometimes, with tails cocked up, they will feed on the ground, but always near reeds. The bearded tit suffers badly in severe winters, but breeds prodigiously (a pair may raise four broods in a season!) and soon builds up its numbers again. After particularly good seasons, flocks 'erupt' from their breeding grounds, and appear in reed beds where they have not been seen for years, if ever. Regular migrations also take place between summer and winter sites, often hundreds of miles apart. Birds may be very faithful to two such sites or ring the changes: it seems likely that they are influenced by others that they encounter – or perhaps by a new mate.

Adult males have 'moustaches', grey heads and black undertail coverts. Females plainer, shape and behaviour distinctive.

Young birds are more golden, with black backs and tail sides; males have yellow bills, females grey, males show black on face.

Long-tailed Tit

Despite appearances, this bird is not really a tit, and may be related to the exotic babbler family: like them it has fluffy plumage and sociable habits. A flock in winter will defend its territory against other flocks and roost communally, the birds huddling together for warmth. In fact this bird seems to like tight places – both adults will roost in the nest with the brood of up to a dozen young! The nest is a wonderful, elastic construction of moss and spiders' webs, disguised with lichen (or even pieces of polystyrene!) and lined with hundreds, perhaps thousands, of feathers. It may be low in a thorn bush or high in a tree, and the adults sometimes take 20 days to build it. After the breeding season, family parties and larger flocks wander through woods and along hedges, often joined by tits and other small birds. Long-tailed tits take mostly insects, but they also peck lichen and green algae from trunks and branches. They are wonderfully acrobatic and will hang upside-down by one foot, holding large food items in the other to eat them. They visit bird-tables only rarely, but when they do decide to do so, they may come regularly, sometimes for more than one winter.

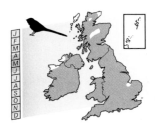

Aegithalos caudatus
14 cm; 8 g
Where to look: hedges, bushes; woods in winter.
Nest: in a bush or in a tree fork. **Eggs:** 8–12, white, spotted with red. **Food:** mainly insects. **Voice:** a thin *zi-zi-zi*; *tup*; a rolling *trrr*: all distinctive. Song rare.

Unique nest is an oval purse of moss, webs and lichen, feather-lined.

An unmistakable 'ball and stick' shape, both perched and in flight.

Adults are black, white and pale pink. Juveniles have dark cheeks, no pink and shorter tails.

Roving bands of these birds move with agility through trees and bushes, crossing gaps in single file and calling ceaselessly as they go.

Marsh Tit

Marsh and willow tits are about as common as each other and, although not rare, are much less frequently seen than blue or great tits. They usually occur in ones and twos and both join nomadic tit flocks in the winter. They pose one of the classic identification challenges and even experts cannot always tell them apart. The two species live subtly different lives. Marsh tits prefer deciduous woodland, rarely occurring in conifer woods or scrub. They regularly drop to the ground, for instance to pick up beech-mast, and they hammer open this and other seeds, such as those of yew, honeysuckle and spindle. Marsh tits usually nest in ready-made holes in trees, walls and banks – perhaps doing a little enlarging work: for some reason they rarely use nestboxes. They come regularly to gardens and bird-tables, from which they can often be seen carrying food away to hide it, usually in crevices under bark, but sometimes in the ground. Such food is regularly recovered, but whether by searching likely places or by precise memory is not yet known.

Parus palustris
11.5 cm; 11 g
Where to look: deciduous woodland, gardens. **Nest:** in a hole, usually in a tree. **Eggs:** 6–10, white, spotted red. **Food:** insects, seeds and fruits. **Voice:** an explosive *pitchu; chika-dee-dee-dee*, etc. Song a repeated *chip-chip-chip*.

Adult male and female marsh tits are alike in colour and pattern. The young bird has a browner cap and bib and is whiter below: it is very like the young willow tit.

In adults the cap is glossy black, the neck is 'slim', the bib neat, and there is little or no pale panel in the wing. The flanks and belly are a similar grey-white.

Marsh tits have strong bills and will hammer at tough seeds, such as beech-mast, while holding them under one foot.

Willow Tit

Parus montanus
11.5 cm; 10 g
Where to look: woods, scrub, gardens. **Nest:** self-excavated, low in a stump. **Eggs:** 6–10, white, spotted red. **Food:** insects, seeds and fruits. **Voice:** a nasal *air-air-air*; high, thin calls, etc. Song is a clear *piu piu*.

The willow tit has the distinction of being the most recent British breeding species to be recognised. It was only separated from the marsh tit at the end of the last century, and the differences between the two species can still be very difficult in practice. Plumage differences are slight, especially in summer when adults have worn feathers: juveniles can be inseparable even in the hand. However, the calls and song are fortunately very distinctive. There are other differences, too. Although they occur more patchily across the country, willow tits live in a wider variety of woods than marsh tits, including conifer plantations. This may explain their slightly finer bills, which could be useful for feeding among bunches of conifer needles. They feed low down, but only very rarely on the ground, nor do they appear to 'hammer' food. Yet they excavate a new nest hole each year, typically in soft, rotten wood, and ignoring older apparently suitable holes, even in the same stump. This may be to avoid a build-up of parasites, which live in old nests. Willow tits will use nestboxes, especially if these are filled with wood chips or polystyrene for the bird to excavate!

The marsh tit's distinctive, sharp, sneezing, *pitchu* sounds annoyed. The willow tit's deliberate, very nasal, *air-air-air* is unique. Both calls are frequent.

Compared with the marsh tit, adults have a duller black cap, a bull neck, a more diffuse bib; in fresh plumage, pale wing panel and bright buff flanks.

The female excavates a new hole each year, low in a rotten stump.

Willow tits do not prefer willows, nor marsh tits marshes! The willow tit is less confined to deciduous woods than the marsh.

Both species sometimes occur in the same wood, and both join roving tit flocks, but it is rare to see them together.

Blue Tit

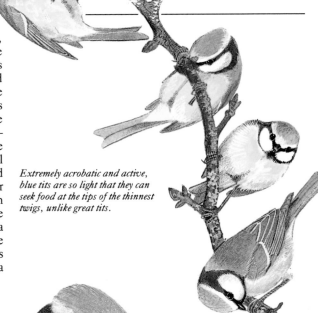

Parus caerulus
11.5 cm; 9–10 g
Where to look: broadleaved woods, especially oak and birch, less in conifers; gardens; widespread in winter. **Nest:** hole in tree, nestbox, almost any kind of cavity. Nest of moss with grass and bark strips, lined with feathers. **Eggs:** 7–13, (smaller clutches in gardens), tiny, white with red-brown spots. **Food:** insects in summer, insects and seeds in winter. **Voice:** high, thin notes, churrs and trills – *tsee, tsee-see-chuchuchuch.*

Blue tits literally put all their eggs into one basket, producing a single brood of chicks each year to coincide with the greatest abundance of juicy, nutritious caterpillars. If that brood fails, there is no second chance. This contrasts with the strategy of the blackbird, whose dependable supply of worms allows three broods of four at a time, spread through the summer. Despite its eagerness to profit from man – quickly discovering a bag of peanuts, searching the window frames of houses for spiders, using an artificial box for nesting – the blue tit is essentially a woodland bird, especially where there is oak or birch. In winter they spread out, even feeding in reed beds and much more open places – almost anywhere, in fact, where food might be available. In a mixed feeding flock in a wood it is interesting to watch the great tits going to the ground using the bigger branches while the blue tits tend to feed out on the slimmer twigs, using their extra agility to the full.

Extremely acrobatic and active, blue tits are so light that they can seek food at the tips of the thinnest twigs, unlike great tits.

A fresh-plumaged, bright blue tit has a vivid blue cap, blue wings and tail and clean yellow breast. In dull light it tends to look rather drab, paler beneath, and the white face with black lines is then the best feature.

Blue tits are clever feeders, and hold food firmly under one foot if necessary, so they are able to deal with hard nuts and seeds, pecking into them with sharp stabs.

The great tit is bigger, with a blacker head; the coal tit has no blue, green or yellow. Blue tits feeding in tree tops with thin, high calls may easily be confused with other tits and goldcrests.

Blue tits may not easily be forgiven for stealing cream from milk bottles, pecking putty or even tearing wallpaper if they get the chance!

Pale yellow underside, with a thin dark streak. Young birds have greener wing coverts.

A bird at a nestbox may look dull and worn after the exertions of finding food for a dozen chicks. Blue tits favour oak trees and feed and nest in them if they can, even preferring nestboxes in oak trees when a choice is available.

Fledglings have greener caps and yellower faces than their parents, but the basic pattern still helps to identify them.

Male glides slowly towards likely nest site in order to attract female to it. Usually flight is more fluttery, looking quite quick in a small space, suddenly 'stopping dead' on perch. In courtship feeding (left) female begs for food by shivering wings, like a fledgling demanding to be fed.

A lively, aggressive little bird with quick, jerky actions. It is by far the commonest species at peanut baskets. It penetrates the cities, where it often roosts in the warm space above street lamps. After nesting, family groups join in widely-roaming flocks, often with a regular 'beat'. Scores may pass through a garden each day.

Great Tit

Great tits are adaptable, taking advantage of unusual nest sites, such as pipes, letter-boxes, etc. Like blue tits, they have learned to open milk bottles and, in experiments, to perform very complex tasks to obtain food.

Scores of different calls have been described for this species.

Most of these calls have a distinctive metallic or ringing quality which helps identify them; in a wood, 'if you don't know the call, it's probably a great tit!'

Parus major
14 cm; 19 g
Where to look: woods, hedges, gardens. **Nest:** in a natural or artificial hole. **Eggs:** 5–12, white with red spots. **Food:** mainly insects, seeds, fruits. **Voice:** very varied; calls are mostly metallic and ringing, such as *chink*. Song, a loud *teacher-teacher-teacher*, very strident.

Great tits are the 'tough guys' of the tit family, as anyone who has watched them at a bird-table can testify. They usually stop short of serious violence, but that stout beak, which can hack open a hazel-nut, is a formidable weapon, and there is evidence that they occasionally kill other birds and may eat portions of them. There is even a remarkable record of one killing a goldcrest and carrying it away in its feet, like a miniature hawk. Despite these unendearing habits, the great tit is a fascinating species. It has been well studied, partly because it nests very readily in boxes, and also because it is reasonably easy to distinguish the male from the female – the black band on his belly is thick and unbroken, especially as it passes between the legs. Males take little or no part in building the nest, but feed the hen while she is laying and incubating the eggs. If disturbed at the nest, she will hiss like a snake and this may frighten predators away, or startle them enough for her to escape. The young are fed, as in other tit species, mainly on caterpillars, and the birds time their families to coincide with peak numbers of these. This peak varies in timing from year to year. But how do the birds know – some weeks in advance – when the peak will be?

Juvenile birds have washed-out, duller colours and their cheeks are yellowish, not white.

The tail is blue-grey with obvious white outer feathers.

Their large size, plus their striking combination of white cheeks, yellow breast, black crown and bib, make great tits unmistakable.

Females have less glossy caps, and less black on the belly.

In autumn and winter, great tits roam the woods in flocks, often with other species. They regularly drop to the ground, where they toss leaves aside and tear up moss and fungi in search of food.

They are aggressive birds, especially when feeding. One threat posture is 'horizontal' with wings and tail fanned, often with the bill open; another is 'vertical', with the chin held high.

Crested Tit

Parus cristatus
11.5 cm; 11 g
Where to look: old pine forests. **Nest:** self-excavated in a stump, etc. **Eggs:** 5–7, white, blotched red. **Food:** insects, seeds and fruit.
Voice: thin calls like other tits and a distinctive, purring *choorrr*, repeated as song.

The favourite nest site is a rotten stump, but a fence post or a hole in the ground may be used.

Although a very few crested tits have occurred in England (probably all vagrants from the Continent), the only place in Britain where there is a realistic chance of seeing them is in the old pine woods of Highland Scotland, particularly in the valley of the River Spey. Even here, there are only a few hundred pairs, and the bird can be very difficult to find. The best approach is to choose a stretch of this ancient Caledonian forest (with plenty of dead wood, which the birds and their insect food love) and to listen for the soft, purring call. The first view may well be of an apparently drab, grey-brown and buff little bird, neck-achingly high in a pine. However, with patience, the 'bridled' face pattern and the upstanding black and white crest may be seen, especially if the bird drops low to inspect some cracked or rotten stump as a possible nest site. If, as modern pine plantations age, more sites become available, or if crested tits learn to use nestboxes more regularly, they may well be able to expand their range.

This is the only small British bird with a crest, but this feature can be surprisingly difficult to see, especially on a bird overhead. Nor is the distinctive face pattern always obvious in brief views.

Males and females look alike. Juveniles are a little duller with shorter crests.

Crested tits often feed by clinging to the trunk of a tree. They will join roving tit flocks, but are usually seen in ones and twos.

Coal Tit

Parus ater
11 cm; 9 g
Where to look: woods, especially coniferous; gardens. **Nest:** in a hole low in a tree, or in the ground. **Eggs:** 7–11, white, spotted red. **Food:** chiefly insects and seeds. **Voice:** bright *peet*; song, great tit-like, faster, softer.

The smallest of the tits, it often looks dumpy and short-tailed.

The coal tit occurs regularly in deciduous woodland, but it is with conifers that most birdwatchers associate it. In a mixed woodland, it will often be found flitting around in the top of a pine. It is even common in conifer plantations, where few other birds may be present. It overcomes the shortage of natural cavities in plantation trees by nesting in a hollow among the roots, or even in a mouse-hole. It often uses nestboxes and, given the choice, prefers one on a conifer to one on a deciduous tree. In the winter, it often visits gardens, where it tends to be dominated by the larger blue and great tits. It manages quite well, however, by taking small pieces of food discarded by the other birds and also by carrying food away and storing it.

The distinctive double wing bar is often easier to see than the nape-patch: at close range the bars show as separate white spots.

Another distinguishing feature is the obvious olive-grey hue of the back.

In Scottish pine forests, distinguish coal tits from crested by the nape-patch, wing bars and lack of crest. Marsh and willow tits rarely feed as high in pines and look browner and more uniform. Blue tits look brighter, even at a distance. The coal tit's clear, single call is also very distinctive.

The large, white patch on the nape is unique and distinctive. The black bib is more extensive than on other small tits.

Males and females look alike, while juveniles have yellower cheeks, nape and wingbars. Fresh plumage clean and bright.

Nuthatch

A big-headed, short-tailed and perky little bird, rather like a miniature woodpecker in shape and actions, always on the move.

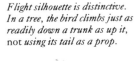

Sitta europea
14 cm; 20–22 g
Where to look: woods, parks. **Nest:** in a tree-hole. **Eggs:** 6–11, white, spotted with red. **Food:** insects, nuts, seeds. **Voice:** a variety of clear, ringing whistles.

The most striking feature is the broad, black eye-stripe.

Flight silhouette is distinctive. In a tree, the bird climbs just as readily down a trunk as up it, not using its tail as a prop.

Nuthatches behave like sparrow-sized woodpeckers, but have the unique ability to climb down trunks and branches as well as up. They do this by moving obliquely, hanging from the upper foot and propped by the lower one. Unlike woodpeckers, they are no carpenters (they nest in ready-made holes), but they are plasterers, and exclude starlings and predators such as weasels with a hard, mud rim to the nest-hole. They even do this to a nestbox hole – and fill in any cracks in the top and sides as well! The young are fed mainly on insects, taken from both bark and leaves. In autumn, nuthatches pick up beech-mast, acorns and hazel-nuts, carrying them to a favoured branch, wedging them in the bark and hacking them open with energetic and noisy whacks of the bill. They sometimes visit bird-tables, and access to this easy food supply may now be helping the bird to extend its range further north and west in England and Wales, though not as yet into Scotland or Ireland.

The birds often plaster the nest-hole entrance with hard-drying mud, to keep out predators and larger competitors for the site.

Blue-grey above, with white cheeks and corners to the tail; buff below. Chestnut flanks are brighter in the male.

Treecreeper

The treecreeper is usually seen flitting across a clearing, landing low on a tree trunk and then jerkily working its way up, propped on the stiff and pointed feathers of its tail. The down-curved, fine-tipped bill is ideal for probing in crevices in the bark. The bird spirals as it goes (quite why is not clear) appearing and disappearing from view, and it climbs along under branches as readily as on top. At any point it may abandon the tree and fly down to the base of another: unlike the nuthatch, it rarely climbs downwards. In winter, treecreepers often join tit flocks; they do not visit bird-tables, but they will sometimes feed on fat if it is smeared into tree bark. Some birds hollow out winter nests in the soft wood of certain tree trunks (Wellingtonias are a favourite). The birds make several hollows, and choose one on the lee side of a tree, according to the weather. Just occasionally treecreepers can be persuaded to breed in a wedge-shaped nestbox with a hole in the side. But beware if you are standing nearby when the young emerge – there is a record of a fledgling mistaking a man for a tree . . . and climbing him!

Treecreepers, nuthatches and woodpeckers all cling to trees. The lesser spotted woodpecker is small enough to confuse, but is obviously black and white. The nuthatch is blue-grey with black eye-stripe. The treecreeper is brown, and thin-billed.

A delicate looking bird, brown above and silvery-white below, with a fine, down-curved bill.

Adults are warm brown above, streaked with buff; juveniles are greyer and more spotted.

Certhia familiaris
12.5 cm; 9 g
Where to look: woodland and parks. **Nest:** in a crack in a tree, or behind loose bark. **Eggs:** 4–8, white, spotted red. **Food:** insects. **Voice:** a thin, high *tsit* or *tsu*. Song is a penetrating *tsip-tsee-tsee-tsee*, ending in a flourish.

Treecreepers usually climb upwards, spiralling round trunk and branches, then drop to the foot of another tree and start again.

Red-backed Shrike

This fascinating bird is suffering a long decline in north-west Europe as cooler, wetter summers affect the availability of large insects, and in Britain the tiny remnant breeding population must soon disappear. This is a great pity, since there is no more colourful sight than a male shrike on a hawthorn spray, pink breast feathers hiding his legs, black-striped head turning and cocking in search of prey. The bird's hooked beak is like a hawk's, and, hawk-like, it sometimes carries prey in its feet. Food may be spiked and stored on thorns, or even barbed wire, which explains the old country name of 'butcher bird'. Nowadays, birdwatchers are more likely to see this species on migration, especially scaly-looking young birds in autumn.

The male bird has a chestnut back, pinkish underparts, grey head and rump, with a black mask, wings and tail, the latter edged white.

Females are red-brown above, and pale below with dark, wavy markings. A few are nearly as bright as males.

Young like female, but more 'scaly'.

In flight: 'too big for a warbler, too small for a thrush'.

Lanius collurio
17 cm; 28–30 g
Where to look: breeds in open areas where there are thorn bushes; coasts on migration. **Nest:** in thorns. **Eggs:** 5–6, very variable in colour. **Food:** insects, small animals and birds. **Voice:** a harsh *shack*, etc. Song a quiet warble, with mimicry.

Great Grey Shrike

A distant white speck on a post, tree or wire may turn out to be this uncommon winter visitor from the north and east. It is, however, often a hard bird to find, even when known to be present, hunting as it does over large areas. Ferocious for its size (about that of a blackbird), it terrorises small birds, pursuing them in flight or dropping on them from a look-out point: voles are also an important food item. The bird will impale prey on a thorn or other spike before eating, and will make 'larders' of several prey items, returning to them from time to time. With its sharp eyesight, the shrike is quick to spot birds of prey and owls and to mob them. In the past, bird-trappers used this behaviour to detect the presence of such birds, so that they could then be lured down and caught. These days a great grey shrike itself tends to be the object of the chase: a regular check of traditional sites or other suitable habitats, especially where small birds roost, may well locate this elusive species.

Grey forehead and crown: black mask, bordered white above in adult.

Females may show dark, wavy bars below: young are browner overall.

Lanius excubitor
24 cm; 60–65 g
Where to look: open country, such as coast, marshes or heaths; often regularly in the same place. **Food:** large insects, small mammals, and especially small birds. **Voice:** a hoarse *check*; quiet warble rarely heard.

Flight is deeply undulating, often low, with a sweep up to perch. Bold, white wing bars are obvious.

A pied bird, typically perched in a prominent place, flaunting its ample tail and scanning for prey.

Jay

Garrulus glandarius
34 cm; 140–190 g
Where to look: deciduous and conifer woods, wooded farmland, parks, gardens.
Nest: well-hidden, of sticks.
Eggs: 4–5, pale bluish, spotted. **Food:** almost anything, especially acorns.
Voice: a harsh *skraaak*; quiet mewing.

Jays are widespread in wooded counties of England and Wales, absent from the southern and northern counties of Scotland, but occur in a band from Argyll to the east coast. They were badly persecuted in the last century, but this is lessening and the bird is now increasing, spreading into suburbs, and into upland areas where coniferous woodland has been created. Jays eat a wide variety of foods, but acorns are the most important and persecution is quite unjustified on the grounds of their eating habits. They are responsible for the large-scale dispersal of acorns in the autumn, probably involving several thousand acorns per bird. This helps to sustain the birds, and is also vital for future survival of oak woods. Jays do not normally move far in Britain, although large movements occur on the Continent in autumn, and in most years some birds reach southern and eastern Britain. Huge movements of jays were recorded in southern Britain in autumn 1983, caused by the widespread failure of the acorn crop both in Britain and on the Continent.

The most colourful of the crows. The body is pinkish, browner above than below, with a white rump and black tail. The wing has a bright white panel and a patch of blue with black bars.

White rump, small red mark on inner black wing feather oddly repeated on bullfinch.

The juvenile has a less streaked crown and smaller 'moustache' than adult. The body is more reddish-brown, the tail shorter.

When flying away, the white rump and black tail are very conspicuous, and flight into or between trees is quick and agile. Often calls loudly when excited or disturbed.

When flying across open spaces, flight is weak and undulating, with irregular flapping action.

Crown is whitish, streaked black, forming a small crest when erect. The 'moustache' is black.

Pinkish-brown body and white and blue wing patches unmistakable when stationary. In flight watch for very conspicuous white rump, white and blue on wings, dark tail and undulating flight. Loud, raucous *skraaak-shraaak* calls in dense woods are most likely to be jays. Compare with 'machine gun'-like '*chak-chak-chak*' call of magpie made from trees along hedgerows.

Jays are easily disturbed and are most often seen flying away.

Jays are secretive and wary, and are probably first heard rather than seen. The loud, raucous calls carry far. The nest is usually low, well hidden in dense cover.

In autumn jays feed on acorns. Excess acorns are buried in soil and dug up when needed.

Jays open acorns by holding them against a perch with both feet, and levering bits from the shell.

Magpie

Pica pica
40–45 cm; 200–250 g
Where to look: farmland, open country with scattered trees or bushes, also increasingly in suburban and urban areas. **Nest:** large, domed, of sticks lined with earth and fine roots. **Eggs:** up to 8, normally 5–6. **Food:** omnivorous. **Voice:** a loud, rapid *chak-chak-chak-chak.*

Unmistakable as this bird is, it is often the call that gives away the magpie's presence. Except for large parts of Scotland, magpies are common in Britain. They are found in many habitats, though their preference is for grassland with thick hedges or scattered trees. Recent years have seen an increase in numbers, especially in towns and suburbs with thick shrubberies, though in eastern England, where many hedgerows have been removed, magpie numbers have declined. The magpie, beautiful and intelligent, is much persecuted, especially in game-rearing areas, and not appreciated in gardens where it is accused of eating too many eggs and chicks of small birds (though it is far less of a nuisance than the domestic cat and eats far fewer birds than protected hawks and falcons!). Magpies eat mostly invertebrates in summer and seeds and berries in the winter. They do not move from their home territories, and no Continental birds arrive in winter.

Flight is rather slow, with rapid wing-beats. It is weaker than other crows, and rather unsteady because of the long tail.

Note the foreshortened and rather broad appearance of the tail when the bird is seen flying away.

Sometimes comical on the ground. Walks with high-stepping gait and often hops or bounces sideways when excited or seeking food.

Noisy groups of birds assemble in winter, chasing around the branches, displaying and calling.

Bill, legs and feet are black, and the eye is dark brown.

On the ground the tail is usually held elevated, and rarely spread.

When observed closely, the wing feathers have a purplish-blue iridescent sheen, and the tail is iridescent green, with a band of reddish-purple near the tip.

The magpie often hoards food. It makes a small hole in the ground with its bill, regurgitates food into it and covers it, reclaiming the cache one or two days later.

Even at a distance the black and white plumage and long, graduated tail are unmistakable, as is the distinctive 'machine gun' call.

Juveniles have very short tails, and lack the brightness and gloss of adults' plumage. Initially the flight is weak, and the birds hide in the foliage. The family party remains together until autumn.

Chough

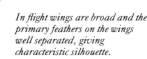
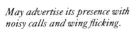

Pyrrhocorax pyrrhocorax
40 cm; 280–360 g
Where to look: sea cliffs, very occasionally inland at rock faces and quarries. **Nest:** of sticks, lined with wool or fine grass, on a ledge or crevice, often high on rock face. **Food:** chiefly invertebrates. **Voice:** *kwee-ow; chee-a!*

Adults have slim, down-curved red bills and red legs. Juveniles' bills are shorter and orange.

In flight wings are broad and the primary feathers on the wings well separated, giving characteristic silhouette.

May advertise its presence with noisy calls and wing flicking.

Choughs are slightly larger than jackdaws, and are the scarcest of Britain's crows. Although once common, they are now confined to the cliff coasts of Wales, the Isle of Man, some of the Inner Hebridean islands, and Ireland. A few pairs breed on inland cliffs in Wales.

Choughs are gregarious, even in the breeding season, often flying along the cliffs in small flocks. Their flight is superbly graceful, agile and buoyant, often with aerobatic swoops and dives. The noisy calls are distinctive and far reaching; though usually pronounced 'chuff', the English name may originally have been 'chow' in imitation of the call. They feed on the maritime heath and pasture above cliff tops. The loss of these areas to arable farming has contributed to the chough's recent decline. About 1,000 pairs breed in the British Isles, the majority found in western Ireland.

Plumage glossy and entirely black. Walks, runs and hops.

Jackdaw

Quicker and more active on the ground than other crows. Flight also quicker, and primary wing feathers only slightly separated. Has pale eye.

Corvus monedula
33 cm; 220–270 g
Where to look: towns, cities, farmland, parkland, woodland, and sea cliffs.
Nest: pile of sticks in holes or crevices in trees, buildings or rocks. **Eggs:** 4–6, blue-green. **Food:** virtually anything.
Voice: *kow, chuk-chuk, jak.*

Noisy and sometimes aggressive. Fluffs out feathers and spreads tail when defending nest site.

Gregarious at all seasons, often roosting and feeding communally with other crows, notably rooks.

Jackdaws are widespread throughout the British Isles, except for parts of Scotland (although numbers have increased and the breeding range has expanded there this century), yet oddly rare in places.

They nest in loose colonies, often using the same nest sites year after year. Almost any suitably large crevice or hole, which the birds fill with a tangle of sticks, might be used as a nest site. Less material is used at cliff sites, where the nest is often in a rabbit burrow. Jackdaws usually eat vegetable matter, especially grain and seeds, and surface-dwelling invertebrates, but will take almost any food. They readily exploit temporary abundances of food, such as the large numbers of leaf-eating caterpillars in woodlands in May or June, or animal foodstuffs. In winter they commonly scavenge at domestic refuse tips. Some migration occurs in winter when British birds move west, sometimes to Ireland, and birds from the Continent arrive on the east and south coasts.

Plumage is entirely black except for the ash-grey sides of the neck, nape and back of the head.

Rook

Corvus frugilegus
46 cm; 460–520 g
Where to look: farmland, grasslands, parks and wooded suburbs. **Nest:** communally in rookeries in trees, re-using stick nest from previous year. **Eggs:** 2–7, usually 4–5. **Food:** omnivorous. **Voice:** a deep *caw* or *kaaah*.

Broad wings show well-separated primary feathers. Tail straight-sided, rounded at tip; beware confusion with raven.

Activity and noise reach a peak at the rookery in early spring. Birds quarrel over territories, make pursuit flights around the rookery, and display by bowing, tail fanning and wing drooping.

What would the countryside be without its lively, noisy, busybody rooks? The very essence of lowland farmland, but less common in the uplands, they are gregarious, quarrelsome birds, nesting in tree-top rookeries which sway precariously in the wind, with anything from a handful to several thousand nests. Life at a rookery is fascinating and easily observed, since nesting begins well before the leaves appear. In winter a rookery may become a traditional roost. Travelling flocks of rooks, using set routes, may amalgamate into spectacular gatherings of several thousand birds. The amiable 'caws' are among the essential countryside sounds. Accused of damaging crops, rooks eat mainly worms and leatherjackets, though grain undoubtedly forms a large part of the diet when they can reach it. On balance, rooks seem to be beneficial and it would be a sad loss if the village rookery or the roaming flocks of big, black birds were to disappear from the rural scene. British rooks are resident, but numbers are boosted by Continental birds in winter.

The communal roost, which may be at a rookery, attracts rooks from several other rookeries, as well as jackdaws and carrion crows.

The face and chin of adults lack feathers, and are pale grey. The base of the bill is also grey.

Juveniles have black, feathered bills and face-patches which do not become bare like the adults' until they are 9–12 months old.

Note deep wing-beats and upturned wingtips when seen from behind.

Walks sedately, probing the soil, picking at invertebrates or seeds. Gregarious when feeding.

The all-black plumage has a purplish gloss, and the long thigh feathers give the 'baggy trousers' appearance.

The iridescent sheen of the feathers gives a silvery effect when viewed against the sun.

Carrion & Hooded Crow

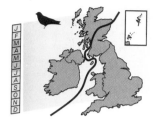

Corvus corone
47 cm; 540–600 g
Where to look: farmland, open woodland, heaths, coasts, towns and parks. **Nest:** usually in trees, made of sticks and earth, lined with wool or hair. **Eggs:** usually 4, greenish, spotted. **Food:** omnivorous. **Voice:** *kaaaw.*

The all-black carrion crow is found throughout England, Wales and most of Scotland. The grey and black hooded crow occurs in north-west Scotland, in Ireland and the Isle of Man. They are distinct forms, or subspecies, of the European crow. Although they have separate breeding ranges and different plumages they are regarded as the same species because they inter-breed freely where their ranges overlap and they produce fertile offspring (often called hybrids). The zone where inter-breeding occurs is rather narrow, which indicates that the hybrids are less successful breeders than either of the pure forms. Both forms are usually resident, although there is some dispersal of young in autumn. Numbers of hooded crows are boosted in winter by the arrival in northern and eastern Britain of birds from Scandinavia. Crows will eat almost anything, and scavenge widely in winter, including at refuse tips and on the shore. They are widely considered to be pests, eating gamebird eggs, or causing damage to trapped sheep or young lambs. Although some damage is caused, it is rarely as serious as often suggested – hoodies eat a lot from tips and cattle troughs!

Pairs with territories nest alone, not in groups like rooks. Birds without territories do not breed, and remain in flocks.

After leaving the nest the brown-black juveniles follow their parents, dependent on them for food for several weeks.

The carrion crow is entirely glossy black. The hooded crow has a largely grey body with black elsewhere. Carrion crow told from jackdaw by larger size, call, and lack of grey on the back of the head; from raven by smaller size, lack of wedge-shaped tail and by call. Best told from rook by the black bill and throat, squarer tail, neater plumage without 'trousers'.

The hooded crow has grey back, breast and underside, and grey underneath the front of the wing.

Both hooded and carrion crows often mob birds of prey, such as this buzzard, and are usually successful in driving them away.

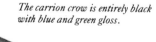

The powerful dagger-like bill is capable of tearing flesh.

The crows often get quite close. Buzzards sometimes respond by striking out with their talons, but they rarely make contact.

Where hooded and carrion crows inter-breed, the young may have mixed black and grey plumages.

The carrion crow is entirely black with blue and green gloss.

Raven

Corvus corax
64 cm; 800–1,500 g
Where to look: sea cliffs, woods and crags on valley sides, mountains and moors. **Nest:** usually on rocky crags and ledges, less often in trees, large and built of small branches and sticks, lined in layers, first with earth and roots, then plant material, mainly moss, then wool, hair and fine grass. **Eggs:** 3–7, (usually 5) laid in March. **Food:** omnivorous, but sheep carrion forms the majority of the diet. **Voice:** a deep croaking *prruk* often repeated. Also an almost bell-like *toc* and quiet, rattling 'song'.

The spectacular raven is an inseparable part of the upland and coastal scene in western and northern Britain and much of Ireland. More widespread at the turn of the century, it has withdrawn westwards due to persecution. There has been a slight recovery since 1914 in places adjacent to ancient strongholds, partly due to a return to tree nesting by birds unable to find a suitable, unoccupied crag. More recently the range has contracted again, and large conifer plantations, which result in the removal of sheep, trigger a decline. In Ireland, where conifer planting is less concentrated and the food supply (largely dead sheep) consequently less affected, ravens may be on the increase. The British and Irish population is still less than 5,000 pairs. Most ravens are crag-nesters, ideally suited to the harsh and expansive upland environment or the windswept sea coast, but trees, quarry faces and old buildings are also used for nesting. Ravens with territories stay in them all year round, but young birds disperse and non-breeders form sizeable itinerant flocks. At a suitable windy crag they dive and roll in the upcurrents in an expression of sheer exuberance in their mastery of a difficult environment.

The larger, heavier and more powerful bill helps distinguish the raven from the carrion crow.

The throat feathers are long and pointed, giving a bearded appearance, or the impression that the head is extra-large.

The largest crow in Britain. Entirely black plumage with blue, purplish and greenish gloss, and black bare parts. Readily told from other crows by large size.

Breeding birds found singly, in pairs, or in family parties in summer. Where numerous, non-breeding birds form small flocks.

Flocks use communal roosts, usually of less than a hundred birds. Fewer birds use such roosts in the breeding season.

Large, and all black. Readily told from other crows by size, large heavy bill, and shaggy throat. In flight, watch for large head and longer neck, and wedge-shaped tail, longer than carrion crow's or rook's. Wingspan is similar to that of buzzard. Often soars, and performs tumbling aerobatics. Deep croaking *prruk prruk* highly distinctive.

At an exceptional food source, ravens may flock in huge numbers — once 800 were recorded feeding on stranded whales in Shetland.

Flight is direct, with deep, heavy wing-beats, rather slower than carrion crow. May spread primary wing feathers, making wing-beats very noisy. Glides, and frequently soars on thermals.

In display, ravens turn upside-down and glide, belly uppermost, for short distances.

In flight, note well-separated tips to primary wing feathers, large head, and long, wedge-shaped tail.

They use the same nest sites year after year. Most pairs have alternative sites in their territory for use if the site of their choice is buried in snow.

Ravens nest early, gathering material in February. Crags are favoured nest sites, but they may be taken over by peregrines.

Only the female incubates the eggs. She is fed by the male, who brings food in his throat pouch.

They sometimes hang upside-down from a thin branch for a few minutes. The reason is not known.

Juvenile ravens can be told from adults by their browner plumage.

Perches on rocks and boulders, also on the ground. Has a stately walk. Hops clumsily when hurried.

Ravens eat small mammals, frogs, lizards, insects and even refuse.

The principal food is dead sheep, which may be abundant after hard winter weather. In the lambing season the placentae are eaten.

Starling

Sturnus vulgaris
22 cm; 75–90 g
Where to look: widespread.
Nest: in hole in building or tree. **Eggs:** 4–6, blue. **Food:** seeds, fruit, caterpillars, leatherjackets, ants. **Voice:** trills, buzzy and screeching calls; a good mimic of birds and of other sounds.

Though familiar in gardens, parks and even town centres, the starling's life-style still holds secrets little known even to the keenest observer of birds. As with so many species, research reveals fascinating facts.

A male in spring, having built his rough nest, sings with puffed-out throat and drooped wings to attract a mate. Should a female come close he will sing in a frenzy of wing-waving with his back hunched and tail fanned. If she stops near by, he will sing from the nest itself, to attract her in, and she will complete the lining. If there are several pairs of starlings in an area, by some unknown means they will synchronise their breeding and start laying eggs at the same time. Some females lay an egg in another's nest and bright blue eggs can often be found on a lawn, mysteriously intact – removed from a nest by a starling, but whether by an intruding female is not known. Some males are polygamous, leaving one mate on eggs while going off with another, often younger, female. The male incubates eggs for a small part of the day, leaving the rest and all night to the female.

The naked chicks need protein and water from caterpillars and insects, but variety of food is essential. Leatherjackets, for instance, are a favourite food, but too many can cause health problems. It is thought that starlings in America (comparable research has not yet been done in Britain) line their nests with certain plants that 'fumigate' the nest and rid it of parasites. There is more to the gorgeous starling than meets the eye!

An old woodpecker hole makes an ideal nest site. Parents make a bee-line back to woodland nest from feeding places outside wood, flying quite high and quickly; as they approach chicks call loudly.

Song is long mixture of trills and rattles, unmusical but full of energy; wings waved vigorously during song. Many starlings mimic other birds and mechanical sounds.

In spring, male is very glossy and colourful with blue base to beak (female has pink patch on bill).

When probing for food open bill lets bird see what it is eating as eyes swivel forward; can also swivel eyes backward to look for possible danger approaching, without raising head.

Food is often abundant, so they can gather in large flocks.

Probing for food and feeding of chicks wears away facial feathers of some birds by late summer.

From December onwards the bill turns yellow and in spring the legs change from dull brown to orange or reddish. Pale feather tips weaken and crumble away to reveal glossy colours beneath, most obvious in males. Females often keep more orange-brown on wings than males in summer.

Starlings spend winter days in small flocks, though sewage farms, places where cattle are fed, and other food sources may attract hundreds of them.

In winter, kitchen scraps and grain become more important in the diet; water is essential.

Flight fast, direct, with fast swoops to ground; short tail, pointed head, triangular wings.

The legs are strong and quite long, but often hidden as the bird fluffs out its feathers and crouches in order to retain warmth. Snow, hard-frozen soil and drought all make feeding difficult in farmland.

After the autumn moult adult has fresh, creamy tips to feathers of head and body. Wing feathers neatly edged orange-brown. Short tail, confident walk and frequent flocking all unlike blackbird; full of life, noise and energy.

Flocks settle for a last-minute feed on their way to roost, to help them through the cold night.

British starlings remain all winter and others fly in from northern Europe each autumn and leave again in spring.

Winter roosts in plantations, reed beds, city centres can be huge, even a million birds, flocks looking like smoke.

When their moult is almost complete the young birds are all spotted except for paler heads; in winter they are spotted all over, but still look dark.

Juveniles just out of the nest are mouse-brown with a black bill and a dark 'mask', but their quick walk, strong legs and short tail are typical of starlings.

By late summer juveniles begin to grow new, glossy wing feathers and spotty body feathers: head colour fades, making them very striking.

House Sparrow

There is no species more closely associated with man than the house sparrow. From the centre of large cities to farm buildings in the most rural settings, this cheerful exploiter of man's rubbish and wastefulness is found in abundance. They are inventive opportunists and have managed to colonise much of the world – especially those areas explored by Europeans. They followed the army camps across the North African desert in World War II, and they take rides on the London Underground and on cross-Channel ferries where discarded food is available. They appear in all kinds of isolated places where man settles – how do they find them?

The normal breeding cycle is May to July, often with three broods, but there has been an increasing trend towards year-round nesting, a sign of a very successful species. Any month with a spell of fine weather triggers breeding activity and nest building, and although many of these out of season attempts are doomed to failure, an unusually long mild spell can result in fledged young being seen in mid-winter.

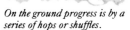

Passer domesticus
14.5 cm; 22–31 g
Where to look: associated with human habitation, rural and urban. **Nest:** untidy grass and straw, in buildings or hedges. **Eggs:** 3–7, greyish, finely speckled. **Food:** varied, mainly seeds and buds. **Voice:** noisy, twittering and cheeping notes.

When perched, a rather 'perky' stance is adopted with chest puffed out and tail cocked.

On the ground progress is by a series of hops or shuffles.

In flight, the males exhibit a striking contrast between the clear grey rump, brown back and wings with white wing-bar and chestnut side of neck.

In winter, farmland sparrows concentrate around buildings and stock pens. In autumn large flocks feed in cereal fields.

The rather drab female and young show distinctive broad pale band over eye; plain underparts (see greenfinch).

In winter the striking contrast of the male plumage is hidden by pale tips to the feathers. In the spring these crumble away and the 'new' plumage is revealed.

Little evidence of migration, but ringed birds have been found over 400 km (250 miles) from place of ringing.

Displaying flocks of males are noisy, active affairs and several will often chase a single female for a considerable distance.

Food provided in gardens will always attract large numbers of house sparrows, which have learnt to feed from peanut feeders.

One of the most familiar of birds – but the very smart, clean appearance of the 'country' sparrow, with warm brown nape and black bib of the male contrasting with almost white under-parts, is very different from the rather grey 'dirty' appearance of town-living birds. Female and young are a rather nondescript grey-buff and brown.

Tree Sparrow

Less widespread than the more familiar house sparrow, the tree sparrow differs in several distinctive ways. It is a smaller, plumper bird than the house sparrow, lively and bold, but less inclined to exploit gardens and human waste, and more characteristic of open woods, parks and farmland with scattered trees. To look at, there is no difference between the sexes and even the recently fledged young resemble the adults.

A hole-nesting species that will frequently take over tit nestboxes in a woodland, it is dominant over any tits using the chosen box. Tree sparrows have even built on top of a brood of young blue tits, which the parents continued to struggle to feed until they were eventually stifled by the accumulating nest material gathered by the sparrows. Another favoured nesting site is within the base material of a larger nest, such as that of a crow, magpie or heron. The owner of the main nest apparently tolerates the squatters quite happily.

Passer montanus
14 cm; 19–25 g
Where to look: areas of open woodland, farms and buildings in winter. **Nest:** in holes, of straw and grass. **Eggs:** 4–6, stippled brown. **Food:** Mainly seeds, but some insects. **Voice:** *cheep* call higher pitched and more metallic than house sparrow, flight note a double *tchur tchur* or *tek tek*.

In flight the shorter tail and rather more bouncy action separates tree from house sparrow.

The distinctive double flight call is somewhat reminiscent of the redpoll.

A regular migrant, there is an annual late-autumn immigration into Britain from continental Europe often associated with other finches.

Smaller than house sparrow, but more active and jerky with tail almost permanently cocked and hopping movements on ground.

Plumage lacks variation between sexes, age and season; these only distinguishable by behaviour.

Ground-feeding birds can appear to have a dark head and white collar as in reed buntings.

In winter, flocks exploit open farmland, often in parties of several hundred, occasionally mixed with other species.

Female is less dominant and is not vocal near the nest site.

After autumn moult, the winter plumage resembles that of summer.

Male and female tree sparrows share incubation, unlike house where the job is female's.

The female is always at the nest during the night, brooding the young until seven days old.

Usually two broods each year, the young quickly moulting out of their juvenile plumage, after which they resemble the adults.

Semi-colonial when breeding, often found in large flocks mixed with finches in winter. A small, 'jerky' bird, often with cocked tail. White cheeks with contrasting black spot very distinctive. Chocolate-coloured crown and double white wingbars are good features.

Comparing Finches

Finches comprise a varied group of seed eating species that have adapted to exploit the varied food supply that is available to them. All are characterised by deep, broad based bills, but some bills are more pointed – goldfinch – while others are blunt and conical – greenfinch – a reflection of the principal items in their diet. In all cases the males are more brightly coloured than the females, a reflection of the necessity for the females, which undertake the majority of the incubation and brooding activities, to remain hidden. The reed bunting often mixes with finches and may visit gardens.

The lightweight goldfinch can feed delicately on small plants.

Redpolls

Flocks of siskins and redpolls rush from tree top to tree top in bounding flight, stop abruptly.

The goldcrest (below) might be confused with a siskin for an instant, but its needle-thin, insect-eater's beak soon gives it away.

In early spring, siskins have discovered peanuts in gardens, but only those in red bags.

Siskins

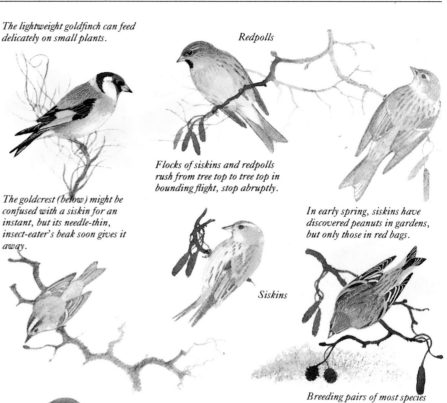

Mixed flocks of tits and finches can often be separated in flight by the different lengths and shapes of wing and tail and bulk of body.

Reed buntings are associated with wetland habitats, the male strikingly marked with black head and broad white collar. The streaky brown female shown below.

Breeding pairs of most species tend to be solitary, but flocks often formed of several species gather at winter feeding sites.

Chaffinches (male above, female below) are the commonest of the British finches.

Greenfinches (left and right) exploit weeds and stubble, berry-bearing shrubs and bird-tables, but are too heavy for slender stems.

Greenfinch flocks swirl round fields, sweep into hedge if alarmed.

Less well marked than the male, female greenfinches (above) still retain a small yellow flash in the wing.

In winter, twites (male above) move in flocks to favoured coastal salt marshes in south and east England.

The twite (female above) is a moorland breeding species found in northern Britain.

Although they may nest in Scotland, bramblings (female above) are winter visitors, favouring beech woods.

Male brambling in winter

Typically a heathland species, the linnet moves to more open areas in winter. Flocks 'disappear' on ground but fly in tight groups.

Linnets often go un-noticed in such unlikely-seeming places as industrial estates and business areas. Female above and winter male above left.

Chaffinch

Winter flocks use a distinctive choop *flight call; no twittering.*

Females show white in the wing; *unstreaked; ground feeders.*

In flight, the distinctive white *outer tail feathers and wingbars are equally apparent.*

The male's contrasting plumage *is highlighted by the pink breast.*

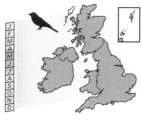

Fringilla coelebs
15 cm; 19–23 g
Where to look: hedgerows, gardens and farmland. **Nest:** in bush or low tree, of grasses decorated with lichen. **Eggs:** 4–5, dark spotted, greenish. **Food:** varied. **Voice:** *spink* call; rattling song ends with flourish; *choop* in flight.

The chaffinch, among the most popular spring songsters, is one of Britain's commonest and most widespread breeding species, with seven million pairs distributed throughout Britain and Ireland. Largely resident, British chaffinches rarely move more than five km (three miles) from home. The numbers are swollen each winter by a marked immigration from northern and eastern Europe. In these cases movements in excess of 2,000 km (1,200 miles) are not unusual. Spectacular migrations can be watched on the east and south coasts during October and November and it is calculated that 10 to 20 million arrive each autumn.

Producing only one brood per year, chaffinches build a beautifully camouflaged nest in the fork of a tree or dense bush. The outside of the nest is covered with lichen stripped from the surrounding bark. They are extremely long lived for small birds, ringing recoveries indicating that individuals may survive for up to 12 years. Where cause of death is known the majority have been killed by traffic or by cats.

Brambling

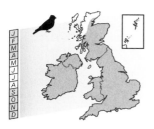

Fringilla montifringilla
14.5 cm; 22–30 g
Where to look: beech woods or farmland. **Nest:** odd pairs may breed in Scotland. **Food:** insects in summer, beech-mast and other seeds in winter. **Voice:** twanging *sweek*; nasal greenfinch-like *dweeee*; hard *chup* in flight.

In shape and behaviour the brambling is very similar to the chaffinch and the two frequently mix in winter flocks. The conspicuous white rump is the most striking field characteristic of bramblings when the birds are in flight and is the best way of spotting them in a finch flock. A more prolonged view will show the orange breastband of both male and female and the pale orange shoulder patch and, in spring, the black head of the male. The black is obscured by pale grey in winter.

In recent years small numbers have been recorded nesting in Scotland and northern England, but there has been little evidence of major colonisation. The species is still principally a winter visitor from northern Europe, arriving each autumn in October and early November in variable numbers. In peak seasons as many as two million may be involved, but this is quite exceptional. A roost site one winter in northern England was estimated to hold over 150,000 individuals. The wintering flocks, however, are very nomadic, wandering erratically, but remaining in each site long enough to exhaust the available food supply. They can be elusive, but a good flock is worth seeking out.

The male is highly distinctive, *with a striking black head.*

Winter flocks may be found in *woods or open farmland.*

In flight, the prominent white *rump is a key feature.*

Both sexes show orange breast *and white belly which distinguish them from the chaffinch.*

Mainly a ground feeder, the *preferred food is beech-mast, but many small seeds are eaten.*

Greenfinch

Carduelis chloris
14.5 cm; 25–31 g
Where to look: open woodland, gardens and farmland. **Nest:** of twigs and moss in hedges and bushes. **Eggs:** 4–6, spotted, off-white. **Food:** mainly seeds and berries. **Voice:** twittering song; drawn out nasal *tsweee*.

Increasingly familiar garden birds, greenfinches have been attracted more and more to bird-tables with sunflower seeds. Together with house sparrows they have quickly learnt how to feed from peanut feeders and, being rather aggressive when competing for food, will drive away other birds, including tits.

The stout bill on this rather heavily built finch enables it to deal with some of the larger seeds that become available, such as sea-buckthorn in the winter. In gardens they like mezereon, yew and cotoneaster berries. In spring they like tall hedges and are happy in big shrubberies and parks, their tinkling trills and wheezy notes livening up a sunny morning.

Flight, in common with all finches, is distinctly undulating, but in the breeding season the very characteristic song-flight of the male consists of a circling pattern on strangely erratic, slow, bat-like wing-beats, during which the bell-like calls are given non-stop. In winter, flocks burst up from the ground with a loud rush, swirling over a field or into the nearest hedge.

Note the very stout bill.

The green plumage of the male is off-set by varying degrees of yellow, brighter on older birds.

Juvenile (right).

The yellow in wings and tail is clearly visible on flying birds.

Although solitary when breeding, flocks form in winter, often mixed with other species in woods and open farmland. In competition will become aggressive.

The duller female is browner with subtle streaking on the underparts. The yellow flashes in wing and tail are more subdued.

Siskin

The bill shape is ideal for extracting seeds of birch, alder and larch.

Very active. Shows a distinct notch in tail in bounding flight.

Often mixed with redpolls.

Feed on twigs like party of tits.

In early spring, siskins will discover the orange string bags containing peanuts.

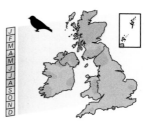

Carduelis spinus
12 cm; 12–18 g
Where to look: mainly conifers when nesting, alders by streams in winter. **Nest:** twigs and moss, high in conifers. **Eggs:** 4–5, deep blue, with pale spots. **Voice:** varied twittering song and shrill *tsewi* flight call.

As a breeding species the siskin is closely associated with conifers, and recent expansion within Britain has almost certainly been the result of increased afforestation and the development of mixed ornamental woodland. At one time confined to Scotland, the species now nests in small numbers in scattered places throughout the British Isles, including several on the south coast.

On the breeding grounds the very musical twittering song, delivered in flight as the males circle the tree tops, is a sure sign of the presence of nesting birds. Indeed the song-flight will continue well after the female has settled to incubate the eggs and consists of very exaggerated wing-beats, the wings appearing to meet above the back. At the same time, the tail is usually spread, flashing vivid yellow patches.

Like the greenfinch, this is predominantly a yellow-green bird, but it is smaller and slimmer and the male has a black chin and throat and yellow rump. The female is very much greyer, lacks yellow and has paler, striped underparts. The neat, complex wing pattern can usually be seen on this tiny bird.

Goldfinch

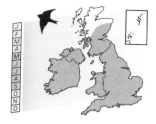

Carduelis carduelis
12 cm; 14–17 g
Where to look: gardens and orchards, rough and open ground. **Nest:** built of wool and moss at end of branch. **Eggs:** 5–6, spotted and streaked, bluish. **Food:** seeds, mainly thistles, and insects. **Voice:** liquid twittering calls and song.

Not a bird-table visitor.

On leaving the nest, young birds lack the face patterns, but acquire these within two months.

One of the most colourful and distinctive of all the British finches, the goldfinch is the 'thistle-finch', with a decided preference for eating the seeds of thistles. It is particularly appropriate that the collective noun for such an attractive bird is 'charm'. Where some finches are ground-feeders and others tree-top feeders, the goldfinch is very much a bird of the lower vegetation, favouring plants of open and waste ground such as teasels and hawkweeds. It can hop on the ground, but is more likely to be seen hanging from the seed-heads in a tit-like manner; flocks also feed in trees.

The striking plumage consists of a mixture of black, white, brown, yellow and red – goldfinches have white rumps, but this is often overlooked among the wealth of other colours. Sexes are similar in appearance, although the red extends behind the eye only in the male. Young birds are 'grey pates' without the colourful head pattern, and slightly streaked beneath.

At one time this was a very popular cage bird – one form of trap for small birds is known as a 'chardonneret' – the French name for the goldfinch.

The striking pattern on the head of all adults is unique. In spring there are patches of brown each side of the breast.

Unforgettable and unmistakable. Identification is easy.

The pointed bill is used to extract seed from thistles and similar plants.

A clever, delicate feeder.

In all plumages the black feathering of the wings is contrasted with the bright yellow flash that gives the bird its name.

Outside the breeding season flocks rarely mix with others, but may be with siskins in alders.

In addition to the band of brilliant yellow, the black wing feathers each have a prominent pale tip.

Black tail feathers have pale tips and oval patches.

A slim, delicate-looking finch, usually seen fluttering in a rather butterfly-like manner among the seed heads of low-growing vegetation. The very liquid quality of the twittering flight call and song is characteristic. Visually striking, with red, black and white patterning on the head; black wing and tail feathers have white spots at the ends and the wings have a prominent yellow band. Although the flight action retains the usual undulations of all finches, the goldfinch has a peculiar bouncing quality in its movements.

Linnet

Breeding pairs gather in suitable nesting bushes and form rather loose scattered colonies. Two or three broods each year.

After breeding, large numbers will flock and settle in an area of food supply. They often feed in the same fields for several days.

White patches in wing and tail are most noticeable in flight.

Carduelis cannabina
13.5 cm; 15–21 g
Where to look: areas of gorse in summer, farmland and shore in winter. **Nest:** grasses near ground. **Eggs:** 4–6, spotted, bluish. **Food:** small seeds and insects. **Voice:** varied, musical twittering song. Rapid flight call.

Widespread throughout Britain, the linnet is often thought of as a bird associated with heaths, commons and gorse bushes. In fact it is also found in open country and farmland far from gorse. A semi-colonial species, small groups of 10 or more pairs can often be located, and then the bird will appear absent for some distance until the next group is found. Large numbers form lively flocks in winter, but can be difficult to locate. All the birds assemble in one place where there is plentiful food, rather than a genuine reduction in numbers taking place, but large areas can seem empty of linnets.

Although quite large numbers and concentrations may be encountered on southern and eastern coasts in late autumn, the amount of migration undertaken by linnets is still something of a mystery. It appears that small numbers of British birds move south for the winter, travelling as far as Iberia; a somewhat larger number from Scandinavia probably arrives to spend the winter in Britain from eastern Scotland southwards.

The male's strongly contrasting plumage of grey head and crimson breast and crown is lost in winter and absent in females.

Linnets often pause to give a chorus of musical twittering.

The linnet is a very widespread species, but is frequently overlooked as it never makes itself particularly obvious.

Open farmland or coastal salt marshes are very much favoured during the winter months. Small seeds are taken all year round.

When breeding, the birds perch very openly on the tops of low bushes. At this time the males, with their chestnut backs, grey heads, white in tail and wing and crimson crown and breast, are most striking. Females are less strongly marked and lack the crimson. Flight is rapid and undulating, bouncing with a dancing action.

Feeds on bushes in summer, but a ground-feeder in winter.

Young males looking like females acquire crimson after one year.

The winter flocks are frequently mixed with other species, usually chaffinches and goldfinches.

The British breeding population probably numbers about one million pairs, with up to three million birds in winter.

Juvenile

Twite

Very linnet-like in appearance, the twite is often known as the 'mountain linnet'. Although very much a bird of the higher ground, mountains and moorland, in summer it is also found nesting at sea level in northern and western Scotland and parts of Ireland. The breeding areas are largely deserted in winter and there is a general movement to coastal localities where it feeds on the seeds of salt marsh plants, often in company with linnets and skylarks.

Flight, behaviour and shape are all reminiscent of the linnet, but this is a slightly smaller bird with a relatively longer tail. Generally much darker, it lacks the chestnut back and red crown of the male linnet. In mixed flocks twites can be distinguished by having pinkish rumps (males) and yellow bills in winter.

Lacking clear-cut identification features, the twite is probably frequently overlooked, but it is estimated that the British breeding population numbers some 20,000 pairs, with perhaps 100,000 individuals present in winter.

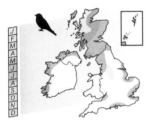

Carduelis flavirostris
13.5 cm; 13–17 g
Where to look: moors and mountains in summer, coasts in winter. **Nest:** built of grass near ground. **Eggs:** 5–6, blue with bold markings. **Food:** seeds. **Voice:** song a linnet-like twittering, call a very nasal *tsooee, dweye*.

Favours open country all year, breeding in Pennines, northern Scotland and western Ireland. Winters on coast.

Colonial as a breeding species, small numbers grouping together. Flocks form in winter months.

Overall appearance of dark tawny brown with bright orange-buff colouring around face and breast; neat tawny wingbar.

The bill is rather greyish in summer, pale yellow in winter.

In flight shows pink rump and very little white in wing.

A ground-feeding species, rarely perching in tall trees.

Redpoll

Feeding in tree tops, their behaviour is very tit-like and agile.

Females lack the pinkish flush; some males vivid in spring. Juvenile (left) lacks red.

Carduelis flammea
13–14 cm; 10–13 g
Where to look: birch and alder woodland. **Nest:** grasses on a twig foundation, usually high in tree. **Eggs:** 4–5, blue, spotted and streaked. **Food:** mainly seeds. **Voice:** trilling unmusical song in flight; call fast *chuchuchuh-uh*.

In winter, redpolls often join siskins in mixed flocks. They feed together in the tops of alder and birch trees, extracting the tiny seeds. Their behaviour is very tit-like, birds often hanging upside down at the very end of the branches. Such flocks are often associated with areas of running water, cress beds or riverside banks. Migrant flocks can be found in open areas of scrub or waste ground, feeding on low clumps of vegetation such as seeding willow-herb. In spring they feed on the ground on fallen birch seeds, bursting up into the trees if disturbed.

The presence of redpolls is frequently first indicated by the distinctive metallic twittering flight call; a close view will reveal the crimson on the forehead and small black chin patch. Some males have a noticeable pink flush to the underparts, but this may be absent from other individuals. Some are very colourful in spring.

Still rather sparsely distributed in south-west England, redpolls have increased and spread quite dramatically since the 1950s and are now widespread throughout the rest of Britain, although numbers fluctuate greatly from year to year.

Variable in size and colour, larger and paler individuals from northern localities are occasional winter visitors.

The bouncy, undulating flight is accompanied by the distinctive three- or four-note flight call.

Breeding birds fly over a large area during display.

Hawfinch

Coccothraustes coccothraustes
18 cm; 48–62 g
Where to look: mixed woods and orchards. **Nest:** roots on foundation of twigs, usually in fruit trees. **Eggs:** 4–6, bluish-green, spotted. **Food:** large seeds and fruit stones. **Voice:** quiet whistling song, robin-like *tick* call.

Mixed woods and orchards are preferred, but beech, hornbeam and wild cherry are most favoured.

Secretive when breeding, a little more obvious in winter when flocks form to roost communally.

The massive bill and rather short tail give the hawfinch a most distinctive silhouette, both in flight and when perched. At times it will appear to be so 'top heavy' that it seems in danger of tipping forwards. The thick neck and large head add to a most striking flight appearance which is quite unlike any other British finch, but clear views are unusual.

Generally considered a shy and secretive species, often difficult to locate, it will frequently perch on the very top-most branches, but obtaining good views is not an easy task for the birdwatcher. The broad white patch on the wing coverts and border to the tail contrasts with the warm brown back and provides a striking pattern as the bird flies away, but other details demand closer study, which in turn requires patience and care.

The exceptional structure of the bill, together with massive jaw muscles, enables the hawfinch to tackle food ignored by other finches. Cherry stones are a regular feature of the diet, but softer seeds are taken and dealt with in a delicate manner.

Scattered populations throughout England, but mainly a south-eastern species.

A bird of tree tops, but will feed on ground when soft fruit is available in orchards.

Bullfinch

Colourful, but easily overlooked.

In spring, rarely welcomed by gardeners concerned for the buds.

White rump striking in flight.

Males with contrasting plumage of grey back, jet-black cap and striking pink-red underparts. Inner flight feathers with red.

Small groups or flocks unusual, mainly seen in pairs.

A sedentary species; movements over 100 km (60 miles) are very unusual.

Unlike the male, the female has pinkish-grey underparts, but retains black cap, white rump. Young birds resemble female, but no black cap.

Pyrrhula pyrrhula
15 cm; 21–27 g
Where to look: undergrowth near woods and gardens. **Nest:** fine twigs, built in thick cover. **Eggs:** 4–5, clear green-blue. **Food:** buds, berries and seeds. **Voice:** a distinctive low, piping *teu*, which carries well.

Throughout orchards and gardens in south-east England bullfinches have a justified reputation for damage to buds on fruit trees, often seriously affecting far more than they eat and reducing the crop. Many birds are trapped and destroyed. Two factors may affect the amount of damage. The number of suitable nest sites near the orchard will determine the population level in the area, and the available 'natural' food supply in late winter controls the change of diet to buds. When the ash-key crop is good, bullfinches remain in the woodland and fruit farmers sleep more easily.

Although males have a remarkably bright plumage, bullfinches can be very secretive. Their presence in an area – and they are far more numerous in south-east England than the rest of the country – is revealed by the distinctive, far-carrying piping call and the prominent white rump which stands out as they fly away.

Never far from dense cover, keeping to bushes and trees, they rarely settle on the ground. When they do, movement is by a series of ungainly hops. Pairs remain together throughout the year, with family parties in autumn and occasionally small flocks in winter.

Crossbill and Scottish Crossbill

Crossbills are the most specialised of all the finches. Most obvious are the crossed mandibles, which enable the birds to extract seeds from pine cones. Other adaptations include particularly strong asymmetrical jaw muscles which assist the twisting movement necessary to extract the seed. In normal circumstances the feeding activity follows a regular routine. The cone is broken from the tree, usually requiring a considerable effort, with the bird apparently making use of every muscle. It is then carried to a convenient branch where it is held firmly by the feet while each seed is extracted in a systematic manner.

The numbers and distribution of crossbills in Britain vary greatly from year to year, for this is an 'invasion species'. Factors as varied as food supply and prevailing weather conditions will control the number of migrants reaching Britain in the autumn, and in many cases the subsequent size of the breeding population early the following year.

The Scottish crossbill is a different but very similar species, found only in Scottish pine woods.

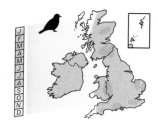

Loxia curvirostra
16–17 cm; 34–48 g
Where to look: conifer woods and plantations. **Nest:** grasses on twig foundation, breeding between January and July. **Eggs:** 4, off-white with bold spots. **Food:** almost exclusively seeds from cones of pine, larch and spruce. **Voice:** loud, persistent *chip chip* flight call. Song of trilling notes followed by greenfinch-like calls.

Winter flocks can include two very rare visitors: the parrot crossbill, large with heavy bill, and two-barred crossbill.

Streaky juvenile.

Bill sizes indicate preferred food. Parrot and Scottish (large) – pine seeds; crossbill – spruce; and two-barred crossbill (small) – larch seeds.

Flocks moving through the tops of the conifers maintain contact with distinctive flight call.

The increase in conifer plantations has produced a wider spread of the common species.

Crossbills are often detected by pine cones, with seeds extracted, lying on the woodland floor.

The crossing of the mandibles can be in either direction, right or left-handed cross! This determines which is the stronger leg!

Young birds resemble females, but with a greyish tinge.

In flight the short deeply-forked tail, together with the heavy neck and bill and distinctive call, readily identify the crossbills.

Early nesting species, some pairs have eggs in January or February.

The Scottish crossbill is confined to the Highlands.

Female

Scottish crossbill (left) is separate species with larger, blunter bill, larger body; Britain's only unique species.

The variation in colour of the red-plumaged males is partly a reflection of age, but many breeding males will not have attained the full red colouration.

The combination of habitat, behaviour, voice and appearance make this one of the easiest species to identify. Many feeding parties tend to be tame and allow close approach, when the rather parrot-like appearance is obvious – a combination of heavy bill, thick neck and short tail. Feeding by using the feet aids the likeness. Adult males are often a bright brick-red, but the intensity of colour varies and some have a golden hue, but most have a pale crimson rump. Females and young are usually a yellowish-green, with a yellower rump.

Yellowhammer

Breeding male most attractive, with brilliant lemon-yellow head and chestnut streaked back. Yellow less bright in winter, feathers with greyish-green tips.

Female much duller than male with suggestion of face stripes. Beware confusion with rare cirl bunting. Note rather upright stance, slim neckless outline.

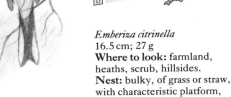

Emberiza citrinella
16.5 cm; 27 g
Where to look: farmland, heaths, scrub, hillsides.
Nest: bulky, of grass or straw, with characteristic platform, low down or on ground in grass clump or bush. **Eggs:** 3–5, pale with dark 'scribbling' and spots. **Food:** cereals, grass seeds; insects in summer. **Voice:** familiar 'little-bit-of-bread-and-no-cheese'.

The derivation of the curious English name becomes clear upon learning that the German for bunting is 'Ammer'. The two languages have a distant common origin. The dark, irregular lines on the eggs have given rise to the country name of 'scribbling lark'.

The 'bread-and-cheese' words recall the song of this familiar bunting only in rhythm: in fact the song is rather variable and sometimes lacks the final (higher or lower) 'cheese'. On drowsy high-summer days it is often the only bird sound accompanying the hum of insects. Aggressive when setting up territory, the male pursues his prospective mate in a rapid, twisting courtship flight. Once paired, both birds often feed together, and indeed gather food for the young, away from their nesting territory. The young are fed almost entirely on green caterpillars and insects.

In winter yellowhammers are social. They may roost in large numbers in rank vegetation, sometimes in reed beds with reed and corn buntings, and even on occasion in snow burrows. Ringing reveals that 70 per cent of adults spend the winter within five km (three miles) of the nest site.

Often makes long, circular flight, returning to a point close to where it took off.

When flying away, the unstreaked rusty rump is very striking in all plumages.

Juveniles are darker, well-streaked, and may show very little yellow, but plumage extremely variable.

Rather slim, long-tailed bird. Except adult male, chief identifying feature is the rusty rump. Often perches prominently, may flick tail, though not as obviously as reed bunting. Feeds on ground. Sociable in winter, often mixed with other buntings and finches. Wing-beats interrupted by brief pauses. Flight call *twick* or *twitick*.

Long, notched tail shows white on sides when spread, less obvious than on reed bunting.

Feeds almost exclusively on ground. When disturbed, flocks fly up into bushes, and come back down in ones and twos when the danger has passed.

Corn Bunting

Britain's largest bunting, this nondescript bird makes up for its drab appearance with a fascinating sex life! It is one of a very few truly promiscuous passerines, both male and female mating with several partners. The males return to the breeding sites in midwinter, the largest birds securing the best territories. The females do not leave the winter flock until April, and they alone deal with all the domestic duties leaving males free to court other hens. Males sing, head thrown back, from a prominent low perch, or from overhead wires, in almost every month of the year, and at any time of day.

Although one of the few species at home in modern agricultural 'prairies', the corn bunting has, for reasons unknown, decreased this century to the point of extinction in much of the west and north. The British population is sedentary, flocking outside the breeding season to feed on stubble and in farmyards. Winter roosts in reed beds or scrub may contain a hundred or more birds. The distinctive flight call is a low-pitched dry but loud *kwit* or *quilp kwit-it*.

Miliaria calandra
18 cm; 44–54 g
Where to look: open farming country. **Nest:** large, loose, of coarse grasses, often in scrape on ground. **Eggs:** 3–5, usually pale with bold, dark scribbles and blotches. **Food:** seeds, insects. **Voice:** unique, discordant jangling.

Shortish tail for a bunting. Sexes alike in plumage.

May fly short distance with legs dangling, on fluttering wings.

A bulky, clumsy-looking, sparrow-like bird. Heavy head and bill, rather neckless appearance. Large, dark eye in rather pale face. No white in tail.

Pursues rivals or prospective mates low over cornfields.

Paler, less buff in summer. Streaking most dense in centre of breast, forming diffuse dark spot.

Cirl Bunting

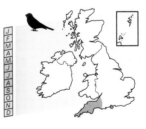

Emberiza cirlus
16.5 cm; 22 g
Where to look: farmland with hedges and tall trees, bushy slopes, cliffs. **Nest:** neat, well-concealed, of moss and grass. **Eggs:** 3–4, bluish-white, boldly marked. **Food:** seeds, insects. **Voice:** metallic rattle on one note.

Not discovered as a British bird until 1800, in Devon, the cirl bunting expanded its range during the 19th century to become widespread, if local, north to the Midlands and Wales. A decline was first noticed in the 1930s, accelerating since the late 1950s to the present precarious position of perhaps 150 pairs, almost all in Devon. The recent colder, wetter springs and summers are probably responsible, for the cirl bunting is essentially a Mediterranean species at the edge of its range in Britain.

The bird is easily overlooked until the song is learnt. Like the other farmland buntings, the song period is long: it may be heard regularly from late February to early September, and occasionally at other times, though bursts may be irregular, even during the main song period. It may recall a distant lesser whitethroat, but with an unmistakable, sharper, bunting quality. The breeding territory is unusually large, and given the bird's relative secrecy, and tendency to fly quite long distances, it can be very elusive. Nevertheless, a recent survey revealed that three out of five territories contained a house or farm building.

Black and yellow head markings make male unmistakable.

Call a soft, penetrating ssi.

Female told by olive-grey rump, buffy rather than yellowish breast, with neat, dark streaks.

In winter, gathers into small flocks, or remains in pairs.

Reed Bunting

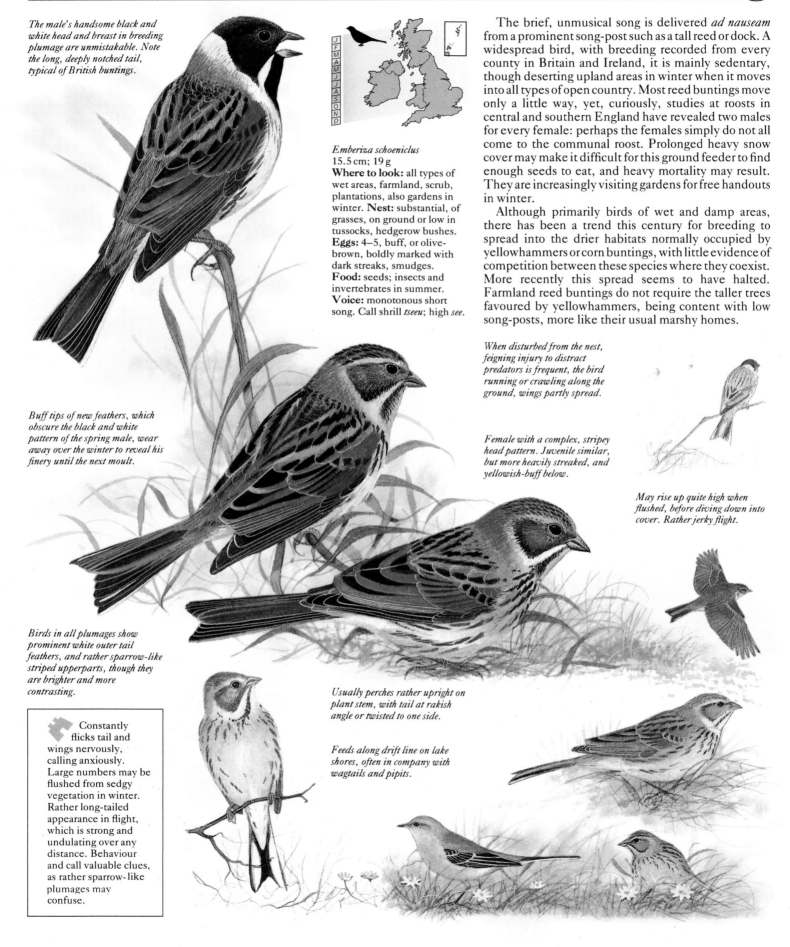

The male's handsome black and white head and breast in breeding plumage are unmistakable. Note the long, deeply notched tail, typical of British buntings.

Emberiza schoeniclus
15.5 cm; 19 g
Where to look: all types of wet areas, farmland, scrub, plantations, also gardens in winter. **Nest:** substantial, of grasses, on ground or low in tussocks, hedgerow bushes. **Eggs:** 4–5, buff, or olive-brown, boldly marked with dark streaks, smudges. **Food:** seeds; insects and invertebrates in summer. **Voice:** monotonous short song. Call shrill *tseeu*; high *see*.

The brief, unmusical song is delivered *ad nauseam* from a prominent song-post such as a tall reed or dock. A widespread bird, with breeding recorded from every county in Britain and Ireland, it is mainly sedentary, though deserting upland areas in winter when it moves into all types of open country. Most reed buntings move only a little way, yet, curiously, studies at roosts in central and southern England have revealed two males for every female: perhaps the females simply do not all come to the communal roost. Prolonged heavy snow cover may make it difficult for this ground feeder to find enough seeds to eat, and heavy mortality may result. They are increasingly visiting gardens for free handouts in winter.

Although primarily birds of wet and damp areas, there has been a trend this century for breeding to spread into the drier habitats normally occupied by yellowhammers or corn buntings, with little evidence of competition between these species where they coexist. More recently this spread seems to have halted. Farmland reed buntings do not require the taller trees favoured by yellowhammers, being content with low song-posts, more like their usual marshy homes.

Buff tips of new feathers, which obscure the black and white pattern of the spring male, wear away over the winter to reveal his finery until the next moult.

When disturbed from the nest, feigning injury to distract predators is frequent, the bird running or crawling along the ground, wings partly spread.

Female with a complex, stripey head pattern. Juvenile similar, but more heavily streaked, and yellowish-buff below.

May rise up quite high when flushed, before diving down into cover. Rather jerky flight.

Birds in all plumages show prominent white outer tail feathers, and rather sparrow-like striped upperparts, though they are brighter and more contrasting.

Usually perches rather upright on plant stem, with tail at rakish angle or twisted to one side.

Feeds along drift line on lake shores, often in company with wagtails and pipits.

Constantly flicks tail and wings nervously, calling anxiously. Large numbers may be flushed from sedgy vegetation in winter. Rather long-tailed appearance in flight, which is strong and undulating over any distance. Behaviour and call valuable clues, as rather sparrow-like plumages may confuse.

Snow Bunting

Winter birds usually show lovely warm rusty-buff wash over crown and breast, reddest on females.

Breeding male black and white, female cold grey-brown and white.

Numbers wintering in Britain vary greatly. Highly sociable, flocks of a thousand or more on record, usually under 50.

Plectrophenax nivalis
16 cm; 30–40 g
Where to look: rare breeder, high mountain tops. Commoner in winter in northern hills, east coast. **Nest:** in crevice. **Eggs:** 4–6, off-white, blotched brown. **Food:** seeds, insects. **Voice:** rippling trill; *tew*.

Breeding right around the Arctic Circle in Eurasia and North America, the snow bunting reaches further north than any other small bird, right up to the summer limit of ice in Greenland. The first British nest was found in 1886. These lovely buntings remain a prize summer find on the barren, hostile tops of the highest mountains, the sweet musical song being uttered in a short display flight. The nest often has a warm lining of ptarmigan feathers.

In winter, they are often delightfully confiding. Sometimes called 'snowflakes', a flock in flight does indeed fancifully recall a flurry of snow as each bird flies in deep undulations, seeming to dance along, then swooping low and fast before landing, flashing white in wings and tail. A feeding flock moves in rolling fashion, each bird running rapidly, pecking, leap-frogging over its companions in short flights, frequently calling.

Inland lowland sightings are unusual, and reports in gardens usually involve partially albino sparrows.

Very long-winged, well-built bird. Flight strong and bouncing.

Yellow bill with dark tip in winter. Some white always visible in the wing in flight.

Lapland Bunting

Calcarius lapponicus
15.5 cm; 25 g
Where to look: in autumn on west coast, islands, but scarce; in winter on east coast stubble, saltings. Very rare breeder. **Food:** seeds, insects. **Voice:** dry, quick rattle *tik-ik-ik-it*; liquid *tew*.

Though breeding widely in the far north in both the Old and New Worlds, a special effort is required to find this bird in Britain. Autumn migrants in the west and Ireland almost certainly originate from Greenland, but whether these or Scandinavian birds form the small east coast British wintering population is unknown.

An unobtrusive species in its winter garb, it would often be overlooked, but for its characteristic *ticky-tick* flight call. On the ground, it looks confusingly like a reed bunting at first glance, though a closer look reveals plumage, structural and behavioural differences. The American name, Lapland longspur, and the scientific name, refer to a further feature – the very long hind claw, also found in other terrestrial birds such as the meadow pipit and skylark. They often consort with skylarks and other finches and buntings in rough pasture and stubble.

Possible breeding was first reported in Scotland in 1974, and very small numbers bred up to 1981. Like the snow bunting, the male has a surprisingly musical song for a bunting, which it also may deliver in a song flight, an adaptation to nesting in open tundra.

Dark triangle corners to rear of ear coverts, and rather beady eye in sandy buff face.

Pale central crown stripe more pronounced than reed bunting's.

Chestnut greater coverts, framed by two narrow, whitish wing-bars; belly clear white.

Longer-winged, larger-headed, shorter-tailed than reed, white tail sides less obvious.

Crouches low, runs quickly and rather jerkily like clockwork toy.

Exotics & Escapes

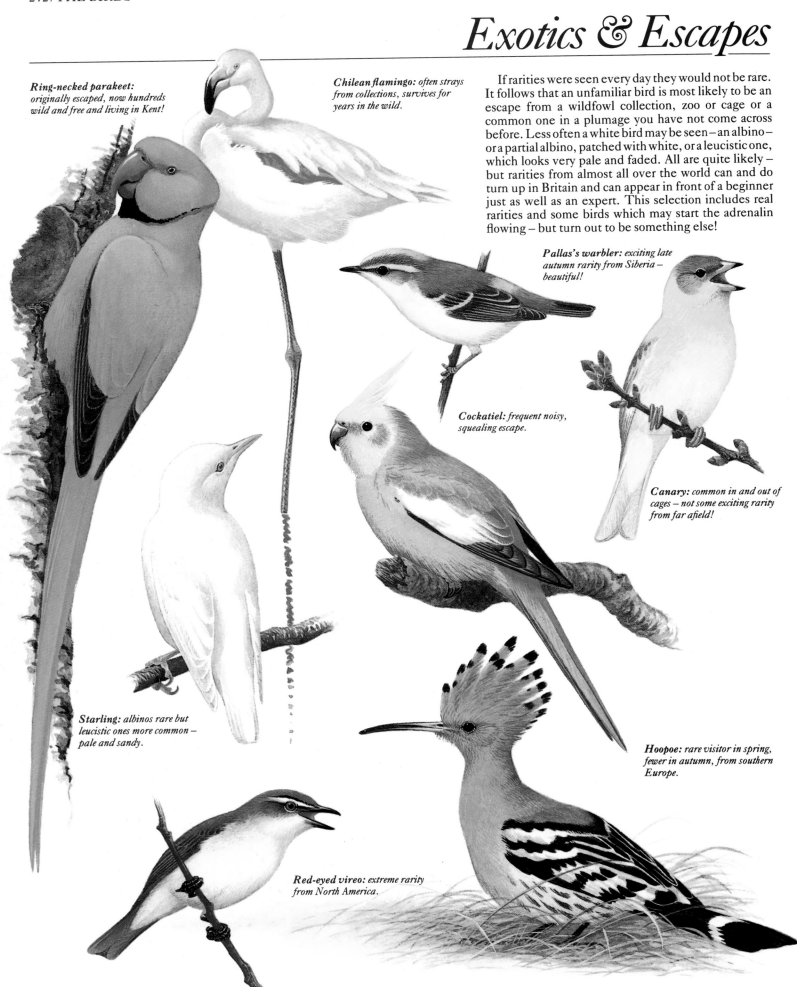

Ring-necked parakeet: *originally escaped, now hundreds wild and free and living in Kent!*

Chilean flamingo: *often strays from collections, survives for years in the wild.*

If rarities were seen every day they would not be rare. It follows that an unfamiliar bird is most likely to be an escape from a wildfowl collection, zoo or cage or a common one in a plumage you have not come across before. Less often a white bird may be seen – an albino – or a partial albino, patched with white, or a leucistic one, which looks very pale and faded. All are quite likely – but rarities from almost all over the world can and do turn up in Britain and can appear in front of a beginner just as well as an expert. This selection includes real rarities and some birds which may start the adrenalin flowing – but turn out to be something else!

Pallas's warbler: *exciting late autumn rarity from Siberia – beautiful!*

Cockatiel: *frequent noisy, squealing escape.*

Canary: *common in and out of cages – not some exciting rarity from far afield!*

Starling: *albinos rare but leucistic ones more common – pale and sandy.*

Hoopoe: *rare visitor in spring, fewer in autumn, from southern Europe.*

Red-eyed vireo: *extreme rarity from North America.*

The West Country

Yellowhammer

*With superb coastal scenery, wild rolling moorlands,
and unspoiled countryside, the West Country is rich in
birds. Exceptional birdwatching places include the
Land's End Peninsula, the Exe Estuary, the area
around Poole Harbour, and the Isles of Scilly, which
are 'musts' for the dedicated birdwatcher*

The West Country

Useful addresses:

RSPB Headquarters: The Lodge, Sandy, Bedfordshire, SG19 2DL
RSPB South-West Office: 10 Richmond Road, Exeter, Devon, EX4 4JA.
Many RSPB reserves have explanatory leaflets. These are often available at the reserve, but in any event the regional office, or RSPB HQ, will supply information on any reserve upon receipt of a stamped, addressed envelope.

Avon Wildlife Trust: The Old Police Station, 32 Jacob's Wells Road, Bristol, BS8 1DR.
Cornwall Trust for Nature Conservation: Dairy Cottage, Trelissick, Feock, Truro, TR3, 6QL
Devon Trust for Nature Conservation: 35 New Bridge Street, Exeter, Devon, EX4 4AH
Dorset Trust for Nature Conservation: 39 Christchurch Road, Bournemouth BH1 3NS
Gloucestershire Trust for Nature Conservation: Church House, Standish, Stonehouse GL10 3EU
Somerset Trust for Nature Conservation: Fyne Court, Broomfield, Bridgwater TA5 2EQ
Wiltshire Trust for Nature Conservation: 19 High Street, Devizes, SN10 1AT
Nature Conservancy Council: South-West Regional Office, Roughmoor, Bishop's Hull, Taunton TA1 5AA
South-West Water Authority: Peninsula House, Rydon Lane, Exeter, EX2 7HR
Wildfowl Trust: Slimbridge, Gloucestershire GL2 7BT

Axmouth/Lyme Regis Undercliff

Devon

The coastline between Axmouth and Lyme Regis is very distinctive, landslips caused by coastal erosion having created a remarkable landscape, much of which is protected as a National Nature Reserve. The mixed habitats of cliffs, open scrub and woodland are attractive to a range of birds, so a summer walk here can be very rewarding. Cliff-breeding gulls and fulmars soar over open slopes where stonechats, linnets and yellowhammers breed, while the woods have a variety of summer migrants, including spotted flycatchers, garden warblers and even nightingales. The wild flowers and butterflies here are exceptional.

Location: between Seaton and Lyme Regis.
Access: at all times to the Undercliff along coast path, away from which access restricted.
Map reference: SY254901

Aylesbeare Common

Devon   `RSPB`

Aylesbeare Common is part of a five-mile heathland ridge known collectively as Woodbury Common. The specialised heathland birds here include nightjars, Dartford warblers, tree pipits and stonechats. Other breeding birds include curlews, redpolls, yellowhammers, grasshopper warblers and green woodpeckers. The common is also a good place for birds of prey, with buzzards, kestrels and sparrowhawks, and the possibility of a sighting of hobbies in summer and hen harriers in winter. The whole area is rich in plants and is especially attractive in late summer. At this time of year the insect life is outstanding, with many dragonflies and damselflies and special butterflies of heathland; in fact Aylesbeare itself can boast the best butterfly list of any RSPB reserve.

Location: heathland ridge west of Newton Poppleford on A3052.
Access: at all times along footpaths. Car park across road from RSPB reserve.
Map reference: SY057898

Bodmin Moor

Cornwall

The largest upland block in Cornwall, the moor is mainly rough grazing with large areas in private ownership without free access. There are fewer moorland birds than

Berry Head

Devon

On the ledges of this limestone headland is the largest breeding colony of guillemots along the entire Channel coast. Between April and July around 400 pairs of these colonial auks can be viewed from the cliff-top. Other breeding seabirds include razorbills, kittiwakes, fulmars, shags and herring gulls. This is a good place to watch for other passing seabirds. Cirl buntings may be present in winter and breed in the surrounding farmland in summer. The country park provides outstanding views across Lyme Bay and has a wonderful show of wild flowers, many of which are limestone specialities. The headland has been used by man since at least as early as Iron Age times, and there are traces of fortifications dating from that time to the 19th century.

Location: clifftop country park just east of Brixham, signposted from town centre.
Access and facilities: open daily. Car park. Toilets. Information centre.
Map reference: SX942564

Berry Head – the cliffs here are excellent for seabirds

Bridgwater Bay – a flock of up to 1,000 whimbrels can gather here in spring during the migration from Africa to Iceland

might be found further north, but good numbers of wheatears, whinchats, snipe, lapwings and curlews are present and birds of prey are often seen. Some of the best birdwatching areas are described below.

1. Upper Fowey and Dozmary Pool

The upper Fowey Valley is one of the best areas of Bodmin, with a mixture of habitats including moorland, rough grazing and damp woodland, where redstarts, tree pipits and grasshopper warblers are summer visitors. The shallow valley bottom, with its fast flowing river, has scattered alders and willows, and here birds include both marsh and willow tits and redpolls. Spring brings willow warblers and chiffchaffs in good numbers, with spotted flycatchers arriving

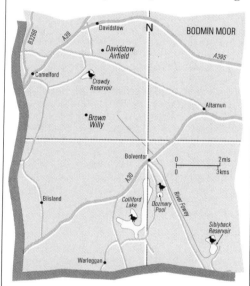

later. The river is frequented by dippers and grey wagtails, and a few sand martins nest in the low banks. Evenings are sometimes enlivened by the presence of a barn owl hunting over the open grassland. Dozmary Pool, set in open moorland at the top of the valley, attracts long-tailed ducks and goldeneyes in winter and has the possibility of a hunting hen harrier or short-eared owl over the surrounding moorland.

Location: south of Bolventor on unclassified roads off A30.
Map reference: SX208740

2. Crowdy Reservoir and Davidstow

The reservoir is set close to open moorland and has some recently felled plantations on its fringes. The shallow nature of this site and its marshy edges is attractive to many birds. Waders include large numbers of lapwings and snipe, and curlews and ruffs occur regularly. Wildfowl are predominantly mallard, teal and wigeon with a few tufted ducks and pochards, although goldeneyes and goosanders are present in midwinter.

Nearby Davidstow Airfield's heavily grazed turf is very attractive to lapwings and usually has a wintering flock of golden plovers. Other waders often occur in autumn, including the occasional dotterel,

and North American species like buff-breasted sandpipers, which are becoming almost regular in October.

Location: east of Camelford on unclassified roads off A39.
Access and facilities: reservoir key and permits from South West Water Authority. Hide. Car park. Reservoir can be viewed from road. Road crosses airfield.
Map reference: SX139834

3. Siblyback Reservoir

Set on Bodmin's south side, this 140-acre reservoir is a flooded valley set in open moorland. Due to its exposed situation wildfowl numbers are not great, but there is usually a good mixture and smews are frequently found in midwinter. The margins attract snipe, and a few jack snipe, while lapwings and golden plovers are regular on the neighbouring farmland. Summer birds are usually restricted to cormorants, grey herons and feeding parties of swallows, martins and swifts, but by late July the first of the autumn waders appear.

Common and green sandpipers are present throughout the autumn, but rarer species can turn up, with American species a distinct possibility.

Location: north of Liskeard, signposted on unclassified roads off B3254.
Access and facilities: car park. Hide (permit from South West Water Authority).
Map reference: SX237707

4. Colliford Reservoir

This recently constructed reservoir is by far the largest in Cornwall and its wildlife potential has yet to be fully realised. Winter wildfowl numbers are higher than on the other Bodmin lakes, with sizeable flocks of wigeon and teal, a few tufted ducks and pochards. Gadwalls, shovelers and pintails are often present, with the western arm the best part to search if wind conditions are suitable.

Location: south of Bolventor, on unclassified roads between A30 and St Neot.
Access and facilities: view from perimeter road. Car park. Toilets.
Map reference: SX164723

Bridgwater Bay

Somerset

Bridgwater Bay National Nature Reserve is one of the major inter-tidal areas of the Severn. The estuary is extremely wide here and has the largest tidal range in the country, so a visit within a few hours of high tide is essential. High numbers of waders and wildfowl occur, with the presence of a summer flock of moulting shelducks of national significance. Several thousand wildfowl – mainly mallard, wigeon and teal – spend the winter here. Among a wide variety of waders are high numbers of dunlins, with black-tailed godwits, grey plovers, curlews and redshanks. A spring passage of whimbrels occurs in April/May with birds flying in to roost on Stert Island at dusk. A good spot to see them is from the sea front at Burnham-on-Sea. The reserve attracts many birds of prey, with peregrine and merlin among them.

At the far end of Fenning Island several lagoons with hides have been provided.

Location: 5 miles north-west of Bridgwater. From A39 Minehead road at Cannington take unclassified roads to Combwich and Steart.
Access: open to foreshore. Car park in Steart.
Map reference: ST276464

Brokers Wood

Wiltshire

This ancient woodland is actively managed as a demonstration woodland, to encourage wildlife and to produce a commercial timber crop. Waymarked paths through the wood provide the chance to see woodpeckers, nuthatches, treecreepers, and in summer a variety of warblers. The insect life is rich, with many butterflies, and there is a host of wild flowers. The Phillips Countryside Museum forms a complex with the wood and has colourful displays on natural history and detailed explanations of forestry practices, making for an interesting day out.

Location: 2 miles north-west of Westbury off unclassified Brokerswood to Standerwick road.
Access: open all year (admission charge), picnic area, museum. Special trail for blind.
Map reference: ST835524

Camel Estuary

Cornwall

The Camel Estuary is the largest on the north coast of Cornwall. Most of the typical estuary waders can be found here, particularly curlews, ringed plovers and redshanks. Hides on both shores of the upper estuary give good views of the salt marshes, and some of the best feeding areas, where greenshanks and spotted redshanks are frequently seen on passage; some may even remain in winter. This is a good estuary for peregrine falcons, which are often responsible for putting the flocks of waders and wildfowl to flight; passage ospreys are regularly seen in August.

On the north shore, part of Amble Marshes, the Walmesley Sanctuary, is a reserve of the Cornwall Birdwatching and Preservation Society and the pools here attract wildfowl in winter. The lower end of the estuary, between Rock and Padstow, is the best place for diving species – attracting both great northern divers and Slavonian grebes in winter.

Location: north of Wadebridge.
Access and facilities: Amble Marshes and northern bird hide are close to Trewornan Bridge on B3314. Southern bird hide and other viewpoints are along public track on converted railway by south shore. (Hide keys are available from Hon Treasurer, Cornwall Birdwatching and Preservation Society, 33 Treworder Road, Higher Redannick, Truro, TR1 2JZ.)
Map reference: SW991724

Channel Islands

Jersey and Guernsey, the main islands, are fairly densely populated and lack the full variety of wildlife habitats. However, the coastlines remain unspoilt and many seabirds breed, while the beaches are often good for waders and the bays shelter wildfowl in winter. Along the clifftops there are areas of gorse which have Dartford warblers and stonechats. One speciality of the woodland areas is the short-toed treecreeper, a continental species which replaces Britain's mainland bird. Both islands attract many migrants in spring, with hoopoes and golden orioles annual visitors.

The smaller islands, especially Alderney, have rather more to offer the birdwatcher. Alderney's cliffs and offshore stacks have outstanding seabird colonies, with breeding gannets probably the highlight. Several thousand of them breed on two rocky islands, one of which is very close to the main island and is a spectacular sight from the clifftop. For the best views of all, it is possible to take a boat trip from Alderney harbour to visit the gannetry and to see puffins, guillemots and razorbills, fulmars and kittiwakes on their breeding ledges (April to July). A large part of the island is open fields with easy access and the chances of seeing migrants are good here, especially in spring, with warblers, flycatchers and chats.

Location: off French coast west of Cherbourg Peninsula. Reached by passenger ferry from Portsmouth all year (Weymouth summer only), or by air. Good inter-island air service.

Chapel Wood

Devon   **RSPB**

This small RSPB woodland reserve is set in a sheltered valley and has a good range of West Country birds. Redstarts and spotted and pied flycatchers are here in summer, while kestrels, sparrowhawks, treecreepers, nuthatches, etc are resident. Ravens and buzzards nest in the valley and are regularly seen circling over the wood; they are most likely to be located in the first place by their distinctive calls.

Location: near north Devon coast north of Barnstaple. Off A361 Barnstaple to Ilfracombe road on unclassified road towards Spreacombe.
Access: at all times by permit from warden: 8 Chichester Park, Woolacombe, Devon – park on verge near entrance.
Map reference: SS483413

Chew Valley Lake

Avon

The largest man-made lake in the region, Chew Valley Lake has a natural shoreline and fringing reed beds. The open water attracts a host of wildfowl in winter and thousands of gulls arrive on winter afternoons to spend the night roosting on the lake. Of particular interest are the large numbers of great crested grebes and the increasing population of ruddy ducks. Winter wildfowl include gadwalls, shovelers, pintails, goosanders, goldeneyes and the occasional smew.

The lake attracts many migrants in spring and autumn and is often one of the best places to find the early martins and swallows. The area near Herriots Bridge is zoned as a nature reserve and suffers less disturbance from sailing and fishing.

The reed beds in this vicinity are used by breeding warblers and in winter can harbour water rail and bearded tit.

Blagdon Reservoir (ST504507) has similar birds and is just to the west near Blagdon village; permit details as for Chew.

Location: 1 mile south of Chew Magna, south of Bristol.

Christchurch Harbour – the view from Warren Hill, Hengistbury Head. A wide variety of migrants has been recorded here

Access and facilities: good views over lake from parking areas on A368 at Herriots Bridge and B3114 at Herons Green. Car parks and picnic areas at Denny Wood and by main dam, where there is a wildlife information centre and toilets. Access to birdwatching hides and reservoir by permit from Bristol Waterworks Co, Woodford Lodge, Chew Stoke, Avon.
Map reference: ST573614

Christchurch Harbour

Dorset

Christchurch Harbour is the estuary of two rivers, the Hampshire Avon and the Dorset Stour. As on most estuaries, the waders and wildfowl are most varied in winter, when they include dark-bellied brent geese, wigeon, shelducks, black- and bar-tailed godwits, and grey plovers. Stanpit Marsh – on the northern shore – is a local nature reserve and one of the better places to view the harbour.

On the south side of the harbour lies Hengistbury Head, which is well known as a migration landfall site, especially in spring. Many interesting migrants have been recorded here, with the attractive hoopoe a distinct possibility in spring and a variety of flycatchers, chats and thrushes in autumn.

Location: just east of Christchurch and south of A35.
Access: Stanpit Marsh is reached on unclassified road towards Mudeford. Hengistbury Head can be reached along coast from Southbourne.
Map reference: SZ173925

Coate Water

Wiltshire

Wiltshire has few sizeable open water areas, and this is one of the largest lakes in the county. It is part of a country park and there are several birdwatching hides along the newer southern arm, which is a nature reserve. The natural shoreline is reed fringed in places. Reed and sedge warblers can be found here in summer and both great crested and little grebes nest. Migration periods attract common sandpipers, and in autumn black terns are regular visitors. In winter the lake attracts good wildfowl populations, especially in times of hard weather. These include teal, wigeon, pochard and tufted duck. The lake margins often have wintering snipe and the occasional jack snipe – offering an opportunity to sort out the differences between these two birds.

Location: on southern side of Swindon, close to M4 motorway, reached from B4006.
Access and facilities: open daily except Christmas. Picnic areas. Birdwatching hides.
Map reference: SU176826

Cotehele

Cornwall

Cotehele is a medieval manor house set in wooded grounds on the western side of the Tamar Valley. Footpaths lead from the attractive gardens down into the valley and the deciduous woodland, which supports excellent bird populations including buzzards and sparrowhawks. In spring, these oak woods are filled with birdsong, with the vibrant trill of wood warbler particularly evident. Pied flycatchers also breed and dippers and grey wagtails are resident along the river.

Within the Cotehele estate is a fascinating array of buildings, ranging from a secluded woodland chapel to beautifully restored early industrial buildings, making walks along the many paths equally interesting for non-birdwatchers.

Location: 8 miles south-west of Tavistock on banks of River Tamar. Signposted off A390 at St Ann's Chapel village.
Access and facilities: National Trust grounds open daily (house April to October). Admission charge. Refreshments. Toilets.
Map reference: SX423685

Dartington

Devon

The Dartington Estate is set in superb surroundings in the wooded lower Dart Valley. A waymarked 'woodpecker trail' extends for three miles and provides the chance to see dippers, grey wagtails, common sandpipers, kingfishers, woodlarks, wood warblers and general woodland species. The valley has good populations of buzzards, sparrowhawks and ravens, any of which might be seen overhead. The Dartington craft workshops are located nearby and provide added interest.

Location: north-west of Totnes off A384/A385 Totnes to Buckfastleigh road.
Access and facilities: car park at Shinners Bridge on junction with A385. Car park and other facilities at Dartington.
Map reference: SX787622

Dartmoor

Devon

Dartmoor National Park covers almost 400 square miles of upland area, the largest in southern England. The high moorland has several breeding birds which are not found elsewhere in the region except, in some cases, on Exmoor. They include dunlin, golden plover, ring ouzel and red grouse. The moorland fringes and combes are good areas to find summer migrants such as redstarts, grasshopper warblers and tree pipits. Lower down, the valley oak woods have rich bird populations with high numbers of wood warblers and pied flycatchers, while the fast running rivers have both grey wagtails and dippers. Throughout the whole of the moor there is exceptionally rich birdlife with buzzards and ravens very much in evidence. The national park has many areas to explore; below are eight examples.

1. Parke

National park headquarters and information

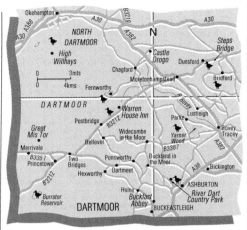

centre set in 200 acres of parkland in the wooded Bovey Valley. There are several walks through woodlands and beside the river. Birds include dippers, grey wagtails, sparrowhawks, buzzards and all three species of woodpecker. A rare breeds farm open from April to October with a pets corner and play area is an additional attraction (admission charge).

Location: west of Bovey Tracey on B3344.
Access and facilities: open all year, information centre open April–October, admission free. Special newspaper Dartmoor Visitor available free each summer.
Map reference: SX806785

2. Warren House Inn

Open moorland around the inn includes some of the best heather areas and both ring ouzels and red grouse can be found here. More typical species are skylarks, meadow pipits, cuckoos and wheatears in summer. In winter the area has been good for great grey shrikes, and in the evening the occasional roosting hen harrier can be seen. Soussons Plantation, just to the south, has typical birds of coniferous woodland including coal tits, sparrowhawks and jays, with the possibility of breeding siskins and crossbills.

Location: on B3212 Moretonhampstead to Princetown road.
Map reference: SX674809

3. Yarner Wood

This rich oak wood is a National Nature Reserve with an excellent complement of woodland birds, especially wood warblers, redstarts and pied flycatchers. The flycatchers nest in nestboxes and can be easily seen in May and June. Other woodland birds include nuthatches, treecreepers and all three species of woodpecker. The reserve is well waymarked, with each path identified with the time required to walk it.

Location: on B3344 Bovey Tracey to Manaton road.
Access: open all year. Walks; access restricted elsewhere.
Map reference: SX786788

4. Dunsford Wood

This valley oak wood beside the River Teign is a Devon Trust for Nature Conservation reserve. A visit in early April is a wonderful experience as the river bank is

Cotswold Water Park

Wiltshire/Gloucestershire

These widely scattered lakes are the result of over 50 years of gravel extraction – which is still continuing. Many of the lakes are used for water sports, but a few are designated as nature reserves and birds can be found on most of them, especially in winter. This is the period when the greatest number of species occurs, particularly diving ducks such as pochards and tufted ducks, which can be found in their thousands. A search could also reveal others such as goldeneye and ruddy duck, while red-crested pochard has been found on a few occasions. In summer the more vegetated lakes support a range of breeding birds, with warblers in the reed and scrub and a few pairs of great crested grebes on the more secluded lakes. Little ringed plovers are sometimes present in the area in summer. At Keynes Country Park there is a range of facilities for all the family, including paddling beaches.

Location: south and south-east of Cirencester, on unclassified road north of Ashton Keynes.
Access: Keynes Country Park open all year.
Map reference: SU028954

Cotswold Water Park

carpeted with wild daffodils which grow in profusion beside the fast flowing river. Most of the birds of the Dartmoor valleys can be found here, including dippers, wood warblers and pied flycatchers.

Location: at Steps Bridge on B3212 Moretonhampstead to Exeter road.
Map reference: SX804883

5. North Dartmoor

The main plateau of high moorland and blanket bog lies to the south of the military road. This is the best area for many of the specialised moorland birds, although they are sparsely distributed. Wheatears and ring ouzels should be present in good numbers in summer, and red grouse, although scarce, are around all year. The lower slopes hold whinchats, stonechats, and tree pipits; snipe and curlews frequent the valley bogs. Although heavily overgrazed, the sheer size of the moor gives it a wilderness feeling and the views are spectacular. A range of interesting wetland plants including cotton grass and sundew is found on the blanket bog; dragonflies are outstanding in summer.

Location: south from Okehampton town centre, signposted Dartmoor National Park.
Access: area is part of Dartmoor Military Ranges, but public access is allowed when firing is not taking place. This includes most weekends and public holidays and summer school holidays. Details are available locally from post offices.
Map reference: SX591932

6. Fernworthy

The large conifer woodland at Fernworthy surrounds a moorland reservoir with a bird hide overlooking the lake. Wildfowl in winter include a few interesting species such as goosander and goldeneye. The forest walks can produce some good birds in spring including crossbills and siskins; nightjars also breed. In late summer the muddy margins of the reservoir can repay investigation for waders including both common and green sandpipers.

Location: signposted from Chagford on unclassified roads.
Access: Forestry Commission car park. Waymarked walks and bird hide.
Map reference: SX669839

7. Burrator Reservoir

Similar to Fernworthy, this Forestry Commission woodland consists mainly of conifers surrounding a large reservoir. Wintering wildfowl include tufted duck, pochard and teal, with a few goosanders and goldeneyes. Other wetland species are coots, grey herons and gulls, including common gull. Among the woodland birds siskins, redpolls and bramblings can be found in winter. There are some areas of deciduous woodland and these attract migrants in summer, including wood warblers and redstarts.

Location: between Yelverton and Princetown off B3212, signposted from Dousland on unclassified roads.
Access and facilities: by permit from South West Water Authority, but not necessary for viewing lake. Car park. Woodland and moorland walks.
Map reference: SX568694.

8. River Dart Country Park

This private country park is set on the banks of the river in the wooded Dart Valley. There are lots of facilities for the whole family including picnic, adventure and play areas. The birdlife covers many of the West Country specialities, such as dippers and buzzards, etc.

Location: just north of Ashburton on unclassified road.
Access: admission charge.
Map reference: SX741698

Exe Estuary

Devon

One of the best estuaries in the West Country, the Exe provides outstanding birdwatching opportunities within a relatively small area. Individual sites are given below.

1. Dawlish Warren Local Nature Reserve

A large sand spit with saltings and mud flats across the mouth of the Exe, the Warren is a nature reserve and an extensive holiday beach all in one. It is owned by the Devon Trust for Nature Conservation and Teignbridge District Council. The reserve information centre is set behind the beach and dunes beyond the car parks. From here paths lead along the beach towards a large hide, facing upriver at the far end of the golf course. The high tide bird roost is exceptional, with thousands of oystercatchers and a good range of other waders. In summer there are usually common and Sandwich terns, while autumn brings curlew sandpipers and little stints, and winter brent geese and wigeon. Many of the smaller waders can often be found along the beach. Offshore in winter there are often a few red-throated divers and Slavonian grebes, while scoters and eiders are frequent. The flowers of the Warren include the very rare warren crocus, along with marsh orchids and autumn lady's tresses.

Location: east of Dawlish Warren Station.
Access and facilities: nature centre. Car park (charge). Toilets.
Map reference: SX978786

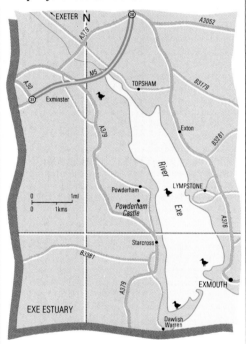

2. Exmouth

One of the major feeding areas for the estuary's waders and wildfowl lies upstream from Exmouth. In late autumn and winter, wildfowl arrive to graze on the extensive eelgrass beds, with 4,000 brent geese and similar numbers of wigeon, plus sizeable groups of pintails and mute swans. Waders here include bar-tailed godwits and grey plovers with a small flock of knots in mid-winter. The main tidal channel runs along the seafront at Exmouth and is a good place to see red-breasted mergansers and shags in winter. At any time of year towards evening gannets can be seen coming to feed on incoming tides.

Sandwich terns are always present in summer.

Facilities: large car park and toilets off Imperial Road near bus station.
Map reference: SX998811

Fernworthy Reservoir – the creation of reservoirs such as this has increased the variety of birds on Dartmoor

Exmoor – pastoral scenery at Tivington Knowle, near Selworthy

3. Powderham

This central part of the estuary is a good area to see curlews, black-tailed godwits, grey and ringed plovers and dunlins. Mid-tide is the best time. Part of the Exe Wildfowl Sanctuary, this area attracts many mallards, teal and wigeon, with a scattering of shovelers, pintails and pochards. At high tide many of the waders roost in Powderham Park. They can be viewed from the road a short way downstream, either on the pools or along the River Kenn. Greenshanks and green sandpipers are regular here. The park has a heronry in its large oaks and a herd of fallow deer can be seen grazing beneath them.

Location: west side of estuary off A379.
Access: small parking area beside railway, further parking available beyond church.
Map reference: SX974845

4. Exminster Marshes   RSPB

The upper estuary is best viewed from the tow path along the Exeter Ship Canal, which is raised above the marshes and estuary. The meadows here include part of an RSPB reserve area and long term management is planned to attract more of the waders to roost on the fields at high tide. Redshanks and lapwings breed and large numbers of black-tailed godwits are often present. The area is good for birds of prey with peregrines and buzzards regularly seen and hen harriers and short-eared owls in winter. Of special interest on the mud flats in winter is the flock of up to 150 avocets. They remain out on the open estuary, floating in a group at high tide, and can

often be seen upstream of the Turf Hotel at the lower end of the ship canal. One of the best ways to view the waders and wildfowl of the estuary and to be sure of a sighting of avocets is to obtain a place on an RSPB 'Avocet Cruise'. These trips run on certain weekends between November and March – full details can be obtained from the RSPB South-West Regional Office.

Location: follow signs for Swans Nest from southern end of Exminster by-pass.
Access: limited parking further along road. Area can also be reached by pedestrian ferry from Topsham (small charge). Keep to footpaths.
Map reference: SX958875

Exmoor National Park

Somerset/Devon

Covering just 265 square miles, Exmoor is one of the smallest national parks in the country. However, within that relatively small size it encompasses a wide variety of habitats for birds. Sea cliffs, high moorland and valley woodland all help to make it an outstanding place for bird-watching. Some of the suggested sites given below are on the eastern side where the majority of heather moor occurs, but many other areas are worthy of exploration.

1. Webbers Post

Set high above the National Trust's Holnicote Estate, this is an excellent place to begin an exploration of Exmoor. The deep wooded valleys lie below, while up above the moor rises towards Dunkery, its highest point. The heather moor has a few pairs of ring ouzels and red grouse, but whinchats and wheatears are more likely. Where the moorland joins the woodland edge, redstarts, tree pipits and cuckoos are found. Birds of prey range from the wooded valley onto the open moor; buzzards and sparrowhawks are frequently seen, while peregrines and merlins are also possible. The Exmoor herd of red deer is large and many visitors see them on the open moor.

Location: on unclassified road from Luccombe to Exford.
Access: free car park.
Map reference: SS902440

2. Horner

The Horner Valley has one of the best oak woods in the West Country, and walking through it alongside the swift running stream is a sheer delight. All the typical birds are present, with especially good numbers of wood warblers and pied flycatchers in summer.

Location: south of A39 Minehead to Porlock road.
Facilities: car park. Toilets. Refreshments.
Map reference: SS897455

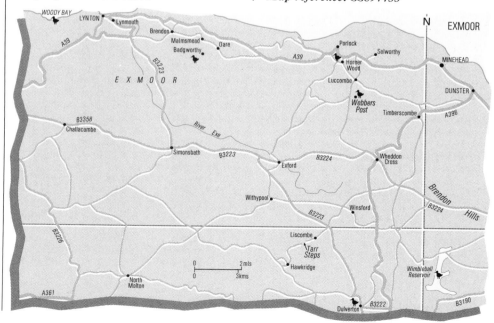

3. Badgworthy

This is the 'Doone Valley' made famous by RD Blackmore. Although very popular with tourists, a walk up the valley in delightful scenery should provide views of whinchats, stonechats and linnets, with other species quite likely the further you go.

Location: south of Malmsmead.
Access and facilities: car park at bottom of valley at Malmsmead. Exmoor Natural History Society have small centre here, open Wednesday and Thursday afternoons.
Map reference: SS791478

4. Woody Bay

Wringapeak, near Woody Bay, is the best area for seabirds along the Exmoor coast. It is necessary to walk down fairly steep paths to get the best views of the breeding colonies. Guillemots and razorbills nest in good numbers, together with a small colony of kittiwakes and many fulmars and shags. Lesser and great black-backed gulls breed on the cliffs here too, along with jackdaws, buzzards, kestrels, and ravens.

Location: west of Lynton on unclassified road along coast toward Martinhoe.
Map reference: SS675490

5. Wimbleball Lake

Set in a wooded valley on the edge of the national park, this reservoir is fairly new. The Somerset Trust for Nature Conservation has a nature reserve on the northern end with a self guided nature trail. Summer birds here include wood warblers, and both species of flycatcher, while at other seasons there are good numbers of wildfowl.

Location: north-north-east of Dulverton, sign-posted from A396 and B3190.
Access and facilities: car parks. 3 picnic areas. Toilets. Nature trail. Information kiosk.
Map reference: SS965308

6. Barle Valley

This superb valley has some of the most extensive oak woods in the national park. All the typical birds mentioned previously are present in outstanding unspoilt country. The bracken slopes above the woods lead up to West Anstey Common, a fragment of the much larger moorland areas which once existed here. A few moorland birds may be found here, with whinchats, cuckoos and tree pipits in summer, and merlins and hen harriers in winter.

Location: on unclassified road to Hawkridge signposted from B3223 Dulverton to Exford road.
Facilities: limited parking along road.
Map reference: SS870290

Fal Estuary Complex

Cornwall

The winding estuary of the Fal and its tributaries has many waders and wildfowl, but local geography makes viewing difficult. High tides are needed to push the waders up from the deep tidal channels, and the well wooded shoreline of the upper estuary obscures the view in some places. Curlews, black-tailed godwits, redshanks, oyster-catchers and dunlins are numerous, and greenshanks and spotted redshanks often remain all winter in the mild climate. Wild-fowl variety is excellent with red-breasted mergansers and goldeneyes among the high-lights. Carrick Roads, nearer Falmouth, often shelters divers and grebes, particularly after gales. Unusual visitors may remain for long periods; little egrets have been known to spend the winter in the sheltered creeks, and ospreys are seen every autumn.

Location: south of Truro.
Access: Tressillian River can be viewed from A39, although better viewing is possible along footpath from St Clement. For Carrick Roads park at Mylor and view from beach. Many other areas can be viewed from minor roads and footpaths.
Map reference: SW830360

Forest of Dean

Gloucestershire   `RSPB`

'The Dean' is one of the few remaining ancient royal forests left in England. Although commercial forestry plantations have replaced much of the original oak woods, there are still a few areas where magnificent oaks over 150 years old can be found. One of these is at the RSPB Nagshead Reserve, which covers some of the best remaining oak woodland and a rich bird community. Summer visitors include wood warblers, redstarts and, increasingly, pied flycatchers, more evident on the reserve nowadays following the success of nestbox schemes. The whole range of woodland species occurs, including all three species of woodpecker, sparrowhawks, treecreepers and nuthatches. Other specialities include cross-bills, which nest early in the year, and a few pairs of shy and elusive hawfinches.

Elsewhere in the Dean another rare species can often be seen under special circumstances. This is the peregrine falcon,

Exmoor (main picture) – in the Doone Valley
Forest of Dean (small picture) – the view to Yat Rock

which after many years has recently returned to breed on Symonds Yat Rock. If a breeding pair is present the RSPB organises a special protection scheme and visitors are encouraged to view the nesting ledge from an observation point. The best time to see these falcons is likely to be from April to early July, although after a successful season birds may still be around much later.

Location: south of Ross on Wye.
Access and facilities: open all year, Forestry Commission. Car parks. Picnic sites. Walks. RSPB Nagshead Reserve immediately west of Parkend village off B4431 to Coleford; keep to waymarked track. Hides. Information centre. Car park. Toilets. Symonds Yat Rock off A40 at Whitchurch.
Map reference: SO612078

Garston Wood

Dorset   `RSPB`

This 84-acre wood is on the edge of Cranborne Chase, once a vast area of woodland. A wonderful place to hear spring birdsong, the reserve consists of mature oak and ash with an understorey of coppiced hazel. The traditional craft of hurdlemaking is still practised here, and the rotational cutting produces ideal conditions for many of the summer migrants.

Breeding birds include nightingales, garden warblers, blackcaps and white-throats, and a visit in May or June is a delight.

Location: north of Sixpenny Handley on unclassified road to Bowerchalke.
Access: RSPB reserve. Keep to footpaths.
Map reference: SU004194

Haldon Forest

Devon

This is Forestry Commission woodland on a long ridge, with extensive views over the surrounding Devon countryside. The various age stages of pines here attract different species of birds; for example, the young conifers have willow warblers, tree pipits and turtle doves while the older stands are good for goldcrests, coal tits and ravens. A few pairs of crossbills and siskins breed in the oldest plantations, and the open areas have an excellent population of nightjars in summer. The ridge is a superb vantage point to watch for birds of prey, with high numbers of buzzards and sparrowhawks all year and hobbies in summer.

Location: south-west of Exeter, signposted off A38 towards Plymouth.
Facilities: free car park, picnic areas and waymarked paths.
Map reference: SX885848

Highnam Wood

Gloucestershire   **RSPB**

Purchased in 1987 as part of the Woodland Birds Appeal, this 300-acre, broadleaved woodland is among the newest RSPB reserves. Nightingales at the very edge of their range are notable among the varied birdlife here. Other summer migrants breeding in the wood include pied and spotted flycatchers and blackcaps. Resident species are all three species of woodpecker, nuthatches, tawny and long-eared owls, buzzards and sparrowhawks. A sight not to be missed here is the spectacular springtime carpet of bluebells.

Location: west of Gloucester, just off A40.
Access: open at all times; car park and marked paths.
Map reference: SO773198

Holt Heath

Dorset

Typical heathland birds are present here, including Dartford warblers and nightjars, together with frequent green woodpeckers, stonechats and redpolls. The open aspects are good for birds of prey with the possibility of merlins and hen harriers in winter and hobbies in summer. There are pools and areas of wet heath which abound in dragonflies in summer.

Location: north of Bournemouth. South-west of B3072 at Three Legged Cross, on unclassified road to Broom Hill.
Access: limited car parking. National Nature Reserve managed by Nature Conservancy Council; open at all times along paths.
Map reference: SU047037

Kingsbridge Estuary

Devon

Many winding creeks give this drowned valley its particular character. It has most of the usual waders, with dunlins, oystercatchers, curlews and redshanks most obvious. On the smaller creeks are greenshanks, spotted redshanks and common sandpipers. Lower down, off East Portlemouth, deeper waters shelter a few sea ducks after winter gales, mainly eiders and scoters. Elsewhere, regular wildfowl consist of wigeon, teal, mallards and pintails with just the chance of a few brent geese, red-breasted mergansers and goldeneyes.

Location: south of Kingsbridge.
Access: from A381 and A379 on footpaths.
Map reference: SX745410

Land's End Peninsula

Cornwall

Many of the outstanding birdwatching localities of this part of west Cornwall are also ideal for the summer visitor. Four are described here.

1. Hayle Estuary and Carnsew Pool

One of the smallest estuaries in the country, Hayle provides good views of waders and wildfowl at any state of the tide. Even in midsummer a few species are present, including redshanks, curlews, ringed plovers and bar-tailed godwits. Autumn and winter bring many gulls, with lesser black-backed and common, and several scarce species. Wildfowl include shelducks, wigeon and teal, while nearby Carnsew Pool often has diving ducks, including long-tailed ducks and red-breasted mergansers. There is a perimeter path around Carnsew Pool, which is on the eastern edge of the estuary, and which may also have dunlins and ringed plovers feeding at low tide and divers and grebes on the main pool. Terns may be seen diving for fish during the summer months, and also flying between here and Porth Kidney Sands, where they roost.

Location: south-west of Hayle at junction of B3301 and A3074 St Ives road.
Access: car parking for RSPB hide at Old Quay House restaurant (patrons only at lunch time).
Map reference: SW546363

2. St Ives Island and Bay

'The Island' is a rocky headland with a coastguard lookout renowned as one of the best seabird watchpoints in Britain. It overlooks the bay and during northerly and north-westerly winds in late summer and autumn many thousands of seabirds pass close by. Watching from here during on-shore winds can be rewarding at any time of year. The variety of seabirds is amazing, with auks, gulls, shearwaters, petrels, terns, skuas and divers, depending on the time of year. Divers and grebes are often present in the bay during winter and spring.

Location: St Ives reached by A3074 from Hayle bypass. The island is on north of St Ives harbour with car park nearby.
Access: park and ride scheme from Lelant operates in summer.
Map reference: SW520413

3. Marazion Marsh and Mounts Bay

This small grazing marsh and reed bed attracts many interesting migrants. Spring is good for swallows and yellow wagtails while autumn brings many reed and sedge warblers and the occasional aquatic warbler. It is also often good in autumn for skulking species such as water rail and spotted crake, which are often more visible here than elsewhere. Breeding birds include reed and sedge warblers but also, and unusually, ground nesting grey herons in the reed bed. Mount's Bay often shelters wintering great northern divers and in summer terns and waders can be seen roosting on the beach.

Location: west of Marazion on coast road.
Access: from car park.
Map reference: SW514312

4. Porthgwarra Valley

This south-facing valley is well known as a refuge for migrant birds. Almost anything can appear, with spotted and pied flycatchers autumn specialities. Birds of prey often turn up here and rarities have included small migrants from America. Seawatching from here on southerly winds is particularly productive in August when Cory's and great shearwaters are often seen.

Location: 3 miles from Land's End off B3315 Land's End to Newlyn road.
Map reference: SW372218

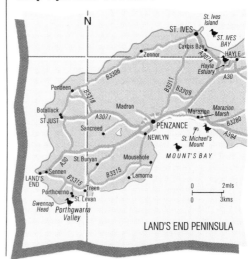

LAND'S END PENINSULA

Leigh Woods

Avon

This 160-acre mixed woodland is owned by the National Trust and managed as a National Nature Reserve by the Nature Conservancy Council. The wood has a typical woodland bird population and its spectacular situation perched high above the Avon Gorge, with the tidal river winding below, makes it well worth a visit. In springtime the birds include redstarts, wood warblers, grasshopper warblers, tree pipits and a few pairs of nightingales. Among the resident species are nuthatches, treecreepers and all three species of woodpecker. The hawfinch is also a resident, but usually difficult to see.

Location: woodland on edge of Avon Gorge just west of Bristol across Clifton suspension bridge (toll). After crossing bridge turn right on to North Road, entrance is on right.
Access: open at all times.
Map reference: ST560730

The Lizard

Cornwall

The windswept peninsula of the Lizard is the southernmost point of Britain and it is chosen as a landfall by many exhausted migrant birds. The high cliffs here are good vantage points to watch for passing seabirds, especially during onshore winds, although gannets are almost always on view.

Winter brings turnstones and purple sandpipers to the rocky shoreline where, in spring, oystercatchers and rock pipits can be found breeding. Most birds occur during migration, with the autumn bringing the biggest variety. Bad weather conditions cause vast numbers of swallows and swifts to congregate, and during overcast weather large numbers of warblers and flycatchers may be found. The area is quite large and the terrain can be difficult, but exploration can often bring good rewards.

Location: from Helston take A3083 to Lizard. Unclassified roads lead from A3083 to various points on peninsula.
Access: public footpaths follow coastline.
Map reference: SW703124

Lundy

Devon

The rugged granite island of Lundy is by far the best seabird breeding site in the West Country. The name means 'puffin island', and puffins can still be found in small numbers on the north-west side of the island. Most numerous of the breeding auks are guillemots, with over a thousand pairs. Razorbills, kittiwakes, fulmars and shags are common, as are great and lesser black-backed gulls. Other birds breeding on the sheer cliffs are buzzards, kestrels and ravens. Manx shearwaters and storm petrels also breed, but are mainly nocturnal, although rafts of shearwaters can often be seen floating offshore in daylight. The island is well known for the variety of migrants which occurs in spring and autumn, making a longer visit at these times a worthwhile enterprise. Lundy has a number of other wildlife species which make it of special interest. These include its own breed of sheep, and among an outstanding flora, the unique Lundy cabbage.

Location: 12 miles north of Hartland Point in Bristol Channel.
Access: reached from Bideford Quay two to three times a week (details of sailings from The Landmark Trust, Shottesbrooke, Maidenhead, Berks. Tel. Littlewick Green 5925).
Map reference: SS140440

Mendip Hills

Somerset

The limestone rock which forms the Mendips has eroded to form several gorges, the best known of which is Cheddar Gorge. Ebbor Gorge, to the south, is smaller and less well known, but is a National Nature Reserve. Both gorges are good places to see birds of prey, with buzzards and kestrels regular throughout the year and peregrine falcons in winter. The open scrub woodland above the gorges attracts many summer migrants including willow warblers, chiffchaffs and whitethroats. The area is excellent for its special limestone flora, with several specialities, perhaps the best known being the very rare Cheddar pink. Other natural attractions are the Cheddar Caves, well worth visiting to view the spectacular rock formations and stalagmites and stalactites. Nearby Cheddar Reservoir is a good birdwatching spot, attracting diving ducks, especially goldeneyes and goosanders, and some waders on migration and in winter.

Location: north-west of Wells. Cheddar Gorge is signposted from M5 motorway.
Access: reserves and waymarked paths open at all times. Cheddar Caves open daily.
Map reference: ST463537

Poole Harbour and Purbeck

Dorset

Around Poole Harbour are some of the most unspoilt wildlife sites in southern England. Especially important are the lowland heaths of Purbeck, which have a variety of birds, reptiles, plants and insects hard to find elsewhere. Poole Harbour is a large estuary with a double tidal system and extensive mud flats, with wildfowl and waders in nationally important numbers. To the west

North Cornwall Coast

Cornwall

From Tintagel northwards stretches some of Cornwall's most impressive and spectacular cliff scenery. The towering cliffs support many seabirds in the breeding season, especially herring and lesser and great black-backed gulls, but also a scattering of fulmars and shags.

On the opposite side of the bay from Tintagel is the best site for breeding auks close to the Cornish mainland. The two offshore stacks known as Long and Short Island harbour good populations of guillemots and razorbills with a few pairs of the now locally scarce puffin. This area – near Trevalga – is the most likely spot on the mainland of Cornwall from which to see puffins, and a visit between April and July is best. They are likely to be swimming in small groups out in the bay or sitting outside their nesting burrows on the grassy slopes of Long Island. This time of year is also best for wild flowers.

Location: between Tintagel and Boscastle.
Access: coastal footpath. Keep to path as cliffs along whole stretch are steep and very dangerous.
Map reference: SX074906

North Cornwall coast – the main picture is of Tintagel Castle; inset is Boscastle Harbour

of Swanage are the limestone cliffs of the Purbeck coast with their breeding seabirds. Much of the area belongs to the National Trust, including the huge Corfe Castle Estate and the whole of Brownsea Island.

Together all these sites make the whole area worthy of an extensive exploration.

1. Arne RSPB Reserve

Set in a peninsula extending into Poole Harbour, the whole area preserves a remote quality. Extensive heathland here has breeding Dartford warblers, nightjars and stonechats. The fringing mud flats have black- and bar-tailed godwits, spotted red-shanks and curlews, together with whim-brels and greenshanks on passage. Wildfowl include shelducks all year, and brent geese,

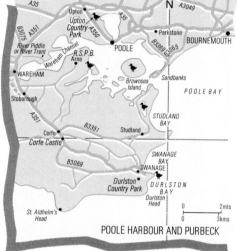

POOLE HARBOUR AND PURBECK

red-breasted mergansers and teal in winter.

Birds of prey include buzzards and spar-rowhawks, with hobbies in summer and hen harriers, peregrines and merlins in winter. The heathland areas look their best in late summer when the purple of the heathers colours the landscape. Among the heathland plant specialities are bog asphodel and marsh gentian, while the dragonflies (22 species) and butterflies are superb. All six British reptile species are found here, and roe and sika deer are often seen.

Location: off A351 Wareham to Swanage road, signposted from Stoborough.
Access and facilities: Shipstall part of reserve open at all times. Car park and toilets at Arne.
Map reference: SY972879

2. Studland National Nature Reserve

This heathland National Nature Reserve is managed by the Nature Conservancy Coun-cil, and together with Godlingstone Heath is one of the largest blocks of this habitat to be found in Britain. The reserve also in-cludes a coastal fresh water lagoon, sand dunes and mud flats. All the heathland birds are present, and the Little Sea Lagoon also attracts reed and sedge warblers in summer and wildfowl and water rails in winter. Brands Bay on the landward side is an important feeding area for both waders and wildfowl and good views can be obtained at mid-tide.

Location: off unclassified road north of Stud-land, or via ferry from Poole.
Map reference: SZ034835

3. Brownsea Island

This 500-acre island is mainly woodland, with some heath and a large man-made lagoon. Half is a nature reserve managed by The Dorset Trust for Nature Conservation. Visitors may explore the island, which has an excellent cross-section of birds, including one of the largest colonies of grey herons in the country and breeding terns on the lagoon. A hide is positioned to view the tern islands and both common and Sandwich terns are present in summer. Many waders can be found on the lagoon, especially at high tide. Of particular interest is the flock of avocets in midwinter. Keen-eyed visitors might spot red squirrels among the pines. They are quite numerous here. Apart from the Isle of Wight, this is their last stronghold in southern England. There are also sika deer on the island, but these are likely only to be seen by quiet and patient visitors.

Location: in Poole Harbour.
Access: by passenger ferry from Poole Quay and Sandbanks. Guided parties at 2.45pm daily July-August.
Map reference: SZ032877

4. Durlston Country Park

The cliffs in this area are limestone and there is much evidence of past quarrying.

There are breeding seabirds here, with a large colony of guillemots, and razorbills, kittiwakes, fulmars and just a few remaining pairs of puffins. This is also a good area for migrants in spring or autumn.

The limestone flowers include several orchids, and the butterflies are outstanding, with specialities like Lulworth skipper and chalkhill blue.

Location: just south of Swanage.
Facilities: car park. Toilets. Information centre open Easter to October.
Map reference: SZ033773

5. Upton Country Park

Situated on the northern shore of Poole Harbour, the grounds of this country park run down to Holes Bay, where there is a large RSPB hide overlooking the salt marsh. It is best visited within a few hours of high tide when the waders are likely to include redshanks, both bar- and black-tailed god-wits, grey and ringed plovers, with whim-brels and greenshanks on migration.

Location: signposted from A35, east of Upton
Access: free. Open daily, car park.
Map reference: ST993928

Savernake Forest – fine beech trees are a major part of its attraction

Quantock Hills

Somerset

Forming an attractive wooded ridge, the Quantocks run roughly west between Bridg-water and Taunton. The ridge is dissected by several sheltered combes, and there are also areas of scattered heathland and rough grazing, all of which are attractive to a range of birds. The oak woodland attracts summer migrants including redstarts and wood warb-lers. Overhead, the mewing of buzzards can be heard in spring and early summer, the time of year when the tops of the combes are the places to find tree pipits and the occasional nightjar. The area is also impor-tant for both red and roe deer. The Forestry Commission has provided several well marked paths and there are a number of parking areas and picnic places. At Fyne Court the Somerset Trust for Nature Con-servation has its headquarters and there are facilities for visitors in the summer.

Location: west of Bridgwater on unclassified roads off A39.
Access and facilities: Fyne Court information centre and shop open daily April-October. Nature trail. Picnic site. Quantock Forest Trail (Forestry Commission) from Seven Wells Bridge or Ranscombe picnic place.
Map reference: ST222321

Savernake Forest

Wiltshire

Once an ancient royal forest, Savernake is now largely converted to commercial conifer plantations, but some areas of mature oaks and beeches remain, and there are also patches of scrub and extensive open rides. Summer is the best time for a visit. The woodland bird population then includes turtle doves and nightingales, summer visi-tors which tend to become scarcer farther west. Warblers include garden warblers, blackcaps and a few pairs of wood warblers. Nightjars nest occasionally, normally being found alongside rides or woodland clearings. The forest has an outstanding butterfly list, with brimstone and white admiral among the highlights.

Location: south-east of Marlborough between A4 and A346.
Access: open all year. Trails. Picnic sites.
Map reference: SY221665

Scilly, Isles of

The islands are famed for their birdlife, particularly the number of rare and unusual species which occur at migration times. They are also among the best places for breeding seabirds in the south-west. Between April and July boat trips can be taken to view the seabirds on the uninhabited islands, especially Annet, although landing is not permitted during the breeding season. Guillemots, razorbills and puffins, together with kittiwakes, fulmars and both great and lesser black-backed gulls are among those that breed. Storm petrels and Manx shearwaters also breed, but are generally nocturnal. Common terns breed on offshore islands and on the island of Tresco.

The spring passage is quieter than the autumn, but migrants from the south at this time can include hoopoes, golden orioles, and even bee-eaters. The superb sandy beaches have a few waders, often very tame and approachable. At this time there are many colourful wild flowers (and relatively few birdwatchers!).

Autumn on Scilly is renowned in birdwatching circles for the vast numbers of migrants seen during certain weather conditions. Many hundreds of keen birdwatchers make an annual pilgrimage, with October being the favoured month. This is the time when North American rarities occur, some – such as blackpoll warbler and gray-cheeked thrush – becoming almost annual. There are good birdwatching spots all over the islands, but many people like to base themselves on the main island of St Mary's from where there is easy access to the other islands. Among these, Tresco possesses the large Abbey Pool and the added attraction of superb sub-tropical gardens. Both St Agnes and St Martin's are also good, with many areas to explore for birds.

Location: 28 miles south-west of Land's End.
Access: by steamer or helicopter from Penzance. Inter-island travel by small passenger boats.
Map reference: SV902109

Slapton Ley and Area

Devon

Slapton Ley is a large fresh-water lagoon enclosed by a long shingle beach, and divided in two by a road bridge. The lower ley – to the south – is the main body of open water. It attracts the majority of wildfowl and other water birds, including great crested grebe, which has its main breeding site in Devon here. A birdwatching hide on the inland side of the lower ley overlooks the main wildfowl roosting area, where wintering diving ducks usually include goldeneyes and red-breasted mergansers, with rarer species at times of hard weather. Slapton is a nature reserve managed by the Field Studies Council, which also organises a range of residential courses from its centre in summer. Local activities also include guided walks – details can be obtained at the Countryside Information Unit based at the centre. The higher ley is mainly reed marsh and scrub and is the site of a bird observatory run by the Devon Birdwatching and Preservation Society. Breeding birds here include reed and sedge warblers and resident Cetti's warblers, whose powerful song can be heard at almost any season. Many migrants occur in spring and autumn and firecrests and chiffchaffs spend the winter here. The ley is good for dragonflies and damselflies in summer and still has two otters.

Offshore, sea birds are often worth checking for, with great northern divers and Slavonian grebes in winter and terns in summer.

Start and Prawle Points, to the south, are major migration spots and provide good birdwatching in the autumn. The coastal farmland in this vicinity is also the area to find the cirl bunting, a bird which has become very scarce nationally. Here it is resident, breeding in the sheltered south-

Slimbridge – ducks at the Rushy Pen, and a greenshank (right)

facing valley hedgerows and coastal scrub. In the breeding season its distinctive song, somewhat like a yellowhammer, can often be heard, while in winter small parties may be found near the coastal headlands.

Location: on south Devon coast between Dartmouth and Kingsbridge beside A379. Field centre and information unit at Slapton village.
Access and facilities: open all year. Information centre. Picnic site and marked trail, hide. Guided walks mid June to mid September.
Map reference: SX828443

Slimbridge Wildfowl Trust, The New Grounds

Gloucestershire

Slimbridge, the headquarters of the Wildfowl Trust, is situated on the south shore of the tidal Severn, where the 'New Grounds' have long been a traditional wintering site for white-fronted geese and Bewick's swans. The establishment of the world's largest collection of ducks, geese and swans which can be fed out of the hand adds to the attraction and makes a visit worthwhile at any time of year.

At the entrance there is a spacious exhibition hall with views through large observation windows over a series of wildfowl pools so that even in the poorest weather birds can be viewed in comfort. In winter, visitors can watch thousands of wild birds from an observatory which borders 'Swan Lake'. Screened walkways lead out to 'The Dumbles', where hides overlook the lagoons and salt marshes.

Here, winter migrants from the Arctic and Siberia include thousands of white-fronted geese, often with the odd bean or pink-footed goose keeping them company, and sometimes including the very rare lesser white-fronted goose. Bewick's swans arrive in hundreds, some returning regularly for many years to enjoy the security of the reserve. A wide variety of wildfowl occurs, especially large flocks of wigeon, pochard, tufted duck and teal. There are usually some waders present, especially curlews and lapwings, but during migration periods redshanks, greenshanks and several species of sandpiper occur. This concentration of birds along the shores of the Severn attracts peregrine falcons in winter, which can often be seen from the hides.

Location: 10 miles south of Gloucester off A38 on unclassified road, signposted from A38 and M5 motorway.
Access: open all year except Christmas. Admission charge for non members. Information centre, nature trails. Hides.
Map reference: SO722048

Somerset Levels and Moors

Somerset

Lying south of the M5 between the Mendip Hills and Taunton are the wide flat expanses of the Somerset Levels and Moors.

The meadows and water-filled ditches still support many interesting wetland birds and a host of wild flowers. In winter the flooded meadows are covered with thousands of lapwings, snipe, redwings and fieldfares, and on the deeper floods, wildfowl include wigeon and teal.

Somerset Levels – Tadham Moors, one of the least changed parts of the Levels

Sizeable flocks of Bewick's swans occur in a few areas. The flooding may be localised so that some exploration is necessary to find a concentration of birds in winter. Spring brings passage waders with ruffs arriving as early as February and a large migration of whimbrels in April and early May. This is the best time for breeding birds; lapwings, curlews, snipe, redshanks, yellow wagtails and whinchats being some of the specialities. The meadow flora is outstand-

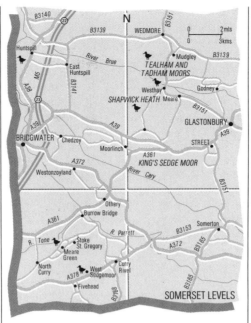

SOMERSET LEVELS

ing, with some of the best remaining fields in the country. These may be covered with the yellow of marsh marigold, or by the delicate pink of lady's smock. The ditches (or rhynes) have many aquatic plants including frogbit, arrowhead and flowering rush, and the insect life includes exotic looking dragon- and damselflies. The whole area repays investigation; the places described here are among the most interesting, and they also offer easy access.

1. West Sedgemoor   **RSPB**

The reserve includes extensive open meadows on the moor and much of the wooded ridge which overlooks the moor. The car park is on the edge of Swell Wood, the site of one of the largest nesting colonies of grey herons in the West Country. A hide is positioned in close proximity to the colony and a visit between April and early June can be an exciting experience. A series of paths leads through the wood where breeding birds include wood warblers, garden warblers and nightingales. At the foot of the hill a second hide looks out over the moor, providing a good vantage point, especially in winter, when floods can attract large numbers of wildfowl and as many as 20,000 lapwings have been recorded.

Other specialities attracted by the shallow floods include a good number of Bewick's swans and birds of prey, including peregrines and hen harriers.

Location: signposted off A378 between Fivehead and Langport.
Access: open to two hides. Car park.
Map reference: ST361238

2. Willows and Wetland Visitor Centre, Meare Green
This visitor centre has been established at the premises of local withy growers and basket makers. Displays cover much of the local history and industry of the Levels. The whole of the upper floor of the centre houses displays on the wildlife of the area created specially by the RSPB.

Location: at Meare Green, on unclassified road

between North Curry and Stoke St Gregory.
Access: open all year. Car park.
Map reference: ST336265

3. Tealham and Tadham Moors
Situated in the Brue Valley, these meadows can be viewed by driving along the road which cuts across the moors, and provides a good vantage point. The area is one of those most prone to shallow floods and so attracts large numbers of lapwings and a flock of golden plovers. Snipe are also numerous, but less obvious since they are hidden low in the hollows; jack snipe are even more difficult to spot.

Among these waders there are often ruffs and even dunlins, which may be joined by large flocks of starlings, redwings and field-fares. Bewick's swans are fairly regular here as are wigeon, teal and shovelers. Breeding waders are present in spring but are not especially numerous although there may be good numbers of yellow wagtails, whinchats and sedge warblers.

Location: off B3151 on unclassified road between Westhay and Wedmore.
Map reference: ST420446

4. Shapwick Peat Workings
The peat workings near Shapwick are creating small areas of marshland and fens and a much larger series of lakes and marshes will gradually come into existence over the next few years as the peat is dug. A number of large lakes for water supply is being proposed and a start has been made on establishing nature reserves. Already the bird interest is increasing with breeding reed, sedge and Cetti's warblers and wildfowl numbers steadily increasing. The alder carr areas are attractive to other migrants, especially whitethroats, garden warblers and blackcaps. The whole area has a tremendous potential for birds, with exciting possibilities for rarer wetland species in due course. The Somerset Trust for Nature Conservation is developing a reserve on a similar area at Westhay (ST456437) where visitor facilities are due to be provided.

Location: from B3151 take unclassified road to Westhay at Shapwick.
Map reference: ST423412

5. The Willows Peat Garden Centre, Westhay
A small information centre at this garden centre includes displays on the archaeological history of the peat moors, the peat industry and the wildlife of the Brue Valley.

Location: along unclassified road between Westhay and Shapwick.
Access: car park and refreshments
Map reference: ST425415

6. New Road Farm, Burnham-on-Sea
A working farm on the edge of the Levels with many facilities for visitors including an information centre and a farm trail.

Location: at Huntspill, 3 miles south-east of Burnham-on-Sea. Signposted from A38; 1 mile south of Highbridge.
Access: open Easter to end of October.
Map reference: ST315460

Tamar Estuary – despite its built-up lower reaches, a fine place for birds

Stithians Reservoir

Cornwall

Cornwall's best reservoir for birds, Stithians has areas of shallows and muddy fringes for waders. Autumn is a good time, when green, wood and common sandpipers stop by and greenshanks, ruffs and spotted redshanks are regular. North American waders have included pectoral sandpipers and long-billed dowitchers. Winter brings a sizeable flock of golden plovers and lapwings to the nearby fields and the margins of the lake have snipe and jack snipe. Wildfowl numbers are usually good in winter with gadwalls and goosanders among the mallards, wigeon and teal.

Location: from A394 Helston to Penryn road follow signs on unclassified roads to reservoir.
Access: good views over lake can be obtained from road. Hides, permits from South West Water Authority.
Map reference: SW715352

Sutton Bingham Reservoir

Somerset/Dorset

This 143-acre reservoir on the Dorset/Somerset border is one of the few large water bodies in the area and it therefore attracts a variety of birds. Wildfowl in winter include goldeneyes, while goosanders, shovelers and pintails are regular; Bewick's swans are also a possibility. Good numbers of waders appear on passage and black terns are often present in August. There is access to a bird hide overlooking a sheltered part of the longest arm, where both great crested and little grebes are often found.

Location: south of Yeovil off A37 on unclassified road to Halstock.
Access: unclassified road crosses reservoir on causeway. There are good views along southern arm from road. Free access to bird hide.
Map reference: ST546114

Tamar Estuary Complex

Devon/Cornwall

A number of rivers join together at Plymouth to enter the sea via Plymouth Sound. These are all good for birds, although the best viewing places are well separated.

1. St John's Lake, Millbrook Lake and Lynher River

After the Exe, this is one of the best estuarine areas in the West Country, with St John's Lake the best place to find many of the wildfowl, including brent geese, shelducks and flocks of several thousand wigeon. Most of the waders are represented, notably knot, one of the birds found less often on most south-west estuaries. There are numbers of both bar- and black-tailed godwits, and a few spotted redshanks and greenshanks remain all winter.

Autumn passage is good here, with little stints, curlew sandpipers and several species of tern.

Location: west of Plymouth.
Access: St John's Lake reached by Torpoint Ferry or A374. Area is best viewed from unclassified roads around its edge: St John's Lake from waterfront at Torpoint and Millbrook Lake from B3247 towards Millbrook village.
Map reference: SX430540

2. Mount Edgcumbe Country Park

Set in the grounds of a large country house, this country park is on the edge of Plymouth Sound. A pleasant spot for a family outing, there are woodland walks here where resident species like treecreeper and nuthatch may be found with warblers in summer. There is also a herd of fallow deer. The coast path leads round to Rame Head, where linnets, stonechats and the occasional Dartford warbler may be found in the coastal gorse. This is a very good spot for migrants and seabird passage at the right time of year.

Location: on peninsula across sound from

Plymouth, reached by pedestrian ferry from Stonehouse, Plymouth or by road as for St John's Lake.
Access: open daily all year. Information centre. Refreshments.
Map reference: SX454524

3. Warleigh Point Nature Reserve

Upstream from the Tamar Bridge, the river becomes more sheltered, with woodland reaching right down to the tideline. At Warleigh Point, near the confluence of the Tamar and Tavy, the Devon Trust for Nature Conservation has a woodland reserve with attractive views over the estuary. At low tide, waders such as redshanks, curlews and oystercatchers are likely to be seen on the mud flats.

Location: north of Plymouth, reached on B3373 through Tamerton Foliat. Beyond railway line.
Access: via lay-by.
Map reference: SX445610

4. Weir Quay

Situated at the top end of the Tamar Estuary, Weir Quay is renowned for the presence of a very large wintering flock of avocets. Between late October and February up to 100 of these elegant waders can be seen feeding near the edge of the tideline. Other waders which may be seen on the upper estuary include redshanks, curlews and greenshanks.

Location: north of Plymouth, reached on unclassified roads west of A386.
Map reference: SX433649

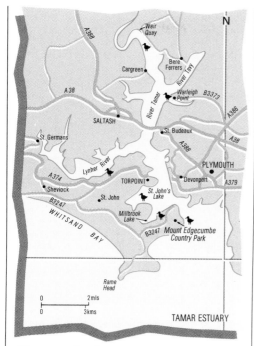

TAMAR ESTUARY

Tamar Lakes

Devon/Cornwall

Both these lakes were originally constructed as reservoirs, but the lower lake is no longer used for this purpose and is now a nature reserve. They lie directly on the Devon and Cornwall border in an area with relatively little open fresh water and so attract a range of wildfowl in winter, including all three

species of sawbill. Waders include green and common sandpipers, and spotted redshanks and ruffs drop in on passage.

Location: north-east of Bude on unclassified roads from A39.
Access and facilities: access to shoreline and paths. Car park. Bird hide on lower lake.
Map reference: SX295110

Taw and Torridge Estuary

Devon   RSPB

This twin estuary of the rivers Taw and Torridge is the only one on the north Devon coast. It has extensive sand banks and mud flats at low tide, and at its mouth there are large dune systems on both sides.

A wide variety of waders can be found, with curlews and ringed plovers particularly numerous. Among the wildfowl, shelducks are likely to be found throughout the year, with brent geese in winter, but of special interest is the presence of eiders. They are usually near the estuary mouth and a small flock of immature birds remains into the summer. As the only estuary in the area, it is attractive to birds of prey, and peregrine falcons are regular outside the breeding season; ravens are also much in evidence. The RSPB reserve at Isley Marsh is mainly salt marsh often frequented by redshanks and greenshanks. It can be easily viewed from the pathway along the converted railway. The dune systems at the mouth of the estuary are also good for birds – especially sanderlings along the tideline. The dunes also have a rich sand flora, with several

species of orchid in late spring. Braunton Burrows is a National Nature Reserve; Northam Burrows is a country park with an information centre and visiting facilities.

Location: west of Barnstaple; bordered by A39 and A361.
Access: Braunton Burrows is reached on unclassified roads from Braunton. Isley Marsh is adjacent to path along disused railway on south side of Torridge. Northam Burrows is off A386 Northam Road, north of Westward Ho!
Map reference: SS475315

Thorburn Museum

Cornwall

A collection of wildlife paintings by Archibald Thorburn is exhibited in an original setting here. He is regarded as one of the pioneering wildlife artists. Many of the vast canvases are displayed, with their game birds, golden eagles and red deer placed in dioramas depicting the remote glens and pine forests where they are normally found. The theme park has a range of other attractions for the whole family including a superb forest railway.

Location: at Dobwalls Theme Park, signposted off A38 at Dobwalls west of Liskeard.
Access: open daily (admission charge). Toilets, car park and refreshments.
Map reference: SX213658

Braunton Burrows – a superb area of dunes and tidal sand. The inset picture is of a sanderling

Weymouth and Portland Area

Dorset

This part of south Dorset possesses outstanding birdwatching localities, all within a few miles of one another, making it an excellent base.

1. Radipole Lake   RSPB

From the information centre at the entrance to this RSPB reserve, part of the tidal lagoon and reed beds can be viewed through the panoramic observation window. Many of the reserve's birds can be seen from the centre in comfortable conditions during poor weather. Level footpaths lead through the reed beds to hides (one for members, two public) overlooking various parts of the lake, where many of the reserve's birds can be seen. The hides are easily accessible to wheelchairs and a tap rail and listening posts also assist disabled visitors. Extensive reed beds support breeding populations of reed, sedge, and grasshopper warblers in spring and summer, and Cetti's warblers and bearded tits are usually present all year and often easier to see here than elsewhere. Many of the water birds are fairly tame because of the regular presence of visitors, and species such as teal, shoveler, cormorant and great crested grebe can often be viewed at very close range. In spring, the early arrivals often include garganey, while in autumn the evening roosts attract many swallows and yellow wagtails. Many scarce visitors arrive here, and together with coots, water rails and mute swans, with a selection of gulls, the sheer variety makes for an exciting visit at almost any time of year.

Location: in Weymouth. Reserve information centre and entrance beside Swannery car park, signposted from seafront.
Access and facilities: open at all times; information centre open daily April–September and at weekends October–March; charge for adjacent car parking, where toilets are available (also includes Lodmoor car park).
Map reference: SY677796

2. Lodmoor   RSPB

Grazing marsh and pools with fringing reed beds make up most of this reserve. In winter the fields are often flooded, attracting large numbers of wildfowl, including teal, wigeon, shoveler, pintail and shelduck. The proximity of nearby rubbish tips is increasing the numbers of wintering gulls on the pools, and scarcer species often include glaucous and Mediterranean gulls. Migration periods attract many rarities, especially waders, including ruff and occasional avocets, Temminck's and little stints, with the possibility of even scarcer species. Breeding birds include reed, sedge and grasshopper warblers, reed buntings, bearded tits and Cetti's warblers in the reed and scrub. Lapwings, redshanks and yellow wagtails breed on the wet meadows.

Location: behind beach road on north-east side of Weymouth.
Access and facilities: from car park at Lodmoor Country Park on A353 Wareham road. Access at all times to perimeter path and hides. Toilets. Parking charge.
Map reference: SY686807

Portland Bill – a place where rarities often turn up

3. Ferrybridge

Where it enters Portland Harbour the Fleet is tidal and the mud flats here often attract waders, including dunlins, redshanks, grey and ringed plovers and bar-tailed godwits. Portland Harbour, on the opposite side of the road, has red-breasted mergansers and goldeneyes, with Slavonian grebes and divers in winter and terns in summer.

Location: off A354 between Weymouth and Portland.
Access: large car park near bridge crossing Fleet entrance and Portland Harbour.
Map reference: SY667760

4. Portland Bill

The 'Bill' extends six miles out into the English Channel and is an outstanding sea watching point and migration landfall spot. The old lighthouse is a bird observatory with accommodation for enthusiasts. As the first landfall for migrants after crossing the English Channel, it has a high reputation for the birds which can be found – from warblers and chats to swallows and martins. Rare birds are frequent, with overshooting birds from the south in spring including such species as hoopoe and golden oriole. Spring seabird passage is often good, with gannets and kittiwakes usually seen and a good sea watch could include Manx shearwaters, and arctic and pomarine skuas. Seabirds breed on the west side of the Bill and can be observed flying out to sea from the tip; they include guillemots and razorbills.

Location: follow 'Portland A354' signs from Weymouth.
Map reference: SY677684

5. Abbotsbury Swannery

Britain's largest colony of breeding mute swans lives here. Visitors can view the nesting swans and their cygnets at close quarters in their protected pens. Adjacent reed beds provide nest sites for moorhens and reed and sedge warblers.

In winter, when the swannery is closed, the Fleet attracts large numbers of wildfowl, especially wigeon. The eelgrass that is found in the Fleet also attracts an increasing number of dark-bellied brent geese. Wintering wildfowl can be viewed from various points on the northern shore.

Location: at Abbotsbury, signposted from B3157 Weymouth to Bridport road.
Access: open May–September daily. Admission charge.
Map reference: SY575841

Willsbridge Mill

Avon

This water mill, set in the sheltered Willsbridge Valley, has been converted into a visitor centre by the Avon Wildlife Trust. It houses a series of displays on the wildlife of the county of Avon and the work of the Trust and is set in pleasant grounds where ponds and other habitats are managed to encourage wildlife.

Location: south-eastern outskirts of Bristol at Willsbridge, just off A431.
Access: open daily.
Map reference: ST664706

South & South-East England

Starling

Despite the urban and suburban character of large parts of this region, there are many exciting birdwatching sites here. They include reservoirs such as Abberton and Tring, and gravel pits such as those at Theale. More 'natural' places include the New Forest, Chichester Harbour and Old Hall Marshes

South and South-East England

Useful addresses

RSPB Headquarters: The Lodge, Sandy, Bedfordshire, SG19 2DL
RSPB South-East Office: 8 Church Street, Shoreham-by-Sea, West Sussex, BN4 5DQ
Many RSPB reserves have explanatory leaflets. These are often available at the reserve, but in any event the regional office, or RSPB HQ, will supply information on any reserve upon receipt of a stamped addressed envelope.

Bedfordshire and Huntingdonshire Wildlife Trust: Priory Country Park, Barkers Lane, Bedford, MK41 9SH
Berkshire, Buckinghamshire and Oxfordshire Naturalists' Trust (BBONT): 3 Church Cowley Road, Rose Hill, Oxford, OX4 3JR
Essex Naturalists' Trust: Fingringhoe Wick Nature Reserve, Fingringhoe, Colchester, Essex, CO5 7DN
Hampshire and Isle of Wight Naturalists' Trust: 8 Market Place, Romsey, Hampshire SO5 8NB
Hertfordshire and Middlesex Trust for Nature Conservation, Grebe House, St Michael's Street, St Albans, Hertfordshire, AL3 4SN
Kent Trust for Nature Conservation: The Annexe, 1a Bower Mount Road, Maidstone, Kent, ME16 8AX
Surrey Wildlife Trust: Hatchlands, East Clandon, Guildford, GU4 7RT
Sussex Wildlife Trust: Woods Mill, Henfield, West Sussex, BN5 9SD
Nature Conservancy Council: South Region, Foxhold House, Thornford Road, Crookham Common, Newbury, Berkshire, RG15 8EL; South-East Region, Church Street, Wye, Ashford, Kent, TN25 5BW
Wildfowl Trust: Slimbridge, Gloucestershire, GL2 7BT
Woodland Trust: Autumn Park, Dysart Road, Grantham, Lincolnshire, NE31 6LL

Abberton Reservoir

Essex

Thousands of wintering wildfowl are attracted to Abberton, as is a wide variety of passing waders and terns, making it one of the country's top reservoirs for birds. This huge expanse of water (over 1,000 acres) can be as bleak and open on a cold winter's day as the nearby coast. Early in the year, sheer numbers can be most impressive. Wigeon (in surrounding fields as well as on the water), mallards and tufted ducks may run into thousands, and there are large numbers of teal, pochard, shoveler, gadwall, pintail and coot. For an inland site the gathering of a few hundred goldeneyes is exceptional. Goosanders and smews are often present, especially in hard weather, and small numbers of ruddy ducks are a recent addition. Bewick's swans and white-fronted geese can sometimes be seen.

Black terns pass through in spring and autumn, dipping over the water with swallows, martins, swifts and sometimes little gulls. Rafts of pochards, coots and great crested grebes form up in late summer and early autumn, when yellow wagtails and common sandpipers hunt the edges for insects.

Of particular interest in the breeding

season is Britain's only tree-nesting colony of cormorants.

Location: 4 miles south of Colchester.
Access and facilities: much can be seen from two causeways crossed by public roads. B1026 south from Colchester to Maldon crosses one of causeways and passes nature reserve, with hide and car park.
Map reference: TL970180

Adur Estuary

West Sussex   RSPB

Shoreham offers easy edge-of-town watching of waders in autumn and winter (but little in spring and summer). The small RSPB reserve here (composed of salt marsh and mud flats) can be circled in about an

Ashdown Forest

hour, with pleasant views of town and downs and a fascinating collection of houseboats. A longer visit could take in the river northwards up to the old tollbridge passing Shoreham Airport and New Salts Farm beside the recreation ground; this is the waders' high tide roost, with a large lapwing flock, often herons and ducks, including wigeon in hard weather. Dunlins, redshanks and ringed plovers are regulars, often with grey plovers, oystercatchers and shelducks.

Location: directly west of Shoreham-by-Sea.
Access and facilities: view from south edge. Car parks north of A259 and at Beach Green; toilets.
Map reference: TQ212047

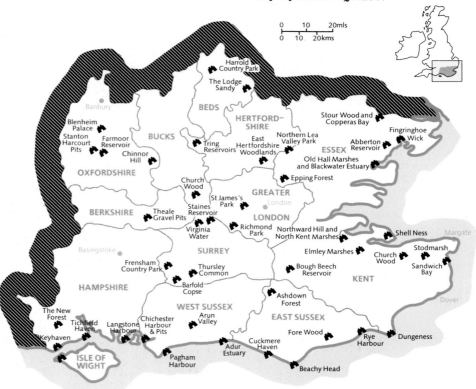

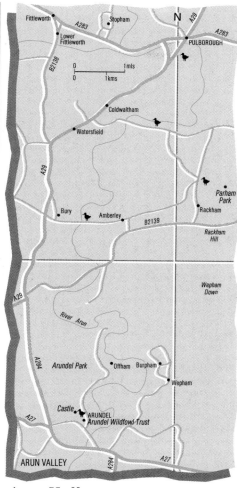

Arun Valley

West Sussex

A hundred or so wintering Bewick's swans are the valley's star attraction, with hundreds of wigeon, teal, snipe and some pintails in support. The herds of swans spend most time around Pulborough, Amberley and Waltham Brooks, but some visit sites further south, including Arundel Wildfowl Trust. Waltham Brooks (east of Coldwaltham), managed by the Sussex Trust for Nature Conservation and wet all year, is a good spot to watch wildfowl in winter; it also has breeding ducks and redshanks, with other waders on passage. For a longer walk take the footpath, often muddy, which runs north across the Wild Brooks from Amberley. As well as waterbirds, watch out in winter for hen harriers and short-eared owls. White-fronted geese, no longer regular, may turn up in bad weather. In summer, the Brooks are important for wetland plants and dragonflies; breeding snipe and yellow wagtails are now sadly scarce.

For a pleasant contrast try the woods by the car park at Rackham and then up to the public footpath across Parham Park. Birds here include woodcock, owls and woodpeckers.

Arundel Wildfowl Trust, well signposted from the attractive town with its castle, has a large captive collection of ducks, geese and swans together with viewing space, a shop and restaurant. Many wild birds visit the pools and reeds, which are overlooked by hides; some of the Trust's mandarins have left to join other water birds at Swanbourne Lake across the road in Arundel Park.

Location: between Pulborough and Arundel.
Access and facilities: to Waltham Brooks and Amberley Wild Brooks via footpaths off A29 and A284 and roads east from A29 and A284. Parham House and park open at certain times. Admission charge. Arundel Wildfowl Trust open all year. Admission charge.
Map reference: TQ035145

Ashdown Forest

East Sussex

Once a royal hunting forest, Ashdown Forest is a splendid mixture of dry, damp and wet heathland with streams, scrub and woodland.

It has a very rich heathland flora and in the wetter sites, where sphagnum mosses abound, common cottongrass, bog asphodel and round-leaved sundew grow prolifically.

The woodlands are varied and include birch, oak, willow and Scots pine, with alder and alder buckthorn growing by some of the streams. Woodland birds include blackcaps, willow warblers and nightingales, which sing in the scrubby areas. Woodcocks may be seen 'roding' at dawn and dusk, while nightjars chur and hawk after insects. Kestrels and sparrowhawks often fly over, along with the occasional hobby. The area has an important population of fallow deer, with badgers, foxes, stoats and weasels.

The wet heaths provide superb breeding sites for a variety of dragonflies, and the forest as a whole is very good for butterflies such as silver-studded blues, graylings, dark green, pearl-bordered, small pearl-bordered and silver-washed fritillaries. Emperor moths can be found in the heathland areas.

Location: east of A22, approximately 4 miles south-east of East Grinstead.
Map reference: TQ432306

Barfold Copse

Surrey   RSPB

Part of a larger block of woodland, Barfold Copse consists principally of oak with an understorey of outgrown hazel coppice. Like most woodlands of its kind, it is home to a good cross-section of woodland birds, including nuthatches, robins and several species of tit. Wild daffodils are the stars of the woodland flora here, while golden-banded dragonflies and white admiral butterflies are particularly notable among the regular insect inhabitants.

Location: ½ mile east of Haslemere, off B2131 Haslemere to Godalming road.
Access: park at second turning (from Haslemere) to Blackdown. Follow public footpath and track to reserve. Keep to woodland paths. Keep clear of derelict buildings.
Map reference: SU914324

Arun Valley – watermeadow at Amberley Wild Brooks

Beachy Head

East Sussex

The white cliffs of Beachy Head provide a vantage point to watch offshore migration of seabirds, waders and wildfowl. Its prominence also makes it a gathering place for migrant landbirds. Sea watching from Birling Gap is usually best in March, April and May, often in the early mornings. Some days produce very little, but on the better days the birds passing up-channel may exceed a hundred per hour; light south-east winds are favourable. Most numerous are common and arctic terns, common scoters and bar-tailed godwits. Sandwich terns and divers are regular; there are sometimes black terns, little gulls and skuas, including pomarine in the first half of May.

Migrant warblers, chats and other passerines can be found in spring. A few nightingales and stonechats breed and there are fulmars on the cliffs. On autumn mornings search fields, scrub and trees for migrants. Warblers in large numbers provide the staple catch in the mist nets of a ringing group which operates in Whitebread Hollow, just south of Eastbourne. Please do not disturb this area when ringing is in progress. Wheatears, yellow wagtails, swallows and martins are numerous, redstarts and pied flycatchers regular; scarcer birds include dotterels, wrynecks and tawny pipits. In late autumn a yellow-browed or even Pallas's warbler might just turn up among the goldcrests and few firecrests which specially like the little wood near Belle Tout. Look out too for birds of prey; among those that might be seen are buzzards, hobbies and harriers.

Location: south-west of Eastbourne.
Access and facilities: along unclassified road leading south from East Dean, along clifftop and back to B2103 on edge of Eastbourne. Parking and toilets at Birling Gap (National Trust); additional parking at Belle Tout, ³/4 mile to east. Footpath along clifftop forms part of South Downs Way.
Map reference: TV595955

Blenheim Palace

Oxfordshire

Built by the Duke of Marlborough in the 18th century, and birthplace of Sir Winston Churchill, the palace is a splendid and historic building surrounded by a fine park. There are lakes, lawns, formal gardens, expansive pastures and varied woodland, making the whole area a very attractive one and good for birds.

While the non-birdwatching members of the family enjoy a picnic overlooking the lake, or a walk around the gardens, or an afternoon in the Palace itself, the bird seeker can explore. Unfortunately, the once magnificent avenue of elms has been totally lost due to disease, but there are still many specimen trees, stands of big conifers, and free-standing oaks in the meadows and natural oak woodland with rich undergrowth.

The lake has great crested grebes, coots, moorhens and Canada geese in summer and pochards, tufted ducks, teal, shovelers and gadwalls arrive in the autumn — a few

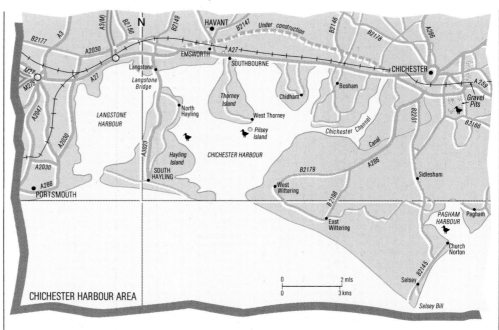

CHICHESTER HARBOUR AREA

gadwalls nest, too, the only ones to do so in the county. There is often a grey heron or a kingfisher and the bridge provides a feeding place for grey and pied wagtails. In summer the lakeside reeds are excellent for reed warblers. The woodland has woodpeckers, nuthatches, treecreepers, coal tits, goldcrests and the chance of a crossbill, and in winter flocks of chaffinches with a few bramblings often mixed with them under the beeches. Hawfinches might also be seen.

Location: off A34, 6 miles north of Oxford.
Access and facilities: from Woodstock village. Open daily mid March to end October. Car park. Toilets. Refreshments.
Map reference: SP440160

Bough Beech Reservoir

Kent

The north-eastern part of this 315-acre reservoir is a reserve managed by the Kent Trust for Nature Conservation. Birds have been encouraged here by the provision of shallow pools and nesting islands, resulting in a list of some 60 species that breed regularly and a great many more that visit.

Among the breeding birds are great crested grebes, shelducks and tufted ducks, while mallard and teal are the most common wintering wildfowl. Waders seen here include greenshanks and sandpipers, with the spotted redshank an uncommon visitor for the lucky birdwatcher. Other unusual birds that have been recorded here include garganey, osprey and red-necked phalarope.

Reserve land adjacent to the reservoir includes some woodland.

Location: 5 miles south-west of Sevenoaks, 3¹/2 miles north-east of Edenbridge.
Access and facilities: viewable only from public roads from Coopers Corner or Winkhurst Green to Bough Beech. No access to lake margins. Information centre (south of Winkhurst Green) open Easter to October, Wed, Sat and Sun. Car park.
Map reference: TQ495489

Beachy Head – the view at Birling Gap

Chichester Harbour and Pits

West Sussex

Together with Langstone Harbour, which adjoins it to the north-west. Chicester Harbour forms one of the largest areas of estuarine mud flats on the south coast of Britain. The massive complex of tidal flats and saltings is of national and international importance to wintering wildfowl and waders. Hence, the best time to visit is autumn and winter.

Dark-bellied brent geese, regularly numbering over 5,000, feed on eelgrass here, having flown in from Arctic Russia and Siberia. There may be as many as 20,000 dunlins at any one time and up to 1,000 knots – the largest south coast flock. Extremely large numbers of redshanks, curlews, bar-tailed and black-tailed godwits,

grey plovers, sanderlings and up to 100 greenshanks may be present at times, with several thousand shelducks, wigeon, mallards, pintails and teal, with goldeneyes and red-breasted mergansers diving in the channels. Slavonian grebes spend the winter months here, while black-necked grebes can be seen on passage. In severe weather pochards and tufted ducks fly in from the inland pits and a flock of white-fronted geese may pay a visit.

Breeding birds include common and Sandwich terns, together with ringed plovers, redshanks and shelducks. The area also boasts the only Sussex breeding colony of black-headed gulls. There is a good population of reed buntings and two of the nearby woodlands house noisy heronries.

A variety of small migrants may be seen outside the breeding season and merlins,

harriers and short-eared owls often fly over.

The best wildfowl are seen at Thorney Deep and the best wader roost is at Pilsey Island – both these spots can be observed from footpaths on Thorney Island.

Chichester's disused gravel pits are of most interest during autumn and winter, when a wide variety of ducks can be seen, and there may be more than 6,000 roosting sand martins.

Location: harbour is 5 miles west of Chichester, off A27 or A286 and B179. Pits are on east side of Chichester.
Access: by public footpaths.
Map reference: SU775005

Chichester Harbour – dark-bellied brent geese gather here in large numbers in winter

Chinnor Hill

Oxfordshire

A reserve of the Berks, Bucks and Oxon Naturalists' Trust, Chinnor Hill consists largely of chalk scrub with woodland and some grassland. The varied cover means it is a good place for an interesting range of birds throughout the year.

The berry-bearing shrubs provide food for fieldfares, redwings and other thrushes in the winter. They also attract other winter migrants. In the summer, quail are often present as are turtle doves, chiffchaffs, willow warblers, garden warblers, lesser whitethroats and blackcaps. Corn buntings, yellowhammers and linnets are present all year round.

There is a fine range of lime-loving trees here, including wayfaring-tree, whitebeam and yew, with scrub species which include juniper, and lovely grassland flowers.

Location: south-east of Chinnor between Chinnor and Bledlow Ridge.
Access and facilities: open. Car park. Nature trail.
Map reference: SP766002

Church Wood

Buckinghamshire `RSPB`

This mixed broadleaved wood is unusual among RSPB reserves in having no warden, but being managed by the Society's great support – volunteers. Along the marked paths a good range of birds can be seen, including all three species of woodpecker, nuthatches, tits, turtle and stock doves, blackcaps and garden warblers.

The mixture of mature trees, including beech, oak and ash, as well as alder and hazel coppice, helps to ensure the diversity of species here. This includes such butterflies as white admiral and purple hairstreak. The reserve also has an interesting variety of plants, among which are butcher's broom and green helleborine. The tiny muntjac deer is sometimes seen here.

Location: 5 miles north of Slough, on outskirts of Hedgerley.
Access: RSPB reserve signposted down farm track in Hedgerley village. No restrictions, but when parking keep to side of track to allow farm traffic to use the private road.
Map reference: SU968873

Church Wood, Blean

Kent `RSPB`

The RSPB's Church Wood reserve is part of a large and important spread of woodland around Canterbury. The best habitats for wildlife are where oak is the dominant tree; and about half of the woodlands are oak, including the majority of Church Wood. There are patches of beech and birch in the reserve; chestnut coppice and conifer plantations remain from previous commercial production, now replaced by careful management to improve conditions for wildlife.

May is a good time to walk the woodland paths and enjoy the songs of nightingales – a local speciality – blackcaps, willow and garden warblers and tree pipits. There are woodpeckers, tits and nuthatches, and three species scarce in the county – redstart, wood warbler and hawfinch.

Location: north-west of Canterbury between A290 and A2.
Access and facilities: open at all times. Down track on north-east side of road through Rough Common. Nature trails. Car park.
Map reference: TR126593

Cuckmere Haven

East Sussex

Seven Sisters Country Park and Seaford Head Nature Reserve make up the area around Cuckmere Haven. The reserve is owned jointly by East Sussex County Council and Lewes District Council. Only three of the Seven Sisters – sheer white cliffs topped by a close green turf – lie within the country park.

The Haven itself is a wide meadow valley where old river meanders form pools beside the new straightened course of the River Cuckmere. A shingle bank, formed mainly from flints which have been washed out of the chalk, has been thrown up in the Haven's mouth. Behind it lies a lagoon with islands which provide nesting sites for ringed plovers and common terns. The lagoon and the marshland beyond are good feeding areas for migrants and winter wildfowl.

Fulmars, herring gulls and jackdaws nest on the cliffs; meadow pipits and skylarks nest on the grassland. The scrub, particularly on Seaford Head, provides a rich habitat for small birds. The western side of the reserve is capped with glacial deposits of sand and mud deep enough to allow dense scrub to develop, providing important shelter for many migrants.

Stonechats are resident, and spring brings chiffchaffs, common and lesser whitethroats, grasshopper and willow warblers, blackcaps, redstarts and a host of other passage birds. Ring ouzels and pied flycatchers pass through on their way to the moors and western woodlands, while more uncommon visitors may include bluethroats, ortolan buntings, red-breasted flycatchers, hoopoes and wrynecks.

The Haven is a welcome resting place for migrants on their return passage in the autumn. Waders using the river as a migration route may pause to feed on the marshes or visit the lagoon and river, where grey herons, cormorants, mute swans and shelducks are commonly seen.

During winter other water birds such as little grebe, mallard, teal, tufted duck and wigeon turn up. Wintering twites can be seen occasionally.

It is an area of contrasts – above Seaford Head the soil conditions are acid enough for emperor and oak eggar moths and on the downland it is chalky enough for chalkhill blue butterflies. All this helps to make it a fascinating place throughout the year with a mixture of superb habitats for a variety of wildlife.

Location: 6 miles west of Eastbourne off A259. Access and facilities: country park open all year; other areas reached on public footpaths. Information centre. Car park. Map reference: TV519995

Cuckmere Valley

Dungeness

Kent   RSPB

The ridges of Dungeness have been made by the sea steadily depositing shingle to build beach after beach – a strange, hard landscape extending windswept Romney Marsh out into the Channel. It is an important migration point and has birdwatching interest all year round.

In winter the flooded gravel pits on the RSPB reserve hold plenty of ducks and have become a regular site for the scarce and attractive smew. Grebes and occasional divers turn up, and there is often a herd of Bewick's swans in the nearby fields. Look out for hunting hen harriers and merlins.

With the wheatears and chiffchaffs of early spring come small numbers of ring ouzels, firecrests and black redstarts. A few pairs of wheatears stay to breed in the shingle; black redstarts at the power station. The many other migrants include occasional hoopoes. Seabird passage can be very impressive with brent geese and ducks, waders – especially bar-tailed godwits – and various seabirds. The 'patch' of warm water outflow from the power station attracts seabirds, so this can be a place to pick out black terns, little gulls, a Mediterranean gull or roseate tern.

The islands of Burrowe's Pit hold hundreds of breeding black-headed gulls and common terns and a few common gulls – the only ones regularly nesting in England. There are great crested grebes, oystercatchers, tufted ducks and ringed plovers too.

With waders, terns and other water birds on the pits, land birds in the patches of scrubby cover and seabirds offshore, autumn brings great numbers and variety of birds. Wrynecks, bluethroats and tawny pipits are possible, and Dungeness turns up real rarities every year.

Location: east of Rye, on unclassified road signposted to Dungeness Peninsula from Lydd. Access and facilities: at Boulderwall Farm track to right leads to RSPB reserve. Parking, toilets and information centre. Hides on reserve overlook flooded Burrowe's Pit and there is trail (with leaflet) round edge. Admission charge to non-members. 9am to 9pm (or sunset), closed Tue.

To reach Dungeness Bird Observatory and sea watching 'patch' continue to old lighthouse. Observatory is nearby in old coast-guard cottage. Map reference: TR063196

East Hertfordshire Woodlands

Hertfordshire

This is a major area of woodland, stretching almost continuously between Potters Bar and Hoddesdon, and very close to the M25 and A10. Much of it is still ancient broadleaved forest, particularly of oak and hornbeam.

A good selection of warblers can be seen, including wood warblers, willow warblers, chiffchaffs and blackcaps. Woodcock can be seen 'roding' on summer evenings, which are also the best times to hear nightingales. Great and lesser spotted woodpeckers, tree-creepers, marsh tits and long-tailed tits are frequent. Redstarts breed in some years, and hawfinches might be seen in the treetops. Open areas attract grasshopper warblers, with many finches around the edges. Redpolls are numerous in winter.

Access details for three areas within this complex of woodlands are given below.

Location: north-east of Potters Bar.
1. Access: Northaw Great Wood Country Park, off 'The Ridgeway' between Cuffley and Brookmans Park. Car park. Trails.
Map reference: TL282038
2. Access: Bencroft Wood, off White Stubbs Lane, from A1170 in Broxbourne.
Map reference: TL333065
3. Access: Broxbourne Woods, south of Brickendon, off Cock Lane from A1170 in Hoddesdon.
Map reference: TL324071

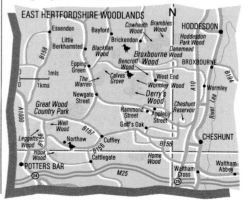

Elmley Marshes

Kent · RSPB

The marshes of North Kent and the Isle of Sheppey, a most important area of rough grazing, with creeks and ditches, have been greatly reduced by drainage and conversion to arable farmland. At Elmley the RSPB has reversed the trend by raising the water level on the marshes. Large lagoons have been created and can be kept wet all year round. Cattle are moved about the grassland to keep the vegetation at the different levels favoured by different birds for feeding and nesting. The improvement for wildlife has been dramatic.

For sheer numbers of birds, midwinter is best. Wrap up well – between hides this place is wide open to the weather! Ducks are present in thousands, sometimes tens of thousands, with wigeon above all, but also mallard, teal, shoveler, pintail, gadwall, pochard and tufted duck. Sheppey's white-fronted geese are often on the reserve, using it frequently as a roost site. Many waders, including curlew, redshank, dunlin, grey and ringed plovers, flock onto the lagoons when high tide covers the rich mud flats of the Swale. Look out for short-eared owls and hen harriers, merlins, and with luck a peregrine. Wader migrants come in fine numbers and variety; there may be little gap between spring and autumn movements, with spotted redshanks in breeding plumage in June and July. Marsh and occasionally Montagu's harriers pass through and there are rarities every year.

Avocets have recently started nesting here. Redshank and lapwing, mallard, shoveler and pochard breed in good numbers. Elmley retains the atmosphere and freedom of coastal birdwatching under big marshland skies, while providing grandstand views of water birds in great numbers and variety from the hides. It is already a top reserve and future management will make it better still.

Location: on southern edge of Isle of Sheppey, approached from A249, 1 mile north of Kingsferry Bridge, down farm track for about 2 miles.
Access and facilities: footpath leads to hides from car park (elderly and disabled visitors may drive nearer hides). Information centre. Toilets. Open from 9am to 9pm or sunset if earlier (closed Tue).
Map reference: TQ926705

Epping Forest

Essex

Queen Victoria gave the Forest to her people of London, and their descendants make great recreational use of it. For wildlife and the naturalist this popularity can present problems, and keen birdwatchers will try to avoid the busiest spots and times.

In different parts the Forest may be predominantly beech or hornbeam – much of it pollarded – or oak. There are patches of birch, thorn scrub, and open plains, glades and slopes. Streams cut through, there are a number of ponds and a lake, Connaught Water, is very popular but attractive to water birds too, including nesting great crested grebes. The Forest has lately gained

Epping Forest – in Great Monk Wood

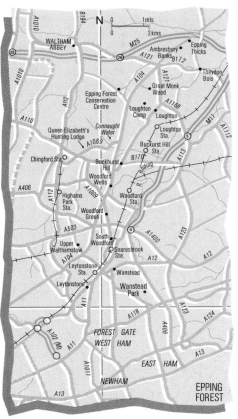

Great spotted woodpecker

breeding mandarins.

Typical woodland species include the three species of woodpecker, nuthatches, treecreepers, tits and finches. The commoner warblers breed with a few nightingales and a very few redstarts.

In winter, redpolls may be joined in the birches by siskins, and large flocks of chaffinches and greenfinches should be checked for bramblings. Hawfinches are shy residents, not easy to watch, but sometimes seen in flocks. They like especially the hard seeds of hornbeam. The Forest's fallow deer are the dark undappled form; they are not tame as in many parks, and can take some finding.

Location: north of Woodford and Chingford on either side of A104.
Facilities: Queen Elizabeth's Hunting Lodge, with museum, near Chingford on A1069. At High Beach, signposted west off A104, Epping Forest Conservation Centre has display area, and educational and scientific activities. Open all year (weekends only November to Easter).
Map reference: TQ397951

Farmoor Reservoirs

Oxfordshire

In spring and autumn these two water supply and river regulation reservoirs near Oxford can attract migrants, the waders variable according to water levels, and in winter wildfowl feed there and gulls roost every night.

The reservoirs are concrete-sided, but set in an area of damp meadows with some trees. They are separated by a causeway, which is a public footpath and gives excellent views. The River Thames runs immediately to the west of them and its valley is well worth exploring, especially in summer.

In winter the gull roost reaches over 10,000 in total, with black-headed being most abundant, but the presence of herring and lesser black-backed gulls also attracts the odd glaucous gull – something to spend time searching for before it gets dark!

Wildfowl include a notable concentration of goldeneyes each winter, and wigeon may reach 1,000 birds. In cold spells all kinds of ducks are possible, with records of smew, long-tailed duck and scoters. Grebes include occasional Slavonian and black-necked and even a great northern diver may appear. Grey herons and cormorants are almost bound to be seen and always provide interesting birdwatching.

Waders on migration include common sandpipers, dunlins and ringed plovers, with several other species possible. Autumn also provides exciting watching in the form of vast roosts of swallows and martins, often attracting a hunting hobby.

Location: west of Oxford, south of B4044 and west of B4017.
Access: main entrance is from B4017 ½ mile from junction at beginning of causeway, which provides excellent views (telescope recommended). Gatehouse issues the essential permit, for which there is a small charge, either for year or for day. Toilets.
Map reference: SP450064

Fingringhoe Wick

Essex

Fingringhoe Wick is a show place reserve and headquarters of the Essex Naturalists' Trust, complete with interpretive centre, observation tower, nature trails and hides, and is an ideal choice for a family day out at any time of year. It is set beside the Colne Estuary with views of mud flats and salt marshes, but it also has fresh-water pools, scrub and woodland. So, as well as winter wildfowl, including brent geese, and waders, there are resident kingfishers and great spotted woodpeckers, and plenty of summer warblers. It is a noted site for nightingales' song in May.

Location: south of Colchester. From Abberton, on B1025, follow unclassified roads signposted Fingringhoe, and then follow signs South Green, to reach entrance track leading to car park.
Access and facilities: open daily except Mon (but at Bank Holidays open Mon), 9am–7pm summer, 9am–4.30pm winter. Information centre. Hides. Nature trails.
Map reference: TM041195

Frensham – reed beds around both the Great and Little Ponds attract many birds, including nesting reed warblers

Fore Wood

East Sussex   RSPB

Fore Wood is an RSPB reserve whose undulating (sometimes muddy) circular nature trails (with leaflet) pass through attractive woodland. The wildlife interest is steadily being improved by management. Many woods in the Weald of Sussex have survived because they were difficult to clear and cultivate. Virtually all had once been used for timber production, including coppicing as at Fore Wood. Since 1976, wardens have revived this practice of cutting hornbeam and chestnut for poles on a rotation basis so that there are open areas recently cut, bushy areas of regrowth, and taller stands ready to be cut again. In spring the open areas are bright with wood anemones, bluebells and early purple orchids. The regrowing coppice gives cover for songbirds including nightingales, blackcaps, garden warblers, willow warblers and chiffchaffs.

Oak grows here in blocks where it is the dominant tree, and as standards (trees left to grow naturally) above the coppice. Thinning the woodland is allowing the trees that are left to grow better, and the undergrowth to develop. Chestnut is being replaced with hornbeam and oak – which have greater wildlife value. As a result the breeding birds are increasing. There are great and lesser spotted woodpeckers, six tit species, nuthatches and treecreepers, sparrowhawks and at least one pair of hawfinches. The creation of glades and rides suits the handsome white admiral butterfly, while mal-lards, moorhens, newts, frogs and dragonflies have colonised the new pond.

Location: ¼ mile north-west of Crowhurst railway station.
Access and facilities: cars should be parked at Crowhurst village hall, opposite church. The two reserve entrances are just up road. Nature trails.
Map reference: TQ756126

Frensham Country Park

Surrey

A mixture of heathland and woodland makes up Frensham Country Park. It also has two ponds – the Great and Little Ponds – which contain reed beds of bulrush, yellow iris, common reed and sweet-flag. They attract a good variety of birds, including a healthy population of reed warblers.

The area is good to visit at all times of the year. Stonechats are always present, as are woodpeckers. In the summer, visitors include garden, willow, wood and reed warblers, whitethroats, lesser whitethroats, redstarts and nightingales. The autumn and winter bring buzzards and possibly a great grey shrike if you are lucky.

It has a range of dry heath with heather, bell heather, bracken, gorse, western gorse, birch and Scots pine. There is also an area of wet heath characterised by purple moor-grass, sphagnum mosses and plants such as bog asphodel, white beak-sedge and the amazing, insectivorous, round-leaved sundew.

Location: south of Farnham, off A287, 2 miles north of Churt.
Facilities: information centre. Nature trails. Car park.
Map reference: SU849406

Harrold Country Park

Bedfordshire

In an area with very few public footpaths, this country park offers an ideal opportunity to get close to the River Great Ouse. As well as the river, there are lakes, osier beds, meadows and woodland here, making a good mixture of habitats for a variety of birds. Breeding birds include reed and sedge warblers, but many would say that the best time to visit is winter, when there are good views of a variety of wildfowl and the chance of waders.

Location: at Harrold, 10 miles north-west of Bedford.
Access: open at all times. Information centre. Car park. Toilets.
Map reference: SP960570

Isle of Wight

The three sites described below are in the west of the island, but a variety of pleasant countryside is packed into this small area – high cliffs and tidal mud flats, river valleys, downland, oak woods and farmland. The island is well placed for observing sea-passage and seasonal migration, particularly at its southern tip, St Catherine's Point.

1. Alum Bay

This popular tourist attraction, with its cliffs of coloured sands, lies near the island's western point. Either side of the amusement park is very attractive countryside and excellent birdwatching. To the south rises West High Down, best reached by fol-

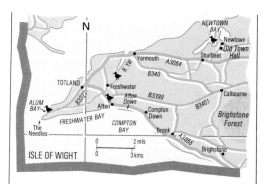

lowing the coast-guard road (no cars; minibus service in summer) to the Needles Battery and lookout. The National Trust downland has open access with wonderful views along the island coast and across to the Purbeck cliffs. Its turf and scrub are good for migrants in spring and autumn; linnets and meadow pipits breed. The 400-foot cliffs on the south side hold breeding auks, fulmar, shag, cormorant and lesser and great black-backed gulls.

To the north of Alum Bay lies Headon Warren, an area of National Trust heath. It holds tits and finches, warblers and stonechat and the south-facing heather slope is particularly good for migrants in season, such as redstarts, wheatears, ring ouzels and whinchats. Headon Hall's garden and sycamore grove are well worth exploring for migrants.

Location: extreme west of island.
Access and facilities: for Alum Bay – car park (charge). Refreshments. Toilets. For Headon Warren – follow track to Headon Hall Tea Rooms. Car park and refreshments at tea rooms.
Map reference: SZ305854

3. Newtown Estuary Local Nature Reserve

Good views across the reserve can be had from the black boat-house, just beyond the long footbridge. Walking much further is difficult because of the erosion of the old sea wall. Conditions underfoot can be very wet in winter and wellingtons are recommended. The Observation Post which stands to the east of the footbridge is usually

open and manned throughout the summer. It gives views of the 'scrape' below.

The extensive tidal mud flats hold large flocks of waders and wildfowl in winter, including golden plovers, black-tailed godwits, pintails, wigeon, shelducks and about 1,000 brent geese. In summer, little and Sandwich terns have bred.

There is a public hide on the east wall of the main marsh, approached from the car park east of the village.

Newtown village itself is full of historical interest and its Old Town Hall (National Trust) is open during the summer.

Location: on north-west coast of island, about 7 miles west of Newport off A3054.
Access and facilities: free; entrance via footpath at west end of village, signposted to Newtown Quay. Hide free. Free parking. Observation Post key from Reserve Centre in village. Parking at signposted entrance. Permit for walk from hide to wood from Warden, School's Reception Centre, Newtown, IOW, PO30 4PA.
Map reference: SZ908420

2. River Yar

This shortest of rivers is best explored by parking near Yarmouth's ferry terminal and then following the nearby riverside walk. The route to the south joins the bridlepath close to the large, old mill. From here one can walk as far as legs or the island's narrow width allow; Freshwater Bay is only three miles to the south, but a shorter circular walk is possible by crossing the river by the first bridge upstream (the Causeway), passing by Old Freshwater Church, and return-

ing to Yarmouth via the signposted Freshwater Way.

In summer the extensive reed beds hold breeding sedge and reed warblers, and the thickets along the paths are good for nightingales. Wintering species include several hundred teal and wigeon, brent geese, goldeneyes, red-breasted mergansers, and grebes. Waders are best seen on the mud flats near Yarmouth; several kingfishers

spend the winter here.

Freshwater Bay's chalk stacks hold a small flock of purple sandpipers in winter.

Location: between Yarmouth and Freshwater Bay.
Access: public footpaths.
Map reference: SZ354896

Freshwater Bay – a perfect mixture of sea and chalk downland

Keyhaven

Hampshire

Keyhaven is an interesting estuary site situated immediately south of the New Forest at the mouth of the Solent near Hurst Castle. Due to changes in vegetation, there is much more exposed mud here than there used to be and the populations of waders and wildfowl have increased accordingly.

Brent geese have become established, with up to 500 feeding on the eelgrass in winter. Most of the birds use the inter-tidal area, but behind the sea wall there are a few pools and muddy fields which form a good area for flocks of wintering waders – grey plovers, black-tailed godwits, dunlins, turnstones and sanderlings. Spotted redshanks are regular, and there may also be up to 180 ruffs.

This area also attracts birds on passage. In the spring, black terns, little gulls, arctic and great skuas, common scoters and red-throated divers often visit. Autumn brings little stints, curlew sandpipers, wood sandpipers, green sandpipers, black- and bar-tailed godwits, greenshanks, grey plovers, spotted redshanks, whimbrels and ruffs. The occasional rarity, such as surf scoter and whiskered tern, has been seen. There is also a large black-headed gull colony and an important population of little terns.

There is a range of interesting wild plants here, especially near Hurst Castle.

Location: south-west of Lymington off A337, east of Milford on Sea.
Access: park at Keyhaven; track leads to sea wall. Keep to rights of way. Solent Way follows coastline either side of Keyhaven and also towards Hurst Castle. Good views from several places, including Hurst Beach.
Map reference: SZ300908

Langstone Harbour

Hampshire   RSPB

This is a most important site for wintering wildfowl and waders; its breeding colony of little terns has lately become one of the largest in Britain. It consists principally of mud flats and marshes with a few small islands. The RSPB owns a large part of the mud flats and low islands here.

Wintering brent geese approach 10,000 at times; there may be over 1,000 shelducks and wigeon and hundreds of teal. Red-breasted mergansers and goldeneyes are regular in smaller numbers and the flock of 30 or 40 black-necked grebes is the largest regular gathering in Britain; look for them at high tide from the top of Hayling Island.

Breeding birds on the low islands have increased greatly since RSPB wardens have stopped people landing by boat in summer. There are now over 100 pairs of little terns, with common and Sandwich terns, ringed plovers, oystercatchers and redshanks. There are many hundreds of waders here in winter.

Location: directly east of Portsmouth.
Access: limited to footpaths round edge. Parking available near A27/A3 roundabout (SU697056) and on Hayling Island near garage (SU718029).
Map reference: SY684045

Langstone Harbour

The Lodge at Sandy – RSPB Headquarters. The grounds form an excellent nature reserve

The Lodge, Sandy

Bedfordshire   RSPB

Headquarters of the RSPB, The Lodge is set on a wooded sandstone ridge. The land around the house forms a 100-acre nature reserve complete with nature trails which take in the gardens (look out for giant carp in the pool behind the house) and open areas of heath, as well as a variety of woodland types – oak, pine, birch – and some good specimen trees. The lake is artificial, but looks natural and there are smaller pools.

The reserve is perhaps most attractive in spring and early summer when the songs of migrants – blackcap, willow and garden warblers, and in the heathland areas tree pipits – join the resident voices. Woodpeckers, nuthatches and treecreepers nest here; there are jackdaws, stock doves, and sometimes kestrels in the quarry, and tree sparrows occupy nestboxes in the pines above (though, mysteriously, sparrow numbers are now greatly reduced). Look here and in other coniferous areas for coal tits and goldcrests.

From the hide by the lake many birds may be watched drinking and bathing. Moorhens nest, and a heron or kingfisher sometimes calls in. Winter brings siskins, redpolls and bramblings to the waterside and birches; some join tits and nuthatches at feeders around the office windows! Two four-legged animals are of special note, the little muntjac deer, well-established since a number escaped from Woburn, and the rare natterjack toad, reintroduced in 1980.

Location: one mile east of Sandy, signposted off B1042.
Access and facilities: reserve open all year 9am–9pm or sunset if earlier. Reception and shop open 9–5 weekdays, 10–5 weekends (except Christmas-Easter 12–4). Car park. Toilets. Shop. Trails. Lodge itself not open.
Map reference: TL192486

The New Forest

Hampshire

The sheer size of its heaths and woodlands, and the long history of their protection, have made the New Forest specially important among the wildlife sites of the south. It is also very popular, with car parks, picnic areas, and caravan and camping sites designed to soak up the enormous number of visitors. Given this easy access to the paths that open the Forest to walkers, the best way to enjoy birdwatching here is to take a large-scale Ordnance Survey map and use it to escape most of the tourists and explore a variety of habitats on foot. It is surprisingly easy to get away from the crowds, but bank holidays and summer weekends should be avoided. The information centre in Lyndhurst has helpful books, maps and leaflets.

The Forest was established as a royal hunting preserve by William I. Since then it has been shaped chiefly by the grazing of deer and the commoners' animals, including the famous ponies; by the cutting of timber, some for the Navy; and by the planting of enclosed woodland. It is now managed by the Forestry Commission.

A major part of the area is open heathland and grassland, with bogs in the valleys. Here men cleared the trees, and animals have prevented much regrowth. In the dry parts, rare sand lizards and smooth snakes survive, and large stretches of heather and gorse are home to stonechats and Dartford warblers. Some wetter areas, important for plants and insects, have nesting curlews.

Substantial remnants of ancient open woodland are particularly rich in wildlife (they can usually be identified on maps since they are called woods rather than inclosures). Here the oaks, beeches and hollies exhibit a full range of ages, right through to decaying wood. This means soft sites for nest-holes and a wealth of insects to feed woodpeckers, nuthatches, treecreepers, tits, redstarts and wood warblers. Churring nightjars and roding woodcocks are rewards for watching woodland edges at dusk, and this can be a good way to see badgers, foxes or deer.

The inclosures are planted woodlands. There are areas of mature oak, and conifer plantations which may hold crossbills and goldcrests, and two scarce, quite recent arrivals, siskins and firecrests.

The Forest is famous for birds of prey, with good numbers of buzzards, sparrowhawks, hobbies and kestrels. Rare honey buzzards and goshawks are much harder to see. On a fine day in early summer settle down at a viewpoint to scan a large tract of woodland and see what comes up. In winter look on the heathland for hen harriers and great grey shrikes.

The pressures on the Forest's wildlife include nest-robbing and disturbance, and some well-known sites are eroded by many feet and tripods. So, treat the Forest and its marvellous wildlife with respect, and keep to the paths.

Location: south-west of Southampton.
Access and facilities: unrestricted. Car parks in many places. Waymarked trails. Information centre in main car park at Lyndhurst.
Map reference: SU298082

Northern Lea Valley Park

Hertfordshire/Essex

The northern part of the Lea Valley Regional Park, stretching north from London along the border between Hertfordshire and Essex, contains many excellent birdwatching sites, managed to encourage wildlife and all with surfaced paths and hides.

Rye House Marsh contains examples of many wetland habitats including muddy scrapes, reed beds, willow scrub and lakes. In summer, reed and sedge warblers, reed buntings and cuckoos can be seen and there is a big colony of nesting common terns. In winter snipe, teal, kingfisher and water rail are present daily, and rarer species such as the bittern are regular visitors. The other valley sites are also rich in wetland birds and other wildlife. This is probably the most important breeding area in the south-east for tufted ducks, and great crested grebes nest on most of the pits. Hobbies are often seen overhead in summer. The scrub and woodland around Turnford and Cheshunt have willow tits and many species of warblers and finches. Hall Marsh and Amwell attract passage waders and have redshanks, lapwings and little ringed plovers breeding.

In the winter, the valley is a regular haunt of short-eared and long-eared owls, and great grey shrikes. Fisher's Green is the best place to see smew, goosander and goldeneye. Access details for five places are given below.

Location: east of A10 between Waltham Abbey and Stanstead Abbots.
1. Access and facilities: **RSPB** *Rye House RSPB Reserve – off Rye Road, 300 yards from Rye House station in Hoddesdon. Car park. Information centre. Toilets. Sat and Sun only.*
Map reference: TL385100
2. Access and facilities: Fisher's Green – off Stubbins Hall Lane, signposted Hayes Hill Farm from B194 north of Waltham Abbey. Car park. Toilets.

Lea Valley – the RSPB's Rye House Marsh reserve.

Map reference: TL376032
3. Access and facilities: Hall Marsh – between Waltham Cross and Waltham Abbey, up towpath from A121. Highbridge Street car park.
Map reference: TL374005
4. Access and facilities: Turnford and Cheshunt Pits – car park across railway from Cheshunt Station, off B176.
Map reference: TL368024
5. Access and facilities: Amwell – between Ware and Stanstead Abbots, footpaths along old railway line or towpath.
Map reference: TL375134

NORTHERN LEA VALLEY PARK

Northward Hill and the North Kent Marshes

Kent   RSPB

Britain's largest heronry is Northward Hill's main claim to fame; hard winters may reduce the total, but it can be over 200 pairs. Disturbance causes breeding failures, so the public paths do not approach too closely. The heronry is in oaks, since Dutch elm disease destroyed its previous site; elm is now regrowing as scrub. Hawthorn covers much of the reserve and needs regular thinning to keep its value for birds, which include many fine singers – nightingales, turtle doves, blackcaps and garden warblers. Woodpeckers, little and sometimes long-eared owls breed; more long-eared owls gather to roost in winter.

Bluebells make a fine show in spring, and later bramble flowers attract many butterflies. This is a top site for the scarce white-letter hairstreak.

The wood overlooks farmland and marshes beside the Thames, which can be reached by tracks to Egypt and St Mary's Bays. White-fronted geese are on the fields in winter, with brent geese and many waders along the shore. Ducks include wigeon and pintail. Hen harriers, short-eared owls and merlins hunt the area.

The sea wall along the North Kent Marshes can also be reached via Allhallows to the east, for waders at Yantlet Creek. To the west are Cliffe Pools, flooded clay pits which hold a variety of dabbling and diving ducks, and sometimes avocets, in winter.

Many wader species and terns pass through and can include the uncommon and really rare. There is still unspoilt marshland at Cliffe and Cooling, but elsewhere much has changed since Dickens set *Great Expectations* in this lonely landscape.

Location: RSPB reserve adjoins High Halstow village, off A228, Rochester to Grain road.
Access: reserve divided in two – paths accessible at all times in public section, but escorted visits only in sanctuary area, by written application to warden (Swigshole Cottage, High Halstow, Rochester, ME3 8SR). Admission charge for non-members. Car park off Northwood Avenue. Access to marshes on roads off A228 or B2000.
Map reference: TQ784559

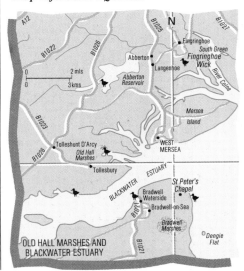

OLD HALL MARSHES AND BLACKWATER ESTUARY

Old Hall Marshes and Blackwater Estuary

Essex   RSPB

Visiting any of the East Anglian estuaries can be a memorable experience, not only for the birds, but also for the huge skies, unique light and flat landscapes dotted with pretty villages. Maldon – with its red-sailed Thames barges – is particularly attractive. Bradwell has an especially fine Saxon chapel. This coast takes the full force of the easterly winds, and these can be bitterly cold, so be prepared to wrap up well.

The whole stretch of wall along the north shore of the Blackwater provides good birdwatching. It is best known for its thousands of wintering wildfowl and waders – brent geese, shelducks, wigeon and teal, dunlins, redshanks, curlews and grey plovers. Boots and waterproofs are frequently needed on the mud flats here. Also useful are a telescope, and good timing, to avoid low tide when birds may be very distant. The estuary has good numbers of goldeneyes, some eiders and mergansers; look out for divers, Slavonian grebes and perhaps long-tailed ducks. Raptors include hen harrier, merlin and short-eared owl; there are big flocks of twites, and sometimes snow buntings.

Behind the sea wall most of the land has been drained for the growing of cereals. Old Hall is the biggest remnant of unspoiled Essex marshland complete with rough grazing, fleets, and reed beds. The typical winter birds of the Blackwater are well represented here, with Bewick's swans too. There are breeding pochards and shovelers, shelducks, redshanks, yellow wagtails and

bearded tits. Many waders pass through and marsh harriers can turn up. The RSPB bought over 1,100 acres in 1985 and leases another 442 acres. As at Elmley in Kent, the wardens are raising water levels and using cattle to manage vegetation. The potential for birds and for people is very exciting.

Location: east of Maldon, south-west of Colchester off B1026.
1. Access: Old Hall Marshes RSPB Reserve – turn east onto unclassified road from B1026 at Tolleshunt D'Arcy. After 1¼ miles turn left up private road to parking at end. Public footpaths, including surrounding sea wall, give good views (walk below the wall to minimise disturbance). Facilities are being planned. Closed Tue.
2. Access: Blackwater Estuary, north shore – footpaths east of Tollesbury village; from Goldhanger; at Heybridge Basin and from Maldon. Southern shore mouth – turn right at church in Bradwell village, park at end of road and walk past St Peter's Chapel to reach Bradwell Bird Observatory and coast.
Map reference: TL950117

Pagham Harbour

West Sussex

An expanse of tidal flats and marshes, Pagham Harbour is an excellent local nature reserve. It is a wonderful place in winter to see wildfowl and waders in fine numbers and variety. They include important gatherings of brent geese, shelducks, grey plovers and black-tailed godwits. A favourite viewpoint is the shingle spit at Church Norton. It is a short walk to the sea to scan for divers, eiders and Slavonian grebes, and along the beach to view the

The view from Old Hall Marshes – East Anglian scenery at its windswept best

reedy pools – the 'Severals'. Here, and especially in the bushes and trees at Church Norton, a good variety of small migrants turn up in spring and autumn.

Little terns nest on an island near the harbour mouth, under protection from the warden. There are shelducks, ringed plovers and oystercatchers too.

Pagham Lagoon is worth checking for smews or sea-ducks in a hard winter. Sidlesham Ferry Pool is always good, giving close views at times of godwits, ruffs, little stints, sandpipers, avocets and broods of ducklings and lapwing chicks.

Location: west of Bognor Regis.
Access and facilities: public footpaths run round edge from Church Norton via Sidlesham to Pagham. Biggest car park, with information centre and toilets, is at Sidlesham Ferry, south of Sidlesham on B2145. Hide. Also parking and access at Church Norton, off B2145, and at Pagham, (reached on B2166 from Bognor Regis) along lane west past church, or through village and right to beach past Pagham lagoon. See map on page 292.
Map reference: SZ856966

Richmond Park

Greater London

Covering an area of 2,358 acres, this is by far the largest of London's royal parks and the most interesting to the birdwatcher. It consists mostly of undulating high grassland and bracken, scattered with an estimated 200,000 trees, many of them ancient oaks.

Even though Richmond is probably the most popular recreational park in London its large size enables a good number of birds to breed each year – they become used to human disturbance. A few redstarts breed in holes in the old trees and there is a colony of jackdaws. Other breeding species include yellowhammers, chiffchaffs, willow warblers, garden warblers, blackcaps, whitethroats and spotted flycatchers. Meadow pipits breed here too, and so do tree pipits, one of the park's special birds. Kestrels can usually be seen flying over, and there are also little and tawny owls.

Great crested grebes and tufted ducks breed on the Pen Ponds; a few pairs of reed warblers breed in the dense vegetation at the southern end of the Upper Pen Pond. The occasional water rail can be seen here too. Rarities, such as black-necked grebes and great grey shrikes, have been seen in recent years on or near these ponds.

During the winter, much of the low-lying land in the park turns to marsh and attracts reed buntings, and snipe and lapwings are frequent visitors at this time. The occasional jack snipe and other more unusual waders occur now and then. Woodcocks inhabit the dense woodland and are most likely to be seen roding at dawn or dusk.

Probably the best area for birds is the Isabella Plantation, a woodland garden which is particularly good during the winter months. Blue, great and coal tits, robins, chaffinches, greenfinches and nuthatches can usually be seen. If you are patient you may also see great spotted woodpeckers, long-tailed and marsh tits, bullfinches, wrens and goldcrests. There is often a flock of redpolls in this area during the winter months. The plantation is also a good place for lesser spotted woodpeckers. You are most likely to see this shy bird in the spring, when its calls draw attention to it.

Over 100 bird species are seen in the park each year and about 60 stay to breed.

One of the main attractions is the relatively large population of fallow and red deer. The best time to see them is during the rut in October, when the bellowing and clashing of the males' antlers can be heard throughout the park. Although the deer appear to be tame, the public are advised to

leave them alone at all times. If driving within the park take extra special care – between 30 and 35 deer are killed by traffic each year.

Location: between Richmond and Kingston upon Thames.
Access: unrestricted. Reached from A305, A306, A307 or A308; also by underground, bus or train.
Map reference: TQ195725

Rye Harbour

East Sussex

Situated at the mouth of the River Rother, Rye Harbour is a reserve of East Sussex County Council and consists of foreshore, shingle, salt marsh, meadows and a gravel pit.

It is the pit, together with the shingle ridges and foreshore, that form the most interesting and important features of the site. The reserve holds a spectacular variety of bird life. In winter, large numbers of waders turn up, including dunlins, lapwings, oystercatchers, golden plovers, curlews, ringed plovers, redshanks, sanderlings and snipe. These can be seen together with good numbers of coot, mallard, pochard, shoveler, tufted duck, wigeon, eider, goldeneye, gadwall, shelduck and teal. In spring bar-tailed godwits, grey plovers, turnstones and whimbrels pay a visit on passage and summer sees the arrival of common and little terns.

Breeding species include ringed plovers, oystercatchers, redshanks, black-headed and herring gulls, little grebes, pochards, shelducks, tufted ducks, yellow wagtails and wheatears. Grey herons nest in the nearby wood and can sometimes be seen stalking their prey at the gravel pit.

Rye Harbour has other animal interest too. It is home to the introduced marsh frog, released on Romney Marsh in 1935, and to the brown-tailed moth, a characteristic south-eastern species which defoliates bramble and hawthorn.

Location: south-east of Rye on unclassified road off A259.
Access: open at all times. Keep to footpaths. Leaflet available from warden.
Map reference: TQ942190

Richmond – the Isabella Plantation

St James's Park

London

Situated within easy walking distance of Whitehall and Trafalgar Square, St James's Park is the most central of London's royal parks. It covers some 93 acres. The habitat is artificial, but an ideal one for many forms of wildlife – over 45 species of bird can be seen here.

Pochards and tufted ducks breed in the park and large numbers visit the lake to feed. Grey herons also frequent the lake.

Woodpigeons, normally very shy and wary birds, have adapted to life in this urban habitat and can be seen feeding on the crusts of bread which visitors love to bring along to feed the birds with. The house sparrows provide good entertainment – they can be attracted down by seed or breadcrumbs. A recent colonist of the park is the herring gull, another example of a bird adapting to the urban environment.

Moorhens and coots inhabit the park and breed regularly in the vegetation around the lake. Other breeding species include blue tits, song thrushes, blackbirds, robins and dunnocks. In some years chaffinches, mistle thrushes and wrens also nest here.

Canada geese often gather in large numbers around the lake. These large birds have established themselves in and around London and fly between the various parks and stretches of open water. There are probably almost 200 of them in central London.

There is a collection of ornamental water birds here, the oldest collection in London.

Location: between Buckingham Palace and Whitehall.
Map reference: TQ295795

Sandwich Bay

Kent

Sandwich and Pegwell Bays form the estuary of the River Stour, immediately south of Ramsgate. The area is ideally situated for interesting migrants and rarities. A bird observatory was founded here in 1961 and operates over 3,200 acres of privately-owned dunes and marshland.

Rarities can turn up at any time of the year, but late spring and particularly late autumn are the most likely periods.

In spring, interesting waders and terns turn up, including occasional rare ones such as gull-billed terns. Garganeys, black redstarts and firecrests arrive in March to be followed by Sandwich terns. The bulk of the passage occurs between April and May, when a number of scarce migrants have been recorded regularly, such as Kentish plover and golden oriole. Such birds, however, may only be present for a day or two – they are not guaranteed for every visit!

August brings the return of the passerine

migrants, mainly chats, warblers and flycatchers. The autumn wader passage begins in mid-July and continues through September. Birds seen regularly at this time include black-tailed godwits, wood sandpipers, curlew sandpipers, greenshanks, ruffs, little stints, chats, flycatchers and warblers. By late autumn there may be falls of goldcrests, robins, thrushes, starlings and finches arriving from the Continent to spend the winter in Britain.

Teal, wigeon, bar-tailed godwits, dunlins, redshanks and sanderlings occur in winter. Red-throated divers can be seen offshore and hen harriers and short-eared owls hunt over the marshes. Golden plovers can be found in the fields together with lapwings, and a variety of waders inhabit the mud flats. Snow buntings are regularly seen on the shore and twites can be found around the estuary.

Behind the coastal dunes lies the famous golf course and inland of that there is an area of grazing marshes intersected by dykes. Waders roost on the fields at high tide. Small areas of fresh water marsh, reed beds, bushes and trees add diversity. To the north the River Stour enters the sea at Pegwell Bay and extensive mud and sand flats and saltings surround the estuary.

Location: east of Sandwich off A256.
Access: to observatory – leave Sandwich east along Sandown Road towards Sandwich Bay Estate. Observatory is at 2 Old Downs Farm, on right shortly after toll gate (charge). Much of area is managed by Kent Trust for Nature Conservation.
Map reference: TR356593

Shell Ness

Kent

On the most easterly point of the Isle of Sheppey, Shell Ness Nature Reserve is well worth a visit at any time of the year. There are good seabird movements during the autumn, especially in strong northerly winds. Gannets, kittiwakes, great and arctic skuas, common, little and Sandwich terns are most commonly seen. Waders mass in their thousands – large flocks of oystercatch-

St James's Park – good for people and for birds

ers, bar-tailed godwits, knots and sanderlings gather to roost at high tide and can be seen feeding on the mud at low tide. They often fly on to the adjacent fields, where flocks of brent geese sometimes occur too.

In September, shelducks can be seen displaying on the inland fields where they breed. Short-eared owls glide over the fields, and hen harriers and other large raptors can regularly be seen in winter. Kestrels are quite common, and a merlin or peregrine visits occasionally.

Wheatears and whinchats occur on migration and yellow wagtails, meadow pipits, redshanks and lapwings breed.

Location: Isle of Sheppey, off B2231.
Access: from Leysdown-on-Sea carry straight on along seafront to Muswell Manor. Car park just past Muswell Manor Country Club. Part of Swale National Nature Reserve. Access restricted to certain areas, but much can still be seen.
Map reference: TR054680

Staines Reservoir

Surrey

The creation this century of reservoirs and flooded gravel pits has been one of the major changes in Britain's wildlife habitats, a great gain for birds and birdwatchers alike. Nowhere has this been more dramatic than around London, in the valleys of the Thames, the Colne and the Lea. Most London reservoirs are obviously man-made, lacking the irregular outlines and natural banks of flooded valleys elsewhere. They have plain functional shapes and concrete sides, they stand above their surroundings and catch the wind. For the urban birdwatcher, however, they are a treasure trove.

Staines Reservoir is the most famous of these waters, partly for the numbers and variety of its water birds, but also because it is the most accessible of the reservoirs, crossed by a public causeway.

In winter it holds great crested grebes, large numbers of wigeon, teal and shoveler, mallard, tufted duck and pochard. There are smaller numbers of goldeneye, goosander, gadwall and ruddy duck, sometimes smew. Look out for the occasional seaduck, diver, Slavonian or red-necked grebe.

Black-necked grebes are often present in autumn, and in both passage seasons Staines attracts waders, terns, yellow wagtails, wheatears, swallows, martins and swifts. Little gulls are chiefly autumn visitors; glaucous and Iceland gulls are winter rarities. Staines is noted for surprises.

It is not specially noted for breeding birds, but the recent provision of rafts for terns is welcome.

Location: north-east of Staines near junction of A30 and A3044.
Access: no formal arrangements for visitors, but parking possible by A3044 and public footpath crosses reservoir on causeway. This path leads to B378 at Stanwell; no path around edge of water.
Map reference: TQ050730

Stodmarsh

Kent

Extensive reed beds make Stodmarsh National Nature Reserve unique in south-east England. This habitat, as well as large lagoons and wet meadows, has developed as a stretch of the Stour Valley, undermined by old coal workings, has sunk and flooded. These features are being managed for wildlife, rather than degrading into the scrub and eventual woodland which now, in patches and fringes, add variety.

May is a favourite time, when the low boom of a bittern might be heard through the chatter of many reed and sedge warblers. If Cetti's warblers have survived the winter, their voices should be loud and clear. Listen for grasshopper warblers and perhaps the rare Savi's warbler.

On a calm day resident bearded tits are more likely to show well, and an osprey or

Stodmarsh — watery habitat for bitterns, warblers, waders and many more

Stanton Harcourt Pits

Oxfordshire

These disused and flooded gravel pits are visible from the roadside, and from public footpaths, and they give varied birdwatching all year round. They have many areas of willow thickets and reeds that are good for warblers in summer, while other shores drop abruptly into deep water. The mixture of habitats allows dabbling ducks to feed in the shallows, while tufted ducks and pochards dive in the open water from autumn to early spring. Kingfishers are worth watching for.

Location: west of Oxford. Stanton Harcourt is on B4449 south of Eynsham. Pits and River Windrush west of village.
Access: view Vicarage Pit from roadside (access off road by permit only); beyond roadside pits footpaths lead to Linch Hill and Standlake, passing close to other pools.
Map reference: SP402056

marsh harrier could drift through. With the regular teal, shovelers, tufted ducks and pochards, there could be migrant garganeys. The wet meadows have breeding lapwings, snipe, redshanks and yellow wagtails; other waders, terns, and many swifts, swallows and martins pass through.

In winter many more ducks gather here, including large numbers of wigeon and some pintails. Bewick's swans and a small flock of white-fronted geese are sometimes around and as the afternoon fades hen harriers may gather to roost.

Location: 5½ miles north-east of Canterbury, take A257 then unclassified road to Stodmarsh.
Access: lane beside Red Lion in Stodmarsh leads to reserve car park. Raised path crosses reserve to River Stour and on to Grove Ferry.
Map reference: TR221605

Stour Wood and Copperas Bay

Essex   RSPB

Stour Wood is chiefly sweet chestnut coppice which is cut by rotation to keep its wildlife value. Trees left to grow on as 'standards' include oaks and other species which give variety. All three species of woodpecker are here, with nightingales and warblers in summer. Whitethroats and reed warblers breed in scrub and reed beds by the estuary.

The wood is important for butterflies, including white admirals, and moths; management provides them with sunny clearings. After the spring carpets of wood anemones and bluebells, bramble and honeysuckle flowers attract the insects; honeysuckle bark provides local dormice with their favourite nesting material.

The shallow and attractive River Stour is internationally important in winter for several species of wader and wildfowl. Copperas Bay is a favourite area and the hides afford good viewing. Up to 1,000 black-tailed godwits make this estuary a major site for these elegant Icelandic visitors. Dunlins and redshanks run into thousands, and there are hundreds of grey plovers and curlews. The wildfowl include thousands of wigeon, hundreds of pintails and brent geese. This is an important winter area for shelduck, with a good number staying to breed. A popular feature further up the river is the herd of mute swans which can be seen around Mistley.

Location: 10 miles east-north-east of Colchester.
Access: parking and entry is in Stour Wood, off B1352 Manningtree to Ramsey road, 1 mile east of Wrabness village. RSPB owns 583 acres of Copperas Bay foreshore and north part of Copperas Wood; the 134-acre Stour Wood leased from Woodland Trust. Access at all times from two waymarked paths through Stour Wood, and ½ mile down to hides overlooking bay.
Map reference: TM189309

Theale Gravel Pits

Berkshire

There are several pits in the area of Theale, many used for sailing, water-skiing or fishing. The Kennet and Avon Canal runs through this area, and its towpath can be a pleasant place to explore. It is worth seeking out quiet spots where birds are allowed to live free from disturbance.

From early autumn, when swifts and later swallows and martins concentrate over the pools and waders begin to move through on passage, to late spring, when the same species are on their return journeys, the area provides varied birdwatching. Autumn waders include common and green sandpipers, ruffs, greenshanks, dunlins and little stints, and ringed and little ringed plovers nest as well as passing through. In dry years with low water levels there are more, but if the levels are high the wader passage may fizzle out altogether. At the same time common terns, with the chance of black terns and little gulls too, call in on their way to and from their nesting areas.

There will usually be grebes, cormorants, grey herons, Canada geese, tufted ducks and a few gulls about, and it is worth keeping an eye out for kingfishers, snipe and grey wagtails. In winter, wildfowl numbers increase, with odd goldeneyes and wigeon among the commoner species. Gull roosts are worth watching carefully in case of a visiting glaucous or Iceland gull. Like most good inland water sites, there is always a chance of 'something good', from a rare grebe or a smew to a diver or rare gull.

Location: west of Reading, beside M4 between junctions 11 and 12.
Access: minor roads and lanes give good views; there are also a number of public footpaths across area.
Map reference: SY676703

Thursley Common

Surrey

Britain's southern heathland is a unique and endangered habitat, threatened by building, overgrazing, afforestation, fire – above all by failure to recognise fully why it is so precious. A fine summer's day at Thursley Common should go a long way to showing that heathland is well worth defending. Here is a lovely area of sandy heath, woodland and bog, carefully managed as a National Nature Reserve, and supporting many of the specialities of these habitats.

Along the woodland edge look out for redstarts, and listen for tree pipits. There are woodpeckers and warblers, stonechats on the heath and the scarce woodlark, which has a liking for patches regrowing after fire. Dartford warblers sometimes nest in the heather and gorse, but they come and go in Surrey as their overall population is affected by hard winters.

Thursley in winter is noted as a place to look out for two elegant hunters from the north – hen harriers and great grey shrikes.

Location: south-west of Godalming and Milford just off A3.
Access: open at all times, but keep to paths. Parking in Thursley or on Thursley – Elstead road.
Map reference: SU904410

Titchfield Haven

Hampshire

A splendid place at all times of the year this attractive Hampshire County Council reserve forms a welcome oasis of quiet between the urban sprawls of Southampton and Portsmouth. It consists of reed beds, marshes, grazing meadows and, where the shingle beach crosses the mouth of the River Meon, there is a fresh water pool surrounded by reeds which attracts a wide variety of bird species.

The meadows and marshes forming parts of the reserve are overlooked by one of the hides. Wintering wigeon feed on the meadows and the marshes are often hunted by kestrels and barn owls.

Another hide overlooks the Meon, where ducks, gulls, grey herons, coots and moorhens can be seen along with the occasional wader on the muddy, tidal shores. In recent years, a ring-billed gull has become an almost regular visitor along with glaucous and the occasional Iceland gull.

The reserve is well-known as an important wintering site for curlews, black-tailed godwits, bitterns, shovelers, mallards, teal and wigeon. Breeding birds include reed and sedge warblers, little grebes and water rails, together with a colony of bearded tits. Spring migrants include a good variety of small birds, together with curlews and greenshanks, and black, common and little terns. Autumn brings the return of spotted redshanks, common and green sandpipers, hobbies and short-eared owls.

The closeness of the reserve to the Solent means there is also the chance of seeing great crested and Slavonian grebes, divers and brent geese in the winter.

Location: on Solent, 4 miles south-west of Fareham. From B3334 take unclassified road to Hill Head then take coast road. Entrance opposite Hill Head Sailing Club car park.
Access and facilities: by permit only by prior arrangement with warden at Haven Cottage, Cliff Road, Hill Head, Fareham. Only open August to March on Fri, Sat and Sun. Guided tours. Information centre. Admission charge.
Map reference: SY533024

Tring Reservoirs

Hertfordshire

Created during the 19th century to supply the Grand Union Canal with extra water, these four reservoirs are of great value for wildlife. Among the breeding birds here are great crested grebes, pochards, shovelers, reed and sedge warblers, mute swans and Canada geese. Many species of migrants visit during the spring and autumn passages, and winter brings thousands of waders and wildfowl. Rarities are almost regular at Tring, so a visit might be very exciting. As well as birds, there are dragonflies and damselflies, an impressive list of aquatic insects, and a broad range of plants, including several species of orchid.

Location: 1 mile north of Tring.
Access and facilities: open all year, on public footpaths only. Hides. Nature trails.
Map reference: SP918137

Virginia Water – snow-laden alders by the lake

Virginia Water

Surrey

A large lake surrounded by old woodland, scrub and parkland, Virginia Water provides an opportunity to see a good variety of woodland and wetland birds. Few places so near to London can boast such rich bird-watching potential.

Its speciality is its population of mandarin ducks, introduced from the Far East. The males are splendidly coloured, but the greyish females are well camouflaged. They are often seen on the lake edge, or resting in small groups under or on overhanging branches.

Tufted ducks are present all year round, and are joined by pochards in the winter. Also present are other water birds such as mallards, great crested grebes and coots. Grey wagtails can be seen at the waterfall area.

Reed and sedge warblers clamber about in the small reed beds fringing the lake during the summer months and the woodlands are full of willow warblers with redpolls and siskins in winter. The dense understorey of rhododendrons attracts blackcaps and garden warblers. Look for crossbills, goldcrests and coal tits in the mature pine trees.

Great and lesser spotted woodpeckers can be seen in the alders and birch, and green woodpeckers are often spotted feeding in the open areas. An exceptionally wide variety of tits, finches and thrushes is present including the occasional hawfinch. Nuthatches and treecreepers can be seen on the mature trees. Kestrels are regular and in the autumn there may be a hobby.

Location: south-west of Egham, off A30.
Access: large car park just north of Wheatsheaf Hotel on A30, almost opposite junction with B389. Go through gates in fence at back of car park and make for lake.
Map reference: SY990687

Central and Eastern England

Knot

*The Norfolk coast is one of the most famous
birdwatching areas in Britain. Here are places, such
as Minsmere and Cley-next-the-Sea, that are full of
exciting birds. There are outstanding sites inland as
well: the Norfolk Broads and the Ouse Washes, and
reservoirs such as Rutland Water and Eyebrook*

Central and Eastern England

Useful addresses:

RSPB Headquarters: The Lodge, Sandy, Bedfordshire SG19 2DL
RSPB East Anglia Office: Aldwych House, Bethel Street, Norwich NR2 1NR
RSPB East Midlands Office: 12 Guildhall Street, Lincoln, LN1 1TT
RSPB Midlands Office: 44 Friar Street, Droitwich, Worcestershire, WR9 8ED
Many RSPB reserves have explanatory leaflets. These are often available at the reserve, but in any event the regional office, or RSPB HQ, will supply information on any reserve upon receipt of a stamped, addressed envelope.

Cambridgeshire Wildlife Trust: 5 Fulbourn Manor, Manor Walk, Fulbourn, Cambridge, CB1 5BN
Derbyshire Naturalists' Trust: Elvaston Country Park, Derby DE7 3EP
Herefordshire Nature Trust: 25 Castle Street, Hereford HR1 2NW
Leicestershire and Rutland Trust for Nature Conservation: 1 West Street, Leicester LE1 6UU
Lincolnshire and South Humberside Trust for Nature Conservation: The Manor House, Alford, Lincolnshire LN13 9DL
Norfolk Naturalists' Trust: 72 Cathedral Close, Norwich, Norfolk NR1 4DF
Northamptonshire Wildlife Trust: Lings House, Billing Lings, Northampton NN3 4BE
Nottinghamshire Trust for Nature Conservation: 310 Sneinton Dale, Nottingham NG3 7DN
Shropshire Trust for Nature Conservation: St George's Primary School, Frankwell, Shrewsbury, SY3 8JP
Staffordshire Nature Conservation Trust: Coutts House, Sandon, Staffordshire ST18 0DN
Suffolk Wildlife Trust: Park Cottage, Saxmundham IP17 1DQ
Warwickshire Nature Conservation Trust: Montague Road, Warwick CV34 5LW
Worcestershire Nature Conservation Trust: Hanbury Road, Droitwich WR9 7DU
National Trust Headquarters: 36 Queen Anne's Gate, London, SW1H 9AS
Nature Conservancy Council: East Anglia Office, 60 Bracondale, Norwich NR1 2BE; West Midlands Office, Attingham Park, Shrewsbury SY4 4TW
Wildfowl Trust: Slimbridge, Gloucestershire GL2 7BT

Blickling Hall

Norfolk

Owned by the National Trust, Blickling Hall is a beautiful, red-brick English country house, surrounded by formal gardens and a park with fine walks through woodlands and past a lake.

The woods have a good variety of birds, including redstarts and hawfinches, and among the waterbirds on the lake are deep water species such as great crested grebe.

Location: 2 miles north-west of Aylsham, off B1354.
Access and facilities: National Trust; open April to end October, closed Mon (except Bank Holiday) and Thu. Shop. Toilets. Refreshments.
Map reference: TG178286

Blithfield Reservoir

Staffordshire

Among the five most important reservoirs in Britain for wildfowl numbers, Blithfield has water of varying depths to suit different waterbirds and, in dry autumns, large areas of exposed mud where waders can feed.

In the autumn there are large numbers of visiting waders, especially dunlins and ringed plovers, and a chance of oddities such as osprey, little gull or a rare wader or tern. In winter, as well as 2,000–3,000 ducks including pochards, goosanders and ruddy ducks, there can be up to 20,000 roosting gulls, often including one or two glaucous or Iceland. The numbers of ruddy ducks can reach over 600, making this the biggest gathering of its kind in Europe.

The reservoir has mostly natural banks and is set in an attractive rural part of Staffordshire; broadleaved and coniferous woodlands, parkland and marshy areas of rush and reed grass add to the variety.

Location: just south of Abbots Bromley.
Access: B5013 Rugeley–Uttoxeter road crosses reservoir. West Midland Bird Club has hides on shore for its members – permit only from Miss M Surman, 6 Lloyd Square, 12 Niall Close, Birmingham, B15 3LX.
Map reference: SK058238

Blickling Hall – house and gardens

Breckland

Norfolk/Suffolk

In the heart of East Anglia, between Swaffham to the north, East Harling to the east, Bury St Edmunds to the south and Lakenheath to the west, lie the 250,000 acres of Breckland. With its low rainfall, hot summers and cold winters, and light, sandy soils, this was once an area of dry, stony plains and heathland, the haunt of strange birds such as the stone-curlew and great bustard. Here and there were beautiful meres – pools with greatly fluctuating water levels, fed by water from the underlying chalk. Fine examples of these oases still survive at the East Wretham National Nature Reserve and at Thompson Common.

Because of exploitation by man – particularly forestry and farming – only about 6,500 acres of heathland now survive, of which about one-fifth is protected as nature reserves. The special birds of the area – stone-curlews, woodlarks and wheatears (great bustards became extinct in Britain in the 19th century) – have declined with their habitat, but can still be seen in a few places, especially the Norfolk Naturalists' Trust reserve at Weeting Heath. Stone-curlews have adapted to changing circumstances to some extent by moving to breed on arable farmland, where local farmers help to protect them.

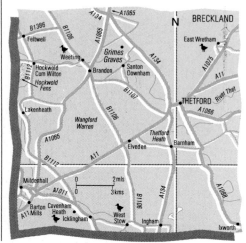

The most noticeable feature of Breckland now is the huge conifer forests – covering some 82 square miles. While the dense forests are not so valuable for birds as the original landscape, they do have their own attractions. Broadleaved trees have been planted around the forest edges where small birds flourish, and in the pines are birds such as crossbills and siskins, with nightjars in the clearings. There are lovely, easy walks along the forest rides, with always the chance of seeing a roe deer or even a red squirrel, and plenty of picnic sites, giving easy parking and access to the forest for a family day out with some good birdwatching. Four sites are described below.

1. Cavenham Heath
One of the finest acid heaths in Breckland, Cavenham is very important for its great range of plants. Damp areas around the River Lark add to the diversity of plants. Among the birds to be seen is a good range of heathland and woodland species, including linnets, tree pipits, whinchats and nightjars, jays, woodpeckers and woodcocks.

Location: 3 miles east of Barton Mills, off A1101 near Icklingham.
Access: open to nature trail and some paths, but certain areas by permit only from Nature Conservancy Council.
Map reference: TL757727

2. East Wretham Heath
A good range of Breckland habitats is found on this National Nature Reserve, including grassland, heath, scrub, woodland and two of Breckland's finest meres. When these are wet, they attract many birds, including gadwall, pochard, shoveler, goldeneye, woodcock, green and wood sandpipers – and also leeches! There are two interesting woods – one of hornbeam which has hawfinches, and ringlet and speckled wood butterflies, and another of old Scots pines, where crossbills and long-eared owls are found.

Location: 4 miles north-east of Thetford on A1075.
Access: open every day except Tue. Permits from Warden's office between 10am and 2pm.
Map reference: TL914886

3. Weeting Heath
This reserve of the Norfolk Naturalists' Trust is a remnant of old Breckland, with special plants such as rue-leaved saxifrage and many butterflies, including the Essex skipper. But its great appeal for birdwatchers is that hides here provide views of breeding stone-curlews. Since these birds are most active at night it might be best to visit as late in the day as possible!

Location: 1½ miles west of Weeting on unclassified roads to Hockwold.
Access and facilities: permits April to August from Warden's caravan. Hides.
Map reference: TL756881

4. West Stow Country Park
Set on the southern edge of Breckland, this country park has some of the heathland which once covered most of this area. Around this is a mixture of broadleaved and coniferous woodland, while one of the park boundaries is formed by the River Lark. There is also a lake. This range of habitats makes for a good mixture of birds. This is one of the places to look for gadwall; these ducks were introduced to Breckland in about 1850.

Another attraction here is a reconstructed Anglo-Saxon village; its foundations were discovered here and the buildings have been remade using appropriate skills. The original village was inundated by sand – a fate which befell many Breckland communities.

Location: 6 miles north-west of Bury St Edmunds, on unclassified road from A1101.
Access and facilities: open all year. Reconstructed village open April to October, Tue to Sat afternoon only, Sun and Bank Holiday all day. Nature trail. Picnic site.
Map reference: TL793715

Breckland – birch and conifers at Thetford Warren. Inset is a long-eared owl

Brockhampton

Hereford and Worcester

Lower Brockhampton manor house is a lovely 14th-century building with a superb 15th-century gatehouse, but the woods around the house are the attraction for naturalists. Walks here pass a small lake and through mixed woodland, where exotic trees such as cedars and Wellingtonias grow alongside oaks, and alders and willows grow in the lower, wetter parts. These damp areas are ideal for attractive plants such as hart's tongue fern and yellow archangel, and for birds such as woodcocks. The woods have a good variety of birds, ranging from pied flycatchers to buzzards and sparrow-hawks, but probably the most exciting bird to watch for at Brockhampton is the raven. On the lake, as well as mallards, you might see a little grebe – not rare but very shy!

Location: 2 miles east of Bromyard just off A44 Worcester road.
Access: National Trust – woods always open but hall of manor house only open April to October, Wed to Sat, Sun mornings and Bank Holiday Mon. Leaflets from Brockhampton Post Office.
Map reference: SO893543

Cannock Chase

Staffordshire

In such a densely populated area, Cannock Chase can be very crowded, so, for bird-watching, weekends are best avoided. However, it has much to offer anyone interested in wildlife. Originally a royal hunting forest, charcoal burning and grazing converted most of the forest to heathland, although some of the ancient forest remains, particularly Brocton Coppice (on an unclassified road between the A513 at Milford and the A34) which has old oaks, birches and hollies. The heath is beautiful in its own right, particularly in late summer when all the heathers are in bloom. The heath is crossed by damp valleys, full of moisture-loving plants such as ferns, orchids and the insect-eating sundew. Also on the heath is a fascinating plant which is a hybrid between bilberry and cowberry, sometimes called the Cannock Chase berry.

Although the Chase is good for birds all year round, a particularly enjoyable time to visit could be a summer evening, when there is a very good chance of hearing nightjars, as this is the best place in the area for this unusual bird. Winter on the heath also has its attractions, when there are often many fieldfares, birds of prey such as merlins and short-eared owls, and great grey shrikes. Ancient woods are always good for birds and these are no exception, with all three species of woodpecker, and tawny owls, but even the much newer pine forests are not without interest, especially where felling has let in light. The birds breeding in the conifers include sparrowhawks, redpolls and a few long-eared owls, and in winter there are sometimes crossbills.

Among the other very varied wildlife which finds sanctuary on Cannock Chase are several species of deer, but especially fallow, and uncommon butterflies such as green hairstreaks and dingy skippers.

Another attraction is the National Trust's Shugborough Park, on the northern edge of the Chase. The house contains the County Museum, with displays covering agriculture, social history, etc. Park Farm has rare livestock, and there are lovely riverside gardens.

Location: between Stafford, Rugeley, Lichfield and Cannock.
Access and facilities: from A513, A51, A460, A34. Country park open at all times. Information centre at Milford (south-west of Stafford on A513). Open Sat, Sun afternoon only. Car park. Nature trails. Forestry Commission Wildlife and Forest Centre. South-west of Rugeley on Penkridge road. Weekdays only. Waymarked walk nearby. Shugborough Park open March to Ocotober; museum and farm park all year (closed Mon except Bank Holiday).
Map reference: SK006171

Clumber Park

Nottinghamshire

As well as parkland, Clumber's 3,700 acres include a fine lake, woodland and farmland, encouraging plenty of birds all year, but the best time for birdwatching is probably winter, when the lake has many wintering wildfowl, including goldeneyes. Resident

Colemere and Ellesmere

Shropshire

In this area, known as Shropshire's Lake District, glaciers retreating at the end of the last Ice Age left behind them enormous hollows which filled with melt-water. Many of these are now the haunt of water birds. At Colemere, meadows and very varied woodlands add to the habitats for wildlife.

The meres have birds such as grey herons, moorhens (originally 'merehens') and even kingfishers all year, and their numbers are swelled during spring and autumn migration and in winter by waders, terns, gulls and wildfowl.

Ellesmere has nine lakes, all of which are accessible for birdwatching, some also for sailing, angling and swimming. Boats can be hired during the summer. For boating enthusiasts, the Shropshire Union Canal runs through Colemere and Ellesmere before joining the Llangollen Canal, one of the most beautiful canals in Britain.

Location: Ellesmere – 7 miles north-east of Oswestry; Colemere Country Park – north of Colemere village, off A528 Shrewsbury road.
Access: always open. Colemere Country Park has meres centre.
Map reference: SJ400348

Ellesmere – Canada geese and admirer

birds include Canada geese, tufted ducks and grebes. The nature trail passes through extensive woods and also along the longest double avenue of lime trees in Europe.

An extra attraction at Clumber recently has been the RSPB's Operation Woodpecker. The Society has set up a special hide during the breeding season to give bird-watchers superb close-up views of a great spotted woodpecker's nest.

Location: edge of Sherwood Forest 2½ miles south-west of Worksop and 4½ miles south-west of East Retford, between A614 and B6005.
Access and facilities: entrances on A57, A614 and B6005. Always open (charge for vehicles). Shop. Refreshments. Toilets. Bicycles can be hired. Nature walk.
Map reference: SK625745

Coombes Valley RSPB reserve

Coombes Valley and Churnet Valley Woods

Staffordshire RSPB

With steep valley sides clothed in woodland, these RSPB reserves are beautiful as well as good for birds. Coombes has a rocky stream which falls 400 feet through a wooded valley, bracken clearings and areas of heath and meadowland. A hide overlooks the stream, which has dippers, kingfishers and grey wagtails, and from another hide high in the trees visitors can watch redstarts, wood warblers and pied flycatchers. Coombes is also excellent for badgers and for butterflies – among the many species here is the high brown fritillary.

The Churnet Valley Woods lie above the river and canal (the Caldon, a branch of the Trent and Mersey) and with their oak, ash, rowan and bird cherry trees, attract many different woodland birds. There are sparrowhawks, many different species of warblers in summer, and in winter siskins and redpolls.

The attractions of these reserves are matched by the surrounding area. To the east lies the spectacular Peak District National Park and to the west, in great contrast, the Potteries with their fascinating museums.

Location: 3 miles south of Leek between A522 (A520) and A523.
Access and facilities: Coombes Valley – turn off A523 towards Apesford; reached in 1 mile. Open every day except Tue, 9 am to 9 pm or

sunset when earlier. Information centre. Toilets. Nature trail. Hides. Churnet Valley Woods off A522 to Consall. Access is on foot from Country Park car park (open at all times). Churnet Valley consists of three woods – Chase Wood, Rough Knipe and Booths Wood, each of which has a waymarked circular walk.
Map reference: SK009534 and SJ990489

Drakelow Wildfowl Refuge

Derbyshire

Set in a great loop of the River Trent, this reserve consists of water-filled gravel pits, scrub and meadowland. Little ringed plovers breed here, pintails are likely to be among the winter wildfowl, and a variety of waders call in during migration.

Locaton: at Drakelow Power Station, immediately south-west of Burton upon Trent, reached from unclassified road to Walton-on-Trent.
Access and facilities: by permit only, in writing, from Central Electricity Generating Board, Drakelow Power Station, Burton upon Trent. Nature trail. Car park.
Map reference: SK227207

Eyebrook Reservoir

Eyebrook Reservoir

Leicestershire

Although not so spectacular as nearby Rutland Water, Eyebrook is worth a visit in winter, when it attracts many wintering wildfowl. Along with the mallards and wigeons there are often goldeneyes and goosanders. There is also a substantial gull roost each evening and occasional Bewick's swans. Autumn can be excellent if the water level is not too high, with many waders calling in on migration and a good variety of ducks in their puzzling 'eclipse' plumages. A good day here could mean the presence of ruffs, green and common sandpipers, dunlins, little stints, greenshanks and spotted redshanks among the waders.

Location: north of Corby, west off A6003 on unclassified road past Stoke Dry.
Access: Stoke Dry road runs over bridge at north tip of reservoir, then runs along west side of reservoir. View from road.
Map reference: SP850960

Felbrigg Hall

Norfolk

Owned by the National Trust, Felbrigg Hall is a fine Jacobean house which boasts a beautiful park with two circular nature walks (1 mile and 1½ miles in length). Two outstanding features of the park are the 500-acre Great Wood, planted 300 years ago on the site of an ancient beech wood, and the lake. There is also a deer park, a heath and a commercial conifer plantation. Old woods like the Great Wood are marvellous for birds because of the variety of feeding and nesting places they offer.

The ideal times for the one-mile Woodland Walk at Felbrigg are spring and early summer, when all the birds are in full voice. In the conifer plantation you may be lucky enough to see the now uncommon red squirrel. The longer Lakeside Walk also goes through a small wood, but then crosses farmland to reach the lake. Here there are always wildfowl such as Canada geese, swans and ducks, but the stocks of fish and especially eels in the lake also attract grey herons. The lake is especially worth visiting during the open days in winter.

Location: 2 miles south-west of Cromer, off A148 to Fakenham.
Access and facilities: open April to October (closed Tue and Fri) plus certain days up to Christmas. Shop. Picnic area. Restaurant.
Map reference: TG193394

Ferry Meadows Country Park

Cambridgeshire

Within this varied country park is a specially created bird sanctuary complete with hides. Three flooded, connecting gravel pits form the basis of the reserve, but the addition of wader scrapes with islands has made this an outstanding area for birds, where some 200 species have been recorded. There are always plenty to be seen. Winter wildfowl numbers vary with the water levels, but there are usually pochards, tufted ducks and teals. Winter is also good for snipe, golden plovers and fieldfares. In spring and autumn many waders call on migration; these have included Temminck's stint and greenshank. The most interesting of the breeding birds are the common terns (26 miles inland!) and little ringed plovers.

The country park forms part of the very much larger Nene Park, which has a wide range of facilities and items of interest, including the Nene Valley Steam Railway. Leisure activities include rowing, sailing, golf and horse-riding. Many miles of walks have been laid out, among the most pleasant of which are along the River Nene itself.

Location: west of Peterborough city centre signposted off A605 between Peterborough and A1.
Access and facilities: free. Hides. Visitor centre. Car park (charge at weekends, Bank Holidays, Easter to October). Picnic area. Refreshments. Shop.
Map reference: TL145975

Frampton Marsh

Lincolnshire   RSPB

On the northern side of the Wash, which is internationally important for its winter bird populations, Frampton has two reserves, one RSPB and the other Lincolnshire and South Humberside Trust for Nature Conservation. It is a huge area of salt marsh and mud flats and, like the rest of the Wash, attracts staggering numbers of waders and wildfowl in winter, while in summer, as well as common terns and redshanks, Frampton has the largest breeding colony of black-headed gulls in Britain. When the tide goes out, the waders spread all over the vast sand and mud flats to feed, making close views difficult, but, as the tide comes in, they are all driven back so that they are much easier to see from the sea wall.

The marshes attract other sorts of birds. Mostly, these come to feed on the seeds produced by plants such as sea purslane, sea aster and sea lavender. There are large flocks of buntings and finches, and also several species of duck. Common seals have their British breeding stronghold in the Wash, so a sight of one may add to the pleasure of a visit here.

See also Snettisham and Gibraltar Point.

Location: 4 miles south-south-east of Boston. Off unclassified road east of Frampton, which is reached from A16 at Kirton.
Access: public footpath along sea wall.
Map reference: TF354384

Fowlmere

Cambridgeshire   RSPB

Amid the intensively farmed countryside of Cambridgeshire, Fowlmere, with its disused watercress beds, reed beds and pools fed by springs, is an oasis for birds. It is at its best in spring and summer when the reed beds are alive with birds – up to 100 pairs of reed warblers, along with sedge warblers, reed buntings, grasshopper warblers and water rails. Flowers such as water forget-me-not, cowslip, purple loosestrife and the strange and beautiful bee orchid add colour. Spring is also a good time to spot the reserve's many toads and few frogs. Other times of year are also worthwhile: kingfishers are seen all year and in autumn waders such as green sandpipers call in.

Fowlmere was bought for the RSPB using money raised by the Young Ornithologists' Club, and so children are especially welcome on this reserve.

Location: 1½ miles north of Melbourn, off A10 Cambridge to Royston road towards Fowlmere village.
Access and facilities: RSPB reserve; always open. Nature trail. Hides. Boardwalk for disabled access.
Map reference: TL407461

Fowlmere – oasis for birds

Gibraltar Point
Lincolnshire

This reserve is a marvellous place to see what interesting and complex places sand dunes can be, and how they can have a remarkably rich variety of plant life. There is also an area of salt marsh here – an equally fascinating kind of habitat. In front of the dunes and salt marsh there are sand and shingle spits and behind them a bank keeps out the sea from an area of fresh water marsh which has wet meadows, ponds and a mere, overlooked by a hide. There are plenty of birds all year. The rarest breeding birds are the little terns which nest on the sand and shingle (no access while nesting) with ringed plovers. Shelducks nest in the dunes and the scrub shelters small birds such as yellowhammers. In the autumn, Gibraltar Point is a stopping off place for many migrating birds, including the redwings and fieldfares which feast on the sea buckthorn berries. The vast sand and mud flats on the shores of the Wash are internationally important feeding grounds for wintering waders and many of these congregate at Gibraltar Point – on a winter's day there can be thousands of curlews, dunlins, and knots, as well as wigeon and pink-footed geese and dark-bellied brent geese. It is also worth watching for snow buntings, which regularly turn up around the Wash in winter.

Location: 3 miles south of Skegness, from where it is signposted.
Access and facilities: Lincolnshire and South Humberside Trust for Nature Conservation reserve and an important bird ringing and field centre. Reserve open all year (car park charge in summer). Visitor centre open daily May to October, weekends only in winter. Picnic area. Nature trail.
Map reference: TF556581

Gibraltar Point – among the breeding birds here are shelducks (inset)

Grafham Water
Cambridgeshire

Such a huge expanse of water (2½ square miles) in an inland county acts as a magnet to birds and there are usually plenty on the water, especially in winter, when there are thousands of ducks, including goldeneyes, wigeons, shovelers and goosanders. In spring and especially autumn, interesting birds often call in; these might include wood sandpipers, ospreys and black terns. Breeding birds include shelducks, great crested grebes and redshanks. Part of the reservoir is a nature reserve which also includes farmland and woodland.

A hide in the reserve looks over creeks specially protected to give sanctuary from boats. This gives a closer view of birds than is otherwise possible – a telescope is needed to view the birds elsewhere as the reservoir is so vast. There is another hide adjacent to Plummer car park. Grafham is also popular with sailors and anglers and tends to be busy on fine weekends. As well as birds, there are always plenty of boats to watch!

Location: 5 miles south-west of Huntingdon; reached on B661 from Buckden, which is on A1.
Access and facilities: part is reserve of Beds and Hunts Wildlife Trust – reached from Mander car park in West Perry. Nature trails. Hides. Toilets. Car parks. Hill Farm car park reached via Grafham village. Nature trail. Plummer car park – hide. Toilets.
Map reference: TL143672

Hardwick Park
Derbyshire

A popular (and sometimes crowded!) family day out, Elizabethan Hardwick Hall, owned by the National Trust, is famous as the home of Bess of Hardwick. Close to the house are fine gardens, while a large country park surrounds the entire property. As well as Millers Pond, where there are moorhens, coots and mallards, the nature trail here passes oak and hawthorn thickets, the famous 400-year-old Hardwick Oak, and a series of fish ponds. In the reeds and sedges around some of these ponds, reed and willow warblers may be seen.

Location: 5 miles north-west of Mansfield. Signposted from A617.
Access and facilities: country park open every day (charge for parking). Information centre. Nature trail. Car park. Picnic area. Hardwick Hall open April to October Wed, Thu, Sat, Sun, Bank Holiday Mon, pm only. Admission charge for non NT members. Refreshments.
Map reference: SK463638

Havergate Island
Suffolk   RSPB

Avocets are the stars of this famous RSPB reserve. Havergate has the largest British colony of this rare wader (over 100 pairs), which returned here to breed during World War II after an absence from Britain of 150 years. Since then, the RSPB has managed the reserve for the benefit of the birds, creating a watery paradise with lagoons where the water level and salinity are carefully controlled, and islands for nesting. As well as avocets, the island has an important nesting colony of Sandwich terns, common terns and even a few arctic terns – very unusual this far south. Other nesting birds include oystercatchers, ringed plovers and shelducks. Short-eared owls do not always nest here, but can usually be seen hunting over the salt marsh. Like nearby Minsmere, Havergate is an exciting place to visit at migration times, when unusual birds turn up. Among the regular visitors are black-tailed and bar-tailed godwits, whimbrels, spotted redshanks and little stints. In winter there are usually still some avocets to be seen, as well as plenty of wildfowl, including wigeon, teal, pintail, shoveler and gadwall. This reserve was particularly badly hit by the severe gale in October 1987, and many of its facilities were damaged.

Location: 16 miles east of Ipswich; south of Orford.
Access and facilities: by boat from Orford quay. Permit only from Warden, 30 Munday's Lane, Orford, Woodbridge, Suffolk IP12 2LX, enclosing £3.50, or £1.50 for RSPB members. Boats leave at 10am and 11.30am on Sat, Sun, Mon and Thu between April and August, and on alternate Thu and Sat September to March (dates available from Warden). Information centre. Hides. Toilets. Picnic site.
Map reference: TM425496

Irchester Country Park

Northamptonshire

Now mainly woodland, this area was mined for ironstone until 1940. This has left attractive, undulating land with dry slopes and boggy dips where many different trees and plants can grow. Although most of the trees are pine and larch, there are also alders, ashes and scrubby areas of bramble and wild rose. Spring is a good time to visit, when the rooks are busily and noisily 'tidying' their nests in the ash trees, and all the other woodland birds – which include goldcrests and long-tailed tits – are in full voice. Other creatures to look for on a walk through the park are grey squirrels and rabbits in the woods and butterflies around the scrub.

Location: 1¾ miles south-east of Welling-borough, off B570, between A509 and Irchester. Access and facilities: open all year. Picnic areas. Nature trail.
Map reference: SP912658

Long Mynd

Shropshire

A vast heather and bracken covered plateau, the Long Mynd rises to nearly 1,700 feet, giving wonderful views as far as Snowdonia, the Cheshire Plain, the Brecon Beacons and the Cotswolds. Much of the Mynd is managed as a grouse moor – also providing a habitat for other upland birds – but this wild desolation is broken by deep, lush valleys, created during the Ice Ages. Here there are cold, clear streams fed by springs; bog plants, and rowan and hawthorn scrub. Walk quietly by these streams and you are likely to see a dipper walking through, and bobbing under, the water, busily searching for food, while yellowhammers sing from the hawthorn bushes. On the moors in summer you may see wheatears and the special thrush of the uplands, the ring ouzel. Buzzards and ravens are often seen soaring overhead.

While it is possible to see some of this beautiful area by car, the best way is to walk, although some parts are very rugged and only suitable for experienced walkers. Three walks of varying length and difficulty start at Carding Mill Valley. For the really energetic, an ancient track, the Port Way, runs the entire 10-mile length of the Long Mynd.

Location: 15 miles south of Shrewsbury, west of Church Stretton.
Access and facilities: much owned by National Trust, including Carding Mill Valley (SO443945) near Church Stretton. Car park. Refreshments. Information centre (open Mon to Sat April to end September; weekends in October).
Map reference: SO425945

Manifold Valley

Staffordshire

Starting from Ilam, the Manifold Valley has walking just as beautiful but far less demanding than much of surrounding rugged Peak District. The Paradise Walk passes the 'boil holes' where the river reappears after flowing underground. Another walk, which

runs along a disused railway to Beeston Tor, starts at Wetton, further north along the valley. A beautiful, wooded dale with sheer limestone cliffs in places, the Manifold is not usually as crowded as the nearby, more famous Dovedale. The clear river is the haunt of dippers, kingfishers and grey wagtails, which nest on the parts not too heavily visited. On the really remote stretches, common sandpipers nest. In the woods are redstarts, wood warblers and woodpeckers, while the crevices and caves in the cliffs, such as those at Wetton Mill, have nesting kestrels, jackdaws and stock doves.

Location: 4 miles north-west of Ashbourne. Reached from unclassified roads off A52 and A515.
Access and facilities: Paradise Walk starts from National Trust's Ilam Hall car park. Information office open April to October; weekends only November to March. Refreshments Easter to September. Picnic site.
Map reference: SX095560

Minsmere

Suffolk   RSPB

One of the RSPB's most important and renowned reserves for birds, Minsmere is also excellent for the visitor, with many pleasant walks. Paths lead through woodland, heath, reed beds and on to the beach. Many of the paths are level and suitable for wheelchairs and pushchairs. Strategically placed hides give excellent, all-weather views of the reserve's huge variety of birds – there is even a hide high in the woodland canopy so that visitors can enjoy watching redstarts, woodpeckers, nuthatches and many other woodland birds. From hides overlooking the muddy lagoons, reed beds and the 'Scrape' – a man-made area of shallow water, islands and mud – there is excellent birdwatching all year. The 400 acres of reed beds are always of interest, with such exciting birds as bitterns, marsh harriers, bearded tits and water rails, as well as many warblers in the breeding season, while the open water has a good variety of wildfowl and other water birds all year. From April to September the Scrape offers endless fascination with its variety of waders. As well as the famous avocets, there can be godwits, spotted redshanks, dunlins, knots, snipe and even occasionally a spoonbill, not to mention many nesting terns and gulls. Plants include ragged robin, bog cotton, yellow rattle, marsh orchids and interesting grasses and sedges. Minsmere's woodland has good numbers of nightingales.

Adjacent Dunwich Heath offers a complete contrast and is well worth a visit in summer. It is crossed by public footpaths and, as well as stonechats and tree pipits, there are many interesting insects including silver-studded blue butterflies and cinnabar moths. In the evenings nightjars are often heard.

Dunwich is itself of interest. Because of cliff erosion, a complete town is now submerged beneath the sea. A museum here tells the story.

Norfolk Broads – inside the Broadlands Conservation Centre at Ranworth, a superb introduction to the wildlife of this unique area

ing plants. These meadows are important breeding grounds for up to 40 pairs of black-tailed godwits (the largest concentration in Britain), occasional ruffs, yellow wagtails, garganey, redshank and snipe.

Because the RSPB and CWT reserves are in the west of the Washes the light is best for birdwatching in the afternoon, while the Wildfowl Trust is in the east and so is better in the morning.

Location: between Ely and March, reached from roads off A1101, and A141.
Access and facilities: RSPB and CWT reserves reached by taking B1093 or B1098 to Manea from A141 Chatteris to March road. Welches Dam (reserve entrance) is signposted from Manea. Access at all times except 24 and 25 December, but Sun preferable during wildfowling season (on adjacent washes) September to January. Information centre. Hides. Car park. Toilets. Wildfowl Trust at Welney is reached via suspension bridge from A1101 south of Welney. Open daily except 24, 25 December. Information centre, Picnic site. Shop.
Map reference: TL480885/TL526940

Ouse Washes – vast numbers of wildfowl gather here in winter

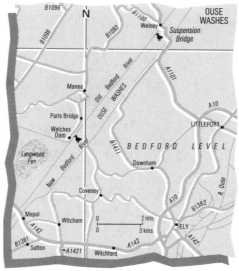

Rutland Water

Leicestershire

With a shore stretching about 24 miles, Rutland Water is one of Europe's largest man-made lakes. When it was created considerable thought was given to making it not only a water supply, but also a habitat for wildlife and a leisure area for people. The result is an area which attracts many birds, alongside human activities such as sailing and fishing. It is now one of the most important places for wildfowl in Britain. On the nature reserve there are areas where the water levels can be controlled to provide ideal feeding conditions for a wide range of waders, dabbling ducks and diving ducks. Around the shore are carefully managed wildflower meadows, and also areas of specially planted trees and scrub. On the northern shore, woodlands near the Barns-

dale car park are full of primroses and bluebells in spring.

There are always plenty of birds on and around the water, but spring and autumn are especially exciting. Since Rutland Water lies on a migration route a long way from the sea, many birds call in, including waders such as godwits and sanderlings in spring and sandpipers and spotted redshanks in autumn. Among the special breeding birds are ruddy ducks, shovelers, oystercatchers and common terns. Winter visitors include short-eared owls and peregrines, which hunt over the grasslands, and several species of divers and grebes. Ducks that might be seen here in autumn and winter include gadwall, pintail, goosander and smew.

Location: south of A606, between Oakham and Empingham.
Access and facilities: 350 acres in west are 2 reserves of Leicestershire and Rutland Trust for Nature Conservation. Lyndon Reserve (with visitor centre) open all year at weekends; from Easter to October also Tue, Wed and Thu. Reached from A6003 south shore. Egleton Reserve open all year – Wed, Sat and Sun. Reached

from A6003 south of Oakham. All permits obtainable on arrival. Hides. Nature Trails. Further information from Warden, Fishponds, Cottage, Stamford Road, Oakham, Leics LE15 8AB. Picnic sites and car parks on northern shore – at Whitwell, Barnsdale (a one-mile nature trail runs between these two), and Sykes Lane (between Whitwell and Empingham). Refreshments Sun and Bank Holidays, afternoons only, at Whitwell, Normanton and Sykes Lane. Car park on south shore, at Normanton.
Map reference: SK897059

Sandringham

Norfolk

Famous as a royal residence, the Sandringham estate also has a country park covering some 300 acres. The park is mainly conifer woodland and heath. In the woods are many rhododendrons, which give a magnificent show of colour in late spring/early summer, but unfortunately are not of much use to wildlife, except the exotic golden pheasant, which shelters in the dense cover. However, the woods do have a good selection of woodland birds such as nuthatches, treecreepers and jays. Some of these have become quite tame and can be seen from the car park, including Sandringham's most interesting bird, the crossbill, which often feeds in the larches around the car park. In winter it is worth watching the fields around the estate for flocks of pink-footed geese which fly in to feed. Sandringham is, of course, very popular with tourists, so for quiet birdwatching peak times are best avoided.

Location: 7 miles north-east of King's Lynn, signposted off A149 to Hunstanton.
Access: country park open all year, but house, church and grounds open only during summer months. Everything closed when Royal Family in residence (telephone King's Lynn 2675 to check). Car park. Refreshments. Shop.
Map reference: TF689287

Ouse Washes – swans at Welney

Sandwell Valley Country Park

Warwickshire ▪RSPB▪

Sandwell Valley is such an oasis that it is very easy to forget the proximity of urban sprawl and two motorways. The RSPB's reserve here is based around the end of a lake, where an island has been specially designed to provide roosting, nesting and feeding areas for birds. Alongside the lake is a marsh with willows and shallow pools and near by many trees and shrubs have been planted to improve the habitat.

The variety of birds this reserve attracts adds to the illusion of being far from the city. Among those nesting here are moorhens, little ringed plovers, lapwings, reed warblers and whitethroats, while winter brings jack snipe and water rails to the marsh, and wigeon and pochards to the lake. Like the rest of the Tame Valley, Sandwell is an important resting place for migrating birds, especially waders, and plenty of mud has been provided for them. The regulars include curlews, dunlins, green and common sandpipers and green-shanks. And birds are not the only wildlife to appreciate the reserve; look out for the frog spawn and the many species of butterflies! The rest of the lake is given over to recreational activities.

Location: 4 miles from centre of Birmingham, west of Hamstead.
Access and facilities: RSPB reserve (open at all times) is reached from Tanhouse Avenue off A4041 in Great Barr. Information centre. Hides. Trails. Toilets.
Map reference: SP036931

Snettisham

Norfolk ▪RSPB▪

With a vast expanse of tidal sand and mud flats, backed by salt marsh, a shingle beach and flooded pits, Snettisham offers ideal conditions for waders and wildfowl. There are always birds to be seen, but in winter the numbers are spectacular. At high tide all the waders which had been spread out over the exposed mud and sand, feeding on buried creatures, are driven back to gather on the banks and islands of the reserve, joining the ducks, geese and swans. There may be tens of thousands of dunlins, knots, oystercatchers, turnstones, grey plovers, redshanks, curlews, bar-tailed godwits and ringed plovers, along with pink-footed and brent geese, shelduck, mallard, wigeon and teal. At night Bewick's and whooper swans fly in to roost. Although the numbers are not so spectacular at other times of year, migration also brings plenty of interest, with waders such as sanderlings and small birds such as wheatears calling in.

In the breeding season, oystercatchers, ringed plovers and redshanks nest along with common terns on the islands, and it is worth looking for immature eiders on the estuary. The reserve has an excellent cross-section of coastal flowers.

Location: on coast between King's Lynn and Hunstanton, reached along signposted road from A149 at Snettisham village.
Access and facilities: RSPB reserve, open at all times. Hides. Public car park; disabled may drive onto reserve itself.
Map reference: TF648335

Sutton Park

West Midlands

While the edges of Sutton Park are heavily used, especially at weekends and bank holidays, it is so big that there are still quiet areas with plenty of wildlife, where it is easy to forget the proximity of the city. In all, this country park covers 2,500 acres, and is entirely surrounded by built-up areas.

Once owned by Henry VIII, the park is mainly undulating heathland, with birch and bracken on the higher ground and attractive boggy areas lower down. The woodlands are mixed, with oaks, birch and rowan, as well as some conifers. Several old mill ponds are an extra attraction. With so many different habitats, there is always a good variety of birds. These range from linnets and stonechats on the heath and nuthatches and redstarts in the woods, to snipe in the bogs and great crested grebes on the mill ponds. Winter too has its attractions, when merlins and hen harriers sometimes hunt over the heath, and the woods are full of thrushes and finches.

A leaflet describing the nature trail is available from City of Birmingham District Council, Council House, Birmingham.

Location: 6 miles from centre of Birmingham, just north-east of M6 motorway (junctions 6 and 7) between Sutton Coldfield and A452.
Access and facilities: open at all times. Nature trail.
Map reference: SP103963

Snettisham – the oystercatcher roost here might contain as many as 13,000 birds

Tame Valley
Warwickshire

Rising in the Black Country near Wolverhampton, the Tame winds its way to Birmingham and then north-east past Tamworth until it joins the Trent. Much of the land on either side is urban or industrial and parts of the Tame used to be very polluted. Recently though it has been cleaned up considerably. The valley is a traditional migration route for birds and so, where there are suitable habitats and access is possible, the birdwatching is good, particularly in spring and autumn.

Some of the industry along the river is of benefit to birds. Power stations which pump out warm water keep areas free of ice in winter, and sand and gravel extraction has created many new pools. Even rubbish tips are productive feeding grounds for gulls. Organisations such as the Central Electricity Generating Board and the Coal Board have created several reserves for wildlife, but these are mainly in areas which it is not possible to open to the general public. There are, however, several other reserves where visiting is possible and two of these are described below.

1. Kingsbury Water Park
Disused gravel pits form the basis of this park. Some are now flooded, but have gravel islands, while others have been filled with ash from local power stations and are now covered with reeds, bulrushes and willow scrub. There are also areas of marsh, rough grassland with hawthorns and brambles and areas of woodland.

With so many habitats, the park is a magnet for birds (and wildlife in general) throughout the year. In spring and summer, it boasts nine breeding species of warbler – including reed and sedge warblers in the reed beds, grasshopper warblers in the brambles and hawthorns and garden warblers in the woods. Another outstanding feature of Kingsbury is the nesting colony of common terns – just one of several coastal species that breed here. On and around the water there are also nesting little grebes, pochards and little ringed plovers, to name but a few. Migration time brings waders to feed on the mud and rest on the islands – usually more in spring than in autumn. Winter, when the park is generally much quieter, is excellent for birdwatching. The open water attracts large flocks of wildfowl – up to 900 ducks (including pochards and goldeneyes), coots, Bewick's and sometimes whooper swans. In the reed beds are snipe and water rails as well as large roosts of finches, thrushes and buntings, while short-eared owls hunt over the grassland.

The northern end of the park has been set aside as a nature reserve with two hides, and the wildlife here is undisturbed. In other parts of the park, despite disturbance, the birdwatching is also good. There is also much here for non-birdwatchers!

Location: 1 mile west of Kingsbury, on unclassified road off A4097 5 miles south of Tamworth.
Access and facilities: Warwickshire County Council Leisure Area, open at all times. Information centre. Nature reserve. Hides.
Map reference: SP204958

2. Alvecote Pools
Colliery subsidence has left several shallow pools with surrounding wet pastures at Alvecote. Reed beds, marsh, alder and willow carr and scrub add to the richness of the area and attract birds all year. It is particularly worth visiting in late summer when up to 200 mute swans gather to moult and in autumn when there are thousands of swallows and sand martins. When the water levels are low and there is plenty of mud, migrating waders call in – up to 30 different species have been recorded. Summer and winter also have their attractions for the birdwatcher. Among the breeding birds are shelducks, redshanks and yellow wagtails, while in winter there are often huge flocks of lapwings, finches and thrushes.

Location: on River Anker, 2 miles east of Tamworth.
Access: reserve of Warwickshire Nature Conservation Trust. Access by permit only, but good views from unclassified road across reserve.
Map reference: SK254047

Tetney Marshes
Lincolnshire　RSPB

Near the mouth of the River Humber, this RSPB reserve is a large area of sand flats, low sand dunes and salt marsh (visitors should keep off the dunes and marsh as they have dangerous tides). It is particularly important as the site of one of the largest colonies of one of Britain's rarest breeding seabirds – the little tern. They nest at the tide's edge. Visitors in the breeding season should take care not to disturb them.

Shelducks, oystercatchers, ringed plovers and redshanks also breed. Migrating waders such as grey plovers and whimbrels call in during autumn, and in winter there are flocks of wildfowl (including brent geese) and waders. High tide is the best time for watching the wintering waders. Grey seals are sometimes seen along this coast.

Location: 5 miles south-east of Cleethorpes, reached on unclassified road to Tetney Lock from A1031.
Access: on foot via entrance or along river bank east of Tetney Lock. Sea wall gives good views.
Map reference: TA345025

Upton Warren

Hereford and Worcester

Upton Warren is particularly interesting because, despite being well and truly inland, it has salt water and salt marsh. This comes from seepage from underlying salt, the past extraction of which has caused subsidence and created shallow pools. As well as these three small pools, whose water levels fluctuate to leave plenty of mud for waders, there are three fresh water pools, including a flooded gravel pit used for sailing and fishing. High hawthorn and blackthorn hedges around pastures add to the variety of habitats. The breeding ducks include an important colony of ruddy ducks, but it is as a staging post for migrating birds that the area is fascinating. Birds which regularly call in include little gulls, all sorts of terns and around 30 different waders including greenshank (autumn) and Temminck's stint (spring). Among the small birds on the reserve are eight breeding species of warblers, and in autumn and winter, many redwings and fieldfares feed on the hedgerow berries.

The nearby Avoncroft Museum of Buildings (near Stoke Heath off the A38) has a fascinating collection of buildings of many sorts and ages, reconstructed to create an open-air museum. It is open from March to November.

Location: midway between Droitwich and Bromsgrove on either side of River Salwarpe. Reached from A38, close to Junction 5 of M5.
Access: permit only from the Worcestershire Nature Conservation Trust, Hanbury Road, Droitwich WR9 7DU
Map reference: SO932674

Walberswick

Suffolk

This National Nature Reserve covers many important habitats, including one of the best remnants of the Suffolk Sandlings, a heath which used to extend from Ipswich to Blythburgh and which is important for birds such as nightjars and stonechats and also for reptiles including common lizards, slow worms and adders. Other habitats include saltings and inter-tidal mud around the inland Blyth Estuary, and most of the Westwood Marshes, including the largest continuous reed bed in Britain. Over 100 species of birds breed here altogether.

A hide overlooks the estuary, which in winter has shelducks, dunlins, redshanks and spotted redshanks, and in spring black-tailed godwits as well as many other interesting waders. A telescope is useful. The reed beds are ideal for special birds such as bearded tits, marsh harriers, bitterns and reed warblers, and also have plenty of pools where there are ducks all year. The marshes are particularly famous for their exciting birds of prey in winter, with up to ten species excluding owls. These include hen harriers, merlins, rough-legged buzzards and sometimes even red kites.

The pleasant seaside town of Southwold is just a few miles to the north. See also Minsmere, which is nearby.

Location: east of A12 off B1387 between Blythburgh and Walberswick.
Access: public footpaths; these are shown on map outside Walberswick village hall. Hide.
Map reference: TM465744

Wicken Fen – remnant of a lost landscape

Wicken Fen

Cambridgeshire

Wicken is an island time capsule, raised above the surrounding land and preserved only by careful management by the National Trust. The windpump here is special in that it pumps water up in to the reserve, rather than out of it. The farmland around is 15 feet lower, its peat having shrunk after hundreds of years of drainage. The reserve, one of the most important of its kind in western Europe, has a feeling of wild remoteness and is particularly fascinating to the all-round naturalist. As well as a list of some 200 birds – including in winter hen harriers, bearded tits and great grey shrikes – there are about 5,000 species of insects (including the beautiful swallowtail butterfly) and 300 flowering plants. The droves through the reserve provide good walking, but stout waterproof footwear is essential. There is a raised walkway for disabled visitors.

Location: 7 miles north-west of Newmarket. On south side of A1123 at west end of Wicken.
Access: open every day except 25 December. Charge for non-National Trust members. Further information from Warden, Lode Lane, Wicken, Ely CB7 5XP.
Map reference: TL563705

Wolves Wood

Suffolk   RSPB

This ancient, broadleaved wood has a rich mixture of tree species, including oak, ash, birch, hornbeam, aspen and hazel, and also some coppiced scrub. It attracts many woodland birds, most famous of which are the nightingales, which nest in the coppice and are in full song in May/June. Also of interest are the many warblers – including garden warblers and blackcaps – great and lesser spotted woodpeckers, marsh and long-tailed tits, and hawfinches, which occasionally nest in the hornbeams. The woodland pools are good places to watch for birds coming to bathe and drink. Adding to the beauty of this woodland are the many interesting plants, including two typical of ancient woodland – herb paris and yellow archangel. The butterflies are good, too! Because of the clay soil and high water table, this is a wet wood, so suitable footwear will make a visit to the reserve very much more pleasant.

Location: 2 miles east of Hadleigh, north of A1071 Ipswich road.
Access and facilities: at all times along waymarked trail. Information centre open weekends April to September.
Map reference: TM054436

Wyre Forest

Hereford and Worcester

One of the largest tracts of ancient forest left in Britain, Wyre is especially valuable because of the variety of habitats it offers. The forest is mainly of oak (both types found in Britain – sessile and pedunculate), but is very varied, with woodlands typical of Wales and East Anglia side by side; new conifers planted by the Forestry Commission; streams, and small pastures. All this variety obviously makes for interesting walking and birdwatching. Where the canopy is dense there are wood warblers; pied flycatchers and redstarts abound, and the streams are ideal for dippers, kingfishers and grey wagtails. The variety also benefits insects, and there is an outstanding range of butterflies including silver-washed fritillaries and purple hairstreaks. So, whether you are a serious naturalist or just enjoy walking in beautiful countryside, the Wyre is ideal for a day or afternoon out.

There are picnic sites throughout the forest, including one at Hawkbatch which is within half a mile of a viewpoint over the River Severn and Trimpley Reservoir. A good path for birdwatching is the one alongside Dowles Brook. A leaflet about the forest is available from the Nature Conservancy Council, Northminster House, Peterborough PE1 1VA, or from the information centre.

Location: west of Bewdley, reached from B4194 and A456.
Access and facilities: Nature Conservancy Council and Forestry Commission, open at all times. Public footpaths. Car park at Callow Hill, on A456. Information centre here open all year, except public holidays. Other car parks along B4194. Picnic sites.
Map reference: SO759766

Wales

Jay

Islands such as Grassholm and Skokholm make the Welsh coast marvellous for seabirds. Estuaries, cliffs and rocky shores increase the variety and interest. Inland, the huge, wild expanses of North and Mid Wales have many special birds, including the red kite

Wales

Useful addresses:

RSPB Headquarters: The Lodge, Sandy, Bedfordshire, SG19 2DL
RSPB Wales Office: Bryn Aderyn, The Bank, Newtown, Powys, SY16 2AB
Many RSPB reserves have explanatory leaflets. These are often available at the reserve, but in any event the regional office, or RSPB HQ, will supply information on any reserve upon receipt of a s.a.e.

Brecknock Naturalists' Trust: Lion House, 7 Lion Street, Brecon, Powys, LD3 7AY
Dyfed Wildlife Trust: 7 Market Street, Haverfordwest, SA61 1NF
Glamorgan Wildlife Trust: Glamorgan Nature Centre, Tondu, Bridgend, Mid Glamorgan, CF32 0EH
Gwent Wildlife Trust: 16 White Swan Court, Church Street, Monmouth, NP5 3BR
Montgomeryshire Wildlife Trust: 8 Severn Square, Newtown, Powys, SY16 2AG
North Wales Naturalists' Trust: 376 High Street, Bangor, Gwynedd, LL57 1YE
Radnorshire Wildlife Trust: 1 Gwalia Annexe, Ithon Road, Llandrindod Wells, Powys, LD1 6AS
Nature Conservancy Council: North Wales Region, Plas Penrhos, Ffordd Penrhos, Bangor, Gwynedd, LL57 2LQ; Dyfed – Powys Region, Plas Gogerddan, Aberystwyth, Dyfed, SY23 3EE; South Wales Region, 44 The Parade, Roath, Cardiff, CF2 3AB

Aber Dysynni

Gwynedd

The shingle and maritime grassland here, between the sea and the Cambrian Coast railway has a breeding bird population which includes little terns, ringed plovers, oystercatchers, lapwings, meadow pipits and skylarks. For botanists, there are interesting plants, including sea holly, yellow-horned poppy and pyramidal orchid.

However, it is as a viewpoint for seabird movements that Aber Dysynni is best known. During the summer, large numbers of Manx shearwaters pass the point; thousands are often seen flying northwards in the early morning (presumably from the Pembrokeshire islands). Smaller numbers fly southwards in the evening. At the same time there are frequently gannets and auks. Just offshore there is a resident flock of eiders, and small numbers of red-breasted mergansers, joined (particularly in winter) by common scoters and velvet scoters, along with all three species of diver. In late summer and autumn there are many Sandwich terns, accompanied by smaller numbers of other tern species and occasional arctic and other skuas. A few waders frequent the sea-washed rocks on the point at all times of the year, but there are much larger numbers on the tidal lagoon of the Broadwater on the east side of the railway.

Location: 2 miles north of Tywyn, on unclassified road.
Access: road ends at river; continue on foot under bridge and along footpath to point.
Map reference: SH565029

Anglesey

Gwynedd

Separated from the mainland only by the narrow channel of the Menai Strait, Anglesey is nonetheless quite different in character from the mountains and valleys of Snowdonia and the Lleyn. It is generally low-lying and much of it is high quality arable land. It has a variety of habitats for birds, and seven especially good places are described below. The island is remarkably rich in prehistoric remains (especially the burial chambers of Bryn-celli-ddu and Barclodiad-y-Gawres) and has at Beaumaris one of the finest castle plans in Britain.

1. Cemlyn Pool

This reserve was originally established as a private wildfowl refuge before World War II by the millionaire egg collector Captain Vivian Hewitt, who built the high brick wall around his house on the west side of the main pool. Today, the estate belongs to the National Trust; the pond is leased to the North Wales Naturalists' Trust.

The water level in the pools is maintained by a weir across the outlet stream by Bryn Aber. The water is brackish, being flooded by the sea at high spring tides and receiving fresh water from several streams and springs. The principal interest at Cemlyn is the breeding colony of common, arctic and Sandwich terns, on the salt marsh islands in the main pool. This is the largest such colony in Wales and the most easily viewable. Other breeding species include black-headed gull, shelduck, red-breasted merganser, oystercatcher, redshank and ringed plover. In winter, the species of wildfowl that can be seen regularly include wigeon, shoveler and goldeneye.

A public right of way follows the shingle ridge which separates the main pool from the sea, but visitors are asked to avoid the crest of the ridge to prevent disturbance to birds on the water and the possibility of treading on nests during the summer. The best vantage point is from the lane which skirts part of the pool.

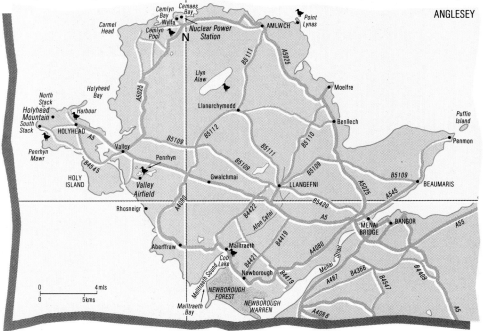

Location: north coast of Anglesey, 1½ miles west of Wylfa nuclear power station. Signposted from A5025 at Tregele.
Access and facilities: car parks at Traeth Cemlyn (east of pool) and Bryn Aber (west).
Map reference: SH331931

2. Cob Lake, Malltraeth

Cob Lake is part of the Newborough Warren/Ynys Llanddwyn National Nature Reserve. It is a shallow pool of brackish water separated from the foreshore of the Cefni Estuary by Malltraeth Cob (an embankment built as a sea defence during the last century by Thomas Telford, the builder of the Menai suspension bridge). The lake has achieved international fame as the setting for many of the late Charles Tunnicliffe's best-known bird paintings and sketches, particularly featured in his book 'Shorelands Summer Diary' ('Shorelands' was Tunnicliffe's home at Malltraeth, overlooking the Cefni Estuary). The species most often seen include shelduck, lapwing, curlew and redshank, but a wide variety of waders has been regularly recorded, particularly when water levels are low. Greenshanks, spotted redshanks, black-tailed and bar-tailed godwits, and ruffs are frequent visitors in autumn, while teal, pintail and other wildfowl occur in winter.

Location: west coast of Anglesey, off A4080 at Malltraeth.
Access: view from A4080 or from top of cob.
Map reference: SH409684

Ruff – male in breeding plumage

3. Holyhead Harbour

Holyhead Harbour is enclosed by a massive breakwater which gives protection against winter storms. It is a splendid site for winter birdwatching, particularly during the period from November to March. To the west of the ferry terminal the harbour is skirted by a road which, elevated well above sea level, provides a first rate and easily accessible vantage point. The total number of birds utilising the sheltered conditions of the harbour is not large, but there is often a most interesting variety of relatively scarce species among the yachts and other vessels. In particular, there is a good chance of seeing several species of divers and grebes, with great northern diver and great crested grebe regularly present. Red-breasted mergansers are also frequent visitors and two or three black guillemots are generally resident during the winter months. As well as the birds to be seen on the open water, small numbers of waders, including turnstones, purple sandpipers, oystercatchers and redshanks can usually be found among the rocks round the periphery of the harbour.

Location: Holyhead is on Holy Island, just off west coast of Anglesey.
Access: at all times.
Map reference: SH245835

5. Llyn Penrhyn   RSPB

This RSPB reserve consists of a reed-fringed fresh water lake (Llyn Penrhyn) and three smaller pools, interspersed with gorse-covered grassland and outcrops of ancient Pre-Cambrian igneous rocks. Although it is close to the Royal Air Force's Valley airfield, this lake is excellent for wildfowl in conjunction with the nearby lakes of Dinam and Traffwll. A wealth of breeding water birds includes great crested and little grebes, mute swans, greylag and Canada geese, ruddy ducks, gadwalls, mallards, shovelers, pochards and tufted ducks. Reed and sedge warblers, reed buntings and stonechats also breed and bitterns and water rails are regular visitors. It is therefore possible to see a good variety of water birds during the breeding season, while numbers build up in the winter with the arrival of teal, wigeon and pintail and on occasions significant numbers of shovelers.

Location: west side of Anglesey off A5. On unclassified road signposted RAF Valley.
Access: reserve entrance is after 1½ miles through white gate on right-hand side just past lake. Track leads from gate and gives good views. Small number of cars can park in lay-by near gate, but ensure that gateway is kept clear.
Map reference: SH314766

4. Llyn Alaw

The eastern end of this reservoir has been declared a wildfowl sanctuary zone by the Welsh Water Authority. There is a visitor centre at the western end of the lake and the water authority has also constructed a hide overlooking the eastern end of the lake, which is much better for birdwatching than the western side. Breeding species include common tern, black-headed gull and tufted duck on the islands in the sanctuary. With low water levels in late summer and early autumn there can be spectacular concentrations of passage waders in the vicinity of the hide, particularly lapwings, curlews, dunlins and golden plovers, but also scarcer species such as pectoral and wood sandpipers. Llyn Alaw is a splendid place to watch winter wildfowl and is one of the top three inland sites in Wales for wigeon and mallard, with good concentrations of teal, tufted duck, pochard and goldeneye. There are greylag geese and whooper swans as well. The rough vegetation around the lake provides a good hunting area for kestrels, hen harriers, short-eared owls and barn owls, and peregrines are frequent visitors, too.

Location: central Anglesey; 1½ miles northwest of Llanerchymedd, off B5112 and B5111.
Access and facilities: unrestricted to visitor centre and hide. Car park. Picnic site. Toilets.
Map reference: SH373856

Llyn Alaw – sanctuary for wildfowl

6. Point Lynas

Choughs, peregrines and ravens, characteristic birds of the north Anglesey coast, are regular visitors to this low headland. It is, however, as an autumn seabird passage watchpoint that it has become well known to birdwatchers, along with Strumble Head in Pembrokeshire and South Stack on Anglesey. Systematic watches of seabirds have taken place each autumn since 1976 and have been well documented in the *Cambrian Bird Reports*. The best movements of seabirds at Point Lynas have been found to take place on mornings with strong or gale force west to north-west winds, particularly when there have previously been long periods of south-west gales. On such mornings seabirds that have been blown into Liverpool Bay pass close inshore as they re-orientate westwards. Movements can involve very large numbers of gannets, kittiwakes, Manx shearwaters and auks during the period August to November, and rarer species such as Leach's petrels, pomarine skuas and Sabine's gulls have been seen on several occasions. The best vantage points are the lee of the foghorn building or from low above the rocks at the extreme northeast tip.

Location: 3 miles east of Amlwch at northeastern tip of Anglesey, reached off A5025 on unclassified road through Llaneilian.
Access: car parking at start of road leading to lighthouse before cattle grid.
Map reference: SH480937

Bailey Einon Wood and Shaky Bridge

Powys

Set on the banks of the Ithon, east of Llandrindod Wells, Bailey Einon Wood is a reserve of the Radnorshire Wildlife Trust. It contains several types of woodland, ranging from ash (with hazel as the shrub layer), wetter patches with alder, and oak-dominated areas with field maple. Dippers, kingfishers and grey wagtails nest along the river and pied flycatchers, redstarts, wood and willow warblers and marsh tits breed in the woodland. There is a nature trail through the reserve, starting from the entrance near Shaky Bridge. The Shaky Bridge Forest Trail through the coniferous plantations of Cwmbrith is complementary to the trail through the broad-leaved woodland of Bailey Einon. The plantations have goldcrests, chaffinches and several species of tit. The trail also embraces some areas of alder, ash and oak, open hill and riverside, which add variety to the walk. On the open hill it is often possible to see ravens, buzzards and kestrels, with wheatears and meadow pipits in summer.

Location: 1½ miles east of Llandrindod Wells. From A483 take Cefnllys Road and Cefnllys Lane.
Access: unrestricted. Entrance at Shaky Bridge. Trails. Car park. Picnic site.
Map reference: SO084612

Bardsey Island

Gwynedd

Bardsey, the only sizeable offshore island in North Wales, is a National Nature Reserve owned by the Bardsey Island Trust and farmed by a small resident community. It is separated from the tip of the Lleyn Peninsula by a turbulent tide race. Bardsey Bird and Field Observatory (the only observatory now in existence in Wales) has, since its foundation in 1953, enabled thousands of naturalists to stay on the island. Basic but homely accommodation is available for up to 12 people at a former farmhouse in the centre of the island. Except when there are specific courses, visitors are expected to cater for themselves.

The island is 445 acres in area, rising abruptly from the sea on its eastern side to a ridge, the mountain sloping gently westwards through furze and bracken slopes to a patchwork of small green fields. The commonest breeding bird is Manx shearwater, with about 3,500 to 5,000 pairs, and there is also an important breeding population of choughs (four to seven pairs). Bardsey is well known as one of the few sites where night migration can actually be observed. Under certain weather conditions following the new moon, migrants are attracted to the revolving beams of the lighthouse, sometimes in thousands. Since 1978 a unique 'false lighthouse' (powerful quartz-iodide lamps on a high mast) has drawn birds safely away from the lighthouse proper. Spring

7. South Stack Cliffs   RSPB

This RSPB reserve consists of two separate areas; the dramatic sea cliffs and heathland of Holyhead Mountain make up the northern part, while the maritime heathland of Penrhosfeilw Common is the southern section. The most numerous seabirds are guillemots (about 3,500 pairs) with about 700 pairs of razorbills, 40 pairs of puffins and an increasing colony of kittiwakes. Six pairs of choughs breed on or adjacent to the reserve and the birds are present all the year round, congregating in a noisy flock in the winter.

The reserve is one of the foremost migration watchpoints in North Wales, both for land birds and seabirds. On most summer days, especially with a westerly wind, Manx shearwaters and gannets may be seen flying past, while in spring and autumn large movements of passerines can be recorded in suitable weather conditions. Hundreds of wheatears and swallows may pass through daily, with smaller numbers of willow and grasshopper warblers, whinchats and ring ouzels. In early winter thousands of starlings, chaffinches and other species pass westward to the warmer climate of Ireland. Rare species recorded recently include red-footed falcon, honey buzzard, dotterel, hoopoe, wryneck and bee-eater. Breeding seabirds are best seen from Ellin's Tower during the period April to mid July.

Location: north-west tip of Holy Island, 2 miles west of Holyhead off unclassified road.
Access and facilities: reserve open all year off unclassified road. Public footpaths. Information Centre (Ellin's Tower) open Easter to mid September. Centre overlooks main seabird colony – telescopes and binoculars provided. Refreshments adjacent to reserve. Car parks at South Stack and Penrhosfeilw. Toilets.
Map reference: SH205823

South Stack – on the coast path

migration on Bardsey is dominated by willow warblers, sedge warblers, whitethroats and spotted flycatchers, while the peak of autumn migration in October is also the best time to see uncommon vagrants – blackpoll warblers and rose-breasted grosbeaks from North America and Pallas's warblers and dusky warblers from Siberia are among the exciting birds that have been recorded in recent autumns.

Location: 2 miles west of the Lleyn Peninsula.
Access: by boat from Pwllheli (boatman: phone Pwllheli 612916). Observatory bookings: phone Newton Abbot 68580. Observatory boat leaves Pwllheli 8.30am Sat March to end November.
Map reference: SH119216

Blackpill

West Glamorgan

Blackpill's mud flats are at the western extremity of Swansea Bay between the mouth of the Tawe and Mumbles Head. A good variety of waders has been recorded here in every month of the year, including oystercatchers, ringed plovers, grey plovers, knots, sanderlings, dunlins, curlews and redshanks. The waders give magnificent views with a rising tide, but great care should be taken not to disturb them at the high-tide roost. Watch from the footpaths and do not go out on to the beach. The site has achieved prominence in ornithological recording annals as the locality in which the first British ring-billed gull was seen, in March 1973. Since that time, through the efforts of a group of gull enthusiasts, this

North American visitor has been found to be of moderately frequent occurrence at Blackpill, mainly in the period from February to May, although it has been recorded in all months of the year. Increasing numbers of Mediterranean gulls also occur in all months of the year, but chiefly in the two periods February to May and July to August. There are also occasional glaucous and Iceland gulls in the large flocks of commoner gull species which frequent the bay. Glaucous and Iceland gulls are seen chiefly in the winter.

Location: off A4067, west of Swansea.
Access and facilities: car park along Mill Lane, which is off A4067 behind beach. Toilets beside main road. Views of foreshore from promenade adjoining A4067.
Map reference: SS618907

The Carneddau

Gwynedd

The Carneddau is the largest group of mountains in Snowdonia. Two peaks, Carnedd Llywelyn and Carnedd Dafydd, top the 3,000ft contour, and there is a substantial plateau above 2,800ft flanked by steep rock outcrops. On the crags and screes of these high tops there is a sparse but characteristic breeding population of peregrines, ravens, ring ouzels and wheatears, birds which are also found on the other Snowdonia peaks. What is special, however, is the regularity with which dotterels occur on migration in May. There are also occasional records from the Carneddau summits in

Llanberis Pass

April and October, but by far the greatest number of records is from the period a week either side of 15 May. At that time small parties of dotterels rest on migration on the high plateaux, favouring the vicinity of Foel Fras. This is very wild country, so an ascent should only be undertaken by well-equipped walkers in good weather, bearing in mind that the weather can deteriorate rapidly in these high places. Map reading can be difficult in mist owing to the absence of well-defined landmarks. There are many possible ascent routes to choose from, ranging from the tough direct ascent from Ogwen Cottage on the A5 to the long walk from Aber Falls, which lie to the south of Aber village on the A55 Bangor to Chester road. Full details of the choice of routes are given in several walking guides to the region (eg *The Welsh Peaks* by W.A. Poucher).

For the birdwatcher who wishes to get a flavour of the breeding birds of the mountains without such a strenuous ascent, there are many much more frequented and less arduous routes, such as the Miner's Track, which leads into the heart of the Snowdon 'horseshoe' of peaks from Pen-y-Pass in the Pass of Llanberis (the A4086, reached from the A5 at Capel Curig). Here, there is a chance of seeing choughs, which breed in the old mine shafts of the area.

Location: east of A5 between Capel Curig and Bethesda.
Access: on tracks and paths. Care required.
Map reference: SH648604

Coed Garth Gell

Gwynedd RSPB

Coed Garth Gell is part of the complex of woodland reserves which the RSPB has built up on both sides of the Mawddach Estuary in the Snowdonia National Park. This wood is on the north side of the estuary and consists of 115 acres of oak and birch on the slopes above the deep gorge of the Afon Cwmmynach. There are also open heather, bracken and boggy areas, the latter with the strongly aromatic bog myrtle. The wood is bounded by a magnificently constructed drystone wall, so characteristic of this part of Wales. The breeding community of birds is characteristic of these western oak woods, with pied flycatchers, redstarts, wood warblers, tree pipits, nuthatches, ravens and buzzards. Black grouse are also seen in small numbers.

A well graded track follows the river past former gold mines and the remains of a gold processing plant and an old smithy, Coed Garth Gell being part of the famous Merioneth goldfield. The mines are water-filled and dangerous. From the top edge of the wood the views along the Mawddach Estuary, with the dramatic outline of Cader Idris in the background, are quite breathtaking.

Directly opposite Coed Garth Gell is the Penmaenpool Wildlife Centre, based in a former Great Western Railway signal box overlooking the river. It is owned by the Snowdonia National Park Authority and operated by the RSPB and North Wales Naturalists' Trust and makes a good preliminary to Coed Garth Gell, providing information on the area as well as a good observation point for watching red-breasted mergansers, oystercatchers, grey herons and other river birds.

Location: 3 miles west of Dolgellau. Coed Garth Gell off A496. Penmaenpool Wildlife Centre off A493 by George III Hotel.
Access and facilities: unrestricted to Coed Garth Gell via public footpath from A496 opposite Borthwnog Hall (on Barmouth side of point where road from Penmaenpool Toll Bridge meets A496). Car parking space along main road. Penmaenpool Wildlife Centre open daily late May to September. Car park. Toilets.
Map reference: SH687191

Connah's Quay Nature Reserve

Clwyd

On land owned by the Central Electricity Generating Board, this 65-acre reserve has been developed through a happy partnership between the board and the Deeside Naturalists' Society. It consists of salt marsh and tidal mud flats, with a 17-acre brackish pool bordering the river created by embanking an area of salting. The pool attracts several species of migrant waders, including greenshank and green sandpiper, as well as herons, kingfishers, and goldeneyes. Two hides have been constructed overlooking the lagoon. A further hide, with disabled access, has been built on a vantage point overlooking Oakenholt Marsh, where spectacular flights of waders to high tide roosts occur in the two hours preceding high water, when the tide is 28ft and above,

particularly from August through to March. Up to 1,200 black-tailed godwits, and up to 100 spotted redshanks, are particular reserve specialities. Large numbers of wildfowl occur in winter, especially wigeon and teal. A nature trail has been developed through an area of rough scrub, and a field studies centre gives information about the habitats of the reserve.

Location: at head of Dee Estuary, west of Connah's Quay, off A548.
Access and facilities: arrangements to visit must be made through secretary, Deeside Naturalists' Society, 38 Kelsterton Road, Connah's Quay, Deeside, Clwyd. Hides. Nature trail. Field Studies Centre.
Map reference: SJ275715

Cors Caron (Tregaron Bog)

Dyfed

Covering 1,950 acres, Cors Caron is one of the best examples of raised bog in England and Wales and one of the largest areas of peat moss in Wales. It is a National Nature Reserve. Breeding birds here include teal, snipe, redshanks, grasshopper warblers, sedge warblers, reed buntings and water rails, but the bog is best known as a winter site for a variety of raptors, especially as a good spot to see red kites, the 'blue riband' birds of the mid Wales hills. In addition to red kites, other regular winter visitors include hen harriers, buzzards, peregrines, merlins, barn owls and short-eared owls. There is also a regular wintering flock of whooper swans and other wildfowl in small pools in and around the reserve.

The nature trail terminates at an observation tower which gives good views of the reserve and overlooks a large pond and scrape.

Top – Cors Caron, a wild landscape with superb birds. Above – Penmaenpool Wildlife Centre (see Coed Garth Gell), housed in an old railway signal box

A winter visit to this reserve should locate several red kites, but if this fails, a drive over the mountain roads from Tregaron to Abergwesyn, from Rhayader to Devil's Bridge, or from Tregaron to Devil's Bridge should give sightings of hunting birds.

Location: 3 miles north of Tregaron, off B4343.
Access: unrestricted to nature trail (reached from lay-by on B4343), but rest of reserve by permit only; details from warden, Minawel, Ffair Rhos, Ystrad Meurig, Dyfed.
Map reference: SN690640

Cwm Clydach

West Glamorgan RSPB

This reserve was established with the invaluable co-operation of local farmers. It consists principally of oak woodland along the banks of the Afon Clydach, and has birds typical of such habitats. Among the nesting birds are buzzards, sparrowhawks, ravens, pied flycatchers, wood warblers and tawny owls. Dippers and grey wagtails are likely to be seen along the river.

Location: 4 miles north of Swansea. Reached on unclassified road from Clydach to Ammanford. Access: limited car parking at Glyneithrym Uchaf Farm. Access only to waymarked path along river.
Map reference: SN682053

Dinas Reserve

Dyfed   RSPB

This 100-acre conical hill is a part of the 1,700-acre RSPB Gwenffrwd reserve. To the north it is bounded by the deep gorge and cataracts of the infant Afon Tywi, just below where it emerges from the massive containing wall of Llyn Brianne, and to the west by the combined waters of the Tywi and the Doethie, which meet at the western corner of the hill at Junction Pool. Oak woods grow on the hill's deeper soils, whereas the boulder-strewn north-western side is covered in gnarled oak and birch, remnants of the ancient forests which once covered most of Wales. The high rainfall gives rise to damp rock faces festooned with luxuriant mosses and ferns.

The hill is famous for the cave which formed a hideaway for Twm Sion Cati, a real-life hero of Welsh folklore who lived here in the 16th century.

Dinas Hill is also famous as one of the erstwhile nesting sites of the small relic population of red kites which maintained a precarious foothold as a British breeding bird in the early years of this century. The well-known photograph of a female kite at the nest taken in 1926 by the late Arthur Brook, doyen of bird photographers, was taken on Dinas Hill. Nowadays kites do not nest on the hill, but, with a much expanded population from the desperate days of the 1920s, they can be frequently encountered over the surrounding valleys in winter and

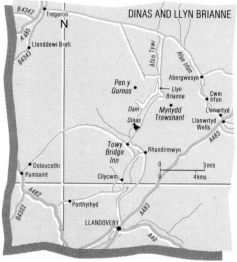

spring. The birdlife of the reserve is dominated in spring and early summer by pied flycatchers, which have taken very readily to the nestboxes erected throughout the woodland. Wood warblers, redstarts and tree pipits are also well distributed through the woods, while buzzards, ravens, sparrowhawks and peregrines are frequently seen. Along the Tywi there are dippers, grey wagtails, common sandpipers and goosanders.

A public footpath runs round the foot of the hill and is connected to an information centre and car park by a wooden boardwalk which takes a quarter-mile route through otherwise impassable bog and alder carr. From the path in spring and early summer it is possible to see all the characteristic breeding birds of the western oak woods as well as being able to look out along the adjacent valley sides for soaring birds of prey. The birdlife is less spectacular at other times of the year, but this circular route goes through some of the most beautiful and spectacular scenery in Wales. The river is very dangerous and visitors should not attempt to cross.

Location: 10 miles north of Llandovery, on unclassified road leading to Llyn Brianne through Rhandirmwyn.
Access and facilities: Dinas Trail open at all times from car park. Information centre open Easter to end August. Toilets at Llyn Brianne. Dogs must be on lead at all times.
Map reference: SN788472

Craig yr Aderyn (Bird Rock)

Gwynedd

The valley of the Afon Dysynni north-east of Tywyn is dominated by the citadel-like outlines of Craig yr Aderyn, which rises steeply from the valley bottom to a height of 720ft above sea level. Although now seven miles inland, in historical times it was lapped by the sea, which perhaps explains the presence of the famous breeding colony of cormorants. The cormorants nest high up on the north-facing cliffs, where their neighbours include choughs, jackdaws, ravens and kestrels. As well as the one or two pairs of choughs which nest here, this is a good spot to see this species outside the breeding season when a small flock often frequents the crag and adjoining grasslands. The best viewing point is from the minor road to the north-west of Craig yr Aderyn, but observers should beware of a stiff neck since the crags rise steeply above the road!

Location: 6 miles north-east of Tywyn.
Access: from B4405 at Abergynolwyn or from A493 at Bryncrug, in either case taking narrow unclassified road along south side of Dysynni Valley.
Map reference: SH643068

Craig yr Aderyn – an inland cliff

Dowrog Common

Dyfed

Dowrog Common is a 200-acre mosaic of wet heathland and fen vegetation with more than 350 species of flowering plants. It is of national importance as an example of a maritime lowland moor and is a reserve of the Dyfed Wildlife Trust. There are several small pools which attract whooper swans and Bewick's swans, wigeon, pintail, teal, pochard and tufted duck in winter, and provide a suitable nesting habitat for water rails. Dowrog was formerly a regular breeding site for Montagu's harriers and merlins; now, sadly, merlins occur only as winter visitors and Montagu's harriers are only seen as very scarce passage migrants, although hen harriers hunt over the common in winter.

Location: 2 miles north-east of St David's.
Access: A487 Fishguard to St David's road crosses southern part of reserve, but best access is from unclassified road to Llanrhian, which turns off B4583 just north of St David's. Just past Gwrhyd Mawr Farm track to right leads to car park on edge of reserve. Open from car park along footpaths and pony tracks.
Map reference: SM773273

Dyffryn Wood

Powys
RSPB

This 65-acre RSPB reserve consists largely of a sessile oak wood lying between 675 and 825ft above sea level, but on the higher slopes the dominant vegetation is bracken, heather and gorse. Grazing animals have been excluded from the southern section of the wood for at least 15 years. Consequently natural regeneration is good here wherever there are gaps in the canopy of the stands of mature trees, with localised dense areas of oak and rowan seedlings and saplings. Holly, hawthorn and honeysuckle are also present in the wood and there is a field layer dominated by bilberry. By contrast, the northern part of the wood was clear-felled for timber during the 1940s and the present

wood has regenerated from the cut stumps, forming a closed and uniform canopy with a very sparse ground flora. Breeding birds of the woodland, particularly the southern area, include high numbers of wood warblers, pied flycatchers and redstarts, while the slopes above hold yellowhammers, whinchats and tree pipits. A visitor trail has been established as a circular route through the reserve, encompassing the woodland and the open heath above. The views over the Wye Valley from the upper parts of the trail are outstanding and there is always a good chance of seeing a variety of soaring birds, particularly buzzards and ravens.

Location: ¾ mile south of Rhayader, off A470 past turning signposted Gigrin Farm Trail.
Access: to reserve and start of trail from lay-by on A470 at north end of wood.
Map reference: SN979672

Elan Valley

Powys/Dyfed

Before the creation of the series of reservoirs which make up the Elan Valley complex, this area was one of the wildest and most remote in Britain. The reservoirs have an undoubted grandeur of their own, and it is still perfectly possible to savour the wind-swept splendour of the open moors. The Elan Valley Estate of the Welsh Water Authority covers about 70 square miles of land comprising the watersheds of the rivers Elan and Claerwen. The average elevation of the estate is more than 1,200ft above sea level and by far the greater part of it consists of a desolate moorland plateau covered by blanket bog or acid grasslands grazed by large numbers of sheep. Other habitats include about 700 acres of coniferous and 300 acres of broadleaved woodland, rocky crags, meadows and a series of reservoirs.

This diversity makes it one of the most important parts of Wales for breeding bird populations. The uplands hold the greatest concentrations of breeding golden plovers and dunlins in Wales, together with other waders such as lapwing, curlew and snipe.

The high numbers of sheep help to support a large population of carrion-feeding birds, including what is probably the greatest density of ravens in Europe, many buzzards and several red kites. The crags which flank the moorland provide nesting sites for peregrines, ravens, kestrels and ring ouzels, while wheatears, stonechats and whinchats breed on the screes and bracken slopes below the crags. In the oak woodlands all the characteristic species occur in good numbers, particularly pied flycatcher, wood warbler, redstart and tree pipit, and there are small numbers of siskins and, occasionally, firecrests in the conifers. Around the reservoirs and the streams which flow into them are breeding grey wagtails and common sandpipers, as well as mallards, goosanders and black-headed gulls.

Location: 2½ miles west of Rhayader, off B4518 to Elan Village and unclassified road leading past series of reservoirs to Rhayader/Cwm Ystwyth mountain road.
Access and facilities: open to estate, but danger of getting lost on upland plateaux in bad weather, so seek advice before attempting to walk in remote parts of area. Visitor centre (west of Elan village) open 10 am to 6 pm daily March to October. Admission charges. Refreshments. Talks. Guided walks May to September. Car park. Toilets. Further information from Head Ranger, or tourist information desk, Elan Valley Visitor Centre, Rhayader, Powys.
Map reference: SN928647

Elan Valley – moorland, woodlands and reservoirs form a rich mosaic of habitats

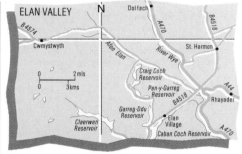

Fronlas Farm, Newtown

Powys

Fronlas is an educational farm serving the Department of Agriculture at Montgomery College of Further Education, and over the last few years it has been developed to show how farming and wildlife can be integrated. A circular trail of about one and a half miles leads from Fronlas to show what can be achieved. Leaflets explaining aspects of the farm can be collected from the information centre at the start of the trail. The Cwm Fronlas Nature Trail follows a woodland dingle with a stream in which breeding birds include pied flycatcher and long-tailed tit. Farming enterprises here include dairy cattle and sheep.

Location: 1 mile south-west of Newtown off A489. Turn off main road opposite Montgomery College of Further Education and then right along Mochdre Lane. Farm entrance is on left.
Facilities: car park. Toilets.
Map reference: SO091901

Glaslyn Nature Reserve

Powys

Situated on the north flank of the Plynlimon uplands, this reserve of the Montgomeryshire Wildlife Trust forms one of the last remaining areas of heather moorland on that massif. The reserve comprises 530 acres, including part of Glaslyn Lake and the scree slopes and gorge of the Afon Dulas. At an elevation of 1,500ft above sea level, this is a site of dramatic vistas with a spectacular view northwards towards the Dyfi Valley. The moorland and gorge provide breeding sites for many species, including wheatear, golden plover, ring ouzel, red grouse and raven. Birds of prey hunting the area regularly include red kite, buzzard and peregrine. In summer several pairs of common sandpipers breed around the lake, while in winter there are small numbers of goldeneyes, tufted ducks and pochards, and occasional whooper swans.

At the nearby village of Dylife the remains of what was a flourishing lead mining industry during the 18th and 19th centuries can be seen. Views from here take in the Plynlimon moors, and, on clear days, Cader Idris.

Location: off unclassified Llanidloes to Machynlleth road, west of Dylife.
Access: track signposted Glyndwr's Way, 1½ miles west of Dylife, leads southward to reserve. Open access to reserve, but visitors are asked not to go into Afon Dulas Gorge because of danger of falling rock and unstable scree slopes.
Map reference: SN825943

Grassholm – there are about 30,000 pairs of gannets on the island. They are so densely packed together in the nesting season that from the air they make half the island seem white!

Grassholm Island

Dyfed   **RSPB**

Grassholm is a small island, about 22 acres in extent, approximately seven miles due west of the two larger islands of Skokholm and Skomer and 10 miles from the mainland coast of Pembrokeshire. It was purchased by the RSPB in 1948 and has been managed as a nature reserve since that date. In a very exposed position, the island is the remnant of a basalt ridge and rises to a plateau at about 150ft above sea level. The steepest cliffs are on the north side, which is where the important gannet colony was first established as far back as 1860, possibly even earlier. Since the 1920s the colony has expanded dramatically to cover the northernmost third of the island, and now numbers approximately 30,000 breeding pairs (more than 28,500 nests were counted from aerial photographs in 1984). As such, it is the second largest gannetry in the British Isles, after St. Kilda. By contrast, the former puffin colony, numbering over 100,000 pairs at the turn of the century, is now deserted. One contemporary account records that in 1893 the breeding population of puffins was so great that it was impossible to make camp on a space clear of them and puffins emerged from their burrows in the tent at night! The desertion of the island by puffins has been quite likely due to the collapse of their extensive burrowing systems in the easily worked *Festuca* peat. The labyrinth of collapsed burrows still makes walking difficult over that part of the island not now covered by the gannets. Besides the gannet colony, other breeding birds include small numbers of kittiwakes, razorbills, guillemots and shags, and a variety of passage migrants has been recorded in the autumn. Up to 120 Atlantic grey seals haul-out on the island, but none breed.

Landings are only possible on the island in calm weather and are only allowed from mid June onwards so that all possible protection is given to the gannets at the crucial earlier period when they have eggs and are vulnerable to predation by gulls. There are still young gannets in the nest well into October, but the best months for a visit are July and August. It is necessary to be fit and active to accomplish a landing on the island. Further details for intending visitors are available from the RSPB Wales Office, Bryn Aderyn, The Bank, Newtown, Powys.

Location: 10 miles west of Dyfed mainland.
Access: by boat from Martin's Haven (details from Dale Sailing Company, telephone Dale 349) from June on. White posts on island to south side of gannet colony denote line beyond which visitors should not go.
Map reference: SM599093

Great Orme, Llandudno

Gwynedd

The Great Orme is a spectacular limestone headland, most of which is a country park and nature reserve administered by Aberconwy Borough Council. The main ornithological interest is the breeding colonies of seabirds, particularly guillemots, razorbills and kittiwakes which nest on the cliffs below the Marine Drive, in the vicinity of the former lighthouse. Other breeding species include raven, rock pipit, stonechat and wheatear. The headland can be interesting at migration times, with passage waders such as dotterel and golden plover, and passerines such as ring ouzel and yellow wagtail. On the summit is a country park visitor centre. A one-way scenic route for cars, the Marine Drive, skirts the headland (a toll system operates).

Location: immediately outside Llandudno.
Access and facilities: by road, footpath, cablecar or tramway. Visitor centre open daily Easter to end September. Car park. Refreshments. Picnic Site. Toilets.
Map reference: SH766834

Kenfig Pool

Mid Glamorgan

A Local Nature Reserve managed by Mid Glamorgan County Council, Kenfig Pool comprises nearly 1,400 acres of fresh water, dune slacks and marsh. It attracts a good variety of winter waterfowl, of which whooper swans, mallard, teal, pochard, gadwall, shoveler, tufted duck and goldeneye are the most regular. Breeding species include sedge, reed and grasshopper warblers, coot, great crested grebe, and mallard, with stonechat, yellowhammer, linnet, reed bunting and whitethroat on the bracken- and scrub-covered dunes.

Location: 2 miles north of Porthcawl, west of M4.
Access and facilities: open all year. Reserve centre (open 9 am to 4 pm weekdays, pm only weekends). Hide at south end of pool. Car park.
Map reference: SS796815

Lake Vyrnwy (Llyn Efyrnwy)

Powys   RSPB

At more than 15,000 acres this is the largest reserve managed by the RSPB. Set deep in the southern part of Berwyn Mountains it encompasses a wide range of habitats, from the lake itself through small meadows, pockets of deciduous woodland, conifer plantations and crags to undulating heather moorland. The lake is somewhat limited in its birdlife, being acid and deep, but it does support a small breeding population of goosanders and great crested grebes as well as common sandpipers round the shoreline and dippers and grey wagtails on the streams that feed the lake. The small meadows hold a variety of orchids and are good for butterflies. In the oak and birch woods there are good breeding populations of pied flycatchers, redstarts and wood warblers. Substantial tree planting schemes will add to the broadleaved woodland canopy in years to come. Siskins and goldcrests are characteristic of the mature conifer plantations and in most years there are a few pairs of firecrests, while crossbills can be very numerous although somewhat unpredictable in their appearances. Breeding birds of prey in the woodland and crags between the lake and the moors include buzzards, sparrowhawks, long-eared owls and peregrines. There are also many pairs of ravens and a very small number of ring ouzels.

The Berwyn Mountains make up the largest remaining area of heather moorland in Wales, and the Vyrnwy upland has more than 2,500 acres of heather. Small numbers of black grouse live along the periphery of

Lake Vyrnwy (main picture).
Inset is the dune system of Kenfig Pool, with flowering restharrow, rattle and thyme

the moorland, and on the high moors breeding species include red grouse, merlin, hen harrier and golden plover.

Spring and early summer are the best times to visit the reserve. In winter the moorland is very bleak, deserted by all but the hardy red grouse, although on the lake the resident wildfowl are joined by small numbers of tufted ducks, pochards and goldeneyes.

Location: 10 miles south of Bala, encircled by B4393.
Access and facilities: information centre, open weekends Easter to Whitsun; daily until end of September. Hides. Car park. Toilets. Several small car parks with picnic tables on road round lake. Refreshments at Lake Vyrnwy Hotel and Post Office.
Map reference: SJ018192

Llandegfedd Reservoir

Gwent

With a fluctuating water level, this 50-acre reservoir is not really suitable for breeding waterfowl, although great crested grebes attempt to nest in some years. It is, however, a major site for wintering and passage waterfowl, and regularly holds large numbers of mallards, teal, wigeon, pochards, tufted ducks and coots, as well as the largest roost of goosanders in Wales. Spring and autumn passage are also rewarding times, with regular arctic, common and black terns and a variety of waders including green and common sandpipers. Most wildfowl congregate at the northern end of the reservoir, but a good variety can still be seen at the more disturbed southern end.

Location: 2 miles east of Pontypool.
Access and facilities: southern end: signposted from A4042 at Lower New Inn. Car park. Picnic site. Toilet. South-west end: reached from Sluvad. Car park. Footpath. Northern end: approached from A472 at Glascoed. Permit for north from Welsh Water Authority, South Eastern Division, Pentwyn Road, Nelson, Treharris, Mid Glamorgan. Car park. Hides.
Map reference: ST328986

Llangorse Lake

Powys

This is the largest natural lake in South Wales, and because its water is both shallow and full of nutrients it is exceptionally rich in wildlife. A wide variety of wildfowl can be seen on the open water, and the reed beds harbour large populations of warblers and other birds. The lake is extremely popular as a water sports centre, which causes disturbance to some birds, while others seem unaffected.

Breeding species of bird here include great crested grebe, coot and mute swan, with 150–200 pairs of reed warblers nesting in the peripheral reed beds. In winter there are good numbers of teal, wigeon and mallards. Through the activities of the Llangorse Ringing Group a substantial amount of data exists to show that the lake is an important 're-fuelling' point for migrant sedge warblers during the period late July to mid September. There is also an important autumn roost for migrating sand

martins from July to early September in the reed beds which fringe the southern shore. A maximum of 10,000 was recorded in 1979 but the current maximum is in the order of 2,000 to 3,000.

The lake is set in the eastern part of the Brecon Beacons National Park. Further east are Mynydd Llangorse and the Black Mountains, rolling hills with few roads and few visitors. To the south-west, beyond the A40, is the Usk Valley. The contrasts in the wildlife of these two landscapes are quite dramatic.

Location: 5 miles south-east of Brecon.
Access: from church at Llangasty-Talyllyn (reached on unclassified road from A40) footpath leads along south side of lake.
Map reference: SO133263

Llyn Brenig

Clwyd

Llyn Brenig is an upland reservoir covering 920 acres in the heart of the wild moorland of Mynydd Hiraethog, 1,200ft above sea level. On the lake itself breeding species include great crested grebe, mallard and teal, with common sandpiper along the shoreline. Adjoining areas of heather moorland, which form part of the Welsh Water Authority estate, have a varied breeding population which includes red and black grouse, snipe, curlew, whinchat, stonechat, wheatear and twite.

Location: 6 miles south-west of Denbigh, 3 miles north of Cerrigydrudion, reached from B4501.
Access and facilities: open at all times. Footpaths. Nature trail. Visitor centre (south-west of reservoir) open daily except winter weekends and Christmas. Car park. Toilets. Hide (northern arm of reservoir). Picnic sites.
Map reference: SH967547

Llyn Mawr and Llyn y Tarw

Powys

A reserve of the Montgomeryshire Wildlife Trust, Llyn Mawr comprises a 20-acre upland lake with a further 10 acres of associated wetland habitats. On the north side the lake is fringed by willow carr, while on the other sides there are marshes, wet heath and gorse scrub. The lake is noted for its wetland birds, which include breeding black-headed gulls, mallards, teal, tufted ducks, coots, Canada geese, great crested grebes, snipe and curlews. Whinchats and reed buntings nest in the fringe habitats. In winter the wildfowl population is augmented by small numbers of pochards, wigeons, goldeneyes and goosanders and occasional visits by the flock of whooper swans which winter in the Severn Valley between Newtown and Caersws. Llyn y Tarw is in a more exposed situation, less than a mile east of Llyn Mawr. It has a substantial breeding colony of black-headed gulls, and redshanks can often be seen in the breeding season. On adjoining grass moorland and improved upland pastures there is a small wintering flock of Greenland white-fronted geese, the only such inland flock in England and Wales.

Location: 7 miles north-west of Newtown, reached from unclassified road off A470 between Pontdolgoch and Clatter.
Access: open. Roadside parking just before bungalow overlooking Llyn Mawr. Access path to lake near bungalow. No physical boundaries demarcate reserve, so visitors are requested to stay as close to lakeside as possible. Footpath leads eastwards to Llyn y Tarw south of bungalow.
Map reference: SO011971

Llangorse Lake

Loggerheads Country Park

Clwyd

Moel Famau, highest peak of the Clwydian range, overlooks this country park, which consists of a limestone escarpment, mixed woodland and a section of the Afon Alyn. The river is shallow and fast flowing and provides an ideal habitat for dippers and grey wagtails. Pied flycatchers, chiffchaffs, treecreepers, green and great spotted woodpeckers breed in the woodland along the river. The path along the river is known as the Leete, taking its name from the watercourse or leat originally constructed to carry water to power water wheels at the lead mines lower down the valley. A little way down the river swallow holes in the limestone bedrock cause some of the river water to disappear underground, sometimes resulting in a completely dry river bed.

Those who climb to the 1,817-ft summit of Moel Famau will be rewarded with superb views (on clear days), as far as the Lake District.

Location: 2¹/₂ miles west of Mold, off A494 Mold to Ruthin road, just past Loggerheads Inn. Access and facilities: open all year. Information centre. Refreshments. Car park. Picnic area. Nature trail. Further information from Clwyd County Council, Shire Hall, Mold, Clwyd. Map reference: SJ198626

Pembrokeshire Coast Path

Dyfed

This path covers 186 miles of the most marvellous coastal scenery, from Poppit in the north to Amroth in the south. The line of the waymarked path is as near to the cliff edge as is practicable. Although over some stretches the path is forced back from the cliff, in making these detours the walker is almost never out of sight of the sea. Two weeks is the ideal time to allow for coverage of the whole footpath but a short walk along any piece of it will always be worth while.

By far the greater part of the Pembrokeshire coast is rocky, much of it with high sea cliffs interspersed with small bays. The variety of habitats along the coast is very marked, however, and includes estuaries with salt marshes, shingle ridges and sand dunes and remnant scrub woodland and thickets where there is some shelter from the prevailing wind. Along the rocky sections of coast there is a resident population of choughs, ravens and peregrines, all of which should be frequently encountered at any time of the year. The chough population of the Pembrokeshire coast numbers about 50 breeding pairs, more than a third of the total Welsh population. Ravens can be counted as commonplace. Thickets along the clifftop provide ideal habitats for breed-

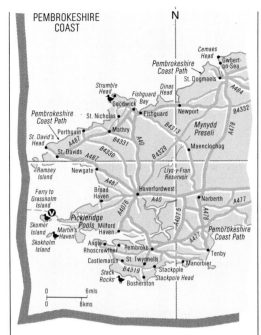

ing birds such as stonechat and whitethroat, while in winter vast numbers of northern birds find shelter in the relatively mild climate of Pembrokeshire.

A comprehensive programme of guided

Oxwich

West Glamorgan

The attractive Oxwich National Nature Reserve is in a particularly beautiful setting on the south coast of the Gower Peninsula. It contains an unusually varied series of habitats ranging from sand dunes and salt marsh on the seaward side, to well-established reed beds, open water and mixed fen, oak and alder scrub and mature broad leaved woodland on the landward side. The reserve totals 700 acres including more than 100 acres of reed swamp, which is the most important habitat for the birds. Notable breeding species of the reed swamp include bearded tit, grasshopper warbler, Cetti's warbler, reed warbler (at least 450 pairs), sedge warbler, water rail, little grebe and pochard. Bitterns and marsh harriers are regular visitors and rarities such as purple

herons and little bitterns have spent the summer at Oxwich. In the woodland breeding birds include buzzards, nuthatches, blackcaps and willow warblers.

Location: 12 miles south-west of Swansea, along unclassified road signposted Oxwich from A4118 Porteynon road. Access and facilities: Oxwich Reserve Centre open all day during school summer holidays, otherwise from 10 am to 12 noon weekends, 9 am to 1 pm weekdays. A variety of leaflets and bird list available from centre, as are permits for access to hide overlooking fresh water marsh. Car park (charge). Toilets. Map reference: SS502865

Oxwich – a beautiful stretch of the Gower Peninsula coastline.
Inset is a purple heron, one of the many rare birds that have been recorded here

walks and events is arranged throughout the year by the Pembrokeshire Coast National Park. Information on these is available from the Information Officer, National Park Department, County Offices, St Thomas Green, Haverfordwest, together with details of the wide variety of accommodation available along the route. Four outstanding areas are described below.

1. Strumble Head

This is the premier spot for watching seabird passage in Wales. An old Ministry of Defence building, with car parking adjacent, provides a sheltered look-out for seawatching enthusiasts. The best season is from late July to the end of October when – if wind conditions are favourable – there can be spectacular movements of seabirds involving arctic, pomarine and great skuas, kittiwakes, gannets and Manx shearwaters, as well as small numbers of rarer species such as sooty shearwater, great shearwater, long-tailed skua, Sabine's gull and Leach's petrel. Rare passerine migrants are also recorded at Strumble – recent sightings including Richard's pipit, yellow-browed warbler and Lapland bunting.

Location: 4 miles north-west of Fishguard, reached on unclassified road to Tresinwen.
Map reference: SM895413

2. Pickleridge Pools

These are coastal lagoons adjacent to the B4327 Haverfordwest to Dale road. This is a good year-round place to watch waders, regularly including oystercatchers, redshanks, dunlins, curlews and greenshanks.

Location: 6 miles west of Milford Haven, near Dale, adjacent to B4327.
Access: from car park at south end.
Map reference: SM812072

3. Stack Rocks

Breeding seabirds on Elegug Stack are the highlights of this section of coast. The near-vertical limestone cliffs of this small off-shore stack provide a breeding site for guillemots, razorbills, kittiwakes, fulmars and small numbers of shags. The scenery here is especially grand.

Location: 6 miles south-west of Pembroke, on unclassified road off B4319.
Access: road closed when Castlemartin Army Range is in use (indicated by signs and red warning flag). View of stack is excellent. Car park.
Map reference: SR925946

4. Bosherston Pools

Formed by blocking their exit to sea, this series of pools was originally intended to hold fish. They now provide a fine haven for wildlife and a beautiful place to visit – especially when the water lilies are in bloom. However, they are best for birds in winter, when they attract a wide range of wildfowl including pochards, goldeneyes, and teal. Grey herons, coots and moorhens are likely to be seen at any time. A network of paths leads around the pools, and these can be good for birds of woodland and scrub. Some of the paths lead to the beach – an excellent one of sand and very popular.

Pembrokeshire Coast Path – for much of its length the path runs along spectacular scenery such as that at St David's Head. A mixture of habitats along the coast makes for an exciting variety of birds

Location: Bosherston, on unclassified road off B4319 south of Pembroke.
Access: at all times; National Trust. Map near car park in village shows footpath network.
Map reference: SR966947

Peterstone Pill

Gwent

Consisting of salt marsh and mud flats on the north side of the Severn Estuary, this is the best site in Gwent for rare species of gulls, terns and waders. It is a reserve of the Gwent Trust for Nature Conservation. A particular feature here is that in the vicinity of Peterstone Pill the rising tide often pushes waders and wildfowl near to the sea wall, where close views can be obtained of them. The main importance of the site is as a winter feeding area for waders, principally dunlins, knots, redshanks, ringed plovers and grey plovers and also wildfowl, notably shovelers and small numbers of scaup and common scoters. Notable passage migrants include garganeys, little ringed plovers, whimbrels, wood sandpipers and little stints, while breeding birds include shelducks and redshanks. The sea wall makes a marvellous vantage point for overlooking the estuary.

Location: 5 miles south-west of Newport, reached on B4239 between Peterstone Wentlooge and St Brides Wentlooge.
Access: from parking space near junction of B4239 and unclassified road from Marshfield. Footpath along lane to sea wall.
Map reference: ST273811

Point of Air

Clwyd `RSPB`

Millions of invertebrates are the key to the importance of this RSPB reserve at the mouth of the Dee. They live in the mud flats here and are food for huge numbers of waders and wildfowl. Regular wader counts have shown that the Point can hold up to 45,000 waders at peak times, although, as with the rest of the Dee (and other UK estuaries), numbers have declined recently. The commonest waders are oystercatchers, knots, dunlins, curlews and redshanks, the total numbers usually peaking in winter at between 15,000 and 20,000 birds. Noisy and dazzling oystercatchers form a very significant proportion of the total Dee population and are a particular feature at the reserve throughout the year, feeding on the mud flats and roosting at high tide on the shingle spit or adjacent areas close to the colliery. Other waders regularly recorded include ringed plover, grey plover, and sanderling. Mallards and shelducks occur throughout the year and are joined by small numbers of teal, wigeon, pintail, shoveler and red-breasted merganser during the winter.

In autumn, large gatherings of terns rest at high tide on the shingle banks, regularly including common, arctic, Sandwich and little terns and occasionally roseate and black terns. Auks and great crested grebes are regular winter visitors and there can be a good passage of seabirds, especially in autumn when arctic, great and pomarine skuas are accompanying the terns in their southward migration. Leach's petrel is a

Skokholm – one of Pembrokeshire's famous bird islands

speciality of this area, and there might be several of them when there are prolonged westerly gales.

There is a regular wintering flock of snow buntings on the shingle spit, along with occasional twites, Lapland buntings and shore larks. The breeding bird population is limited by the beach's popularity with holidaymakers, so the best time for a visit is in autumn or winter. The best viewpoint is from the sea wall (the Llanasa Embankment) at the end of Station Road at Talacre. An exciting period is when waders are flying in to roost an hour or two before high water, especially on the highest spring tides.

Location: 3 miles east of Prestatyn, reached on unclassified road through Talacre, off A548.
Access: at all times, but care required on flats or salt marsh when tide rising. Do not disturb the high tide wader roosts. Limited parking on landward side of sea wall.
Map reference: SJ125848

Skokholm Island

Dyfed

Naturalist Ronald Lockley made Skokholm famous through such books as *Way to an Island*, *Dream Island Days* and *The Island*. The island lay derelict, visited only by fishermen and rabbit trappers, when Ronald Lockley took a lease in 1927. He repaired the farmhouse and buildings and lived with his family for 12 years as a shepherd until compelled to leave at the outbreak of World

War II. In 1933 he established Skokholm as Britain's first Bird Observatory, constructing a Heligoland-type trap for the ringing of birds as an aid to the study of migration. In addition, he conducted pioneer studies of puffins and Manx shearwaters, including fascinating experiments on the remarkable homing abilities of shearwaters when transported thousands of miles from the island during the breeding season. The observatory continued to operate successfully until 1976, when bird ringing ceased. Today, the island is leased and managed as a nature reserve by the Dyfed Wildlife Trust.

The island is particularly important for its breeding seabird population, with more than 35,000 pairs of Manx shearwaters and up to 7,000 pairs of storm petrels, as well as large numbers of puffins and smaller numbers of guillemots and razorbills.

Location: 2 miles south-west of Marloes Peninsula, west of Milford Haven.
Access and facilities: by boat from Martin's Haven. Island open April to September, Sat to Sat, on weekly basis. Up to 15 visitors can be accommodated. Full board. Educational courses each year. Day visits only possible on Mon from late May to late August; bookings through Pembrokeshire Coast National Park authority. All arrangements to stay must be made through the Dyfed Wildlife Trust.
Map reference: SM735050

Skomer Island

Dyfed

Skomer consists principally of a tableland 180 ft above sea level intersected by ridges of rock. Round the perimeter the sea cliffs and steep slopes hold the finest seabird colonies in south-west Britain, with puffins, guillemots, razorbills, kittiwakes and fulmars nesting in large numbers. The most numerous breeding species is Manx shearwater (over 100,000 pairs), which nests on the plateau along with smaller numbers of storm petrels. Other notable breeders include peregrines, short-eared owls (which prey on the unique and endemic Skomer vole), curlews, oystercatchers, stonechats and wheatears. The ponds on the island prove attractive to many species of wader and wildfowl, and many rare passerine migrants have been recorded.

The island is leased by the Dyfed Wildlife Trust from the Nature Conservancy Council.

Location: 1 mile west of Marloes Head, west of Milford Haven.
Access and facilities: by boat from Martin's Haven. Open every day, except Mon (Bank Holidays excepted), March to September 10 am to 6 pm. Cars can be left, for a fee, at National Trust car park, Martin's Haven. Boat service enquiries: Dale Sailing Company (telephone: *Dale 349) or to DWT, 7 Market Street, Haverfordwest (telephone Haverfordwest 5462). No food or shelter available on island. No toilet facilities on island but toilet at Martin's Haven. Accommodation available for up to 6 people wishing to stay on reserve. To stay overnight it is necessary to be member of Trust; details from Islands Booking Officer of DWT (telephone: Haverfordwest 5462). No dogs. Nature trail.*
Map reference: *SM725095*

The Spinnies, Aber Ogwen and Lavan Sands

Gwynedd

The hide here overlooks a shallow brackish lagoon on one side and the mouth of the Afon Ogwen on the other. The lagoon is a

high tide roosting site for greenshanks on passage, and winter visitors include kingfishers, water rails, teal, shovelers and gadwalls. Herons are frequent visitors all the year round, while mallard and moorhen are regular breeding species. The mouth of the Ogwen is an outstanding site for birds, with hundreds of waders and wildfowl in autumn and winter. In summer there are family parties of shelducks and red-breasted mergansers offshore and black-necked and Slavonian grebes are specialities in winter.

The car park itself is also a good vantage point, overlooking as it does the Lavan Sands Local Nature Reserve. The reserve is internationally important for waders, and there are notable build-ups of great crested grebes in autumn, and to a lesser extent in spring, as well as a substantial population of red-breasted mergansers all year round. The Spinnies is a reserve of the North Wales Naturalists' Trust.

Location: 2 miles east of Bangor, off A5122/ A55.
Access and facilities: from A5122 take lane leading north, east of Penrhyn Castle. Car park at end of lane. Gate short distance back up lane leads to hide. Open at all times.
Map reference: *SH613722*

Arctic terns** (left) – autumn visitors to **Point of Air. Below – Skomer Island

Whiteford Burrows and Llanrhidian Marsh

West Glamorgan

Collectively known as Whiteford National Nature Reserve, these two areas on the north coast of the Gower Peninsula consist of an extensive sand dune system and salt marsh. They represent a considerable contrast to the Gower's south coast, which has impressive cliff scenery. A good variety of waders is present here in every month of the year, notably oystercatchers, curlews, redshanks and dunlins, numbers of which are augmented in winter and at times of passage. A few pairs of ringed plovers breed. Bar-tailed godwits, grey plovers and knots are recorded in good numbers in winter, as are brent geese, wigeon and other wildfowl. Eider ducks are seen all year in the vicinity of the mussel scar at the old lighthouse at Whiteford Point, while Slavonian grebes and black-necked grebes are recorded quite regularly in the period from October to March.

Location: north coast of Gower Peninsula, reached on unclassified roads off B4295 from Llanrhidian.
Access and facilities: parking available on roadside beyond Cheriton Church. From there footpath leads down Frog Lane and across salt marsh to track along Whiteford Burrows to Berges Island. Also footpath from Cwm Ivy, further west, joining up with Frog Lane route. Access to reserve only along signposted footpaths and on beach. Access to other areas by permit only, obtainable from Nature Conservancy Council, Oxwich Reserve Centre, Oxwich, Swansea. Hide at Berges Island – no permit required. Organised parties must obtain a permit to visit any part of reserve.
Map reference: SS445953

Ynys-hir

Dyfed   RSPB

This RSPB reserve is exceptionally diverse in habitats, from estuarine salt marshes through fresh water pools and ditches, peat bogs, reed beds, rivers, broadleaved and coniferous woodland, to bracken and gorse-covered hillsides culminating in an upland moor at a height of more than 1,050 ft above sea level. The range of species reflects this diversity and the reserve is an excellent place to visit at any time of the year. In terms of bird conservation the most important habitat is the salt marsh, which is the main feeding area for about 3,000 wigeon in winter, together with one of the two remaining flocks of Greenland white-fronted geese in England and Wales, numbering about 100 birds. About 1,000 curlews use the estuary during early spring and late summer migration and many other waders visit Ynys-hir, particularly between August and October. The woodlands have a rich breeding community of birds characteristic of western oak woods, namely pied flycatchers, redstarts and wood warblers. Other notable species include lesser spotted woodpecker and nuthatch. Breeding birds of other habitats here include reed warblers, grey herons, teal, buzzards, ravens, sparrowhawks, kestrels, barn owls, grasshopper warblers, tree pipits and whinchats. Winter can be a particularly good time for birds of prey, especially peregrines, hen harriers, merlins and red kites.

Location: 5 miles south-west of Machynlleth, off A487. Signposted in Eglwysfach village.
Access and facilities: open all year 9 am to 9 pm or sunset when earlier. Admission charge for non RSPB members. Information centre. Hides. Car park. Toilets.
Map reference: SN683962

Ynyslas

Dyfed

Waders, wildfowl and terns are easily viewed from this part of the Dyfi Estuary, which is part of a National Nature Reserve covering over 5,000 acres. The sand dunes here are of high botanical interest and demonstrate all the stages involved in dune formation and growth. Breeding birds of the dunes include meadow pipits, skylarks and wheatears. In July and August the mouth of the Dyfi is notable for an influx of terns on passage. Common, arctic, and little terns are regularly seen in small numbers, but the commonest species is Sandwich tern, with peaks of over 200 birds. Wintering ducks, mainly wigeon, mallard, teal, shelduck and pintail, can be seen on the salt marsh and foreshore to the east of the dunes where the Afon Leri enters the estuary. Waders feed on the shore at low tide and congregate at high tide roosts on the shingle bank north of the dunes. Dunlins are present almost throughout the year, with several hundred at peak times.

Golden plovers are often present in winter in Ynys Tachwedd fields, east of the approach to Ynyslas. These fields form part of Cors Fochno, a huge expanse of marshy land stretching alongside the estuary. Only one road crosses this bleak and lonely landscape.

Location: 10 miles north of Aberystwyth, on unclassified road off B4353 Borth to Tre'r ddol road.
Access and facilities: visitor centre open every day Easter to end of September, 9.15 am to 5.30 pm. Car park (charge). Toilets.
Map reference: SN610941

Ynyslas – excellent for birds and for plants

The North Country

Little Owl

Some of Britain's finest estuaries are in the North. They include the Ribble, Morecambe Bay, Teesside and the Humber. Not to be missed are the seabird colonies on the Farne Islands. The coast is matched by such spectacular inland areas as the Lake District, the Yorkshire Dales and the North Yorkshire Moors

The North Country

Useful addresses:

RSPB Headquarters: The Lodge, Sandy, Bedfordshire, SE19 2DL
RSPB North of England Office: 'E' Floor, Milburn House, Dean Street, Newcastle-upon-Tyne, NE1 1LE
RSPB North-West England Office: Imperial House, Imperial Arcade, Huddersfield, West Yorkshire, HD1 2BR
Many RSPB reserves have explanatory leaflets. These are often available at the reserve, but in any event the regional office, or RSPB HQ, will supply information on any reserve upon receipt of a stamped addressed envelope.

Cheshire Conservation Trust: c/o Marbury Country Park, Northwich, CW9 6AT
Cleveland Nature Conservation Trust: The Old Town Hall, Mandale Road, Thornaby, Stockton-on-Tees, TS17 6AW
Cumbria Trust for Nature Conservation: Church Street, Ambleside, LA22 0BU
Derbyshire Wildlife Trust: Elvaston Castle Country Park, Derby, DE7 3EP
Durham County Conservation Trust: 52 Old Elvet, Durham, DH1 3HN
Lancashire Trust for Nature Conservation: The Pavilion Cuerden Valley Park, Bamber Bridge, Preston, PR5 6AU
Northumberland Wildlife Trust: c/o Hancock Museum, Barras Bridge, Newcastle-upon-Tyne, NE2 4PT
Yorkshire Wildlife Trust: 3rd Floor, 10 Toft Green, off Micklegate, York, YO1 1JT
Nature Conservancy Council: North-East Region, Archbold House, Archbold Terrace, Newcastle-upon-Tyne, NE2 1EG; North-West Region, Merlewood Research Station, Grange-over-Sands, Cumbria, LA11 6JU
Wildfowl Trust: Slimbridge, Gloucestershire, GL2 7BT

Bempton Cliffs

Humberside   RSPB

These spectacular 445ft chalk cliffs hold the largest breeding colony of seabirds in England and form one of the RSPB's most celebrated reserves. Eight species breed here, the commonest being the kittiwake, with over 80,000 pairs on the whole headland. Fulmars are very obvious as they glide along on up-draughts at the top of the cliffs, and the loud calls of herring gulls make them just as noticeable.

Many thousands of pairs of guillemots nest on the eroded cliff ledges, together with smaller, but still impressive, numbers of razorbills. Crevices in the chalk are the nest sites for thousands of puffins, while a small population of shags nests in the sea caves at the foot of the cliffs. The most famous of Bempton's seabirds is the gannet. About 700 pairs make up the colony, the only one in England, and the only mainland colony in Britain.

The prominent position of the headland on the east coast attracts passing migrants, particularly in the autumn. Regulars such as ring ouzels, redstarts, pied and spotted flycatchers, and uncommon ones such as bluethroat and greenish warbler, are all

recorded here. Sea-watching can be exceptionally good, especially in the autumn, when the terns are moving south, along with skuas, and on occasions large numbers of shearwaters.

The narrow band between the cliffs and the cliff-top fields is an excellent place for wild flowers.

Location: north of Bridlington, stretching from Flamborough Head to Speeton. Reached on unclassified road from Bempton off B1229.
Access and facilities: access at all times to cliff-top path, where there are four safe observation barriers giving excellent views of birds. Visitors must keep to footpath and observation points because cliffs are dangerous. Footpath from Filey to Flamborough Head runs along entire length of reserve. Information centre open during breeding season. Car park.
Map reference: TA197741

Blacktoft Sands

Humberside   RSPB

Set on the Humber Estuary, this RSPB reserve comprises a large tidal reed bed, fringed by salt marsh, with an area of shallow, brackish water lagoons. The reed beds contain a considerable proportion of the British population of bearded tits, as well as several hundred pairs of reed warblers. Water rails shelter in the reeds, and the dense litter at their base provides good nest sites for shelducks, while sedge and grasshopper warblers, as well as large numbers of reed buntings, nest at the edge of the bed. Marsh harriers nest on the reserve occasionally, and up to three pairs of short-eared owls breed each year.

A number of open lagoons have been created here, and mallards, teal and gadwalls nest on islands on these, together with lapwings, snipe, redshanks and little ringed plovers. Water levels on the lagoons are lowered in the autumn to provide mud and shallow water conditions for passage waders. Among those often attracted here are spotted redshanks, greenshanks, wood sandpipers, little stints and curlew sandpipers. In recent years ruffs have been seen in large numbers through the autumn, with small parties staying to the end of the year.

Some species of ducks, notably teal, like these autumn conditions and are sometimes present in large numbers, with up to 1,000 flying in at high tide. Common waders such as redshank and dunlin also fly into the lagoons. Out on the Humber mud flats several hundred pink-footed geese are present in winter.

Hen harriers arrive in late autumn to stay over the winter and use the reed bed as a roost site, while merlins are regularly seen hunting small birds here during the winter months.

Location: 6 miles east of Goole, at confluence of rivers Ouse and Trent. Reached from A161 through Reedness and Ousefleet.
Access and facilities: open every day except Tue, 9am to 9pm or sunset when earlier. Admission charge for non-RSPB members. Hides approached along firm footpaths. Car park. Picnic area.
Map reference: SE843232

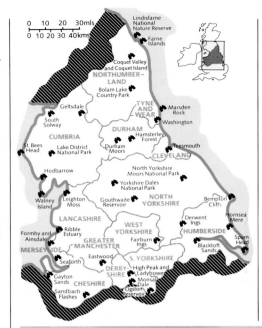

Bolam Lake Country Park

Northumberland

In spite of its name, the main birdwatching interest here is with woodland species. The range of habitats is wide, with large broad-leaved and coniferous trees, dense stands of rhododendrons and open grassland. The lake itself adds the finishing touch, making this a beautiful and varied place to visit.

A long history of feeding birds in the car parks, particularly in the one which contains the information centre, has produced a population of birds more than willing to feed from the hand. On any winter's day, but especially at weekends when there are more visitors, large numbers of birds come down to feed. They include blue tits and great tits, as well as dainty little marsh tits, robins, chaffinches, blackbirds and song thrushes, and colourful nuthatches. One or two jays are brave enough to come for the food, and great spotted woodpeckers and the occasional green woodpecker also put in an appearance.

The lake has goldeneyes and tufted ducks, with a few pochards, in the winter, and water rails live in the rushes at the western end. In spring, a walk along the park trails produces a wide range of breeding birds, including willow warblers, garden warblers, blackcaps, redstarts, spotted flycatchers and many more.

There are roe deer in the park; most visitors are likely to see these only if they visit early in the morning or at dusk, although roe deer will feed in the open in broad daylight if it is quiet. Easier to see are the red squirrels – which even come to the car parks to feed!

Location: 2 miles north of Belsay on unclassified road off A696.
Access and facilities: open all year. Information centre. Picnic area. Car parks.
Map reference: NZ080819

Robin (top) – constant companion in parks and gardens
Blacktoft Sands (main picture)
Bolam Lake (bottom) – alders in the water

The Coquet Valley and Coquet Island

Northumberland   `RSPB`

A journey down the Coquet from the high Cheviots close to the border with Scotland to the North Sea offers a wide variety of birds, particularly in spring and summer. A particularly picturesque road follows the river from Alwinton high up into the head-waters at Blindburn.

In spring, the high moors are wonderful places for that typical bird of Northumberland, the curlew, symbol of Northumberland National Park. Ring ouzels and whin-chats are also found here, but as the river descends into the main valley and its groups of small woodlands, the range of birds changes. Redstarts are a feature of the oak woods and pied flycatchers nest in the alder groves. The river has dippers, grey wagtails and common sandpipers, as well as oyster-catchers on the shingle beds. There are many good birdwatching areas along the Coquet Valley, but a particularly good place is the Caistron Quarry, owned by Ryton Gravel Co Ltd. This is a working gravel quarry being developed as a nature reserve by the company as the gravel is worked out. The reserve has won several major conservation awards in recent years. A series of lakes with islands and extensive shallow areas attracts large numbers of birds throughout the year. A number of well positioned hides give excellent views of waterfowl such as tufted ducks, teal, shovelers and goldeneyes as well as a small flock of wintering greylag geese. The shallow areas are very good for a variety of waders during the passage seasons, particularly in the late summer and autumn.

The other major site of the Coquet, although not in the valley, is the RSPB reserve of Coquet Island, a mile or so off the mouth of the river at Amble. The island has large summer populations of Sandwich, arctic, and common terns as well as a few roseates. Over 3,000 pairs of puffins nest on the island as well as several hundred pairs of eider ducks. The large numbers of terns attract skuas in late summer and all can be watched at close range from the sand dunes immediately to the south of Amble. This area is also good for divers and sea ducks during the winter months.

Location: valley, east and west of Rothbury, reached on B6341, B6344 and unclassified roads into Cheviots. Caistron, 3 miles west of Rothbury, off B6341. Coquet Island 1 mile east of Amble.

Access: Caistron Quarry by arrangement only with Reserve Manager (tel Rothbury 40284). Coquet Island viewed from boats – no landing permitted. Details from Tourist Information Centre, Amble.
Map reference: NU060017

Derwent Ings

North Yorkshire/Humberside

The Ings comprise the flat floodplain land alongside the Derwent as it wends its way to its confluence with the River Ouse. As the volume of water in the river increases in winter and early spring so the Ings become flooded. Expanses of shallow water running the length of the valley attract large numbers of waterfowl, with all the common species here in impressive gatherings. Without doubt, the greatest winter attraction is the herd of Bewick's swans. Up to 200 may be present and a very good place to see them and many of the waterfowl is Derwent Bridge, near the village of Bubwith. Another good vantage point is at Aughton. The ancient church here, standing on a

Coquet Island – families of Sandwich terns on the middle of the island

raised knoll above the Ings, is an attractive feature of the Derwent Valley, and its churchyard affords good views across the adjacent flooded areas.

In spring, when the water has dropped off the Ings, but the land is still wet, the conditions are ideal for breeding waders. Large numbers of redshanks, snipe and lapwings are present, and some of the less common waders such as black-tailed god-wits and ruffs are regularly seen. In autumn, the Ings are used by migrating waders including wood and green sandpipers, spotted redshank and all of the common species.

Location: south-east of York off B1228.
Access: private farmland, except Yorkshire Wildlife Trust's Wheldrake Ings reserve, so access strictly limited, but B1228 from Elvington to Bubwith, then A163 to North Driffield, then unclassified roads north to Wheldrake give excellent views.
Map reference: SE703440

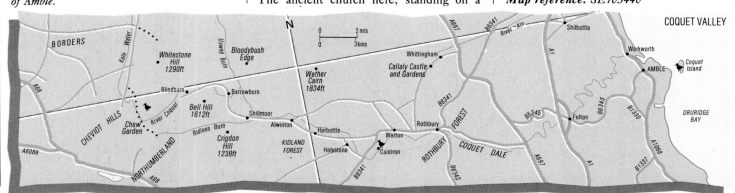

COQUET VALLEY

Durham Moors

Co Durham

Both Teesdale and Weardale are renowned for their dramatic scenery. In between stretch the Durham Moors, billowing uplands often shrouded in rain or mist. Because of well managed heather, the dominant vegetation of much of these moors, red grouse are plentiful here. They can often be seen close to the road, perhaps standing prominently on a rock or raised piece of ground. Indeed the management is vital, not only for grouse (the reason for the management) but also for many of the other typical birds of these moors.

Upland waders are numerous in the damper areas during the breeding season and include snipe, redshank, lapwing, curlew and a few dunlins. Small birds are not abundant, the exception being meadow pipits, which are the principal breeding season food of merlins. The Durham Moors are an important area for these small birds of prey. Peregrines occur in a few places, and kestrels can often be seen hovering above the ridges.

In the deep valleys of the Wear and Tees, riverside woods hold good populations of woodland birds, including pied flycatchers and redstarts. The rivers are good for dippers, common sandpipers and grey wagtails as well as a few goosanders. Blackcock leks may be found in higher parts of the dales.

Location: 12 miles west of Bishop Auckland.
Access: along B6277 (Teesdale), B6278 (Stanhope to Eggleston), and footpaths including Pennine Way. Actual moors privately owned and managed. Snow often blocks roads well into spring.
Map reference: NY997308

Eastwood

Greater Manchester   RSPB

This woodland reserve is set in a steep-sided valley with a stream and pools at its bottom. Among the trees are oaks, wych elm, beech and ash. Woodland birds such as nuthatches, treecreepers and tawny owls nest here, while river birds that might be seen include grey wagtails, kingfishers and grey herons.

Location: east edge of Manchester, reached from A6018 in Stalybridge; beside Cheetham Park, south of junction with A635.
Access: educational reserve; RSPB members and public can visit first and third Sun of month, or by appointment with Warden: 12 Fir Tree Crescent, Dukinfield, SK16 5EH. Reached on foot from car parks in Trinity Street; entrance is by Priory Tennis Club.
Map reference: SJ972977

Fairburn Ings

West Yorkshire   RSPB

Extending along the Aire Valley from Fairburn village, this reserve comprises large shallow lakes, washes, scrub and flood-pools formed by mining subsidence, together with deciduous woodland by the river. It is particularly important for its wildfowl, all the commoner species being present throughout the year, and the winter months bringing the greatest variety. Mallard, teal, shoveler, pochard, tufted duck, goldeneye, and goosander are all here, together with very large numbers of coots. Up to 100 whooper swans roost on the reserve each winter, feeding on nearby farmland.

During spring and autumn passage, common, arctic and black terns, as well as little gulls, are regular after easterly winds. The main footpath across the reserve – known as the Cut – is bounded by hawthorns and leads to a section of reclaimed slag bank with a good cover of silver birch and other vegetation. This area is a stronghold of willow warblers and other summer visitors such as blackcap, garden warbler and lesser whitethroat. The reserve has a number of small reed beds and several pairs of reed warblers nest in them.

A roost of thousands of swallows is a feature of most autumns, while in winter large flocks of gulls roost on the slurry ponds, and glaucous gulls are regular.

Location: immediately west of A1 north of Ferrybridge, signposted Fairburn, along unclassified roads.
Access: at all times to public hides, reached by causeway and footpath below Fairburn village. Information centre 1 mile west of village. Hide. Raised boardwalk. Toilets. Open weekends throughout year 10am to 5pm. At other times good views from lay-bys along road.
Map reference: SE450275

Durham Moors – High Force in Teesdale. Inset is a cock red grouse

The Farne Islands

Northumberland

Because of the large numbers of birds breeding here, together with their approachability, and the rugged beauty of the islands themselves, a visit to the Farnes is one of Britain's outstanding wildlife experiences.

Early in the season is the time to see the handsome black and white eider drakes displaying, but to see the terns for which the Farnes are famous, June and early July are best. All the British terns, except little, nest here, including hundreds of pairs of Sandwich, common and arctic, as well as a

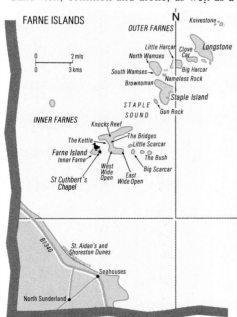

few pairs of roseate terns. It is advisable to wear a hat when visiting the tern islands such as Inner Farne from late June onwards. Arctic and common terns are particularly aggressive in defending young chicks beside the footpaths and will regularly strike the tops of visitors' heads with their sharp beaks. In fact, be prepared for a continual bombardment if you visit at this time! It is well worth the discomfort, for there are few places where birds and their chicks can be watched at such close quarters.

Several thousand pairs of puffins have their nesting burrows on the main islands, and when the young are being fed the sky seems to be full of these colourful little birds racing back and forth with glistening sand eels in their beaks.

Massed ranks of guillemots cover the tops of the Pinnacles off Staple Island, and suitable cliffs elsewhere, and very large numbers are seen alongside the boats as they move between the islands and below the guillemot cliffs. Staple Island is also the best place to see many of the several hundred pairs of shags which nest on the Farnes. Kittiwake Gully is famous for its nesting kittiwakes, but this species has now extended to other parts of the island, and provides visitors with a continuous and memorable sound accompaniment to their visit.

Gannets are regularly seen fishing around the islands, while in the summer months particularly, Manx and sooty shearwaters are seen on passage. The winter months bring good concentrations of divers and sea ducks, such as common scoters and long-tailed ducks, to the area.

The islands also have a large colony of Atlantic grey seals, which are present throughout the year. The boat journey itself

Farne Islands – the guillemot colony on the Pinnacles, off Staple Island

is very exciting, with tremendous views of birds and seals, but the weather can change very quickly, so waterproofs should be taken.

Location: off coast, 2 miles north-east of Bamburgh.
Access: by boat from Seahouses (on B1340). Boats leave hourly from 10 am during breeding season – April to June. Landing allowed on two islands – Inner Farne and Staple – landing charge for non-National Trust members. Not suitable for disabled visitors. Car parking and toilets in Seahouses.
Map reference: NU238375

Formby and Ainsdale

Merseyside

This vast area of dunes and beach offers a surprising remoteness just a few miles north of the great city of Liverpool. The remoteness is welcomed by a wide range of species including the shelduck, which breeds here in good numbers among the marram grass. Sanderlings twinkle up and down on the shore as they catch food brought by each successive wave, while other waders probe for food in the softer parts of the shore. Oystercatchers are here in large numbers, feeding on cockles.

Stands of pines among the dunes provide good cover and breeding sites for goldcrests, coal tits and a few other species, while the stands of sea-buckthorn around the dune slacks are attractive to stonechats and whinchats.

The dune slacks, or low-lying damp hollows within the dune systems, contain a great variety of plants and animals. Among the unusual animals found there are sand lizards, and one of Britain's endangered species, the natterjack toad.

A spring day at Formby and Ainsdale can be memorable – with skylarks singing from first light, migrant waders moving along the shoreline, and migrant passerines, such as wheatears, swallows, sand martins, and many others, feeding among the dunes and woodlands. After dark the singing of the male natterjack toads makes a fitting end to the day.

Location: 3 miles south of Southport. Reached from unclassified roads off A565 at Formby and Ainsdale.
Access: free, but visitors should keep to marked footpaths, particularly in National Nature Reserve. Southern part of site owned by National Trust, while over 1,200 acres of northern part is National Nature Reserve owned by Nature Conservancy Council.
Map reference: SD275080

Geltsdale

Cumbria   RSPB

An important area of the North Pennines, the fells of the King's Forest of Geltsdale form part of a large RSPB reserve. The reserve also includes several woods in the nearby valleys of the rivers Gelt and Irthing.

The high moorland contains an excellent range of upland bird species, with red grouse, golden plover, curlew, ring ouzel and lapwing nesting on the lower pastures in spring and summer. This is a particularly exciting time of year on the reserve because of migrants such as pied flycatcher, redstart

Geltside – in Lower Gelt Wood

and wood warbler, as well as the very common willow warbler, returning to the woodlands. These are also good places to see sparrowhawks, because of the high numbers of small birds.

The woodlands are mainly on the steep valley sides of the main rivers, the Gelt and Irthing, and these hold very good populations of dippers, grey wagtails, common sandpipers and goosanders.

In the winter months, a visit to Tindale Tarn is worthwhile for the opportunity to see over-wintering whooper swans and goldeneyes as well as other wildfowl. Although the woods are quieter at this time of year they are worth exploring for parties of titmice, particularly long-tailed tits, and for great spotted woodpeckers busily searching for grubs in dead trees.

Location: south-east of Brampton, off A69, A689 and B6413.
Access and facilities: no access to Geltside moorland, but bridleways at Jockey Shield, off B6413 east of Castle Carrock, or along old railway track from Tindale, off A689. Parking. Waymarked path through Lower Gelt Woods, off A69 1½ miles south-west of Brampton, or by railway viaduct west of B6413, 3 miles south of Brampton. Open all year. Car park.
Map reference: NY606556

Gayton Sands

Cheshire   RSPB

Almost half of this RSPB reserve is a wilderness of salt marsh dissected by numerous creeks. Beyond the salt marsh are extensive sand banks and mud flats that comprise the remainder of the Dee Estuary reserve.

The reserve is particularly important for spectacular gatherings of shelducks, with peak numbers in the autumn. Pintails are present in large numbers during the winter months, and this is the time of year when the marshes are home to many mallards, teal and wigeon.

In spring and autumn the estuary is a staging post for thousands of waders which stop here to feed on their way between wintering areas in Africa and breeding grounds in the high Arctic. Sanderlings, dunlins, and ringed and grey plovers feed on the inner mud flats, while greenshanks, spotted redshanks and ruffs visit the upper salt marsh pools.

As well as for wildfowl, the salt marsh seeds are a very important food source for the numerous finches and buntings. Chaffinches, greenfinches, linnets and reed buntings are regular winter visitors, often joined by large flocks of bramblings. A small flock of twites spends the winter on the marsh. Birds of prey, including sparrowhawks and kestrels from nearby farmland, hunt over the marsh, and hen harriers, peregrines, merlins and short-eared owls are also seen during the winter months.

One of the most interesting species found on the reserve is the water rail. More often heard than seen, this inhabitant of the dense *Spartina* grass is best looked for when tides are at their highest. On these occasions the rails are regularly forced out onto adjacent land, such as the Parkgate promenade.

Location: south-west side of Wirral, west of Neston, reached on B5135 off A540 Chester to Hoylake road.
Access: parking available in Old Baths car park; adjacent public footpath near Boathouse Restaurant. Good birdwatching can be obtained from both these locations, especially at high tide. Visitors are strongly advised not to walk onto salt marsh because of very dangerous tides.
Map reference: SJ274790

Gayton Sands

Gouthwaite Reservoir

North Yorkshire

This long, narrow reservoir is managed by the Yorkshire Water Authority as a private nature reserve, largely because of its ornithological interest. There is good tree cover along much of the shore-line, so that small birds are abundant, particularly in spring and summer. Willow warblers, blackcaps, garden warblers, and lovely wood warblers are present, as well as spotted flycatchers and redstarts. Other woodland specialists such as great spotted woodpeckers, nuthatches and the occasional green woodpecker are all found here, together with many commoner species.

In winter, after the summer migrants have gone, the area around the reservoir is good for fieldfares and redwings, and in some years, another attractive Scandinavian migrant, the brambling.

On the reservoir itself, Canada geese are always to be seen, and are joined during the autumn and winter by a good variety of wildfowl. Goosanders and goldeneyes accompany commoner ducks such as mallard, tufted duck and pochard. These are frequently joined by whooper swans from Iceland. The reservoir is an ideal place to see these birds at close range.

Winter is a good time for birds of prey, with hen harriers, merlins, peregrines, sparrowhawks, kestrels, an occasional rough-legged buzzard and even golden eagle being seen around the reservoir and the high ground above it. Ospreys are sometimes seen as they make their way north in the spring and on their return journeys in late summer and autumn.

Nearby attractions include the extraordinary rock formations at Brimham Rocks, to the east of Pateley Bridge, and Studley Royal Park, two miles west of Ripon on the B6265, with its 300-acre deer park and herds of fallow, red and sika deer.

Location: in Nidderdale, 2 miles north-west of Pateley Bridge, on unclassified road off B6265. Access: no public access to reservoir surrounds, but good views from road which runs length of western side.
Map reference: SE127693

Hamsterley Forest

Co Durham

County Durham is dominated by its high moors, but there are excellent areas of woodland, and by far the largest of these is Hamsterley, owned by the Forestry Commission. Although commercially grown conifers predominate, the forest has a very wide variety of broadleaved woodland as well, and along with the deep valleys of the Bedburn Beck and high moorland, is a good place for birds. The Commission has way-marked a range of walks in the forest varying in length from a few hundred yards to a few miles, all of which give plenty of opportunities to see the typical birds of the forest.

Because of the conifers, two of the specialities here are crossbill and siskin. Crossbills are early breeders and are particularly active and easier to see in the early spring. Where there are stands of larch, the smaller, colourful siskins are common at times during the winter and breed throughout the forest. The clear-felling and re-planting of parts of the forest as part of the timber-growing operation produces a variety of ages in the conifers and the younger growth can be attractive to many small birds such as willow warblers, goldcrests, whinchats, chaffinches and wrens.

Where the broadleaves predominate, especially where there is a good shrub layer, blackcaps, garden warblers, redstarts and spotted flycatchers are all here in good numbers. Kestrels, sparrowhawks and tawny owls all breed at Hamsterley and so does the much more secretive long-eared owl.

The Bedburn Beck has dippers, common sandpipers and grey wagtails and is a feeding and bathing place for many other birds. In addition to the birds, the forest has a good population of red squirrels, as well as many roe deer and a few badgers. The roe deer are most likely to be seen along the woodland rides or at the forest edge. It is possible to get quite close to them as long as you are quiet and down-wind. Badgers are only likely to be seen at twilight as they begin their nightly perambulations.

Location: west of Bishop Auckland and A68, reached by following unclassified roads from A68 to Hamsterley. Forest is 1½ miles west of village.
Access and facilities: open all year. Visitor centre. Forest drive. Car parks. Picnic sites. Toilets.
Map reference: NZ092312

Ladybower Reservoir. The inset pictures are of a crossbill and of a typical Peak District view with its drystone walls and open moor

The High Peak and Ladybower

Derbyshire

These high moorlands of northern Derbyshire, known as the Dark Peak because of the black peat and dark weathered gritstone which are their principal constituents, comprise the high plateaux of Kinder Scout and Bleaklow.

Spectacular, but inhospitable in winter, the moors have a very specialised range of birds, including several species of waders. Spring and early summer is the best time of year for birds and it is a good time for the typical sounds as well as sights. The long bubbling call of the curlew, the plaintive piping of golden plovers, the 'drumming' of snipe, and the 'reeling' of dunlin can all be heard as the birds display. A few twites breed here, and ring ouzels can be found in many places from March to September. Another migrant, the wheatear, is commonest on well-grazed, boulder-strewn slopes, and meadow pipits seem to be everywhere.

Where heather moorland is well managed, principally by burning, there are good populations of red grouse, and the same conditions are very good for the smallest of Britain's birds of prey, the merlin. Short-eared owls occur in some places. Lower down, on poorer farmland, lapwings are found, while whinchats like the bracken covered slopes, and skylarks are abundant.

Along the River Derwent to the east of Bleaklow is a chain of reservoirs, the largest and most visible of which is Ladybower. Largely dominated by conifers planted on the surrounding hillsides, Ladybower can be an interesting place, with the highest numbers of waterfowl occurring during hard weather. The woodlands have goldcrests, coal tits, redpolls and crossbills, and where there are remnants of the old semi-natural oak woods, woodpeckers and a wide range of common species.

Location: south-east of Glossop, reached from A57 (Snake Pass). Kinder is south of road, Bleaklow north. Ladybower is at junction of A57 with A6013, 11 miles west of Sheffield.
Access and facilities: unclassified road follows western side of Ladybower; closed to motor vehicles beyond Fairholmes on summer Sun and Bank Holidays. Minibus service provided beyond this point. Moorlands are Peak Park Planning Board public access areas, and Pennine Way traverses moors from its beginning in Edale. Some of these areas are wild and remote, and the weather can change very fast. Suitable clothing and footwear essential.
Map reference: SK113905

Hodbarrow

Cumbria   RSPB

Hodbarrow, an RSPB reserve on the northern shore of the Duddon Estuary, is the result of deep shaft mining for iron-ore, an industry which ceased operations here in 1968. Subsidence has created humps and hollows and a large lagoon cut off from the sea by a sea wall.

During late spring and summer great crested and little grebes, red-breasted mergansers and shelducks, together with mallards, tufted ducks, coots and moorhens are all breeding on or around the lagoon, while an extensive slag bank inside the sea wall is attractive to ringed plovers and oystercatchers. This area is also used by a few common and arctic terns, and little terns are always present.

The limestone grass and scrub areas on the reserve are good for willow and sedge warblers as well as blackcaps and whitethroats. Swifts breed in the abandoned lookout building and stone lighthouse.

Barn owls are a particular feature of the reserve and can often be seen hunting in the middle of the day. Kestrels and sparrowhawks can also be seen on the reserve. Late autumn and winter brings large concentrations of wildfowl, with wigeon and teal being particularly numerous, but there are also good gatherings of goldeneyes, pochards and mallards.

Location: immediately south of Millom, off Mainsgate Road.
Access: open at all times. Entrance track forks left from Mainsgate Road. Public footpaths cross reserve; one follows sea wall.
Map reference: SD175785

Hornsea Mere

Humberside   RSPB

The largest natural fresh water lake both in Humberside and Yorkshire, Hornsea Mere is reed-fringed, bordered by mixed woodland and farmland, and is close to the sea – altogether an excellent assemblage of habitats.

The winter population of wildfowl on the mere is spectacular, with mallard, teal, wigeon, pochard, tufted duck and goldeneye here in their hundreds, with smaller numbers of shovelers and gadwalls, and an occasional pintail or goosander. Hard weather brings over 1,000 coots to the reserve, as well as divers, grebes and sea-ducks. Another winter feature is the roost of 50 or more cormorants.

Mallards breed, as well as small numbers of pochards, tufted ducks, shovelers and gadwalls on occasions. The fringe of reeds has breeding reed and sedge warblers as well as reed buntings, and in winter many water rails, small numbers of bearded tits, and an occasional bittern.

The woodlands have great spotted woodpeckers, treecreepers, tawny owls and jays, as well as all the common species. Woodcocks are sometimes numerous in hard winters. Sparrowhawks breed on the reserve and are often seen chasing starlings at the late summer and autumn roosts around the mere.

A large gathering of moulting mute swans is a feature of the mere in late summer, and at the same time as many as 50 little gulls may be seen on the reserve, making it one of the best places in England for this delicate gull.

Because Hornsea Mere is so close to the coast, small migrants such as wheatears and whinchats, and waders such as ruff, greenshank and spotted redshank, and all the commoner terns as well as black terns, are recorded annually.

Location: immediately west of Hornsea, signposted off B1242, south of B1244.
Access and facilities: RSPB information centre (east end of mere). Car parking at Kirkholme Point (permission of Hornsea Mere Marine Co). Refreshments. Toilets. Public footpath from Hull Road, on south side of mere, provides good views – no other access.
Map reference: TA190470

Lake District National Park

Cumbria

This huge area of mountains, lakes and woodlands is very good for birds at any time of the year, but particularly so during spring and summer.

The high mountains, even with the millions of visitors to the park annually, offer remoteness which is attractive to some of Britain's rarer birds of prey. Peregrines breed at a higher density here than anywhere else in the world. The birds are particularly obvious in the central fells. England's only golden eagles breed in the park, the site being wardened each year by the RSPB. Often confused with golden eagles, buzzards are common over much of the Lake District, soaring on the thermals or perched on crags and trees close to the

Hornsea Mere

roads. They are often first noticed by their mewing call. Another typical sound is the deep *cronk, cronk* of the raven, a bird which begins its breeding season very early in the year among the ice and snow of late winter.

The lower slopes of the mountains are home to attractive summer migrants, with ring ouzels on hillsides with broken crags and good vegetation cover, while wheatears prefer more open, sheep-grazed hillsides with scattered boulders. Where streams come tumbling down the hillsides and along the valley floor dippers can regularly be seen perched on boulders; often on tree-lined

streams rather than the bare-sided rocky rivers where many people expect to see them.

The oak woodlands of the hillsides and around many of the lakes are very good for redstarts, pied flycatchers, great spotted and green woodpeckers, as well as many other woodland species. The lakes can be disappointing, but in winter hold very large numbers of waterfowl, although they tend to be widely dispersed.

A few areas might be picked out as being worth exploring. Grizedale Forest, between Coniston Water and Windermere, has numerous marked walks and trails, and a visitor and wildlife centre. Friar's Crag Nature Walk leads from just south of Keswick along the shore of Derwent Water, with good views of waterfowl, and of woodland birds in Great Wood. Loughrigg Fell can be reached from Ambleside. The walk passes rivers, broadleaved and coniferous woodland, bogs and open hillside – a superb range of habitats with excellent views.

It is easy to get away from the crowds, but the best-known beauty spots, and most roads, are extremely busy during the summer holiday season.

Location: west of M6, reached by leaving Junction 36 or 37 for southern lakes and Junction 40 for northern lakes.
Facilities: information centres at Kendal, Windermere and Keswick; National Park Centre at Brockhole near Windermere gives excellent introduction to park.
Map reference: NY390010

Lake District – grandeur at Langdale Pikes

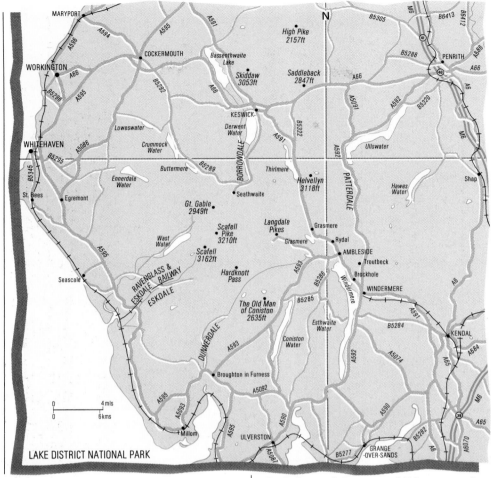

LAKE DISTRICT NATIONAL PARK

Leighton Moss and Morecambe Bay

Lancashire `RSPB`

Leighton Moss RSPB reserve occupies the floor of a small, attractively wooded valley which was once an arm of nearby Morecambe Bay. The shallow meres which make one of the major features of the reserve are surrounded by extensive reed beds. An interesting variety of wildfowl breeds on the reserve, including teal, shoveler, tufted duck, mallard and occasionally garganey. The small islands in the meres are favoured by black-headed gulls, as well as ducks, coots, moorhens and lapwings.

The major attractions during the breeding season are bearded tits and Britain's largest concentration of bitterns – with up to a dozen pairs present. Reed and sedge warblers are plentiful, and in the willows among the reeds are grasshopper warblers. Around the edge of the fen, wrens, willow warblers, reed buntings and whitethroats are all common. Marsh harriers are regular in spring and nested in 1987.

Large numbers of starlings and pied wagtails roost in the reeds for much of the year, and in spring and autumn swallows and sand martins are here in very large numbers. The large roosts attract sparrowhawks and the occasional peregrine.

On the limestone slopes above the valley floor, hawthorn, blackthorn and ash scrub gives way to typical limestone woodland of ash, oak and yew. The resident thrushes, robins, wrens and tits are joined in summer by migrant warblers, including blackcaps and garden warblers.

With the water levels of the meres at the right level in spring and autumn, waders on passage, such as greenshank, common and spotted redshank and many others are regularly present. Grey herons hunting for the abundant eels are a feature of the mere edges throughout the year. Otters are regularly seen on the reserve, as well as roe and red deer.

The nearby RSPB reserve on Morecambe Bay gives the opportunity to see very large numbers of waders of many species, particularly at high tide at Hest Bank.

Location: Leighton Moss 3 miles north-west of Carnforth on east edge of Silverdale village off unclassified road to Yealand Redmayne. Morecambe Bay off A5105 Morecambe to Carnforth road.
Access and facilities: open every day except Tue, 9am to 9pm or sunset. Admission charge for non-RSPB members. Public causeway crosses reserve and is always open, free of charge. Hides.
Map reference: SD478751/SD468666

Lindisfarne National Nature Reserve (Holy Island)

Northumberland

An area of 7,000 acres is covered by Lindisfarne National Nature Reserve, including most of Holy Island, the inter-tidal mud flats to the south and west, Ross Back Sands and Budle Bay. Good birdwatching is available all year round, but the really outstanding time is during the autumn and winter from October to March. Large numbers of wildfowl and waders, including geese, use the reserve during this period. Wigeon are particularly numerous, and are the main quarry species of the wildfowlers who shoot here under licence. Eiders are common along the shoreline and the entrance to Budle Bay has a regular wintering flock of red-breasted mergansers. Thousands of waders feed on the mud flats during these colder months of the year and include bar-tailed godwits, curlews, redshanks, grey plovers and dunlins.

Several thousand greylag geese overwinter in the fields adjacent to Lindisfarne, but the major attraction is the population of pale-bellied brent geese from Svalbard, with up to 3,000 in some winters.

Apart from its wintering birds, Lindisfarne is outstanding as a migration watch point, particularly in autumn when just about anything can turn up. Vagrants from northern Europe and Asia are regularly

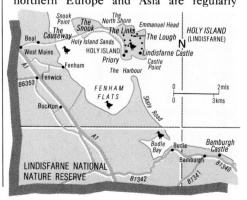

LINDISFARNE NATIONAL NATURE RESERVE

found here through September and October, together with annual thrush migration involving hundreds of thousands of fieldfares, redwings, and blackbirds.

While not featuring the vast populations of the nearby Farne Islands, Lindisfarne nevertheless has an interesting range of breeding birds including fulmars on the north shore cliffs, and shelducks among the sand dunes. The dunes are also rich and exciting places for those who like wild flowers, and harbour several rare and beautiful species, including carpets of orchids in some areas.

Lindisfarne Castle, which was restored by Sir Edwin Lutyens in 1903, belongs to the National Trust and is regularly open, while Lindisfarne Priory ruins are open at most times. Along with the seaside, these make Holy Island an interesting outing for all. On the mainland is Bamburgh Castle, one of the most splendid in England.

Location: 9 miles south-east of Berwick-upon-Tweed, reached off A1.
Access and facilities: B1342 runs alongside Budle Bay part of reserve. Car parks. Access to Holy Island by paved causeway reached by leaving A1 at Beal Crossroads. Causeway is covered by water at high tide and care should be taken to check safe crossing times displayed on prominent notice boards at both ends of the causeway. These times are also given in local newspapers, or can be obtained from coastguard. Car parks. Toilets. Access to much of National Nature Reserve freely available, but care should be taken to read regulations displayed on Nature Conservancy Council signs and maps placed at access points around reserve.
Map reference: NU126420

Marsden Rock

Co Durham

About 4,000 pairs of kittiwakes breed on the mainland cliffs and stack here and are easily watched at close range from the cliff tops and the beach. Fulmars also breed and can be seen drifting along on the air currents within a few feet of the path.

The flat top of Marsden Rock contains one of the most important concentrations of cormorants in England, with over 80 pairs breeding. The stack is only 300 yards off

shore and the spectacular cormorants are at eye-level from the cliff-top car park.

Guillemots and razorbills collect in small numbers around the stack during the breeding season, but do not breed, while Sandwich, common, arctic and little terns can all be seen fishing in the area, particularly during spring and autumn passage. Gannets, as well as Manx and sooty shearwaters, are regularly seen in summer.

The cliffs are backed by extensive areas of mown grassland known as The Leas, and in the autumn they can be covered in thrushes on migration from Scandinavia. Fieldfares and redwings are here in very large numbers, as well as blackbirds and smaller numbers of song and mistle

Lindisfarne – sand dunes being colonised by plants

thrushes. This is also a very good area in winter for snow buntings and the occasional shore lark.

The Magnesian limestone stack and adjacent cliffs of Marsden Bay are owned by the National Trust; the RSPB has a temporary countryside classroom here from May to July each year.

Location: 2 miles south-east of South Shields, off A183.
Access and facilities: open all year. Stairway and lift to beach. Car park. Toilets.
Map reference: NZ403648

Monsal Dale and Cressbrook Dale

Derbyshire

These lovely wooded limestone dales in the White Peak area of the Peak District National Park offer wonderful birdwatching opportunities. An important part of the beautiful scenery of Derbyshire, the dales are very accessible by using the Monsal Trail. At Monsal Head a footpath drops steeply down through woodland to the floor of the dale and along the course of the River Wye. Monsal Dale lies to the south and Cressbrook Dale, which is a National Nature Reserve, to the north. The trail itself follows the route of the old Midland railway so that the walking is easy, with many opportunities to see birds. This area is very popular at weekends.

The woodlands are good for a whole

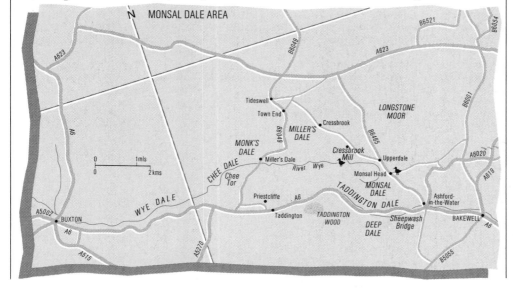

MONSAL DALE AREA

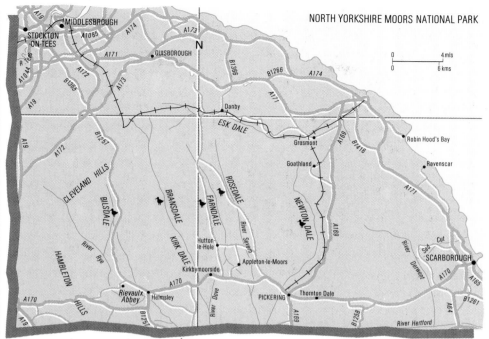

NORTH YORKSHIRE MOORS NATIONAL PARK

Location: 2 miles north-west of Bakewell. Monsal Head reached on B6465 from A6 at Ashford-in-the-Water. Alternative access to Monsal Dale is from car park at southern tip of Dale on A6 3 miles west of Bakewell.
Access and facilities: along Monsal Trail. Car parking and toilets at Monsal Head.
Map reference: SK183715

North Yorkshire Moors National Park

North Yorkshire

The park is a place of great variety, with high heather moorland, deep dales, sandstone cliffs, woodlands and, on its eastern side, the spectacular North Sea coastline. Because of this variety of habitats the range of birds is very wide indeed.

The heather moorlands are excellent places in spring for those typical upland birds, the curlew and golden plover, as well as for several others such as ring ouzel, whinchat, and wheatear. They are also a stronghold for merlins, which rely to a great extent on the well-managed heather, as well as on the good small bird populations. The deep dales which cut into the moorland plateau, especially where there are woodlands, contain a very good range of species including redstarts, pied flycatchers, blackcaps, garden warblers, and many others. Nightjars are found in a number of places.

The dales are important in most winters for a few rough-legged buzzards, winter visitors from Scandinavia which find the conditions much better even in Britain's worst winters than in the winter on their own breeding grounds. Winter is also the best time to see short-eared owls. The dales offering the best birdwatching are Bilsdale, Bransdale, Farndale, Rosedale and Newtondale – the best is Bransdale.

The streams, or becks, which run through them are good for dippers, common sandpipers, and grey wagtails, while the drystone walls which divide the fields on the valley floors provide a good home for many pairs of pied wagtails.

The coastline is dominated mainly by very high cliffs, including the highest on the east coast of England at Boulby Head, where they rise to over 680ft. The structure of the cliffs limits the numbers of birds present. Herring gulls and kittiwakes are the main breeding birds and there are several small cormorant colonies. The cliffs are excellent places to watch the movement of terns, skuas and shearwaters along the North Sea coast in late summer and early autumn.

There are many places of interest, including Rievaulx Abbey, and the white horse at Kilburn. A ride on the North York Moors Railway from Pickering to Grosmont passes through some of the most spectacular scenery in the park.

range of warblers, in particular willow warblers, but there are also garden warblers, blackcaps and that woodland speciality the wood warbler. Redstarts and pied flycatchers are also here, and so too are spotted flycatchers. Tree pipits 'parachute' down onto the tops of the trees in their display flights, and in some places woodcocks perform their unusual 'roding' flights during the breeding season.

Common species such as wrens, robins, blackbirds, blue tits and great tits abound, as do linnets in scrubby areas.

The range of birds along the river is also very good, with grey wagtails and dippers usually to be seen and sometimes a common sandpiper or kingfisher. Little grebes are regularly seen on the river, and large numbers of swifts and house martins, as well as smaller numbers of sand martins and swallows, catch aerial insects low over the water.

Monsal Dale – the Monsal Viaduct

Location: southern part of park reached from A170 to Helmsley and Pickering road; northern part reached from A172 Stokesley road and A171 Whitby road. Unclassified roads give access to central section of park.
Facilities: information centre at Moors Centre, Danby.
Map reference: NP716084

St Bees Head

Cumbria   RSPB

One of the largest seabird colonies on the west coast of England is to be found at this RSPB reserve. The cliffs which make up the reserve are 300ft high and composed of red sandstone. The main breeding birds are the auks, with very large numbers of guillemots, and smaller numbers of razorbills and puffins, as well as kittiwakes, fulmars and herring gulls. The reserve's speciality, however, is the black guillemot, St Bees being the only place in England where this bird breeds. The population is small, so that time needs to be spent looking for the birds, usually on the sea below the main cliffs.

Apart from the breeding seabirds, many others are seen on passage or feeding close inshore. Gannets are regularly seen searching for fish, and even more numerous are the Sandwich, common and arctic terns which pass along this coast on their way to and from their breeding colonies further north. They are followed on their way south in the late summer and autumn by arctic and great skuas. Summer is also a good time to see Manx and sooty shearwaters on passage.

Although the main interest of the reserve is the seabird colony, there is nevertheless an interesting range of land birds because of the areas of rough grassland and gorse along the cliff top. Stonechats, whitethroats, willow warblers and wrens are among the breeding birds, while on the cliffs themselves ravens regularly breed. Peregrines also frequent these cliffs, and kestrels can be seen hunting the fields immediately inland.

Location: south-west of Whitehaven, off B5345 to St Bees village.
Access and facilities: public footpath from car park on sea front at St Bees leads north along steep path to 4 safe observation points on cliffs. Cars with disabled visitors may use private road to St Bees Head lighthouse from Sandwith. Warden present on reserve from April to August.
Map reference: NX962118

St Bees Head – with the Isle of Man in the background

Ogston Reservoir

Derbyshire

More species have been seen at Ogston than at any other site in Derbyshire, and because of that it is the most popular spot in the county for birdwatchers.

The reservoir is set in very pleasant farmland and small woodlands, with Ogston Woodlands along part of the western shore being a Derbyshire Wildlife Trust reserve. The reservoir is good for birds throughout the year, with particularly large numbers there in winter. Several species of wildfowl occur and include wigeon, teal, pochard and tufted duck as well as goosander. Herons regularly stalk the water's edge in search of eels and fish, and kingfishers are also seen. A very large roost of several thousand gulls assembles in late winter. Careful checking of the roost shows that glaucous and Iceland gulls turn up from time to time.

As winter moves into spring goldeneyes move through on their way north, and this is a very good place to look for the first swallows and martins of the year as they arrive from Africa. Skylarks are common on sunny days, while the lovely song of the willow warbler, together with the monotonous call of the chiffchaff, is typical of the woodlands at this time of year.

The margins can be very good in late summer for a wide variety of waders moving south before the onset of winter. They include common ones such as dunlin, redshank and ringed plover, as well as the less common such as greenshank, green sandpiper, and wood sandpiper. Terns are also regularly seen at this time of year.

Location: 5 miles east of Matlock, off B6014, or from A61 Sheffield to Derby road. At Stretton take B6014 signposted Matlock.
Access and facilities: no access to water's edge, but reservoir and surrounding land can be easily seen from car parks and roads. Access to Ogston Woodlands by permit only. Car parks at the northern end of reservoir, and on western shore, reached from unclassified road to Woolley and Brackenfield.
Map reference: SK376610

Ribble Estuary

Lancashire

The estuaries along the west coast of Britain are outstanding for the great volume of birds which use them either on passage or as comfortable wintering areas with an abundant food supply.

The Ribble is one of the very best, with not only large numbers of birds present, but a wide variety as well. At times there are over 100,000 waders present – the spectacle of the huge flocks whirling above the tidal flats is one to remember for a very long time!

Black-tailed godwits are uncommon wintering birds in Britain, but over 2,000 can be seen here in some winters, accounting for over a quarter of the British population. Even greater numbers of bar-tailed godwits spend the winter on the estuary, with over 10,000 present in some years.

Many thousands of knots, grey plovers, dunlins and redshanks feed on the mud at low tide, and roost on the upper salt marsh and on adjacent fields at high tide. The Ribble is by far the most important site in Britain for that lovely little wader, the sanderling, with about 2,000 here in winter, and many thousands more on spring passage, particularly in May.

Along with the winter spectacle of waders is the enormous concentration of pink-footed geese which spend the winter on the South Lancashire Mosses. Well over 20,000 of these lovely geese can be seen flying in and out of the estuary, depending upon the tide. The estuary is also a good place for smaller wildfowl, with many thousands of wigeon, teal, and smaller, but still impressive, numbers of shelducks and pintails.

With such large numbers of birds present, birds of prey are attracted to the estuary, with peregrines, hen harriers, merlins and sparrowhawks, as well as short-eared owls, being regularly seen.

Of further interest is Martin Mere, a Wildfowl Trust reserve 10 miles south of Southport at Burscough, near Ormskirk. It has a large collection of captive wildfowl, but contains a 300-acre wild refuge, where wintering whooper and Bewick's swans, as well as other wildfowl, may be seen. Numbers of teal can be most impressive, and there are large numbers of pintail. Thousands of pink-footed geese visit the area in winter.

Location: west of Preston, reached from A59. Access and facilities: main area for seeing birds is on south shore, owned by the Nature Conservancy Council. Reached by following A59 from Preston to Tarleton, then A565 to Southport. Then take unclassified roads to Hundred End and Crossens. Public footpaths giving views of marsh from embankment lead north from this road. Best views of estuary and birds can be obtained from Coast Road on northern edge of Southport. No other access to marshes. Martin Mere open daily 9.30am to 5.30pm.
Map reference: SD370210

Sandbach Flashes

Cheshire

Subsidence ponds formed by mining of one sort or another are a feature of many parts of northern England and they are known by different names in different places. In some areas they are known as 'swallow' ponds, but here in Cheshire they are called 'flashes' and those at Sandbach – caused by salt mining – are outstanding for their ornithological interest. There are four large stretches of water, together with marshy areas and wet pasture.

There is always something to see, but because of the ideal conditions that abound here for waders, spring, late summer and early autumn can be particularly good. Northbound waders in the spring use the flashes briefly as a staging post, but on the return journey in the late summer and autumn they stay longer and it is then that the greatest variety occurs.

All the common waders occur, but they are joined by many others including greenshanks, green and wood sandpipers, curlew sandpipers, ruffs, little stints, and that most elegant wader, the spotted redshank. During the summer several of the common waders breed around the flashes, including redshanks and common sandpipers. The great crested grebe, another spectacular bird of the area, is much in evidence at this time of the year, with several pairs breeding on the flashes.

The sheltered waters are attractive to wildfowl in winter when good numbers of tufted ducks, pochards, wigeon and goldeneyes can be present.

The whole area is worth exploring in the spring when the migrants begin to return, and not only the water birds and waders are present. Swallows, martins and swifts hawk for insects, whitethroats are in the hedgerows, and pied wagtails seem to be everywhere.

Location: between Sandbach and Middlewich, reached from A533. Flashes are between A533 and River Wheelock, reached on unclassified roads to Moston Green, Warmingham, Occlestone Green, etc.
Access: none to flashes themselves, which are managed by Cheshire Conservation Trust, but good views from roads.
Map reference: SJ720620

Seaforth Nature Reserve

Merseyside

For those seeking rare gulls, this is one of the best reserves in the country. Its mixture of salt and fresh water pools, marshy areas and rubble mounds regularly attracts Mediterranean, ring-billed and little gulls. Other birds recorded here include Leach's petrels, black terns, little stints and ruffs. Breeding birds include shelducks, ringed plovers and yellow wagtails. It may look an unprepossessing place at first, but the birdwatching rewards can be great.

Location: 5 miles north-north-west of Liverpool City Centre. Reached from A565 through Freeport entrance at Crosby Road South.
Access: open daily 8am to sunset; closed Christmas and New Year. Pedestrians only.
Map reference: SJ315972

South Solway

Cumbria   RSPB

With its spectacular views across the Solway Firth to the Galloway Hills of south-west

Scotland, the road along the southern shore of this splendid estuary would be worth driving even if there were no birds to be seen from it. Fortunately, there are enormous numbers of birds at most times of the year, with the best times of day being when the tide is high, bringing the birds close to the road.

The Solway is particularly important for its wintering and passage waders, with very large numbers of oystercatchers, ringed plovers, golden plovers, grey plovers, lapwings, knots, dunlins, bar-tailed godwits, curlews and redshanks. Because the road is so close to the shore over much of its length the high water roosts can be watched from very close range. There are several roost sites, but two of the best are on the RSPB reserve of Campfield Marsh just west of Bowness-on-Solway. Many thousands of oystercatchers gather here, particularly at the most westerly of the two roosts opposite Maryland Farm. In addition, there are large numbers of curlews, grey plovers, dunlins and knots. The birds are easily watched from the road and visitors should not venture on to the marsh. Not only does this disturb the birds, but the marshes are dangerous places, with hidden channels and fast rising tides.

As the road leaves Campfield it begins to follow the shore of Moricambe Bay, a major inlet of the southern Solway. This is an important area for shelducks, as well as mallards and wigeon, and at the outer reaches of the bay, scaup. A fine vantage point for the outer bay is Grune Point, on the other side of the bay. It is reached by following the B5302 to Calvo and then the road to Skinburness. From here a footpath leads out to the point. This is a good spot for birds at any time of year.

Apart from the ducks and waders, other important winter visitors to the Solway are herds of whooper swans, large flocks of pink-footed geese, and the entire Spitsbergen population of barnacle geese.

Location: 12 miles west of Carlisle.
Access: for Bowness 'island' – follow unclassified road from Burgh by Sands through Bowness-on-Solway to Anthorn. For Grune Point – take B5307 from Kirkbride, then B5302 and unclassified roads to Skinburness.
Map reference: NY215628

Spurn Head

Humberside

Few places are better for seeing large numbers of migrant birds than this unusual place. It is a sand and shingle spit projecting four miles out into the mouth of the Humber, and is subject to everything the North Sea weather can throw at it.

On the estuary side of the spit there are salt marshes, while on the side facing the sea are narrow beaches of sand and shingle with some sand dunes.

Because of its prominent position, and because it is such a narrow peninsula, Spurn is a wonderful place for seeing birds during the migration seasons, but particularly in the autumn. Spurn Bird Observatory at the north end of Spurn Head is managed by the

Spurn Head – old sea defences

Yorkshire Wildlife Trust, and annually among the huge numbers of common migrants records some of the rarest birds seen in Britain.

Shorebirds, gulls, terns, and other seabirds can be seen from the Head at different times of the year, but it is the small passerines for which Spurn is famous. If the weather conditions are right, producing a 'fall' of migrants along this part of the east coast, almost anything can turn up. These are birds which have been moving southwest along the mainland shore of Europe and have become disorientated, usually after meeting adverse weather conditions over the sea, and birds such as wrynecks, bluethroats, shrikes, barred and icterine warblers and many others can be found in these conditions. September and October are the principal months, and every day seems to bring something different. Particularly spectacular are mornings of the thrush migrations when tens of thousands of Scandinavian thrushes make landfall, after crossing the North Sea overnight.

Location: 18 miles south-east of Hull, reached by taking A1033 to Patrington and then B1445 to Easington. From here take unclassified road through Kilnsea. Road to Spurn Head is private, but public footpath runs along spit.
Access and facilities: Most of Spurn Head is nature reserve managed by Yorkshire Wildlife Trust. Open all year. Information centre. Admission charge for cars.
Map reference: TA420150

Teesmouth

Cleveland

In spite of the ravages of industry, the mouth of the Tees continues to attract a large variety as well as large numbers of birds. Only about 400 acres of the inter-tidal mud flats known as Seal Sands remain following in-filling by the Port Authority, but they still provide a rich food source for many thousands of migratory waders and wildfowl. Although Seal Sands holds the greatest numbers of birds, there are plenty of other places at Teesmouth where birds can be seen.

Waders use Seal Sands in both spring and autumn, with many spending the winter here. Bar-tailed godwits, golden plovers and grey plovers can be particularly prominent, and as the tide covers the mud a variety of wildfowl moves in to the shelter and food

supply of the inner estuary. Shelducks winter in large numbers and can often be seen flying against the background of industry. Winter is the time of year to watch sanderlings twinkling up and down in front of the waves on the sands of the South Gare.

Sea-watching at the mouth of the estuary can be very rewarding with large numbers of terns passing by, particularly in autumn when they are harried by skuas. Gannets are often seen fishing just off shore, and divers use Tees Bay as a feeding area throughout the winter.

Location: just north of Middlesbrough.
Access: for views over Seal Sands park in car park on Cowpen Marsh on north side of A178 midway between Middlesbrough and Hartlepool. Footpath beginning on opposite side of road leads along embankment of Greatham Creek to hide overlooking Seal Sands. Adjacent to A178 just beyond Seal Sands roundabout are Saltholme Pools and nearby Reclamation Pond, which can be viewed from road, but care should be taken because of traffic. North Gare can also be reached from A178 by walking south along beach from Seaton Carew. South Gare reached by following unclassified road from Redcar northwest towards British Steel works, or by walking along Coatham Sands.
Map reference: NZ530260

Yorkshire Dales – Swaledale under snow

Walney Island

Cumbria

The southern tip of Walney Island is a reserve of the Cumbria Trust for Nature Conservation, and there is also a bird observatory here. The mixture of open water, marshes, dunes and sandy beaches attracts a

variety of birds, both resident and migratory. Residents include large colonies of herring gulls and lesser black-backed gulls, and there are nesting eiders. Terns, skuas and divers are seen in autumn, while winter brings wildfowl and waders.

Location: 4 miles south of Barrow-in-Furness; reached by following A5087 on to island, then unclassified road through Biggar.
Access and facilities: reserve open Tue–Sun and Bank Holiday Mon, 10am to 5pm; permit available on site. Admission charge. Nature Trail. Observatory closed Mon. Hides.
Map reference: SD212623

Washington Waterfowl Park

Tyne and Wear

A superb collection of captive wildfowl from every corner of the world is the main attraction here. At the southern end of the park is a Wild Refuge, with open water and low woodland. This has numerous resident birds, and also attracts a good many migrants.

Location: east of Washington, 3 miles west of Sunderland, off A1231.
Access: Wildfowl Trust Reserve, open daily 9am to 5pm; closed Christmas. Admission charge for non-members. Information centre. Picnic area. Nature Trail. Hides. Toilets.
Map reference: NZ330565

Yorkshire Dales National Park

North Yorkshire

This National Park is dominated by the high Pennines lying along its western side, but visitors probably know it best because of the two main dales – Swaledale and Wensleydale. Both dales are farmed, but in a way which makes them good places for birds.

The rivers are excellent for common sandpipers during the spring and summer and for dippers the year round. Grey wagtails are common in some areas, and the wetter and more traditionally farmed riverside meadows are good for yellow wagtails.

Lower down the dales the older woodlands can be very good for all the common species, along with good numbers of redstarts and pied and spotted flycatchers.

The farming system means that waders such as lapwing and curlew are common, and in late summer particularly large concentrations can be found. Other waders such as redshank, snipe, golden plover and dunlin breed on the high Pennine ridge. This part of the park, particularly in the far western corner, contains some of the wettest, bleakest and most remote country in England, ideal for these birds.

Location: between Richmond and Kendal.
Access: A6108 from Scotch Corner on A1 leads through Richmond and entrance to Swaledale; B6270 turns west off this road 4 miles beyond Richmond and follows Swale along the length of dale. By following A6108 to Leyburn and then turning west on A684 whole of Wensleydale is reached. Many unclassified roads give access between and beyond these dales. Footpaths give access to higher and more remote areas of park. Pennine Way winds north near western edge.
Map reference: SD875898

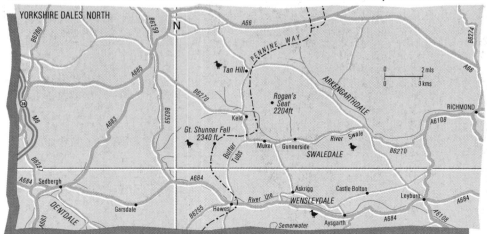

Scotland

Buzzard

Unrivalled mountain and moorland wildernesses give Scotland its principal character. Here golden eagles soar over some of the most precious wildlife areas in Europe. The lochs and islands have special birds of their own. Among the most outstanding sites are the Orkneys and the Shetlands

Scotland

Useful addresses

RSPB Headquarters: The Lodge, Sandy, Bedfordshire, SG19 2DL
RSPB Scottish Headquarters: 17 Regent Terrace, Edinburgh, EH7 5BN
Many RSPB reserves have explanatory leaflets. These are often available at the reserve but in any event the regional office, or RSPB HQ, will supply information on any reserve upon receipt of a stamped addressed envelope.
Scottish Wildlife Trust Headquarters: 25 Johnston Terrace, Edinburgh, EH1 2NH
National Trust for Scotland: 5 Charlotte Square, Edinburgh, EH2 4DU
Nature Conservancy Council: South-east Scotland Region, 12 Hope Terrace, Edinburgh, EH9 2AS; South-west Scotland Region, The Castle, Loch Lomond Park, Balloch, G83 8LX; North-east Scotland Region, Wynne Edwards House, 17 Rubislaw Terrace, Aberdeen, AB1 1XE; North-west Scotland Region, Fraser Darling House, 9 Culduthel Road, Inverness, IV2 4AG

Argyll Forest Park

Strathclyde

A vast area of hills, mountains, lochs and sea lochs with mainly coniferous woodland, this Forest Park is well worth exploring. It stretches from Inveruglas on Loch Lomondside in the north, to Strone Point on Holy Loch in the south; and from the shores of Loch Long to its western boundary near Strachur on Loch Fyne. There are many trails and signposted walks. The area includes some oak woods, many of them coppiced, of which the best are at Loch Eck on the A85. Here, redstarts, great spotted woodpeckers and occasional pairs of wood warblers breed. The coniferous areas of sitka and Norway spruce, with some larch and various North American species, have a few patches of Scots pine. Crossbills, siskins, coal tits, goldcrests and chaffinches flourish here. The Younger Botanic Garden and Arboretum at Benmore in the south has nature trails, and the gardens themselves are beautifully laid out.

Flocks of eiders, with red-breasted mergansers and the common ducks swim on Loch Long and occasionally divers appear, particularly in winter. There are good numbers of dunlins and other waders, especially oystercatchers, curlews and redshanks. Buzzards perch on almost every electricity pole and there are tantalising glimpses of peregrines and golden eagles.

Location: west of Loch Long.
Access: car ferry from Gourock to Dunoon, or by road from north, via Arrochar. Good access points are at Ardgarten off A83 (at NN275030), at Lochgoilhead on B839 (at NN200015), at Kilmun on the A880 (at NS160826), and at Glenbranter at the north end of Loch Eck on the A815 (at NS113980). Younger Botanic Garden is on the A880 north of Dunoon (at NS145853). Open April to October. Admission charge. Information about park is obtainable from the Forestry Commission.
Map reference: NS143946

Ariundle Oakwoods

Highland

This National Nature Reserve has a well-surfaced trail leading through ancient sessile oak woodland. The rich variety of mosses and lichens, including the green seaweed-like lungwort, is witness to the mild, moist climate and the unpolluted air. The best time for a birdwatching visit is May and June for a good variety of woodland birds, including summer visitors such as spotted flycatchers, redstarts, tree pipits and wood warblers. Grey wagtails and dippers bob and feed along the river.

The reserve is set in a wild area with few roads and scattered villages; its very remoteness gives it a special quality. To the west is Ardnamurchan Point – the most westerly on the British mainland.

Location: between lochs Sunart and Shiel.
Access: from Strontian village on A861 at the east end of Ardnamurchan peninsula, take minor road north for a mile. Turning to reserve is on right.
Facilities: nature trail.
Map reference: NM830635

Ariundle Oakwoods

The Ayrshire and Renfrewshire Clyde Coast

Strathclyde

The whole of the coastline south of Gourock is worth visiting, particularly in the winter, when good numbers of the common sea and shore birds can always be seen. The chance that various species of divers or grebes might be spotted can add to the pleasure. Waders can be plentiful, and the autumn passage often turns up uncommon birds. Five sites are described below.

1. Bogside Flats, Irvine

This area of salt marsh and mud at the mouth of the River Garnock provides good birdwatching from the early autumn passage time at the end of July, right through until the spring. Odd rarities turn up on passage, but there are good views of waders such as dunlin, golden plover and curlew at most times during this period. Whooper swans appear in winter, when there are also wigeon and teal. Iceland and glaucous gulls make an occasional appearance, so the gull flocks ought not to be neglected.

Location: just west of Irvine. Follow signs to Magnum Leisure Centre south-west of town.
Access: harbour wall gives good views, as does racecourse on north side of flats.
Map reference: NS310385

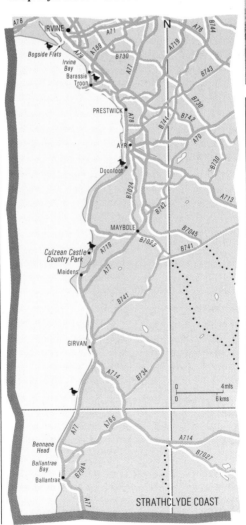

STRATHCLYDE COAST

2. Barrassie

This vantage point is especially good for passage waders; bar-tailed godwits are sometimes seen. Barrassie is effectively part of Troon, which lies just to the south. The rocky headland at Troon juts well out to sea and might provide a good viewpoint.

Location: 3 miles south of Irvine, off A78; reached on B746.
Map reference: NS336337

3. Doonfoot

In winter this is an excellent place to see waders, particularly redshank, oystercatcher and plovers, especially where the burn flows onto the beach. Gulls and wildfowl abound. In summer, gannets from the breeding colony on Ailsa Craig feed offshore, in company with common, arctic and Sandwich terns. At migration, particularly in August, interesting waders appear on passage, and wheatears can be seen on the beach. Other places of interest nearby include, at Alloway, the cottage where Robert Burns was born, and the Auld Kirk, the site of Tam O'Shanter's vision. In fact, this part of Scotland is full of Burns connections.

Location: 4 miles south of Ayr. At roundabout on A719 turn off towards coast, opposite Alloway turn, and follow unclassified road.
Facilities: short path to beach. Car park. Toilets.
Map reference: NS315194

4. Culzean Country Park

A castle designed by Robert Adam forms the centrepiece of this 560-acre country park, which is owned and administered by the National Trust for Scotland. The extensive grounds have a variety of habitats, with semi-natural woodland as well as plantings of exotic conifers and other trees. There are formal gardens as well as cliff and beach areas. In the woodlands, summer brings willow and garden warblers, chiffchaffs and blackcaps, as well as treecreepers, goldcrests and long-tailed tits. Common woodland and garden species are abundant and, with luck, sparrowhawks will show themselves. Mute swans breed on a lake in the grounds.

On the beach, all the common shore birds of the Ayrshire coast appear, while the clifftop is a summer habitat for whitethroats.

The Park Centre, adapted from the old Home Farm, has display and exhibition areas, and there are tape slide programmes available. Various other estate buildings, such as the Gas House and the Ice House can be visited in the grounds. A visit here would be incomplete without a tour of the castle, since it is one of Adam's masterpieces.

Location: 12 miles south of Ayr off A719.
Access and facilities: country park open all year. Castle open April to end October. Information centre. Car park. Toilet. Refreshments. Picnic areas.
Map reference: NS234103

Culzean Castle

5. Girvan to Ballantrae Bay

From Girvan the A77 southwards skirts the coast for over a dozen miles, giving excellent views of a variety of beaches and rocky foreshores and out to the imposing shape of Ailsa Craig. Various minor roads head inland over moorland and along small valleys into the higher ground east of the A714. The area is worth exploring in winter, when divers are often offshore and there are sizeable groups of eider and goldeneyes.

Greylag geese are frequent in the area. There are often gannets offshore even in the winter and the rockier parts of the coast are notable for purple sandpipers, with a few black guillemots just out to sea.

Location: between Girvan and Ballantrae, off A77.
Map reference: NX150130

Barons Haugh

Strathclyde   RSPB

An outstanding area of wetland and open water, with marsh and some mature woodland falls within this RSPB reserve. Winter is the best time for a visit, especially since the open water rarely freezes over. At this time, flocks of whooper swans and many wigeon, teal, mallards, pochards and tufted ducks are usually visible from the hides.

But other times can be good for birdwatching; for example, during the late summer passage ruffs, green sandpipers and other uncommon waders occur, when they may be seen along with breeding waterbirds such as little grebes, common sandpipers and redshanks.

Breeding birds of the woods and banks of the river include garden, sedge and grasshopper warblers, with tree pipits and whinchats. The Haugh has a surfaced path around it, part of the trail leading along the bank of the Clyde, where the lucky visitor may see a kingfisher.

Another path leads through to Strathclyde Country Park, where the open water attracts smews in the winter, as well as good numbers of commoner water birds.

The loch here is nearly two miles long – nothing very special about that, except that it is entirely artificial (including two beaches), part of a scheme which created this park from an industrial landscape.

Location: south of Motherwell, signposted from Airbles Road, which runs between A723 and A721.
Access and facilities: RSPB reserve open at all times. Car park. Disabled access from Warden, at 9 Wisteria Lane, Carluke, Strathclyde. Country Park open at all times. Information centre and Mausoleum open daily Easter to September; October to March weekends only. Trails. Picnic area.
Map reference: NS755552

Beauly Firth

Highland

This large estuary dries out almost completely at low tide, attracting waders and wildfowl in large numbers. In winter, thousands of greylag and pink-footed geese feed on the fields around the firth, and on still January days they can be heard calling for several miles. Snow geese are recorded most years and some at least seem to be genuine vagrants rather than escapees.

Some thousand or so Canada geese from the breeding populations in Yorkshire and the English midlands migrate here each summer to moult. The first birds arrive in late May; all but a few stragglers are gone by the end of September.

Passage or wintering waders include large numbers of bar-tailed godwits, knots, oystercatchers, curlews and redshanks. Ospreys sometimes fish over the Firth in summer, and two or three pomarine skuas overwintered here in the freak winter of 1985–1986. In fact, almost anything could turn up on this vast expanse of little-watched mud flats.

Large flocks of sea-ducks can be seen off Inverness and east of the Kessock bridge. Among these, goldeneye, common scoter, velvet scoter and an occasional smew are particularly obvious. Flocks of goosanders and red-breasted mergansers are found well up the River Ness, as well as on the Firth itself.

Location: just north-west of Inverness.
Access: easily watched from surrounding roads. The Inverness sea-front, just west off Kessock Bridge, and Tarradale in north-west corner of Firth, are particularly good points from which to make observations.
Map reference: NH600480

Benbecula and North and South Uist

Outer Hebrides, Western Isles

Set in the wild Atlantic 30 miles from the Scottish mainland, this string of islands is one of the most exciting wildlife havens in Britain. The ancient crofting way of life is still continued, and it is the continuation of this tradition, which enhances rather than destroys the environment, that has allowed such birds as the corncrake to find a refuge here. The whole western edge of these islands has been officially designated an ESA (Environmentally Sensitive Area), highlighting its value for both wildlife and agriculture. The coastal strip, known as the machair, has been enriched over many years by shell sand blown from the beaches. This not only provides a perfect habitat for a spectacular array of wild flowers, but includes marshy areas supporting a large population of breeding waders. Among these, dunlins and ringed plovers have their highest breeding densities in Britain.

The islands are reached by car ferry from Oban to Lochboisdale on South Uist or from Uig on Skye to Lochmaddy in North Uist. Good roads serve all three islands, and from these it is possible to see most of what they

have to offer. The two reserves described below show the tremendous contrast between the fertile western coasts and the acid moorlands of the east.

1. Balranald Reserve, North Uist RSPB
Sandy beaches and rocky foreshore as well as machair, marshes and a small loch give this RSPB reserve a wide variety of habitats typical of the islands' western sides. The best time to visit is summer, when breeding waders include lapwings, snipe, oystercatchers, ringed plovers and dunlins. Sometimes the increasingly-rare red-necked phalarope also breeds. Teal, shoveler and gadwall nest in the marshes. Little and arctic terns, twites and wheatears also breed, as does the corncrake. Its monotonous *crek-crek* call may often be heard, particularly at dusk, and frequently all night as well!

Location: west of A865 on west side of island. On unclassified road signposted to Hougharry, 3 miles north of Bayhead.

Beinn Eighe

Highland

More than 10,500 acres are covered by this National Nature Reserve. Included in this huge area are superb tracts of mountain and moorland scenery, and some rare fragments of the pine and birch forests which once covered much of the Highlands. Among the breeding birds here are both red- and black-throated divers, golden eagles, peregrines, ptarmigans, crossbills and black grouse.

Location: off A832, 1 mile north-west of Kinlochewe
Access and facilities: restricted in autumn. Visitor centre (at Anancann Field Station) open June–September. Car parks, with picnic site and nature trail, beside Loch Maree.
Map reference: NG000610

Black Wood of Rannoch

Tayside

The Black Wood is an extensive tract of ancient Caledonian pine forest which still holds most of the classic birds of that very special habitat, including capercaillies, black grouse, siskins and Scottish crossbills, although not (as yet) crested tits. Summer visitors such as redstarts, spotted flycatchers and tree pipits are common. Contrast the beautiful ancient pine woods with new, regimented plantations and you will see how wonderful a pine wood *should* be!

Location: 20 miles west of Pitlochry. Reached from B846 at Kinloch Rannoch; follow minor roads along southern shore of loch.
Access: along tracks and waymarked walks.
Map reference: NN600570

*Access and facilities: free at all times, but keep to waymarked paths to avoid disturbing ground-nesting birds. Visitor reception (Warden present only from April to August) is at Goular, near Hougharry.
Map reference: NF706707*

2. Loch Druidibeg, South Uist

Lying on the fringe of the acid, eastern side of the islands, this National Nature Reserve presents a perfect contrast to places like Balranald. It is a stronghold of greylag geese. These are native wild birds, unlike those introduced to more southerly areas.

*Location: off A865 5 miles south of the South Ford Bridge between Howmore and Stilligarry. Access: permits required during breeding season (from Warden, Stilligarry, South Uist) but loch can be viewed from road.
Map reference: NF790375*

North Uist – corn marigolds at Tigharry village. The inset is of Sidinish, also on North Uist

Cameron Reservoir
Fife

This is one of the best places to be at dusk, in mid to late autumn, for it is then that great flocks of pink-footed geese – up to 5,000 – fly honking in to roost. Greylags come in smaller numbers, to join the pink-feet and a flock of whooper swans. There are gadwalls as well as numbers of the commoner ducks. An Edwardian country house, Hill of Tarvit, two miles out of Cupar on the A916 is worth a visit.

*Location: 3½ miles south of St Andrews, reached on track west off A915.
Access and facilities: free. Hide for members of Scottish Ornithologists' Club and also of Scottish Wildlife Trust.
Map reference: NO479123*

Carron Valley Reservoir
Central

Much of the area around this reservoir is Forestry Commission sitka spruce plantation, but as there is variation in the ages of the trees there is a pleasing variety of birds. Crossbills nest here in the early part of the year, and there are flocks of siskins, chaffinches and coal tits. The open water has good numbers of the commoner duck species throughout the winter, but the greatest attraction here is the flock of 40 to 50 bean geese which visit the south side of the loch in October. These elegant, dark geese are scarce in Britain.

*Location: 12 miles west of Falkirk, off B818. Access and facilities: views over loch are possible from roadside, but good stopping places are few. Track leads along southern shore, through plantations, with access to the water possible at various points. Car park, with toilets, at east end of reservoir.
Map reference: NS722838*

Clyde Estuary
Strathclyde

Birdwatchers have tended to undervalue the Clyde in the past, but it is now recognised as an important wintering ground for shelducks and flocks of redshanks, lapwings, oystercatchers and dunlins, as well as many other species. On the open water there are goldeneyes, eiders, pintails, wigeon, mallards and teal, with some red-breasted mergansers and common scoters.

1. South Shore
Good views can be had of the birds on the stretch of coast between Erskine and West Ferry.

*Location: west of Erskine.
Access and facilities: free and unrestricted at*

Clyde Estuary – a wild side and a suburban side

*all times. Leave M8 motorway westbound from Glasgow at junction 31, signposted Bishopton, and follow round roundabout to West Ferry, where there is car parking space. Alternatively leave motorway at junction 30, follow signs to Erskine hospital, then go towards AA HQ and take a turning left to coast and car park. It is possible to walk from one end to the other of this stretch of coastline, on fairly good pathways.
Map reference: NS390730*

2. North Shore: Ardmore Point
There is a nature trail around this Scottish Wildlife Trust reserve. It leads round the coast from mud flats at the eastern end, where huge flocks of oystercatchers and other waders congregate at low tide in winter. Further round the coastline becomes rocky, with the famous geological fault between Upper and Lower Old Red Sandstone which marks the Highland Line. Scrub and grassland lie inland, and the trail leads back to the beginning past salt marshes and through stretches of woodland; the going is rough and wet in some places. The best time to visit is in winter when there are large numbers of waders (including turnstone and dunlin) in the muddy areas. In the western bay, pink-footed and greylag geese feed with whooper swans on the salt marshes. The rocky shore is a good vantage point for seeing divers and grebes at sea, and there are eiders and other sea-ducks. In the scrubby areas sedge and willow warblers nest, together with reed buntings and yellowhammers. Snipes breed in wetter patches among the orchids. An old fish yair is visible in the west bay.

*Location: off A814 between Helensburgh and Cardross.
Access: free at all times.
Map reference: NS315785*

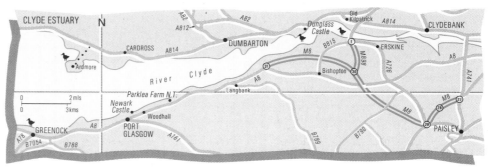

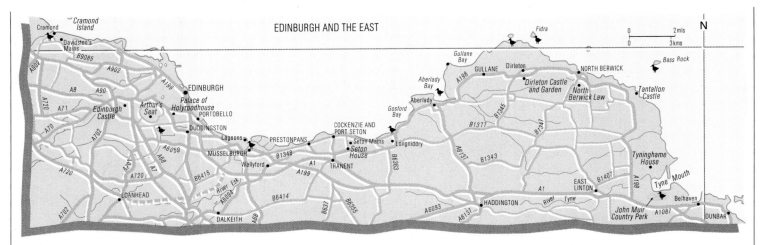

EDINBURGH AND THE EAST

Eden Estuary

Fife

This is one of the best places for winter birdwatching in Fife, or indeed Scotland. Acres of mud and sand are exposed at low tide and, backed by salt marshes and arable fields, they provide safe feeding and roosting areas for very large numbers of waders and wildfowl. There are wigeon and teal, and the area is of national importance (*ie* with more than one per cent of the total population) for bar-tailed and black-tailed godwits, as well as oystercatchers, ringed plovers, dunlins and redshanks. There are usually some grey plovers. Flocks of curlews, lapwings and golden plovers congregate with greylag and pink-footed geese, and there are many shelducks and whooper swans. Sea ducks appear, too, with eiders and red-breasted mergansers. During the autumn passage rarer migrants such as greenshank, spotted redshank and little stint occur.

Location: 4 miles north-west of St Andrews, off A91.
Access: Local Nature Reserve. Ranger service. Southern shore has easiest access, with car parking. Bridge at Guardbridge on A91 is a good viewpoint, but further east it is possible to get nearer shore on disused railway line.
Map reference: NO455188

Edinburgh and the East Lothian Coast

Lothian

The city of Edinburgh has attractions beyond the ornithological for the tourist, but there are a number of sites in or near the city which amply repay investigation by the birdwatcher. Its many parks and open spaces support the healthiest urban population of raptors in Britain, with over 40 pairs of kestrels and 35 pairs of sparrowhawks proved breeding in recent years. A small colony of fulmars is to be found on Salisbury Crags, only a few hundred yards from the city centre. Given below is a selection of birdwatching places close to the city.

1. Cramond

A picturesque little village at the mouth of the River Almond, Cramond is rich in historical interest. For the singleminded birdwatcher, however, its main interest lies in the large inter-tidal flats to the west of the causeway connecting Cramond Island with the mainland. These hold large numbers of wading birds overwintering and on passage. These are mainly knots, redshanks, curlews and oystercatchers, but greenshank and whimbrel are frequently recorded and rarities are not unknown. The waters around Cramond Island hold fair numbers of sawbills, such as goosander in spring, as well as eider and shelduck. In summer, terns fish near the esplanade. Examine them closely in the hope of detecting a roseate tern from the RSPB's Inchmickery reserve a couple of miles offshore.

A small passenger ferry operates in daylight hours at the mouth of the Almond plying between Cramond village and the Dalmeny Estate. A gentle stroll through the parklands here may reveal a rich variety of breeding woodland birds.

Location: 3 miles west of Edinburgh centre off A90.
Map reference: NT190770

2. Duddingston Loch

A superb little wildlife sanctuary within only a few hundred yards of Edinburgh city centre, Duddingston Loch has a variety of breeding, passage and wintering birds unrivalled in any other town in Scotland.

Breeding birds include great crested grebe and little grebe, sparrowhawk and

Duddingston Loch

kestrel, mute swan and grey heron, as well as several species of ducks and warblers. A flock of feral greylag geese breeds near the loch, on the Scottish Wildlife Trust's Bawsinch reserve, and these can often be seen flying in the area or feeding on nearby golf courses or school playing fields.

Location: between Holyrood Park and Craigmillar, reached along Old Church Lane from A1.
Access and facilities: part of northern shore open to public. Car park on Duddingston Road west or by Holyrood Park gates. Keys to hide in Bawsinch reserve available from visitor centre in Holyrood Park.
Map reference: NT284725

3. Musselburgh Lagoons

As romantic in name as they are unprepossessing in appearance, the lagoons are proof positive to the birdwatcher that appearances can be deceiving. These grubby-looking impoundments have attracted as many rarities as any comparable site on the Scottish mainland.

The treacherous surface of the lagoons, filled with fly ash from a nearby power station, promises security from predators, and they are used as safe roosts overnight and at high tide by large numbers of gulls, terns and waders. It is worth checking through the flocks bird by bird in the hope of turning up something really exotic, such as a Forster's tern, a lesser crested tern, Sabine's gull or perhaps a pectoral sandpiper. All of these unusual birds have been

6. Tyninghame and the John Muir Country Park

Along this coast throughout the summer months gannets from Bass Rock can be seen fishing off-shore and there are also seals and dolphins. Tyninghame House Estate holds the largest heronry in Lothian Region and the estuary of the River Tyne is second only to Aberlady Bay in the numbers of passage and wintering waders it holds. John Muir Country Park, which includes much of this coastline, has woodland, scrub and grassland as well as cliffs, dunes and salt marsh.

Location: north-west of Dunbar.
Access: Tyninghame area reached on unclassified roads off A198. Car parks for country park are at Belhaven Bay, off A1087.
Map reference: NT640800

Bass Rock – inset are some of the gannets for which the island is famous

recorded here in the very recent past.

A good selection of commoner birds is also to be seen at close quarters, allowing the finer plumage details to be distinguished. Just off the embankment in late winter, long-tailed ducks are to be seen in full breeding plumage – closer at hand and more easily viewed perhaps than anywhere else in Britain. A trip to the lagoons rarely disappoints and often astounds. In winter the hinterland has flocks of mixed small birds, often including snow bunting and twite, and even Lapland bunting.

Location: east of Musselburgh town centre. Cut back sharply to left just before racecourse and follow the Esk downstream as far as possible.
Access: along sea wall around lagoons.
Map reference: NT345735

4. Seton Sands and Gosford Bay

The four or five miles of coastline stretching from Port Seton to Craigielaw Point (the western corner of Aberlady Bay) offer perhaps the best opportunity in Britain to see all five common species of grebe; from late July for a couple of months, red-necked grebes in particular can be seen in full breeding plumage just a few yards offshore.

Good numbers of waders (bar-tailed godwits, redshanks and ringed plovers) frequent the largely sandy coastline: turnstones and occasionally purple sandpipers are to be found mainly on the many patches of rock. Inevitably, the birds haunting this

attractive and popular stretch of coastline are frequently disturbed.

Fortunately, the birds offshore are indifferent to human pressure. Alongside the grebes are good-sized flocks of eiders, and common and velvet scoters as well as mallards and the occasional sawbill.

Location: 14 miles east of Edinburgh centre.
Access: from B1348 and A198.
Map reference: NT420760

5. Aberlady Bay and coast to North Berwick

A wader site second to none in Scotland, because of the huge expanse of mud flats left exposed at low tide, Aberlady also attracts good numbers of owls, raptors and passerines during the spring and autumn passage.

Greenshanks are to be seen in the bay throughout August and September. Grey plovers, infrequent elsewhere in Scotland, can readily be seen on passage and some stay on throughout the winter. Perhaps half of Lothian's ringed plovers breed on the reserve and some can be seen at any time of year. For a few days each year during migration many hundreds are passing through. It is difficult to think of a wader on the British list which has not turned up at Aberlady Bay at one time or another, and that perhaps is its principal charm: the ever-present possibility of the totally unexpected.

The salt marsh here attracts many birds in winter, including both snow and Lapland buntings, twites, and, occasionally, shore larks.

A path runs from Aberlady to Gullane, and an information board provides topical information. The shoreline between Gullane Point and North Berwick consists mainly of long stretches of golden sand; a holidaymaker's dream, but lacking in interest for the birdwatcher in summer. Terns and a few auks, mainly puffins and guillemots, breed on Fidra, Eyebroughty and the Lamb. Although there is no public access to these small islands, the birds can be seen from the mainland with the aid of a telescope. In winter, the walk from the Timber Bridge at Aberlady Bay round the coast to North Berwick is well worth undertaking. Offshore, east of North Berwick, is the Bass Rock, perhaps best-known for its large colony of gannets. The species takes part of its scientific name *Sula bassana* from the island. The rock also holds good numbers of kittiwakes and guillemots as well as puffins.

Location: between Aberlady and North Berwick, off A198.
Access and facilities: Aberlady Bay is a Local Nature Reserve. Car park. Toilets. Permits for car park from East Lothian District Council, Brunton Hall, Musselburgh. Footpath access to rest of coast.
Map reference: NT472805

Fair Isle

Best known as a migration watchpoint, Fair Isle also has breeding seabirds in good numbers. The hostel attached to the bird observatory offers comfortable accommodation as well as a chance to keep in touch with anything happening on the bird front.

Skuas, auks and waders breed, making Fair Isle a great place to visit in summer, but it is in late spring and again in autumn that migrants appear in astonishing numbers and variety. Nothing is ever guaranteed, and weather conditions have a crucial influence, but the appearance one morning of a tiny stray from America, south-east Europe or eastern Siberia is always simply magical.

Location: between Orkneys and Shetlands.
Access: by ferry (Good Shepherd) 3 times weekly from Grutness in South Mainland of Shetland. Also air services.
Map reference: HZ218719

Falls of Clyde

Strathclyde

Here the River Clyde tumbles through a narrow gorge in broadleaved woodland. Until recently there was considerable conifer plantation, but much of this has been extracted to make the area more attractive for wildlife. Breeding birds in the woodland include garden warblers, chiffchaffs, spotted flycatchers, great spotted and green woodpeckers and willow tits. The river provides a feeding and nesting area for grey wagtails and dippers – the symbol of the reserve.

The town of New Lanark, one of the birthplaces of the industrial revolution, is being gradually refurbished, and some of the mills restored. There is an area where craft workers live and work. The whole area is ideal for a family day out.

Location: 1 mile south of Lanark on unclassified road, signposted New Lanark, off A73.
Access and facilities: open at all times. Visitor centre open weekdays April to October, admission charge. Ranger: telephone Lanark 65262.
Map reference: NS882415

Fife Ness

Fife

The Ness is a mecca for dedicated birdwatchers, but may be rather hard work for the more casual visitor. Reaching out into the North Sea, it is an excellent spot during the migration periods, both spring and autumn, particularly after a period of easterly wind, rain and fog! Among the more interesting species so far recorded are bluethroats, redstarts, pied flycatchers and whitethroats as well as other, rarer migrants. The autumn passage is the best time for skuas, both pomarine and arctic; shearwaters, and common, arctic and Sandwich terns can also be seen.

Location: between St Andrews and Crail, at end of unclassified road off A917 from Crail.
Access: car park near golf club (charge).
Map reference: NO635100

Findhorn Bay

Grampian

A large, nearly land-locked tidal estuary, the bay holds large wintering flocks of the usual waders with good chances of more uncommon birds on passage. In late summer there are good views of hunting ospreys; as many as a dozen birds have been seen in the air or diving into the water at one time. Terns, including Sandwich terns, fly in and out of the bay, and the sandy beaches provide views of common waders. The disused air strip south of the village has a good variety of warblers and common birds.

Location: north of Forres, off B9011.
Access: to west bank by foot through Culbin Forest. B9011 to Findhorn offers good views in places. Findhorn itself is a good vantage point.
Map reference: NJ042641

Fowlsheugh

Grampian
RSPB

Donated to the RSPB by its junior section, the Young Ornithologists' Club, this attractive reserve holds one of the largest seabird colonies in mainland Britain. In summer the noise of tens of thousands of guillemots, kittiwakes and razorbills can be deafening. Puffins can be watched at the entrances to their burrows from a few feet away. Other breeding birds include eiders, fulmars and jackdaws, while peregrines are often to be seen hunting along the cliffs.

Location: 4½ miles south of Stonehaven at Crawton, which is off A92.
Access: at all times along cliff-top path.
Map reference: NO880796

Glasgow – Kelvingrove Park

Glasgow

Strathclyde

Although Glasgow is a modern, bustling city, there are several places within its limits which are rewarding for the birdwatcher. Even the huge early evening starling roost in Sauchiehall Street has its attractions, and a walk alongside the River Kelvin in Kelvingrove Park near the Art Galleries has been known to yield a kingfisher. A selection of sites near to the city centre is given below.

1. Hogganfield Loch
This small loch to the east of the city is primarily a boating pond and a place where families come to feed the ducks. However, in winter it attracts whooper swans and greylag and pink-footed geese, as well as a variety of ducks including goldeneye. Even goosanders are occasionally seen.

Location: on south side of A80 Glasgow/Stirling road just west of Steps.
Access: unrestricted.
Map reference: NS645675

2. Gadloch
The farmer at Loch Farm keeps geese which often mingle with winter visiting greylags, pink-feet and whooper swans. There are Canada geese and a variety of ducks: teal, mallard, wigeon and shoveler. The occasional rarity like green-winged teal turns up, and there are good views of waders.

Location: 3 miles north-east of city centre on south side of B819 south of Lenzie.
Access: to east end of loch is from path crossing field. It is possible to walk along south shore. Car parking space nearby.
Map reference: NS650710

Glencoe

Strathclyde

The two main reasons for visiting this area are for its association with the massacre of the MacDonalds by the Campbells in the late 17th century, and for hillwalking. The scenery is spectacular and the chance of seeing ptarmigan on the high tops may well attract people of an optimistic mind, and energetic bent. Eagles and ravens can be seen, and south-east of the main glen on Rannoch Moor near Loch Ba, breeding waders including curlew and golden plover can sometimes be viewed from the roadside. Other wildlife in the glen includes red

deer, and much, much smaller, plants such as mossy saxifrage and alpine lady's mantle. Hillwalking should not be attempted by the inexperienced or without adequate equipment and clothing.

Location: 12 miles south of Fort William on A82.
Access and facilities: most of area is National Trust for Scotland estate. Visitor centre near Clachaig, open April to October. Admission charge. Nature trails. Refreshments. Toilets. Car park. Picnic area. Ranger service.
Map reference: NN171568

Glencoe

3. Hillend Reservoir

This reservoir is worth a look, particularly during autumn and winter. During the autumn passage, ruffs, black-tailed godwits, green sandpipers and little stints have all been seen in recent years. There are breeding ringed plovers and mallards as well as other ducks. In the winter barnacle geese and the occasional pintail visit, and there should be goldeneyes and goosanders for much of the time.

Location: 2 miles east of Airdrie off A89.
Access: view from road.
Map reference: NS832672

4. Possil Loch and Marsh

A Scottish Wildlife Trust Reserve near the Forth and Clyde Canal, this is an area of shallow water surrounded by marsh and willow scrub. In summer there is a variety of breeding birds such as snipe, coot and moorhen, and reed buntings and willow warblers in the scrubby trees. Wintertime brings large numbers of ducks and other wildfowl, and long-eared owls have been known to roost in the scrub.

Location: 3 miles north of city, off A879.
Access: cars can be parked in cemetery just opposite reserve, or a little further south in Skirsa Street.
Map reference: NS585700

Glen Trool

Dumfries and Galloway

The glen is part of the Galloway Forest Park, owned by the Forestry Commission. Much of the area is afforested and here the usual conifer-loving birds appear: siskins, goldcrests and coal tits, as well as crossbills. There is also old oak woodland, and here there are wood warblers, redstarts and pied flycatchers breeding, as well as woodcocks. Various birds of prey appear, including the elusive peregrine and hen harrier – buzzards are common, as they are throughout western Scotland. Summer is the best time to visit.

It is possible to walk right round the loch, on the 4½-mile Loch Trool Trail, which begins at Caldon, but the more adventurous may prefer hillwalking to the top of 2,764ft Merrick, the highest mountain in the Southern Uplands. To the south-west is Clatteringshaws Loch, with fine scenery and reasonable birdwatching, and the added bonus of the Galloway Deer Museum. Both red and roe deer are common throughout the park, but, despite their size, can be difficult to spot on the open hillsides.

Location: north of Newton Stewart, signposted from A714 at Bargrennan.
Access and facilities: unrestricted. Galloway Deer Museum open daily April to end September.
Map reference: NX400790

Handa

Highland RSPB

A small but spectacular island, just over one square mile in area, Handa's main ornithological interest lies in its huge seabird colonies. Visit the island in summer (May through to mid-July) and thrill to the sight and sound of tens of thousands of breeding guillemots, kittiwakes and razorbills. Puffins, fulmars and black guillemots occur in lesser numbers and there are other breeding birds including red-throated divers and skuas (great and arctic). A procession of gannets dives in the bays.

Non-breeding birds to be seen offshore, particularly on passage in early May and August, include great northern and black-throated divers as well as sooty and Manx shearwaters.

Location: off west coast of Highland north of Scourie.
Access and facilities: day trips to island are run by fisherman from village of Tarbet April to early September, but not on Sun. RSPB members may stay overnight in bothy on Handa with prior permission from RSPB Scottish Headquarters.
Map reference: NC150480

Handa – one of the fulmars

The Hirsel

Borders

This is a private estate belonging to the Earl of Home. It is best visited in May and June if the visitor is to appreciate to the full its variety of breeding woodland birds. Many such birds, relatively common in England, reach their northern breeding limit here, and many others are found far more commonly here than further north. Look out for green woodpeckers, marsh tits, blackcaps and garden warblers. The lake has several types of breeding ducks and grebes.

Location: 1½ miles north-west of Coldstream off A697; signposted.
Access and facilities: Car park. Exhibition centre. Toilets.
Map reference: NT825405

Islay, Inner Hebrides

Strathclyde

This strangely-shaped island has a rich and varied birdlife and is worth a visit at any time of year, though, as with many areas renowned for water birds, winter is the best birdwatching season. Its habitats include moorland, small patches of woodland, farmland, extensive sea lochs and sand dunes, as well as some cliffs. Each has something to offer.

Birds of prey, including golden eagle and possibly white-tailed eagle, are visible at times; buzzards are common and hen harriers, merlins, peregrines and short-eared owls all breed. In winter up to 20,000 barnacle geese arrive from Greenland, along with good numbers of white-fronted geese. Islay is the main wintering ground for these two species, and they may be seen grazing and roosting at many places on the island. Islay is one of Scotland's few breeding sites for choughs, and Machir Bay near Kilcho-

man (NR215632) is a good place to see them. They are also found at the Mull of Oa in the south. Corncrakes still find some suitable habitats on the island.

Other places of interest on the island are the various malt whisky distilleries, such as Lagavulin, Laphroaig, Talisker, and Bowmore.

Islay is reached by ferry from Kennacraig to Port Ellen and Port Askaig. Two outstanding places are described below.

1. Loch Gruinart [RSPB]

This RSPB reserve, largely farmland with dairy cattle, attracts the major part of the wintering Greenland barnacle geese to its pastures from October to April. Whooper swans may also be seen here along with white-fronted geese. Many birds of prey, including hen harriers, buzzards and peregrines hunt over the moorland. Teal, redshank, snipe and curlew are among the breeding species.

Location: west side of island. Reserve lies south and west of loch on both sides of B8017 northwest of Bridgend.
Access: visitors are asked not to enter the fields, but good viewing points are found both from B8017 and unclassified road to Ardnave. Cars may be parked at Aoradh Farm to avoid blocking the road.
Map reference: NR276673

2. Loch Indaal

The A847 skirts this sea loch and affords views of eiders, common scoters and other seabirds such as divers and grebes. In winter there is usually a flock of scaup, and always goldeneyes. Many waders feed on the coastal area.

Location: west of Bowmore, skirted by A847.
Access: view from road.
Map reference: NR270600

Islay – barnacle geese at Loch Gruinart

Isle of Arran

Strathclyde

Arran is an ideal holiday island for those not looking for sophisticated pursuits. It offers hill and coast walking, and mountain climbing for the more adventurous, while Brodick Castle and its famous gardens, together with the wide range of other habitats, provide excellent birdwatching. The gentler moorlands to the south of the island are hunting grounds for merlins, and young plantations provide for hen harriers. Sparrowhawks and peregrines breed, buzzards are common and there is usually a pair of golden eagles.

Whitethroats, wood warblers, tree pipits and woodcocks are found in the woodlands, and the rougher ground is home to whinchats. Red-throated divers are found in some favoured lochans. Waders feed along the coast in winter and breed on moorland. There are some seabird colonies and the winter seas are frequented by divers, grebes and other ducks including scaup.

Location: Firth of Clyde, west of mainland.
Access and facilities: by ferry from Ardrossan; also ferry summer only from Claonaig to Lochranza. A good road (A841) circumnavigates the island. Brodick Castle garden open daily all year. Castle April to September daily, early Oct Mon, Wed, Sat all pm.
Map reference: NR950400

Isle of Arran – boats at Brodick

Ken-Dee Marshes

Dumfries and Galloway [RSPB]

Autumn and winter are the best times to visit this RSPB reserve. The shallow lagoon formed by a dam on the River Dee is bordered by marshes which provide a feeding ground for several hundred Greenland white-fronted geese. Along with them are

greylags and flocks of wigeon, teal, mallards and shovelers. Whooper swans visit from Iceland and specialities are pintail and goosander. In summer redshanks and other waders breed, as do some of the ducks and the elegant great crested grebe.

There is also an area of broadleaved and mixed woodland where there are willow tits and other common woodland species, along with the summer visitors, pied flycatcher and redstart. Crossbills and siskins are sometimes seen. Birds of prey, including hen harriers, buzzards and merlins, hunt over the marshes: an occasional peregrine may show itself.

Other sites nearby include Threave Wildfowl Refuge, belonging to the National Trust for Scotland. It is signposted from the A715 one mile west of Castle Douglas.

Location: south of New Galloway, between it and Castle Douglas, off A713.
Access: by escorted party only (charge for nonmembers) by prior arrangement with the Warden, Midtown, Laurieston, Castle Douglas DG7 2DP. Track through the woods is rough in places. For those who find walking difficult it may be possible to take a car. Good views of marshy areas can be had from A762 between New Galloway and Laurieston and its side roads, and from the A713 on the east side of Loch Ken.
Map reference: NX648704.

Kintyre

Strathclyde

A wide range of habitats makes the Kintyre Peninsula an exciting place to explore and gives it a rich collection of wildlife. The northern end of the peninsula has a variety of woodland with coniferous plantations of various ages: there are also mixed broad-leaved trees on the west side of Loch Sween. The area at the west end of the Crinan Canal and near the site of the Old Crinan Ferry consists of a large area of mud flats at low tide, providing conditions for a variety of shore birds.

In summer the mixed woodland of Taynish National Nature Reserve holds breeding wood warblers, redstarts, tree pipits and blackcaps, with occasional garden warblers, particularly in rhododendron thickets.

Common and arctic terns fish, and occasionally breed on the coasts, as do eiders and red-breasted mergansers. Hen harriers are found in young conifer plantations. In winter, greylag geese feed at Crinan, and there are flocks of wigeon and other ducks; whooper swans gather on Loch Sween. Golden plovers roost and feed in considerable numbers, and there are dunlins, oystercatchers and ringed plovers.

The southern half of the peninsula is renowned for holding good numbers of Greenland white-fronted geese in winter.

Other places of interest include the Crinan Canal, where in summer a stream of boats passes through a number of lochs to avoid the long voyage around the Mull of Kintyre. Further north around Kilmartin is a fascinating complex of stone circles and cairns. Finally, there are excellent forest walks in Knapdale Forest.

Location: 50 miles west of Glasgow.
Access: to north of Kintyre from Lochgilphead, turning off A83 at Cairnbaan on B841. Taynish is reached from B8025, west of Cairnbaan. South – along A83 Tarbert to Southend road.
Map reference: NR720200

Largo Bay

Fife

This is a large bay stretching from Earlsferry in the east to the industrial areas of Leven and Methill in the west. Winter is the time to walk along the sea wall at Leven, or on the beach. Out to sea is the main site for scaup in Scotland, and there are many long-tailed ducks, goldeneyes and common and velvet scoters as well as tufted ducks and eiders. Cormorants perch on various offshore structures, and there are red-breasted mergansers and grebes as well as a few divers – red-throated is always the commonest. Waders feed on the shore, and sanderlings can often be seen. The rocks below the power station at Leven have purple sandpipers and turnstones, and the mouth of the river is full of gulls. The occasional glaucous and Iceland gulls have been known to appear among them.

Location: 10 miles north-east of Kirkcaldy off A915.
Facilities: car park and toilets east of mouth of River Leven and Leven power station.
Map reference: NO382005

Linlithgow Loch

Lothian

Perhaps the best place in Scotland to see the spectacular courtship display of the great crested grebe at close quarters, Linlithgow Loch also holds wintering ducks in fair numbers. Despite a motorway running immediately to the north, the loch maintains a rural atmosphere enhanced by the picturesque ruins of Linlithgow Palace situated on a lochside knoll. Mary Queen of Scots was born in the palace.

Location: just north of Linlithgow.
Access: signposted car park west of palace provides easy access to footpath encircling loch.
Map reference: NT010770

Loch Fleet

Highland

At low tide several square miles of mud and sand are exposed here, attracting large numbers of waders, both overwintering and on passage. The loch is best known however for its ducks: common and velvet scoters, long-tailed ducks, red-breasted mergansers and eiders. One or two individuals of both king eider and surf scoter are probably resident and are likely to be seen at any time, though some enjoyable searching may be required. Offshore, between Golspie and Embo, there are usually small numbers of overwintering divers and a few grebes, mainly Slavonian and red-necked. Look out, too, for white-winged gulls in winter – glaucous and less commonly, Iceland gulls.

Location: 5 miles north of Dornoch east of A9.
Access: unclassified road running south from Golspie to Littleferry provides limited access to loch's northern shore.
Map reference: NH780970

Loch of Kinnordy

Tayside   RSPB

This shallow loch has attractions for the birdwatcher at any time of the year. In winter: a sizeable duck and goose roost, with short-eared owls and hen harriers often to be seen hunting. In summer: the most obvious breeding bird is the black-headed gull – several thousand nest each year – but others include gadwall, ruddy duck, shoveler and water rail. The small passage of waders in spring and autumn features ruff and greenshank.

Location: 1 mile west of Kirriemuir off B951.
Access and facilities: open daily April to August; Sun only September to November; closed December to March. Hides.
Map reference: NO361540

Loch Leven and Vane Farm

Tayside   RSPB

This National Nature Reserve is a superb birdwatching area in autumn, when huge flocks of pink-footed and greylag geese arrive from their breeding grounds in Iceland and Greenland. They feed here before dispersing to their wintering grounds. Some remain all winter, and are joined by Bewick's and whooper swans, goldeneyes, pochards and many other visiting wildfowl.

The best place from which to view the loch is Vane Farm Nature Centre.

On the RSPB reserve here there is a large hide from where visitors have a closer view of the water birds.

A nature trail with some steep and stepped stretches climbs through birch woodland where a good variety of common birds breeds.

Open moorland provides a habitat for meadow pipits and the occasional red grouse. In winter, snow buntings are sometimes seen, and there may be glimpses of peregrine falcons at any season.

Location: at Kinross. Reserve is off B9097 Glenrothes road south-east of Kinross.
Access and facilities: Vane Farm Nature Centre open daily 10am–5pm. Hide. Nature trail. Parking. Refreshments weekends. Reserve always open. Loch Leven NNR: access at Burleigh Sands (north shore), Kirkgate Park in Kinross and Findatie (south-east shore). Car parks. Toilets at Findatie in summer.
Map reference: NT160991

Loch Leven

Loch Lomondside

Central

Popular as a sightseers' destination since Victorian times, Loch Lomond has a fully justified reputation for beauty and grandeur. The main tourist route, the A82, runs along the west side of the loch, but the quieter eastern shore has a road only as far as Rowardennan, where there is a pleasant hotel. From there, the West Highland Way walking route continues to the north of the loch and beyond. The whole area has mixed woodland and forms part of the Loch Lomond National Nature Reserve. Trees, mainly oak, dominate the strip of land running between the loch shore and the heather-covered slopes of Ben Lomond, the most popular mountain climb in the area. Further south and east there are excellent wetland areas providing good birdwatching, particularly in winter. Three areas are described below.

1. Inversnaid   `RSPB`

In summer this RSPB reserve is an excellent part of the lochside woodland for seeing breeding migrants like redstart, wood warbler and pied flycatcher. On the moorland slopes, blackcocks congregate at traditional 'leks' on early spring mornings. Eagles are possible anywhere in the area, and as in most of western Scotland, buzzards are common.

The loch itself is home to many wildfowl, and great crested grebes; common scoters have been known to breed. Grey wagtails and dippers feed along the burns leading into the loch.

Location: east side of loch on unclassified road off B829 west of Aberfoyle.
Access and facilities: access along West Highland Way through reserve. Car parking and toilets available at Inversnaid Hotel, which can also be reached by pedestrian ferry from Inveruglas on west side of loch.
Map reference: NN337088

2. Inchailloch

This wooded island is ideal for a family visit. It has a nature trail, bluebell woods, an old churchyard and a sandy bay for swimming. Apart from birds typical of the area, fallow deer can sometimes be seen.

Location: south-east shore of loch.
Access: open all year; by boat from Balmaha.
Map reference: NS410905

3. Endrick Mouth

The River Endrick enters Loch Lomond north of the area accessible on foot, and the marshy ground near its mouth is the focal point for birdwatchers in winter. Flocks of greylag geese, with occasional white-fronted and pink-footed geese, whooper swans and large numbers of ducks make it a memorable sight. A little to the east is a small loch where big rafts of ducks are often seen.

Location: south-east corner of loch from A811 at Gartocharn, take unclassified road. Reserve off track leading from Townhead of Aber.
Access: permission to visit reserve should be obtained from Warden at 22 Muirpark Way, Drymen. No facilities, but cars can be parked near Aber postbox.
Map reference: NS425872

Loch Lomond – main picture and inset

Loch of Strathbeg

Grampian   `RSPB`

Best known as a wintering ground for tens of thousands of greylag and pink-footed geese as well as hundreds of whooper and mute swans, this loch and much of the surrounding land is an RSPB reserve. Breeding birds include water rails, shelducks and sparrowhawks, and regular passage migrants include green sandpipers, ruffs, black-tailed godwits, ospreys and marsh harriers. Cranes, spoonbills and glossy ibis have all been recorded – just to show what can happen at this splendid place. The loch is separated from the sea by sand and grass, with breeding fulmars in unusual surroundings. Several species of skua and shearwater can be seen in spring and autumn.

Location: off A952 Peterhead to Fraserburgh road near Crimond.
Access and facilities: permit necessary at all times, as access is through MOD property. For visiting arrangements contact Warden, The Lythe, Crimonmogate, Lonmay, Fraserburgh, AB4 4UB. Information centre. Hides. Boardwalk. Parking. Toilets.
Map reference: NK053568

Lochwinnoch

Strathclyde   `RSPB`

A well surfaced, level nature trail leads from the car park at this RSPB reserve through mixed woodland to two hides overlooking Aird Meadow. In summer there is a profusion of wild flowers here, particularly in the marshy habitat. Great crested grebes breed, as do snipe, shovelers, pochards and tufted ducks. There is also a colony of black-headed gulls. Interesting waders may occur on passage, particularly in August, but the best time to visit is winter, when whooper swans, greylag geese and goldeneyes appear, together with large numbers of commoner ducks. There is a second hide on the Barr Loch; ask for access directions at reception in the nature centre.

The centre has an observation tower with telescopes and an area of wildlife displays.

Location: on north side of A760 Largs to Paisley road, 1/2 mile south-east of Lochwinnoch.
Access and facilities: open 9am to 9pm or sunset. Information centre; charge for non-RSPB members. Nature trail. Hides. Refreshments at weekends. Parking. Toilets.
Map reference: NS359581

Montrose Basin

Grampian

At low tide, the estuarine waters of the River South Esk empty into the North Sea, leaving behind extensive mud flats exposed for the attentions of large flocks of wintering waders, predominantly redshanks, oystercatchers, knots and dunlins. Much of the area is a Scottish Wildlife Trust reserve and holds wildfowl in good numbers – whooper and mute swans, greylag and pink-footed geese, shelducks, wigeon and pintail. Unusual waders often turn up on passage, particularly in autumn: look out for spotted redshanks and curlew sandpipers. A public hide offers good views of the birds.

On the coast, Scurdie Ness, just south of the South Esk as it enters the North Sea, is a good vantage point for autumn seawatches. Keep an eye open for skuas and shearwaters.

Location: just west of Montrose.
Access: A92, A934 and A935 offer good views over basin from north, east and south. Unclassified road to Bridge of Dun provides access to western flank of basin. Car parks.
Map reference: NO700580

Nairn Bar and Culbin Forest

Highland/Grampian · RSPB

Culbin Forest, although planted rather than natural, holds good numbers of the classic birds of pine forest: crested tit, crossbill, capercaillie and siskin, etc. Long-eared owls, sparrowhawks and buzzards may also be seen. A network of footpaths transects the forest from east of Nairn along to the west side of Findhorn Bay. Access points are at Wellhill and Cloddiemoss and from the shores of the Moray Firth. The RSPB's Culbin Sands reserve occupies the seaward flank of Culbin Forest. The area is best in winter for wintering waders and sea-ducks (velvet scoters and long-tailed ducks are regular). Surf scoters and king eiders are as frequent as anywhere in mainland Britain.

Location: east of Nairn. RSPB reserve reached on footpath from Kingsteps, on unclassified road beyond Nairn Golf Course. Forest reached from Kintessack, on unclassified road north of A96.
Access: at all times, along footpaths.
Map reference: NH901573

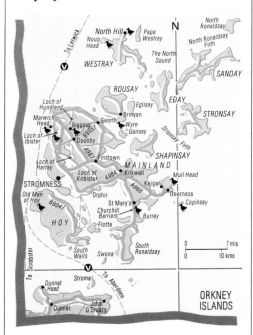

Orkney

Orkney is a collection of 65 islands, only half of which are inhabited. Set in the North Atlantic between the Scottish mainland and the even more remote Shetlands, Orkney has many Scandinavian characteristics, reflecting its past history. The landscapes here vary from bleak moorland to rich farmland; the coastlines are unfailingly spectacular. The islands hold nationally important breeding populations of several species of birds including hen harrier, curlew, guillemot and arctic tern. They are also full of archaeological and historical interest. For example, the Pictish burial chamber of Maeshowe was plundered by the Vikings some 1,000 years ago and the Norse graffiti have since provided historians with valuable insights into the social conditions in Orkney at the end of the first millennium AD.

Regular sea and air links make travel between the various islands straightforward. Descriptions of the better and/or more accessible birdwatching sites are given below.

1. Marwick Head · RSPB

An RSPB reserve, Marwick Head's 300ft high cliffs hold, in the summer months, many tens of thousands of breeding guillemots and kittiwakes as well as smaller but substantial numbers of shags and razorbills. At the reserve's highest point a pillar has been erected to the memory of Lord Kitchener, who was drowned some miles offshore in 1916 while travelling to Russia aboard *HMS Hampshire*, when it was torpedoed. The Kitchener Memorial can be seen from many parts of western Orkney and well out to sea.

Location: reserve lies on west coast of Orkney Mainland north of Marwick Bay. Reached on unclassified road from B9056.
Access: at all times along paths. Great care needed on cliffs. Parking.
Map reference: HY225247

2. The Loons · RSPB

Another RSPB reserve, the Loons is a sizeable marsh holding a variety of breeding waders and ducks, including pintail and shoveler in most years. These birds and others, such as corncrakes, can be seen from the RSPB roadside hide. Visitors should under no circumstances enter the reserve as this disturbs the breeding birds.

Locations: on Mainland 3 miles north of Dounby, off A986 along unclassified road north of Loch of Ibister.
Access: to hide at all times – no access to reserve itself.
Map reference: HY250240

3. Mull Head

East of Kirkwall in the Deerness Peninsula, Mull Head is a fine seabird colony holding good numbers of guillemots, kittiwakes and razorbills, all of which can be seen at close quarters without undue disturbance to the birds. On the way out to the Head you will be unable to avoid noticing arctic skuas vigorously defending their territory against human intruders!

Location: on Mainland, off B9050 at Skaill on unclassified road.
Map reference: HY595097

4. Graemeshall and the Churchill Barriers

The small loch at Graemeshall holds grey heron and several species of breeding ducks in the largest reed beds on Orkney. The Churchill Barriers connect the Orkney mainland with the islands of Burray and South Ronaldsay and were built to protect the naval anchorage in Scapa Flow from U-boat attack. They can be good places for watching for certain kinds of birds – sea-ducks and divers are often seen.

Location: on Mainland, reached on A961 leading to South Ronaldsay.
Map reference: HY490020

5. Copinsay · RSPB

Colonies of cliff-nesting seabirds are the star attractions here. Kittiwakes, guillemots, razorbills and fulmars form the largest groups, but there are also shags, puffins, black guillemots and cormorants. Among other birds that nest here are arctic terns, rock doves, eiders, twites and ravens, making a remarkable tally for an island little more than a mile long.

Location: island is 7 miles south-east of Mainland.
Access: by boat from Skail. (Telephone 085-674 252.) Excellent views of cliffs from boat.
Map reference: HY610010

Orkney moorland This specialised habitat of low-lying maritime heath is peculiar to Orkney, in particular to the Orkney Mainland and to Rousay. Much of it is now owned or managed by the RSPB. Rich in breeding waders, especially curlews, golden plovers and dunlins, the moorlands are perhaps best known for hen harriers, merlins and short-eared owls. Two reserves are described below.

6. Hobbister · RSPB

This reserve holds most of the typical bird species of Orkney moorland, including hen harrier, short-eared owl, merlin, red-throated diver and twite. Black guillemots and ravens nest on the coast.

Location: on either side of A964 Kirkwall to Stromness road near Loch of Kirbister.
Access: much may be seen from road. Rough track leads to Waulkmill Bay and then through much of rest of reserve.
Map reference: HY396070

7. Birsay Moors and Cottasgarth · RSPB

This reserve is perhaps best visited in May or June when breeding birds include hen harriers. Perhaps more easily seen here than anywhere else in Britain are great skuas, arctic skuas and a fine variety of waders – curlews, oystercatchers, golden plovers and dunlins – as well as several duck species. Red-throated divers may be seen on a loch in full view of the Burgar Hill hide.

Location: on Mainland, north-east of Dounby between A986 and A966.
Access: hides at Cottasgarth (HY368183) and Burgar Hill (HY340260). Other public access points are at Durkadale (HY293252) and from B9057.
Map reference: HY325260

Red-throated diver

8. Trumland [RSPB]

Heather moorland is the dominant habitat on this reserve. Among the breeding birds are red-throated divers, hen harriers, kestrels and golden plovers. Short-eared owls, merlins and both great and arctic skuas might be seen. There is a mixed colony of herring gulls and lesser black-backed gulls on the moorland.

Location: above Trumland House at southern end of Rousay. Island reached from Tingwall on Mainland by passenger ferry.
Access: access at all times, but visitors are asked to contact summer warden (April–August) at Trumland Mill Cottage, who will escort them.
Map reference: HY427276

9. Noup Head, Westray [RSPB]

Noup Head is the very north-western tip of the Orkney archipelago, reaching into the rich fishing grounds north of Scotland and west of Orkney and Shetland. It is, therefore, no surprise to find large seabird colonies on Westray and its neighbouring island of Papa Westray.

The RSPB's Noup Cliffs reserve comprises two miles of cliff, over 200ft high in places, which hold spectacularly large numbers of guillemots and kittiwakes, as well as smaller numbers of other breeding seabirds such as razorbills, black guillemots, puffins and fulmars.

Location: north-west tip of Westray.
Access: by passenger ferry from Kirkwall. Reserve reached on track from Noup Farm. Close gates. Care needed on cliffs.
Map reference: HY393501

11. North Hoy [RSPB]

A large reserve (15 square miles in area) owned by the RSPB, North Hoy's spectacular cliff scenery includes the famous Old Man of Hoy and St Johns Head, at 1,100ft the highest sheer cliff in Britain.

Breeding birds include great and arctic skuas, golden plovers and twites, as well as the largest colony of great black-backed gulls in Britain.

Guillemots, razorbills, kittiwakes, shags, peregrines and ravens nest on the cliffs and in late summer evenings Manx shearwaters can often be seen circling offshore at Rack Wick.

Location: north-west part of Hoy.
Access: by passenger ferry from Stromness to Moness. From Moness road to Rackwick runs through southern part of reserve. Public footpath north of Ward Hill takes in much of northern moorland. From Rackwick village another footpath leads out towards the Old Man of Hoy. Take great care on cliffs.
Map reference: HY218008

The Old Man of Hoy

10. North Hill, Papa Westray [RSPB]

The island is perhaps most noted for its huge breeding colony of arctic terns, with well over 6,000 pairs breeding in some years. As with many of these northern tern colonies, numbers and breeding success fluctuate wildly from year to year, and the reasons why this should be are the subject of an RSPB study.

Breeding among the terns and, to a large extent, parasitic upon them, are around 100 pairs of arctic skuas. The interaction between the two species can be better observed on Papa Westray than anywhere else in Britain.

A variety of waders breed on the reserve, including oystercatchers, snipe and ringed plovers, and the low cliffs on the east coast of the island at Fowl Craig, ancient haunt of the great auk, are now home to the smaller auks, guillemots, razorbills and black guillemots (tysties) as well as fulmars, shags and kittiwakes.

Location: northern end of Papa Westray.
Access: by ferry from Kirkwall. Visitors to reserve should contact summer warden at Gowrie, near reserve entrance.
Map reference: HY496549

St Abb's Head

Borders

A large and accessible seabird colony, St Abb's Head is a notable migration watch-point with one of Scotland's voluntary Marine Reserves just offshore. It is of most interest to birdwatchers between May and October. Guillemots, razorbills and kittiwakes all breed, as do puffins in much smaller numbers. Non-breeding purple sandpipers and turnstones are present for much of the year.

The reserve attracts a fine selection of migrants in spring and autumn; particularly noteworthy among them are wrynecks, red-breasted flycatchers and red-backed shrikes.

St Abb's Head is a National Nature Reserve jointly managed by the Scottish Wildlife Trust and the National Trust for Scotland.

Location: north of Coldingham on unclassified road off B6438.
Access: official car park, coffee shop and reserve centre are a few hundred yards west of St Abb's.
Map reference: NT914688

Shetland

The Shetland Islands are too varied, and rich in birdlife, to do more here than touch on six sites which are accessible by car and likely to be rewarding in the main tourist season.

1. Sumburgh Head

One of the best sites in Shetland for close-at-hand views of breeding seabirds without too much walking, the Head is also an excellent vantage point for seawatching. In summer, gannets, puffins, guillemots and razorbills are all easily seen.

Location: southern point of Mainland Shetland.
Access: park car near lighthouse (do not obstruct access). Take care near the cliff edge.
Map reference: HU408079

2. Loch of Spiggie [RSPB]

An RSPB reserve, Spiggie is excellent for breeding and wintering wildfowl with chances of red-necked phalarope.

Location: southern end of Mainland, west of Scousburgh, off B9122.
Access: do not enter reserve as this disturbs birds. Good views of loch can be obtained from road at north end, separating loch from sea.
Map reference: HU373176

3. Noss National Nature Reserve

This superb seabird colony has over 80,000 birds, including gannets, kittiwakes, fulmars, puffins, arctic skuas and great skuas, and vast rafts of guillemots below the sheer cliffs.

Location: Isle of Noss lies east of Bressay and Lerwick.
Access: by ferry from Lerwick to Bressay. Cross Bressay by car or on foot; reach Noss by dinghy May to August. Check with tourist office, Lerwick, for opening times.
Map reference: HU545405

4. Fetlar [RSPB]

A large part of the island is owned or managed by the RSPB as a reserve. Fetlar is outstanding for breeding waders (including whimbrels and red-necked phalaropes), seabird colonies (featuring accessible Manx shearwaters and storm petrels) and spring and autumn passage migrants. It is best known as the erstwhile breeding place of

Skye

Highland

Skye is a large island in the Inner Hebrides, with a wide range of habitats, from high mountains to sea lochs. The scenery is spectacular, and there are good, but sometimes narrow, roads to all parts of the island.

At low tide the shores of all the sea lochs – especially Ainort, Slapin, Sligachan and Harport – provide good views of shore birds, such as grey herons, oystercatchers, common sandpipers in summer, and redshanks. Turnstones and ringed plovers occur on many coasts, and near Isle Ornsay is a good site for greenshanks. Waterloo, near Broadford, has a good variety of ducks and waders in early autumn, with bar-tailed godwits, shelducks and dunlins.

Woodland species are found in the old and interesting woodland at Tokavaig and also in the wooded policies at the Clandonald Centre near Armadale. This centre has a shop and displays available, as well as nature trails in the grounds. The island has many other places of interest, including Dunvegan Castle and a museum of life on Skye, at Carbost.

Location: reached by ferry from Kyle of Lochalsh or Mallaig. Good roads serve whole island.
Map reference: NG500200

Skye – Kyleakin and Castle Moil

snowy owls. Although the owls no longer breed here, individual birds – all female – can still be seen.

Location: reserve is on western side of island, off B9088. Ferry from Gutcher on Yell (booking essential).

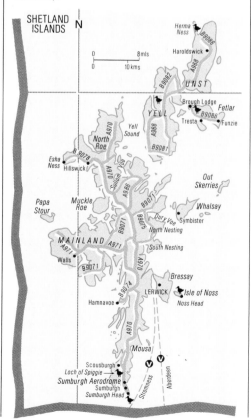

Access: visitors welcome, but in summer must report to warden at Bealance (near reserve entrance) who gives guided tours.
Map reference: HU604916

5. Hermaness National Nature Reserve

This is one of the finest pieces of coastline in Britain. The main sea-cliffs are reached by a three mile walk north from Burrafirth along a well marked path through breeding dunlins, golden plovers and 800 pairs of great skuas. Puffins, guillemots, kittiwakes and a large gannetry are the main ornithological attractions. A black-browed albatross has summered in the gannetry faithfully (and fruitlessly) for some years now. The reserve is best in high summer (May, June, July). Protective clothing is recommended at all times.

Location: northern most point of Unst; off B9086 at Burrafirth.
Access: limited parking near lighthouse.
Map reference: HP600180

6. Lumbister   RSPB

Occupying some 4,000 acres, this reserve consists of moorland dotted with many small areas of water. There is also a gorge leading to the grass-topped cliffs and rocky shore of Whale Firth. Red-throated divers are among the birds resting on the waters, while merlins and both arctic and great skuas are the special nesting birds of the moorland. Black guillemots, puffins, ravens and wheatears nest on the cliffs

Location: west side of Yell, between Whale Firth and A968 to Gutcher.
Access: good views from A968. Pedestrian access from lay-by 4 miles north of Mid Yell, but

visitors are asked to be careful not to disturb birds.*
Map reference: HU509974

The Small Isles: Rhum, Canna, Eigg, Muck

Highland

It is well worth taking a trip around these islands, with their varied scenery and birdlife on and over the sea. Eiders, Manx shearwaters, common and arctic terns, guillemots, black guillemots, razorbills and fulmars are common. Seals, whales and dolphins sometimes swim in view of the boat. The island of Rhum, a National Nature Reserve, has interesting birdlife including eagles and red-throated divers. It is the site of the reintroduction of the white-tailed eagle after an absence of many years, with young birds imported from Norway. There are large Manx shearwater colonies on the upper slopes of the hills, particularly Hallival and Askival. Long-term experiments and observations on red deer are carried out on the island, and there is a programme of planting new woodlands with native species. The castle is an amazing red sandstone building, erected in the last century by the Bullough family and now used as a hotel and self-catering accommodation.

Location: south of Skye.
Access: to Rhum and the other islands by boat from Arisaig, or Mallaig. Permission to stay overnight on Rhum and information about accommodation must be obtained from the Chief Warden, The White House, Isle of Rhum, Inverness-shire.
Map reference: NM400995

Speyside

Highland

A mecca for birdwatchers throughout the year, the Spey Valley between Kingussie and Grantown has something for everyone. Oak woods in the main strath hold pied flycatchers and green woodpeckers, while native pine woods nearer the Cairngorms are home to crested tits, Scottish crossbills and capercaillies. Breeding goldeneyes and Slavonian grebes are to be found on or near the many burns and lochs, with ptarmigan, dotterels and snow buntings up on the hill-tops. Three areas which are of outstanding birdwatching interest are described below. Great care should be taken in the wilder areas.

1. Insh Marshes   RSPB

The Spey Valley floor between Kingussie and Loch Insh is liable to seasonal flooding, attracting ducks and waders of many species, as well as good numbers of whooper swans in winter. Management of much of the land as an RSPB reserve has increased its attractiveness to birds and birdwatchers throughout the year.

Hen harriers and buzzards, tree pipits and redstarts are often seen from the several hides on the reserve and there is always the chance of an osprey or golden eagle or even something more unusual – cranes, marsh harriers and spotted crakes have all been recorded more than once.

Location: 1½ miles south-east of Kingussie, on B970 to Insh village.
Access and facilities: always open, except Tue. Information centre. Hides. Car park.
Map reference: NH775998

2. Loch Garten and Garten Wood   RSPB

A must for any visitor to Speyside, this RSPB reserve is most famous for its breeding ospreys, but is also home to many of the characteristic birds of loch, marsh and – perhaps most importantly – Caledonian pine forest. There are only three major tracts remaining of this unique habitat and the RSPB now owns a large part of one of them, Abernethy Forest. Thanks to the RSPB, Garten Wood is held in trust for future generations to thrill to crested tit, Scottish crossbill, goldeneye, capercaillie and many more fascinating, and, in some cases, endangered species.

The ospreys can normally be seen from the end of April until the middle of August but the reserve is well worth a visit at any time of the year. Much of its bird life is best appreciated during February or early March when the snow is on the ground and crossbills are seen to be carrying nesting material. You might be lucky enough to hear or see the amazing display of the male capercaillie or come across some of the unusual wintering birds which frequent the reserve, such as waxwing or great grey shrike.

Location: east of Boat of Garten off B970 on unclassified road.
Access and facilites: reserve has large viewing hide with telescopes trained on osprey nest. Shop. Shop and hide open April to August, 10am to 8pm. Other parts of reserve open at all times, but keep to paths.
Map reference: NH978184

3. Cairngorms National Nature Reserve

This is a group of large estates, some privately owned, others in the hands of the Nature Conservancy Council. The Cairngorms National Nature Reserve extends from very close to the River Spey to the high tops of the Cairngorm Mountains more than 4,000ft above sea-level, and includes an area of ancient Caledonian pine forest. Heather moor, lochs, marshes, burns and mountain grasslands are all found on the reserve. The birdlife is equally varied and the reserve probably has a greater number of species than any other area of equivalent size in Scotland.

Location: between A9 and B970, east of Aviemore.
Access: A9 and B970 skirt reserve to east and west, but to cover area properly it is necessary to take well-marked footpaths into heart of reserve. This should not be attempted without adequate footwear and clothing. Hill walking should never be undertaken lightly.
Map reference: NH989989

The Solway Coast

Dumfries and Galloway

The whole of the northern coast of the Solway, as far along as the Mull of Galloway, is an excellent place for watching wildfowl in the winter and should not be missed by anyone interested in seeing huge flocks of geese and waders. The birds are attracted here by the vast tracts of intertidal mud and sand, with large areas of salt marsh and fields lining the coast, which provide excellent feeding areas. Some areas are open to wildfowlers in the shooting season, but there are many relatively undisturbed places. Some of the best places to visit are mentioned below.

1. East Park Farm, Caerlaverock

This Wildfowl Trust reserve includes part of the Caerlaverock National Nature Reserve; as well as its bird interest it is the northernmost limit of the rare natterjack toad, which breeds in shallow pools here.

Flocks of whooper and Bewick's swans can be seen as can many wigeon, tufted ducks, teal and mallards together with smaller numbers of pintails, shovelers and goldeneyes. This is one of the best places in Scotland to observe birds at close quarters, and unlike other Wildfowl Trust refuges, Caerlaverock has only wild, unpinioned birds. There is easy access for disabled visitors to this hide.

In addition there are three large tower hides and a number of smaller ones placed along the banking which separates the flat pathways from the reserve lands. From the hides there are long views over the marsh to the flocks of up to 10,000 barnacle geese from Svalbard, as well as large numbers of pink-footed and greylag geese. The wet meadows hold flocks of teal and other ducks as well as many waders; sightings of a hunting peregrine, merlin or hen harrier are by no means infrequent.

Location: 7 miles south-east of Dumfries off B725 on unclassified road, signposted East Park.

Access: Wildfowl Trust reserve open September to April. Admission charge. Guided tours 11am and 2pm. National Nature Reserve open at all times.
Map reference: NY051656

2. Caerlaverock Castle

This castle, in the National Nature Reserve, has a nearby area of woodland and a car park with access to the foreshore, from where the ducks, waders and geese can also be seen. The woodland is likely to receive its visiting summer birds much earlier than the rest of Scotland.

Location: 7 miles south-east of Dumfries off B725.
Access: open Mon to Sat all day, Sun pm only. Admission charge.
Map reference: NY026657

3. Southerness Point and Carsethorn

Southerness Point is a rocky area, and purple sandpipers and turnstones winter there; it is also a good vantage point for seawatching with the chance of divers and grebes. Among the many sea-ducks, scoters and scaup should be looked for. Carsethorn Creek is an excellent place for waders, including bar-tailed godwits; it is particularly worth a visit during the spring and autumn passage.

Location: south of Kirkbean, off A710.
Map reference: NX978541

4. Mull of Galloway   RSPB

This is an RSPB clifftop reserve, consisting of a small nesting seabird colony on the granite ledges. There are guillemots, razorbills, fulmars and shags breeding on the cliffs and black guillemots among the shoreline boulders. From the cliff, where there is a car park, views of feeding gannets off Scar Rocks are frequent in summer, and it is a good vantage point for passing seabirds, including Manx shearwaters.

Location: 20 miles south of Stranraer. Take A716 to Drumore and then B7041. Unclassified road leads to the lighthouse and cliffs.
Access: at all times.
Map reference: NX157304

Wood of Cree

Dumfries and Galloway   RSPB

Set alongside the River Cree, this reserve consists largely of old coppice. It is one of the largest broadleaved woods in the south of Scotland, its trees mostly oak, birch and hazel. Nesting birds here include sparrowhawks, buzzards, woodcocks, garden warblers, tree pipits, wood warblers and redstarts. Several small streams tumble through the wood, and dippers, common sandpipers and grey wagtails are likely to be seen along these. As well as birds, this is a place to watch for otters, and there is a good butterfly population.

Location: 4 miles north-west of Newton Stewart. Reached from unclassified road from Minnigaff running north parallel with A714.
Access: open at all times along woodland track from roadside pull-off.
Map reference: NX382708

Northern Ireland

Lapwing

From the sparkling waters of Lough Neagh to the bright air of the Mourne Mountains, and from the lake country of Fermanagh to the woodlands of Glenariff, Northern Ireland has a wonderful mixture of birdwatching places. The coastline has its regular birds and can also turn up surprises

Northern Ireland

Useful addresses

RSPB Headquarters: The Lodge, Sandy, Bedfordshire SG19 2DL
RSPB Northern Ireland Office: Belvoir Park Forest, Belfast, BT8 4QT.
Many RSPB reserves have explanatory leaflets. These are often available at the reserve, but in any event the regional office, or RSPB HQ, will supply information on any reserve upon receipt of a stamped addressed envelope.
Ulster Trust for Nature Conservation: Barnetts Cottage, Barnetts Demesne, Malone Road, Belfast, BT9 5PB
National Trust Northern Ireland Office: Rowallane House, Saintfield, Ballynalinch, Co Down, BT24 7LH

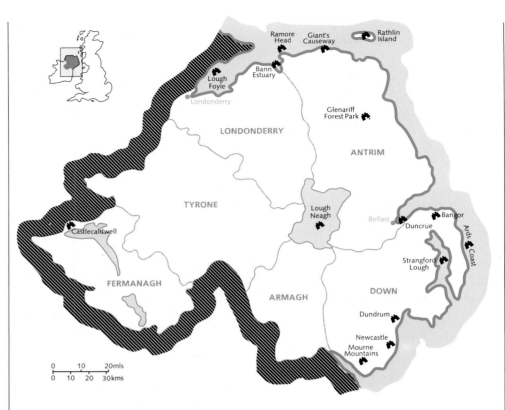

Ards Coast

Co Down

This is a low-lying coastline, with long stretches of sandy beach separated by rocky outcrops. Most of the commoner waders can be watched here, especially in winter, as they feed along the beach or roost on the rocks. There are oystercatchers, ringed plovers, redshanks, bar-tailed godwits and curlews and, on the rocky places, turnstones and purple sandpipers. On adjoining meadows there are usually flocks of lapwings and golden plovers. Stonechats are often to be seen and wheatears pass through in spring and autumn. On or over the sea, at appropriate times of year, gannets, divers, eiders and red-breasted mergansers, shags, black guillemots and a variety of gulls and terns can be found. The gulls are always worth a close look, as rarities have been found in recent years.

Location: east of Belfast, stretching between Bangor and Ballyquintin Point. Reached from A2.
Facilities: car parks at Templepatrick Strand, 2 miles south of Donaghadee; Drumfad Bay, 1 mile from Millisle; Ballywalter harbour (toilets); John's Port, 1 mile south of Ballyhalbert pier; Portavogie; Cloughy (toilets) and Granagh Bay.
Map reference: J364370

Bangor

Co Down

The seafront here holds interesting species, including black guillemots nesting in the pier. A good variety of gulls includes kittiwakes and occasional rarities, with glaucous now regular; waders include purple sandpipers in winter. Eiders, red-breasted mergansers, odd long-tailed ducks and, in winter, great northern divers appear offshore and gannets, common, arctic and Sandwich terns dive for fish in summer. Castle Park has common suburban birds, but goldcrests, treecreepers and coal tits add interest. Ward Park, with its ornamental lake, has mallards, tufted ducks, shelducks and Canada geese, a rookery and a large winter starling roost.

Location: east of Belfast.
Map reference: J350382

Bann Estuary

Londonderry

At the mouth of the River Bann are two headlands – Barmouth to the east and Castlerock to the west; Castlerock Strand is a long, sandy beach with sand dunes behind it, a golf course and a handy pier. Barmouth has marshes adjacent to the estuary, with a National Trust hide, in front of which the waders move towards their roost with a rising tide. Autumn is the best time to be here, especially in a spell of north-westerlies when seabirds move offshore and divers, auks, kittiwakes, grebes and eiders feed in the surf. Waders may include the usual wintering species plus migrant whimbrels, little stints and curlew sandpipers; there are usually knots and sanderlings. Snow buntings arrive in the autumn and gulls may include good ones such as glaucous, and even Mediterranean or Sabine's from time to time. Wintering wildfowl include goldeneye, teal and wigeon in good numbers.

Location: on coast north of Coleraine.
Map reference: C278436

Castlecaldwell

Fermanagh   RSPB

Castlecaldwell Forest RSPB reserve is good for seeing the important population of breeding common scoters on Lough Erne, with a variety of other ducks, gulls and terns. There are great crested and little grebes, too. The forests have sparrowhawks, long-eared owls and siskins.

Location: 4 miles east of Belleek, off A47.
Access: via shoreline paths. Hide in Castle Bay. Car park. Information centre. Toilets.
Map reference: H009603

Bangor – Stricklands Glen

Duncrue, Belfast

Co Antrim

This is an arm projecting into Belfast Lough, with a rubbish tip, a sewage farm and a marsh – not the most attractive place in the world, but good for birds. Shelducks, moorhens, lapwings, sedge warblers and others nest here and a variety of waders can be found in the autumn. Some rarities have been found, along with commoner migrant waders. The tip has many gulls, often including glaucous in winter, when snow buntings, twites and many other finches are to be found. This area has the habit of turning up oddities!

Location: north-east edge of Belfast.
Access: leave Belfast northwards along York Street. Turn right in to Duncrue Street. Follow Duncrue Street round to left after 3/4 mile, then take first right into Duncrue Road; park after 300 yds and walk along path to right.
Map reference: J336377

Dundrum

Co Down

Dundrum Bay is a very sheltered estuary, so shallow as to be nearly drained at low tide, when it becomes an expanse of mixed sand and mud flats. Autumn and winter are best here. Passage waders include greenshanks and common sandpipers and, from time to time, ruffs, black-tailed godwits, spotted redshanks, little stints and curlew sandpipers. The bay has a good variety of wildfowl, with the odd whooper swan and occasional brent geese.

South of Dundrum village is Murlough Nature Reserve, a National Trust property, with excellent birds all year – from cuckoos, long-eared owls and grasshopper warblers in summer, to gatherings of redwings and fieldfares (in sea buckthorn thickets) in autumn and snow buntings in winter.

Location: 3 miles north-east of Newcastle, on A2.
Access: inner bay is landlocked estuary with National Trust coastal footpath giving good views. Park beside A24 south of Dundrum. Toilets at Slidderyfords Bridge, from which footpaths lead around bay and into reserve.
Map reference: J342336

Giant's Causeway

Co Antrim

Cliffs and rocky shores, including the famous Giant's Causeway formations, provide a variety of habitats for birds and a fascinating place for a walk. You may well find buzzards, sparrowhawks, kestrels and peregrines here, and there are rock doves, rock pipits, stonechats, twites, ravens and choughs. Look out over the sea in summer and expect gannets, Manx shearwaters, cor-

morants and shags; guillemots, razorbills and black guillemots should be evident and kittiwakes and fulmars fly by offshore. In autumn and winter there are waders, including the two that specially like rocky shores, turnstones and purple sandpipers.

Location: west of Ballycastle, off A2 on B146.
Access: causeway well signposted; other car parks at Dunseverick Castle and Harbour, Whitepark Bay and Ballintoy. Wheelchairs can be transported by minibus from car park to causeway in summer. National Trust information centre.
Map reference: C296445

Glenariff Forest Park

Co Antrim

The high Antrim plateau here drops steeply to the floor of the Glenariff Valley, making it one of the most spectacular places in Northern Ireland. Streams cascade into the head of the valley in superb waterfalls; the upper valley is enclosed by conifer woodland, but, lower down, as the valley broadens towards the sea, farmland takes over and adds variety to the habitats available for birds. Rocky crags and steep, windswept slopes create ideal conditions for birds of prey, and kestrels, buzzards, sparrowhawks and peregrines are all likely. On the streams are dippers, and both pied and grey wagtails. The conifer plantations are not specially good for birds, but the more open mixed and broadleaved woods have most of the commoner woodland species.

Location: north-east of Ballymena, reached on A43, or A2 coast road. Signposted.
Facilities: Car parks. Toilets. Footpaths.
Map reference: J320420

Lough Foyle

Co Londonderry `RSPB`

The RSPB has a 3,300 acre reserve on the lough foreshore, with sand and mud flats, mussel beds and salt marsh. It is a stunning place for birds and is of great importance for migrating waders and wildfowl.

In the autumn, wigeon numbers reach 26,000 here and nearly 1,000 brent geese feed in the estuary. Pintail, gadwall, teal, shoveler, mallard and other species are found and waders are even more varied. All kinds of migrants can be seen, especially on a windy autumn day, when skuas, petrels, shearwaters and others sometimes seek shelter. In winter the fields behind the sea wall attract large numbers of whooper and Bewick's swans, making the scene even more spectacular, and a few greylag and white-fronted geese appear. In winter it is well worth visiting the remote National Nature Reserve of Magilligan Point, which cuts across the mouth of the estuary. Great northern and red-throated divers, great crested grebes, black guillemots and various sea ducks feed in the channel and sweep up and down with the tide.

Location: north-east of Londonderry.
Access: take A2 between Londonderry and Limavady; road to Longfield Point, 7 miles from Derry, and Ballykelly Marsh make suitable points for viewing. Cross railway line with great care. 4 miles north of Limavady River Roe enters lough; take B69 signposted to Downhill from Limavady. Magilligan Point reached by turning off A2 5 miles west of Downhill; park after 3 miles, beyond prison. Keep out of firing range.
Map reference: C545237

Giant's Causeway

Lough Neagh

Co Antrim [RSPB]

Several lanes follow the east shore of Lough Neagh. The surrounding farmland, with its orchards, woods and thick hedges, makes birdwatching rewarding if, from the point of view of rarities, unremarkable. The water has great crested grebes, shelducks, black-headed gulls and common terns and, in winter, visiting goldeneyes and Bewick's swans. Watch for siskins and redpolls in the loughside alders at this season.

On the north-east shore is Randalstown Forest, part coniferous plantations and part oak wood. There is a National Nature Reserve along the reedy shore. In winter there are many ducks, especially pochards, tufted ducks and goldeneyes, but look also for teal and scaup. Another NNR is Oxford Island, about four miles from Lurgan – in winter there are often whooper and Bewick's swans and many wildfowl here.

Shane's Castle is an RSPB reserve on the north-east shore of the lough between Antrim and Randalstown. There is mixed woodland and marsh along the edge of the lough and the mature woodland is especially valuable, being a scarce habitat in Ulster. The ruined castle of the O'Neills gives a raised vantage point for looking out across the lough, where flocks of wildfowl are present in winter – mainly tufted ducks and pochards, but with scaup, gadwalls, teal and goldeneyes to search for. There is a nature trail and hides and the area provides interesting walking. Birds include blackcaps, long-tailed tits, treecreepers, siskins, woodcocks, long-eared owls, kingfishers, grey wagtails, dippers and water rails.

Location: south-west of Antrim.
Access and facilities: reach Oxford Island from M1 at junction 10. Signposted. Information centre. Car park. Toilets. Hides. Randalstown Forest 3 miles west of Antrim, 2 miles from Randalstown; take Staffordstown road from B53, sign to Forest on left; permit necessary, from Forester's house. Shane's Castle RSPB reserve open Easter to September (but subject to change) and by arrangement with warden. Reserve is 1 mile west of Antrim off A6. Admission charge. Car park.
Map reference: J315362/J309387

Mourne Mountains

Co Down

Dominating the whole of south Co Down, the Mourne Mountains extend from Newcastle to Rostrevor. They are largely of granite rocks and give a range of habitats from rock and crag to rough pasture, with heather moorland and high-level bog. There are a few rapid streams and several reservoirs, with patches of coniferous plantation. Kestrels, merlins, peregrines, buzzards and sparrowhawks all occur, and there are some red grouse in the heathery places. In damp places there are snipe and curlews, and stonechats, wheatears, skylarks and meadow pipits all breed commonly. One typical and spectacular bird is the raven, which nests on crags very early in the year.

Location: south-west of Newcastle.
Map reference: J327323

Newcastle

Co Down

Newcastle is a popular resort with a beautiful setting, between the Mourne Mountains and a long, broad sweep of golden sand. To the south the beach changes gradually to shingle and then rocks and cliffs. Except in summer, the shore usually has some birds and it can sometimes be really rewarding. Waders and gulls feed and loaf about on the sands and make for good birdwatching, with the chance of an exciting discovery always adding extra spice. Brent geese feed on the beach, and divers, grebes and ducks feed offshore. In autumn, skuas chase terns and kittiwakes over the waves and there may be gannets and other passing seabirds. Out on the sea in autumn and winter there will be a large flock of common scoters, with a scattering of velvet scoters with them. You may have to wait for one to flap its wings or fly up to show the white patches and identify itself.

Location: at Newcastle, 30 miles south of Belfast.
Map reference: J338332

Mourne Mountains

Ramore Head

Co Antrim

This low cliff with a grassy top juts out to the west of the Giant's Causeway near Portrush. It is the place to be on a windy autumn day – north-westerlies often bring superb passages of seabirds, and red-throated and great northern divers, fulmars, Manx and sooty shearwaters, storm petrels, gannets and various gulls, terns and auks can be seen. Great, pomarine and arctic skuas all turn up from time to time, either beating their way purposefully offshore, or pausing to chase the terns and gulls in order to steal their food. Gulls should be examined carefully as several rare ones have been seen, including glaucous (quite regular), Iceland, little, Sabine's and Mediterranean. In late autumn, wildfowl will be on the move and all kinds may fly by the headland – from barnacle, brent and greylag geese to wigeon, eider and red-breasted merganser. If the winds are not right for productive seawatching, there will still be some birds

about – often snow buntings and purple sandpipers in winter and various terns in summer.

Location: immediately north of Portrush.
Map reference: C286441

Rathlin Island

Co Antrim [RSPB]

With high cliffs of chalk and basalt, and varying landscapes inland, from heather moor and rough grassland to green pastures and small marshes, this large and beautiful island makes an excellent destination. There is an RSPB reserve and a National Nature Reserve which, between them, contain the bulk of the breeding seabirds – kittiwakes, razorbills, guillemots and puffins in particular. There are also black guillemots, buzzards, peregrines, ravens and choughs, making one of the most varied and exciting lists of coastal birds one can find. Rock doves are common, and skylarks, meadow pipits, stonechats and wheatears make the island seem alive with birds.

Location: off Antrim coast.
Access: by boat from Ballycastle in summer. Further details available from RSPB Northern Ireland office.
Map reference: D313452

Strangford Lough

Co Down

This is a predominantly muddy sea lough, an inlet of the Irish Sea that is of great importance for birds. The northern mud flats have most of the bird life and a rising tide brings many of them within close range. There are many good places and each of them deserves exploration.

Castle Espie, two miles south-east of Comber, has a National Trust hide along the Mahee Island road. There are brent geese from September to April, often at close range in big numbers. With them will be wigeon, shelducks and many waders.

Reagh Island is five miles south-east of Comber, beyond Castle Espie on the same road. There is a car park and a hide. There are fewer birds here, but black-tailed godwits, greylag geese and pintails are especially good. Island Hill, north-east of Comber, is reached along Ringcreevy Road from the A21 one mile from Comber. It is an excellent place for watching brent geese, and there are also mergansers, golden plovers, greenshanks and godwits.

The Maltings, a mile and a half south of Newtownards on the A20, where a lay-by gives good views, is good for most of the area's birds with brent geese, whooper swans, pintails and golden plovers.

Greyabbey is on the east shore, seven miles from Newtownards, and has most of the typical species. Like many other spots it is at its best in winter, being slightly disappointing in summer except for a few fishing terns. The whole area is worthy of lengthy exploration; much of it is protected by the National Trust, with many hides, information displays and car parks.

Location: 10 miles south-east of Belfast.
Map reference: J355360

Helping
The Birds

Nightingale

Included on these pages is advice on gardening for birds, notes on choosing binoculars, basic birdwatching tips, the answers to some regular bird-related questions, organisations to join, and much more. A complete checklist of British birds follows the index

Gardening for Birds & Wildlife

Gardens in the United Kingdom cover a staggering 670,000 acres – 100,000 acres more than the combined area of Britain's nature reserves. This goes to show the importance of gardens for all sorts of wildlife. And, of course, the potential is there to increase that importance – and everyone can do something to help, whatever the size of the garden.

Nancy and John Dawson's garden in Ickwell, Bedfordshire, is not typical. Firstly, it covers two acres and, secondly, it has been a winning garden in a best wildlife garden competition. The secret of its success is not so much its size, but the number of different habitats they have created within it. This was a deliberate policy when they moved in to their medieval house with its derelict garden 30 years ago. 'Our aim has been to build a low labour garden that is pleasing to the eye,' Nancy explained, 'and we have tried to create a maximum number of wild-life habitats.'

Not many people will have a garden of this size, but there is still plenty you *can* do to help the local wildlife. Why not select as few or as many as you can of the habitats from those in Nancy and John's garden to recreate in your own? You will find you are offering something that many species of birds, mammals, butterflies and other insects will find irresistible.

Short grass
Most gardens have a lawn, its main use often being for a bird-table during the winter. However, it can attract more wildlife in summer if it is not sprayed with weedkillers. Nancy and John's lawn is rich in small wild flowers, including germander speedwell, celandine, creeping buttercup, daisy, cuckoo flower, selfheal and red and white clovers. This mosaic of colour buzzes with bees on hot, sunny days. The grass is cut regularly but the cuttings are spread evenly, not removed. This mulching encourages earthworms, and these attract blackbirds, song thrushes, starlings, dunnocks and pied wagtails to feed on them.

Long grass
These areas can be full of colour almost all year round – not only flowers, but also the hordes of butterflies and bees attracted to them. However, the creation of such an area should be viewed as a long term project, so do not expect instant results! The good news is that it will get better each year. Unlike the short grass, this only needs cutting twice a year to ensure the flowering plants set their seeds. John uses a traditional scythe to make the first cut at the beginning of July and the second is done with a rotary mower as late as possible in November. Remember to remove all the cuttings. This is very important as the idea is to impoverish the soil to prevent the grass from overpowering the flowering plants.

In spring, the long grass areas in Nancy and John's garden are a carpet of primroses, celandines and dandelions, which provide nectar for early bees and butterflies. These are followed in May and June by cuckoo flower, oxeye daisy, lupin, columbine, yellow rattle, sorrel, cow parsley, bird's foot trefoil and several species of wild geraniums.

Herbaceous beds
Wildlife gardeners are a relaxed bunch on the whole and one reason is that many of the chores normally associated with flower beds are made redundant or greatly reduced. In fact, herbaceous borders are a good way to introduce yourselves to the joys of wildlife gardening. Firstly, convince yourself that it is not necessary to have bare patches of soil around each plant and encourage self-sown wild plants to grow – even rampant species can be used if thoroughly hemmed in by shrubs. Secondly, allow the flowering plants to go to seed at the end of the season and do not cut the seed heads until March. These will provide food for birds throughout the winter and insects, such as earwigs, will find a safe refuge in the dead stalks. Thirdly, aim to have a selection of plants and shrubs which flower from February through to November. A good proportion of these should be native, insect-pollinated species (single rather than double flowered species), or should produce berries for birds or cover in the winter. Nancy's flower beds are full of such plants as junipers, berberis, spindle, cotoneasters,

Borders like this look wonderful and are usually excellent for wildlife while adding varied colour and form to the garden

viburnums, shrub roses, sedums, asters, primulas, honesty, foxglove, herb-robert, forget-me-nots and alyssum, all helping the local bird, insect and butterfly populations.

Hedges
The Dawsons' evergreen yew hedge is in three sections. One is close trimmed on both top and sides in the autumn and its dense foliage makes it a safe place for early breeding birds to nest in March and April. The second has the sides trimmed but the top is allowed to grow into trees. The abundant glistening pink fruits are eagerly eaten by mistle thrushes. Finally the end section is allowed to grow up and out (unless obstructing a path) and its bushy growth offers even the shy goldcrest a secure place to raise a family. Nancy and John also have holly and beech hedges. The former is only trimmed in winter when the birds have stripped the berries and in May is visited by the beautiful holly blue butterfly. The 30-year-old beech hedge is cut in September after dunnocks, linnets, bullfinches, blackbirds and thrushes have all finished nesting.

Mature trees
As you might expect, Nancy and John's garden has a number of mature trees. The seeds from the alders are eaten by goldfinches and siskins, jays eat the acorns and bullfinches the ash keys. Small mammals, such as mice, voles and squirrels, feed on the beech-mast and pine seeds which fall to the ground. Great spotted woodpeckers excavate nesting holes which are then taken over by starlings. And birds such as turtle doves, cuckoos and kestrels use a dead-top pine as a look-out post. This variety is exceptional; more often gardens have only one or two mature trees at most. Supplement what you do have by providing nestboxes as additional nest sites, leave piles and stumps of dead wood lying around to provide cover and to encourage insects such as wood-boring beetles, and allow ivy to climb in a hectic tangle up the trunks providing both shelter and food for many birds and insects.

Rockeries and stone walls
One easy habitat to provide is a series of nooks and crannies in a rockery or low brick wall surrounding a raised flower bed. Turn over one of these moss- or lichen-covered stones and you could discover a sleeping toad, a hibernating newt, a cluster of snails' eggs, a wriggling pack of woodlice or other invertebrates. Birds such as wrens can often be seen working their way along the low walls looking for insects.

Working with wildlife
Nancy and John have put a tremendous amount of effort into their garden over the years, but Nancy is keen to emphasise that they have 'not tamed the wilderness, but entered into a relationship with it'. You must look at gardening for wildlife from the wildlife's point of view – try to link the different habitats with ground covering plants to create paths and passageways for creatures which do not like to come out into the open, and endeavour to have some secluded corners in your garden which could be no-go areas, as humans can be just as disturbing as the neighbour's cat!

A Cambridgeshire garden
'A labour of love.' This is how Ray and Pam Matthews of Little Paxton in Cambridgeshire view their gardening for wildlife. When they moved into their house nine years ago, the garden consisted of rubble the builders had left behind, a high brick wall down one side, an unattractive chain-link fence running down the other and a few mature trees as the house had been sited on an old arboretum. Quite a contrast with the Dawsons' large plot.

Although their early intention was not to plant a garden for wildlife, but to have the usual combination of formal flower and vegetable beds, Ray did plant a native hedge of hornbeam, hawthorn, beech, wild cherry, holly, rowan and oak to hide the chain-link fence. Over the years the hedge has become festooned with bramble and wild bryony, giving it a natural, well established look. Native plants generally provide homes to many more insects than introduced plants. These, in turn, attract larger numbers of birds.

Starlings, toads and hedgehogs

Five years ago Ray and Pam dug a pond and created a bog garden behind it. They immediately saw that the area of open water with its natural grass edges not only looked good but also proved a magnet to wildlife. Hordes of chattering starlings took to visiting it for a winter evening's bathe; other garden birds flew down for a daily drink and the highlight was the sight of a black redstart enjoying a splash one May morning. Toads breed in the pond each year and hedgehogs come to

drink. A colourful profusion of water plants includes common rush, brook-lime, meadowsweet, purple loose-strife, water mint, marsh marigold and water plantain (all available from garden centres). Dragonflies and damselflies come to lay their eggs on the emergent leaves.

Gradually the formal flower beds are disappearing, but there is still plenty of colour throughout the year, with buddleia, sedum, foxgloves and Michaelmas daisies all vying for the attention of discerning butterflies and bumble bees. In the spring the mini woodland area under the mature holly and hazel trees is carpeted yellow, blue and purple with primroses, bluebells and violets.

But the creation of habitats is one of the aspects of wildlife gardening which Ray enjoys. 'You can do what you like in a wildlife garden,' he enthuses 'and *you* decide how much time and effort you put in.' One of his many current projects is creating a hedge of flowering plants, including moon daisy, red campion, lady's

bedstraw, hedge woundwort, shining cranesbill and bird's foot trefoil, where the 'woodland' meets the lawn. And it is easy to achieve results with a ready-made mix as Ray and Pam have done.

Ivy

'It is important to realise the advantages of wild flowers and foliage. Appreciate these plants for what they are and do not forget that native plants have a longer flowering period and are hardier than cultivated flowers.' And while extolling the benefits of native plants, Ray is quick to tell you how useful ivy is to the wildlife gardener. Although often distrusted when growing on houses, ivy does no damage at all to trees and Ray allows his to run riot up and round the trunks and along the high wall. In spring this provides a safe home for families of robins and blackbirds, ivy-covered stumps hold nesting wrens and deep in the tangle of ivy around tree roots a dunnock's nest is hidden. Later in the season

the tiny ivy flowers attract swarms of insects and late autumn butterflies and the Matthews have seen both birds and bats making the most of this inviting supply of food. And as well as the ivy's evergreen leaves providing shelter to birds in winter, the bounty of black berries in February is gobbled up by hungry blackbirds, song and mistle thrushes, starlings, woodpigeons and, in mild winters, blackcaps. A useful plant indeed and one which requires little looking after.

A project which will take more effort is the wild flower area and nursery. Here Ray is growing cowslips, meadow buttercups and meadow cranesbills for transplanting to other areas, and plans to grow others from seed. But he is keen to emphasise that gardening should not become a chore, and as he puts it he 'dabbles'. Dabble or not, the local wildlife has certainly benefited and the Matthews are enjoying being the wardens of their own mini nature reserve.

Planting for Wildlife with Geoffrey Smith

Geoffrey Smith, *well-known broadcaster and writer about gardening, explains why gardening for wildlife is increasingly important and suggests some plants that will attract birds, bees and butterflies.*

On an autumn day not long ago I sat on a limestone outcrop high up in the hills above Wharfedale. Warm sunlight combined with the intense quiet encouraged a mood of reflection. The scene below me had changed very little in the 30 years I had known it. Serene, lovely, inviolate, as everlasting as the hills themselves.

Ten years ago I would have had no doubts. Assuredly this will remain a sanctuary for those for whom such a scene provides healing for the mind. Then I thought of other pieces of wilderness which in those 30 years have disappeared under plough and concrete.

While campaigning energetically for conservation, I am more than ever aware that, in my own garden, a habitat, albeit small, can be provided for a fascinatingly varied wildlife. Birds, butterflies and other insects can all find a home. Contrary to popular belief, it is possible to have a garden which is beautiful and yet at the same time offers the right conditions to attract wildlife which is in serious peril in a highly mechanised, chemical infested world.

Having established that a garden, even the smallest one, forms an increasingly important link in the conservation chain, the choice of what to plant is an easily adjusted compromise between what gives pleasure to the human eye and satisfactory harbourage to wild flora and fauna. *Daphne mezereum*, lovely when the sweetly scented pink flowers wreathe the naked branches in spring, is not often mentioned as a suitable forage plant, yet the

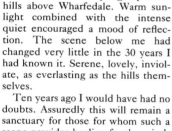

greenfinches guzzle the berries avidly, usually while they are yet unripe. That the mezereum grows in any soil shows an amiable disposition on the part of this handsome native shrub.

Pyracantha, the firethorn, I would always include in the design, particularly as a wall shrub. A bush of the orange-red fruited *Pyracantha coccinea* 'Lalandei' partially covers the garage wall, giving protection to the blue tit nesting holes which were left when the walls were built.

Cotoneasters are notable berrying shrubs, and yet the birds show inexplicable preferences in the species they eat. I grow the herring-bone patterned *Cotoneaster horizontalis*

across a dry-stone wall and this makes an excellent nesting site for blackbirds and thrushes. On a warm day in early spring the abundant small flowers offer hospitality to bees and winter-worn small tortoiseshell butterflies. In autumn, the patterned branches become a panoply of autumn colour, leaf and fruit. Yet I have found that the berries remain untouched long after other cotoneasters have been stripped.

Berberis are obvious choices as berrying shrubs to provide food. And the evergreen *Berberis darwinii* provided nesting sites for long-tailed tits for over 20 years in my last garden.

There are two plants which I would say were essential 'tempters',

veritable sirens to the insect population. Buddleia, particularly the familiar *davidii* hybrids, which open long racemes of fragrant flowers in July and August, are very attractive to butterflies and bees. To extend the season of interest from the gardening aspect, I bed the buddleia round with the other essential, *Sedum spectabile* 'Brilliant' or 'Autumn Joy'. As the shrub goes out of bloom, the deep pink flowers of the sedum open over the grey, fleshy leaves, giving colour and food for butterflies through late summer.

Flowers of the pink corncockle (*Agrostemma*) and the yellow and cream 'foam of the meadow' (*Limnanthes*) are quite excellent as are the blue bells of *Phacelia campanularia*. Carpets of thyme, boscages of lavender and, later in the summer, hyssop, offer solace to the hard-working bee. An over-emphasis on insects as opposed to birds is not intended. The degree of interdependence between the collective whole is, on reflection, obvious yet not always appreciated. Insects bring birds.

Anyone who maintains a garden of any sort will by that very act invite visitors. Even as the spade enters the soil, a robin will be there, head cocked on one side in expectation. Plant a shrub and soon a dunnock will cast an investigating shadow. Bees will follow the flowers as the seasons unfold, and when the planted sapling has grown a season, the blackbird will perch on a branch to greet the sun. Those who cultivate plants in a garden spend time outdoors and see much more than just the fruits of their own labours.

Helping the birds

Feeding birds

Feeding birds in winter is a tradition in Britain dating back many years. It makes us happy to feel that we are helping to keep them alive during the coldest months of the year. However, very often this only means throwing a few crusts of bread out of the back door. These are certainly appreciated, especially by pigeons, house sparrows and starlings, but if you want to attract a wider variety of species you will need to have a selection of different foods on offer!

Where to put food

The best place is on a bird-table. You can buy one from the RSPB or a garden centre, but they are quite simple to make. Think carefully about where you are going to put it – near enough the house so that you can watch all the comings and goings from the comfort of your armchair, but not so close that the cat can have a flying start from some vantage point. Position it somewhere in the open, but with a perch or washing line nearby so that the birds can land there and scan the surrounding area for predators before feeding. Perhaps put it somewhere close to a bush for birds to dive into when danger threatens. Some birds, such as dunnocks and thrushes, prefer to feed on the ground, so do not forget to scatter food around the base of the bird-table. Do not worry if you have not got a big enough space for a bird-table – you can adapt one to fit on a window sill. There is also a wide range of nutfeeders and titbells available – even containers with suckers to stick on windows.

When to feed

You should only provide food between October and April. After that there should be sufficient natural food for the birds to find. Tired parent birds might be tempted to feed their young on indigestible food such as peanuts which could kill them. If you do begin feeding them, it is important to continue doing so throughout the winter as the birds come to depend upon you. Spread the food around so allow the maximum numbers of birds to feed at any one time – their energy is wasted if they are having to compete for every crumb. The best times to put out food are early in the morning and late afternoon.

Maintenance

It is a good idea to move the bird-table periodically to prevent disease; also the accumulation of droppings over several months could affect your lawn. For the same reasons clean the table regularly while it is in use. During the autumn give it a thorough going over, replacing any rusty screws and giving it a coat of wood preservative – allow this to dry completely before using.

Bird food ideas

Nuts	Cooked rice	Oats and oatmeal
Raisins and sultanas (soaked)	Uncooked pastry	Tinned cat and dog food
Fruit	Fresh coconut (**do not** put out desiccated	Meat bones
Sunflower seeds	coconut as this will swell	Suet (the best way to use this is to spread it into
Mealworms	up inside the bird)	the nooks and crannies of
Bread (moistened first)	Cheese	bark, where it will attract
Bacon rinds (cut into small pieces)	Baked potato	birds that do not visit bird-tables)
Peanuts (**not** salted ones)	Melon seeds	
	Stale cake	

Water

Birds need water to drink and bathe in, but the creation of a pond will attract more than birds as a host of other creatures depend on water for at least part of their life cycle.

Is your garden too small for a pond? Do not worry, an upturned dustbin lid or an old sink filled with water will still act as a magnet for thirsty birds or a frog looking for somewhere to spawn. Remember that small birds and amphibians need a shallow edge so they do not get trapped, so you will probably need to build up one side with stones. Position your lid or sink in the open so that the birds cannot be surprised by predators and try to provide a perch nearby to allow them to scan the area before landing. And to make a sink look more natural, why not add a few water plants?

It is important that the water is kept ice-free during the winter, so you could place a nightlight in a draught-free position under the dustbin lid or submerge an aquarium immersion heater, covering it and the thermostat with gravel; or float an easily removable ball or piece of wood on the surface. Do not add salt, glycerine, alcohol or anti-freeze to the water to prevent freezing as this will harm the birds and other animals.

Making a pond

The creation of a pond is a laborious process, but your efforts will be well rewarded as it will be excellent for wildlife. So here is a 12 point plan to a perfect pond ...

1 First, think about how big a pond you want – remember any size will do, although the larger it is the more diverse the wildlife – and buy your liner.

Its shape is an important factor – complex shapes use much more liner, and also mean that you will have lots of liner left over – it is far too expensive to waste! So keep the shape simple. You may also wish to have a 'bog' area beside the pond; this will need a liner, too, if your garden has dry, well drained soil, so take that into account (see No 10).

Thick butyl lining is best and to find out the width, add twice the greatest depth to the width of the pond. Similarly, for the correct length add twice the greatest depth to the length. You could use a pre-formed glass-fibre pond if desired, although the sides are usually rather steep.

2 Plan where you want the pond to go. Ideally, do not make it directly beneath trees as the shade can stunt the growth of plants and the fallen leaves in autumn can reduce the amount of oxygen in the water. Consider also the dangers of flooding in winter and also the risks to small children. Finally, ensure that there is sufficient space to put the soil you have dug.

3 Mark the edges with pegs and string so that you do not get carried away when digging and find that the liner you have bought is now insufficient!

4 Now dig the hole and place the soil well away. You will need to make the pond deeper at one end, shelving gradually to the shallow end. You may wish to leave some shelves to take pots of water plants. The pond should be at least 60 cm (24″) deep to ensure it does not freeze in winter (even that may not be enough for the very hardest weather). Remember to allow extra depth for the liner and a layer of soil on top.

5 Line the hole with either thick layers of newspaper, sieved soil, sand or old carpet to prevent stones from tearing the liner.

6 Put the liner in the hole and allow 12″ of overlap around the edge as a considerable amount of slack will be taken up when the pond is filled.

7 Put in a layer of soil. Make sure the sides are not too steep since the soil will not stick to a steep gradient. Place a couple of smooth stones in the pond as shelters for pond animals. Sharp stones should be on plastic dishes. Some plants could be put in at this stage; these should either be placed in soil in special pond tubs (cheap from garden centres) or firmly anchored to stones.

8 Fill with water. Allow the water from the hose to run gently into the pond.

9 Trim and bury the edges of the liner. Use either paving stones (but make sure these do not overhang the edge) or grass turfs for a more natural look. You may want to kneel at the edge of the pond to peer into its depths; in that case turfs all round may not be a good idea as you will always get wet knees! It is important to cover the plastic as it may deterio-

rate in sunlight, although most liners should last at least 15–20 years.

10 While you are waiting the few days for the water to clear, use the spare soil to create a rockery or adjacent flower bed or bog garden. Some remnants of the butyl liner under the soil will help trap any water – and moisture-loving plants could be planted here. Think carefully if building a rockery. Nothing looks worse than a pile of earth with stones poking out of it; it will never look natural. Try to make its contours fit the contours of your garden; make any stones look like a natural outcrop rather than a pile of rubble!

11 After a week has passed put in oxygenating plants such as hornworts, starworts, arrowhead, quillwort and water violet and a selection of emergent plants such as rushes, water forget-me-not, water mint, bogbean, purple loosestrife, water plantain, flag iris and others. All these will either need to be planted in pond pots, or firmly anchored to stones or weighted with lead ties. Plants are best collected from friends with overgrown ponds, or garden centres. Never dig up wild ones.

12 Next comes the introduction of animal life. Again, a friend or garden centre may have some snails or frog spawn to get you going. A bucket of water from an established pond will contain all sorts of microscopic creatures. Soon you will find that other visitors will turn up of their own accord, such as diving beetles, pond skaters, damselflies, dragonflies and, if you are lucky, frogs, newts and toads.

One of the best things about a pond is that it begins to look natural only a short time after it has been made. If it is dug in March you should be reaping your rewards a few months later.

Nestboxes

Hole-nesting birds such as great and blue tits, nuthatches and starlings take readily to nestboxes, as very often the mature trees full of holes and crevices they need are not available in gardens. In fact, over 60 species of birds are known to have used nestboxes. You may not be able to aspire to as many as that in your garden, but given the right garden, it is possible to encourage the species already mentioned as well as robins, wrens, pied wagtails, spotted flycatchers, treecreepers, house and tree sparrows, swifts, house martins and even kestrels and tawny owls by providing a suitable nestbox.

Position

A nestbox should not face into strong sun or the wettest weather, so it is best facing north, east or south-east unless there are trees and buildings which give shelter. Try to fix it about 2-5 metres (8–15 feet) high so it is as safe as possible from cats and human disturbance. Angle the nestbox slightly forward by wedging a piece of wood between it and the tree or wall. If you place it on a wall make sure it is hidden from view by vegetation – do not worry, the birds will be able to find it! The nestbox should not be placed too close to a bird-table as the birds may spend all their time chasing other birds attracted to the food rather than getting on with nesting. Finally, two boxes of the same kind should not be put up too close together.

Predator prevention

Nestboxes prove inevitable targets to predators such as cats, stoats, weasels, rats, mice, squirrels, great spotted woodpeckers and members of the crow family. A metal plate fixed around the nest hole should help prevent many predators from enlarging it to get at the eggs or chicks. And barbed wire or gorse or rose cuttings fixed to the tree above and below the nestbox should discourage even the most determined predator. Another way is to hang the nestbox from wires – use four so that it does not spin.

Maintenance

It is a good idea to clean out the nestbox once a year with boiling water as parasites often lay eggs in the nesting material. Remember that the young birds may return to roost for a while after they have left the nest, so leave cleaning the box for a few weeks. If you replace it quickly it may be used as a winter hibernation or roost site by some insects, mammals or birds – once 64 wrens were found roosting in a standard nestbox! This is also the time to treat the outside of the box with creosote or other wood preservatives such as Cuprinol, but a coat of clear polyurethane varnish is quite adequate. If unhatched eggs are found in the box these may only legally be removed between October and January and must be disposed of.

Nesting material

Now you have put up all your different types of nestbox around the garden, you could help the birds even more by providing a selection of nesting material from March onwards. It could be fun to find out the preferences of the individual species. The nets that you used for peanuts during the winter could be filled with dried grass, hair, small feathers, short lengths of wool and moss raked from the lawn. Remember to avoid bright colours or shiny objects as the nests should be camouflaged. Leave some dried leaves under your shrubs – and how about creating a muddy edge to your pond or a puddle to encourage house martins and swallows to build their nests close by? If you do that, ensure that cats cannot pounce on the birds while they are engrossed in mud collecting.

A leaflet about nestboxes, giving precise building instructions, is available from the RSPB.

Birdwatching – some tips for a beginner

Having bought a book and binoculars, dressed up in some comfortable old clothes, and filled his or her head with jumbled identification features of likely species, the time must come when a beginner has to go outside and look for some birds!

Oddly enough, this most enjoyable pursuit, the object of the whole exercise, can be very daunting indeed.

Most books fail to say that it is not always easy. Learning the plumage details of a goldcrest is fine, but tracking one down, spotting it high up against the sky in the depths of an ornamental conifer, then getting to see its pattern and recognise its call, is a very different proposition. Nevertheless, the learning stage is one of the most exciting periods in any birdwatcher's career, when birds are fresh and new and the initial discovery of even the commonest species gives a pump of adrenalin difficult to recapture after years of familiarity.

Take out a notebook and learn to use it; take a field guide, having done your homework beforehand. Always remember that practice makes perfect, so there is never any substitute for watching real birds, but regular swotting up on identification is just as important to a birdwatcher as rehearsal is to a musician, or training to an athlete. So read.

Take a plastic bag folded up in a pocket – handy for sitting on a wet grassy bank. Make sure that binoculars are clean and that the eyepiece setting is correct. Leave the case at home. Taking binoculars for a walk inside a case is pointless, as you will always miss the bird that flashes by in an instant. You need to be ready, with binoculars round your neck, on a strap that is shorter rather than longer (it is more comfortable that way and you are less likely to damage the binoculars, or yourself, when climbing over a stile or jumping a ditch). Be dressed for the occasion – and that means light and comfortable clothes for a hot sunny day just as much as wet weather gear in the winter. Many birdwatchers mindlessly conform to an 'image' and wear big boots and waterproof jackets when everyone else is in shorts and a 'T' shirt. It is unnecessary.

Go out with a knowledgeable friend, or on a bird club or RSPB members' group outing if you can. Even if there is no expert there to help, you can learn from each other's mistakes. Try to visit a lake or park where birds will stay in view – or a reserve such as Minsmere, or Slimbridge, where there will be plenty to

see and you can sit comfortably in a hide while trying to sort out what is what. In a hide, listen to others and learn from them – or decide that they know less than you do!

Train yourself to notice movement, even in the corner of your eye, a flicker in a bush that is not a shaking leaf, something moving left when all the windblown grasses are moving right – even shadows crossing the ground. Keep looking about you, look up into the sky and high tree tops. This is how 'experts' spot birds that most people miss.

Most of all, try not to jump to conclusions. Most competent birdwatchers will say that the commonest source of mistakes is misuse of a book – seeing a picture that is vaguely right and assuming that 'that must be it', probably without reading the text – or leaping to a conclusion and then closing the mind to the possibility that the initial diagnosis was wrong. Keep an open mind and check again, and be willing to learn.

Binoculars and telescopes

Binoculars are virtually essential for birdwatching in the field and very useful even if you simply wish to watch birds in your garden. Telescopes are becoming more and more popular with birdwatchers, but are by no means essential.

Binoculars

At first, the choice of binoculars seems bewildering. What are all these names, numbers and specifications? However, it is not as complicated as it looks and it is certainly worth the trouble of getting the right pair – they will then be a pleasure to use for many years.

If you have inherited or been given a pair, check them carefully and compare them with new ones. They may have been invisibly damaged, which could spoil your enjoyment and even strain your eyes. They may need an overhaul or internal cleaning.

If you are buying a pair, you will obviously be influenced by price. At several hundred pounds a pair, the very best makes of binoculars do seem expensive, but most serious birdwatchers use them. If you are sure about your interest and can reasonably afford them, they can be recommended without more ado. They can sometimes be bought secondhand and, if undamaged, might well prove a bargain.

The majority of people taking up birdwatching will begin with something cheaper, but do avoid very cheap binoculars. 'Amazing offers' in newspapers and the cheapest models in high street stores are likely to be unsuitable for regular birdwatching.

Between the two extremes there is a vast range of binoculars. How to choose? The first thing is to decide the magnification you need. The commonest is eight times ($8\times$) and this is an excellent choice. Many birdwatchers do use $10\times$, but the extra magnification is often of little use and the natural shake of our hands may begin to be obvious at $10\times$. Other magnifications include $7\times$ and more rarely $8.5\times$ and $9\times$: all are suitable for birdwatching. 'Zoom' binoculars (ie with variable magnifications) are usually not good enough.

The second important choice is the size of the large 'object' lenses since this governs the amount of light available. For an $8\times$ binocular 30 mm is the minimum acceptable (except with very expensive binoculars when the rule can be relaxed); for a $9\times$ it is 35 mm and for a $10\times$, 40 mm. So, you might well choose an 8×30, a 9×35 or a 10×40 binocular. Some binoculars have larger object lenses, for instance 7×50 and 10×50. These will tend to give better viewing in poor light conditions. They will always be heavier, however, adding to problems of shake and handling/carrying comfort, especially at the end of a long day in the field. You will need to look at a range of binoculars and compare them. The best place to do this is at a specialist dealer, rather than at a high

Presumably the first blue tit to discover that milk bottles hold delicious liquid did so by mistake. Now most blue tits steal milk when they can

street chain store. These dealers advertise in birdwatching and photography magazines, and they offer a wide choice and expert advice, and competitive prices.

Look at as many pairs of binoculars as possible within your price range. You may find you have a choice between conventional ('step-shaped') and roof-prism ('straight through') designs: judge them on their merits, not just looks. Next, consider field of view. This should be indicated somewhere on the binoculars or their packaging. Some binoculars have an especially wide field – this is useful, but it may mean an inferior image, so do check.

Take each pair of binoculars and adjust them to your own eyes. If you wear glasses, try each process both with and without your spectacles: long and short sight, but not astigmatism, are automatically corrected by binoculars. First bend the two halves together or apart, so that when you look through you see a single, circular image. Next, cover the large right-hand lens with a piece of card or your hand, and focus on a distant object using the central wheel. When you have a sharp image, cover the left lens and focus on the same object, this time using the focus on the right hand eyepiece. The object should now look sharp when viewed with both eyes and focusing for different distances can now be done with the central wheel. You will not need to touch the eyepiece again, but you will use the central wheel all the time. Do the eyepiece and the wheel move smoothly? If not, reject the binoculars.

Look at a distant object against the sky – an aerial, flagpole or dead branch are ideal. In the middle of the field of view this object should be sharp and crisp and you should feel no sense of strain in looking at it. Nor should it have any obvious 'colour fringes'. As you move the binoculars sideways you will see that the object will appear to bend, become unsharp and perhaps take on colour fringes. These things are acceptable at the edge, but not in the centre, of the field of view. Reject any binoculars accordingly.

Peer into the binoculars through the object lenses; inspect carefully every surface you can see. Are there any bubbles, cracks, marks, dirt or other flaws? If so, reject them.

See how closely the remaining pairs will focus: everything else being equal, the closer they will focus the better. It is a real nuisance to have to move away from a bird because it is too near to get into focus.

Having checked these things, all now depends on your own appreciation of the image you see through the binoculars. Do the colours appear true to life (many binoculars add a yellow or green cast)? If in doubt, check out your choice against an expensive pair. Make reasonable allowance for price; if it compares favourably you will probably be satisfied with it.

Telescopes

More birdwatchers are buying telescopes and there is no doubt that they add an extra dimension to the hobby. In open country they make the identification of distant dots possible, and they give superb and intimate views of birds which are already close. They do need a tripod to be fully effective, and although this can conveniently be carried on a sling over the shoulder, the extra weight is considerable. Good telescopes are also expensive. On the whole, it is probably not a good idea to buy a telescope when taking up birdwatching, but to get used to binoculars first and consider buying a 'scope later.

Old-style brass telescopes are rarely seen these days, but modern draw-tube telescopes (cylindrical in shape), are readily available. The alternative type is the prismatic telescope, with its characteristic 'stepped' shape. Draw-tube telescopes can be used more easily without a tripod. Prismatic scopes are more weatherproof and they are much more adaptable: interchangeable lenses allow different magnifications to be chosen (these are better optically than 'zoom' lenses, by the way), and some models can be used for photography. Both types are capable of excellent optical performance.

In choosing a telescope, similar test procedures should be followed as for binoculars. However, the likelihood is that you will have 'field-tested' several models among your birdwatching friends already and have a good idea of what you want. A magnification of between 20× and 30× is ideal and the object lens should be at least 60 mm across.

Baby birds

During the spring and summer months the RSPB is inundated with calls from people who have brought home an apparently deserted baby bird and want to know how to look after it properly. It is a sad fact that many will die when this happens, so it is better to leave them alone. The parent birds are much better able than we are to provide everything the young bird needs. If you find a 'lost' bird in your garden or on an open path do not be tempted to take it home, but place it somewhere safe nearby. In most cases, the parents will be close at hand, probably finding food, and will return to feed it when you have gone. Only if the bird is certainly orphaned should you consider looking after it, but bear in mind that this will take an enormous amount of time and effort and may not be successful.

Wild Birds and the Law

The Wildlife and Countryside Act came into force in 1981. It gives protection to all of Britain's rare and endangered species of mammals, birds, reptiles, insects and wild plants. With regard to birds, the 1981 Act supersedes the 1954 Protection of Birds Act. All birds, their nests and eggs are protected by law, and it is an offence, with certain exceptions, intentionally to:

• kill, injure or take any wild bird

• take, damage or destroy the nest of any wild bird while it is in use or being built

• take or destroy the egg of any wild bird

• have in one's possession or control any wild bird (dead or alive) or any part of a wild bird which has been taken in contravention of the Act or the Protection of Birds Act 1954

• have in one's possession or control any egg or part of an egg which has been taken in contravention of the Act

• have in one's possession or control any live bird of prey of any species in the world (except Old World vultures) unless it is registered and ringed in accordance with the Secretary of State's regulations

• have in one's possession or control any bird of a species occurring on Schedule 4 (see page 382) of the Act unless registered (and in some cases ringed) in accordance with the Secretary of State's regulations

• disturb any wild bird listed on Schedule 1 while it is nest building, or at a nest containing eggs or young, or disturb the dependent young of such a bird.

Baby birds, such as this robin, often look lost and sound forlorn, but the parents are usually close by, so it is best to leave them alone

What should I do if ...?

Answers to some frequently asked questions about wild birds and the law.

I know someone who traps finches and keeps them in an aviary. Is this illegal?

Yes. Not only is it an offence to take British wild birds, but keeping them would also be illegal.

I have found an injured bird. Can I look after it?

Yes, but you must release it when it has recovered. In the case of Schedule 4 birds (see list on page 382) you must inform the Department of the Environment and register the bird.

My neighbour keeps a bird of prey. Does he need a licence?

No, but all birds of prey (excluding owls) must be registered with the Department of the Environment at Tollgate House, Houlton Street, Bristol. Keeping a bird of prey taken from the wild is, of course, illegal.

Is it an offence to possess wild birds' eggs?

Yes, if they were taken after 28 September 1982 – the day the Wildlife and Countryside Act came into force.

I have a nestbox in my garden and last year the birds deserted their eggs. Is it all right to clean the box out ready for the next season?

Yes, but only if carried out during October, November, December or January. And remember, you are not allowed to keep the eggs.

I have found a dead tawny owl on the road. Can I have it stuffed and keep it?

If the bird has died of natural causes you can pay a taxidermist to stuff and mount it for you to keep. You cannot sell the bird to a taxidermist. Only a person registered with or licensed by the Department of the Environment can sell dead wild birds. Also, the dead birds must themselves be registered. If you have the bird mounted as a service then no sale has taken place and it will not need to be registered, unless you wish to sell it. This applies only to legitimate specimens. If the bird had been killed illegally, then possessing it would be an offence.

Every year house martin nests on a local building are destroyed by workmen. Is this legal?
No; all wild birds' nests are fully protected and it is an offence to destroy them while in use or being built. In the case of house martins and swallows, a nest will remain in use throughout the summer and until the birds leave on their autumn migration. Only after they have all left (some time towards the end of October) can the nests be removed.

What can I do about youths with airguns shooting at birds in our local park?
They are committing a serious firearms offence by using an airgun in a public place. Inform the police immediately. With the exception of 'pest' species, gamebirds and certain waterfowl (which may be killed or taken by authorised persons or during the open season) it is illegal to shoot at any birds.
Further information on wild birds and the law is available in a booklet from the RSPB.

Pests

We spend time and effort in the garden to create the ideal conditions for birds to come and share it with us – we provide food, a place to drink and bathe, and somewhere safe to nest and roost. Sometimes we also play host to unwelcome visitors, such as cats, grey squirrels, grey herons and magpies. All these are 'problem species' to many people and the RSPB is often asked for advice on deterring them. However, a garden is simply a smaller version of the world outside it and to an extent nature must run its course, although there are certain precautions you could consider taking.

Cats

The cat is probably the greatest predator of garden birds as its natural instinct is to hunt, hungry or not. This is particularly galling if it is your neighbour's cat which is to blame, but if you own a cat it would be best to think twice about encouraging birds in to your garden. You could persuade your neighbour's cat to keep out with a high, galvanised wire fence (coated with bitumen to make it less obtrusive) or plant a hedge of holly or hawthorn. Fill in the gaps with bramble, thorns or holly leaves.

Grey squirrels

Although attractive, grey squirrels can be a nuisance during the winter, eating everything on the bird-table or in the nutfeeders, and in the breeding season they will try to gnaw their

way into nestboxes. Try putting an inverted metal cone or biscuit tin under the tray of the bird-table. The squirrel will climb the post but should be unable to get round the obstacle. One way to protect your nutfeeders is to cut the end off a plastic lemonade bottle and hang it over the basket – the open end should still allow the tits to feed but the squirrel will have lost its footholds.

Herons

The sight of a grey heron in your garden one early morning or at dusk would be spectacular – but the reason for its appearance is probably the presence of goldfish in your pond. The occasional raid is forgivable, but frequent visits could leave your pond with no fish at all. The best solution is to have two parallel strings set 15 cm (6 in) from the edge of the pond with the upper one at 35 cm (14 in) high and the lower at 20 cm (8 in). They prevent the heron approaching the pond. You could cover the pond with netting, but this would not be so pleasing to the eye and would lessen the value to other wildlife.

Magpies

Magpies have shown a marked increase in numbers probably because of a decrease in persecution. They are most obvious in spring when they raid the nests of songbirds. It is not pleasant to have every nest in your garden attacked by magpies, but census work over the last 20 years by the British Trust for Ornithology has shown no major declines in numbers of garden birds – there are fluctuations, but these are usually associated with habitat change or the effects of severe winters.

If magpies do seem to be a problem in your garden, the law does permit the landowner, or someone with the landowner's permission, to destroy the nests of magpies while they are being built.

Rather than destroy the magpies' nest you could think about planting some dense hedges or bushes of laurel, yew, ivy or hawthorn to provide the small birds in your garden with somewhere safer to nest. And always remember that magpies kill far fewer birds than cats, cars, sparrowhawks or peregrines!

Treatment of injured birds

Injured birds are difficult to look after – often the shock of being handled affects them more than the injuries received. Once you have decided that a bird needs help you must try to capture it causing the minimum of distress. Usually covering it with a box or cloth will quieten it enough to allow capture. If the bird is beyond recovery it is best to destroy it humanely. A vet will need to treat more serious injuries and you should seek expert advice before

attempting treatment yourself.

Handling should be firm, but gentle, with the wings held close to the body to prevent fluttering and possible further injury. Clean small wounds with water and a mild antiseptic. Then put the bird in a covered box in a warm, quiet place like an airing cupboard and leave for an hour or so. This treatment also applies to birds in shock, following collision with a window for example. Such birds may need just warmth and quiet, before being released – do not attempt to force food into them. Do not keep them near pet birds, and wash your hands after handling.

Birds should be released as soon as possible, early in the morning near where they were found. If they can be left quietly for an hour or two before release then so much the better. If you have had them in captivity for a while you may need to feed them at regular times for a day or two.

Finally, if you come across an oiled bird you must not attempt to clean it yourself, but contact the RSPCA. All birds of prey (except owls) and Schedule 1 (see page 382) birds are required by law to be kept by a registered keeper; again contact the RSPCA.

For further information on looking after sick and injured birds a joint RSPB/RSPCA leaflet is available from the RSPB.

Stop the Massacre

The killing and catching of migratory birds has been a way of life in Mediterranean countries for centuries and the number of hunters far exceeds the conservationists – in some countries by thousands to one. Each year *hundreds of millions* of birds are shot, trapped, caged or netted for fun, eating or taxidermy and much of this is done illegally. The worst areas are in Portugal, Spain, France, Italy, Malta, Cyprus and the Lebanon. Although there are legal restrictions to such activities in most of these countries, the law is rarely enforced.

How can I help?

The RSPB is often asked by birdwatchers whether they should boycott countries where this slaughter takes place. The Society does not encourage this as conservationists may then be viewed as hostile rather than constructive, but would ask travellers, if they see any evidence, to complain to that country's tourist association. If the incident takes place in an EEC country write to your European Parliament Member (address at the local library). Point out that your major reason for visiting that country was to enjoy the wildlife and that the wholesale slaughter is lessening the attraction for potential visitors.

Another way you can do something is by donating unwanted binoculars

or European field guides to the Stop the Massacre Committee, c/o The Lodge, Sandy, Bedfordshire, SG19 2DL. This Committee organises the distribution of these to places where they can be of most use. Many wardening schemes, school teachers and information officers all over Europe and Africa have already benefited.

You may also wish to help directly by joining an international bird protection society or the one in the country you are visiting – the addresses of which can be obtained from the RSPB at the address above.

Indexes

Index of Birds

Figures in bold italic type refer to full illustrated entries. Figures in italics refer to illustrations additional to these entries. References within the regional guides have not been indexed.

Index of Places

Figures in italics refer to illustrations without accompanying text.

Index of Subjects

British and Irish Bird List

The following is the complete British list as at July 1986. It is arranged in the sequence of orders, families and species used by major ornithological bodies, and is the arrangement adopted in this book.

Some birds have a bracketed number (1) after their name. These appear on Schedule 1, Part 1 of the Wildlife and Countryside Act 1981 and are protected by special penalties at all times. A licence is needed to photograph these species at or near a nest (licence available from Nature Conservancy Council, Northminster House, Peterborough PE1 1UA). Birds which have (1, 4) after their names also appear on Schedule 4 of the same act. All these species must be registered with the Department of the Environment if kept in captivity. Schedule 4 also includes all birds of prey in the world with the exception of Old World vultures.

There are four blank boxes beside each bird's name. These are so that species can be ticked off as they are seen. One box might be for your garden list, another for your life list, and so on. Lists are personal things – they may interest you, or become an obsession, or leave you cold. Most people just 'like to know what they have seen', so keep a simple 'life list'.

GAVIIFORMES
Gaviidae
Red-throated Diver □□□□
Gavia stellata (1, 4)
Black-throated Diver □□□□
G. arctica (1, 4)
Great Northern Diver □□□□
G. immer (1, 4)
White-billed Diver □□□□
G. adamsii (1, 4)

PODICIPEDIFORMES
Podicipedidae
Pied-billed Grebe □□□□
Podilymbus podiceps
Little Grebe □□□□
Tachybaptus ruficollis
Great Crested Grebe □□□□
Podiceps cristatus
Red-necked Grebe □□□□
P. grisegena
Slavonian Grebe □□□□
P. auritus (1, 4)
Black-necked Grebe □□□□
P. nigricollis (1, 4)

PROCELLARIIFORMES
Diomedeidae
Black-browed Albatross □□□□
Diomedea melanophris

Procellariidae
Fulmar □□□□
Fulmarus glacialis
Capped Petrel □□□□
Pterodroma hasitata
Bulwer's Petrel □□□□
Bulweria bulwerii
Cory's Shearwater □□□□
Calonectris diomedea
Great Shearwater □□□□
Puffinus gravis
Sooty Shearwater □□□□
P. griseus
Manx Shearwater □□□□
P. puffinus
Little Shearwater □□□□
P. assimilis

Hydrobatidae
Wilson's Petrel □□□□
Oceanites oceanicus
White-faced Petrel □□□□
Pelagodroma marina
Storm Petrel □□□□
Hydrobates pelagicus
Leach's Petrel □□□□
Oceanodroma leucorhoa (1, 4)
Madeiran Petrel □□□□
O. castro

PELECANIFORMES
Sulidae
Gannet □□□□
Sula bassana

Phalacrocoracidae
Cormorant □□□□
Phalacrocorax carbo
Shag □□□□
P. aristotelis

Fregatidae
Magnificent Frigatebird □□□□
Fregata magnificens

CICONIIFORMES
Ardeidae
Bittern □□□□
Botaurus stellaris (1, 4)
American Bittern □□□□
B. lentiginosus
Little Bittern □□□□
Ixobrychus minutus (1, 4)
Night Heron □□□□
Nycticorax nycticorax
Green Heron □□□□
Butorides striatus
Squacco Heron □□□□
Ardeola ralloides
Cattle Egret □□□□
Bubulcus ibis
Little Egret □□□□
Egretta garzetta
Great White Egret □□□□
E. alba
Grey Heron □□□□
Ardea cinerea
Purple Heron □□□□
A. purpurea (1)

Ciconiidae
Black Stork □□□□
Ciconia nigra
White Stork □□□□
C. ciconia

Threskiornithidae
Glossy Ibis □□□□
Plegadis falcinellus
Spoonbill □□□□
Platalea leucorodia (1, 4)

ANSERIFORMES
Anatidae
Mute Swan □□□□
Cygnus olor
Bewick's Swan □□□□
C. columbianus (1)
Whooper Swan □□□□
C. cygnus (1)
Bean Goose □□□□
Anser fabalis
Pink-footed Goose □□□□
A. brachyrhynchus
White-fronted Goose □□□□
A. albifrons
Lesser White-fronted Goose □□□□
A. erythropus
Greylag Goose □□□□
A. anser
Snow Goose □□□□
A. caerulescens
Canada Goose □□□□
Branta canadensis
Barnacle Goose □□□□
B. leucopsis
Brent Goose □□□□
B. bernicla
Red-breasted Goose □□□□
B. ruficollis
Egyptian Goose □□□□
Alopochen aegyptiacus
Ruddy Shelduck □□□□
Tadorna ferruginea

Shelduck □□□□
T. tadorna
Mandarin □□□□
Aix galericulata
Wigeon □□□□
Anas penelope
American Wigeon □□□□
A. americana
Gadwall □□□□
A. strepera
Baikal Teal □□□□
A. formosa
Teal □□□□
A. crecca
Mallard □□□□
A. platyrhynchos
Black Duck □□□□
A. rubripes
Pintail □□□□
A. acuta
Garganey □□□□
A. querquedula (1)
Blue-winged Teal □□□□
A. discors
Shoveler □□□□
A. clypeata
Red-crested Pochard □□□□
Netta rufina
Pochard □□□□
Aythya ferina
Ring-necked Duck □□□□
A. collaris
Ferruginous Duck □□□□
A. nyroca
Tufted Duck □□□□
A. fuligula
Scaup □□□□
A. marila (1)
Eider □□□□
Somateria mollissima
King Eider □□□□
S. spectabilis
Steller's Eider □□□□
Polysticta stelleri
Harlequin Duck □□□□
Histrionicus histrionicus
Long-tailed Duck □□□□
Clangula hyemalis (1, 4)
Common Scoter □□□□
Melanitta nigra (1, 4)
Surf Scoter □□□□
M. perspicillata
Velvet Scoter □□□□
M. fusca (1, 4)
Bufflehead □□□□
Bucephala albeola
Goldeneye □□□□
B. clangula
Hooded Merganser □□□□
Mergus cucullatus
Smew □□□□
M. albellus
Red-breasted Merganser □□□□
M. serrator
Goosander □□□□
M. merganser
Ruddy Duck □□□□
Oxyura jamaicensis

ACCIPITRIFORMES
Accipitridae
Honey Buzzard □□□□
Pernis apivorus (1, 4)
Black Kite □□□□
Milvus migrans
Red Kite □□□□
M. milvus (1, 4)
White-tailed Eagle □□□□
Haliaeetus albicilla (1, 4)
Egyptian Vulture □□□□
Neophron percnopterus
Griffon Vulture □□□□
Gyps fulvus
Marsh Harrier □□□□
Circus aeruginosus (1, 4)
Hen Harrier □□□□
C. cyaneus (1, 4)
Pallid Harrier □□□□
C. macrourus (1, 4)
Montagu's Harrier □□□□
C. pygargus (1, 4)
Goshawk □□□□
Accipiter gentilis (1, 4)
Sparrowhawk □□□□
A. nisus
Buzzard □□□□
Buteo buteo
Rough-legged Buzzard □□□□
B. lagopus
Spotted Eagle □□□□
Aquila clanga
Golden Eagle □□□□
A. chrysaetos (1, 4)

Pandionidae
Osprey □□□□
Pandion haliaetus (1, 4)

FALCONIFORMES
Falconidae
Lesser Kestrel □□□□
Falco naumanni
Kestrel □□□□
F. tinnunculus
American Kestrel □□□□
F. sparverius
Red-footed Falcon □□□□
F. vespertinus
Merlin □□□□
F. columbarius (1, 4)
Hobby □□□□
F. subbuteo (1, 4)
Eleonora's Falcon □□□□
F. eleonorae
Gyrfalcon □□□□
F. rusticolus (1, 4)
Peregrine □□□□
F. peregrinus (1, 4)

GALLIFORMES
Tetraonidae
Red (Willow) Grouse □□□□
Lagopus lagopus
Ptarmigan □□□□
L. mutus
Black Grouse □□□□
Tetrao tetrix
Capercaillie □□□□
T. urogallus

Phasianidae
Red-legged Partridge □□□□
Alectoris rufa
Grey Partridge □□□□
Perdix perdix
Quail □□□□
Coturnix coturnix (1, 4)
Pheasant □□□□
Phasianus colchicus
Golden Pheasant □□□□
Chrysolophus pictus
Lady Amherst's Pheasant □□□□
C. amherstiae

GRUIFORMES
Rallidae
Water Rail □□□□
Rallus aquaticus
Spotted Crake □□□□
Porzana porzana (1, 4)
Sora Rail □□□□
P. carolina
Little Crake □□□□
P. parva
Baillon's Crake □□□□
P. pusilla
Corncrake □□□□
Crex crex (1, 4)
Moorhen □□□□
Gallinula chloropus
Allen's Gallinule □□□□
Porphyrula alleni
American Purple Gallinule □□□□
P. martinica
Coot □□□□
Fulica atra
American Coot □□□□
F. americana

Gruidae
Crane □□□□
Grus grus
Sandhill Crane □□□□
G. canadensis

Otididae
Little Bustard □□□□
Tetrax tetrax
Houbara Bustard □□□□
Chlamydotis undulata
Great Bustard □□□□
Otis tarda

CHARADRIIFORMES
Haematopodidae
Oystercatcher □□□□
Haematopus ostralegus

Recurvirostridae
Black-winged Stilt □□□□
Himantopus himantopus (1, 4)
Avocet □□□□
Recurvirostra avosetta (1, 4)

Burhinidae
Stone-curlew □□□□
Burhinus oedicnemus (1, 4)

Glareolidae
Cream-coloured Courser □□□□
Cursorius cursor
Collared Pratincole □□□□
Glareola pratincola
Black-winged Pratincole □□□□
G. nordmanni

Charadriidae
Little Ringed Plover □□□□
Charadrius dubius (1, 4)
Ringed Plover □□□□
C. hiaticula
Semipalmated Plover □□□□
C. semipalmatus
Killdeer □□□□
C. vociferus
Kentish Plover □□□□
C. alexandrinus (1, 4)
Greater Sand Plover □□□□
C. leschenaultii
Caspian Plover □□□□
C. asiaticus
Dotterel □□□□
C. morinellus (1, 4)
American Golden Plover □□□□
Pluvialis dominica
Pacific Golden Plover □□□□
P. fulva
Golden Plover □□□□
P. apricaria
Grey Plover □□□□
P. squatarola
Sociable Plover □□□□
Chettusia gregaria
White-tailed Plover □□□□
C. leucura
Lapwing □□□□
Vanellus vanellus

Scolopacidae
Knot □□□□
Calidris canutus
Sanderling □□□□
C. alba
Semipalmated Sandpiper □□□□
C. pusilla
Western Sandpiper □□□□
C. mauri
Little Stint □□□□
C. minuta
Temminck's Stint □□□□
C. temminckii (1, 4)
Long-toed Stint □□□□
C. subminuta
Least Sandpiper □□□□
C. minutilla
White-rumped Sandpiper □□□□
C. fuscicollis
Baird's Sandpiper □□□□
C. bairdii
Pectoral Sandpiper □□□□
C. melanotos
Sharp-tailed Sandpiper □□□□
C. acuminata
Curlew Sandpiper □□□□
C. ferruginea
Purple Sandpiper □□□□
C. maritima (1, 4)
Dunlin □□□□
C. alpina
Broad-billed Sandpiper □□□□
Limicola falcinellus
Stilt Sandpiper □□□□
Micropalama himantopus
Buff-breasted Sandpiper □□□□
Tryngites subruficollis
Ruff □□□□
Philomachus pugnax (1, 4)
Jack Snipe □□□□
Lymnocryptes minimus
Snipe □□□□
Gallinago gallinago
Great Snipe □□□□
G. media
Short-billed Dowitcher □□□□
Limnodromus griseus
Long-billed Dowitcher □□□□
L. scolopaceus
Woodcock □□□□
Scolopax rusticola
Black-tailed Godwit □□□□
Limosa limosa (1, 4)
Hudsonian Godwit □□□□
L. haemastica
Bar-tailed Godwit □□□□
L. lapponica
Little Whimbrel □□□□
Numenius minutus
Eskimo Curlew □□□□
N. borealis
Whimbrel □□□□
N. phaeopus (1, 4)
Curlew □□□□
N. arquata
Upland Sandpiper □□□□
Bartramia longicauda
Spotted Redshank □□□□
Tringa erythropus

Redshank / *T. totanus* □□□□
Marsh Sandpiper / *T. stagnatilis* □□□□
Greenshank / *T. nebularia (1, 4)* □□□□
Greater Yellowlegs / *T. melanoleuca* □□□□
Lesser Yellowlegs / *T. flavipes* □□□□
Solitary Sandpiper / *T. solitaria* □□□□
Green Sandpiper / *T. ochropus (1, 4)* □□□□
Wood Sandpiper / *T. glareola (1, 4)* □□□□
Terek Sandpiper / *Xenus cinereus* □□□□
Common Sandpiper / *Actitis hypoleucos* □□□□
Spotted Sandpiper / *A. macularia* □□□□
Turnstone / *Arenaria interpres* □□□□
Wilson's Phalarope / *Phalaropus tricolor* □□□□
Red-necked Phalarope / *P. lobatus (1, 4)* □□□□
Grey Phalarope / *P. fulicarius* □□□□

Stercorariidae
Pomarine Skua / *Stercorarius pomarinus* □□□□
Arctic Skua / *S. parasiticus* □□□□
Long-tailed Skua / *S. longicaudus* □□□□
Great Skua / *S. skua* □□□□

Laridae
Great Black-headed Gull / *Larus ichthyaetus* □□□□
Mediterranean Gull / *L. melanocephalus (1)* □□□□
Laughing Gull / *L. atricilla* □□□□
Franklin's Gull / *L. pipixcan* □□□□
Little Gull / *L. minutus (1)* □□□□
Sabine's Gull / *L. sabini* □□□□
Bonaparte's Gull / *L. philadelphia* □□□□
Black-headed Gull / *L. ridibundus* □□□□
Slender-billed Gull / *L. genei* □□□□
Ring-billed Gull / *L. delawarensis* □□□□
Common Gull / *L. canus* □□□□
Lesser Black-backed Gull / *L. fuscus* □□□□
Herring Gull / *L. argentatus* □□□□
Iceland Gull / *L. glaucoides* □□□□
Glaucous Gull / *L. hyperboreus* □□□□
Great Black-backed Gull / *L. marinus* □□□□
Ross's Gull / *Rhodostethia rosea* □□□□
Kittiwake / *Rissa tridactyla* □□□□
Ivory Gull / *Pagophila eburnea* □□□□

Sternidae
Gull-billed Tern / *Gelochelidon nilotica* □□□□
Caspian Tern / *Sterna caspia* □□□□
Royal Tern / *S. maxima* □□□□
Sandwich Tern / *S. sandvicensis* □□□□
Roseate Tern / *S. dougallii (1, 4)* □□□□
Common Tern / *S. hirundo* □□□□
Arctic Tern / *S. paradisaea* □□□□
Aleutian Tern / *S. aleutica* □□□□
Forster's Tern / *S. forsteri* □□□□
Bridled Tern / *S. anaethetus* □□□□
Sooty Tern / *S. fuscata* □□□□
Little Tern / *S. albifrons (1, 4)* □□□□
Whiskered Tern / *Chlidonias hybridus* □□□□

Black Tern / *C. niger* □□□□
White-winged Black Tern / *C. leucopterus* □□□□

Alcidae
Guillemot / *Uria aalge* □□□□
Brunnich's Guillemot / *U. lomvia* □□□□
Razorbill / *Alca torda* □□□□
Black Guillemot / *Cepphus grylle* □□□□
Little Auk / *Alle alle* □□□□
Puffin / *Fratercula arctica* □□□□

PTEROCLIDIFORMES
Pteroclididae
Pallas's Sandgrouse / *Syrrhaptes paradoxus* □□□□

COLUMBIFORMES
Columbidae
Rock Dove / *Columba livia* □□□□
Stock Dove / *C. oenas* □□□□
Woodpigeon / *C. palumbus* □□□□
Collared Dove / *Streptopelia decaocto* □□□□
Turtle Dove / *S. turtur* □□□□
Rufous Turtle Dove / *S. orientalis* □□□□

PSITTACIFORMES
Psittacidae
Ring-necked Parakeet / *Psittacula krameri* □□□□

CUCULIFORMES
Cuculidae
Great Spotted Cuckoo / *Clamator glandarius* □□□□
Cuckoo / *Cuculus canorus* □□□□
Black-billed Cuckoo / *Coccyzus erythrophthalmus* □□□□
Yellow-billed Cuckoo / *C. americanus* □□□□

STRIGIFORMES
Tytonidae
Barn Owl / *Tyto alba (1)* □□□□

Strigidae
Scops Owl / *Otus scops* □□□□
Eagle Owl / *Bubo bubo* □□□□
Snowy Owl / *Nyctea scandiaca (1)* □□□□
Hawk Owl / *Surnia ulula* □□□□
Little Owl / *Athene noctua* □□□□
Tawny Owl / *Strix aluco* □□□□
Long-eared Owl / *Asio otus* □□□□
Short-eared Owl / *A. flammeus* □□□□
Tengmalm's Owl / *Aegolius funereus* □□□□

CAPRIMULGIFORMES
Caprimulgidae
Nightjar / *Caprimulgus europaeus* □□□□
Red-necked Nightjar / *C. ruficollis* □□□□
Egyptian Nightjar / *C. aegyptius* □□□□
Common Nighthawk / *Chordeiles minor* □□□□

APODIFORMES
Apodidae
Chimney Swift / *Chaetura pelagica* □□□□
Needle-tailed Swift / *Hirundapus caudacutus* □□□□
Swift / *Apus apus* □□□□

Pallid Swift / *A. pallidus* □□□□
Pacific Swift / *A. pacificus* □□□□
Alpine Swift / *A. melba* □□□□
Little Swift / *A. affinis* □□□□

CORACIIFORMES
Alcedinidae
Kingfisher / *Alcedo atthis (1, 4)* □□□□
Belted Kingfisher / *Ceryle alcyon* □□□□

Meropidae
Blue-cheeked Bee-eater / *Merops superciliosus* □□□□
Bee-eater / *M. apiaster (1, 4)* □□□□

Coraciidae
Roller / *Coracias garrulus* □□□□

Upupidae
Hoopoe / *Upupa epops (1, 4)* □□□□

PICIFORMES
Picidae
Wryneck / *Jynx torquilla (1, 4)* □□□□
Green Woodpecker / *Picus viridis* □□□□
Yellow-bellied Sapsucker / *Sphyrapicus varius* □□□□
Great Spotted Woodpecker / *Dendrocopos major* □□□□
Lesser Spotted Woodpecker / *D. minor* □□□□

PASSERIFORMES
Alaudidae
Calandra Lark / *Melanocorypha calandra* □□□□
Bimaculated Lark / *M. bimaculata* □□□□
White-winged Lark / *M. leucoptera* □□□□
Short-toed Lark / *Calandrella brachydactyla* □□□□
Lesser Short-toed Lark / *C. rufescens* □□□□
Crested Lark / *Galerida cristata* □□□□
Woodlark / *Lullula arborea (1, 4)* □□□□
Skylark / *Alauda arvensis* □□□□
Shore Lark / *Eremophila alpestris (1, 4)* □□□□

Hirundinidae
Sand Martin / *Riparia riparia* □□□□
Swallow / *Hirundo rustica* □□□□
Red-rumped Swallow / *H. daurica* □□□□
Cliff Swallow / *H. pyrrhonota* □□□□
House Martin / *Delichon urbica* □□□□

Motacillidae
Richard's Pipit / *Anthus novaeseelandiae* □□□□
Blyth's Pipit / *A. godlewskii* □□□□
Tawny Pipit / *A. campestris* □□□□
Olive-backed Pipit / *A. hodgsoni* □□□□
Tree Pipit / *A. trivialis* □□□□
Pechora Pipit / *A. gustavi* □□□□
Meadow Pipit / *A. pratensis* □□□□
Red-throated Pipit / *A. cervinus* □□□□
Rock Pipit / *A. petrosus* □□□□
Water Pipit / *A. spinoletta* □□□□
American Pipit / *A. rubescens* □□□□
Yellow Wagtail / *Motacilla flava* □□□□
Citrine Wagtail / *M. citreola* □□□□

Grey Wagtail / *M. cinerea* □□□□
Pied Wagtail / *M. alba* □□□□

Bombycillidae
Waxwing / *Bombycilla garrulus* □□□□

Cinclidae
Dipper / *Cinclus cinclus* □□□□

Troglodytidae
Wren / *Troglodytes troglodytes* □□□□

Mimidae
Brown Thrasher / *Toxostoma rufum* □□□□

Prunellidae
Dunnock / *Prunella modularis* □□□□
Alpine Accentor / *P. collaris* □□□□

Turdidae
Rufous Bush Robin / *Cercotrichas galactotes* □□□□
Robin / *Erithacus rubecula* □□□□
Thrush Nightingale / *Luscinia luscinia* □□□□
Nightingale / *L. megarhynchos* □□□□
Siberian Rubythroat / *L. calliope* □□□□
Bluethroat / *L. svecica (1, 4)* □□□□
Red-flanked Bluetail / *Tarsiger cyanurus* □□□□
Black Redstart / *Phoenicurus ochruros (1, 4)* □□□□
Redstart / *P. phoenicurus* □□□□
Whinchat / *Saxicola rubetra* □□□□
Stonechat / *S. torquata* □□□□
Isabelline Wheatear / *Oenanthe isabellina* □□□□
Wheatear / *O. oenanthe* □□□□
Pied Wheatear / *O. pleschanka* □□□□
Black-eared Wheatear / *O. hispanica* □□□□
Desert Wheatear / *O. deserti* □□□□
White-crowned Black Wheatear / *O. leucopyga* □□□□
Black Wheatear / *O. leucura* □□□□
Rock Thrush / *Monticola saxatilis* □□□□
White's Thrush / *Zoothera dauma* □□□□
Siberian Thrush / *Z. sibirica* □□□□
Hermit Thrush / *Catharus guttatus* □□□□
Swainson's Thrush / *C. ustulatus* □□□□
Gray-cheeked Thrush / *C. minimus* □□□□
Veery / *C. fuscescens* □□□□
Ring Ouzel / *Turdus torquatus* □□□□
Blackbird / *T. merula* □□□□
Eye-browed Thrush / *T. obscurus* □□□□
Dusky (Naumann's) Thrush / *T. naumanni* □□□□
Dark-(Red-, Black-)throated Thrush / *T. ruficollis* □□□□
Fieldfare / *T. pilaris (1, 4)* □□□□
Song Thrush / *T. philomelos* □□□□
Redwing / *T. iliacus (1, 4)* □□□□
Mistle Thrush / *T. viscivorus* □□□□
American Robin / *T. migratorius* □□□□

Sylviidae
Cetti's Warbler / *Cettia cetti (1, 4)* □□□□
Fan-tailed Warbler / *Cisticola juncidis* □□□□
Pallas's Grasshopper Warbler / *Locustella certhiola* □□□□

Lanceolated Warbler / *L. lanceolata* □□□□
Grasshopper Warbler / *L. naevia* □□□□
River Warbler / *L. fluviatilis* □□□□
Savi's Warbler / *L. luscinioides (1, 4)* □□□□
Moustached Warbler / *Acrocephalus melanopogon* □□□□
Aquatic Warbler / *A. paludicola* □□□□
Sedge Warbler / *A. schoenobaenus* □□□□
Paddyfield Warbler / *A. agricola* □□□□
Blyth's Reed Warbler / *A. dumetorum* □□□□
Marsh Warbler / *A. palustris (1, 4)* □□□□
Reed Warbler / *A. scirpaceus* □□□□
Great Reed Warbler / *A. arundinaceus* □□□□
Thick-billed Warbler / *A. aedon* □□□□
Olivaceous Warbler / *Hippolais pallida*
Booted Warbler / *H. caligata* □□□□
Icterine Warbler / *H. icterina* □□□□
Melodious Warbler / *H. polyglotta* □□□□
Marmora's Warbler / *S. sarda* □□□□
Dartford Warbler / *Sylvia undata (1, 4)* □□□□
Spectacled Warbler / *S. conspicillata* □□□□
Subalpine Warbler / *S. cantillans* □□□□
Sardinian Warbler / *S. melanocephala* □□□□
Ruppell's Warbler / *S. rueppelli* □□□□
Desert Warbler / *S. nana* □□□□
Orphean Warbler / *S. hortensis* □□□□
Barred Warbler / *S. nisoria* □□□□
Lesser Whitethroat / *S. curruca* □□□□
Whitethroat / *S. communis* □□□□
Garden Warbler / *S. borin* □□□□
Blackcap / *S. atricapilla* □□□□
Green Warbler / *Phylloscopus nitidus* □□□□
Greenish Warbler / *P. trochiloides* □□□□
Arctic Warbler / *P. borealis* □□□□
Pallas's Warbler / *P. proregulus* □□□□
Yellow-browed Warbler / *P. inornatus* □□□□
Radde's Warbler / *P. schwarzi* □□□□
Dusky Warbler / *P. fuscatus* □□□□
Bonelli's Warbler / *P. bonelli* □□□□
Wood Warbler / *P. sibilatrix* □□□□
Chiffchaff / *P. collybita* □□□□
Willow Warbler / *P. trochilus* □□□□
Goldcrest / *Regulus regulus* □□□□
Firecrest / *R. ignicapilus (1, 4)* □□□□

Muscicapidae
Spotted Flycatcher / *Muscicapa striata* □□□□
Red-breasted Flycatcher / *Ficedula parva* □□□□
Collared Flycatcher / *F. albicollis* □□□□
Pied Flycatcher / *F. hypoleuca* □□□□

Timaliidae
Bearded Tit / *Panurus biarmicus (1, 4)* □□□□

Aegithalidae
Long-tailed Tit / *Aegithalos caudatus* □□□□

Paridae
Marsh Tit / *Parus palustris* □□□□